THE PHYSICS OF ELECTRICITY AND MAGNETISM

Wiley International Edition

THE PHYSICS OF ELECTRICITY AND MAGNETISM
Second Edition

WILLIAM TAUSSIG SCOTT
Professor of Physics, University of Nevada

John Wiley & Sons, Inc.   NEW YORK   LONDON   SYDNEY

TOPPAN COMPANY, LTD.   TOKYO, JAPAN

Wiley International Edition

This book is not to be sold outside the country
to which it is consigned by the publisher.

Printed in Japan

By TOPPAN PRINTING COMPANY, LTD.

To Ann

PREFACE

The text for the second edition of *The Physics of Electricity and Magnetism* has been modified in four principal ways. I have taken account of the higher level of sophistication which most physics students now bring to this subject, embodied some new insights concerning the displacement current and phenomena related to the Fermi level, included the important electromagnetic background for plasma physics and magnetohydrodynamics, and made several improvements in order, smoothness, and clarity.

The aim of the book is still to cover the *physics* of the subject in both its mathematical and phenomenal aspects. I have resisted the growing trend to write electricity and magnetism texts almost entirely for prospective theorists, although I have continued to present the theory of the subject in a sound and complete way. Instead of emphasizing electromagnetic radiation and other parts of Maxwell field theory to the almost total exclusion of the properties of conductors and the fields in and around them, I have tried to balance the two sides of the subject. Both experimental and theoretical physicists need to think in physical terms about circuits, contact potential, impedance, and many similar matters which are now disappearing from modern texts at the junior-senior and even at introductory levels. I trust that the unified approach used in this text will not only appeal to undergraduate physics majors, but will also be appreciated by prospective electrical engineers and physical chemists.

Certain of the more mathematical aspects of the subject are introduced earlier in this edition than in the first, without raising the basic level of the derivations. The added theoretical material, such as the discussion of the Lienard-Wiechert potentials, uses straightforward arguments of a type similar to those used elsewhere in the text.

Relativity theory has been shifted to the end of Chapter 7, where it follows naturally after the consideration of Maxwell's equations. The complex vector method for a-c circuits is now self-contained in Section 9.4. A basic introduction to second-order linear differential equations is still provided in the last section of Chapter 8.

Introductory material on plasma physics, including plasma oscillations, Debye-Hückel theory, particle motions, adiabatic invariants, flux transport, magnetohydrodynamics, and Alfvén waves, has been inserted at places where it follows naturally from principles which it illustrates. A separate chapter for all this material would involve considerable recapitulation of earlier material, and might give the misleading impression that the subject had been adequately covered, rather than merely introduced.

The so-called displacement current has been deduced directly from the differential form of the Biot-Savart law, following up a remark in the first edition concerning the connection of these two principles. The clarity and directness of this approach seem to me to outweigh the advantages of the customary procedure.

The material on electron levels in conductors has been considerably simplified, especially by use of the concept of the Fermi potential of a conductor. The electrochemical matters have now been more fully concentrated in Chapter 6.

Gaussian units are still used in a secondary way, but all references to them are now in small-type paragraphs, mostly at the end of each section. All formulas not specifically labeled are in MKS units.

Some of the problems have been improved and a few added. The lengthier and less interesting have been scrapped. All numerical values have been changed, and a selection of answers provided in the Appendix.

For many helpful suggestions on order, content, and expression, I am grateful to Drs. Robert M. Eisberg, Donald Ginsburg, Peter Lindenfeld, G. G. Wiseman, Arnold Strassenburg, and R. Edwin Worley. Acknowledgment is hereby given to several others who have furnished useful comments. Drs. Robert Manhart and Eugene Kosso, of the University of Nevada Electrical Engineering Department, have been especially helpful in guiding me to up-to-date reference material for all parts of the text. Mr. B. Jeffrey Anderson assisted with new drawings, and Mr. Ping-lei Wang modified the numerical values in all the problems and carefully worked out new answers. I owe thanks to my daughter Jennifer and to Mrs. Steven Kaylor for help in typing.

My greatest thanks, however, go to my wife, Ann, who read the entire text and made many improvements in style, smoothness of language, and clarity of presentation.

William Taussig Scott

Reno, Nevada
April 1966

PREFACE TO
THE FIRST EDITION

This text was written because, like many other teachers of physics, I was dissatisfied with available texts in the field traditionally called "Electricity and Magnetism." I felt that there was need for a text on electricity and magnetism suitable for juniors, seniors, and first-year graduate students that had the following characteristics:

1. It should present a good balance between theory and experiment, training the reader's physical intuition by use of careful physical and mathematical reasoning—i.e., it should represent the physics of the subject in the complete sense of that word.

2. It should be fairly complete as far as the topics from which most instructors would draw material for students of physics, chemistry, mathematics, and engineering. The book should have somewhat more material than can be covered in an average year course, for different instructors will wish to cut out different sections, and non-student readers will naturally have a variety of interests within the general framework. (See below for suggestions on the material to be used for various groups of readers.)

3. It should be suitable for a first course in physics involving an extensive use of the calculus and of vectors, as well as for use following courses in analytical mechanics, etc. Assuming the reader to have had a good previous grounding in the mathematics of differential and integral calculus, it should develop with some care the physical application of this branch of mathematics.

4. It should be logically accurate, with a rock-bottom minimum of "it can be shown" statements. Material not covered in detail should be left out altogether or mentioned without deriving consequences from it. The mathematical level of the proofs should be as elementary as possible, consistent with the requirements of logic. Proofs general enough to include all exceptional cases are best avoided.

5. Certain concepts, such as the vector potential, multipoles, etc., should be introduced in a more elementary way than is usually the case, so that the reader can gain the advantages of using these concepts without having to meet them first in terms of existence proofs or boundary value calculations.

6. It should primarily stress the force rather than the energy point of view, because physical intuition is better trained starting in this way. The energy point of view must however be introduced and in a way that is integral with the rest of the subject.

7. The book should be modern in two particular respects: (*a*) It should be up to date as regards recent developments in the classical theory itself or in the presentation of it

(cf. the material on the non-closure of lines of **D** in Section 3.6 and of **B** in Section 7.7, and the method of introducing the magnetic field); (*b*) It should make full use of modern training at the elementary college level in atomic physics, both to help the reader's imagination and to allow explanation of electrical matters that depend on atomic structure, such as chemical emfs, ferromagnetism, and semiconductors. In addition, reference at least should be given to such recent technical developments as ferrites and transistors.

This text was written in accordance with these prescriptions. Some of its special features and the reasons for them are worth reviewing here.

The concepts of field, flux, and potential, as produced by given charge distributions, are introduced in Chapter 1. Each concept is developed and examples given before the next one is taken up, a general principle which is followed throughout. Sections on div **E**, **curl E** and $\nabla^2 V$ are included, to be used either on first reading or postponed until later as the instructor desires. (The first two are needed in Chapter 3.) The added complication of the determination of charge distributions by conductor arrangements is taken up first in Chapter 2. Conductors are introduced with a qualitative description of the band theory of conduction and the Fermi level, to be used as an aid to the imagination for electrostatics and as a base for the material of Chapters 5 and 6. The concept of the cavity potential of a metal is introduced to provide logical exactness and pedagogical clarity in discussing the work function and contact potential difference. Electroscopes, ice pails, etc., are discussed briefly with the full use of the potential and flux concepts rather than in the traditional way at the beginning of the course.

Chapter 3 introduces dielectric behavior by starting with the dipole field and then considering how a given set of dipoles acts as a whole, using the analysis first given by Poisson for magnetism. Idealized electrets are discussed in detail, both to give a thorough understanding of the vectors **E**, **D**, and **P**, and to prepare the way for magr   lculations in Chapter 8. Ideal dielectrics are then introduced, together with the permitti v..y concept, and the limitations on the usual force formula for charges in a dielectric medium are clearly demonstrated.

Chapter 4 includes image calculations, an introduction to boundary-value calculations and a discussion of energy and forces in a system of conductors. This material is arranged so that all or part of it can be omitted without influencing the study of what follows. The conjugate function method has been omitted as best reserved for readers who have had a course in complex function theory.

Chapter 5 includes standard material on direct currents and also a discussion at the beginning on the electrostatic fields in such circuits, so that the field ideas so necessary for modern high frequency work are introduced at the start. The electrical mechanism of the production of chemical emfs is established by use of the Fermi level, together with qualitative ideas concerning quantum levels in solutions. This method has proved itself capable of readily explaining phenomena that are usually dismissed with the assertion that "non-electric" forces are involved. It is hard in my viewpoint to justify training readers to deal with emfs and leaving their origin a mystery.

Chapter 6 presents material on semiconductors, thermoelectricity, and chemical effects. Thermoelectric effects are described in terms of the recently developed thermodynamics of irreversible processes; the semiconductor material is a brief introduction to the basic level structure and a description of a *p-n* junction for students who may otherwise miss this important topic. The treatment of electrolytic conduction and Faraday's laws emphasizes the electrical rather than the chemical aspects of the subject.

Chapter 7 introduces the magnetic field **B** in terms of the Lorentz force law, treated as a fundamental law of physics. Several consequences of the law are deduced, and then

Ampère's law for the production of **B** by a system of currents is brought in, first in the directly verifiable solid-angle form and later in the Laplace rule form, the circuital form, the vector-potential form, and the Maxwell equation form (including the displacement current). Faraday's law is brought in as an extension of Ampère's law based on simple relative-motion considerations. As a consequence of this development, all of Maxwell's equations have been discussed by the end of this chapter. Their consequences for waves, however, are postponed until Chapter 10, to allow a period of assimilation. Inductance and some of the difficulties with its calculation are brought in near the end of Chapter 7. The vector potential concept is used to explain the paradox of a toroidal solenoid producing no magnetic field outside itself and yet inducing current in an exterior coil.

Chapter 8 introduces Ampère's law in the magnetic dipole form and shows how the pole fiction can be used to calculate magnetic fields. The earlier calculations on electrets and dielectrics can then be taken over directly without repetition. A clear definition of the vector **H** is given, followed by a discussion of magnetic materials. In addition to the usual treatment of hysteresis, etc., there is a discussion of the formation of permanent magnets. Galvanometers, with their differential equations, are brought into this chapter because of their connection with magnetic testing methods.

Chapter 9 gives a standard treatment of alternating-current theory based on the complex-number method. Transformers and a small amount of work on filters are included. Pulse analysis and Fourier analysis are included, with a section on Laplace transforms for those who wish to study them.

Chapter 10 introduces radiation with a discussion of signal propagation along coaxial conductors. Waves in free space, retarded potentials, the energy and momentum theorems, dipole radiation, physical optics, waves in pipes and cavities, and a section on the four-vector notation and special relativity are included.

The Appendix gives a rather complete section on vector analysis (A.2) and another on vector invariance (A.4), plus short review sections on advanced calculus concepts (e.g., Taylor's theorem in several variables), differential equations, determinants, and complex numbers, and tables of units and of physical constants.

A list of symbols and abbreviations precedes the index.

Each chapter is quite long, and so problems are inserted at the end of appropriate sections. The fact that this points the reader to the section of the book relevant to each problem does not seem to detract from the benefit he obtains in trying to work it.

I should like to express my appreciation to certain of my colleagues and to the several classes of Smith College girls who patiently, energetically, and with considerable clarity studied the material as I prepared it, found errors in writing and in logic, and asked a large number of penetrating and helpful questions. Women who elect physics do so against a prevailing fashion; such students have on the average considerable interest and ability in physics and considerable independence and desire to learn, for all of which I am duly grateful.

In particular, I should like to thank the following for the help they have given me. The late Professor David C. Grahame of Amherst College suggested the use of the cavity-potential concept and in various ways stimulated my initial efforts at writing this book. Dr. W. J. Hamer of the National Bureau of Standards made helpful comments on an early draft of the electrochemistry sections. Mrs. Gunther K. Wertheim was particularly helpful at various stages of the work in constructively criticizing both the writing and the physics. Others who helped in these regards were Mrs. Richard H. Walters, Mrs. David Willey and the Misses Catharine H. Stevens, Blanche E. Leatherman, Louise F. Clark, Mrs. A. David May, and Judith J. Snow. The last two individuals also assisted with the preparation of the figures, along with Mr. George Gardiner, Miss

Anne M. Shea, whose assistance in this aspect was particularly valuable, and Mr. W. Thompson Lawrence. Appreciation is also due Mrs. Jonathan Hoxie for her very considerable help in the typing; some valuable typing assistance was also obtained from Mrs. Vincent Erikson and Mrs. Melvin Prouser; the Misses Lindsey A. Cairns and Edith M. Christian helped in checking the manuscript, and Miss Helene Blodgett assisted in the preparation of the index. And finally, I owe a great debt to my wife and children for their patience and encouragement, without which this book would never have been written.

William T. Scott

Smith College
February 1959

CONTENTS

* Starred sections may be omitted without loss of continuity. Specific information about continuity is contained in footnotes to Sections 2.6, 5.5, 7.6, 7.15, 7.19, 8.9, 9.1, and in the text of Section 6.1.

Chapter 1

CHARGE, FIELD, AND POTENTIAL

1.1 Atomic Structure

It is the purpose of this book to present the fundamental laws of electrical and magnetic phenomena that are valid in the macroscopic, or non-atomic, realm. Although it would be perfectly logical to develop the theory without reference to the atomic nature of matter, the use of modern notions concerning atoms and their constituents is of great help in clarifying and illuminating these macroscopic principles. Hence, we assume the reader to be acquainted in a general way with the modern concept of the structure of matter. We give here a brief summary of the relevant material.

Matter is composed of atoms roughly 10^{-10} m in diameter, each containing a nucleus of dimensions of the order of 10^{-14} m. Electrons move about the nucleus of each atom, and it is their electrical influence on the electrons of other atoms that effectively defines the atomic dimensions. Regardless of where they are found, electrons are negatively charged and are all alike, each bearing a charge of $-e = -1.602 \times 10^{-19}$ coulomb.

Most of the mass of an atom is contained in its nucleus. Each nucleus bears a positive charge, numerically equal in electronic units to the atomic number of the atom in question, that is, to its ordinal number in the periodic table of the elements.

Thus there are two kinds of electrical charge in matter, positive and negative. Like charges repel; unlike attract. Because of the attraction of unlike charges, each atom or molecule in its normal state has as many electrons as it has units of positive charge in its nucleus or nuclei, and thus is electrically neutral.

Nearly all the large-scale effects of electricity arise from the fact that electrons may become separated from their atoms under appropriate circumstances, thus leading to a separation of positive and negative charges by distances appreciably greater than atomic dimensions. As far as is known, the entire universe contains equal amounts of positive and negative electricity, with the result that an excess of one sign at any place implies the location elsewhere of an equal and opposite charge. Furthermore, net amounts of electric charge can neither be created nor destroyed (law of conservation of charge).

Isolated positive and negative charges will attract one another, and this attraction will result in a flow of charge if a conducting path is available. The flow of charge may consist of the motion of electrons (as in metals), the motion of ions (as in solutions), or the motion of bare atomic nuclei (as in cyclotrons, etc.). The motion of positive charge in one direction has the same effect on the increase or decrease of excess (unneutralized) charge anywhere as has the motion of negative charge in exactly the opposite direction. We shall see later that the magnetic effects of moving charges are also symmetric in this way. Certain combinations of electric and magnetic fields affect positive and negative charges differently (cf. Section 7.5), but for most of our results the fact that it is only the electrons that move in metallic conductors has no bearing, other than being a help to the imagination.

1.2 Coulomb's Law and Electric Field Strength

Our subject begins with electrostatics, which is the study of charges at rest (in the macroscopic sense) in a particular frame of reference, such as the laboratory system. All of electrostatics is derived from the experimentally verifiable Coulomb law for the electrostatic force between a pair of point charges or elementary particles, and from certain specific properties of matter. We shall write Coulomb's law as follows:

$$\mathbf{F} = \frac{q_1 q_2}{4\pi\epsilon_0 r^2} \mathbf{1}_r \qquad (1.2\text{--}1)$$

where $\mathbf{F}$ is the force between point charges of magnitude q_1 and q_2 situated a distance r apart (a point charge is one which occupies a region of space small compared with the error in the measurement of distances). The force is a vector or directed quantity and will be represented by bold-face type, like other vectors in this book.[1] The magnitude of the force, denoted by F, is the scalar $q_1 q_2/4\pi\epsilon_0 r^2$, and its direction is that of the unit vector $\mathbf{1}_r$, a vector of unit length drawn from the charge considered to be the agent

[1] Appendix A.2 gives a summary of vector analysis.

toward the charge upon which the force is calculated, i.e., in the r direction (see Fig. 1.2a). The power of r in the denominator has been shown to be 2 within an accuracy of one part in 10^8, by an experimental method to be discussed in Section 2.8.

The forces between charges at rest obey Newton's third law, equality of action and reaction, so the force of q_2 on q_1 is $-\mathbf{F}$. We shall see in Section 7.6 that the third law is no longer valid for charges in motion. However, conservation of momentum is not violated (Section 10.4).

The quantity ϵ_0 is a constant the value of which depends on the units used for q; it is generally called the "permittivity of free space." In this book we shall use primarily the meter-kilogram-second (MKS) system of

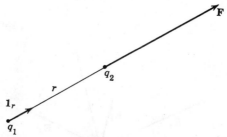

Fig. 1.2a.   The force of q_1 on q_2 lies in the direction of $\mathbf{1}_r$.

units,[2] with force in newtons (1 newton $=$ 1 kg-m/sec^2 $=$ 10^5 dynes), and shall measure q in coulombs, to be defined later in terms of forces between currents (see Section 7.8). For this system, $\epsilon_0 = 8.85 \times 10^{-12}$ coulomb^2/newton-m^2, approximately.[3] For many calculational purposes involving Coulomb's law, the value $1/4\pi\epsilon_0 = 9 \times 10^9$, good to 0.14%, is convenient. The 4π which appears to complicate matters here will be seen to disappear in certain practical formulas to be derived later.

The electrostatic system of units, part of the 'Gaussian system to which we shall refer in small-type paragraphs, is based on the centimeter-gram-second system of mechanical units. In this system, $4\pi\epsilon_0 = 1$. Equation 1.2–1 then is not only the elementary law of force but also the equation that defines the unit of charge, called the esu of charge or the statcoulomb. One statcoulomb is equal to 3.34×10^{-10} coulomb, or 2.08×10^9 electron charges. One coulomb $=$ 3.00×10^9 statcoulomb $= 6.24 \times 10^{18}$ electron charges.

Equation 1.2–1 is the fundamental law of force. *The force it represents is completely unaffected by the presence of other charges or materials.* The effect of other charges is not to change $\mathbf{F}$ but to provide additional forces

[2] See Appendix A.7 for a table of units.
[3] We shall see later that $\epsilon_0 = 10^7/4\pi c^2$, where c is the velocity of light, 3.00×10^8 m/sec. Precise values of ϵ_0, c, and other physical constants are given in Appendix A.8.

on q_1 and q_2. In general, the force on a charge is the vector sum of the separate forces exerted on that charge by all other charges taken independently. This is the principle of superposition, which may be treated as an implicit part of Coulomb's law, or as an independent, experimentally verified physical principle.[4]

The additivity of electric forces, and also of the magnetic forces to be taken up in Chapter 7, has as a consequence the linearity of the basic equations of electricity and magnetism, a matter of the utmost importance. Almost the whole development of physics has depended on linearity—we can hardly imagine what physics would be like if nature provided us with non-linear effects of any appreciable magnitude.

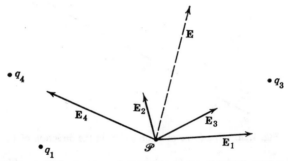

Fig. 1.2b.   The vector **E** is the sum of the fields produced at $\mathscr{P}$ by the charges shown.

The superposition principle allows us to define the electric field strength or intensity **E**, frequently called electric field for short (although the word "field" by itself usually connotes a *region*). In fact, the force on a charge q at a point $\mathscr{P}$ may be written

$$\mathbf{F} = q\mathbf{E} \qquad (1.2\text{--}2)$$

where **E** is a vector given by

$$\mathbf{E} = \frac{1}{4\pi\epsilon_0} \sum_n \frac{q_n}{r_n^2} \mathbf{1}_n = \sum_n \mathbf{E}_n \qquad (1.2\text{--}3)$$

In Eq. 1.2–3, the summation is over all charges q_n near enough q to have an appreciable force on the latter; r_n is the distance from q_n to the point $\mathscr{P}$, and $\mathbf{1}_n$ is a unit vector in the direction defined by a line from q_n to $\mathscr{P}$. $\mathbf{E}_n$ is the field strength at $\mathscr{P}$ due to q_n alone. (See Fig. 1.2b.) The sum is a vector sum in the usual geometrical sense. The respective vectors of lengths $q_n/4\pi\epsilon_0 r_n^2$ may be added successively tail-to-head; alternatively each of the three rectangular components of **E** may be found as the

---

[4] For a detailed discussion of the logical meaning of Coulomb's law, see the article by the Coulomb's Law Committee, *Am. J. Phys.* **18**, 1 (1950), especially pp. 5 and 6.

algebraic sum of the corresponding components of $\mathbf{E}_n$. Vector addition is commutative and associative—it does not matter in which order the several vectors are added.

For instance, a sphere of uniformly polarized dielectric contains molecules whose positive and negative charges are all separated by the same amount. The field at a point outside the sphere may be calculated in one of two ways. We may first add the contributions of all the positive charges, then those of the negative charges, and finally add the two nearly opposite resultant fields. Alternatively, we may first combine the effects of positive and negative charges in each molecule, and then add the effects of all the

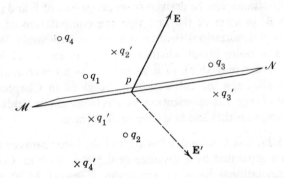

Fig. 1.2c. The field $\mathbf{E}$ of the charges q_1 to q_4 of Fig. 1.2*b* and the field $\mathbf{E}'$ of the same set of changes reflected in the plane $\mathcal{M}\mathcal{N}$ and labeled q_1' to q_4'. The vector $\mathbf{E}$ obeys the law of reflection.

molecules (see Section 3.6 and Problem 3.6*h*). The results must be the same for the two calculations.

The field strength $\mathbf{E}$ obeys the reflection properties of any true or so-called "polar" vector. For instance, if a plane is passed through the point of observation $\mathscr{P}$ and a new physical arrangement of charges is constructed that is a reflection of the old one in that plane, the vector $\mathbf{E}$ for the new set will be the mirror image of the original set, as shown in Fig. 1.2*c*. The component of $\mathbf{E}$ perpendicular to the plane changes its sign whereas the components parallel to the plane are unchanged. We shall see in Chapter 7 that the magnetic vector $\mathbf{B}$ does not behave in this way.

In the MKS system, E is measured in newtons/coulomb or joules/meter-coulomb, which we will identify later with volts/meter.

We are considering here forces exerted by charges at rest. In Eq. 1.2–2 we assume $\mathbf{E}$ to remain constant when the magnitude of q is changed, or when q is removed. Actually, in most cases a change in the magnitude or position of q would cause a shift or motion in the other charges q_n. To be precise, we shall define the field strength **E** at any point in space as the force per unit charge that *would* be exerted on a test charge put there, *if* this charge did not affect the neighboring charges. We shall normally assume that we can introduce an appropriately small test charge, which is possible in principle in the macroscopic realm, but not in the realm of atomic magnitudes.

In introducing the field concept, we have divided the problem of forces between charges into two problems: that of the sources of electric field, given by Eq. 1.2–3, and that of the effect of the field on the local charge q, given by Eq. 1.2–2. (Both of these equations will be generalized in Chapter 7.) It is an enormous simplification to make this division. Many results of importance can be derived from properties of **E** and its magnetic counterpart **B**, in spite of the fact that the computation of fields from 1.2–3 and its generalizations is often difficult or impossible. We need say nothing at this point about whether **E** exists as an actual independent entity—the reader may think of it as real or as a convenient device for calculation—although the calculation to be given in Chapter 10 of the transport of energy and momentum by electromagnetic fields will give a strong presumption that the fields are really "there."

Problem 1.2a. Use Coulomb's law to find the force between an electron and a proton separated by a distance of 0.529×10^{-10} m. Compare this with the gravitational force of attraction $F = GM_pM_e/r^2$ where $G = 6.67 \times 10^{-11}$ newton-m^2/kg^2, the electron mass is 9.11×10^{-31} kg, and the proton mass is 1837 times greater.

Problem 1.2b. Find the relation between q and θ when two pith balls hung from a common point on light strings of length l stand apart from each other at an angle θ. Each has a mass m and a charge q and is small enough to be treated as a point.

1.3 Calculation of Field Strengths

The simplest cases are those in which only a few source charges are present and the vector sums can be found directly. The reader is urged to try one or more of Problems 1.3a, b, c, and d.

An interesting and important case is that of two equal and opposite charges, $+q$ and $-q$, separated by a short distance δl. We shall calculate the field at a point $\mathcal{O}$ at a distance from either charge which is large compared to δl. From such a distant vantage point, the pair of charges is called a dipole. Let us denote the distances of $\mathcal{O}$ from $+q$ and $-q$ by r and r' as in Fig. 1.3a, the angle between $\mathbf{1}_r$ and δl by θ, and that between $\hat{\mathbf{i}}_r$ and $\mathbf{1}_r'$ by α.

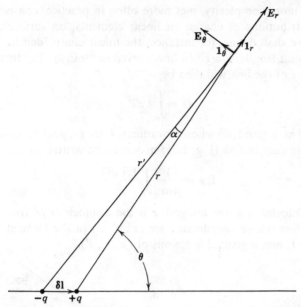

Fig. 1.3a. Illustrating the calculation of the field produced by a pair of charges at a distance r large compared to their separation δl.

Then we have

$$r'^2 = r^2 + \delta l^2 + 2r\,\delta l\cos\theta$$

$$\sin\alpha/\delta l = \sin\theta/r'$$

The field at $\mathcal{O}$ perpendicular to $\mathbf{1}_r$ is produced entirely by $-q$ and has the magnitude $(q/r'^2)\sin\alpha$, which to the first power of δl is

$$E_\theta = \frac{q\,\delta l\sin\theta}{4\pi\epsilon_0 r'^3} \simeq \frac{q\,\delta l\sin\theta}{4\pi\epsilon_0 r^3} \qquad (1.3\text{-}1a)$$

Since $\cos\alpha$ differs from 1 by the second and higher powers of δl, we can write the field along r as

$$4\pi\epsilon_0 E_r = \frac{q}{r^2} - \frac{q}{r'^2}\cos\alpha \simeq \frac{q}{r^2} - \frac{q}{r'^2} \simeq \frac{q}{r^2} - \frac{q}{r^2}\left(1 - \frac{2\,\delta l}{r}\cos\theta\right)$$

using the binomial theorem (see Appendix A.1). We have finally

$$E_r = \frac{2q\,\delta l\cos\theta}{4\pi\epsilon_0 r^3} \qquad (1.3\text{-}1b)$$

The vector field at $\mathcal{O}$ may then be written

$$\mathbf{E} = \frac{q\,\delta l}{4\pi\epsilon_0 r^3}(2\cos\theta\,\mathbf{1}_r + \sin\theta\,\mathbf{1}_\theta) \qquad (1.3\text{-}1c)$$

Another calculation of this result is given in Section 3.1, Eq. 3.1-7.

Cases of more complexity, met more often in practice, consist of continuous distributions of charge on linear elements, on surfaces, and in volumes. We shall define, for instance, the linear charge density λ as the charge per unit length on a given line, curved or straight. The total charge on a length l of the line will then be

$$Q = \int_l \lambda \, dl' \tag{1.3–2}$$

The field at a point $\mathscr{P}$ whose coordinates are (x, y, z) produced by a linear charge distribution (Fig. 1.3b) may then be written as

$$\mathbf{E}_{\mathscr{P}} = \frac{1}{4\pi\epsilon_0} \int_l \frac{\mathbf{1}_r \lambda \, dl'}{r^2} \tag{1.3–3}$$

where the integral is a line integral, r is the distance to $\mathscr{P}$ from a point $\mathscr{P}'$ on the line whose coordinates are (x', y', z') in the element dl', and both λ and $\mathbf{1}_r$ are in general functions of (x', y', z').

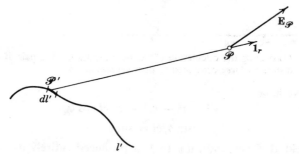

Fig. 1.3b.   The field at $\mathscr{P}$ is given by a vector integral over a curved path l'.

Of course, no distribution of atomic charges can actually be continuous. We can, however, treat certain distributions as if they were continuous, provided that we deal only with macroscopic phenomena. To be more specific, we can use the notion of continuity if the distance of $\mathscr{P}$ from the nearest charge is very much greater than the distance between charges.[5] Appendix A.1 gives a mathematical definition of densities for continuous distributions, and Appendix A.2 contains a discussion of vector integrals such as 1.3–3.

Let us as a first example find the field at a distance R from a straight, infinite, uniformly charged, thin wire with a constant charge density λ (Fig. 1.3c). To evaluate the integral in this case, we can use the distance x' of $\mathscr{P}'$ from the foot of the perpendicular from $\mathscr{P}$ as the independent variable. Then we have $dl' = dx'$ and $r^2 = R^2 + x'^2$.

[5] A careful discussion of the application of ideas of continuity to actual matter is given by R. B. Lindsay and H. Margenau, *Foundations of Physics*, Dover, New York, 1963, Sec. 1.7.

The unit vector 1_r is variable in direction, so we shall write it as a linear combination of two constant unit vectors. As shown by the small diagram in the figure, we have

$$1_r = -1_x \sin \theta + 1_R \cos \theta$$

As x' varies from $-\infty$ to $+\infty$, $\sin \theta$ takes on first negative values and then positive values. It is easy to show by considerations of symmetry that the integral $\int \sin \, dx'/r^2$ vanishes. Physically this is equivalent to saying that the components of field strength parallel to the wire produced by elements at x' and at $-x'$ will just cancel.

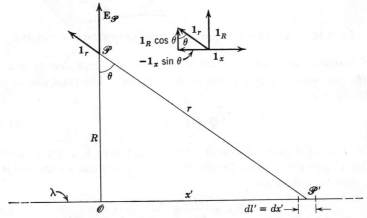

Fig. 1.3c.   Illustrating the evaluation of Eq. 1.3–3 for a long straight wire.

We have then only the term $1_R \cos \theta$ to consider. Since $\cos \theta = R/(x'^2 + R^2)^{1/2}$, we have

$$E = \frac{\lambda 1_R}{4\pi\epsilon_0} \int_{-\infty}^{\infty} \frac{R \, dx'}{(x'^2 + R^2)^{3/2}} = \frac{\lambda 1_R}{2\pi\epsilon_0 R} \qquad (1.3\text{–}4)$$

The integral in Eq. 1.3–4 may be most easily carried out if one uses the angle θ as a new variable, writing $x' = R \tan \theta$. Such a trigonometric substitution suggested directly by the geometry of the problem is often useful in evaluating integrals of this sort.

To illustrate Eq. 1.3–4, suppose we have 3.0×10^{-6} coulomb/m on a long straight thin wire. The field strength at a distance of 0.1 m from the wire is $E = 18 \times 10^9 \times 3.0 \times 10^{-6}/0.1 = 5.4 \times 10^5$ newtons/coulomb (or volts/meter). The force on an electron at this point would be $5.4 \times 10^5 \times 1.60 \times 10^{-19} = 8.64 \times 10^{-14}$ newton, and its acceleration $8.64 \times 10^{-14}/9.11 \times 10^{-31} = 9.48 \times 10^{16}$ m/sec², since the mass of an electron is 9.11×10^{-31} kg.

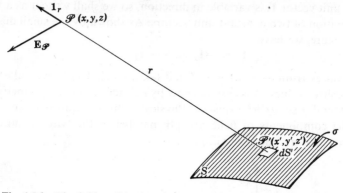

Fig. 1.3d. The field at $\mathscr{P}$ is given by a vector integral over the surface S.

In a similar way, we may define the surface charge density σ as the charge per unit area at a point $\mathscr{P}$ on a surface. The total charge on a surface S will be

$$Q = \int_S \sigma \, dS' \tag{1.3-5}$$

The field at a point $\mathscr{P}$ whose coordinates are (x, y, z) produced by a surface charge distribution (which may or may not contain the point $\mathscr{P}$) may then be written as

$$\mathbf{E}_{\mathscr{P}} = \frac{1}{4\pi\epsilon_0} \int_S \frac{\mathbf{1}_r \sigma \, dS'}{r^2} \tag{1.3-6}$$

where the integral is a surface integral over the surface S (Fig. 1.3d), r is the distance to $\mathscr{P}$ from a point $\mathscr{P}'$ whose coordinates are (x', y', z') in the surface element dS', and both σ and $\mathbf{1}_r$ are as before general functions of the variable point (x', y', z').

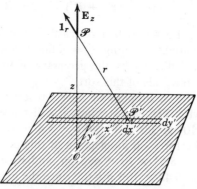

Fig. 1.3e. Illustrating the calculation of the field outside an infinite charged plane.

Let us find the field at a point $\mathscr{P}$ a height z above an infinite plane distribution of uniform density (Fig. 1.3e). For the element dS' in Eq. 1.3–6 we shall use $dx'\,dy'$, where x' and y' are the Cartesian coordinates of a point $\mathscr{P}'$ in the plane, with the origin $\mathscr{O}$ at the foot of the perpendicular from $\mathscr{P}$. We see that $r^2 = x'^2 + y'^2 + z^2$ and that the vertical component of $\mathbf{1}_r$ is z/r. Hence we may write

$$E_z = \frac{\sigma}{4\pi\epsilon_0} \int_{-\infty}^{\infty} dy' \int_{-\infty}^{\infty} \frac{z\,dx'}{(x'^2 + y'^2 + z^2)^{3/2}}$$

The x'-integration is the same as in the last problem (if we set $R^2 = y'^2 + z^2$) and we find

$$E_z = \frac{\sigma}{4\pi\epsilon_0} \int_{-\infty}^{\infty} dy' \frac{2z}{y'^2 + z^2} = \frac{\sigma}{2\epsilon_0} \tag{1.3–7}$$

The x and y components of $\mathbf{E}$ vanish, by symmetry. We note that the field strength $E_z(=E)$ at a point $\mathscr{P}$ outside an infinite plane distribution of charge is independent of the distance z of $\mathscr{P}$ from the plane. However, the field is in the opposite direction on the other side of the plane, and hence suffers a discontinuity at the plane.

As a third example, let us find the field strength on the axis of a disk of radius a, at a distance z from the center $\mathscr{O}$ (Fig. 1.3f) when the surface density σ on the disk at a distance r' from $\mathscr{O}$ is given by $\sigma = br'$ coulomb/m^2, with b a constant.

For reasons of symmetry, we calculate only the axial component, E_z. We shall let $dS' = r'\,dr'\,d\phi'$ and must take the variation of σ into account. We have

$$\begin{aligned}
E = E_z &= \frac{1}{4\pi\epsilon_0} \int_0^a \frac{br' \cdot r'\,dr' \cdot z}{(r'^2 + z^2)^{3/2}} \int_0^{2\pi} d\phi' \\
&= \frac{bz}{2\epsilon_0} \int_0^a \frac{r'^2\,dr'}{(r'^2 + z^2)^{3/2}} \\
&= \frac{bz}{2\epsilon_0}\left(\ln \frac{a + (a^2 + z^2)^{1/2}}{z} - \frac{a}{(a^2 + z^2)^{1/2}} \right)
\end{aligned} \tag{1.3–8}$$

The total charge on the disk is

$$Q = \int_0^a br' \cdot 2\pi r'\,dr' = \tfrac{2}{3}\pi b a^3$$

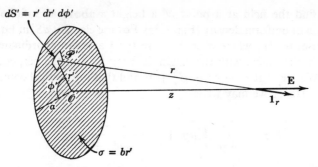

Fig. 1.3f. Illustrating the calculation of the field produced by a charged disk.

The case of volume distributions can be treated in the same way. We shall denote by ρ the volume charge density, i.e., the charge per unit volume at a point $\mathscr{P}'$. The total charge in a volume τ is given by

$$Q = \int_\tau \rho \, d\tau' \tag{1.3-9}$$

Then if ρ is known as a function of the coordinates of $\mathscr{P}'$, we can find $\mathbf{E}$ at $\mathscr{P}$ from

$$\mathbf{E}_\mathscr{P} = \frac{1}{4\pi\epsilon_0} \int_\tau \frac{\mathbf{1}_r \rho \, d\tau'}{r^2} \tag{1.3-10}$$

where $d\tau'$ is an element of volume at $\mathscr{P}'$ (Fig. 1.3g), τ is the entire volume containing the charge, and $\mathbf{1}_r$, ρ, and r are taken at the point $\mathscr{P}'$ at which $d\tau'$ is taken. (The Greek τ, tau, is used for volume since V will generally be used for potential, and v for velocity.)

The field at an arbitrary point outside a uniformly charged spherical shell is a more difficult example than the three above. Although the calculation is straightforward, and the interested reader may work it for himself, we shall postpone this example until we have developed two simpler methods. However, it is interesting to note that this problem is essentially the same as calculating the gravitational field outside a spherical body such as the earth or moon. It is reported that Newton had his gravitational

Fig. 1.3g. The field at $\mathscr{P}$ is a vector integral over the volume τ.

theory ready to publish except for proving that a spherical body acts like a point mass located at its center. It took him twenty years to develop the calculus to the point where he could prove this fact by integration, and only then did he publish his now famous theory.[6]

Problem 1.3a. Point charges of $+4.0$ and $+6.0$ microcoulombs, respectively, are located at the origin and at the point $(0.50$ m, $0)$ in an x–y plane. Find the direction and magnitude of **E** at the points $(0.50$ m, 0.90 m), $(1.0$ m, $0)$, and $(1.0$ m, -0.3 m$)$. Calculate the result for the last point both by components and by trigonometry.

Problem 1.3b. Find where **E** $= 0$ in the situation of Problem 1.3a. Also find where **E** $= 0$ if the $+6.0$ microcoulomb charge is changed to -6.0 microcoulombs.

Problem 1.3c. Charges of $+q$ and $-q$ are separated by a distance l. Find **E** at points a distance $r > \frac{1}{2}l$ from the midpoint of the line joining the charges (a) on the perpendicular bisector of this line; (b) on the extension of this line through the positive charge. Use your results to verify Eqs. 1.3–1.

Problem 1.3d. Find the direction and magnitude of **E** at the origin in an x–y–z space, if point charges are located as follows: -4.0 microcoulomb at $(0.15$ m, $0, 0)$; -5.0 microcoulomb at $(0, 0.40$ m, $0)$; and $+3.0$ micro-coulomb at $(0.20$ m, 0.20 m, 0.35 m$)$.

Problem 1.3e. Find E just outside a plane distribution of charge of effectively infinite extent that carries 1 electronic charge per square Ångstrom unit $(1 \text{ Å} = 10^{-10}$ m$)$. What acceleration would an electron experience in this field (mass of electron $= 9.11 \times 10^{-31}$ kg$)$? How long would it take the electron to acquire a velocity of 3×10^8 m/sec under this acceleration (neglect any relativity effects)?

The reader who has studied the Bohr theory of the hydrogen atom will find it instructive to compare this acceleration with the centripetal acceleration of an electron in the lowest state of a Bohr hydrogen atom.

Problem 1.3f. Find a formula for the field at a point on the axis of a uniformly charged circular disk of radius a. Show that as $a \to \infty$ the infinite plane result is obtained. Find E if $\sigma = 1.77 \times 10^{-8}$ coulomb/m^2, $a = 6$ cm, and z (distance of point from center) $= 8$ cm.

Problem 1.3g. Show that when z is very large, the formula of problem 1.3f is approximately the same as the result for a point charge (Coulomb's law).

---

[6] See, for instance, Sir William C. Dampier, *A History of Science*, 4th ed. Cambridge 1949, pp. 150–154; and Arthur Koestler, *The Sleepwalkers*, Grosset and Dunlap, New York, 1963, pp. 507–8.

Problem 1.3h. Suppose that the disk of Fig. 1.3f has a radius of 20 cm and carries a total charge of 3×10^{-9} coulomb. Find the field strength on the axis at a point 80 cm from the center of the disk.

Problem 1.3i. Find the field at a point on the axis of a disk of radius a, if $\sigma = br'^{-1} \cos^2 \phi$.

Problem 1.3j. Consider a general surface distribution σ, continuously variable on a continuously curved surface. Because of continuity, about any point $\mathscr{P}$ on the surface a circle of radius a can be drawn such that (1) σ varies by less than $\frac{1}{3}\%$ within the circle and (2) the maximum distance of points on the surface within the circle from a tangent plane constructed at $\mathscr{P}$ is less than $\frac{1}{3}\%$ of a. Hence the field at a height h above the surface produced by the charge within the circle differs from the uniform disk result by less than $\frac{2}{3}\%$ (actually considerably less, in general).

Find h so that the difference between the uniform disk result and the infinite plane result is less than $\frac{1}{3}\%$, so that the actual field is within 1% of Eq. 1.3–7.

Problem 1.3k. Prove explicitly that the horizontal components vanish in the calculation of Eq. 1.3–4 in the text.

1.4   Flux and the Gauss Flux Law

The first new method for calculating fields involves the concept of flux. With this concept we shall prove a general law, credited to Gauss, which is both of great use in calculating symmetrical fields and also a powerful tool for establishing some of the properties of conducting media.

The electric flux Φ_E through an elementary area S is defined as the product of the area and the component of field strength normal to that area. One direction through the surface must be specified as the positive normal (Fig. 1.4a). That is, $\Phi_E = ES \cos \theta$, where S is the area in square meters and θ is the angle between the direction of E and the positive normal to S. The MKS unit of flux is the newton-m²/coulomb.

The Gaussian or electrostatic unit of field strength is the dyne/statcoulomb, so the Gaussian unit of flux is the dyne-cm²/statcoulomb.

For instance, a rectangular surface of 0.20 m × 0.30 m (Fig. 1.4b) placed with its normal at an angle of 30° in a uniform field of 2000 newton/coulomb would have passing through it a flux of $0.06 \times 2000 \times \cos 30° = 60\sqrt{3} = 104$ newton-m²/coulomb.

It is customary and convenient to attribute the positive normal direction to the quantity S itself, and to write S as a vector $\mathbf{S}$, pointing in the direction defined as positive by an appropriate convention (Fig. 1.4c).

Then θ is the angle between two vectors, and the flux can be written as a scalar product of the two vectors[7]

$$\Phi_E = \mathbf{E} \cdot \mathbf{S}$$

If S is large or $\mathbf{E}$ varies considerably over it, we must break S into elementary areas ΔS, calculate for each one the flux $\Delta\Phi_E = \mathbf{E} \cdot \Delta\mathbf{S}$, and sum over all the $\Delta\mathbf{S}$. As a result, we define the flux through a general surface, plane or curved, by the integral

$$\Phi_E = \int_S \mathbf{E} \cdot d\mathbf{S} \qquad (1.4\text{--}1a)$$

For closed surfaces the outward direction is taken as positive; for bounded surfaces the sign convention is more or less arbitrary.

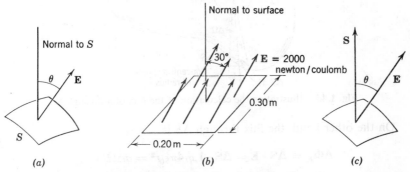

Fig. 1.4a,b,c. Illustrating electric flux Φ_E.

The real justification of any definition is its use in later work, and the usefulness of the concept of flux will appear shortly. However, we might say here that the name "flux" and the notion of adding elements of it together to get a total as in Eq. 1.4–1, are derived by analogy with the flow of a liquid or gas. If we substitute for the vector $\mathbf{E}$ a vector $\mathbf{v}$ representing the velocity of the particles of fluid at the point in question, the expression $\Delta\Phi_v = \mathbf{v} \cdot \Delta\mathbf{S}$ is equal to the product of the displacement per second perpendicular to the area ΔS, and the area. We see that $\Delta\Phi_v$ is the volume flowing per unit time through ΔS and that Φ_v is the volume flowing through S.

"Flux" is the Latin word for "flow" and describes here an accurate mathematical analogy. There is, of course, no actual motion associated with $\mathbf{E}$.

Let us consider a single point charge q. The field at a distance R from it is $\mathbf{E} = q\mathbf{1}_R/4\pi\epsilon_0 R^2$. On any sphere S_R drawn with q as center (Fig. 1.4d), $\mathbf{E}$ is normal to the surface, and E is constant all over the sphere.

[7] Cf. Appendix A.2, Eqs. A.2–5 to A.2–11.

Hence the total flux Φ_E through the sphere in the outward direction is $(q/4\pi\epsilon_0 R^2)(4\pi R^2) = q/\epsilon_0$, a result independent of R.

One would expect the same answer for an arbitrary closed surface S surrounding q. To show that this expectation is correct, divide all the space surrounding q into elementary conical volumes or elements of solid angle,[8] one of which is $\Delta\Omega$ in Fig. 1.4d. Let ΔS in Fig. 1.4d be the area cut out by $\Delta\Omega$ on the arbitrary surface S. Now ΔS is not in general oriented with its normal along the axis of the cone. The projection of ΔS along the axis, ΔS_r, is $\Delta S_r = \Delta S \cos\theta = \mathbf{\Delta S} \cdot \mathbf{1}_r$ and is equal to the area cut by $\Delta\Omega$ on a concentric sphere of radius r. Thus $\Delta\Omega = \mathbf{\Delta S} \cdot \mathbf{1}_r/r^2$, and is independent of the value of r.

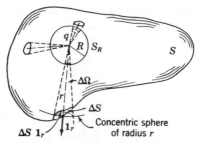

Fig. 1.4d. Illustrating the calculation of the flux of q through S.

On the other hand, the flux through ΔS is

$$\Delta\Phi_E = \mathbf{\Delta S} \cdot \mathbf{E} = \mathbf{\Delta S} \cdot \mathbf{1}_r q/4\pi\epsilon_0 r^2 = q\Delta\Omega/4\pi\epsilon_0$$

and in place of Eq. 1.4–1a we can write the flux through a finite portion of S in terms of the solid angle Ω subtended at q by that portion:

$$\Phi_E = \int d\Phi_E = q\Omega/4\pi\epsilon_0 \qquad (1.4\text{–}1b)$$

The entire flux through S is obtained by replacing $\Delta\Omega$ with $\int d\Omega = 4\pi$, regardless of the size or shape of the surface.

$$\Phi_E = \int d\Phi_E = q(4\pi)/4\pi\epsilon_0 = q/\epsilon_0$$

If q is negative, Φ_E is negative and inwardly directed.

---

[8] A solid angle Ω (Greek capital omega) is measured by the area it cuts out on a concentric sphere of unit radius. Since the area cut out on any sphere will be proportional to the square of the radius, we can alternatively say that $\Omega = S/R^2$, where S is the area cut out by the cone on an arbitrary sphere whose radius we denote by R. The entire solid angle around a point is one that includes an entire sphere, $\Omega = 4\pi R^2/R^2 = 4\pi$.

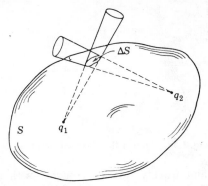

Fig. 1.4e.   Flux produced by two charges inside S.

By the distributive law of the scalar product and the principle of super-position, we can add the fluxes through any dS due to several distinct charges $q_1, q_2, \cdots$ (Fig. 1.4e):

$$\mathbf{E}_1 \cdot \mathbf{\Delta S} + \mathbf{E}_2 \cdot \mathbf{\Delta S} + \cdots = (\mathbf{E}_1 + \mathbf{E}_2 + \cdots) \cdot \mathbf{\Delta S} = \mathbf{E} \cdot \mathbf{\Delta S}$$

Hence we have the Gauss flux law, namely that the total flux through any closed surface due to any number of charges inside is

$$\Phi_E = \int\limits_{\text{closed } S} \mathbf{E} \cdot \mathbf{dS} = \frac{1}{\epsilon_0} \sum_n q_n \qquad (1.4\text{--}2)$$

$\sum_n q_n$ is to be replaced by appropriate integrals $\int \rho \, d\tau$, $\int \sigma \, dS$, or $\int \lambda \, dl$ for the various types of continuous distributions or by a combination of sums and integrals in complex cases, such as the case of a single point charge or a dipole outside a charged disk. Note that flux may be thought of as originating or "starting" on positive charges ("sources") and ending on negative charges ("sinks"), even though no motion is involved.

If a particular solid angle cuts a surface three or more times, as $\Delta\Omega'$ in Fig. 1.4f, the calculation will involve a cancellation of inwardly and outwardly directed parts in pairs. Charges outside the surface contribute nothing to Φ_E (Fig. 1.4g). The surfaces ("Gaussian surfaces") to which Eq. 1.4–2 applies are imaginary surfaces to be placed at the convenience of

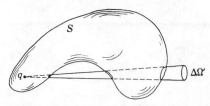

Fig. 1.4f.   Flux counted only once when $\Delta\Omega'$ intersects the surface more than once.

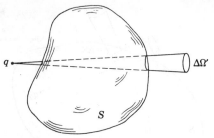

Fig. 1.4g.   No net flux from q external to S.

the investigator, and usually do not coincide with any real material surfaces.

Equation 1.4–2 can be used in cases of high symmetry to make simple and elegant calculations of fields. For instance, an isolated sphere of radius r_0 bearing a symmetrically distributed surface or volume charge of total amount Q must have a spherically symmetric field (Fig. 1.4h). Here E is a function of $\mathbf{r}$ only, and we have for a Gaussian sphere of radius $r > r_0$, $\Phi_E = E(4\pi r^2) = Q/\epsilon_0$ leading   to $E = Q/4\pi\epsilon_0 r^2$. The vector equation reads

$$\mathbf{E} = \frac{Q\mathbf{1}_r}{4\pi\epsilon_0 r^2} \qquad (1.4\text{–}3)$$

The field outside such a sphere is the same as that of a point charge equal in magnitude to the total charge on the sphere and located at its center. This is the theorem Newton waited so long to prove.

By Newton's third law of motion, which holds for charges at rest, we can also show that the force on a symmetrical spherical distribution of charge

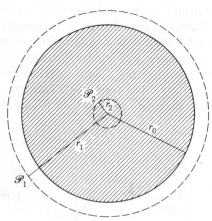

Fig. 1.4h.   Gaussian surfaces for a sphere, of radii r_1 and r_2 for points $\mathscr{P}_1$ and $\mathscr{P}_2$.

in any external field is the same as the force on the same total charge located at the center of the sphere (cf. Problem 1.4*a*).

Equation 1.4–3 applies, of course, to a point charge as a special case, and thus we have derived Coulomb's law from Gauss'. The two laws are logically equivalent. Note that the proof of Gauss' law combines the inverse square law for field strengths and the r^2 variation of the area included in a solid angle.

In contrast to 1.4–3, the field at a point inside the sphere is not the same as that for a point charge Q. Consider a new Gaussian surface of radius $r < r_0$. The same calculation as before now leads to

$$\mathbf{E} = Q_r \mathbf{1}_r / 4\pi\epsilon_0 r^2 \tag{1.4-4}$$

where Q_r is the total amount of charge within the Gaussian surface. That is to say, the charge lying between the spheres of radii r and r_0 produces

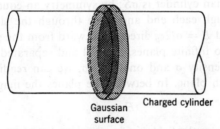

Fig. 1.4*i*. Gaussian surface for a cylinder.

no field within the radius r. In particular, a uniformly charged spherical surface has no field anywhere in its interior. On the other hand, if the charge density ρ is constant within the sphere, $Q_r = \frac{4}{3}\pi r^3 \rho$ and

$$\mathbf{E} = \rho r \mathbf{1}_r / 3\epsilon_0 \tag{1.4-5}$$

The interior field strength is proportional to the radius in this case.

For an infinite symmetrically charged cylinder, a Gaussian surface as in Fig. 1.4*i* may be used, and the field shown to be

$$\mathbf{E} = \lambda \mathbf{1}_r / 2\pi\epsilon_0 r \tag{1.4-6}$$

where λ is the total charge per unit length carried by the cylinder, and we have therefore the same result as in Eq. 1.3–4 (Problem 1.4*b*).

The result of Eq. 1.3–7 for a uniform, infinite plane distribution of charge ($\sigma = $ constant) may also be obtained in a simple way by use of the Gauss flux law. Let us use as a Gaussian surface a cylindrical surface perpendicular to the plane in question that cuts it in some area S and is capped by two planes each of the same area, parallel to the distribution of

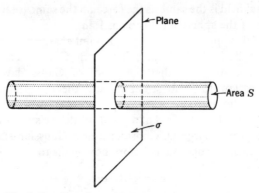

Fig. 1.4j. Gaussian surface for an infinite plane.

charge and equidistant from it on opposite sides (Fig. 1.4j). The charge inside the Gaussian cylinder is σS; by symmetry an equal amount of flux passes out through each end and none through the sides. Thus $\Phi_E = 2ES = \sigma S/\epsilon_0$ and $E = \sigma/2\epsilon_0$ directed outward from the surface.

If we have two infinite planes, parallel and separated by a distance h, one of charge density σ and one of $-\sigma$, we can readily add the fields produced by each plane. In between the planes the magnitudes add and

$$E = \sigma/\epsilon_0 \qquad (1.4\text{--}7)$$

Outside either plane the fields are in opposite directions and the resultant is zero (see Fig. 1.4k). This is the result for the field far from the edges in an ordinary plane-parallel condenser, to be treated in more detail later.

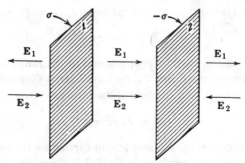

Fig. 1.4k. Combination of fields produced by two infinite planes.

Problem 1.4a. By considering first the force of a symmetrically charged sphere on a single external point charge, develop a rigorous argument for the statement that the force of *any* external field *on* such a sphere is the same as if all the charge in the sphere were at the center.

Problem 1.4b. Prove Eq. 1.4–6 for the field outside a cylindrically symmetric charge distribution.

Problem 1.4c. Find the field strength at a distance r from the axis of a ·cylindrically symmetric charge distribution when (a) ρ is constant out to a radius $r_0 > r$ and (b) ρ is proportional to the radius, out to a radius $r_0 > r$.

Problem 1.4d. Describe the symmetries of a sphere, an infinite right circular cylinder, and an infinite plane by giving the changes of coordinates (rotations, translations, reflections) that can be made without changing the signs and magnitudes of any physical quantities that may be associated with these figures. Use this description and the method of *reductio ad absurdum* to demonstrate the assertion in the text that the field outside a spherically symmetric charge distribution is directed along the radius and depends in magnitude only on R.

Problem 1.4e. Noting the result that a uniform spherical shell of charge has no field within it, use the Gauss flux law to derive directly a relation between the surface charge density and the field just outside the surface.

Problem 1.4f. Find the flux through a circle of radius a produced by a charge q on the axis of the circle at a distance z from its center, by integration over the circle. Use the result to prove that the solid angle subtended by the circle at q is $2\pi(1 - \cos\theta)$, where θ is the angle between the axis and a line from q to any point on the circle.

Problem 1.4g. Solve problem 1.4f, but take the integration over the portion of a spherical surface whose center is at q, bounded by the edge of the circle.

Problem 1.4h. Find the flux through the curved side of a right circular cylinder of length $2z$ and radius a, produced by a single charge q at its center.

Problem 1.4i. Find E at an arbitrary point inside a sphere of radius r_0 if $\rho(r) = br^2$, where b is a constant.

1.5 Differential-Equation Form of the Flux Law

For the case of volume distributions of charge, including the case $\rho = 0$ (vacuum), we can apply Gauss' flux law to an infinitesimal volume of space and obtain a relationship between the partial derivatives of the components of E with respect to the coordinates of a point in that volume and the charge density ρ at that same point. It is clear that each component of E can vary with all three coordinates. For instance, E_x for Eq. 1.4–3 is $Qx/4\pi\epsilon_0 r^3$ (components of $\mathbf{1}_r$ are given by Eq. A.2–4).

As shown in the appendix, the flux out per unit volume at a point is given by the divergence of a vector, Eq. A.2–21. Hence Gauss' law becomes

$$\text{div } \mathbf{E} = \mathbf{\nabla} \cdot \mathbf{E} = \left(\frac{\partial E_x}{\partial x} + \frac{\partial E_y}{\partial y} + \frac{\partial E_z}{\partial z}\right) = \frac{\rho}{\epsilon_0} \qquad (1.5\text{–}1)$$

In empty space, of course,

$$\mathbf{\nabla} \cdot \mathbf{E} = 0 \qquad (1.5\text{–}2)$$

The differential equation 1.5–1 will find uses in later sections in connection with the motion of charge in vacuum tubes and semiconductors, in which volume distributions of electrons give rise to variations of electric field. It is, of course, an expression of Coulomb's law and is one form of the first of Maxwell's famous equations for electromagnetic radiation.

At present, we wish to show that Eq. 1.5–2 holds in two cases we have considered. In the first place, a uniform plane distribution of charge produces a uniform field so that E_x, E_y, E_z are constants with respect to variations in x, y, and z. Hence all their derivatives vanish and div $\mathbf{E} = 0$. An exception to this rule occurs at the charged plane, where the field abruptly changes from $\sigma/2\epsilon_0$ in one direction to the same value in the opposite direction. If the normal to the plane is in the z-direction, we then have the result that $\partial E_z/\partial z$ is infinite at the plane, assuming the charge to be in a layer infinitesimally thin. However, the volume density of charge will also be infinite, and Eq. 1.5–1 is not violated. The case of a layer of finite thickness is considered in Problem 1.5a.

A second example is the field near a point charge or a symmetrically charged sphere, Eq. 1.4–3. The three components are $E_x = Qx/4\pi\epsilon_0 r^3$; $E_y = Qy/4\pi\epsilon_0 r^3$, $E_z = Qz/4\pi\epsilon_0 r^3$. To calculate div $\mathbf{E}$, note that

$$\partial r/\partial x = \frac{\partial}{\partial x}(x^2 + y^2 + z^2)^{\frac{1}{2}} = x/(x^2 + y^2 + z^2)^{\frac{1}{2}} = x/r$$

with corresponding relations for y and z. Hence

$$\frac{\partial E_x}{\partial x} + \frac{\partial E_y}{\partial y} + \frac{\partial E_z}{\partial z} = \frac{Q}{4\pi\epsilon_0}\left[\left(\frac{1}{r^3} - \frac{3x}{r^4}\cdot\frac{x}{r}\right) + \left(\frac{1}{r^3} - \frac{3y}{r^4}\cdot\frac{y}{r}\right)\right.$$
$$\left. + \left(\frac{1}{r^3} - \frac{3z}{r^4}\cdot\frac{z}{r}\right)\right]$$
$$= \frac{Q}{4\pi\epsilon_0}\left[\frac{3}{r^3} - \frac{3}{r^5}(x^2 + y^2 + z^2)\right] \equiv 0$$

It is interesting to reconstruct Gauss' law Eq. 1.4–2 from Eq. 1.5–1. Using the divergence theorem, Eq. A.2–22, we have on the one hand

$$\int_\tau (\mathbf{\nabla} \cdot \mathbf{E})\, d\tau = \int_S \mathbf{E} \cdot d\mathbf{S} = \Phi_E$$

and on the other, using Eq. 1.5–1,

$$\int_\tau (\nabla \cdot \mathbf{E})\, d\tau = \int_\tau \frac{\rho}{\epsilon_0}\, d\tau = \frac{Q}{\epsilon_0}$$

where Q is the total charge enclosed in the volume τ bounded by the surface S.

Problem 1.5a. A pair of parallel infinite planes which are separated by a distance $2z_0$ contain between them a uniform distribution of charge of density ρ. Using the Gauss law, find $\mathbf{E}$ at points inside and outside the pair of planes. Test the relation div $\mathbf{E} = \rho/\epsilon_0$ for your solution. Graph the magnitude of $\mathbf{E}$.

Problem 1.5b. Prove that the fields of Eqs. 1.4–5 and 1.4–6 obey Eq. 1.5–1.

Problem 1.5c. Find the charge density at a point (x, y, z) for the fields given by (a) $\mathbf{E} = b_1(x\mathbf{1}_x + y\mathbf{1}_y + z\mathbf{1}_z)/(x^2 + y^2 + z^2)^{\frac{1}{4}}$ and (b) $\mathbf{E} = b_2(x\mathbf{1}_x + y\mathbf{1}_y + z\mathbf{1}_z)(x^2 + y^2 + z^2)$ where b_1 and b_2 are constants.

Problem 1.5d. Solve problem 1.5c for the field $\mathbf{E}$

$$\mathbf{E} = b_3(\mathbf{1}_x \cos \alpha + \mathbf{1}_y \sin \alpha)(x \cos \alpha + y \sin \alpha)$$

where b_3 and α are constants.

Problem 1.5e. Prove that $\nabla \cdot \mathbf{1}_r = 2/r$ and that $\nabla \cdot \mathbf{r} = 3$.

1.6 Lines and Tubes of Force

A graphic representation of the electric field strength in a given region may be obtained by use of the concept of lines of force. Through any point in a field we may draw a short segment of a line having the direction of the field vector. If we imagine space to be filled with such segments, they will fit together to form continuous lines that are tangent to the field vectors $\mathbf{E}$. Alternatively, a single such line may be started at any point and continued until a discontinuity in the field is reached, which by Eq. 1.2–3 can only occur at the locations of charges. These lines are called lines of force ("lines of field" would be better but the historical terminology is generally adhered to).

A concept that is sometimes useful is that of a tube of force, which is a region bounded by a cylinder-like surface whose walls are composed of lines of force. A tube of force may have a regular or an irregular cross section (Fig. 1.6a).

The special significance of such a tube derives from the flux theorem. In a region free of charge ($\rho = 0$), the net flux through the sides and two ends of a section of such a tube is zero. The sides being lines of force and tangent to $\mathbf{E}$, there is no flux through them. Thus the flux in through one end of the tube is equal to the flux out through the other. Flux bears an analogy to the volume or mass flow of liquid through a pipe—it is "conserved" along a tube in charge-free regions of space. We can thus get a quantitative and graphic description of a field by considering all space to be occupied by such tubes, each carrying one unit of flux (or some convenient multiple, such as 10^{-4}, 10^{-8}, etc.). Each charge q thus is the "source" or starting point of q/ϵ_0 tubes, and each $-q'$ is the "sink" or end-point of q'/ϵ_0 tubes. Since the flux is a constant we can write, if each tube is sufficiently thin, $\Phi_E = ES = 10^{-8}$ say, where S is the cross-sectional area of a tube, so that $E = 10^{-8}/S$, or the field strength is inversely

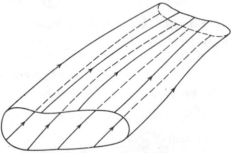

Fig. 1.6a.   A tube of force.

proportional to S. In fact, E can be measured by the number of tubes of flux per square meter.

Another method of representation is to draw a line of force down the center of each tube and count the lines per unit area. Since each line represents a definite amount of flux, the number of lines per unit area will be proportional to the flux density, that is to E itself. The tubes are not needed at all in this case. This method has the advantage that in certain cases one can actually draw diagrams with lines of force spaced quantitatively. The disadvantage of the use of lines is the difficulty of thinking of a fractional line, in contrast to the ease of imagining a tube of fractional flux content. However, the concepts of lines and tubes of force are chiefly of use as aids to the imagination, and the choice between them may be left to the reader.[9] It is important to note that in combining two fields by the principle of superposition, there is no simple geometric relation between the lines of force in the two separate fields and those of the combined fields.

[9] The line-of-force concept runs into the difficulty of indefinite circulation without closing when used for fields that have a circulatory or non-source character, such as the electric field of magnetic origin (Section 7.14), the magnetic induction **B** (Section 7.12), the displacement field **D** (Section 3.6), the magnetic field **H** (Section 8.5), and the vector potential **A** (Section 7.10).

Tubes of flux can be more readily combined than can lines of force, since flux is a scalar. However, the graphical superposition of fields is best carried out by methods to be described in Section 1.11.

In concluding this section, it is well to note that if Coulomb's law were not true, flux would not be conserved along a tube. In that case although we could still define the concepts of flux, of lines, and of tubes, they would lose much of their usefulness. Note also that a line of force gives the direction of the force and hence of the *acceleration* that would be experienced by a small charge if free to move at the point in question, but that the motion of the particle is in general along a quite different path, owing to inertia. In fact, particles moving in a uniform electric field follow parabolic

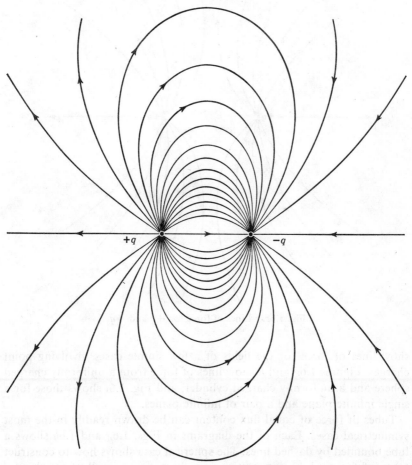

Fig. 1.6b.   Lines of force for $+q$ and $-q$.

paths in precise analogy to the motion of a mass point in a uniform gravitational field. (Cf. Problems 1.6a and 1.6b.) Note finally that a line of force can never intersect itself or any other line, for the direction of a line (the direction of the field) is uniquely defined at every point.

Careful study of accurately drawn field diagrams can provide considerable qualitative insight into the physics of electric fields. Figures 1.6b–f

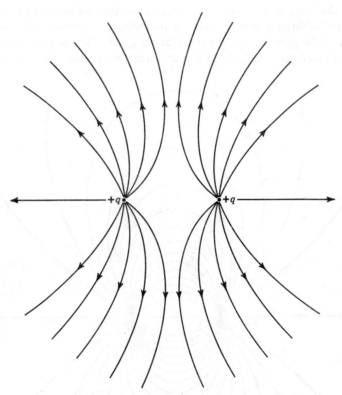

Fig. 1.6c.   Lines of force for $+q$ and $+q$.

show lines of force for the fields of a few simple cases involving point charges. Figures 1.6g and h show lines of force from a uniformly charged sphere and a uniformly charged cylinder, and Fig. 1.6i shows those for a single infinite plane and a pair of infinite planes.

Tubes of force of equal flux content can be drawn readily in the most symmetrical cases. Each of the diagrams in Figs. 1.6g and 1.6h shows a tube bounded by dashed lines. The spherical case shows how to construct tubes of force whose intersections on the sphere are all of equal area,

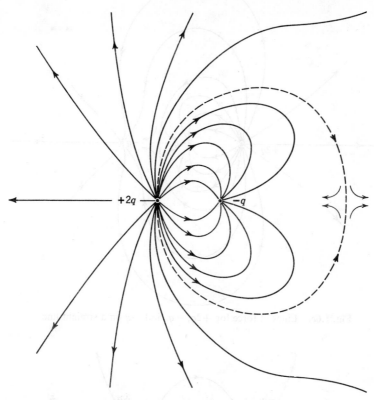

Fig. 1.6d.   Lines of force for $+2q$ and $-q$.

sides of these intersections being formed by planes through a common diameter of the sphere, equally spaced in angle, and by planes perpendicular to this diameter, equally spaced along it.

Problem 1.6a. A beam of electrons moving with a speed of 20×10^5 m/sec passes between a horizontal pair of plates that carry charge densities, plus and minus, of 5.0×10^{-10} coulomb/m^2 respectively. Assume that the field is the same as for an infinite set of plates, that the beam moves originally parallel to the plates, and that the beam leaves the field after passing a horizontal distance of 1 cm in it. What is the vertical deflection of the beam as it leaves the space between the plates, and what is its direction?

Problem 1.6b. A beam of electrons constrained to move parallel to the x–z plane enters through a narrow slit into a uniform field $\mathbf{E} = E_z \mathbf{1}_z$, at $z = 0$. At the entrance point the angular width of the beam is 1°. If the beam follows parabolic paths back to the plane at $z = 0$, at what average

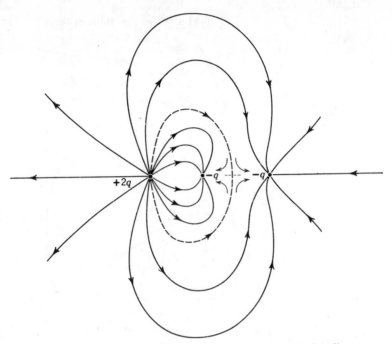

Fig. 1.6e. Lines of force for $+2q$, $-q$, and $-q$ on a straight line.

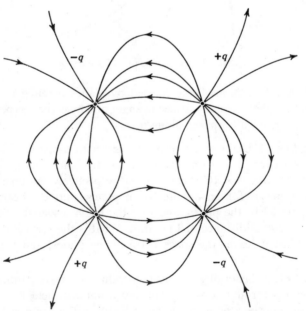

Fig. 1.6f. Lines of force for $+q$, $-q$, $+q$, $-q$ on the corners of a square.

28

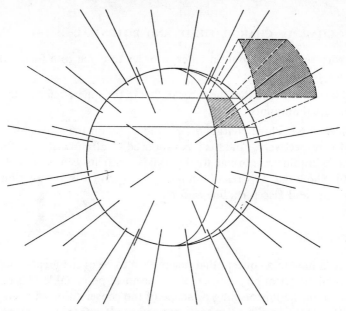

Fig. 1.6g. Lines of force and tube construction for a uniformly charged sphere.

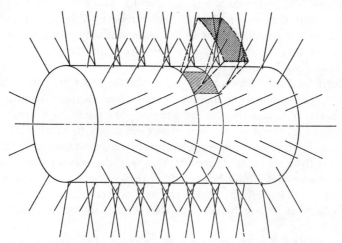

Fig. 1.6h. Lines of force and tube construction for a uniformly charged infinite cylinder.

Fig. 1.6i. Lines of force for one plane and for two oppositely charged planes.

angle with the z-axis should it enter in order to come to a focus when it gets back to $z = 0$?

Problem 1.6c. Prove that the tubes of flux in the sphere referred to above contain equal amounts of flux.

Problem 1.6d. Three charges q_1, q_2, and q_3 lie on the x-axis at $x = x_1$, x_2, and x_3 respectively. Find the flux produced by all three charges through a circle of radius r, normal to the x-axis, with its center at the point $(x, 0, 0)$. Show that this relation among Φ_E, r, and x is an equation for a tube of flux and also for a line of force.

1.7 Potential

We turn now to a concept that has proved to be of the greatest value in the field of electrical phenomena: the concept of potential.[10] This concept makes use of the far-reaching principle of the conservation of energy and leads to great simplification for a number of otherwise complicated calculations. The potential is a scalar quantity and is frequently easier to compute than the vector electric field strength, although it must be emphasized that calculations with the latter quantity can yield the same information that is contained in a knowledge of the former, since in general each can be found from the other.

We have used the field vector **E** to describe the space around a distribution of charge where other charges can experience forces. We now introduce a scalar V to describe the same region. The potential V at any point $\mathscr{P}$ is defined as the *work per unit charge* necessary to bring a small test charge to $\mathscr{P}$ from an arbitrary reference or zero point, usually taken as a point far from all other charges. It is, in fact, the added *potential energy per unit charge* that would be present in the system if a test charge were placed at $\mathscr{P}$. (The test charge should be small enough that the charges whose effects at $\mathscr{P}$ are being calculated would not be disturbed by its presence.)

Our definition of potential makes no mention of the path by which the test charge is brought from the reference point to $\mathscr{P}$. The fact that the work is independent of the path is equivalent to the fact that the law of conservation of energy applies here, and this will be proved in the next paragraphs.

---

[10] This concept was given its name by the mathematician George Green, in *An Essay on the Application of Mathematical Analysis to the Theories of Electricity and Magnetism.* T. Wheelhouse, Nottingham, England, 1828; reprinted by Stig Ekelöf, Göteborg, Sweden, 1958; also in *Mathematical Papers of the late George Green*, N. M. Ferrers, editor, Macmillan, London, 1871.

The reader will recall that work is defined as force times distance, provided the force is in the direction of the displacement. That is, if a force **F** acts on a body while the body suffers a displacement **dl**, the work dW is $(F \cos \theta) \, dl$; θ is the angle between **F** and **dl** so that $F \cos \theta$ is the component of **F** responsible for the work done. Note that we may also say that dW is F times the component of **dl** in the direction of **F**. We thus have another important physical application of the scalar product: $dW = \mathbf{F} \cdot \mathbf{dl}$, or for a path of finite length,

$$W = \int_l \mathbf{E} \cdot \mathbf{dl}$$

where the integral is a line integral taken along the path over which the body is moved.

For the electric case, the work per unit charge is to be calculated from the force per unit charge. Furthermore, in calculating potential energy we must remember that the work is done by a mechanical force that opposes the electric force. (In order to avoid consideration of any kinetic energy that might be acquired by a moving charge, we shall assume that the mechanical and electrical force just balance each other, once the charge has been set into motion.) Thus we must replace **F** by $-\mathbf{E}$, and write

$$V_{\mathscr{P}} = - \int_{\mathscr{P}_0}^{\mathscr{P}} \mathbf{E} \cdot \mathbf{dl} \qquad (1.7\text{--}1)$$

$\mathscr{P}_0$ is the reference point, and $\mathscr{P}$ is the point at which the potential is desired. The unit of potential in the MKS system is the joule/coulomb, which is called a volt[11]

It will be noted that it is really potential difference (PD) that is defined and measured. In fact, we can derive from 1.7–1 an expression for any two points $\mathscr{P}$ and $\mathscr{P}'$:

$$V_{\mathscr{P}} - V_{\mathscr{P}'} = - \int_{\mathscr{P}'}^{\mathscr{P}} \mathbf{E} \cdot \mathbf{dl} \qquad (1.7\text{--}2)$$

The potential at a point involves an arbitrariness due to the freedom of choice of the reference point $\mathscr{P}_0$, but potential difference has no such arbitrariness. The minus sign in Eqs. 1.7–1 and 1.7–2 can most easily be

---

[11] In most considerations dealing with the atomic aspect of matter, it is convenient to measure charge in units of e and potential in volts. This leads to the introduction of a new energy unit, the electron-volt (abbreviated ev), which is the work done in taking a charge e through a PD of one volt. Clearly 1 ev = 1.602×10^{-19} joule = 1.602×10^{-12} erg.

kept in mind if we remember the analogous case of gravity: potential energy increases as we go up, in a direction opposite to the force.

Let us calculate the potential at a point $\mathscr{P}$ near an isolated point charge q, using for $\mathscr{P}_0$ an arbitrary point. (See Fig. 1.7a.)

We may write $\mathbf{E} \cdot \mathbf{dl}$ as $E(dl \cos \theta) = E \, dr'$ where dr' is the change in the distance from q of the test charge δq. Thus

$$V = -\int_{\mathscr{P}_0}^{\mathscr{P}} \mathbf{E} \cdot \mathbf{dl} = -\int_{r_0}^{r} E \, dr' = -\int_{r_0}^{r} \frac{q \, dr'}{4\pi\epsilon_0 r'^2}$$

$$= \frac{-q}{4\pi\epsilon_0}\left(-\frac{1}{r'}\right)\Big|_{r_0}^{r} = \frac{q}{4\pi\epsilon_0}\left(\frac{1}{r} - \frac{1}{r_0}\right)$$

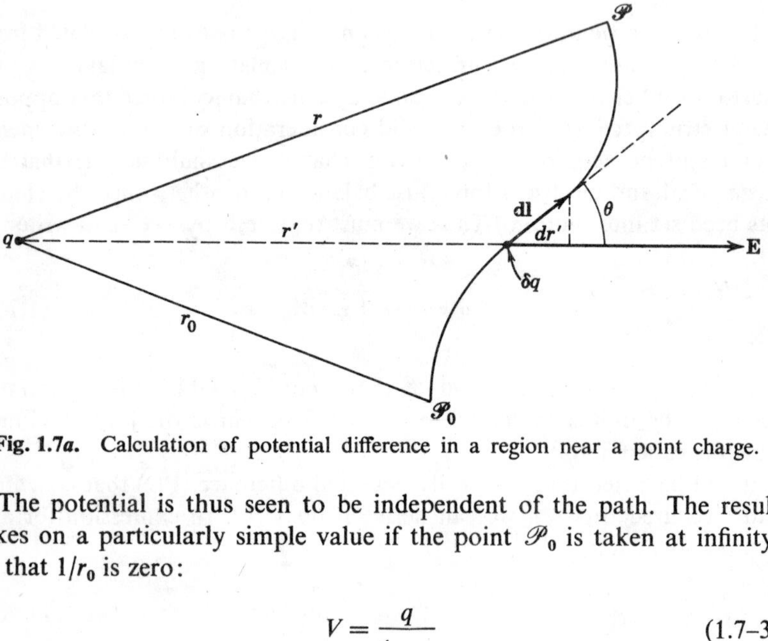

Fig. 1.7a. Calculation of potential difference in a region near a point charge.

The potential is thus seen to be independent of the path. The result takes on a particularly simple value if the point $\mathscr{P}_0$ is taken at infinity, so that $1/r_0$ is zero:

$$V = \frac{q}{4\pi\epsilon_0 r} \qquad (1.7\text{--}3)$$

This convention for $\mathscr{P}_0$ will be generally used whenever feasible. In practice, it means that in dealing with a system of charges, infinity is taken to be any point situated at a distance sufficiently large compared to the dimensions of the system (which must include all points at which values of V and $\mathbf{E}$ are desired) that resulting errors are less than the desired limits of experimental accuracy.

The potential at a point $\mathscr{P}$ in a system of charges is the algebraic sum of the potentials produced by each charge separately, as can be seen by using the superposition principle for $\mathbf{E}$ in 1.7–1. When $\mathscr{P}_0$ is taken at infinity, the summation becomes especially simple, so we write in general

$$V = -\int_{\infty}^{\mathscr{P}} \mathbf{E} \cdot d\mathbf{l} \tag{1.7–4}$$

and find

$$V = -\int_{\infty}^{\mathscr{P}} \left(\sum_n \frac{q_n \mathbf{1}_{rn}}{4\pi\epsilon_0 r_n'^2} \right) \cdot d\mathbf{l} = \frac{-1}{4\pi\epsilon_0} \int_{\infty}^{\mathscr{P}} \left(\sum_n \frac{q_n\, dr_n'}{r_n'^2} \right)$$

so that

$$V = \frac{1}{4\pi\epsilon_0} \sum_n \frac{q_n}{r_n} \tag{1.7–5}$$

In these expressions, r_n' is the variable distance of the test charge δq from the nth charge q_n of the given system, and r_n is the distance of point $\mathscr{P}$, the final position of δq, from q_n. This result shows that V is independent of the path used to calculate it regardless of the number of charges and thus proves the validity of the energy conservation law for all distributions of charges at rest.

If we consider two different arbitrary paths from $\mathscr{P}_0$ to $\mathscr{P}$, we can calculate a closed-loop line integral of $\mathbf{E} \cdot d\mathbf{l}$ by reversing the sign for one of the two chosen paths. The result is a more direct expression of the law of conservation of energy:

$$\oint \mathbf{E} \cdot d\mathbf{l} = 0 \tag{1.7–6}$$

where the $\oint$ sign refers to a closed-loop line integral and applies here to an *arbitrary* loop. In general, the integral $\oint \mathbf{A} \cdot d\mathbf{l}$ for any arbitrary vector $\mathbf{A}$ is called the circulation of $\mathbf{A}$ around the path in question. The circulation of $\mathbf{E}$ is always zero, which means that any charged particle that executes motion in a closed loop under the action of electrostatic forces will suffer no net change in energy.

The significance of the conservation property of V may be seen by comparison with frictional work. We can write for the latter $W = \int_{\mathscr{P}_0}^{\mathscr{P}} \mathbf{F} \cdot d\mathbf{l}$, and since the friction force $\mathbf{F}$ always opposes the motion, $\mathbf{F} \cdot d\mathbf{l}$ is always negative, regardless of which direction is followed along a given path. Furthermore, since F is often roughly constant, the amount of frictional work will be larger for the more circuitous routes from $\mathscr{P}_0$ to $\mathscr{P}$. The integral around a closed loop obviously cannot vanish—friction forces do not conserve mechanical energy.

Equation 1.7–5 can be written in forms suitable for continuous distributions of charge, exactly as in the case of Eqs. 1.3–3, 1.3–6, and 1.3–10 for the field strength. For line, surface, and volume charge densities λ, σ, and ρ, we have

$$V = \frac{1}{4\pi\epsilon_0} \int_{\text{line}\,l} \frac{\lambda\,dl'}{r'} \qquad (1.7\text{–}7a)$$

$$V = \frac{1}{4\pi\epsilon_0} \int_{\text{surface}\,S} \frac{\sigma\,dS'}{r'} \qquad (1.7\text{–}7b)$$

$$V = \frac{1}{4\pi\epsilon_0} \int_{\text{volume}\,\tau} \frac{\rho\,d\tau'}{r'} \qquad (1.7\text{–}7c)$$

We shall illustrate the formulas in Eq. 1.7–7 by finding the potential due to a spherically symmetrical distribution of charge, without using the known value for $\mathbf{E}$ in this case, Eqs. 1.4–3 and 1.4–4.

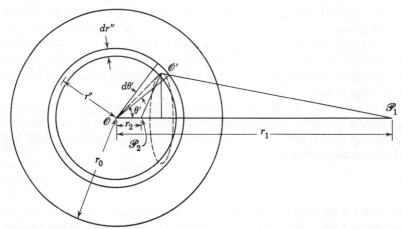

Fig. 1.7b. Calculation of the potential for a spherical distribution of charge.

Consider a sphere of radius r_0, filled with charge of density $\rho(r'')$, a function of r'' only. We calculate the potential at a point $\mathscr{P}_1$ (Fig. 1.7b) at a distance $r_1 > r_0$ from the center, and at $\mathscr{P}_2$ a distance $r_2 < r_0$ from the center. Let us first divide the sphere into spherical shells and calculate the potential produced by one of them of radius[12] r'' and thickness dr''. The charge per unit area of this shell is $\rho(r'')\,dr''$, so if we write $\rho\,dr'' = \sigma$, we have a surface distribution problem with σ uniform over the sphere and could use Eq. 1.7–7b.

We can specialize still further and divide the shell into rings, coaxial with the line $\mathscr{O}\mathscr{P}_2\mathscr{P}_1$ of cross section $r''\,d\theta'\,dr''$ and radius $r'' \sin\theta'$ (see

---

[12] For clarity in what follows, we shall temporarily assume $\mathscr{P}_2$ to be inside the shell ($r'' > r_2$). The reader can readily handle the case $r'' < r_2$ which we shall shortly need, by using the treatment for $\mathscr{P}_1$.

Fig. 1.7*b*). For such a ring, the linear density $\lambda = \sigma r'' \, d\theta' = \rho r'' \, dr'' \, d\theta'$; for this case, we can use Eq. 1.7–7*a*. The value of r', that is of $\mathcal{O}\mathcal{P}_2$ or $\mathcal{O}'\mathcal{P}_1$, may be found from the law of cosines. Since r' is constant for all points along a ring, the integral to be calculated is just $\int dl$, the circumference of the circle, so the potential of the ring at $\mathcal{P}_1$ is

$$
\begin{aligned}
V_{\text{ring},1} &= \frac{\lambda(2\pi r'' \sin\theta')}{4\pi\epsilon_0(r''^2 + r_1{}^2 - 2r''r_1\cos\theta')^{\frac{1}{2}}} \\
&= \frac{\rho r''^2 \sin\theta' \, d\theta' \, dr''}{2\epsilon_0(r''^2 + r_1{}^2 - 2r''r_1\cos\theta')^{\frac{1}{2}}}
\end{aligned}
\tag{1.7–8}
$$

with r_2 instead of r_1 for $V_{\text{ring},2}$.

To get the potential produced by the whole shell, we must integrate this result over θ' from 0 to π, which will result in covering the entire sphere just once by ring elements. We have

$$
\begin{aligned}
V_{\text{shell},1} &= \frac{\rho r''^2 dr''}{2\epsilon_0} \int_0^\pi \frac{\sin\theta' \, d\theta'}{(r''^2 + r_1{}^2 - 2r''r_1\cos\theta')^{\frac{1}{2}}} \\
&= \frac{\rho r''^2 \, dr''}{2\epsilon_0}\left[\frac{(r''^2 + r_1 - 2r''r_1\cos\theta')^{\frac{1}{2}}}{r''r_1}\right]_0^\pi
\end{aligned}
\tag{1.7–9}
$$

wherein r_1 is to be replaced by r_2 to get $V_{\text{shell},2}$. When we evaluate the indefinite integral in brackets at the indicated limits, we have the problem of which sign of square root to take. We must remember that the r' in Eq. 1.7–7 is always a positive number, so that the radicals in Eq. 1.7–9 must be positive. When $\theta' = \pi$, the expression is $(r''^2 + r_1{}^2 + 2r''r_1)^{\frac{1}{2}}$, clearly equal to $r'' + r_1$. When $\theta' = 0$, we have $(r''^2 + r_1{}^2 - 2r''r_1)^{\frac{1}{2}}$, which is either $r'' - r_1$ or $r_1 - r''$. To get a positive result for $\mathcal{P}_1$ we use $r_1 - r''$, whereas for $\mathcal{P}_2$ we use $r'' - r_2$. Thus

$$
V_{\text{shell},1} = \frac{\rho r''^2 \, dr''}{2\epsilon_0}\left[\frac{(r_1 + r'') - (r_1 - r'')}{r''r_1}\right] = \frac{\rho r''^2 \, dr''}{\epsilon_0 r_1} = \frac{q}{4\pi\epsilon_0 r_1}
\tag{1.7–10a}
$$

and

$$
V_{\text{shell},2} = \frac{\rho r''^2 \, dr''}{2\epsilon_0}\left[\frac{(r_2 + r'') - (r'' - r_2)}{r''r_2}\right] = \frac{\rho r'' \, dr''}{\epsilon_0} = \frac{q}{4\pi\epsilon_0 r''}
\tag{1.7–10b}
$$

using $q = \int\sigma \, dS = 4\pi r''^2\rho \, dr''$ for the total charge on the shell. We see that outside a shell the potential is the same as that of a single point charge at $\mathcal{O}$, whereas inside the potential is *constant*, i.e., independent of r_2. It is everywhere equal to the value it has at the surface of the shell where $r_2 = r''$. This result agrees with that of p. 19 for such a shell—if $\mathbf{E}$ is zero inside, no work would be done on moving a small test charge about. Such a region of constant potential is called an *equipotential volume*. A surface of constant potential, such as, in this case, any spherical surface with center at $\mathcal{O}$, is similarly called an *equipotential surface*.

The extension of the calculation to the entire sphere of Fig. 1.7*b* is now easy. For a point $\mathcal{P}_1$, we can add all the shells into which the sphere can be divided and find

$$V_1 = \frac{Q}{4\pi\epsilon_0 r_1}; \qquad r_1 \geqslant r_0 \qquad\qquad (1.7\text{--}11)$$

where Q is all the charge in the sphere. For $\mathcal{P}_2$, we have two parts for V:

$$V_2 = \frac{Q_2}{4\pi\epsilon_0 r_2} + \frac{1}{\epsilon_0} \int_{r_2}^{r_0} \rho(r'')r''\,dr''; \qquad r_2 \leqslant r_0 \qquad (1.7\text{--}12)$$

where the first term includes all the charge Q_2 situated within a radius r_2 and the second is an integral over Eq. 1.7–10*b* for $r'' \geqslant r_2$. The details of

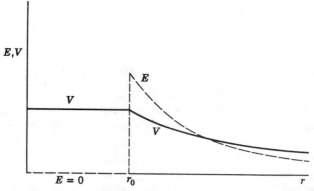

Fig. 1.7c. E and V plotted against r for a spherical shell.

the calculation are not particularly instructive, and specific examples are left to Problems 1.7*c* and *d*.

We have shown in this example the power of the integral calculus to provide in a straightforward way an answer to a physical problem in which a discontinuity appears—E is discontinuous at the surface of the shell, and the derivative of V with respect to r is discontinuous. More advanced work in electromagnetic theory involves many such integrals. Figure 1.7*c* shows a plot of E and V against r for a uniformly charged spherical shell.

There are some occasions when it is desired to find V directly from its definition Eq. 1.7–1, instead of from the charge distributions as in Eqs. 1.7–7. The case of the point charge, Eq. 1.7–3, is of course the simplest example. Sometimes the field **E** is already known; sometimes it is easier to calculate than V. As examples we shall take the infinite plane and infinite line distributions dealt with in Eqs. 1.3–7 and 1.3–4 respectively. If for the plane we choose as origin a point $\mathscr{P}_0$ at a distance z_0 from the plane, we find that at a point $\mathscr{P}$, whose distance is z on the same side of the plane,

$$V = -\int_{z_0}^{z} E_z\, dz = -\frac{\sigma}{2\epsilon_0}(z - z_0) \qquad (1.7\text{–}13)$$

As z_0 approaches infinity, this result becomes infinite, a difficulty that reflects merely the impossibility of having a truly infinite plane distribution of charge! However, as illustrated in Problem 1.3h, a finite plane has, to any desired approximation, the same field as an infinite plane for points sufficiently close to the plane compared to their distance from its edges. Equation 1.7–13 is thus valid if z and z_0 are both small enough.

If z is on the other side of the plane, we have to calculate the integral in two parts because of the discontinuity at the plane. It is left to the reader to get an expression for this case (Problem 1.7f).

For the case of an infinite line of charge, a similar difficulty arises about the potential at infinity. For finite points at distances r_0 and r from the line, it is easy to prove from Eq. 1.3–4 that

$$V = -\int_{r_0}^{r} \mathbf{E} \cdot \mathbf{dl} = \frac{\lambda}{2\pi\epsilon_0} \ln \frac{r_0}{r} \qquad (1.7\text{–}14)$$

Suppose we have two long parallel wires with charge densities $+\lambda$ and $-\lambda$. By symmetry, the plane that is the locus of points equidistant from the two wires is an equipotential. This plane extends to infinity and hence may properly be taken as the zero equipotential. Using Eq. 1.7–14 for the two wires, with r_0 equal to one-half the distance between them, we find that the potential at a point $\mathscr{P}$, at a distance r_1 from the positive wire and r_2 from the negative, (Fig. 1.7d) is given by:

$$V = \frac{\lambda}{2\pi\epsilon_0} \ln \frac{r_2}{r_1} \qquad (1.7\text{–}15)$$

Clearly the potential is positive for points nearer the positive wire, and vice versa.

The calculation of the equipotentials and lines of force for this case is of considerable importance and will be taken up in Chapter 4 in connection with calculations involving charged conducting surfaces.

Let us note in conclusion of this section that the existence of the potential does *not* depend on the inverse square law but does depend on the principle of superposition and on the existence of a force law giving a radial force that depends only on the distance r between point charges. Potentials can be defined, for instance, for inverse cube fields or any other power.

In addition to the existence of the potential, the fact that makes the law of conservation of energy hold in electrostatics is that one charge can move about without necessarily having work done on the other charges—they only need to be sufficiently fixed in position. When uniquely defined scalar potentials do not exist, it also happens that one system (charge or

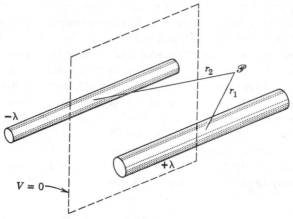

Fig. 1.7d. Illustrating the calculation of the potential for a pair of infinite cylinders.

current) cannot move without work necessarily being done on other systems (see Section 7.18).

The electrostatic and Gaussian unit of potential is the erg/statcoulomb or statvolt. One statvolt is readily seen to be equal to nearly 300 v—more exactly, 299.793 v.

Problem 1.7a. Find the potential at the points in problem 1.3a at which **E** was to be calculated.

Problem 1.7b. Find the value of V at the point at which $\mathbf{E} = 0$ when point charges of $+4.0$ and $+6.0$ microcoulombs are located at $(0, 0)$ and $(0.50m, 0)$ in the x–y plane, as in Problem 1.3b. Find also the value of V at the four points which are 0.02 m away from the point where $\mathbf{E} = 0$, in the positive and negative x and y directions. Describe the variation of V in the neighborhood of this point.

Problem 1.7c. Find the potential at an arbitrary point inside a uniformly charged sphere, by evaluating Eq. 1.7–12.

Problem 1.7d. Find the potential at an arbitrary point inside a symmetrically charged sphere when (a) $\rho(r'') = b_1 r''$, $r'' \leqslant r_0$; (b) $\rho(r'') = b_2/r''$,

$r'' \leqslant r_0$; and (c) $\rho(r'') = b_3 r'' e^{-b_4 r''}$, $r'' \leqslant r_0 [\rho(r'')$ is to be taken as zero for $r'' \geqslant r_0]$.

Problem 1.7e. Calculate the potential on the axis of a uniformly charged disk (cf. problem 1.3f).

Problem 1.7f. Complete the calculation referred to in the text for the PD between two points on opposite sides of an infinite uniformly charged plane. For an arbitrary z_0, sketch a plot of V against z as z varies from $-2z_0$ to $+2z_0$. Also plot E_z for this case.

Problem 1.7g. Find the potential as a function of z for the thick infinite slab of charge described in Problem 1.5a, taking $V = 0$ at the center of the slab. Sketch a graph of $V(z)$.

Problem 1.7h. Two parallel infinite wires carry equal and opposite uniform line distributions of charge. The wires are 10 cm apart. If the PD is 8 v between two points whose distances to the two wires are respectively 6 cm and 8 cm, and 8 cm and 6 cm, find the value of λ.

Problem 1.7i. A "double layer" at an electrode-solution interface in a certain chemical cell consists of plane layers of positive and negative charge, each of surface density 1.0 electronic unit per 100 square angstroms (1 angstrom = 10^{-10} m) separated by a distance of 1.2 Ångstroms. Find the PD between the two layers.

Problem 1.7j. A sphere of radius 2.0 m is uniformly filled out to half its radius with negative charge of density 9.1×10^{-6} coulombs/m³. The remainder is filled uniformly with positive charge of density 1.3×10^{-6} coulomb/m³. Find the potential as a function of r, inside and outside the sphere. Find the work done in taking an electron from the center of the sphere to its edge.

Problem 1.7k. Suppose **E** is given by $\mathbf{E} = (300x + 500y)\mathbf{1}_x + (500x - 400)\mathbf{1}_y - 300z\mathbf{1}_z$. Find the PD between the origin and the point $(0.90m, -0.60m, 0)$ using two different paths of integration.

Problem 1.7l. Find the potential at a point $(x, y, 0)$ outside a line of charge of constant density λ which extends along the x axis from $x = 0$ to $x = a$.

Problem 1.7m. Find the work done in taking an electron from the point $(2a, 0, 0)$ to the point $(0.5a, 2a, 0)$ in the example of Problem 1.7l, if $\lambda = 8.85 \times 10^{-12}$ coulombs/m and $a = 50$ cm.

Problem 1.7n. What fraction of the work done in taking an electron to infinity from the surface of a spherical distribution of total charge Q and radius a is performed in taking the electron to a radius na where $n > 1$?

Problem 1.7o. Find the potential for the same circumstances and by the same method as were involved in Eqs. 1.3–1.

1.8   The Curl of E

We have considered in Section 1.5 the differential-equation expression for the flux law. We turn now to a similar expression for the conservative property expressed in Eq. 1.7–6, namely the vanishing of the circulation $\oint \mathbf{E} \cdot \mathbf{dl}$.

In Appendix A.2 it is shown that for any vector $\mathbf{A}$ that varies from point to point, another vector called **curl A** can be constructed whose component in any direction is the circulation of the vector $\mathbf{A}$ per unit area around a small area whose normal is in that direction. If $\oint \mathbf{E} \cdot \mathbf{dl} = 0$ for any closed path, **curl E** must vanish. Using Eq. A.2–41a for the Cartesian components, we can write

$$\left.\begin{aligned}
(\text{curl } E)_x &= \frac{\partial E_z}{\partial y} - \frac{\partial E_y}{\partial z} = 0 \\[6pt]
(\text{curl } E)_y &= \frac{\partial E_x}{\partial z} - \frac{\partial E_z}{\partial x} = 0 \\[6pt]
(\text{curl } E)_z &= \frac{\partial E_y}{\partial x} - \frac{\partial E_x}{\partial y} = 0
\end{aligned}\right\} \tag{1.8–1}$$

In terms of the vector operator ∇, we write, simply,

$$\textbf{curl E} = \nabla \times \mathbf{E} = 0 \tag{1.8–2}$$

Using Stokes' theorem, (A.2–42), we can reverse the argument and show that, if **curl E** $= 0$, then $\oint \mathbf{E} \cdot \mathbf{dl} = 0$ around any closed path. In fact, we have

$$\oint_l \mathbf{E} \cdot \mathbf{dl} = \int_S \nabla \times \mathbf{E} \cdot \mathbf{dS} = 0 \tag{1.8–3}$$

In the previous section we said that we can define a potential whenever the field depends only on the vector distances from the point charges that are its sources. We can now generalize by saying that the vanishing of **curl E** is the condition that a potential exists, i.e., that the line integral $\int_{\mathscr{P}_1}^{\mathscr{P}_2} \mathbf{E} \cdot \mathbf{dl}$ between two points $\mathscr{P}_1$ and $\mathscr{P}_2$ is independent of the path.

As a simple example, let us assume that $\mathbf{E}$ lies entirely in the x direction in a certain region. Then from Eq. 1.8–1 we find, setting $E_y = E_z = 0$,

$$\frac{\partial E_x}{\partial z} = \frac{\partial E_x}{\partial y} = 0$$

so that E_x cannot vary in the y and z directions. If ρ is also zero in this region, then from $\nabla \cdot \mathbf{E} = 0$ we have

$$\frac{\partial E_x}{\partial x} = 0$$

so that E_x does not vary with x either. If the electric field has a constant direction in a certain region, it also has a constant magnitude throughout the region.

It is not hard to verify Eq. 1.8–1 for the various fields we have already calculated (cf. Problems 1.8a, b, c).

Problem 1.8a. Using Cartesian coordinates, verify Eq. 1.8–1 for the field of a uniform spherical volume distribution of charge, both inside and outside the radius r_0 of the sphere.

Problem 1.8b. Solve Problem 1.8a for a long uniformly charged cylinder.

Problem 1.8c. Repeat Problems 1.8a and 1.8b using, respectively, spherical and cylindrical coordinates.

Problem 1.8d. Test for vanishing of **curl E**, the fields given by (a) $\mathbf{E} = b_1\{3x^2yz\mathbf{1}_x + [x^3z + yz^2(yz)^{1/2}]\mathbf{1}_y + [x^3y + y^2z(yz)^{1/2}]\mathbf{1}_z\}$, (b) $\mathbf{E} = b_2(y\mathbf{1}_x - x\mathbf{1}_y)$, and (c) $\mathbf{E} = b_3[y\mathbf{1}_x/(x^2 + y^2)^{3/2} - x\mathbf{1}_y/(x^2 + y^2)^{3/2}]$. ($b_1$, b_2, and b_3 are constants.) Evaluate **curl E** in the cases in which it does not vanish.

Problem 1.8e. Find the charge density ρ at a point (x, y, z) for each of the fields given in Problem 1.8d.

Problem 1.8f. Calculate $\int \mathbf{E} \cdot \mathbf{dl}$ from the origin to a point x_0, y_0 in the x-y plane for the field $\mathbf{E} = b_2(y\mathbf{1}_x - x\mathbf{1}_y)$ along three different rectilinear paths: (a) from $(0, 0)$ to $(0, y_0)$; (b) from $(0, 0)$ to $(x_0, 0)$ to (x_0, y_0); (c) from $(0, 0)$ along a radius directly to (x_0, y_0).

Problem 1.8g. Solve Problem 1.8f, but use cylindrical coordinates and choose two different paths composed of radii and arcs of circles.

1.9 Potential Gradient

We have seen how to find the potential V if the field $\mathbf{E}$ is known (Eq. 1.7–1) and how to find V if the charge distribution is known (Eqs. 1.7–5, 1.7–6, and 1.7–7). We have also shown how to find $\mathbf{E}$ from the charge distribution (Eqs. 1.3–1, 1.3–2, and 1.3–4). Let us show how to find $\mathbf{E}$ if V is known.

The field $\mathbf{E}$ is a vector, whereas V is a scalar. We should hence be able to calculate *components* of $\mathbf{E}$ from a knowledge of V. In fact, if we wish to know the force per unit charge in a given direction at a given point, we may imagine a small test charge δq to move a distance dl in the given direction. Then, using our knowledge of V as a function of position, we calculate the change dV in the potential energy per unit charge. If the field component is E_l, we have $dV = -E_l\,dl$ (potential *decreases* in the direction of the field). Hence, $E_l = -dV/dl$, or as it is usually written to indicate that only one specific direction is involved,

$$E_l = -\frac{\partial V}{\partial l} \qquad (1.9\text{-}1)$$

We see that the component of field strength in a given direction is the negative of the directional derivative of the potential in that direction, evaluated at the point in question. Equation 1.9–1 is the inverse of Eq. 1.7–1.

In particular we can find the Cartesian components of $\mathbf{E}$:

$$E_x = -\partial V/\partial x, \qquad E_y = -\partial V/\partial y, \qquad E_z = -\partial V/\partial z \qquad (1.9\text{-}2)$$

and hence may construct the vector $\mathbf{E}$:

$$\mathbf{E} = -\left(\mathbf{1}_x\frac{\partial V}{\partial x} + \mathbf{1}_y\frac{\partial V}{\partial y} + \mathbf{1}_z\frac{\partial V}{\partial z}\right) \qquad (1.9\text{-}3a)$$

$$= -\left(\mathbf{1}_x\frac{\partial}{\partial x} + \mathbf{1}_y\frac{\partial}{\partial y} + \mathbf{1}_z\frac{\partial}{\partial z}\right)V \qquad (1.9\text{-}3b)$$

$$= -\nabla V \equiv -\mathbf{grad}\,V \qquad (1.9\text{-}3c)$$

in accordance with Eqs. A.2–15. The name "gradient" is derived from the analogy of gravitational potential, as expressed in our use of the gradient for the slope of a hillside. It is clear from Eqs. 1.9–3, as well as from the definition of the volt, that the units in which E is measured may be called volts/meter, which is in fact the most common designation.

In terms of the gradient, we can write for any component E_l,

$$E_l = -\frac{\partial V}{\partial l} = -\nabla V \cdot \mathbf{1}_l \qquad (1.9\text{-}4)$$

(see Eq. A.2–18) and conversely for a differential or increment of V, corresponding to a vector displacement $\mathbf{dl}$,

$$dV = \nabla V \cdot \mathbf{dl} = -\mathbf{E} \cdot \mathbf{dl} = -E_l\,dl \qquad (1.9\text{-}5)$$

(see Eq. A.2–19).

An important proposition, generally referred to as Earnshaw's theorem,[13]

---

[13] S. Earnshaw, *Trans. Cambridge Phil. Soc.*, **7**, 97–112 (1842), showed that particles in an elastic medium cannot be held in equilibrium by inverse-square forces. J. C. Maxwell, *Treatise on Electricity and Magnetism* 2nd or 3rd ed., Clarendon Press, Oxford, 1881 and 1904, Dover, New York, reprint, 1962, article 116, applied the theorem to electrostatics, including application to forces on conductors. Cf. W. T. Scott, "Who Was Earnshaw?", *Am. J. Phys.* **27**, 418–9 (1959).

states that an isolated charge cannot remain in stable equilibrium under the action of electrostatic forces only. In other words, there can be no maximum or minimum of the potential function $V(x, y, z)$, in free space. For suppose there were a minimum at a point $\mathscr{P}$ where no charge resides. Then just outside $\mathscr{P}$ the gradient of V would everywhere be directed away from $\mathscr{P}$, and the electric field would be directed toward $\mathscr{P}$. Application of the flux theorem shows that a negative charge must exist at $\mathscr{P}$, contrary to the assertion that $\mathscr{P}$ was in free space. It is possible for the gradient

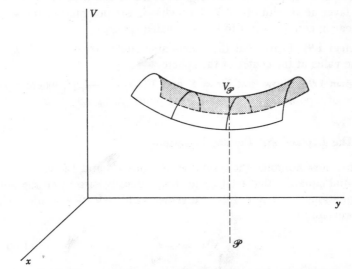

Fig. 1.9a. Graph of a two-dimensional potential $V(x, y)$ in neighborhood of a point $\mathscr{P}$ of unstable equilibrium.

to be zero at $\mathscr{P}$ (field zero), but we cannot have V increase in all directions away from $\mathscr{P}$. Any such zero-field point is therefore one of unstable equilibrium. A graph of $V(x, y)$ for a two-dimensional case would show a "saddle point" at $\mathscr{P}$ (Fig. 1.9a) and the three-dimensional case is similar but harder to picture. Problem 1.7b is a quantitative example.

In a region of continuous charge distribution ρ, a maximum or minimum could exist, but a continuous distribution is an idealization. We have to consider each electron or proton as an isolated charge, so that pure electrostatic equilibrium is impossible.

Problem 1.9a. Use Eq. 1.9–1 to find the field outside a symmetrically charged sphere if the potential is given by Eq. 1.7–11.

Problem 1.9b. Find the potential at a point (x, y) produced by the charges in Problem 1.3a, and from the expression find the x and y components of the field. Use the result to check the answers for Problem 1.3a.

Problem 1.9c. Find the field strength at an arbitrary point inside each sphere in Problem 1.7d.

Problem 1.9d. Find the field strength in the sphere of Problem 1.7j at a point 1.50 m from its center.

Problem 1.9e. In fair weather, an upward potential gradient of about 100 v/m is observed at the earth's surface. Assuming the earth to carry a uniform distribution of charge on its surface and none in its interior, find the value of σ. If an equal and opposite charge distribution $-\sigma$ exists in a thin layer at an altitude of 20 km, what is the potential at the surface of the earth, considering it to be an isolated sphere?

Problem 1.9f. Prove that the potential found in Problem 1.7c has an extreme value at the center of the sphere.

Problem 1.9g. Show that $\nabla r = 1_r$ and $\nabla(1/r) = -1_r/r^2$, where r is the distance of a point (x, y, z) from a fixed point (x_0, y_0, z_0).

1.10 The Laplace and Poisson Equations

We can now combine the results of Sections 1.5 and 1.9, and obtain a differential equation that relates the charge density directly to the potential. Equations 1.5–1 and 1.9–3c together yield $-\nabla \cdot \nabla V = \rho/\epsilon_0$, which we abbreviate to

$$\nabla^2 V = -\frac{\rho}{\epsilon_0} \tag{1.10–1a}$$

or

$$\frac{\partial^2 V}{\partial x^2} + \frac{\partial^2 V}{\partial y^2} + \frac{\partial^2 V}{\partial z^2} = -\frac{\rho}{\epsilon_0} \tag{1.10–1b}$$

The operator $\nabla \cdot \nabla = \nabla^2$ is frequently written as Δ and is called the Laplace operator, or Laplacian. Equation 1.10–1 is a partial differential equation for the scalar potential function $V(x, y, z)$ in terms of the "source" ρ of this potential and is called Poisson's equation. From Section 1.7, it is clear that knowledge of the function $\rho(x, y, z)$ and the special cases of surface and line densities and isolated point charges is sufficient to determine V uniquely. It has been proved by Dirichlet and others that the corresponding purely mathematical problem is similarly determined. That is, if ρ is given everywhere, there is one and only one V that satisfies Eq. 1.10–1. In fact, the solution is just 1.7–7c when no line or surface distributions are present.

In most cases of interest, however, conductors are involved (Chapter 2) and surface distributions of charge prevail (although σ is not usually given in advance). The solution becomes Eq. 1.7–7b, and in the space outside the conductors, the equation becomes the Laplace equation:

$$\nabla^2 V = 0 \tag{1.10-2}$$

Every potential function derived from any electrostatic distribution whatsoever must obey this equation in free space.

It is not hard to prove the uniqueness of the solution to 1.10–2 for a given region of space when the charge all lies on equipotential surfaces (conductors) that bound the region and have known values of potential. Suppose there are two functions $V_1(x, y, z)$ and $V_2(x, y, z)$ that satisfy Laplace's equation and reduce to the known values on the given surfaces. Then since Laplace's equation is linear, the difference $V_{12} = V_1 - V_2$ will satisfy it, and will reduce to zero at each given surface. Let us apply Green's theorem in the form of Eq. A.2–29, with $u = v = V_{12}$:

$$\int_S V_{12} \, \nabla V_{12} \cdot \mathbf{dS} = \int_\tau \nabla V_{12} \cdot \nabla V_{12} \, d\tau \tag{1.10-3}$$

where we have used the fact that $\nabla^2 V_{12} = 0$. The volume τ is bounded by a surface S consisting of the given equipotential surfaces and a sphere of radius R much larger than the dimensions of the charge-bearing surfaces. Since V_{12} must fall off with increasing R as R^{-1} or faster, and ∇V_{12} as R^{-2} or faster, the surface integral over the large sphere will vanish as $R \to \infty$. Furthermore, $V_{12} = 0$ on the remaining parts of S, so the left side of 1.10–3 is zero.

The integrand on the right side of 1.10–3 is a quantity $|\nabla V_{12}|^2$ which is either positive or zero, so we must have $\nabla V_{12} = 0$ at every point if the integral is to vanish. If the gradient vanishes, V_{12} itself must be constant, and therefore equal everywhere to the zero value it has on S. Thus $V_1 \equiv V_2$ and only one solution of 1.10–2 is possible subject to the given boundary conditions.

The uniqueness theorem may be applied to the expression 1.7–5 for the potential due to a collection of discrete charges, for each charge q_n can be imagined to be located on a very small spherical conductor of radius a and potential equal to $q_n/4\pi\epsilon_0 a$ plus the contribution of the rest of the charges which is relatively very small if $1/a$ is large enough. Thus 1.7–5 is verified as the unique solution of Laplace's equation in the space surrounding the given set of charges.

We can also assert the uniqueness of the integrals in Eqs. 1.7–7a and b as solutions to Laplace's equation in the space surrounding linear and surface distributions of charge. The formula for a volume distribution, 1.7–7c, is a solution of Poisson's equation rather than Laplace's and may be considered as a limiting case of Eq. 1.7–5.

We may also show directly, without attempting mathematical rigor, that 1.7–7c satisfies 1.10–1. If we carry out the operation ∇^2, we can write

$$\nabla^2 V = \frac{1}{4\pi\epsilon_0} \int_\tau \rho(x', y', z') \, d\tau \left(\frac{\partial^2}{\partial x^2} + \frac{\partial^2}{\partial y^2} + \frac{\partial^2}{\partial z^2} \right) \frac{1}{r'} \quad (1.10\text{–}4)$$

where the integral is over all space in which ρ does not vanish.

The second derivatives with respect to x, y, and z may be replaced by those with respect to x', y', and z' since r' depends only on x–x', y–y', and z–z'. However, $\nabla^2(1/r') = 0$ (Problem 1.10a) except where $r' = 0$. The integrand vanishes except for the point where $x' = x$, $y' = y$, and $z' = z$, where it becomes infinite. Let us therefore write the integral over all space as the sum of an integral over a small sphere of radius R about the point (x, y, z), and a vanishing integral over the rest of space. If R is small enough and if ρ is a continuous function of x', y', and z', we can approximate $\rho(x', y', z')$ by $\rho(x, y, z)$ and write

$$\nabla^2 V \simeq \frac{\rho(x, y, z)}{4\pi\epsilon_0} \int_{r' < R} \nabla'^2 \left(\frac{1}{r'} \right) d\tau'$$

which by using the divergence theorem A.2–22 becomes

$$\nabla^2 V \simeq \frac{\rho(x, y, z)}{4\pi\epsilon_0} \int_{r' = R} d\mathbf{S} \cdot \nabla' \left(\frac{1}{r'} \right) = \frac{\rho(x, y, z)}{4\pi\epsilon_0} \int_{r' = R} r'^2 \, d\Omega' \, \frac{\partial}{\partial r'} \left(\frac{1}{r'} \right)$$

The integral is taken over elements of solid angle $d\Omega'$ of the spherical surface of radius R. Since the integrand is -1, the integral is -4π. If now we let $R \to 0$, the approximation sign may be replaced by an equality and we arrive at Eq. 1.10–1a.

The uniqueness of the solution may be seen from the fact that the difference of two solutions of Poisson's equation must satisfy Laplace's, with zero potential on any boundaries, and so by the argument above must vanish.

A further consequence of the uniqueness theorem is that any field vector whose curl and divergence both vanish identically and which falls off as $1/R$ or faster at distant points must itself be identically zero throughout space. Suppose that we have

$$\nabla \times \mathbf{E} = 0 \quad (1.10\text{–}6)$$

$$\nabla \cdot \mathbf{E} = 0 \quad (1.10\text{–}7)$$

In Section 1.8 we showed that if **curl E** $= 0$, **E** is derivable from a potential, so we have

$$\mathbf{E} = -\nabla V$$

and by Eq. (1.10–7)

$$\nabla^2 V = 0$$

The argument above shows that ∇V must vanish identically throughout space, which proves the assertion.

One direct application of Eq. 1.10–2 is to make a new proof of Earnshaw's theorem. A maximum or minimum of $V(x, y, z)$ requires that the three second derivatives

$$\frac{\partial^2 V}{\partial x^2}, \quad \frac{\partial^2 V}{\partial y^2}, \quad \frac{\partial^2 V}{\partial z^2}$$

be all of one sign (or zero). This is patently impossible from Eq. 1.10–2 unless all are simultaneously zero, a condition not met with in practice unless V is constant, when of course there is no *stable* equilibrium at any point. A higher-order minimum or maximum involving the simultaneous vanishing of these three derivatives is in fact impossible, but the proof will not be considered here.[14]

Plane Diode with Space Charge. An interesting application of Poisson's equation occurs in the steady flow of electrons between a plane cathode and a plane anode in a diode vacuum tube. The potential and charge density in this case will be functions only of x, where x is the coordinate perpendicular to the planes. If v is the electron speed at x, then ρv is the rate of flow of charge per unit area, or current density. Steadiness of flow implies that charge does not pile up anywhere, so ρv must be a constant independent of x (cf. Section 5.2). Hence ρ will be inversely proportional to v.

The sum of the kinetic and potential energies of each electron will be constant,

$$\tfrac{1}{2} M_e v^2 - eV = \text{constant}$$

and the constant will be zero if V is measured from a point where v is zero. Such a point, x_1, will be shown in Section 5.2 to exist at a minimum of $V(x)$, so that we have

$$v(x_1) = 0: \qquad V(x_1) = 0; \qquad \left(\frac{dV}{dx}\right)_{x=x_1} = 0 \qquad (1.10\text{–}8)$$

Consequently, we can write Poisson's equation as

$$\frac{d^2 V}{dx^2} = \frac{a}{[V(x)]^{1/2}} \qquad (1.10\text{–}9)$$

where a is a positive constant (since ρ is negative). (Ordinary derivatives are used because only one independent variable enters.)

[14] See, for instance, Sir James Jeans, *Mathematical Theory of Electricity and Magnetism*, Cambridge University Press, Cambridge, 1946, paperback 1961, Art. 50, p. 42; also W. R. Smythe, *Static and Dynamic Electricity*, 2nd ed., McGraw-Hill, New York, 1950, p. 13.

This equation can be integrated if we multiply each side by $2(dV/dx)$, since

$$\frac{d}{dx}\left(\frac{dV}{dx}\right)^2 = 2\,\frac{dV}{dx}\frac{d^2V}{dx^2}$$

and

$$4a\,\frac{d}{dx}(V^{\frac{1}{2}}) = 2aV^{-\frac{1}{2}}\frac{dV}{dx}$$

We therefore find on integrating that

$$\left(\frac{dV}{dx}\right)^2 = 4a[V(x)]^{\frac{1}{2}} + \text{constant}$$

The constant of integration must be zero if Eq. 1.10–4 is to be valid for $x = x_1$. For points $x > x_1$, beyond the minimum, $dV/dx > 0$, and we can take the positive square root of each side:

$$\frac{dV}{dx} = 2a^{\frac{1}{2}}[V(x)]^{\frac{1}{4}} \qquad (1.10\text{--}10)$$

or, separating the variables,

$$\frac{dV}{V^{\frac{1}{4}}} = 2a^{\frac{1}{2}}\,dx$$

and

$$\tfrac{4}{3}[V(x)]^{\frac{3}{4}} = 2a^{\frac{1}{2}}(x - x_1) \qquad (1.10\text{--}11)$$

where the second constant of integration has also been set by reference to Eq. 1.10–4. From this result, it is possible to find the way in which E, ρ, and v all vary with x (Problem 1.10e). Volume-charge distributions that appear in connection with currents in vacuum tubes or semiconductors are frequently called space-charge distributions.

The application of Poisson's equation to a simplified model for a semiconductor rectifier is given in Problem 1.10g, and to a different model in Section 6.2.

Problem 1.10a. Show that $V = q/4\pi\epsilon_0(x^2 + y^2 + z^2)^{\frac{1}{2}}$ satisfies the Laplace equation.

Problem 1.10b. Show that the potential of Problem 1.7c satisfies the Poisson equation.

Problem 1.10c. Show that the potentials of Problem 1.7d satisfy the Poisson equation.

Problem 1.10d. Show that the solid angle subtended by an arbitrary curve at a point $\mathscr{P}(x, y, z)$, namely $\Omega = \int d\mathbf{S} \cdot \mathbf{1}_r/r^2$, satisfies Laplace's equation.

Problem 1.10e. Find how E, ρ, and v vary with x in the electron-flow example of the text.

Problem 1.10f. Solve the Laplace equation for the potential in the space between the planes $x = x_1$ and $x = x_2$, given that the potential is a constant V_1 for $x = x_1$ and a different constant V_2 for $x = x_2$. Assume that V is a function of x only. (Ideal parallel-plate capacitor.)

Problem 1.10g. A simplified model of a so-called rectifying barrier layer at the surface of certain semiconductors consists of a negative surface distribution of charge of density $\sigma = -\sigma_1$ and a positive volume distribution of density $\rho = \rho_1$ below the surface to a depth $x = b$ (the problem can be treated as one dimensional). Beyond the point $x = b$, we have $E = 0$ and $V = V_0$. Find an expression for the potential as a function of depth below the surface, and the PD between the interior of the semiconductor and a point just outside its surface, treating these idealized charge distributions as the only sources of electric field.

1.11 Equipotential Surfaces

Just as lines of force provide a graphic description of the variations of field in a given portion of space, so can equipotential surfaces describe the variations of potential. An equipotential region is the locus of points all at the same potential. We have met in the case of the uniformly charged spherical shell an equipotential *surface*, which is the shell itself, and an equipotential *volume*, which is its interior. The volumes are special cases, however (although important ones!), and for the most part we are concerned with surfaces. An equipotential surface can be drawn through any point in an electric field. Since the field strength is the negative of the potential gradient and has the direction of the greatest space rate of change of the potential, it must everywhere be perpendicular to the equipotential surfaces, which contain the directions of zero change of potential. Another way of showing the same fact is to remark that by definition it takes no work to move a small test charge around on an equipotential surface, so that there must be no component of force on the charge parallel to the surface, leaving the force and field to be necessarily normal to the surface.

If lines of force have been drawn, equipotentials can be drawn perpendicular to them. In simple cases, the equations of equipotentials can be obtained, and the surfaces described analytically. For instance, for a point charge or a sphere, by Eqs. 1.7–3 and 1.7–11, we have $r = q/4\pi\epsilon_0 V$; if we keep V constant, we obtain the polar-coordinate equation of a sphere whose radius depends on the value of V. For a line of charge, Eq. 1.7–14, we have cylinders whose radius for a given V is $r = r_0 e^{-2\pi\epsilon_0 V/\lambda}$. For a

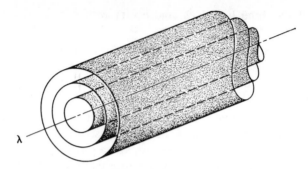

Fig. 1.11a.   Equipotentials about a line of charge.

plane, the equipotentials are parallel planes, with $z = z_0 - 2\epsilon_0 V/\sigma$. Figures 1.11a and 1.11b show lines of force and equipotentials for the latter two cases, drawn for equal intervals of potential.

It is, of course, possible to draw equipotential surfaces for any values of V whatsoever and, in fact, to fill all space with them. But the most graphic description occurs when equal intervals of potentials are used as in these figures. In fact, if the equipotentials are close together, we may write

$$E = -\left(\frac{\partial V}{\partial l}\right)_{\text{normal}} \simeq -\frac{\Delta V}{\Delta l}$$

where ΔV is the potential interval between adjacent surfaces, and Δl is the distance, measured along a normal. If ΔV is the same for a whole family of surfaces, we see that Δl is inversely proportional to the field strength.

We have also seen that the number of lines of force per unit area is proportional to E. In the so-called "two-dimensional cases," or cases of cylindrical symmetry, where all lines of force lie in planes parallel to one given plane and form the identical pattern in each of these planes, we can take tubes of force bounded by a pair of such planes (Fig. 1.11c). A picture of the lines in one of the parallel planes thus will have the linear separation of the lines of force (that is, the width of the tubes) inversely proportional to E. Hence the equipotential lines in the diagram will have spacings proportional to those of the lines of force.

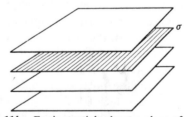

Fig. 1.11b.   Equipotentials about a plane of charge.

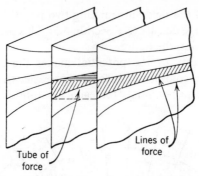

Fig. 1.11c.   Illustrating "two-dimensional" field patterns.

In a region in which the direction and magnitude of **E** are constant, a group of parallel lines of force and the straight equipotentials perpendicular to them will form a set of identical small rectangles. By proper choice of the intervals in flux and potential at which the lines are drawn, these rectangles can be made into squares. If these same lines are continued into regions of variable **E**, we obtain a set of curved figures that resemble squares, so-called "curvilinear squares." They are illustrated in Fig. 1.11*d*,

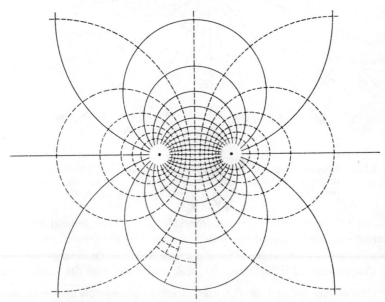

Fig. 1.11d.   Equipotentials (dashed) and lines of force (solid) about two parallel wires with equal and opposite charge densities. (Taken from *Electricity and Magnetism*, Milan Wayne Garrett, University Litho-printers, Ypsilanti, Mich., 1941, p. 51, Fig. 4,12.)

which gives part of the field surrounding two parallel wires of equal and opposite linear charge density (see Section 4.5). This property is of material assistance in sketching the figures.

The scalar property of the potential makes the construction of the equipotentials for a complex case somewhat easier than the construction of lines of force. Equipotentials for each separate charge are drawn for

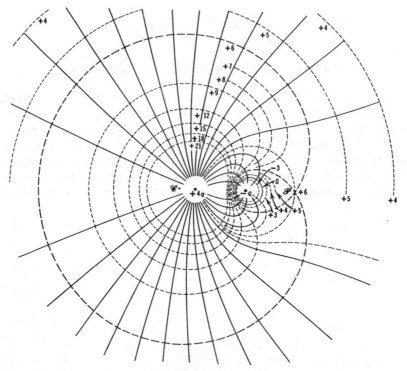

Fig. 1.11e. Equipotentials and lines of force for $+4q$ and $-q$. The light dashed line through P separates flux that passes from $+4q$ to $-q$ from flux that passes from $+4q$ to infinity. (From Garrett, *op. cit.*, p. 48, Fig. 4,7.)

a considerable number of equal intervals of V. Then several points of intersection can be joined for which the sums of the separate values are some one given value. Lines of force are sketched in when the equipotentials are thus completed.[15] Problems 1.11a, b, and c will give the reader some

[15] Lines of force and equipotentials can be located experimentally using electrostatic voltmeters and small probes, or using straws or bits of hair to give the field direction. Cf. E. Weber, *Electromagnetic Fields: Theory and Applications;* Vol. 1, *Mapping of Fields*, John Wiley, New York, 1950, Vol. I, Chapter 5, and W. H. Hayt, *Engineering Electromagnetics*, McGraw-Hill, New York, 1958, Ch. 6.

practice in such construction and more familiarity with such field maps. Figure 1.11e shows the field of charges $+4q$ and $-q$.

There are several properties of equipotentials and lines of force which are important because, as we shall see in Chapter 2, when conductors are present the equipotential surfaces are determined by the construction of the conductors. Hence it becomes natural to consider the accompanying charge distributions as derivable from the equipotentials, in contrast to the treatment we have given so far in which we consider the locations of the charges to be known and the potential distributions to be derived from this knowledge. The properties we shall consider are the following:

I. The potential V varies continuously as a function of x, y, and z, with discontinuities appearing only at charged points and lines (where

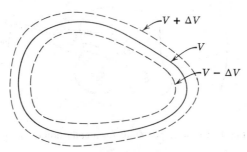

Fig. 1.11f. Three adjacent equipotentials.

V becomes infinite).[16] As we have seen, we arrive at the same values of V at (x, y, z) when we start from a zero reference point and consider the variation of V from the reference point to (x, y, z) over any path whatsoever; i.e., V is single valued. Among the consequences of continuity are:

(a) No two equipotentials can intersect each other, since then a single point would have two values of V.

(b) Within any region where the field strength is not zero there must be equipotentials just inside and just outside any given equipotential that differ only infinitesimally from the given one. One of these must correspond to a higher value of V, and one to a lower value (see Fig. 1.11f). Lines of force pass through a surface in the direction of lower potential values.

(c) As we let our consideration travel from one equipotential surface to the next, we can imagine a rubber sheet or balloon that is gradually and

---

[16] A true electric "double layer," where two equal and opposite, infinitely strong, surface distributions of charge are located an infinitesimal distance apart, would be the location of a finite discontinuity in V. However, such double layers are idealizations that will not be dealt with in this book.

continuously being deformed passing from coincidence with one equipotential to coincidence with another. This process can be continued until a discontinuity or a surface bounding an equipotential volume (field-free region) is reached; if neither occurs, we can go to "infinity."

(*d*) In any given field, there can be at the most just one equipotential surface that extends from nearby points to infinity, namely, a surface whose potential is equal to the value assigned to infinity (usually zero). The zero surfaces in Figs. 1.7*d* and 1.11*d* are examples. Problems 1.11*a* and 1.11*f* will give further examples.

II. The equipotentials at a great distance from a collection of charges whose total sum is not zero are approximately spheres. This follows from

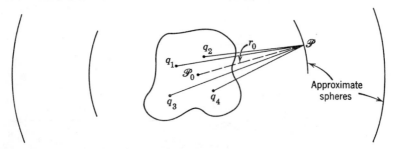

Fig. 1.11g.   Equipotentials for a collection of charges.

Eq. 1.7–5, since the r_n's for all the charges will be nearly the same and may be taken as approximately equal to the distance r_0 measured from some average or representative point $\mathscr{P}_0$ near the center of the collection (see Fig. 1.11*g*). The value of the potential will, of course, be approximately that of a single point charge equal to the sum of the original collection. (More accurate approximations to the field far from a collection of charges will be discussed in Sections 3.1 and 3.3.) It then follows that there can be an equipotential surface that extends from finite points to infinity only if the sum of all charges at finite points is zero.

III. From our remarks in Section 1.1 concerning the neutrality of the universe and from the statement in Section 1.6 that lines of force start on positive charges and end on negative, we conclude that whenever we have a finite distribution that does not add up to zero, there is "at infinity" a charge equal and opposite to the net excess in the given distribution. This charge may be thought of as distributed uniformly on the inside of an infinitely large sphere. Any charge at infinity that relates to other distributions that are disregarded as being far from the one under consideration may clearly be disregarded itself. For actual experimental situations, the infinite sphere may be replaced by the walls of the laboratory.

IV. If an equipotential surface is isolated—i.e., if it does not form part of an equipotential volume—and is closed, it must contain a net excess of charge, either on or inside itself. This is seen to be true from the flux theorem because there must be a potential gradient just outside the surface of a constant sign with respect to the outward normal, and hence a net positive or negative flux through the surface. We can then prove that:

(a) Any closed equipotential surface that is known to contain no net charge inside itself (e.g., that contains a vacuum or completely neutral atoms) must enclose an equipotential volume (Problem 1.11d).

(b) Any region that is known to be an equipotential volume must contain no net charge at any place within it, for if it contained any type of distribution whatever, there could be found small regions containing charge of one sign which will have net flux out through their boundaries and hence non-vanishing potential gradients. (Remember that we shall consider only regions which are large compared to atomic dimensions.)

(c) If it is known that a certain surface is the outermost boundary of an equipotential volume, it must be true that some charge resides on the surface. There is clearly no field inside the surface although obviously there must be a variation of potential outside or the surface would not be the boundary. Thus flux must end *at* the surface, on charges residing there.

V. At a point $\mathscr{P}$ where **E** vanishes and only at such a point the equipotential surface intersects itself.[17] As we have seen on p. 47, at least one of the second derivatives $\partial^2 V/\partial x^2$, $\partial^2 V/\partial y^2$, and $\partial^2 V/\partial z^2$ must be positive and one must be negative. If we consider the variation of V along lines through $\mathscr{P}$ in these two directions (say the x and y directions), then V will be a minimum at $\mathscr{P}$ along one line and a maximum at $\mathscr{P}$ for the other, as in Figure 1.11h. In a plane containing these directions there are four regions in between these lines, *each* of which must contain a line of constant V equal to $V_{\mathscr{P}}$. Thus the equipotential surface through $\mathscr{P}$ intersects itself, either in a line or a point.

(a) Whether the surface consists of two parts, as in Problem 1.11f, or only one, as in Fig. 1.11e, is another matter. Note the lines of force in Fig. 1.11i and their asymptotes, which are the lines of greatest rate of increase and decrease, respectively, of V.

(b) The asymptotes are perpendicular to each other. Without proving this we shall make it evident by noting that, if the second derivatives do not vanish, V in the neighborhood of $\mathscr{P}$ is approximately a quadratic function of x, y, and z. Intersections of the equipotentials in the plane of Fig. 1.11i

---

[17] We consider points where the first derivatives of V vanish but not the second derivatives. The argument in the text can be modified without much difficulty so as to handle the exceptional cases. See Problem 1.11g for such a case.

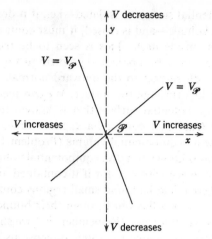

Fig. 1.11h. Variation of V near a point of equilibrium, two-dimensional case.

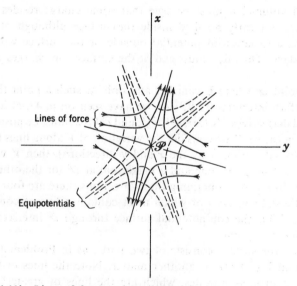

Fig. 1.11i. Lines of force and equipotentials near a point of equilibrium.

will therefore be conic sections—in fact, hyperbolas—whose axes are the lines in question and are mutually perpendicular.

Problem 1.11a. Make a careful drawing of the lines of force and equipotentials for two equal and opposite charges.

Problem 1.11b. Draw equipotential curves for charges of 3×10^{-8} coulomb and -1×10^{-8} coulomb separated by 0.10 m.

Problem 1.11c. Draw equipotential curves for charges of 3×10^{-8} coulomb and 1×10^{-8} coulomb separated by 0.10 m.

Problem 1.11d. Prove that a closed equipotential surface known not to contain net charge anywhere within itself must enclose an equipotential volume.

Problem 1.11e. Under what conditions can there be adjacent to an isolated equipotential of value V one of value $V + \Delta V$ on each side of $V(\Delta V > 0)$?

Problem 1.11f. Sketch equipotentials for four equal charges, two plus and two minus, placed alternately around the corners of a rectangle 4 cm $\times$ 8 cm in dimension.

Problem 1.11g. Four charges, of magnitudes $-8q$, q, q, and $-8q$, are placed on the x-axis at values of x equal respectively to $-2x_1$, $-x_1$, x_1, and $2x_1$. Write a formula for V at a point (x, y) in the x–y plane, and expand this result in powers of x and y up to fourth-degree terms. Discuss the behavior of V near the origin.

Chapter 2

METALLIC CONDUCTORS

2.1 Electric Conduction

In Chapter 1 we were concerned with fields and potentials produced by various given charge distributions. We are now ready to consider the properties of matter that help to determine the charge distributions and that are involved in measurement of fields and potentials. The most relevant property of matter is conduction, the ability to move charge over macroscopic distances, which we explain by the mobility of charged particles within a material substance. Materials vary in this property all the way from the good conductors (metals) to the very poor conductors (insulators). Metallic conductors are by far the most important class of materials, and we shall deal mostly with them. Brief attention will be given to electrolytes and semi-conductors in Chapter 6; the discussion of conduction in gases is left to more specialized textbooks, although some properties of plasmas are considered in Sections 3.5, 6.5, 10.5, and 10.10.

Metals are conductors because electrons in them are free to move when electric fields of macroscopic extent are applied. A classical picture of metallic structure would describe electrons as small charged points or spheres, flying about at random under the influence of thermal agitation in the interstices between the atoms. The influence of an electric field that has value $\mathbf{E}$ when averaged over distances large in proportion to the sizes of atoms is to produce a drift velocity $\mathbf{v}$ proportional to $-\mathbf{E}$ (negative because the electron charge is negative).

The quantum theory, on the other hand, gives electrons a combined wave-particle character and describes their motion in terms of energy levels. A typical energy-level diagram for a metal is given in Fig. 2.1a. A level in such a diagram is an explicit or implicit horizontal line whose height above a reference level indicates a particular quantized energy value which an electron can take. The figure shows two bands which each contain many possible levels for conduction-electron motion. The spacing of levels is so close that it can be taken as continuous—the lower band in Fig. 2.1a might for instance consist of 10^{24} distinct levels!

According to the Exclusion Principle, enunciated by Pauli in 1925, no more than one electron may occupy each physically distinct level. Alternatively, we may describe each level as "empty" if no electron "occupies" it,

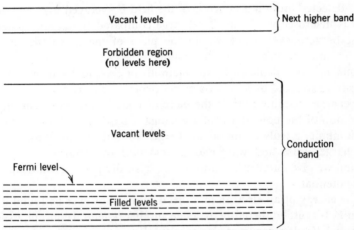

Fig. 2.1a.   The band structure of a metal. The actual spacing of levels is so close as to appear continuous. The Fermi level represents the top of the filled group, except for the effects of thermal agitation.

and "filled" if one electron does. Electrons naturally tend to move toward the lowest levels, and in a metal, as in Fig. 2.1a, the lowest band is only partly filled. Except for the fluctuations produced by thermal agitation, there is a definite level called the "Fermi level" representing the top of the filled group. Just above the Fermi level there are levels into which electrons can be lifted either by thermal agitation or by a field **E**, no matter how small in magnitude. Excitation by thermal agitation makes no change in the completely random directionality of electron motions although of course it leaves some levels vacant below the Fermi level and fills some levels just above.[1] The effect of an electric field, however, is to produce a

[1] The function that describes the relative occupation of a level at any temperature T above absolute zero is the so-called Fermi distribution function, $F(U) = [1 + e^{(U-U_F)/kT}]^{-1}$ where U is the energy of the level in question, U_F is the Fermi level energy, and k is Boltzmann's constant.

net electron drift **v** proportional to $-\mathbf{E}$, just as predicted by classical theory. More specifically, a field **E** will set up a continuous process of electrons jumping into empty levels, corresponding to flow in the $-\mathbf{E}$ direction and away from levels of the opposite kind. At the same time, collisions with grain boundaries, crystal imperfections, impurity atoms, and thermally-agitated atomic nuclei will produce backward jumps that counteract the effect of **E**. Thus a steady state of flow is reached in a very short time for each value of **E**, the mean free time t_m for an electron in a state of regular motion being about 10^{-14} second. The proportionality of **v** and $-\mathbf{E}$ is the basis of Ohm's law, and holds over a ratio of 10^{12} or more in values of E.[2]

When electrons in a piece of metal are at rest as far as any macroscopically-detected motion is concerned, the field **E** averaged over any domain that is macroscopically small yet large compared to atomic dimensions must be zero everywhere within the piece of metal, so that its entire interior must be an equipotential volume. The value of the potential in this volume can be calculated by the methods of Section 1.7 from the charge densities produced by an excess or deficiency of electrons, as well as from any charges residing outside the piece of metal. This statement implies a definition of the potential V of a conductor based on taking to the metal from infinity a truly infinitesimal charge, without the quantum properties of charge, mass and wave-nature possessed by electrons. In the next section we give an alternate and more physically meaningful definition of this potential.

The energy of an electron in a metal cannot however be found directly from V. It is useful therefore to define another potential concept, the Fermi potential V_F. If a group of electrons is taken into a metal under the usual conditions of constant temperature and pressure, they will fall into a set of levels just above and below the Fermi level and their average energy will be equal to the Fermi energy U_F. Similarly, when some electrons are removed and those remaining readjust themselves, the average energy loss is just U_F per electron.

The Fermi energy U_F has both kinetic and potential energy components but on a macroscopic scale it may be treated as if it were all potential energy. Let us call the energy per unit charge for an electron in a metal at the Fermi level the Fermi potential, V_F. We have

$$V_F = -\frac{U_F}{e} \tag{2.1-1}$$

[2] An excellent and relatively elementary presentation of the theory of the electrical conductivity of metals is given by V. F. Weisskopf, *Am. J. Phys.*, **11**, 1–12, (1943); for a brief account, see R. L. Sproull, *Modern Physics, The Quantum Physics of Atoms, Solids, and Nuclei*, 2nd ed., John Wiley, New York, 1963, Sec. 9.6.

The Fermi potential V_F differs from the electrostatic potential V by an amount depending on the local atomic, that is chemical, structure. This difference is almost constant for a given type of metal with a given surface treatment under given conditions of temperature and pressure, and is called the "work function."

$$\phi = V_F - V \tag{2.1-2}$$

When V_F is more positive than V, ϕ will represent the work necessary to take an electron from inside the metal to an evacuated space where the potential is V, thus accounting for the name work function.

Changes in the electrostatic surroundings or conditions of a metallic conductor will not change ϕ but will change V_F and V together. Consequently when differences or gradients of potential are concerned, V_F and V may be used interchangeably. Nevertheless it is well to bear in mind that it is V_F whose gradient really determines whether electrons will flow, but V which can be calculated from given charge distributions.

2.2 Conductors with Charges at Rest

The electric field that produces an average drift of electrons in a particular direction is an average field, produced by largescale excesses or deficiencies of electrons in or on the conductor or elsewhere. It is of fundamental importance to note that any motion of charge is always in the direction that automatically leads to a reduction of the field that produces the motion. As electrons move in a certain direction in an isolated conductor, one side of the conductor must become negatively charged and the other side positively charged, thus giving rise to a contribution to the field that would by itself produce the opposite motion. This process of the separation of positive and negative charges is called *induction.*

If a conductor is placed in an electric field $\mathbf{E}_0$, its electrons will continue to move until they produce a field $\mathbf{E}_1$ that just cancels the original at all points within the conductor, so that $\mathbf{E}_1 + \mathbf{E}_0 = 0$. No matter how complicated the shape of the conductor, the field within it will be zero everywhere when all charges have come to rest. For most metals, the time for equilibrium to be established is extremely small, of the order of 10^{-19} sec. (Section 5.2.) It takes far less time for moving electrons to reduce $\mathbf{E}$ than for the same electrons to undergo collisions and change their motion.

As stated in the previous section, when charges are at rest on a conductor, the entire space occupied by conducting material is an equipotential volume. It was proved in Section 1.11 that there can be no net (macroscopic) charge density within such a volume—all the charge, if any, must reside on the surface. Problems 2.2*d* and 2.2*f* illustrate how small an excess or deficiency of electrons in a metallic surface can be expected in practice. The potential $V(x, y, z)$ calculated from $\int \sigma \, dS/4\pi\epsilon_0 r$ for a collection of statically charged conductors (see Fig. 2.2*a* for an example) will be a variable function for points (x, y, z) in the field-occupied space outside the conductors but will be constant throughout the volume of each conductor. The gradient of V will therefore be normal to the conducting surfaces at each point, and there will be no field tangent to any surface tending to

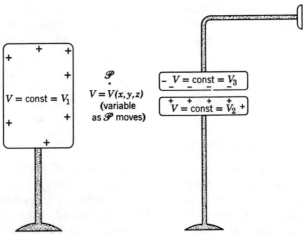

Fig. 2.2*a*.   The potential is variable in the space surrounding the conductors but is constant within each one.

move the surface charges about, a condition that is essential if the distribution is to remain in equilibrium. It is evident that σ must in general have a very complex variation over the surfaces of the conductors and may even have opposite signs at different points on the same conductor. In fact, it is possible to calculate its value only in cases of considerable symmetry.

The various properties of equipotential surfaces and volumes discussed in Section 1.11 are immediately applicable to conductors in which the charges are at rest. If a conductor lies in an external field, its surface will be the boundary of an equipotential volume and so must contain charge.[3] Let us use the flux theorem to calculate the charge density in terms of the field just outside the surface. We construct a Gaussian surface in the form of a small pill box with sides that are perpendicular to the metal surface and

---

[3] We treat the surface as having strictly infinitesimal thickness. Actually, the excess or deficiency of electrons will move around in a layer of the order of an angstrom in thickness, producing on the average a volume density of charge in a thin layer, too thin to be of macroscopic importance.

of infinitesimal height, with the bottom of the box just inside the surface of the conductor and parallel to it, and with the top in the field just outside. (Fig. 2.2b.) There is no field inside the surface, and the field outside is parallel to the sides of the box, so there is no flux through the bottom of the box or its sides. The flux leaving the surface all passes through the top of the box and is equal to the charge inside divided by ϵ_0. Calculating flux and charge per unit area, we have

$$E = \frac{\sigma}{\epsilon_0} \tag{2.2-1}$$

where E refers to the limiting value of the field strength as the point of observation approaches the surface from the outside. The direction of **E** is, of course, normal to the surface.

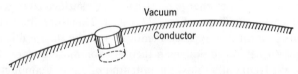

Fig. 2.2b.   A Gaussian surface at a conductor boundary.

The Uniqueness Theorem.   We referred above to the complicated way in which charge distributes itself on an arbitrary set of conductors. Let us show in an elementary way that, if the n conductors of a given set are each given prescribed net charges $Q_1, Q_2 \cdots Q_n$, there is only *one* way in which these charges can distribute themselves over the conductors and reduce the field to zero in each one. This theorem is a special case of the general uniqueness theorem of electrostatics; if it were not true, it might be possible, for instance, to get different results by charging the objects one after another in different orders.

The proof uses the superposition principle. Consider two differently obtained equilibrium distributions of the same charges $Q_1 \cdots Q_n$, and suppose temporarily that the charges are spread out differently on some of the conductors in the two cases. Each makes all the conductors equipotential volumes.

Now let us imagine calculating for each point on each conductor the difference between the two values σ' and σ'' for the two arrangements. With the values $\sigma' - \sigma''$ we can next imagine making a third arrangement in which we place at each point on each conductor a charge density $\sigma''' = \sigma' - \sigma''$. Since the first two charge arrangements produce potential distributions V' and V'' which are constant inside each conductor, the third one $V''' = V' - V''$ will also. Thus it will be an equilibrium arrangement and there will be no forces that can vary σ'''. Once in place, the charge density σ''' will remain.

If σ''' is not zero everywhere, there will be flux leaving various points on the conductors. However, since the *total* charge on each conductor was the same for σ' and σ'', it will be zero for the third arrangement. Any conductor that has σ''' different from zero anywhere must have *both* positive and negative values of σ''' and must have flux both entering and leaving. Since a line of force begins and ends at different potentials, each line that enters or leaves a conductor must have its other end on *another* conductor. Thus each conductor that bears a non-vanishing σ''' is intermediate in potential between two other conductors.

Even if we include "infinity" as a conductor (which is not necessary if all the Q's are zero, for then no flux passes to infinity), it is impossible for *all* the conductors to be intermediate in potential. Any "highest" one would only have flux leaving it, which is also impossible. So the set of conductors with zero net charge must have zero surface charge density at every point and *no field anywhere*, $\nabla V''' \equiv 0$. Therefore the two original distributions of σ must have been identical, and the theorem is proved.

Let us now treat the uniqueness theorem for more general boundary conditions. We frequently know the potential of a given conductor, rather than the charge on it. For simplicity, we may think that each conductor we have to consider is connected to one terminal of a set of batteries that have their other terminals grounded, so that the conductors are individually maintained at definite potentials $V_1, V_2 \cdots V_n$. The mechanism whereby batteries can maintain these potentials is irrelevant here (it will be discussed in Sections 5.3 and 6.4).

The conditions for our general uniqueness theorem are that we are given the charges $Q_1, Q_2 \cdots Q_n$ on n conductors and the potentials $V_{n+1} \cdots V_{n+m}$ on m other conductors. We may further allow the presence of any number of fixed and known point charges $q_a, q_b \cdots$. The theorem we wish to prove states that under these given conditions there is one and only one way in which charge is distributed over all the conducting surfaces, with therefore one and only one resulting field in the entire region under consideration.

Consider first the case in which we have the V's known for all the conductors, with empty space between them. (This case has already been proved by use of Green's theorem in Section 1.10.) Suppose we have two fields, the potential for each of which reduces to the appropriate value at the surface of each conductor. For instance, the batteries might have been connected in different orders, or one field might have been obtained experimentally by connecting the conductors to the batteries in some arbitrary order and plotting the field by the straw needle or gypsum crystal line-of-force method, or the probe and electrostatic voltmeter method (see footnote on p. 52). The other field might then be a mathematically invented one—e.g., derived from a potential function $V(x, y, z)$ that was constructed in a mathematical fashion so as to yield the correct V's at each conductor, and at the same time to provide in the intervening space a field $-\nabla V$ that obeys the flux law. We can then calculate the corresponding local charge densities on each conductor from $\sigma = -\epsilon_0(\nabla V)_n$.

Now, if the two fields $\mathbf{E}'$ and $\mathbf{E}''$ differ from each other at any points in the intervening space, we subtract the two at each point to get a hypothetical third one $\mathbf{E}''' = \mathbf{E}' - \mathbf{E}''$. The potential V''' of this hypothetical field will be zero on all conductors, but from the given conditions there may be nonvanishing charge densities $\sigma_1 \cdots \sigma_n$. However, application of the flux law will show that this is impossible. Both given fields obey this law, so the difference must. Flux cannot begin and end on a single conductor. In this case, it also cannot begin on one conductor and end on another or at infinity because all are at zero potential. So there can be no flux or field anywhere, and the two original fields and corresponding charge distributions are identical.

Now suppose we have m conductors with V's given and n with known Q's. Again consider two possible fields, of which one might be a mathematically constructed one, this time with $Q_i = \epsilon_0 \int_{S_i} \mathbf{E} \cdot d\mathbf{S}$ specified in each case on the surface S_i of the ith conductor with known charge. The subtraction yields a set of m conductors of zero potential, and another set

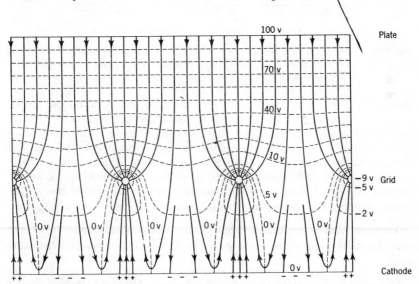

Fig. 2.2c. Lines of force and equipotentials in a plane triode, shown in cross section (moderately negative grid). The cathode is assumed to be cold (no electron emission).

(of n conductors) with unknown potentials but zero net charges. The same argument used above applies here—namely, that there can be no highest or lowest potential among the n conductors, so that all $n + m$ must be at zero potential, and we can then use the argument of the previous paragraph to prove that the field is zero.

The addition of fixed point charges does not affect the arguments above because both the charges and the fields in their neighborhoods cancel on subtraction. Thus we have proved the theorem in quite a general way. The only extension left to consider is to the case in which the space between the conductors is filled with dielectric material. This case will be taken up in Section 3.8.

An interesting example of field and potential distributions around a system of conductors is given in Fig. 2.2c. (See also Problem 2.2d.)

Electron Lens. Another example is the two-cylinder electron lens shown in Fig. 2.2d. Some lines of force will pass between the insides of the cylinders near

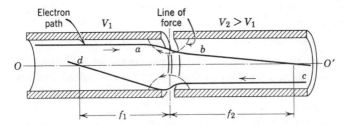

Fig. 2.2d. Two cylinders at different potentials from a converging electric lens, whose focal lengths are f_1 and f_2. (From J. R. Pierce, *Theory and Design of Electron Beams*, D. Van Nostrand Co., Princeton, N.J., 1954.)

their ends. If an electron follows a path such as ab, it will have more kinetic energy and higher speed in the positive potential region near b than in the negative region near a, and will therefore spend less time in region b than in a corresponding part of region a regardless of which way it goes along the cylinder. The force on the electron when it is near a is directed toward the axis, while the force near b is directed away. Hence the electron will receive a larger impulse toward the axis in region a than away from the axis in region b. For each direction of travel, therefore, the opening between the cylinders acts like a converging lens.[4]

Problem 2.2a. Prove that in a set of charged, isolated conductors there must be at least one whose surface charge density has everywhere the same sign.

---

[4] For more details, the reader is referred to J. R. Pierce, *Theory and Design of Electron Beams*, 2nd ed., D. Van Nostrand, Princeton, N.J., 1954; and Zworykin, Morton, Ramberg, Hillier, and Vance, *Electron Optics and the Electron Microscope*, John Wiley, New York, 1945.

Problem 2.2b. Prove that, if an insulated, uncharged conductor is placed near a charged conductor and no other conductors are present, the uncharged body must be intermediate in potential between that of the charged body and that of infinity.

Problem 2.2c. Make a sketch of a circumstance in which a positively charged body certainly has a negative potential with respect to ground.

Problem 2.2d. Prove that, if a single isolated charged conductor is near a grounded one, the two conductors have opposite charges and the distribution on each is of one sign only.

Problem 2.2e. Write the field and potential just outside the surface of an isolated charged conducting sphere in terms of the charge density on the sphere. Do the same for the field and potential at a distant point.

Problem 2.2f. The field strength at which normal air becomes conducting is approximately 3×10^6 v/m. What charge density on the surface of a conductor will produce this field? How many excess electrons per square angstrom will there then be? Find the same quantities for a tungsten surface which just begins to emit electrons under the influence of the surface field ("field emission") when $E = 3 \times 10^9$ v/m.

Problem 2.2g. Sketch lines of force and equipotentials for the triode structure of Fig. 2.2c, in the cases (a) when the grid is sufficiently negative that no flux passes from plate directly to cathode and (b) when the grid is· at zero potential. In each case, the plate is to remain highly positive in potential.

Problem 2.2h. Figure 2.2e shows a disk with a hole in its center between two regions of different field strength. Sketch lines of force and equipotentials on both sides of the hole in the central disk and show that, for certain circumstances, electrons passing through the hole will be focussed toward the axis of the figure.

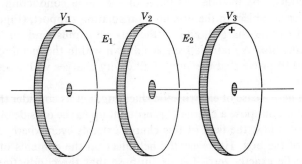

Fig. 2.2e. A three-disk electron lens. The center disk lies between two regions of different fields, $E_2 > E_1$.

2.3 Cavities in Conductors

Let us now consider conductors with cavities in them. A completely closed metal box is a good example. (Fig. 2.3*a*.) The inner surface of such a cavity is of course an equipotential surface. If the box is empty (strictly, if it contains no non-conductors and no disconnected or insulated conductors), we have the case of a closed equipotential surface known to have no charge within itself; the enclosed space is an equipotential volume. There must also be no charge *on* the inside surface, for if so there would be flux within the enclosure. Another way of seeing this result is to note that

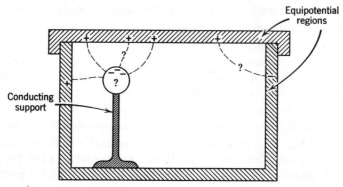

Fig. 2.3*a*. A conductor with a cavity containing no isolated charges can have no inner charge or flux.

since no flux can pass into the metal itself, any flux present must begin and end on the surface. But the two ends of a line of flux cannot be at the same potential, and so the existence of flux would lead to a contradiction.

Any conductors placed in the box that make electrical contact with it must, of course, be included as parts of the same conducting volume.[5] But consider an object in the box on an insulating support. (Figure 2.3*b*.) This object can be charged, and all the flux on it must end on the inside surface of the box. A Gaussian surface drawn within the metal of the box can be used to prove that the sum of all cavity charges within and on the cavity surface is zero.

We have here a case of electrostatic shielding. Let us consider the matter in more detail. Suppose a charge Q is brought up to the outside of the box. By Coulomb's law, the field of this charge extends everywhere, even into the inside of the box. However, the net effect on the contents of the box will always be exactly zero. Let us suppose that the conducting objects

---

[5] Provided they are made of the same material. See Section 2.6.

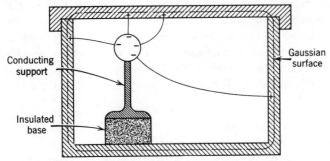

Fig. 2.3b.   An insulated object in a cavity can have a charge.

inside the box remain fixed in position. Then consider the two circum-stances: (*A*) in which the external charge *Q* is absent (Fig. 2.3*c*) and (*B*) in which it is present (Fig. 2.3*d*). Consider a third charge distribution (Fig. 2.3*e*) obtained by subtracting at each point the charges or charge densities that were present in cases *A* and *B* respectively. The potential at any given point will then be the difference $V_B - V_A$ between the values for (*A*) and (*B*). The inside of the box will then have no net charge on any isolated object. Thus it will be an equipotential volume. (The reader should be able to show (Problem 2.3*b*) that an insulated conducting object in the cavity could not have a positive charge on one part of its surface and an equal negative charge on the other.) Therefore there can be no charge density anywhere in the cavity, and the two original distributions of cases *A* and *B* must have been identical. The inside of the box is thus said to be "shielded" or "screened" from outside influences. The result of bringing up the external charge *Q* is merely to induce on the outside of

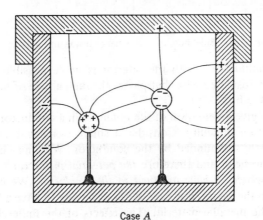

Case *A*

Fig. 2.3c.   Shielding, case *A*. Charge inside, none outside.

the box a charge distribution that exactly cancels the field that Q itself produces inside the box.

In a similar way it can be shown that motion of charges inside a cavity or changes in their magnitudes can have no external effect, provided that the total charge on the outside of the hollow conductor does not change. (Problems 2.3a and 2.3c.) It may be assumed in either of these cases that

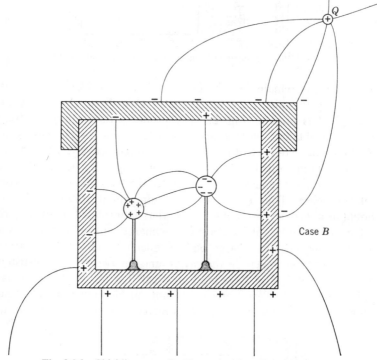

Fig. 2.3d. Shielding, case B. Charge inside and outside.

electrical communication with the interior is made possible through an arbitrarily thin, insulated wire that passes through a hole of negligible size in the side of the box.

We can now give a definition of the potential in a conductor that avoids the work-function difficulty. Consider a small, evacuated cavity of any shape completely surrounded by the conductor. With no charge inside, there will be no field, and therefore *the potential in the cavity will be the same as that which we have assigned to the conductor.* We can measure the potential in the cavity, however, without having to have a test electron taken inside the metallic material. The effects of the finite charge of an electron can be made negligible by making the cavity spherical with radius *r* large enough that the potential $e/4\pi\epsilon_0 r$ produced at the surface by an electron in the center is small compared to the errors of measurement. *Thus we define the potential V of a piece of metal as the potential in a suitable cavity in that piece of metal.*[6] When it is necessary to emphasize this point, we refer to *V* as the cavity potential. It makes the most appropriate zero for energy diagrams such as Fig. 2.1*a*.

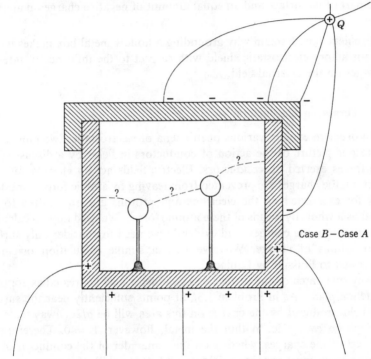

Fig. 2.3*e*. Shielding, case *C*. Subtraction of surface densities for cases *A* and *B*.

Communication with the outside may be made in principle by imagining a very slender cylindrical channel connecting the cavity with the outside, narrow enough that the unavoidable field distortions at its two openings have negligible effect. One can also imagine taking an electron into the metal through the outer surface and out through the inner, canceling the work-function effect.

[6] A point "just outside" the conductor can be used if distances of atomic size are not considered, and many authors define the potential in such terms. The use of a cavity avoids all difficulties involved in imagining a limiting process that stops outside the surface "somewhere" beyond distances of atomic size. The author is indebted to the late Prof. D. C. Grahame of Amherst College for suggesting the use of a cavity in this way.

Problem 2.3a. Prove the theorem stated in the text to the effect that changing or moving charges inside a cavity in a hollow conductor can lead to no external effect if the net charge on the outside of the conductor is unchanged.

Problem 2.3b. Show that an insulated conductor situated within an enclosed cavity in another conductor cannot have some positive charge on one part of its surface and an equal amount of negative charge on another part.

Problem 2.3c. Explain why grounding a hollow metal box makes it into a satisfactory electrostatic shield with respect to the influence of internal charges on the external field.

2.4   Forces on Conductors

In order to explain various phenomena of electrostatics, we must complete our picture of the action of conductors in fields by a discussion of the forces exerted on conductors. Electric fields act on charges. In conductors, the charges are prevented from leaving by atomic forces, and thus any forces exerted on the electrons and protons are transmitted to the solid as a whole by means of these atomic forces. We need only to calculate the forces on the charges, and evidently we need to consider only surface distributions of charge. We give here a simple calculation originally suggested to Poisson by Laplace.[7]

Any small area on the surface of a conductor may be treated as approximately a plane. As in Problem 1.3j, at points sufficiently near the surface the field produced by the charge on this area will be $\sigma/2\epsilon_0$ away from the surface on *each* side. Within the metal, however, $\mathbf{E} = 0$. Therefore all the rest of the charges, whether on the remainder of the conductor or on other bodies, must produce a field (the "distant field") that exactly cancels the "local field" $\sigma/2\epsilon_0$ inside the metal (Fig. 2.4a). The local field reverses sign without change of magnitude as one goes through the surface. However, the distant field must be continuous. Therefore the two fields just outside the metal surface are each $\sigma/2\epsilon_0$ in the same direction. In adding them we have found another proof for Eq. 2.3–1.

As an example, consider a point charge q lying at a distance h above an infinite conducting plane (Fig. 2.4b). There will clearly be negative induced charge on the plane, with σ strongest just under q. At a point $\mathscr{P}$ in the

[7] S. D. Poisson "Mémoire sur la Distribution de l'Electricité à la Surface des Corps Conducteurs," *Mem. Classe Sci. Math. Phys. Inst. Imp. France*, Année 1811, p. 30 (separate pagination for this article). See also Sir E. T. Whittaker, *A History of the Theories of Aether and Electricity*, Thomas Nelson, London, 1951, and Harper and Row, New York, 1960, Vol. I, p. 62.

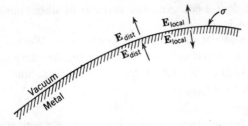

Fig. 2.4a. Distant and local fields at the surface of a conductor.

plane whose distance is s from $\mathcal{O}$, the foot of the perpendicular from q, the distant field will consist of the contribution from q, $\mathbf{E}_q = q\mathbf{1}_r/4\pi\epsilon_0 r^2$ and a contribution parallel to the plane from all the surface charge outside a small circle of arbitrary size at $\mathcal{P}$ that we choose to be the source of the local field. If we take this circle to be small enough that σ is constant to, say, $\frac{1}{2}\%$ within it, and consider points above and below $\mathcal{P}$ to be sufficiently close, the local field will be $\sigma/2\epsilon_0$ to an accuracy of 1%. As shown in the diagram, the distant field normal to the surface has the magnitude $qh/4\pi\epsilon_0 r^3$ downward. Inside the metal, therefore, the field $\sigma/2\epsilon_0$ must have this magnitude but be upwardly directed. Therefore, we must have

$$\sigma = -\frac{qh}{4\pi\epsilon_0 r^3} = -\frac{qh}{4\pi\epsilon_0(s^2 + h^2)^{3/2}} \qquad (2.4\text{-}1)$$

Above the plane, the local field will be downward and the total field normal to the surface will be $\sigma/\epsilon_0 = -qh/2\pi\epsilon_0 r^3$. The field of all the distant surface charge must integrate to a value equal and opposite to the horizontal component from q, namely, $qs/4\pi\epsilon_0 r^3$, but the integrals are not easy to

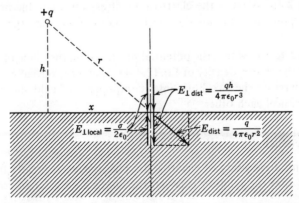

Fig. 2.4b. Local and distant fields on the surface of an infinite plane conductor in the presence of a point charge $+q$.

perform (cf. Problem 2.4c). Another method of obtaining this result is given in Section 4.3.

Now let us consider the force on surface charges. We have divided the field into a local part that can exert no force on the charge producing it[8] and a distant field that can act on the local charges. Since $F = qE$, the force per unit area is σE_{dist} or

$$f_S = \sigma^2/2\epsilon_0 \tag{2.4-2}$$

We use a small f for the stress or force density, with a subscript to indicate that it is calculated per unit area. (A force per unit volume would be written f_r.) Then f_S is always outward, since, if σ is positive E_{dist} is directed outwardly and if σ is negative, the field is inward but the force outward.

In terms of field strength just outside the surface, Eq. 2.2–1, we have

$$f_S = \tfrac{1}{2}\epsilon_0 E^2 \tag{2.4-3}$$

This result is chiefly used to find the total force on a given conductor by integration:

$$\mathbf{E} = \int f_S \, d\mathbf{S} \tag{2.4-4}$$

It may also be used for deformable conductors along with their mechanical properties to determine the equilibrium shape they take in the given electrical circumstances.

Problem 2.4a. A certain kind of brass has a tensile strength of 7.5×10^4 lbs/in² or 5.25×10^8 newtons/m². What charge density on this material will be enough to break it by electrostatic forces? How many excess electrons per square angstrom will there then be? How many coulombs on a brass sphere of diameter 10 cm? What is the value of E just outside the surface?

Problem 2.4b. What is the electrostatic stress on a conductor charged just to the point that the air outside becomes conducting? (Cf. Problem 2.2c.)

Problem 2.4c. Show that the potential produced on the plane of Fig. 2.4b by $+q$ and the charge density of Eq. (2.4–1) together is zero at every point, and that therefore the two horizontal components of field shown in Fig. 2.4b must cancel each other.

2.5   Capacitance

The quantitative study of electrostatic phenomena is greatly facilitated by the fact that the relation between the charges on a set of conductors

---

[8] The electrons or protons in the surface layer exert forces on each other parallel to this layer, in equal and opposite pairs that add up to zero.

and the resulting potentials depends only on the geometric arrangement of the conductors. This result is a consequence of the uniqueness theorem.

Let us first consider a single, isolated conductor of any shape. If we place a charge Q on it, the charge will distribute itself in some particular equilibrium pattern on the surface of the conductor. The distribution obtained from this one by multiplying σ everywhere by a fixed constant m would also be an equilibrium arrangement, since the potential would then be m times greater (m would factor out of the equation $V = \int m\sigma \, dS/4\pi\epsilon_0 r$). This therefore must be the unique way in which a charge mQ would distribute itself if placed on the conductor. Thus the potential of the conductor would be multiplied by m, and we see that V is proportional to Q. We write

$$Q = CV$$

and call the constant of proportionality C the capacitance[9] of the conductor. Capacitance is measured in coulombs/volt, which are called *farads*.

In particular, if the conductor is a sphere of radius R_0 we have $V = Q/4\pi\epsilon_0 R_0$ from Eq. 1.7–11, so that

$$C = 4\pi\epsilon_0 R_0 \qquad (2.5\text{--}1)$$

With R_0 measured in meters and $\epsilon_0 = 8.85 \times 10^{-12}$ farads/m, most capacitances of isolated conductors are numerically very small (the values for non-spherical objects will be of the same order of magnitude as those for spheres of comparable size), so that the microfarad (μf) $= 10^{-6}$ farad and the micromicrofarad or picofarad ($\mu\mu f$ or pf) $= 10^{-12}$ farad are the units in common use.

The electrostatic unit of a capacitance is called the statfarad; it is, of course, a statcoulomb/statvolt. Since in electrostatic and Gaussian units $4\pi\epsilon_0 = 1$, we see by 2.5–1 that the capacitance of a sphere in these units is equal to its radius in çm (cf. Problem 2.5a).

The flux that leaves an isolated body goes to infinity. If the amount Q is changed, the flux pattern will change its density but not its shape. The same thing will happen if we have a pair of conductors so arranged that all the flux from one conductor, say conductor 1, passes to the other one. Such a pair of conductors is called a condenser or capacitor. Changing the charge on conductor 1 involves an equal and opposite change on conductor 2. The result is a change of potential difference without a change in the relative way the change is distributed. Except for the scale, there is no change in the flux pattern. We again have the charge and potential difference proportional to each other and write

$$Q = C(V_1 - V_2) \qquad (2.5\text{--}2)$$

[9] The term "capacity" is also used, but of course no reference to how much charge a conductor can "hold" is intended.

C is again called the capacitance. Q represents the amount of charge on one of the conductors, usually the one taken arbitrarily as positive. Note that an isolated body together with "infinity" may be considered as a special case of a condenser with $V_2 = 0$.

A simple way to ensure that all the flux from conductor 1 passes to condensor 2 is to enclose conductor 1 in a cavity in conductor 2. The spherical condenser is the most symmetrical example. A spherical metal ball is enclosed in a hollow spherical shell and kept in its central position

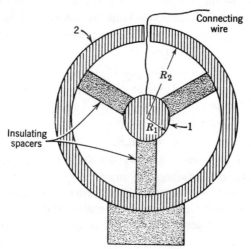

Fig. 2.5a.   Spherical condenser.

by suitably spaced insulating spacers. (Fig. 2.5a.) Ignoring the influence of these spacers (cf. Chapter 3), we can readily find the capacitance of this condenser. The field inside the space between the ball and the shell is $\mathbf{E} = Q\mathbf{1}_R/4\pi\epsilon_0 R^2$ (this is a special case of Eq. 1.4–4) and hence

$$V_1 - V_2 = -\int_{R_2}^{R_1} \frac{Q}{4\pi\epsilon_0 R^2}\, dR = \frac{Q}{4\pi\epsilon_0} \int_R^{R_2} \frac{dR}{R^2} = \frac{Q}{4\pi\epsilon_0}\left(\frac{1}{R_1} - \frac{1}{R_2}\right)$$

Hence

$$C = \frac{Q}{V_1 - V_2} = 4\pi\epsilon_0 \frac{R_1 R_2}{R_2 - R_1} \qquad (2.5\text{–}3)$$

Note that although all the flux from conductor 1 passes to conductor 2, the reverse is not true. A proper way of using such a condenser to measure either Q or $V_1 - V_2$ when the other is known would be to ground the outer shell and measure the charge and potential on the central ball by means of the thin wire passed through the shell.

For most uses, it is not necessary to have *all* of the flux from one conductor pass to the other. The parallel-plate condenser is a good approximation to a perfect capacitor. Two parallel metal plates of the same shape (usually rectangular) are placed in close proximity. Suppose as in Fig. 2.5*b* that conductor 2 is connected to ground and conductor 1 is given a charge. For the pair of plates to act as a condenser, plate 1 and its wire must be remote from the ground. Then if this plate is given a positive charge, it will be at a positive potential V. Since the distance from plate 1 to plate 2 is small, there must be a relatively strong field between the plates, since $V = -\int \mathbf{E} \cdot \mathbf{dl}$ over this short distance. On the other hand, there must be a much

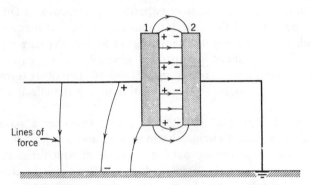

Fig. 2.5*b*.   Parallel-plate condenser, showing "stray" flux.

weaker field between plate 1 with its wire and the ground itself, because $\int \mathbf{E} \cdot \mathbf{dl}$ over the long path must also equal V. Therefore nearly all the flux passes from plate 1 to plate 2. That part of the flux that passes directly to ground may be attributed to another capacitance, generally called the "stray capacitance," of the edges and back of plate 1 and its connecting wire.

Ignoring the stray capacitance for a moment, let us calculate C for a parallel-plate condenser of area S and plate separation d. We have also to ignore the fact that flux near the edges is not perpendicular to the plates (the so-called fringing field), although the field near the center is the same as that for two infinite planes and is in the perpendicular direction. The field in the center is thus given by Eq. 1.4–7, $E = \sigma/\epsilon_0$. Therefore $V_1 - V_2 = Ed = \sigma d/\epsilon_0$. Insofar as we can neglect the effects of the fringing field, we can assume that σ is constant over the area S, and write $Q = \sigma S$. Dividing these last two equations, we find for the capacitance of a parallel-plate condenser (in vacuo)

$$C = \frac{\epsilon_0 S}{d} \qquad (2.5\text{–}4)$$

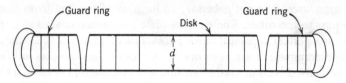

Fig. 2.5c.   Guard-ring condenser, cross-sectional view. The field in the center is uniform, with cylindrical symmetry.

A simple physical interpretation of ϵ_0 can be derived from these results, namely that ϵ_0 is the capacitance per square meter of a plane-parallel condenser of 1 m separation.

Consideration of the details of capacitor construction is left to other texts; the behavior of the dielectric materials with which capacitors are usually filled is considered in Chapter 3. Let us consider here only certain forms of standard capacitors, operated generally in air or in a vacuum. The spherical condenser is one form of standard; two other forms depend for accuracy on an ingenious method of avoiding the effects of fringing fields.

The method is that of the "guard ring." Consider a parallel-plate condenser made with a circular bottom plate and a top plate consisting of two parts—one a ring the outside diameter of which matches that of the bottom plate, and the other a disk, smaller than the lower plate, that just fits inside the ring, leaving a small ring-shaped slot for insulation. Figure 2.5c shows a cross section of such a condenser. The ring and disk are always charged to the same potential but are discharged separately so that the charge Q on the disk itself may be measured (for instance, by a ballistic galvanometer, discussed in Section 8.9). The fringing field is now at the outside edge of the ring. Thus, as indicated in the figure, E and hence σ are uniform over the area of the disk. We correct for the finite width of the slot by using the geometric mean of the inner and outer radii of the slot for calculating the area S.[10] Guard-ring capacitors are

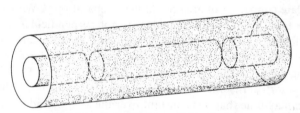

Fig. 2.5d.   Cylindrical guard-ring condenser.

[10] For accuracy, the width of the ring should be at least 4 or 5 times the spacing d. A more accurate correction can be made by using a formula given by F. K. Harris, *Electrical Measurements*, John Wiley, New York, 1952, p. 683.

made with capacitances ranging from 5 $\mu\mu$f down to 0.1 $\mu\mu$f, and are described in detail by Harris in the reference given in the footnote.

A similar arrangement can be made in the cylindrical condenser, shown in Fig. 2.5d. Two coaxial cylinders constitute a condenser, with a center section of the inner cylinder cut apart from its two guard-ring ends. It is left to the reader (Problem 2.5b) to show that when the outer cylinder is grounded, the capacitance of the central portion is

$$C = \frac{2\pi\epsilon_0 l}{\ln \dfrac{R_2}{R_1}} \tag{2.5-5}$$

where R_1 is the radius of the central cylinder and R_2 is the inner radius of the outer cylinder. The same formula, of course, gives approximately the capacitance of an ordinary coaxial condenser without guard rings.

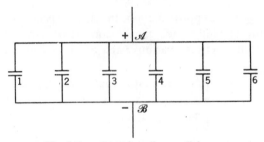

Fig. 2.5e. Capacitors in parallel.

If a group of condensers are connected together and two connections made to the combination, the latter may be treated as a single condenser. If charge Q is added to one terminal and removed from the other, then the capacitance of this condenser is the ratio of Q to the resulting potential difference. The two simple methods of connection are the *series* and *parallel* arrangements.

The parallel arrangement is shown schematically in Fig. 2.5e. When a potential difference is applied to the two terminals $\mathscr{A}$ and $\mathscr{B}$, all the condensers acquire the same potential difference, and the charge put into the combination at $\mathscr{A}$ is the sum of the charges on each condenser. That is

$$Q = Q_1 + Q_2 + \cdots = C_1 V + C_2 V + C_3 V + \cdots$$

and

$$C = \frac{Q}{V} = C_1 + C_2 + C_3 + \cdots \tag{2.5-6}$$

If the condensers are connected as in Fig. 2.5f, we have a series connection. If all the condensers are initially uncharged, and then charges $+Q$ and $-Q$ are applied to $\mathscr{A}$ and $\mathscr{B}$, a charge of amount $-Q$ will appear on the opposite plate of C_1, leaving a charge of $+Q$ on the first plate of C_2, and so forth. Every condenser will have the same charge Q. By virtue of the series connection, however, the potential difference V will be the sum of the separate PD's. Thus

$$V = V_1 + V_2 + V_3 + \cdots = \frac{Q}{C_1} + \frac{Q}{C_2} + \frac{Q}{C_3} + \cdots = Q\left(\frac{1}{C_1} + \frac{1}{C_2} + \cdots\right)$$

so that

$$C = \frac{Q}{V} = \frac{1}{\dfrac{1}{C_1} + \dfrac{1}{C_2} + \cdots}$$

or

$$\frac{1}{C} = \frac{1}{C_1} + \frac{1}{C_2} + \frac{1}{C_3} + \cdots \tag{2.5-7}$$

To a fair degree of approximation, the stray capacitances of connecting wires, outsides of plates, etc., can be considered as small separate condensers connected between various parts of the circuit and ground. They

Fig. 2.5f. Capacitors in series.

will thus frequently be in parallel with the principal capacitance, adding only a small amount to its value. We shall see later (Chapter 10) that when the charges and currents vary with great rapidity, it is no longer possible to think of the stray capacitance in this fashion as "lumped," but a more careful analysis of its "distributed" nature is required.

The parallel-plate guard-ring condenser can be used to measure a potential difference in terms of force and length. In this case we do not try to measure the charge Q on the disk, but rather the force. The disk is movable and connected to a balance of some type so that the force of attraction exerted by the field on its lower side can be balanced by a known weight. By Eq. 2.4–3 we can write

$$F = \epsilon_0 E^2 S / 2$$

Furthermore $V = Ed$, so we have

$$F = \epsilon_0 V^2 S / 2d^2$$

or, finally,

$$V = d\left(\frac{2F}{\epsilon_0 S}\right)^{\!\!1/2} \tag{2.5-8}$$

A precise measure of the difference of two potentials can be made by maintaining F constant and changing d by means of a micrometer screw that moves the lower plate. Such an instrument is called an "attracted-disk" or "absolute" voltmeter, the word absolute referring to the measurement of an electrical quantity in mechanical terms.

There are several other forms of electrostatic voltmeter. They all have the advantage of drawing no steady current in operation and the disadvantage of requiring especially good insulators, careful suspensions, etc. The forces involved are not as easy to calculate as in the absolute instrument just described, but, since the field at a particular point in a system of conductors is proportional to the PD applied, F will still be proportional to V^2. (This proportion is only approximate for instruments in which the moving element is subjected to different fields and presents a different area or length along which the force acts when it is in different positions.) These various instruments all require calibration against a standard.[11]

Problem 2.5a. Prove that the electrostatic unit of capacitance has the dimensions of centimeters, and derive the ratio between the centimeter and the picofarad. Show also that the dimensions of ϵ_0 in the MKS system are farads/meter as stated in the text.

Problem 2.5b. Prove Eq. 2.7-5.

Problem 2.5c. Consider that an ideal condenser is charged up by taking small increments ΔQ of positive charge from one plate to the other. Show that the total work done is $Q^2/2C$ and express this work in terms of Q and V and in terms of V and C, where Q and V are the final values of charge and potential. Make an argument to show that this work can be interpreted as potential energy.

Problem 2.5d. A condenser of 1200 μf is charged to 350 v and discharged through a photo-flash lamp. If one flash is produced every two seconds, what average power (joules/second) is needed to recharge the condenser?

Problem 2.5e. Two small metal spheres, of radii a and b, are separated by a distance c between their centers. Show that the capacitance of the condenser formed by the two is $4\pi\epsilon_0/(1/a + 1/b - 2/c)$, when c is large enough that the charge on each can be assumed to be distributed symmetrically and the potential of each sphere produced by the charge on the other can be taken as the value produced at the center of the former.

Problem 2.5f. Two coaxial cylindrical air capacitors are made with pieces of the same brass stock of 0.380 cm wall thickness. The inner cylinder has an inside diameter (i.d.) of 7.471 cm; the outer cylinder has an i.d. of 8.563 cm. The two cylinders of one capacitor each have a length of 13.70 cm; the other cylinders are 26.20 cm long. Find the difference between the capacitances of the two condensers.

[11] For details on electrostatic voltmeters, see Harris, *op. cit.*, pp. 443–454, and D. E. Gray, ed., *American Institute of Physics Handbook*, 2nd ed., McGraw-Hill, N.Y. 1963, sec. 5c.

Problem 2.5g. A cathode-ray tube has a pair of parallel deflection plates in the form of rectangles 1.50 cm × 3.00 cm, separated by 3.00 mm in vacuo. Find their capacitance approximately.

Problem 2.5h. Find the shape of the plates of a variable air condenser (e.g., find r as a function of θ, using polar coordinates) if the capacitance is to vary with angle of turning θ according to

$$C = \frac{a}{(b + \theta)^2}$$

Problem 2.5i. Find the capacitance of the earth, in farads.

Problem 2.5j. Find the capacitance between a concentric pair of metal spheres of which the larger has an inside diameter of 1.0 m and the smaller has an outside diameter of 0.80 m. Compare your answer with the result of using Eq. 2.5–4 as an approximation.

2.6   The Work Function and Contact Potentials[12]

We saw in Section 2.3 that the work necessary to remove an electron from a metal can be defined without considering electrostatic fields outside the metal if we imagine taking the electron into a cavity. The potential energy of an electron at the Fermi level in the metal is $-eV_F$,[13] which by Eq. 2.1–2 we may write

$$-eV_F = -e\phi - eV \tag{2.6–1}$$

which states that the Fermi energy per electron is the sum of the work-function potential energy, which is a property of the metal itself, and the macroscopic electrostatic potential energy, which depends on the charge and capacitance of the piece of metal and its electrical environment. As indicated in Section 2.1, when the net charge on a piece of metal is changed, $-eV$ and $-eV_F$ change together, leaving $-e\phi$ constant. A shift ΔV in V produces a shift of all the energy levels together of amount $-e\Delta V$.

In most cases of external fields, the variation of potential outside the metal is gradual enough that there is a considerable region beyond the range of the atomic fields where the potential is closely equal to the cavity value V. Hence Eq. 2.6–1 applies to taking an electron to any point in this region without appreciable error. (Cf. Problem 2.6a.)

Figure 2.6a gives a simple energy-level diagram that is adequate for our purposes.

[12] The material of this section is referred to in Chapter 6. If that chapter is to be skipped, this section may be omitted without loss of continuity.

[13] It is customary in physical chemistry to denote $-eV_F$ by $\bar{\mu}$, the "electrochemical potential" or "Gibbs free energy," often taken per mole of electrons rather than per electron.

The work function ϕ is of importance in the photoelectric effect, as it represents the difference between the amount of energy given to an electron by a photon which may fall on a metal surface and the maximum kinetic energy with which the electron can emerge. The study of the photoelectric effect was one of the crucial steps in the establishment of the quantum theory, and is described in any text on modern atomic physics.

Another phenomenon related to the work function is thermionic emission. When the temperature of a metal is raised sufficiently, electrons may

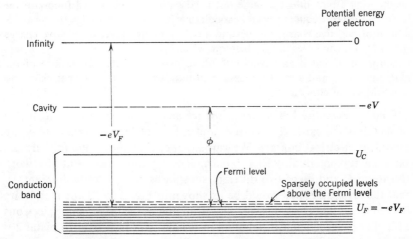

Fig. 2.6a. Energy levels in and outside of a piece of metal. The quantities V_F, V, and ϕ are positive as shown.

not only jump up into any of the conduction levels, but also they may get enough energy to leave the metal completely. This is the principle of operation of the various electron-emitting surfaces used in vacuum tubes.[14]

It is also possible to apply a strong enough field to a piece of metal to produce emission at lower temperatures than would otherwise be needed. Fields at a surface of the order of 3×10^9 v/m can produce copious emission at room temperature. This effect is called "field emission." Problem 4.3m involves a simplified calculation dealing with this effect.[15]

[14] T. S. Gray, *Applied Electronics*, 2nd ed., The Technology Press, M.I.T., and John Wiley, New York, 1954, pp. 75–95; K. R. Spangenberg, *Fundamentals of Electron Devices*, McGraw-Hill, New York, 1957, Chapter 8.

[15] See C. Herring and M. H. Nichols, *Revs. Mod. Phys.*, **21**, 185 (1949), especially pp. 220–223, for a discussion of the details and difficulties of the measurement of ϕ from the photoelectric effect. See also W. B. Nottingham, "Thermionic Emission," *Encyclopedia of Physics*, Vol. XXI, Springer-Verlag, Berlin, 1956, pp. 1–175. See R. H. Good, jr. and E. W. Mueller, "Field Emission," *ibid*, pp. 176–231, for up-to-date material on this subject.

It is possible to define a potential for the interior of a piece of metal as the average of the electrostatic potential over all the space in and around the atoms. This potential is sometimes misnamed the Galvani potential V_G, galvanic effects having to do with currents being fundamentally dependent on V_F rather than on V_G. In contrast, the cavity potential V is sometimes called the Volta potential. The Galvani potential differs from V because a piece of metal has in general a permanent surface double layer (cf. Problem 1.7i) with a resulting potential difference across it, generally called the χ-potential (χ is a small Greek chi). The reason for this is that the electrons at the edge of the metal are not forced by neighboring atoms into the same restricted paths as they would follow in the interior; they consequently spend enough time just outside the edge to constitute a layer of negative charge out beyond a corresponding layer of positive charge (i.e., of "electron holes"). We therefore write $V_G = V - \chi$.

Unfortunately, it is extremely difficult to make accurate calculations of the magnitude of χ and almost impossible to measure it, so that we can make no practical use of either χ or V_G.

Contact Potential Difference. Now let us consider two different pieces of metal at the same temperature and ask what happens when they are placed in electrical contact. We can suppose that they have initially the same cavity potential V; its value makes no difference. But the work functions ϕ_1 and ϕ_2 of two different substances are generally different, so that the level diagrams would be as shown in Fig. 2.6b. If the metals are in contact so that electrons can pass from one to the other, some electrons of higher electrochemical potential in metal 1 will pass over to metal 2.[16] The passage of a few electrons to metal 2 will make V_2 more negative and leave V_1 more positive. Thus the energies of all the electrons in metal 2 will be raised, and those in the other metal lowered. The process will continue until the Fermi levels of the two metals are equal, when equilibrium will set in (Fig. 2.6c). The condition for no current between two adjacent metals in contact is clearly

$$V_{F1} = V_{F2} \qquad (2.6\text{--}2)$$

It will be seen both from Fig. 2.6c and Eq. 2.6–1 that the resulting difference of potential between the two metals is equal to the difference in work functions; that is,

$$V_1 - V_2 = \phi_2 - \phi_1 \qquad (2.6\text{--}3)$$

The difference of potential $V_1 - V_2$ is called the *contact potential difference* of the two metals. Its sign can be remembered from the fact that the metal

---

[16] It might appear that an electron must acquire energy $e\phi_1$ to get out of metal 1 before it can enter metal 2, that is, that it must over a "barrier." This is not a strict requirement, however, for the wave properties of electrons allow them to pass narrow barriers without having enough energy to go over them.

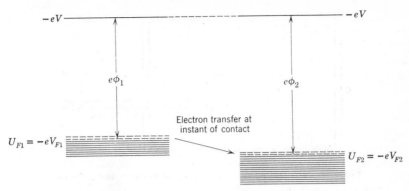

Fig. 2.6b.   Energy levels for adjacent metals at the same V, not in contact.

with the largest work function gives up electrons the least readily and becomes the more negative.

Absolute voltmeters and other electrostatic devices are affected by contact potential differences if not made of homogeneous materials with clean surfaces. Consider the condenser plates in Fig. 2.6d made of, say, copper and zinc. Each has a wire attached to it of the same material, with a junction at $\mathcal{O}$. Temporarily suppose that all the surfaces are clean. Zinc gives up electrons more readily than does copper, so that zinc has the lower ϕ and is positive with respect to the copper. Therefore, there must be an electric field as shown between the plates and of course a force of attraction. The amount of charge on the plates will be determined by the capacitance C and the contact potential difference:

$$Q = C(V_{Zn} - V_{Cu}) = C(\phi_{Zn} - \phi_{Cu}) \qquad (2.6\text{--}4)$$

The Fermi potential V_F of the electrons is constant throughout the system.

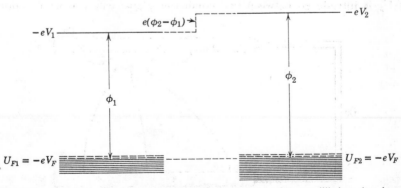

Fig. 2.6c.   Energy levels for adjacent metals in contact when equilibrium has been established (Fermi levels coincident).

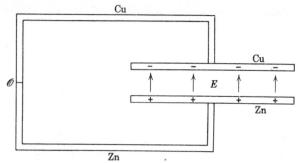

Fig. 2.6*d*.   Contact potential difference between copper and zinc.

If a copper or a zinc wire is connected to the plates and placed in the space between them, *no current will flow* (except that involved in the change of C produced by the introduction of the wire). Then V_F in the wire will become equal to V_F for the rest of the system, regardless of the material of which the wire is made. In fact any number of conductors of other materials can be connected between the plates, or inserted in series at the point $\mathcal{O}$, without changing $V_{Zn} - V_{Cu}$.

Although extraneous materials that are electrically connected between two metals do not affect their contact potential difference, dirt or other materials on the surfaces of condenser plates can affect the fields between them. Figure 2.6*e* shows a case with two similar materials, one bearing an exaggerated lump of "dirt," which could also be a region of the same composition as the copper plate but different crystal structure. We have taken as example a lump more negative than the copper. This figure shows why electrometers must have meticulously clean and homogeneous surfaces.

If by means of a potentiometer (Section 5.8), a measurable difference ΔV_F is introduced between two condenser plates whose work-function

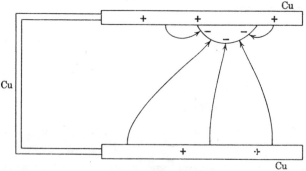

Fig. 2.6*e*.   Two similar metal plates with contamination, showing lines of force.

difference is $\Delta\phi$, the charge on the capacitor will be $Q = (\Delta\phi + \Delta V_F)C$. If now, furthermore, the capacitance is made to vary in time, by mechanical vibration of one condenser plate, a current

$$i = dQ/dt = (\Delta\phi + \Delta V_F)(dC/dt)$$

will flow in and out of the condenser. The quantity $\Delta\phi$ can be measured if, using a suitable current detector, ΔV_F is adjusted until $i = 0$, for then $\Delta\phi = -\Delta V_F$.

Ordinary voltmeters and potentiometers, of course, measure V_F and not V and cannot be used for contact potential differences.

Triboelectricity, an effect produced by contact potential differences between insulating materials, can result in rather large residual charges. The lack of conductivity means that each small section of one insulator (e.g., a piece of fur) that comes into contact with the other (e.g., hard rubber) will acquire its own local charge and potential. In order to have any considerable amount of charge transferred, there must be a large area of contact, which normally requires rubbing the two substances together. This is the origin of the common but fallacious notion that friction is necessary to produce a separation of electric charge. (The word triboelectricity comes from the Greek "tribein," to rub.)

A detailed study of this oldest-known manifestation of electricity[17] would involve complexities beyond the concern of this book, but we can list here in Table 2.6A the so-called "triboelectric series," a list such that, if any two materials on it are rubbed together, the first mentioned will become positive. The reader will recognize that the list is therefore in order of increasing work function. Numerical values of work functions are difficult to obtain because of variability in surface conditions. Values for certain clean metal surfaces are given in Table 2.6B.

A useful and also traditional method of obtaining a negative charge for electrostatic experiments is to wipe a rod of resinous material or hard rubber with fur or wool. The rod becomes negative and the fur positive. Positive charges are readily obtained on a piece of glass by contact with silk. It was Benjamin Franklin[18] who gave the negative and positive signs respectively to what had been called "resinous" and "vitreous" electricity and whom the reader can blame for the confusion attendant on the attachment of the minus sign to the common type of charge carrier.

---

[17] Amber, in Greek "elektron," was the earliest substance used for triboelectricity—probably by rubbing on cloth—and has provided us with names for our subject matter and our negative elementary charge.

[18] I. B. Cohen, ed., *Benjamin Franklin's Experiments*, Harvard University Press, Cambridge, Mass., 1941, p. 175. Franklin assumed a one-fluid theory of electric charge, intending "positive" to refer to an excess and "negative" to a deficiency of the hypothetical fluid.

Table 2.6A   The Triboelectric Series

Each substance on this list will become more positive than one below it, on
contact under average conditions. (*Smithsonian Tables*, 9th ed.)

Asbestos	Woods, Iron
Rabbit's fur	Tinned Iron
Glass	Cork, Ebony
Mica	Amber
Wool	Slate
Quartz	Resins
Calcite	Cu, Ni, Co, Ag, Sn, As, Bi, Sb, Pd, C,
Cat's fur	Brass
Ca, Mg, Pb	Para rubber
Silk	Sulfur
Al, Zn, Cd, felt, human skin	Pt, Au
Cotton	Celluloid
Rock salt	India rubber

Table 2.6B   Work Functions for Clean Metal Surfaces

(Mean or recent values,* measured in volts)

Potassium	2.15	Aluminum	4.20
Sodium	2.27	Silver	4.35
Barium	2.29	Iron	4.36
Lithium	2.39	Copper	4.46
Calcium	2.76	Mercury	4.52
Magnesium	3.46	Wolfram (100 plane)	4.59
Zinc	3.74	Nickel	4.74
Lead	4.00	Carbon	4.83
Silicon	4.02	Platinum	5.29
Tin	4.11		

* From D. E. Gray, ed., *American Institute of Physics Handbook*, 2nd ed.,
McGraw-Hill, New York, 1963, Sec. 9*j*.

Problem 2.6a. If the work function ϕ of a piece of tungsten is 4.5 ev
and a field of 1.5×10^6 newtons/coulomb is applied to its surface, within
how many angstrom units from the metal is the variation of potential
less than 0.1 % of ϕ?

Problem 2.6b. A beam of electrons is accelerated through a PD of 5.0
volts and then passed on the way to a scattering chamber down a wide
rectangular pipe made of clean nickel. If one of the wider sides of the pipe
inadvertently is given a clean coating of magnesium along 10 cm of the
beam path, and the depth of the pipe is 0.8 cm, by what angle will the
beam be deflected on its journey down the pipe?

2.7   Experimental Electrostatics[19]

We are now in a position to describe and explain some of the experimental aspects of electrostatics that are usually used as introductions to the subject, as well as for experimental proofs of our basic assumptions (Coulomb's law, superposition, and the free mobility of charges in conductors). Although electroscopes and similar pieces of demonstration apparatus are used to illustrate the material of this section, the same arguments may be applied to the study of Wimshurst and Van de Graaff generators and many other kinds of apparatus.

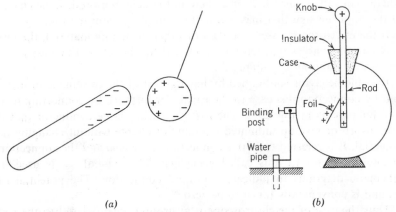

(a)   (b)

Fig. 2.7a and b.   (a) Why a pith ball is attracted to a charged rod. (b) Schematic diagram of an electroscope.

If a negatively charged rod is brought near a light ball of pith, rendered conducting by a coating of aluminum, the ball will be attached to the rod. This is because of inductive separation of the charges on the surface of the pith ball, required to reduce the field inside the ball to zero. There will be positive charge near the rod and an equal amount of negative on the far side (Fig. 2.7a). The attraction of the negative rod for the positive induced charge is larger than the repulsion on the negative because of the different distances, so that the conductor as a whole is attracted. We may refer to the ball as having been "polarized," a term of which we shall make much use in Chapter 3.

For the same reason a positive rod will also attract the pith ball, but with the signs of all charges reversed. If the pith ball touches the rod in either case, it may acquire enough of the charge on the rod that the repulsion of like charges overcomes the attraction due to polarization and the

---

[19] The remainder of this chapter may be omitted without loss of continuity.

ball flies away. The ball may be discharged by contact with a large, uncharged conductor—e.g., a human body—and the attraction by polarization repeated.

Electroscopes are primitive forms of devices for measuring charge and potential. A typical electroscope is shown in Fig. 2.7b. If a charged conducting body is connected to the knob, charge will flow into rod and foil, and the foil will stand out from the rod at such an angle that the gravitational and electrical forces on it just balance. The electrical forces are partly those of mutual repulsion of the charge on the rod and that on the foil, but other forces act as well, as can be seen by the following considerations. The flux that leaves (or enters) the charges on rod and foil must end elsewhere. Thus there must be, somewhere in the neighborhood, some charge of the opposite sign that may *attract* the foil away from the rod.

If the electroscope case is of glass or other insulating material, the flux may end on charges that have accumulated by chance on the glass or go off to some laboratory "infinity."

Reliable behavior is obtained by having part of the case made of metal and by connecting this case to the earth, for instance by connecting it to a water pipe as in Fig. 2.7b. The earth is such a large conductor that it can absorb or give up unlimited amounts of charge without changing its potential. It is referred to in this connection as *ground* and the connection of any conductor to it is called *grounding*. The symbol $\equiv$ is used in schematic diagrams to indicate a ground connection. The potential of ground is conveniently taken to be zero.[20]

Thus the case of the electroscope is at ground potential. When the rod and foil are positively charged, the region surrounding them rises in potential. The case only remains at ground potential if a counter-acting negative charge appears on its inside. That is, the field in the grounding wire produced by the plus charge on the rod will move electrons up to the case until their minus charge cancels this field. There will still be some flux from the rod and foil to more distant grounded points, since the metal case does not usually surround the rod if visual observation is to be allowed, but, if no other conductors are near the case, the amount of this flux ("stray field") will be very small.

A given deflection of the foil corresponds to a given amount of charge on it and hence to a given strength and distribution of the field between rod and case. The capacitance between foil and case will change by a small amount as the foil moves, but nevertheless a given deflection involves a corresponding *potential* of rod, foil, and knob. The electroscope as

[20] In actual practice, there is usually no conflict between this zero for potential and the "infinity" discussed on pp. 32 and 54, since experiments with isolated conductors must be performed with all extraneous objects including walls at a considerable distance.

generally used is essentially a potential-difference-measuring device (see Problem 2.7a).

Another method of charging the electroscope (or for that matter, any conductor) is to use the process of induction. Suppose the knob and rod to be uncharged and hence at ground potential. Bring, say, a negatively charged conductor C (Fig. 2.7c) to the neighborhood of the knob, but do

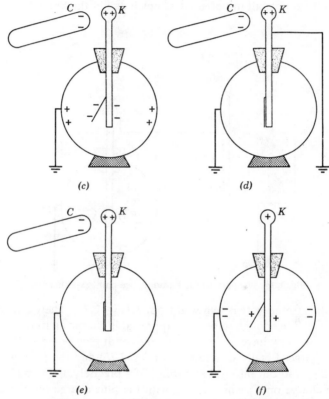

Fig. 2.7c to f.   Charging an electroscope by induction.

not make contact. The negative conductor will be at a negative potential since some of the lines of force that end on it must start on grounded objects.[21] The knob will have positive charge induced on it, and there will be an equal negative charge distributed on rod and foil. Consideration of the field inside the case shows the knob and rod also to be at negative potential. Consideration of the knob K and the conductor C shows that

---

[21] The reader will observe the deductive nature of this and the following statements.

C is the more negative. Now the knob is grounded (Fig. 2.7*d*) *without* removing *C*; *K* goes to zero potential, the foil drops, and there is no field inside the case. The potential difference between *K* and *C* must increase, since *K* is at zero.

The field between *C* and *K* being larger, more flux passes from *C* to *K* than before (increasing the positive charge on *K*) and less flux therefore passes from *C* to ground. This means that *C* is less negative than it was, although it cannot fall in potential as much as did the knob *K*.

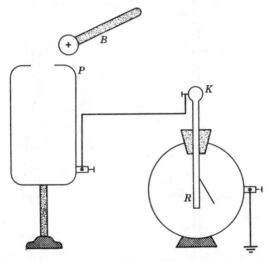

Fig. 2.7g.   Apparatus for Faraday "ice-pail" experiments.

Now the ground wire is removed from *K* (Fig. 2.7*e*). There is no change if the wire is thin enough to bear no appreciable charge on its own surface. Note that we now have an isolated conductor at zero potential with a net positive charge. Finally *C* is removed (Fig. 2.7*f*) and the positive charge on *K* will spread out into rod and foil. More precisely, the removal of the negative charge on *C*, which acting with the plus charge on *K* produced zero potential on the latter, enables the potential of *K* to rise to a positive value. The foil deflects in accordance with this potential, and the electroscope has been positively charged by a method far more convenient and reliable in practice than the method of direct contact. It should be remarked that *C* need not be a conductor but could be an insulator—e.g., a charged rubber rod. All the foregoing argument will apply except that the rod will not be an equipotential volume and reference will have to be made to some average value of its potential.

We turn now to the experiments that Faraday performed with an ice pail and that are still referred to as "ice-pail experiments." Our "ice pail" will be a hollow conductor with a small opening which allows objects to be put in and removed without touching the sides. For practical purposes, the opening need only be small compared to the dimensions of the conductor, but for use of the experiments for precise verification of theory (e.g., of the conclusions of Section 2.3), the opening should have a cover, which can have insulating strings hanging from its under side to support the objects to be inserted.

Let us connect the pail to the knob of an uncharged electroscope, as in Fig. 2.7g. Let us take a small positively charged metal ball or disk B mounted on an insulating handle—a so-called proof plane—and insert it into P without touching the latter. The electroscope leaf diverges, and it is clear that there will be a negative charge on the inside of P and a positive charge divided between its outside and KR, each of the same magnitude as that on B. Motion of B inside the hollow will produce no effect on the electroscope. The potential of P remains constant during such motion. That of B is higher and variable as its position is changed.

Now let B touch the inside of P. While in contact it becomes part of the equipotential volume made by the material of P. According to the discussion of Section 2.3, B will be completely discharged, neutralizing the negative charge inside P and making no change on the outside of P or on KR. If B is now removed, no change takes place in the electroscope. We have clearly charged the pail and the electroscope combination with a charge equal to that originally on B.

The fact that B has no charge when removed after touching P is an *experimental proof* that the space inside P is an equipotential volume. If it were not, electrons would move on or off B to make the latter an equipotential volume. (It is logically possible that for certain special positions of B the state of equilibrium could be established by a polarization that did not involve any net charge; but this could not happen for all points of contact and various shapes of P and B, as is experimentally observed.)

Problem 2.7a. Using the concept of capacitance, describe the difference between the circumstance in which an electroscope is primarily a potential-measuring device and one in which it is primarily a charge-measuring device.

Problem 2.7b. Relate the various changes of charge and potential discussed in the text for the induction-charging of an electroscope to the capacitances among C, K, and ground, and their variation.

Problem 2.7c. A metal electrophorous disk is placed on a somewhat rough sulfur plate which has been charged negatively. The disk is grounded; the ground is removed; the disk is then touched to an insulated sphere;

finally it is returned to the sulfur plate. Describe the changes of potential and capacitance that occur during each stage of the charging process. What limits the charge that can be placed on the sphere? What other shape of insulated collecting object would not have this limitation?

Problem 2.7d. Show how to get a charge on a pail-electroscope combination that is *opposite* to that on a proof plane, but equal in magnitude.

Problem 2.7e. How can the Faraday ice pail be used to show that no net charge is created in triboelectricity?

Problem 2.7f. Show how to use a small pail that fits inside a large one and an insulated ball with a charge Q on it to get a charge on the large pail equal to nQ where n is any positive or negative integer.

Problem 2.7g. Discuss the evidence from experiments discussed in Section 2.7 and in the above problems for the validity of the principle of superposition.

Problem 2.7h. Discuss in terms of potential what happens when (a) a positively charged object and (b) a negatively charged object are each brought near the knob of a positively charged electroscope.

2.8 Indirect Proofs of Coulomb's Law

Coulomb[22] in 1785 established the law that bears his name by means of difficult but direct measurements of the force between two small charged spheres. He used a torsion balance and was not able to get very great accuracy. Actually, Priestley[22] (1766) and Cavendish[22] (1771) each had established the same law before this date by consideration of the field inside a hollow conductor. The discussions in Sections 1.11 and 2.3 concerning the absence of charge in an equipotential volume, etc., all depend on the flux law which is equivalent to Coulomb's inverse square law. A proof of the inverse square law, or the flux law, can be made if (a) we establish experimentally that hollow charged conductors have no charges inside their cavities and (b) we can show that *only* the inverse square law can lead to this result.

The ice-pail experiments in the previous section (and indeed any electrostatic-screening experiments) show that there is no charge on the inner surface of a hollow conductor when the cavity itself is empty. They also show that in this case the cavity itself is an equipotential volume. That the interior of the metal is equipotential follows solely from the free mobility of charge.

From the fact that the above-mentioned experiments work for ice pails and proof planes of any shape and size, we can deduce that the interior

---

[22] Whittaker, *op. cit.*, pp. 53–59.

of the metal must also have no charge, unless within a distance from the outer surface less than the least thickness of any material yet used in any screening experiment. Otherwise a suitably shaped proof plane would surely be able to remove some charge—e.g., make the proof plane in the form of a flexible foil and temporarily line the cavity with it.

These experiments, however, are not particularly sensitive. On the other hand, Plimpton and Lawton[23] have made an extremely accurate test for the non-existence of a charge within a completely enclosed conductor. They used a five-foot diameter spherical conductor, for mathematical reasons to be mentioned below, and mounted a galvanometer with a sensitive battery-operated amplifier permanently inside the sphere, so as to avoid any errors due to work-function difficulties. This detector measured the flow of charge to or from a 4-foot hemisphere concentric with the 5-foot sphere. Observation of the galvanometer was made through a window consisting of a glass cup set into the sphere and filled with conducting liquid (salt water) so as to make a closed conducting surface. The outside of the sphere was slowly and regularly charged and discharged to a maximum of 3000 v. The galvanometer was shown in another experiment to be capable of detecting charge corresponding to a potential on the hemisphere of 10^{-6} v. If the inverse-square law were not true, the inner hemisphere would have to bear a charge if it were at the same potential as the outer sphere, and conversely, if it did not bear a charge, it would have *not* been at the same potential, as the proof we are about to give makes clear.

No detectable motion of the galvanometer could be seen through the window. The method was sensitive enough that blowing some of the salt water from the cup introduced a noticeable effect and was used to test the operation of the apparatus!

The theory of these results is considerably more difficult than that used in Chapter 1, where the inverse-square law was assumed to be true. There are two simple cases that can be handled, the sphere and the plane. Laplace proved, using differential equations, that if the field is everywhere zero inside a uniformly charged spherical shell, the law of force must be the inverse square.[24]

A simpler proof, due to Poynting,[25] is as follows. Figure 2.8a shows the

[23] S. J. Plimpton and W. E. Lawton, *Physical Review*, **50**, 1066–71 (1936).

[24] Laplace's proof can be found in J. C. Maxwell, *Electricity and Magnetism*, 2nd or 3rd ed., Clarendon Press, Oxford, 1881 and 1904, Dover, New York, reprint 1964, article 74e; in A. G. Webster, *Theory of Electricity and Magnetism*, Macmillan, New York 1897, Part II, article 129; in J. H. Jeans, *Mathematical Theory of Electricity and Magnetism*, Cambridge, 1946, paperback 1961, article 47; and in R. M. Whitmer, *Electromagnetics*, 2nd ed., Prentice-Hall, Englewood Cliffs, N.J., 1952, Chapter 2.

[25] J. H. Poynting, *Scientific Papers*, Cambridge, 1920, pp. 165–7.

cross section of a uniformly charged spherical shell, of charge density σ. The field at any point $\mathscr{P}$ is calculated by dividing up the space around $\mathscr{P}$ into double-ended cones, each of solid angle $d\Omega$, cutting the sphere at $\mathscr{M}$ and $\mathscr{N}$. Since the chord $\mathscr{M} \mathscr{P} \mathscr{N}$ cuts the sphere at equal angles at $\mathscr{M}$ and $\mathscr{N}$, the charges intercepted by the cone are equal respectively to $\overline{\mathscr{M} \mathscr{P}}^2 \sigma \, d\Omega \sec \theta$ and $\overline{\mathscr{N} \mathscr{P}}^2 \sigma \, d\Omega \sec \theta$. If the inverse-square law is true, the fields at $\mathscr{P}$ due to these two charge elements will cancel, as the reader can readily prove. If the law is not true, suppose first that the more distant

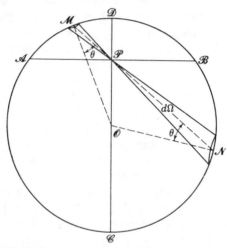

Fig. 2.8a.   Illustrating Poynting's proof for the inverse-square law.

charge always gives the greater (or the least) field. Then all the resultant fields produced as $\mathscr{N}$ swings over the entire part of the sphere below $\mathscr{A} \mathscr{B}$ will be upward (or downward) and cannot add to zero, which is contrary to experiment. Suppose then that the more distant charges give a larger result for certain distances and smaller for others in such a way that the resultant field is zero. There must then be some particular position of $\mathscr{N}$ between $\mathscr{B}$ and $\mathscr{C}$ for which the two contributions cancel. For this particular $\mathscr{N}$, the ratio of fields produced per unit of charge on the surface is inversely as the square of the distance, and so we have proved that there must be at least *one* ratio $\overline{\mathscr{M} \mathscr{P}}/\overline{\mathscr{N} \mathscr{P}}$ for which the inverse square law is true.

But $\mathscr{P}$ can be at any position, for we understand as experimentally proved that there can be no field *anywhere* inside the sphere. For each value of $\mathscr{P}$ there will clearly be a *different* particular ratio $\overline{\mathscr{M} \mathscr{P}}/\overline{\mathscr{N} \mathscr{P}}$ for which the inverse-square law must surely hold. For instance, if $\mathscr{P}$ is near $\mathscr{D}$, $\overline{\mathscr{M} \mathscr{P}}$ will have to be small and $\overline{\mathscr{N} \mathscr{P}}$ large. If $\mathscr{P}$ is near $\mathcal{O}$, the two distances

will be nearly equal. Thus the inverse-square law holds for all experimentally accessible ratios. Finally, the experimental result holds for spheres of
any size, and so the inverse-square law holds for all actual distances as
well as all ratios. Q.E.D.

The other simple case is that of a uniform plane distribution of charge.
If we let the potential $V(r)$ at a distance r from an isolated charge q be
$q/4\pi\epsilon_0$ times an unknown function $f(r)$, it is easy to show that the field
outside a uniform plane distribution of density σ is

$$E_z = \frac{\sigma}{2\epsilon_0} zf(z) \qquad (2.8\text{--}1)$$

where z is the perpendicular distance from the plane to the point at which
the field is calculated. (See Problem 2.8a.)

Now if we take as established the fact that the charge resides on the
surface of a conductor and divide the field just inside the surface into local
and distant fields, as in Section 2.4, we must as before have the distant
field constant over a sufficiently small region and the total field zero inside
the surface. Thus the local field, Eq. 2.8–1, must be constant for small z,
which can only be true if $zf(z)$ is a constant, or $f(r) = \text{constant}/r$, which
proves Coulomb's law (the mathematical properties of f are independent
of the symbol used for the independent variable). To make this proof more
rigorous would require a consideration of the deviation of the surfaces
used from planarity. (The larger the radius of curvature of the surface,
the larger the values of z over which $zf(z)$ is constant.)

Although any deviation from the inverse-square law should probably
not be considered as simply a change from one power of r to another,[26]
one can express the result of Plimpton and Lawton's work in such terms.
If the exponent in the force law is $2 \pm \alpha$, the correction α was shown by
them to be less than 2×10^{-9}. No experiments of this sort, of course,
can detect any variation within atomic distances. However, Rutherford's
famous alpha-particle scattering experiment with which the atomic nucleus
was discovered amounts also to a sensitive test of Coulomb's law down
to distances of the order of 10^{-13} m or better; modern experiments in the
scattering of electrons of a billion or more electron-volts carry the range
of validity down to 10^{-15} m or even less.

Problem 2.8a. Find the field of a uniform plane distribution of charge
at a point $\mathscr{P}$ at a distance z from the plane, if the formula for the potential
of a charge q is $(q/4\pi\epsilon_0)f(r)$.

---

[26] If it is taken as established that similar figures have similar electrical properties
when only the scale of dimensions is changed (for instance, that lines-of-force patterns
remain similar), then the law of force must be a power law. See Maxwell, *loc. cit.*, and
Problem 4.7h.

Hints: Find the resultant field directly, without calculating the potential. Use polar coordinates, and use as the variable in the integration the distance from $\mathscr{P}$ to the charge element. It must be assumed that $f(\infty) = 0$.

Problem 2.8b. Discuss the logical distribution between the assertions (*a*) that there is no charge within the material of a conductor and (*b*) that there is no field there.

Problem 2.8c. Does the experiment of Plimpton and Lawton prove the inverse-square law only for repulsions between charges of like sign, or does it also include the attractive forces?

Problem 2.8d. Find how the capacitance of an arbitrary condenser will vary if all its dimensions are increased by the same factor k, and the law of force between two charges contains r to the power $-(2 + \alpha)$.

Chapter 3

DIELECTRIC
MATERIALS

3.1 The Dipole Field

An insulator is a substance whose electrons or ions cannot move about under the influence of an applied electric field. In general such substances consist of neutral polyatomic molecules, except for the rare gases (helium, neon, argon, xenon, and radon) which are monatomic in nature and some crystals whose energy gaps are so large that their semiconducting properties are negligible. There are no *perfect* insulators, as all substances have some measurable conductivity, but we shall deal here with those materials whose conductivity is extremely small and shall omit for the time being the consideration of any effects resulting from their conductivity.

Insulators also have the property of *molecular polarizability*. That is, the presence of an electric field may shift the positive and negative charges within a molecule away from their average positions, so that an inductive redistribution of charge occurs that is quite similar to the inductive effect on the small pith ball discussed in Section 2.7. Insulators are called "dielectrics"[1] when their polarizability is under consideration. Strictly speaking, all substances are polarizable, but the effects of polarizability are readily observed only in the absence of appreciable conductivity.

Now the redistribution of charges on the pith ball or on any conductor involves the transfer of a very small amount of charge in terms of electronic units per atom (see Problems 2.2f and 2.4a), over macroscopic distances. Molecular polarization, on the other hand, involves the motion of one or more electrons per atom over subatomic distances. This chapter is devoted

---

[1] The word "dielectric" was coined by M. Faraday, *Experimental Researches in Electricity*, Taylor and Francis or B. Quaritch, London, 1838, Dover, N.Y., reprint 1965, vol. I, §1168.

to a study of the macroscopic effects of such transfers. We shall first calculate the magnitude of the effects involved for single atoms or molecules, and then consider matter in bulk.

Let us think of a molecule as consisting of a collection of positive and negative point charges all located within distances of the order of 10^{-10} m of each other. We are interested in the field at large distances from the molecule—say 10^{-4} m or more. To a first approximation, we may neglect altogether the intramolecular distances and following the discussion on p. 54 write the potential as

$$V = \frac{1}{4\pi\epsilon_0} \sum_i \frac{q_i}{r_i} \simeq \frac{1}{4\pi\epsilon_0 r_0} \sum_i q_i \qquad (3.1\text{--}1)$$

where r_i is the distance to a point of observation from the ith charge, and r_0 is the distance from some central point in the molecule.

This formula is the one we will normally use for the molecules that have a net charge, because these molecules usually appear separated by distances large compared to their dimensions. On the other hand $\Sigma q_i = 0$ for neutral molecules; to get a value of V different from zero, we will need a closer approximation than that made above.

To make such an approximation, let us pair off each electron with a nuclear proton. We can then use the dipole calculation of pp. 6–7 and Problem 1.7o for the field and potential produced by each of these pairs. We shall show that a calculation made in this way, with neglect of the spatial separation of the various pairs in a molecule, constitutes a completely adequate approximation for dealing with dielectrics.

Let us rederive the dipole potential by a more elegant method that yields directly an especially useful form for V, and is of material help in discussing the qualitative features of quadrupole and higher fields. Consider an electric dipole consisting of a positive and a negative charge, each of value q, separated by a small distance $\boldsymbol{\delta l}$, as in Fig. 3.1a.

The potential at $\mathcal{O}$ is given by

$$V_{\mathcal{O}} = \frac{1}{4\pi\epsilon_0}\left(\frac{q}{r} - \frac{q}{r'}\right) = V_{+q,\mathcal{O}} + V_{-q,\mathcal{O}}$$

which is the same as the *difference* between the potential $V_{+q,\mathcal{O}}$ that $+q$ produces at $\mathcal{O}$ and $V_{+q,\mathcal{O}'}$ that $+q$ produces at $\mathcal{O}'$; from the figure we can see that V produced by $-q$ at $\mathcal{O}$ (i.e., $V_{-q,\mathcal{O}}$) equals $-V_{+q,\mathcal{O}'}$. We assume that the separation δl between the two charges is so small in comparison to r that we may treat it as a differential. (The symbol δ is used to indicate a quantity small enough to be a differential, but one that we need not let go to zero.) We can now calculate the difference $V_{\mathcal{O}} = V_{+q,\mathcal{O}} - V_{+q,\mathcal{O}'} = \delta V$ by use of the gradient (Eq. A.2–19). The negative sign must be used

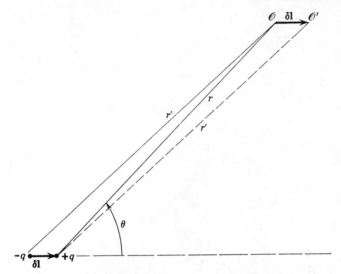

Fig. 3.1a. Illustrating the calculation of the dipole potential.

because **δl** is directed toward $\mathcal{O}'$. We have

$$V_{\mathcal{O}} = \delta V = -(\nabla V_{+q}) \cdot \boldsymbol{\delta l} = \frac{-q}{4\pi\epsilon_0}\left(\nabla \frac{1}{r}\right) \cdot \boldsymbol{\delta l}$$

so that the potential at point $\mathcal{O}$ produced by the pair is given by

$$V_{\mathcal{O}} = \frac{-q\,\boldsymbol{\delta l} \cdot \nabla\left(\dfrac{1}{r}\right)}{4\pi\epsilon_0}$$

The quantity $q\,\boldsymbol{\delta l}$ is the vector that determines the strength of the dipole pair. It is called the *electric dipole moment* and will be given the symbol **p**. Thus we can write, dropping the subscript,[2]

$$V = -\frac{1}{4\pi\epsilon_0}\,\mathbf{p} \cdot \nabla\left(\frac{1}{r}\right) \tag{3.1-2}$$

It is easy to show (Problem 1.9g) that

$$\nabla\left(\frac{1}{r}\right) = -\frac{\mathbf{r}}{r^3} = -\frac{\mathbf{1}_r}{r^2} \tag{3.1-3}$$

---

[2] A true mathematical dipole occupies a point and is the limit of $q\,\boldsymbol{\delta l}$ as $\boldsymbol{\delta l} \to 0$ and $q \to \infty$ in such a way that the quantity **p** remains constant. The potential of Eq. 3.1–2, which approximates that of an actual charge pair, is exact for a true dipole. As far as is known, no true electric dipoles exist, and we do not need to consider them.

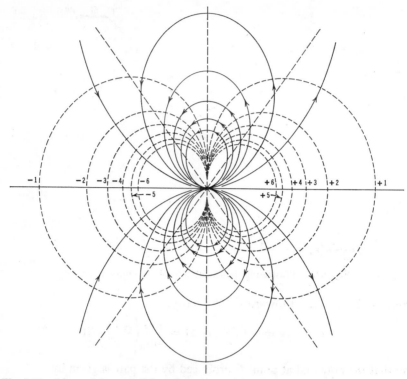

Fig. 3.1b. Lines of force (solid) and equipotentials (dashed) of a horizontal dipole. The numbers represent potential values (in arbitrary units). The dashed straight lines are loci of points where the field direction is vertical. (Taken from *Electricity and Magnetism*, Milan Wayne Garrett, University Lithoprinters, Ypsilanti, Mich., 1941, p. 29, Fig. 3,4.)

Another expression for the dipole potential is therefore

$$V = \frac{\mathbf{p} \cdot \mathbf{1}_r}{4\pi\epsilon_0 r^2} \qquad (3.1\text{–}4)$$

and if we write $\mathbf{p} \cdot \mathbf{1}_r = p\cos\theta$ we have an expression without vectors:

$$V = \frac{p\cos\theta}{4\pi\epsilon_0 r^2} \qquad (3.1\text{–}5)$$

V is inversely proportional to the square of the distance along any radius drawn from the center of the dipole.

The equipotential surfaces are clearly surfaces of revolution about an axis through the dipole. Their intersections in a plane containing the axis are curves whose polar coordinate equation can be written

$$\cos\theta = Kr^2 \qquad (3.1\text{–}6)$$

with $K = 4\pi\epsilon_0(V/p)$. We see that $\theta = \pm 90°$ when $r = 0$, so that all curves pass through the dipole at right angles to its axis. The zero equipotential is that for which $\cos\theta = 0$ for all r, i.e., the entire plane through the origin normal to $\mathbf{p}$. The largest values of r for $\cos\theta = +1$ when K is positive ($\theta = 0°$) and for $\cos\theta = -1$ when K is negative ($\theta = 180°$). Figure 3.1b shows some of the equipotential curves given by Eq. 3.1–6, along with lines of force.

The field of a dipole at a point $\mathcal{O}$ is found by taking the negative gradient of V. It is most convenient here to use polar coordinates and Eq. 3.1–5. The radial component of $\mathbf{E}$ is given by a directional derivative with $dl = dr$. The component normal to the radius, in the direction of increasing θ, is

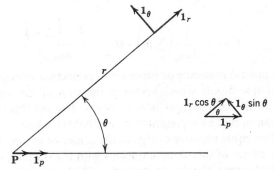

Fig. 3.1c. Showing the relation between the unit vectors $\mathbf{1}_r$, $\mathbf{1}_\theta$, and $\mathbf{1}_p$.

that for which $dl = r\, d\theta$. There is, of course, no component of $\mathbf{E}$ normal to the plane containing $\mathcal{O}$ and $\mathbf{p}$.

We obtain for the field at $\mathcal{O}(r, \theta)$ the same results as given in Eqs. 1.3–1:

$$E_r = -\frac{\partial V}{\partial r} = \frac{2p\cos\theta}{4\pi\epsilon_0 r^3} \tag{3.1-7a}$$

$$E_\theta = -\frac{1}{r}\frac{\partial V}{\partial\theta} = \frac{p\sin\theta}{4\pi\epsilon_0 r^3} \tag{3.1-7b}$$

A useful vector form for $\mathbf{E}$ can be derived from 3.1–7 or 1.3–1 by using the relation $\mathbf{1}_p = \mathbf{1}_r\cos\theta - \mathbf{1}_\theta\sin\theta$ (see Fig. 3.1c) to eliminate $\mathbf{1}_\theta$. We find

$$\mathbf{E} = \frac{1}{4\pi\epsilon_0 r^3}[3(\mathbf{p}\cdot\mathbf{1}_r)\mathbf{1}_r - \mathbf{p}] \tag{3.1-8}$$

The field strength E is

$$E = \sqrt{E_r^2 + E_\theta^2} = \frac{p}{4\pi\epsilon_0 r^3}\sqrt{\sin^2\theta + 4\cos^2\theta}$$

$$= \frac{p}{4\pi\epsilon_0 r^3}\sqrt{1 + 3\cos^2\theta} \tag{3.1-9}$$

It is evident that E falls off as r^{-3} along any radius vector. The lines of force all pass from the positive end of the dipole around to the negative end, as is easily seen by comparing Fig. 3.1b with Fig. 1.6b. Note that the field is directed along the radius for $\theta = 0°$ and $\theta = 180°$ and perpendicular to it for $\theta = \pm 90°$.

The potential produced by a molecule with several electron-proton pairs can be found by adding the potentials due to each pair. The same degree of approximation will be involved in neglecting the distances between the centers of the various dipoles as was involved in treating the length of a single dipole as an infinitesimal. From the vector expression Eq. 3.1–2 or Eq. 3.1–4 we see that the sum of the potentials is given by replacing $\mathbf{p}$ by the sum $\sum_i \mathbf{p}_i$ of the moments for all the pairs so that

$$V = -\frac{1}{4\pi\epsilon_0}\left(\sum_i \mathbf{p}_i\right) \cdot \nabla\frac{1}{r} = \frac{\mathbf{1}_r \cdot \left(\sum_i \mathbf{p}_i\right)}{4\pi\epsilon_0 r^2} \qquad (3.1\text{–}10)$$

Thus any neutral molecule or other small collection of charges is equivalent to a simple dipole whose vector is the sum of the separate dipole vectors for all the charge pairs in the system. The net dipole strength of each atom can in fact be represented by a dipole consisting of the positive nucleus and an equal negative charge at the center of the electronic charge cloud. If the center of this cloud coincides with the nucleus, as in the case of symmetrical atoms, the dipole strength will of course be zero. The fact that the electrons are continually in motion is taken into account by making a time average for the charge cloud.

Another representation of the dipole moment for an atom or molecule, using a continuous mean distribution ρ, is given below in Eq. 3.3–4.

Problem 3.1a. Write Eq. 3.1–6 in Cartesian coordinates, and show that the equipotentials are not spheres.

Problem 3.1b. Write Eq. 3.1–5 in Cartesian coordinates, and show that the potential satisfies Laplace's equation.

Problem 3.1c. Find the Cartesian components of $\mathbf{E}$ from $-\nabla V$ and also from Eq. 3.1–7. Find the locus of points for which the lines of force are perpendicular to the direction of $\mathbf{p}$.

Problem 3.1d. Show that all the lines of force from a dipole meet any given radius vector at the same angle, and similarly for the equipotentials. Find the direction of that radius for which the intersecting lines of force make an angle of 45° with $\mathbf{p}$.

Problem 3.1e. Calculate the flux from a dipole that passes through a spherical cap whose axis is collinear with $\mathbf{p}$ and whose edge is made by the circle generated when the point $\mathcal{O}(r, \theta)$ is rotated about the axis. How must θ vary with r to keep this flux constant? Obtain in this way the equation of a line of force, and check by comparing its direction with that given in Eq. 3.1–7. Show that each line of force is closed.

Problem 3.1f. Using polar coordinates, prove that **curl E** $= 0$ for the dipole field.

3.2   Forces and Torques on Dipoles

Before we proceed to consider polarized molecules in bulk, let us find expressions for the torque $\mathscr{T}$ and the force **F** on a dipole in an arbitrary external electric field. The net force on a dipole is zero if the field is the same at the two ends, for then we have two equal and opposite forces. Thus the force must depend on the variation of the field. More specifically, the net force in the x-direction F_x depends on the difference of the x-components of the field, the y-force F_y on the difference of the E_y's and the same for F_z and E_z. For instance, $F_x = qE_{x,+q} - qE_{x,-q}$. The difference for any component of **E** can be calculated by the differential formula A.2–19 involving the gradient, since each component is a scalar function of position. Thus the components of the force on the dipole are given by

$$F_x = q\ \delta \mathbf{l} \cdot \nabla E_x = \mathbf{p} \cdot \nabla E_x = p_x \frac{\partial E_x}{\partial x} + p_y \frac{\partial E_x}{\partial y} + p_z \frac{\partial E_x}{\partial z}$$

$$F_y = \mathbf{p} \cdot \nabla E_y$$

$$F_z = \mathbf{p} \cdot \nabla E_z$$

These three equations can be combined into a single vector formula if we treat $(\mathbf{p} \cdot \nabla)$ as a special scalar differential operator. We have

$$\mathbf{p} \cdot \nabla = p_x \frac{\partial}{\partial x} + p_y \frac{\partial}{\partial y} + p_z \frac{\partial}{\partial z} \qquad (3.2\text{–}1)$$

and can write corresponding formulas in cylindrical and spherical coordinates if we are careful to note the variation of the unit vectors with the polar angles. (Cf. Problem 3.2c.) Then we may write:

$$\mathbf{F} = (\mathbf{p} \cdot \nabla)\mathbf{E} \qquad (3.2\text{–}2)$$

This formula is convenient for calculation, but a form more convenient for later development can be obtained by transforming this expression using the conservative field property expressed by Eqs. 1.8–1 or 1.8–2. The derivatives $\partial E_x/\partial y$ and $\partial E_x/\partial z$ in the expression above for F_x can be replaced by their equals $\partial E_y/\partial x$ and $\partial E_z/\partial x$, giving

$$F_x = p_x \frac{\partial E_x}{\partial x} + p_y \frac{\partial E_y}{\partial x} + p_z \frac{\partial E_z}{\partial x} = \frac{\partial}{\partial x}(\mathbf{p} \cdot \mathbf{E})$$

since **p** and its components are constants. Therefore, F_x is the x-component of a gradient, and we can write for **F** the expression[3]

$$\mathbf{F} = \nabla(\mathbf{p} \cdot \mathbf{E}) \tag{3.2-3}$$

To derive the torque expressions, consider a dipole of length δl with charges $+q$ and $-q$, in an electric field **E** that makes an angle θ with **δl**. Referring to Fig. 3.2a, we readily find the torque $\mathscr{T}$ about the center of the dipole to be $2 \cdot qE \cdot \frac{1}{2}\delta l \sin \theta = q \, \delta l E \sin \theta$, so that

$$\mathscr{T} = pE \sin \theta$$

which in accordance with Eq. A.2–37 we can write as a vector:

$$\mathscr{T} = \mathbf{p} \times \mathbf{E} \tag{3.2-4}$$

If **E** is not uniform in the neighborhood of the dipole, so that its value at $-q$ is different from that at $+q$, an average value taken at the center will be a good approximation. The reader can readily show that for the

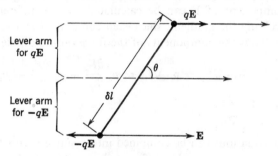

Fig. 3.2a. Torque on a dipole.

case of uniform **E** the torque $\mathscr{T}$ is the same if any other point is chosen as the center. If the field is not uniform, the torque about a distant center due to the force 3.2–2 must be added to Eq. 3.2–4.

Just as the force per unit charge is the negative gradient of the potential energy per unit charge, so also is any conservative force the negative gradient of a potential energy. We see from Eq. 3.2–3 that the potential energy U of the dipole can be written

$$U = -\mathbf{p} \cdot \mathbf{E} \tag{3.2-5}$$

Let us corroborate this by calculating the potential energy by means of the torque formula. Imagine bringing the dipole from infinity to the point where its energy is to be evaluated in such a way that $+q$ and $-q$ are at all times on the same equipotential (**p** is always perpendicular to **E**). The

---

[3] This result can be calculated in vector terms by expanding $\mathbf{p} \times (\nabla \times \mathbf{E}) = 0$. Cf. Problem A.2l.

work done on $+q$ will therefore exactly cancel that on $-q$. Now rotate the dipole from $\theta = 90°$ to the chosen θ. (See Fig. 3.2a.) The work done by the electric field, which lowers the potential energy, is given for an angular displacement $d\theta$ by $\mathscr{T}\, d\theta = pE \sin\theta\, d\theta$. Hence the total work done is $-\int_{\pi/2}^{\theta} pE \sin\theta\, d\theta = pE \cos\theta = \mathbf{p} \cdot \mathbf{E}$, where the minus sign is used because the direction of the torque is that of decreasing θ. This is the entire work done by the field in moving the dipole from ∞ to the position in question, so the potential energy must be its negative, as given by Eq. 3.2–5.

The potential energy of a dipole $\mathbf{p}_1$ arbitrarily located in the field of another $\mathbf{p}_2$ can be found by using 3.2–5 and 3.1–8:

$$U = -p_1 \cdot E_2 = \frac{1}{4\pi\epsilon_0 r^3}[\mathbf{p}_1 \cdot \mathbf{p}_2 - 3(\mathbf{p}_1 \cdot \mathbf{1}_r)(\mathbf{p}_2 \cdot \mathbf{1}_r)] \qquad (3.2\text{–}6)$$

a formula which is unchanged if $\mathbf{p}_1$ and $\mathbf{p}_2$ are interchanged and $\mathbf{1}_r$ is changed to $-\mathbf{1}_r$. This energy U is called the "dipole-dipole interaction energy."

Problem 3.2a. Assume that the $+q$ and $-q$ of a dipole are located in a nonuniform field at positions $\mathbf{r}_1$ and $\mathbf{r}_2$ with respect to an arbitrary origin. Derive a formula for the torque on the dipole about the origin.

Problem 3.2b. Show that the effect of non-uniformity in the field on 3.2–4 depends in lowest order on δl and on the second derivatives of $\mathbf{E}$.

Problem 3.2c. Write $\mathbf{p} \cdot \nabla$ in spherical coordinates. Using the results of Problem A.2d, calculate $(\mathbf{p} \cdot \nabla)\mathbf{E}$ and interpret each term geometrically for a small but finite δl.

Problem 3.2d. A dipole of strength 4.8×10^{-18} statcoulomb-cm is situated 5×10^{-8} cm from a nucleus of charge equal to $+3$ electronic units. Find the force and torque on the dipole (a) when it is oriented along a radius from the nucleus, positive end further away; (b) when it is at right angles to a radius; (c) when it makes an angle of $45°$ with the radius, positive end towards the nucleus. *Hint:* Use Cartesian coordinates or the answer to Problem 3.2c.

Problem 3.2e. Two dipoles of strengths respectively 3×10^{-13} coulomb-m and 5×10^{-13} coulomb-m are located 2 cm apart. Find the force between them (a) when both dipole vectors point in the same direction along the line joining them; (b) when one dipole points towards the other, and the second points at right angles to the line of centers; (c) when both point at right angles to the line of centers, and in the same direction; (d) same as (c) but pointing oppositely. Verify in each case that Newton's law of action and reaction holds.

Problem 3.2f. Find the torques of each dipole of Problem 3.2e on the other. Can you resolve the apparent difficulty entailed in the failure of these torques to obey the law of action and reaction in some of the cases given?

Problem 3.2g. Find the force and torque on a dipole located at a radius r outside a uniformly charged infinite cylinder of density λ coulomb/m when **p** is oriented at an angle θ with **r**, in the plane containing r and the axis of the cylinder.

3.3 Closer Approximations to Molecular Fields

Although the dipole field calculated in Section 3.1 will turn out to give a completely adequate account of dielectric phenomena, it is of interest to see how higher approximations can be calculated, partly in order to be able to estimate the error involved in using the dipole field and partly because the same calculations are important in dealing with radiation from antennas, from molecular systems, and from nuclei, as well as in considering forces that act on atoms, molecules, and nuclei.

We shall begin with a step beyond the calculation of Section 3.1. Suppose that the dipole moments of a given molecule add to zero. A next approximation would start with a pair of equal and opposite dipoles, separated by a displacement $\delta\mathbf{l}'$. Just as the potential was previously found by use of the gradient formula for a differential, $V = -\delta\mathbf{l} \cdot \nabla(V_{+q})$, we have now $V = -\delta\mathbf{l}' \cdot \nabla(V_{+p})$, so that using Eq. 3.1–2,

$$V = -\delta\mathbf{l}' \cdot \nabla\left(\frac{-\mathbf{p} \cdot \nabla\dfrac{1}{r}}{4\pi\epsilon_0}\right) \tag{3.3-1}$$

We shall leave the details of the expansion of this expression to Problems 3.3a and b and shall shortly give an alternate calculation. Let us meanwhile discuss the results qualitatively.

The two dipoles may be situated with respect to each other in various ways, as shown in Fig. 3.3a. Any of these configurations is called an "electric quadrupole." Symmetry considerations often allow only the form in which the two dipoles are collinear. Since the dipole potential varies inversely as the square of the distance from the molecule and the quadrupole potential involves another differentiation, the latter will evidently vary as $1/r^3$, with the quadrupole field varying as $1/r^4$.

Similarly, we might have a cancellation of the quadrupole field and be led to make another differentiation, obtaining the *octupole field*, with $V \propto 1/r^4$ and $E \propto 1/r^5$. Higher multipole fields are generally called 16-pole, 32-pole, etc.

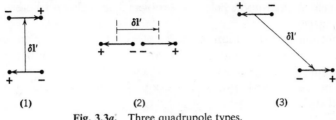

Fig. 3.3a. Three quadrupole types.

Now let us consider the error made by use of the true dipole formula for a dipole of finite length. One can relate r and r' in Fig. 3.1a by the law of cosines as in Section 1.3, or more symmetrically by using the distance r_0 from $\mathcal{O}$ to the center of the dipole. Then if an expansion is made in powers of $\delta l/r_0$ by means of the binomial theorem, one gets a series with terms that vary as $1/r^2$, $1/r^4$, etc., giving the actual potential as a sum of dipole, octupole, 32-pole terms (Problem 3.3c).

Another way to see that this must be so is to replace the dipole by a group of dipoles including fictitious positive and negative charges whose combined effect is zero. One such combination that is equivalent to $+q$ and $-q$ separated by δl is shown in Fig. 3.3b. If the dipole of length $\frac{1}{2}\delta l$ and charge $2q$ be superimposed on the two quadrupoles, all the fictitious charges cancel, and we are left with the original dipole. The shorter dipole has the same moment, and the two quadrupoles together form an octupole, so that an actual dipole of a given length is equivalent to one of the same strength but half the length plus an octupole whose displacements are $\frac{1}{2}$ and $\frac{1}{4}$ the original length. If the process were to be continued, we would continue to add octupole moments until we reached the limiting value that is obtained in the series referred to above.

Similarly, higher actual multipoles can be reduced to a series of ideal multipoles, generally in more than one way. We may also consider more complex combinations of charges as the sum of a "monopole" field, a

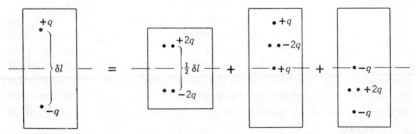

Fig. 3.3b. One dipole and two quadrupoles that are equivalent to a single dipole. If the three figures on the right are slid together along the dashed line and superimposed, they will give the figure on the left.

dipole field, a quadrupole field, etc. Problem 3.3c deals with a case of three point charges.

A continuous distribution of charge $\rho(x, y, z)$ located near an origin $\mathcal{O}$, at a distance small compared to the coordinates (x_0, y_0, z_0) of a point of observation, gives rise to a potential which can be expressed in multipole orders by use of the binomial expansion. We have, integrating over the charged region,

$$
\begin{aligned}
V &= \frac{1}{4\pi\epsilon_0} \int \frac{\rho \, dr}{[(x_0 - x)^2 + (y_0 - y)^2 + (z_0 - z)^2]^{\frac{1}{2}}} \\
&= \frac{1}{4\pi\epsilon_0} \int \frac{\rho \, d\tau}{[(\mathbf{r}_0 - \mathbf{r}) \cdot (\mathbf{r}_0 - \mathbf{r})]^{\frac{1}{2}}} \\
&= \frac{1}{4\pi\epsilon_0} \int \frac{\rho \, d\tau}{[\mathbf{r}_0 \cdot \mathbf{r}_0 - 2\mathbf{r}_0 \cdot \mathbf{r} + \mathbf{r} \cdot \mathbf{r}]^{\frac{1}{2}}} \\
&= \frac{1}{4\pi\epsilon_0} \int \frac{\rho \, d\tau}{r_0 \left[1 - \dfrac{2\mathbf{r}_0 \cdot \mathbf{r}}{r_0^2} + \dfrac{r^2}{r_0^2}\right]^{\frac{1}{2}}}
\end{aligned}
\tag{3.3-2}
$$

which by the use of the binomial expansion becomes, letting $\mathbf{r}_0/r_0 = \mathbf{1}_{r0}$ and carrying the expansion only to quadratic terms in r,

$$
V = \frac{1}{4\pi\epsilon_0} \int \frac{\rho \, d\tau}{r_0} + \frac{1}{4\pi\epsilon_0} \int \frac{\rho \mathbf{r} \cdot \mathbf{1}_{r0}}{r_0^2} \, d\tau + \frac{1}{4\pi\epsilon_0} \int \rho \, \frac{3(\mathbf{r} \cdot \mathbf{1}_{r0})^2 - r^2}{2r_0^3} \, d\tau + \cdots
\tag{3.3-3}
$$

The first term is clearly the potential that would be produced by the total charge if it were placed at the origin. If we place an equal negative charge at the origin and combine it with the second term, we see that to each $\rho \, d\tau$ at a displacement $\mathbf{r}$ from the origin we can associate $-\rho \, d\tau$ at the origin and consequently an elementary dipole potential.

The total or net dipole moment is thus seen to be given by the integral

$$
\mathbf{p} = \int \rho \mathbf{r} \, d\tau
\tag{3.3-4}
$$

and so the second term of Eq. 3.3–3 represents the dipole potential of the distribution. The third represents the quadrupole potential, as is apparent from dimensional arguments. An explicit demonstration of this assertion requires the definition of the quadrupole moment as a two-subscript affair (i.e., a tensor):

$$
Q_{xx} = \int \rho x^2 \, d\tau; \qquad Q_{xy} = \int \rho xy \, d\tau; \qquad \text{etc.}
\tag{3.3-5}
$$

and the evaluation of the field produced by each of the nine combinations by use of Eq. 3.3–1. For each element of charge $\rho \, d\tau$ which has a dipole moment $\rho \mathbf{r} \, d\tau$ there is assumed to be an opposite dipole at the origin. The details are left to the reader. (Problem 3.3*b*.)

Now we can explain why quadrupole and higher moments are not important for a discussion of dielectric materials. Dipole moments are important because, although the dipole fields are much weaker than monopole fields, there are many more dipoles than free monopoles in any ordinary piece of material. Quadrupole fields, however, must be compared to dipole fields as produced by the *same* number of molecules. Hence the macroscopic effects of atomic quadrupoles are expected to be small in the same ratio as that for the field of a single molecule, for which the quadrupole contributions has an added factor of about the size of the molecule in the numerator, and one higher power of the distance of observation in the denominator.

Forces on multipoles clearly involve higher derivatives of the electric field—second derivatives for quadrupoles, third for octupoles, in general Nth derivatives for 2^N poles. An important example is that of many nonspherical atomic nuclei. The protons in these nuclei are apparently arranged in such a way that in addition to the monopole field there is a substantial symmetrical quadrupole contribution. There are thus forces on nuclei that depend on the second derivative of the average molecular field; experiments involving the absorption of high-frequency radiation "tuned" to the quadrupole moment thus give a measure of this second derivative at the position of the nucleus.

Problem 3.3a. Obtain explicit formulas from 3.3–1 for quadrupoles of types (1) and (2) in Fig. 3.3*a*.

Problem 3.3b. Find the potential produced by a linear octupole in which the displacements $\delta\mathbf{l}$, $-\delta\mathbf{l}'$, and $\delta\mathbf{l}''$, are all parallel.

Problem 3.3c. Write r and r' for the dipole of Fig. 3.1*a* in terms of the distance r_0 from the center of the dipole to the point of observation and the angle θ between $\mathbf{r}_0$ and $\mathbf{p}$. Use the binomial theorem to calculate the dipole and octupole potentials for this physical dipole.

Problem 3.3d. Complete the demonstration mentioned in the text that the last term of Eq. 3.3–3 is indeed the quadrupole potential. Write an expression for this term when the z-axis is an axis of rotational symmetry for the distribution ρ.

Problem 3.3e. Charges of value $+q$ each are located at two corners of an equilateral triangle, and a charge of value $-q$ is located at the other vertex. Show how the resulting field can be calculated in two ways as the sum of monopole, dipole, and quadrupole fields.

Problem 3.3f. Show that a charge distribution that is symmetric with respect to an inversion through the origin must have zero dipole moment. Show that such a distribution with a single axis of rotational symmetry will usually have a quadrupole moment, but that a spherically symmetric distribution cannot.

3.4 The Field Produced by Polarized Dielectric Material

In general, nearly every molecule of a dielectric is polarized and contributes through its dipole moment to the total field. Some molecules are permanently polarized for chemical reasons, and are called "polar molecules." Materials composed of them are called "polar substances." The molecular agitation due to heat usually distributes these dipoles in a random way, so that their net effect is zero, but the presence of an external electric field will tend to line them up in some given direction. The resulting equilibrium between the thermal agitation and the external force means that each molecule contributes to the total field during some small fraction of the time. In a few polar substances, called "ferroelectrics," there is a strong tendency for the dipoles to keep each other lined up in spite of the random heat motion.

There are also a few substances in which the polar molecules can be lined up in a strong field in such a way that a permanent over-all polarization is frozen in. These substances are called "electrets" and, although their actual behavior is complex and they are not much used in practice, their theoretical resemblance to bar magnets makes them of considerable importance for this book. We shall discuss idealized electrets in Section 3.6, and some properties of real ones in Section 3.10.

Finally, a great many molecules are normally unpolarized and become polarized under the influence of an external field. Polar molecules will also have their dipole strengths changed by an external field. In both these cases, the electrons are shifted more or less as a group toward one side of the molecule or atom, so that the center of the electron cloud is displaced relative to the nucleus.

Before considering further the physical properties of molecules, we wish to calculate the external field produced by an arbitrary piece of polarized material. It will not matter how the polarization came about—in fact, the calculation will apply perfectly well to a plasma in which the ions and electrons at a given instant of time happen to be separated. We shall make the calculation first in a somewhat idealized but simple fashion that helps to provide a concrete explanation of the results, and shall then repeat the process in a general and straightforward way originally introduced by Poisson.

If we consider any small volume $d\tau'$ in the dielectric, we can add the dipole moments of all the molecules within and use for r in the potential formula 3.1–9 a radius drawn from (x', y', z'), a point in $d\tau'$, to the point of observation. The sum of the moments will be proportional to the number of molecules (as long as there are enough to be a representative sample for the purpose of averaging) and hence to the volume $d\tau'$. Let us call it $\mathbf{P}\, d\tau'$, so that

$$\sum_i \mathbf{p}_i = \mathbf{P}\, d\tau' \tag{3.4–1}$$

where the summation is over all individual dipoles in the volume $d\tau'$. The vector $\mathbf{P}$ is called the *electric polarization;* more explicitly it is the electric

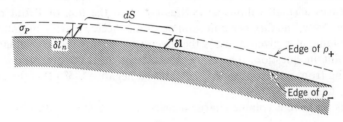

Fig. 3.4a.   Surface polarization charge.

dipole moment per unit volume. It is generally a function that varies in both direction and magnitude from point to point.

Let us idealize the dielectric by assuming that all molecules in a given region are polarized identically, each by the motion of a charge $+q$ through a displacement $\boldsymbol{\delta l}$ ($+q$ is for instance the charge on a nucleus or group of nuclei). Let the number of molecules per unit volume be N. Then we have $\mathbf{P} = Nq\, \boldsymbol{\delta l}$. We shall furthermore consider all the positive and negative charges separately and replace the discrete distributions of the two signs by continuous charge clouds. Thus we assume there to be a positive charge density $\rho_+ = Nq$, and a negative one $\rho_- = -Nq$. When the dielectric is unpolarized, these distributions are everywhere equal and opposite. Polarization involves the displacement of the entire positive charge distribution with respect to the negative one. We may allow ρ_+, ρ_-, and $\boldsymbol{\delta l}$ to vary from place to place.

Now at the surface, the edges of the negative and positive clouds coincide before polarization occurs. If the positive cloud moves out by a displacement $\boldsymbol{\delta l}$, there will be a positive excess of charge at the surface. (If $\boldsymbol{\delta l}$ is inward, a negative excess is left behind.) The amount of excess in an area dS is given by ρ_+ times the volume of a cylinder of base dS and slant height δl (Fig. 3.4a). Let the height of this cylinder, which is the component of δl normal to the surface, be called δl_n. Then the volume is $\delta l_n\, dS$ and we can describe the excess charge by a surface density σ_P, given by

$$\sigma_P\, dS = \rho_+\delta l_n\, dS = Nq\, \delta l_n\, dS = P_n\, dS = \mathbf{P} \cdot \mathbf{dS},$$

or

$$\sigma_P = \mathbf{P} \cdot \mathbf{1}_S = P_n \qquad (3.4\text{--}2a)$$

where $\mathbf{1}_S$ is normal to the surface, and P_n denotes the normal component of $\mathbf{P}$. The surface charge is seen to result from a lack of cancellation of ρ_+ and ρ_- at the boundary.

There will also be a net volume charge inside the dielectric if the displacement δl varies from place to place. We note by the calculation just given that $\mathbf{P} \cdot \mathbf{dS}$ represents the amount of charge that passes through a surface element $\mathbf{dS}$ when polarization occurs. The net amount of charge that leaves a small volume $d\tau$ is thus equal to the flux of $\mathbf{P}$ out of the surface. Now, the flux per unit volume of any vector leaving an infinitesimal volume at a given point is the divergence of this vector evaluated at the point in question. Therefore, the charge decrease per unit volume resulting from polarization is $\nabla \cdot \mathbf{P}$, and its negative $-\nabla \cdot \mathbf{P}$ is the charge added, or ρ_P.

Thus we have a volume charge density resulting from polarization,

$$\rho_P = -\nabla \cdot \mathbf{P} \qquad (3.4\text{--}2b)$$

The field and potential produced at a point anywhere outside the dielectric can be calculated from 3.4–2 since these distributions represent the net uncanceled effect of all the molecular charges in the material.

Let us verify this conclusion by Poisson's method. The potential produced at an external point (x, y, z) by the dipoles in a volume $d\tau'$ may be written by Eqs. 3.1–9 and 3.4–1 as

$$dV = -\frac{1}{4\pi\epsilon_0}\, \mathbf{P} \cdot \nabla\left(\frac{1}{r}\right) d\tau'$$

The potential produced by the entire piece of dielectric is therefore the integral

$$V = -\frac{1}{4\pi\epsilon_0}\int_\tau \mathbf{P} \cdot \nabla\left(\frac{1}{r}\right) d\tau' = +\frac{1}{4\pi\epsilon_0}\int_\tau \mathbf{P} \cdot \nabla'\left(\frac{1}{r}\right) d\tau' \qquad (3.4\text{--}3)$$

The ∇ in the expression contains derivatives with respect to x, y, and z, the coordinates of the point of observation, whereas ∇' contains derivatives of x', y', and z'. Derivatives of $r = [(x - x')^2 + (y - y')^2 + (z - z')^2]^{1/2}$ with respect to the primed coordinates have an opposite effect to those taken with respect to unprimed coordinates,[4] so that $\nabla = -\nabla' = -[\mathbf{1}_x(\partial/\partial x') + \mathbf{1}_y(\partial/\partial y') + \mathbf{1}_z(\partial/\partial z')]$.

---

[4] If r increases for a certain displacement of the point (x, y, z), it will be decreased if the same displacement is applied to (x', y', z').

We shall now perform a type of integration by parts. A generalization of the formula $u\,dv = d(uv) - v\,du$ that applies to our case is the following vector identity (see Table A.2B, p. 633, item 2):

$$\mathbf{P} \cdot \mathbf{\nabla}\left(\frac{1}{r}\right) = \mathbf{\nabla} \cdot \left(\frac{\mathbf{P}}{r}\right) - \frac{1}{r}\,\mathbf{\nabla} \cdot \mathbf{P}$$

which can be proven easily by writing out components. Thus we have

$$V = \frac{1}{4\pi\epsilon_0} \int_\tau \mathbf{P} \cdot \mathbf{\nabla}'\left(\frac{1}{r}\right) d\tau' = \frac{1}{4\pi\epsilon_0} \int_\tau \mathbf{\nabla}' \cdot \left(\frac{\mathbf{P}}{r}\right) d\tau' - \frac{1}{4\pi\epsilon_0} \int \frac{\mathbf{\nabla}' \cdot \mathbf{P}}{r}\,d\tau'$$

Transforming the first integral of the last expression by the divergence theorem, Eq. A.2–22, we get

$$V = \int_S \frac{\mathbf{P} \cdot d\mathbf{S}'}{4\pi\epsilon_0 r} - \int \frac{\mathbf{\nabla}' \cdot \mathbf{P}}{4\pi\epsilon_0 r}\,d\tau' \tag{3.4–4}$$

This expression is exactly the same as the formula for the potential due to a combined surface and volume distribution of amounts given by Eqs. 3.4–2, but no assumption of uniformity of q or δl need be made.

We have proved that a polarized piece of dielectric or body of ionized gas with zero net charge produces electric field as if it had a charge density on its surface equal in magnitude to the normal component of the polarization at the surface and a volume distribution throughout its interior equal at every point to the negative divergence of the polarization at that point. These charge densities are sometimes called "fictitious," but they are not. However more common and less misleading names are "bound charge" or "polarization charge." Charge acquired by a dielectric as a result of triboelectricity or by any contact with an already charged object is called "free charge," a name used generally for any charge other than polarization charge.

We have implicitly assumed here that the dielectric material ends abruptly at its surface. By P_n we mean the limiting value as we approach the surface from an interior point. For some purposes it is convenient to avoid the resulting discontinuity between P_n inside the surface and that just outside by imagining the surface of the dielectric to be slightly diffuse—that is, we think of P_n as changing from its interior value to zero in a very thin but finite layer at the surface. In this case we will have a concentrated volume distribution of charge in the thin layer and a large value of div $\mathbf{P}$, but no surface charge σ and no limiting P_n. This amounts to shifting all the contribution of the first term of Eq. 3.4–4 into the second. However, for most physical interpretations, the infinitesimal surface layer is the most useful concept.

The average field and potential at a point in the interior of dielectric material may also be calculated from 3.4–4. To see that this is so, we must convince ourselves that a time-and-space average for V will result in canceling out all the local fluctuations produced by moving electrons and atoms.[5]

Consideration of suitably-shaped cavities in the material allows an easy demonstration that 3.4–4 may be used to calculate potential differences between points in a dielectric, but a direct proof that this formula gives the correct average takes some calculation, which the reader may or may not wish to pursue.

An explicit calculation for the average can best be done in terms of the field rather than the potential. As we consider a point O in the medium, we can divide

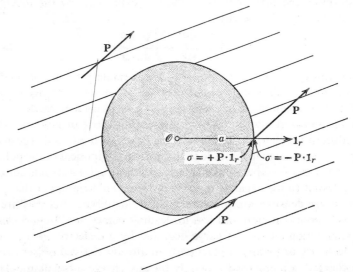

Fig. 3.4b.   Illustrating the calculation of the average field at a point O in a dielectric medium.

the material into two parts, the one a small sphere of radius a drawn about O and the other the remainder (Fig. 3.4b). The sphere is to be large enough to contain a good average representation of the molecules in their various states of polarization. The potential and field produced at O by the dipoles outside the sphere are given by Eq. 3.4–4, including the field produced by the polarization surface charge P_n on the inside of the sphere (the magnitude of this field is calculated in section 3.9). Taking $\mathbf{1}_r$ as outward on the spherical surface (i.e., into the material) we can write P_n as $-\mathbf{P} \cdot \mathbf{1}_r$.

Now we need to calculate the field at O produced by the material *in* the sphere and to average it for different positions of O. Consider the volume integral of the

[5] It was pointed out for metals on p. 84 that V_G calculated from the charges on the surface and outside and from the double-layer χ potential was an average field for points inside the metal. For dielectrics, any such double-layer will automatically be included in **P**.

field $d\mathbf{E}$ produced by the $N\, d\tau$ molecules in each volume element $d\tau$ of the sphere. This field depends only on the relative coordinates of the point $\mathcal{O}$ and the center of the group of $N\, d\tau$ molecules. The integral $\int d\mathbf{E} = N\int \mathbf{E}_P\, d\tau$ where $\mathbf{E}_P$ is the field of a single dipole, is $N\tau$ times the integral one would get by placing one molecule at the center of the spere—τ being the total volume—and calculating the *average* field produced by it in the sphere, which is $(1/\tau)\int \mathbf{E}_P\, d\tau$. Each infinitesimal contribution to this integral has the same value corresponding to the same relative coordinates as the corresponding contribution to the integral we started to calculate. Furthermore, averaging over all points near the single dipole will give a result corresponding exactly to a space-and-time average for different points $\mathcal{O}$.

Now, since for a single molecule $\mathbf{E}_P = -\nabla V_P$ where V_P is the dipole field, we can use the theorem given by Eq. A.2–24 and write

$$\int_\tau \mathbf{E}_P\, d\tau = -\int_\tau \nabla V_P\, d\tau = -\int_S V_P\, d\mathbf{S}$$

and

$$N\int_\tau \mathbf{E}_P\, d\tau = -N\int_S V_P\, d\mathbf{S} = -\int_S \frac{N\mathbf{p}\cdot \mathbf{1}_r}{4\pi\epsilon_0 r^2}\, d\mathbf{S} = -\int_S \frac{\mathbf{P}\cdot \mathbf{1}_r}{4\pi\epsilon_0 r^2}\, d\mathbf{S} \qquad (3.4\text{–}5)$$

Since we have chosen a sphere with center at $\mathcal{O}$, $d\mathbf{S} = \mathbf{1}_r\, dS$. As above, $\mathbf{1}_r$ points away from $\mathcal{O}$. Taking into account this direction for $\mathbf{1}_r$, we see that Eq. 3.4–5 gives the same field as that which a layer of charge $+\mathbf{P}\cdot \mathbf{1}_r$ on the spherical surface would produce. Thus the contributions from the material inside and outside cancel exactly.

We have proved that our original result Eq. 3.4–4 gives from its gradient the average field within the material. The potential itself can only differ from 3.4–4 by a constant, as is to be expected.

At points in a dielectric medium, it is best to make a direct operational definition of $\mathbf{E}$ and V in terms of cavities within which, at least in principle, some experimental apparatus can be placed. *Such cavities are to be imagined as having no effect on the polarization existing before they were made.*

Now, a cavity will in general have components of $\mathbf{P}$ normal to its surfaces and thus carry a charge σ_P. But if its dimensions are small, the potential gradients produced by this extra surface charge will have only a small effect on V. Thus we shall assume that Eq. 3.4–4 also applies to the potential in any small cavity.

We must be careful in calculating the field from the gradient of Eq. 3.4–4 since the cavity surface charges can produce an appreciable field even when their dimensions are infinitesimal. There is one shape and orientation of cavity, however, for which the cavity charges are negligible. Consider a very thin, cylindrical, needlelike cavity or drill hole, parallel to $\mathbf{P}$ (see $\mathscr{A}\mathscr{B}$ in Fig. 3.4c). Now P_n will be zero along the sides of this cavity. If the cylinder is sufficiently thin compared to its length, the field produced at its center by the polarization charges on its ends will be negligible (Problem 3.4e). Thus the field inside the cavity at its center will be given by the gradient of a potential calculated from Eq. 3.4–4 and from any extended charges present. Therefore the field in a needlelike cavity parallel to **P** may be taken as an exact operational definition of the field at an average point in the medium itself.

If the drill hole is not parallel to **P**, there will be a contribution to the field from the surface polarization, but near the center of the cavity these contributions will be perpendicular to its length, so that *the parallel component of* **E** *in such a cavity is equal to the component in the same direction in the medium.* Therefore, we can imagine calculating $\int \mathbf{E} \cdot \mathbf{dl}$ along the

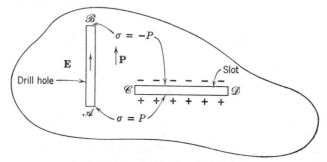

Fig. 3.4c. Cavities in a dielectric.

paths through the dielectric by locating the paths in needle-like tunnels. The result for the PD across an entire piece of dielectric is of course independent of the path, but this argument shows that we may indeed use Eq. 3.4–4 for all observable potential differences.

Let us consider another simple cavity shape. $\mathscr{CD}$ in Fig. 3.4c is a cross section of a flat coin-shaped cavity or slot with top and bottom perpendicular to **P** and lateral dimensions large compared to its thickness. Such a cavity will have a plane distribution of charge on top and bottom, and a field inside produced by this charge of magnitude $E_P = \sigma_P/\epsilon_0$ in the same direction as **P** itself. Thus the total field strength in the slot (far from the edges) is

$$\mathbf{E}_{\text{cavity}} = \mathbf{E} + \sigma_P \mathbf{1}_P/\epsilon_0 = \mathbf{E} + \mathbf{P}/\epsilon_0 \qquad (3.4\text{–}6)$$

where $\mathbf{1}_P$ is a unit vector in the direction of **P**, and **E** denotes as before the field inside the dielectric (whose sources are the external charges and all the polarization volume and surface charges, *except* those on the walls of the cavity).

Problem 3.4a. What surface density of charge will appear on a slab of dielectric which is polarized normal to the surface in an amount corresponding to a shift of one electron per molecule through a distance of 6×10^{-10} cm? Assume 4×10^{22} molecules/cm³ in the material.

Problem 3.4b. Suppose that in a certain medium **P** is entirely in the x-direction and is variable. Suppose that the resulting volume charge density corresponds to one extra electron per million molecules. Find $\partial P_x/\partial x$. If $P_x = 0$ when $x = 0$, find P when $x = 10^{-6}$ m. Find the corresponding displacement of charge in this region, if one electron in each molecule actually shifts. Assume 3×10^{22} molecules/cm^3.

Problem 3.4c. Calculate the total dipole moment of a piece of dielectric, $\int \mathbf{P}\, d\tau$, from ρ_P and σ_P by use of Eq. 3.3–4 and the equivalent surface integral. (*Hint:* Use Eq. A.2–25.)

Problem 3.4d. If one electron per cubic Ångstrom moves when a certain piece of dielectric is polarized, how far does it move when σ_P on a surface normal to **P** is equal to the value found in Problem 2.2f?

Problem 3.4e. A drill hole parallel to **P** in uniformly polarized material is a circular cylinder of radius r and length l. Find a formula for **E** at its center, taking the fields produced by the bound charges on the two ends as (a) uniform disk fields and (b) point charge fields. Show from (a) how to get both the result for a coin-shaped cavity of infinitesimal height and that for a drill hole of infinitesimal radius.

3.5 Application of the Flux Law to a Dielectric Medium

A particular form of the flux law that is useful when dealing with dielectrics can be obtained by dividing the total charge inside an arbitrary Gaussian surface into free and bound parts. If the Gaussian surface lies entirely outside a piece of dielectric, the total bound charge inside is zero, and we have nothing new (except of course if the piece of dielectric is so shaped as to destroy symmetry otherwise present and prevent any practical use of Gauss' law).

Consider a Gaussian surface that lies partly or wholly in a dielectric medium. In accordance with the calculations made in the last section, we can find the polarization charge that has been transferred *into* the surface by calculating the integral $q_P = -\int P_n\, dS = -\int \mathbf{P} \cdot d\mathbf{S}$ over the surface. (There is no contribution from any part of the surface not lying in the dielectric since **P** will be zero on these parts.) Let us write Eq. 1.4–2 again, denoting the *free* charges inside the surface by $\sum_n q_{n,\text{free}}$ and the total polarization charge by q_P,

$$\epsilon_0 \Phi_E = \epsilon_0 \int_{\text{closed } S} \mathbf{E} \cdot d\mathbf{S} = \sum_n q_{n,\text{free}} + q_P = \sum_n q_{n,\text{free}} - \int \mathbf{P} \cdot d\mathbf{S}$$

or, transposing and combining terms,

$$\int_S (\epsilon_0 \mathbf{E} + \mathbf{P}) \cdot d\mathbf{S} = \sum_n q_{n,\text{free}}$$

We can now write a flux law that *that does not contain the polarization charge explicitly* if we define a new field vector and a new flux. We write the new vector, in the MKS system,

$$D = \epsilon_0 E + P \qquad (3.5\text{-}1a)$$

We shall call D the "electric displacement" (a name introduced by Maxwell) and its flux,

$$\Phi_D = \int\limits_{\text{any } S} D \cdot dS \qquad (3.5\text{-}2)$$

will be called the flux of displacement. In empty space, it is equal to $\epsilon_0 \Phi_E$. Now we can write the flux law for dielectrics:

$$\Phi_D = \int\limits_{\text{closed } S} D \cdot dS = \sum_n q_{n,\text{free}} \qquad (3.5\text{-}3a)$$

The differential equation form of this law, corresponding to Eq. 1.5–1, is

$$\nabla \cdot D = \rho_{\text{free}} \qquad (3.5\text{-}4a)$$

which is another form of Maxwell's first equation (cf. Section 1.5).

In free space, D is equal to $\epsilon_0 E$, and we can draw lines or tubes of displacement that coincide with lines or tubes of force. In dielectrics for which P is parallel to E (see Section 3.7 below), D is also, although the density of lines of displacement will differ from that of the lines of force in a way that depends on the relation of P to E. In general, however, P may have a direction different from that of E, and D will point in still a third direction.

Maxwell interpreted D in terms of his theory of "aether strains" but for our purposes it is best to think of it as a convenient, auxiliary vector that is useful when we do not want to take the locations and magnitudes of the polarization charges into explicit account. We can define D in an operational way by making it equal to ϵ_0 times the field in a disk-shaped cavity normal to P, in accordance with Eq. 3.4–6.

In the Gaussian and electrostatic systems, we write

$$D = E + 4\pi P \qquad \text{Gaussian} \quad (3.5\text{-}1b)$$

The flux law becomes

$$\Phi_D = \int\limits_{\text{closed } S} D \cdot dS = 4\pi \sum_n q_{n,\text{free}} \qquad \text{Gaussian} \quad (3.5\text{-}3b)$$

and the first Maxwell equation

$$\nabla \cdot D = 4\pi \rho_{\text{free}} \qquad \text{Gaussian} \quad (3.5\text{-}4b)$$

For this system, $D = E$ and $\Phi_D = \Phi_E$ in free space. The field in a disk-shaped cavity in a dielectric is $E + 4\pi P$, equal to D without a multiplying factor.

A simple application of Eq. 3.5–3 which is of quite a general nature is to derive a condition on the values of **D** on the two sides of a boundary of a dielectric medium or an interface between two different media. Let us construct a Gaussian pillbox of infinitesimal height with its top on one side of the interface and its bottom on the other, just as we did for the surface of a conductor (see Section 2.2). Assuming there be *no free charge* at the boundary, we deduce that the displacement flux into the bottom of the box is equal to that out through the top or that the normal component of **D** is the same on the two sides.

$$D_{n1} = D_{n2} \text{ (at a dielectric boundary with no free charge)} \quad (3.5\text{–}5)$$

The flux law gives us no information about the components of **D** parallel to the boundary. However, we can easily get a relation between the tangential components of **E** from considerations similar to those for the needle-like cavities of the last section. It is clear from the discussion in Section 2.4 of local and distant fields at the surface of a conductor that the only difference in **E** that can occur between two points on opposite sides of a charged surface must be a difference in the normal components, since a layer of charge (polarization charge in this case) does not produce a local field parallel to itself. Thus the tangential component of **E** is the same on the two sides,

$$E_{t1} = E_{t2} \text{ (at a dielectric boundary with no free charge)} \quad (3.5\text{–}6)$$

Another way of seeing the same result is to note that V will be continuous across any boundary,[6] and therefore its derivative *along* the boundary will be the same on each side. The result, although not this second argument, is still valid for electric fields in non-static cases.

It is evident that the lines of force and of displacement will have changes in direction at dielectric boundaries (see Problem 3.8a).

Plasma Oscillations. Another application of Eqs. 3.5–1 and 3.5–3 is to electric oscillations in a plasma, which is a gaseous body of ions and electrons of sufficiently low density that considerable charge separation is possible. Because of the mobility of charge, a plasma is normally neutral and free of electric field in its interior, just like a metallic conductor. However, the electrons and ions may oscillate about their mean positions, the electrons being, of course, much more mobile than the ions.

Now if a sudden disturbance, such as an external electric field applied for a short time, displaces each electron by an average amount ξ in the x-direction, the result is a polarization **P** given by

$$\mathbf{P} = -Ne\xi \quad (3.5\text{–}7)$$

[6] Except for *localized* dipole layers, which could scarcely affect the tangential derivatives to any appreciable extent and which we shall ignore.

where there are N electrons per unit volume. If all the ions and electrons are thus counted as "bound charge," the "free charge" density ρ_{free} is zero, so $\nabla \cdot \mathbf{D} = 0$.

Furthermore, all the distant charges produced a zero displacement $\mathbf{D}$ equal to $\epsilon_0\mathbf{E}$ before the disturbance, so after the disturbing field has gone, $\mathbf{D}$ itself will still be zero. Thus we have

$$\mathbf{E} + \frac{\mathbf{P}}{\epsilon_0} = 0 \qquad (3.5\text{–}8a)$$

or

$$E_x = \frac{Ne\xi}{\epsilon_0} \qquad (3.5\text{–}8b)$$

Since the electrons are quite free to move, the field given by 3.5–8 will be the principal force acting on them and we can write to good approximation for each electron

$$F_x = -eE_x = M_e \frac{d^2\xi}{dt^2} = -\frac{Ne^2}{\epsilon_0}\xi \qquad (3.5\text{–}9)$$

This is the well-known equation for simple harmonic oscillation, whose solution is

$$\xi = \xi_0 \sin(\omega_p t + \varphi) \qquad (3.5\text{–}10)$$

The angular frequency ω_p, the so-called "plasma frequency," is given by

$$\omega_p = (Ne^2/\epsilon_0 M_e)^{1/2} \qquad (3.5\text{–}11)$$

If $N = 10^{18}$ electron/m³, $\omega_p = 2\pi \times 9.0 \times 10^9$ sec⁻¹. These plasma oscillations can, of course, be induced by imposing alternating external fields of the right frequency, as well as by pulse-like disturbances such as we assumed above.

It is possible to have electric oscillations of a plasma whose amplitude and phase vary from place to place. In fact, oscillatory traveling waves can be set up. In this case, the frequency is somewhat higher than ω_p by an amount that depends on the mean square speed of the electrons associated with their thermal motion.[7]

Problem 3.5a. Find boundary conditions that hold at an interface between two dielectrics for the *tangential* component of $\mathbf{D}$ and the *normal* component of $\mathbf{E}$.

3.6 Ideal Electrets

As we remarked in Section 3.4, there are a few substances which can be put into a state of permanent polarization. The complicated physical

[7] Cf. C. L. Longmire, *Elementary Plasma Physics*, Interscience, New York, 1963, Sec. 6.2; and J. D. Jackson, *Classical Electrodynamics*, John Wiley, New York, 1962, Sec. 10.9.

characteristics of actual electrets will be discussed briefly in Section 3.10 in connection with other properties of dielectrics. The calculation of field and displacement for an ideal, uniformly polarized electret is on the other hand straightforward and relatively simple. It will serve as a good first application of the theory of Sections 3.4 and 3.5, and the calculations we make here will be easily transferable to the corresponding magnetic cases in Section 8.4.

Let us consider first a long slender cylindrical bar of dielectric that is uniformly and permanently polarized with the constant vector **P** parallel to the axis, as shown in Fig. 3.6a. According to our theory, the field **E** at any point inside or outside the bar can be calculated from the surface

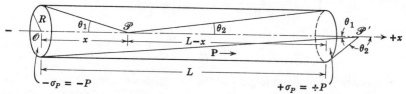

Fig. 3.6a. Diagram for the calculation of **E** on the axis of a uniform bar electret, at points inside and outside the bar

densities $\sigma_P = P$ and $-\sigma_P = -P$ at the ends of the bar. The value of **E** on the axis can be found from the answer to Problem 1.3f, namely, that the field on the axis of a uniformly charged disk of radius R, at a point a distance x from the center, is

$$E = (\sigma/2\epsilon_0)[1 - x/(x^2 + R^2)^{1/2}]$$

Thus at a point $\mathscr{P}$ on the axis x meters from the origin $\mathcal{O}$ at the negative end of the bar with $x < L$, the field is

$$E_{\text{axis}} = \frac{-P}{2\epsilon_0}\left(1 - \frac{x}{(x^2 + R^2)^{1/2}}\right) - \frac{P}{2\epsilon_0}\left(1 - \frac{L - x}{[(L - x)^2 + R^2]^{1/2}}\right) \quad (3.6\text{--}1)$$

This formula can be written in terms of θ_1 and θ_2 as shown in Fig. 3.6a

$$E_{\text{axis}} = \frac{-P}{\epsilon_0} + \frac{P}{2\epsilon_0}(\cos\theta_1 + \cos\theta_2) \quad (3.6\text{--}2a)$$

For a point $\mathscr{P}'$ outside the bar, where $x > L$, the contribution from the right-hand end must have its sign changed, yielding

$$E_{\text{axis}} = \frac{-P}{2\epsilon_0}\left(1 - \frac{x}{(x^2 + R^2)^{1/2}}\right) + \frac{P}{2\epsilon_0}\left(1 - \frac{x - L}{[(x - L)^2 + R^2]^{1/2}}\right)$$

$$= \frac{P}{2\epsilon_0}(\cos\theta_1 + \cos\theta_2) \quad (3.6\text{--}2b)$$

since $\cos\theta_2$ is negative in this case.

For point $\mathscr{P}$, $\mathbf{D} = \epsilon_0\mathbf{E} + \mathbf{P}$, and for $\mathscr{P}'$, $\mathbf{D} = \epsilon_0\mathbf{E}$. In both cases we find the same formula

$$D_{\text{axis}} = \tfrac{1}{2}P(\cos\theta_1 + \cos\theta_2) \tag{3.6–3}$$

Just inside the negative end of the bar, the field is

$$E_{x=0+} = \frac{-P}{2\epsilon_0} - \frac{P}{2\epsilon_0}\left(1 - \frac{L}{(L^2 + R^2)^{\frac{1}{2}}}\right)$$

If R is much smaller than L, the parenthesis can be simplified by the use of the binomial theorem

$$1 - \frac{L}{(L^2 + R^2)^{\frac{1}{2}}} = 1 - \left(1 + \frac{R^2}{L^2}\right)^{-\frac{1}{2}}$$

$$= \frac{R^2}{2L^2} - \frac{3R^4}{8L^4} + \cdots \simeq \frac{R^2}{2L^2} \tag{3.6–4}$$

The error resulting from neglect of the fourth-power term is about 2.5% if the diameter of the bar is equal to its length, and $\frac{1}{16}$ of this for half this diameter. $R^2/2L^2$ itself is less than 1% if R is less than about $L/7$. Thus for any reasonably long thin bar the field on the axis near the negative end is just $-P/2\epsilon_0$, namely, the value for an infinite plane distribution $-\sigma_P$, and similarly it can be readily seen that the field near the positive end is also $-P/2\epsilon_0$. The fields just *outside* the two ends are each obviously $+P/2\epsilon_0$. At the center, on the other hand, $x = L/2$ and

$$E = \frac{-P}{\epsilon_0}\left(1 - \frac{L/2}{[(L/2)^2 + R^2]^{\frac{1}{2}}}\right) \simeq \frac{-P}{\epsilon_0} \cdot \frac{R^2}{2(L/2)^2} = \frac{-2PR^2}{\epsilon_0 L^2}$$

a value very much smaller than at either end.

Lines of force and equipotentials are shown in Fig. 3.6b. They are continuous across the sides of the bar because there is no surface charge there ($P_n = 0$).

Let us now consider the electric displacement. We see immediately that $\mathbf{E}$ and $\mathbf{P}$ are in exactly opposite directions on the axis and approximately so elsewhere in the bar. Just inside each end, on the axis, $D = \epsilon_0(-P/2\epsilon_0) + P = P/2$, using the approximation that $E \simeq -P/2\epsilon_0$, or by noting that one of the cosines in 3.6–3 is zero and the other is nearly one. The same value clearly holds just outside each end. At the center, D is approximately P, since E is so small. Thus $\mathbf{D}$ is in the same direction as $\mathbf{P}$ along the axis, and in contrast to $\mathbf{E}$, it has its greatest value at the center. Furthermore, since no *free* charge is present, there can be no beginning or ending of the flux of $\mathbf{D}$, so the lines of $\mathbf{D}$ must be *closed* curves in cases of ideal symmetry like this one. (Since the field far from the electret must resemble that of a single dipole, the only lines of **D** that can go to infinity must be those exactly on the axis.) Outside the bar the lines of force and of displacement coincide except for density or scale factor. Lines of **D** are shown in Fig. 3.6c. Note that these lines show sharp breaks at the edge of the electret, in contrast to those of **E**. Note also that the flux of **D** at the center of the

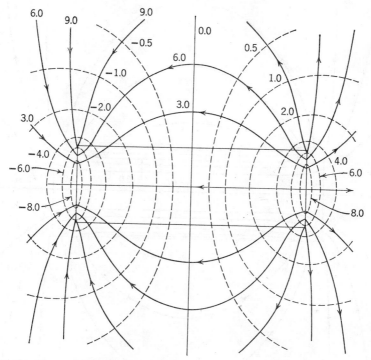

Fig. 3.6b. Lines of **E** and equipotentials for a uniform bar electret. The numbers represent flux Φ_E contained in surfaces of revolution and potential values (arbitrary scales).

bar is approximately $\pi R^2 P$, whereas at the ends it is approximately $\frac{1}{2}\pi R^2 P$; half the flux of **D** leaves the bar through its sides and half through its ends.

At distances from the bar large compared to R but not to L, one can approximate the field **E** by replacing the distribution on each end by a point charge

$$Q = \pm\sigma_P(\pi R^2) = \pm\pi R^2 P$$

and one has a field like that of the two opposite point charges in Fig. 1.6b. Thus great distances from the bar (large compared to L), **E** is approximately the field of a dipole of strength $\pi R^2 \sigma_P L = \pi R^2 PL$, which is the product of P and the volume of the bar.

The closing of the lines of **D** depends on idealizing the symmetry of the problem. In actual cases the lines of **D** are not closed, even though they have no physical ends and do not pass to infinity.

Consider for instance a uniform bar electret which has been given a slight bend or twist. Then a line of **D** will not leave one end at exactly the

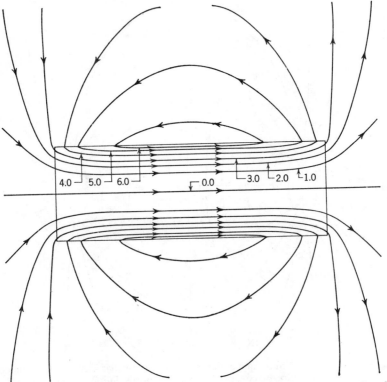

Fig. 3.6c.   Lines of **D** for a uniform bar electret. The numbers represent flux Φ_D contained in surfaces of revolution (arbitrary scale).

same radius and azimuthal angle at which it entered at the other end. When it passes around outside the bar, it will undergo very little "twist," tending to remain in one plane, and so will not come back on itself when it reenters the bar. (Fig. 3.6*d*).

In this way, a line of **D** clearly will circulate a number of times unless we deliberately terminate it at some arbitrary point. In fact, it could only close on itself if after some number of circulations it exactly came back to the starting point. Although in exceptional cases it might come very close after a few circulations, the inevitable limits of precision in any physical situation prevent its ever being truly closed. One line, in fact, can be drawn with enough circulations to fill out, as densely as we please, any given surface through which it passes.

The number of lines of **D** per unit area can thus be made to measure **D** only if each one is restricted by arbitrarily ending it in some way so as to have not more than one circulation. Such a restriction can be called a "topological restriction"; one can assume whenever necessary that topological restrictions have been introduced.[8]

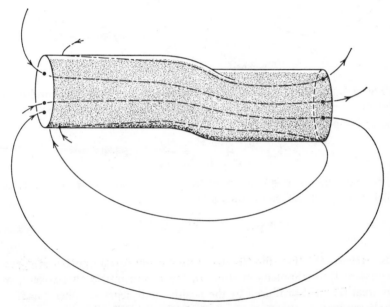

Fig. 3.6*d*. Unclosed lines of **D** for a distorted bar electret (schematic).

Consider next a sphere of dielectric of radius *a* with a constant polarization throughout. (Fig. 3.6*e*). One can make the calculation most readily by considering separately the fields produced by the positive and the negative charges on the dipoles. Since **P** is constant in direction and magnitude, the charge separation δl must also be constant. Thus we are led to finding the fields of a positive and a negative sphere of uniform volume density $\pm \rho = \pm Nq$. We calculated the field at an internal point of one such sphere in Section 1.4; by Eq. 1.4–5, it is

$$\mathbf{E}_+ = \frac{\rho_+ r \mathbf{1}_r}{3\epsilon_0} = \frac{\rho_+ \mathbf{r}}{3\epsilon_0}$$

[8] Cf. Joseph Slepian, "Lines of Force in Electric and Magnetic Fields," *Am. Journ. Phys.*, **19**, 87 (1951).

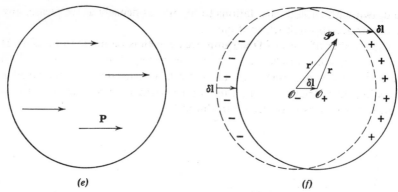

(e)   *(f)*

Fig. 3.6e-f. A spherical electret.

In Fig. 3.6*f*, we have indicated the vectors **r** and **r**′ that determine **E** for the two spheres, whose centers are respectively at $\mathcal{O}_+$ and $\mathcal{O}_-$. The resultant field at the point $\mathcal{P}$ is

$$\mathbf{E} = \frac{\rho_+ \mathbf{r}}{3\epsilon_0} + \frac{\rho_- \mathbf{r}'}{3\epsilon_0} = \frac{Nq}{3\epsilon_0}(\mathbf{r} - \mathbf{r}')$$

From the figure, $\mathbf{r} - \mathbf{r}'$ is equal to the displacement from $\mathcal{O}_+$ to $\mathcal{O}_-$ which is $-\boldsymbol{\delta}\mathbf{l}$. Therefore the field at $\mathcal{P}$ is

$$\mathbf{E} = -\frac{Nq\,\boldsymbol{\delta}\mathbf{l}}{3\epsilon_0} = -\frac{\mathbf{P}}{3\epsilon_0} \tag{3.6-5}$$

It is a remarkable fact that the field inside a uniformly polarized sphere is constant throughout its interior. In the region outside the sphere, we may treat the field produced by the positive and negative spheres as if all the charge were at the center and obtain the field of a dipole of strength

$$\mathbf{p} = \tfrac{4}{3}\pi a^3 \rho_+\,\boldsymbol{\delta}\mathbf{l} = \tfrac{4}{3}\pi a^3 \mathbf{P} \tag{3.6-6}$$

Similarly, the force and torque on such a sphere in an external field may be calculated by the use of this equivalent dipole, in accordance with Newton's third law of motion for static charges (cf. pp. 18–19 and Problem 1.4*a*).

Third, let us consider a thin disk of dielectric with a uniform polarization perpendicular to its surface (Fig. 3.6*g*).

To find the field at a point $\mathcal{O}$, consider a small area dS of the disk. Let t be the thickness of the disk. Then the total dipole moment in the volume of area dS and thickness t is $\mathbf{P}t\,dS$. The potential at $\mathcal{O}$ produced by this dipole is, by Eq. 3.1–4,

$$dV = t\,dS\,\frac{\mathbf{P}\cdot\mathbf{1}_r}{4\pi\epsilon_0 r^2} = tP\,\frac{d\mathbf{S}\cdot\mathbf{1}_r}{4\pi\epsilon_0 r^2} = P_S\,\frac{d\mathbf{S}\cdot\mathbf{1}_r}{4\pi\epsilon_0 r^2} \tag{3.6-7}$$

since the vectors $\mathbf{dS}$ and $\mathbf{P}$ have the same direction. The quantity $tP = P_S$ is the dipole moment per unit area of the disk. But $\mathbf{dS} \cdot \mathbf{1}_r/r^2 = d\Omega$, the solid angle subtended by dS at $\mathcal{O}$. Thus, we have $dV = P_S \, d\Omega/4\pi\epsilon_0$, or integrating,

$$V = P_S\Omega/4\pi\epsilon_0; \qquad P_S = Pt \qquad (3\text{-}6\text{-}8)$$

where Ω is the solid angle subtended by the boundary of the disk at $\mathcal{O}$, a result which applies to any shape of boundary and even to "disks" that are not plane. Thus the calculation of $\mathbf{E}$ outside the disk can be reduced to calculating a solid angle and taking its gradient. Note that as the point $\mathcal{O}$ moves around from the positive to the negative side of the disk, Ω reduces

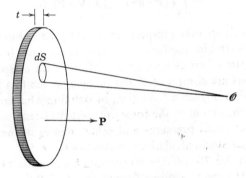

Fig. 3.6g. A disk electret.

to zero and then must take on negative values if Eq. 3.6–8 is to be of general validity. It is a remarkable fact that V depends *only* on the boundary and on P_S but not on the shape of the surface.

Inside the disk, we have the field of two plane charge distributions. Discounting the fringing effects near the edges, we have approximately $E = -\sigma_P/\epsilon_0 = -P/\epsilon_0$ and $D = \epsilon_0 E + P = 0$. The surprising result occurs that the displacement is nearly zero inside the dielectric.

This result can, however, be readily found from the fact that E and consequently D must be approximately zero just outside the disk (except near the edges) and from the condition 3.5–5 that D is the same on both sides of the boundary.

An accurate value for a point on the axis of the disk can be found from Eq. 3.6–3. It is left to the reader (Problem 3.6b) to show that on the axis just outside a disk of "length" $L = t$ and radius a, D is approximately given by

$$D = P_S/2a \qquad (3\text{-}6\text{-}9)$$

Now let us consider in general the action of an external field on an electret or in fact on any piece of dielectric material. The total force on an electret is equal to the sum of the forces on all the charges of which the dipoles are composed. We have seen that these charges combine to give a resultant volume distribution $\rho_P = -\nabla \cdot \mathbf{P}$ and a surface distribution $\sigma_P = P_n$. Therefore we should expect that the force exerted by an external field on an entire piece of dielectric should be obtainable by calculating the forces of that field on these polarization charge distributions. That is, we should be able to write for the force

$$\mathbf{F} = \int_S \sigma_P \mathbf{E} \, dS + \int_\tau \rho_P \mathbf{E} \, d\tau$$
$$= \int_S \mathbf{E}(\mathbf{P} \cdot d\mathbf{S}) - \int_\tau \mathbf{E}(\nabla \cdot \mathbf{P}) \, d\tau \qquad (3.6\text{--}10)$$

where the integrals are taken respectively over the entire surface and entire volume of the electret in question. Note that we have not tried to calculate the forces on part of an electret or a portion of an extended dielectric. Such calculations are complicated and involve, in the first place, making a careful definition of such a force (i.e., by defining what sorts of possible motions under the action of the force are contemplated), and second, the problem of mechanical pressures and other stresses in the medium. We shall not consider such calculations in this book.[9]

A proof of Eq. 3.6–10 could be constructed by Newton's third law, as in Problem 1.4a. However, a direct formal proof of this equation may be obtained by adding up the forces on each dipole. By Eq. 3.2–2, the force on any one of the dipoles is given by $\mathbf{F} = (\mathbf{p} \cdot \nabla)\mathbf{E}$. The total force on an electret is to be obtained by adding up for each dipole only that part of $\mathbf{F}$ resulting from the external field. (The internal forces will cancel out in equal and opposite pairs in this addition.)

For a small volume $d\tau$, we can write

$$\mathbf{dF} = \sum_i (\mathbf{p}_i \cdot \nabla)\mathbf{E} = \left[\left(\sum_i \mathbf{p}_i \right) \cdot \nabla \right] \mathbf{E}$$
$$= (\mathbf{P} \cdot \nabla)\mathbf{E} \, d\tau$$

since $\mathbf{P} \, d\tau = \sum_i \mathbf{p}_i$ taken over all the dipoles in $d\tau$. Now, the transformation that was made from Eq. 3.2–2 to Eq. 3.2–3 assumed that $\mathbf{p}$ was a constant. On the other hand, $\mathbf{P}$ may vary from point to point. Let us make a transformation of $(\mathbf{P} \cdot \nabla)\mathbf{E}$, utilizing the fact that ∇ may operate on both $\mathbf{P}$

[9] Some calculations of this sort are made in G. P. Harnwell, *Principles of Electricity and Electromagnetism*, 2nd ed., McGraw-Hill, New York, 1949, pp. 69–73; W. R. Smythe, *Static and Dynamic Electricity*, 2nd ed., McGraw-Hill, New York, 1950, sections 1.14 and 1.17; W. K. H. Panofsky and M. Phillips, *Classical Electricity and Magnetism*, Addison-Wesley, Reading, Mass., 2nd ed., 1962, pp. 107–116.

and **E**. Let us, in fact, use the convention adopted in the appendix that the quantities to the right of ∇ upon which it is to operate are indicated by a superior bar where necessary to avoid ambiguity. Then (cf. Appendix Table A.2*B*, item 3) the product rule for derivatives becomes

$$\overline{(\nabla \cdot \mathbf{P})\mathbf{E}} = (\mathbf{P} \cdot \nabla)\mathbf{E} + \mathbf{E}(\nabla \cdot \mathbf{P}) \qquad (3.6\text{--}11)$$

so that **dF** becomes

$$d\mathbf{F} = \overline{(\nabla \cdot \mathbf{P})\mathbf{E}}\, d\tau - \mathbf{E}(\nabla \cdot \mathbf{P})\, d\tau \qquad (3.6\text{--}12)$$

The second term of this expression yields the second term of Eq. 3.6–10 on integration. To calculate the integral of the first term, we can use the vector theorem A.2–27 in the form

$$\int_\tau \overline{(\nabla \cdot \mathbf{P})\mathbf{E}}\, d\tau = \int_S \mathbf{E}(\mathbf{P} \cdot d\mathbf{S}) \qquad (3.6\text{--}13)$$

a result which shows that the first term of Eq. 3.6–12 integrates to the first term of Eq. 3.6–10.

The calculation of the torque of an external field upon an electret can be carried out in a similar way, but we shall not perform the calculation here, postponing it to the corresponding magnetic case in Section 8.4.

Problem 3.6a. Discuss the field of a disk electret at a distance which is large compared to its lateral dimensions. Sketch lines of **E** and **D** for small and large distances.

Problem 3.6b. Prove Eq. 3.6–9 by an appropriate expansion from Eq. 3.6–3. When is Eq. 3.6–9 exact?

Problem 3.6c. Find **D** inside the uniform spherical electret, and sketch lines of **D** and **E** for this case. Calculate the radial and tangential components of **D** just inside and outside the surface, at a point whose coordinates are (r, θ).

Problem 3.6d. Prove Eqs. 3.6–11 and 3.6–13 by using Cartesian components instead of vector notation.

Problem 3.6e. Find the total dipole moment of a bar electret of length L and cross-sectional area S, for which **P** is parallel to the axis of the bar, of magnitude $P = b(L^2 - 4x^2)$ where x is the distance along the axis from the center. Calculate σ_P and ρ_P.

Problem 3.6f. A sphere of radius a contains dielectric material in which $\mathbf{P} = k\mathbf{r}$, where **r** is a vector from the center of the sphere. Find ρ_P, D, and E as functions of r.

Problem 3.6g. Find **E** just outside a spherical electret at a point (a) on a diameter parallel to **P** and (b) on a diameter perpendicular to **P**. Find E_r and E_θ just inside and just outside the electret at a point (r, θ).

Problem 3.6h. Calculate $\mathbf{E}$ inside and outside a spherical electret directly from Eq. 3.4–4.

Problem 3.6i. If a diamond were polarized so that $P = 8.0 \times 10^{-6}$ coulomb/m², by what distance would the center of the cloud of 6 electrons on each carbon atom be shifted from the nucleus, assuming that all the carbon atoms were polarized alike? The density of diamond is 3.51 g/cm³ and 12 g of carbon contain $N_0 = 6.02 \times 10^{23}$ atoms.

3.7 Parallel-Plate Capacitor with Dielectric; Dielectric Constants

Polarization generally occurs only with applied fields. As a simple case involving an outside source of field, let us consider an ideal parallel-plate condenser with charge Q, area S and separation d, in which the space is

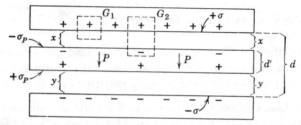

Fig. 3.7a. A plane slab of dielectric between two metal plates.

partly filled with a dielectric of uniform polarization everywhere normal to the planes of the plates. We shall assume that $\mathbf{P}$ points toward the negative plate (Fig. 3.7a); the direction of $\mathbf{E}$ will also be toward the negative plate, so that $\mathbf{E}$, $\mathbf{P}$, and $\mathbf{D}$ are all parallel. A Gaussian surface such as G_1 with one end in the metal plate and the other in the evacuated space x–x can be used to show that E in this space is the familiar value $E = \sigma/\epsilon_0 = Q/S\epsilon_0$. Since $P = 0$ here, we have $D = \sigma$.

A surface like G_2 can be used with the flux Φ_D to show that D in the dielectric is also equal to σ, which of course also follows from the continuity of $\mathbf{D}$. Since $D = \epsilon_0 E + P$, E in the dielectric is $(\sigma - P)/\epsilon_0$. We can also see this by noting that the upper surface of the dielectric appears to bear a charge density $\sigma_P = -P$, and the lower surface a charge $\sigma_P = +P$. The field of these two surface densities has a value P/ϵ_0 upward inside the dielectric and zero elsewhere. The E inside the dielectric is thus the resultant of the fields produced by two pairs of plane-parallel surface densities.

We can draw lines of force and displacement to illustrate this discussion (Fig. 3.7b). The displacement is continuous across the surface of the dielectric, so the lines run from one plate to the other and are exactly the same as if no dielectric were present. Lines of E leave the positive plate,

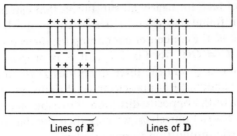

Lines of **E**   Lines of **D**

Fig. 3.7b. Lines of **E** and **D** for Fig. 3.7a.

some running to the negative charge on the dielectric, and some running through the dielectric to the other plate.[10] Of course, lines also leave $+\sigma_P$ on the lower side and pass to $-\sigma$. The reduction of E inside the dielectric is clearly shown in the resulting diagram.

Let us calculate the potential difference between the plates. Denoting by x and y the two distances between plates and dielectric and by d' the thickness of the dielectric slab, we have

$$V = V_1 - V_2 = \int \mathbf{E} \cdot \mathbf{dl} = (\sigma/\epsilon_0)x + (\sigma - P)\,d'/\epsilon_0 + (\sigma/\epsilon_0)y$$

$$= [\sigma(x + y) + (\sigma - P)\,d']/\epsilon_0$$

In terms of the charge $Q = \sigma S$, we have, using $d = x + y + d'$,

$$V = \frac{Q\,d}{\epsilon_0 S} - \frac{P\,d'}{\epsilon_0} \qquad (3.7\text{-}1)$$

The arguments presented above are also valid if $\mathbf{P}$ is uniform throughout the material but is not perpendicular to the plane of the plates. We only need to use P_n, the component of $\mathbf{P}$ in the perpendicular direction, in the various formulas above.

Now suppose we do not know the value of $\mathbf{P}$ but put a homogeneous[11] slab of dielectric in the position indicated, place charges Q and $-Q$ on the two plates, and ask what value of $\mathbf{P}$ results. Because of the homogeneity and symmetry of the material we can deduce that $\mathbf{D}$ and $\mathbf{E}$ must also be homogeneous in the condenser (except near the edge) and must be directed normally to the plate. $\mathbf{P}$ will also be the same throughout. If the material is also isotropic[12] one can conclude from symmetry considerations that the other components of $\mathbf{P}$ must vanish. Its value can be found from Eq. 3.7-1 by measuring Q and V.

[10] We assume here that $\sigma_p < \sigma$.

[11] Homogeneous means having the same properties at each point.

[12] Isotropic means that at any point in the material, the properties are the same in all directions.

As a matter of fact, for nearly all substances that can be placed in such a condenser, it is found that Q and V are strictly proportional over a wide range of V. That is, the condenser containing the dielectric has a meaningful capacitance $C = Q/V$. By Eq. 3.7–1, if V is proportional to Q, P is also proportional to Q and the three quantities D, E, and P are all proportional to one another. For non-electrets, $\mathbf{P}$ is always in the same direction as $\mathbf{E}$, never in the opposite direction. For isotropic media, to which we shall largely restrict ourselves, we may then say that the vectors $\mathbf{D}$, $\mathbf{E}$, and $\mathbf{P}$ vary in strict proportion to one another.

The most fundamental expression of this relation would be to relate $\mathbf{P}$ to the field that acts on the molecules and polarizes them. This field, however, is not the average field $\mathbf{E}$ in the medium, since this average includes the field produced by the very molecule on which we might calculate the external force. The correct expression for the average field acting *on* a molecule will be calculated in Section 3.9.

It is, however, still useful to consider how $\mathbf{P}$ is related to $\mathbf{E}$. When they are proportional, we write

$$\mathbf{P} = \chi\epsilon_0\mathbf{E} \tag{3.7–2a}$$

where the constant χ (Greek chi) is called the "electric susceptibility" and characterizes the material in question. It is always positive, is generally a function of temperature, and may be a function of position.

From this relation we can find one between $\mathbf{D}$ and $\mathbf{E}$. We have $\mathbf{D} = \epsilon_0\mathbf{E} + \mathbf{P} = \epsilon_0(1 + \chi)\mathbf{E}$, which we write

$$\mathbf{D} = \epsilon\mathbf{E} \tag{3.7–3a}$$

where ϵ is another constant called the "permittivity" of the medium and is always greater than ϵ_0. Like the latter, ϵ is measured in farads/m. We also use κ (Greek kappa) as the dielectric constant or relative permittivity,[13] defined as a dimensionless number greater than one by

$$\kappa = \epsilon/\epsilon_0 \tag{3.7–4}$$

The relation between susceptibility and dielectric constant is clearly

$$1 + \chi = \kappa \tag{3.7–5a}$$

In Gaussian units we write

$$\mathbf{P} = \chi\mathbf{E} \qquad \text{Gaussian} \tag{3.7–2b}$$

---

[13] Also called "specific permittivity" or "specific inductive capacitance." Because it is not a constant with respect to temperature, some authors call it the "dielectric coefficient." The name dielectric constant appears to be firmly established by long tradition and common usage.

In these units $\mathbf{D} = \mathbf{E} + 4\pi\mathbf{P}$, and we write

$$\mathbf{D} = \kappa\mathbf{E} \qquad\qquad \text{Gaussian} \quad (3.7\text{-}3b)$$

which defines κ, so that we have

$$1 + 4\pi\chi = \kappa \qquad\qquad \text{Gaussian} \quad (3.7\text{-}5b)$$

It is important to note that $\mathbf{D}$ and χ are defined differently in the two systems so that it is not possible to change them from one to the other by merely setting $\epsilon_0 = 1/4\pi$.

Any medium for which a dielectric constant exists—that is, in which $\mathbf{D}$, $\mathbf{E}$, and $\mathbf{P}$ are proportional—may be referred to as linear. The theorem of superposition can be applied in such cases for all three vectors (provided bound as well as free charge is taken into account). All gases and liquids are linear and isotropic. Solids are generally linear but frequently are not isotropic; in fact, only amorphous solids and cubic crystals are reasonably isotropic. They are often non-homogeneous by virtue of non-uniform mechanical strains set up in the process of crystallization or of machining, if not by virtue of being chemically inhomogeneous. For single crystals, the relation 3.7–3 can be replaced by a more complicated relation connecting each of the various components of $\mathbf{D}$ with all those of $\mathbf{E}$. We shall not consider such relations here.

Another type of limitation on dielectric constants comes when extremely large fields are applied. It is to be expected that materials will become non-linear under these circumstances because there should be some limit to the degree to which molecules can be polarized. This effect has indeed been observed, but only to an extent of a few parts per million at the very highest fields available.[14] Still another consideration has to do with the rate at which the fields $\mathbf{E}$ and $\mathbf{D}$ are made to change; that consideration is discussed in Section 3.10. Table 3.7A lists the values of κ for several substances, measured for static fields.

Let us note further that for a homogeneous linear medium, there can be no volume polarization charges. We have $\mathbf{P} = \mathbf{D}(1 - 1/\kappa)$ and $\nabla \cdot \mathbf{P} = \nabla \cdot [\mathbf{D}(1 - 1/\kappa)]$. If κ is a constant, so that its x, y, and z derivatives vanish, then

$$\rho_P = -\nabla \cdot \mathbf{P} = -(1 - 1/\kappa)\nabla \cdot \mathbf{D} = -(1 - 1/\kappa)\rho_{\text{free}}$$

Since dielectric materials do not usually have free charge distributed anywhere within them, ρ_P is also zero.

Finally, observe that although $\mathbf{P}$ produced by $\mathbf{E}$ is parallel to $\mathbf{E}$ in an ideal medium, the field $\mathbf{E}_{\text{pol}}$ produced by $\mathbf{P}$ is in general not parallel to $\mathbf{P}$, as shown by the calculations in Section 3.6.

[14] See for instance, J. H. Van Vleck, *Electric and Magnetic Susceptibilities*, Clarendon Press, Oxford, 1932, p. 87. Ferroelectric materials show non-linearities at lower fields; cf. A. von Hippel, *Dielectrics and Waves*, John Wiley, New York, 1954, pp. 204–5.

Table 3.7A   Dielectric Constants*

	Temp. °C	Dielectric Constant κ		Temp. °C	Dielectric Constant κ
			Gases at 760 mm pressure		
Air	25	1.000536	Hydrogen	25	1.000254
Argon	25	1.000517	Oxygen	25	1.000495
Carbon dioxide	25	1.000922	Water (steam)	100	1.0126
Helium	25	1.000065	Water (steam)	140	1.00785

	T. °C	κ		T. °C	κ
			Liquids		
Ammonia	25	16.9	Castor oil	15	4.7
Benzene	20	2.284	Cottonseed oil	14	3.10
Ethyl alcohol	25	24.3	Transformer oil	25	2.22
Glycerol	25	42.5	Water	25	78.54
Hydrogen	−253	1.23	Water	200	34.6

	κ		κ
		Solids at Room Temperature	
Corning Glass 0010	6.68	Pyrex 7070	4.00
Corning Glass 0080	8.30	Foamglas	90.0
Pyrex 7050	4.88	Quartz (fused)	3.75–4.1
Barium nitrate	5.9	Red Glyptal	4.9
Beryl, ⊥ optic axis	7.02	Mica	2.5–7.0
Beryl, ∥ optic axis	6.08	Neoprene	6.70
Diamond	5.5	Hevea Rubber	2.94
Lead nitrate	37.7	Polystyrene	2.56
Naphthalene	2.85	Amber	2.65
Ruby, ⊥ optic axis	13.27	Beeswax, yellow	2.9
Ruby, ∥ optic axis	11.28	Paraffin wax	2.1–2.5

* Mostly from D. E. Gray, ed., *American Institute of Physics Handbook*, 2nd ed., McGraw-Hill, New York, 1963, Sec. 5d.

3.8 Ideal Dielectrics

Dielectric materials that are homogeneous, isotropic, and linear have a number of simple and useful properties, and we shall hereafter refer to such material as "ideal dielectrics." As indicated above, any actual material that approximates an ideal dielectric will almost certainly be a liquid or gas. We shall deal in this section with a number of applications of interest.

Consider first the capacitance of the condenser discussed in the last section. We have $P = (\kappa - 1)\epsilon_0 E$, where $E = D/\kappa\epsilon_0 = Q/S\kappa\epsilon_0$ is the field inside the dielectric. Thus Eq. 3.7–1 becomes

$$V = Q\left(d - \frac{\kappa - 1}{\kappa}d'\right)\bigg/\epsilon_0 S$$

so that the capacitance Q/V is

$$C = \frac{\kappa\epsilon_0 S}{\kappa d - (\kappa - 1)d'} \tag{3.8–1}$$

Now, if $x = y = 0$ so that the entire space is filled with dielectric, $d = d'$ and we have

$$C = \kappa\epsilon_0 S/d \tag{3.8–2}$$

We note that the effect of the dielectric is to multiply the capacitance of the *completely filled* condenser by κ over the value it has when the space is evacuated.

This property is quite a general one, as we shall now show. Consider the plane case a bit further. Just below the layer of charge σ on the top plate is a layer of polarization charge $-\sigma_P = -P$ on the adjacent dielectric. Since

$$P = (\kappa - 1)D/\kappa$$

we have

$$\sigma_P = (\kappa - 1)\sigma/\kappa$$

and the *sum* of the two adjacent distributions is

$$\sigma_{net} = \sigma - \sigma_P = \sigma/\kappa$$

Therefore the field everywhere between the condenser plates is that produced by an effective charge of $1/\kappa$ times the charge actually on the plates, so that the PD between the plates is likewise multiplied by a factor $1/\kappa$, thus accounting for the larger capacitance. (The presence of the dielectric does not, of course, change the amount of free charge on an insulated conductor.)

Now consider a condenser of arbitrary shape. If it is filled completely with a dielectric medium with dielectric constant κ, then at every point on the surface of either conductor, a charge density σ will produce fields **E** and **D** just outside it of the same values as those which hold throughout in the parallel-plate case, so that the same charge density $-\sigma_P$ will be induced on the adjacent dielectric. If σ varies from point to point, so will σ_P. Thus the net charge at the surface is σ/κ, whatever the value of σ. Now, the charge will distribute itself so as to make all conducting surfaces into equipotentials. This will occur with the same relative distribution as in the case of the empty condenser; for if and only if this is so, will the field and potential be everywhere equal to those produced by a charge density $1/\kappa$ times that of the one actually on the conductors. All equipotentials will thus have the same shape and have the values of their potentials divided by κ.

It is this property that allows us to extend the uniqueness theorem proved in Section 2.2 to the case in which the space between the condensers is filled with ideal dielectric. The property of superposition stated in the last section allows us further to include the cases of partial filling and of varying κ.[15]

If a condenser has a fringing field, as in the parallel-plate example, the proportionality of C to κ will only hold exactly if the dielectric material extends beyond the edges to allow all the fringing flux to pass through it, since otherwise there will be polarization charges at the extraneous boundaries that destroy the exact geometric similarity of the field patterns with and without the dielectric. Furthermore, if there is any stray flux passing to distant conductors and this flux passes out of the dielectric material, a similar result will hold. In most practical cases, however, this effect is small.

Let us consider a spherical condenser filled with an ideal dielectric. At the inner surface of radius R_1 there will be a charge density $\sigma = Q/4\pi R_1^2$ on the conductor and a net charge density $\sigma_{net} = Q/4\pi\kappa R_1^2$. The displacement D in the space between the conductors obeys the formula $D = Q/4\pi r^2$; the field is $E = Q/4\pi\kappa\epsilon_0 r^2$ where r is the radial coordinate of any point between the two conductors. Consequently P is also variable and is given by $P = (\kappa - 1)Q/4\pi\kappa r^2$. The charge densities on the outer dielectric surface and the inner surface of the outer conductor (radius R_2) are thus smaller in magnitude than at the inner surface, with $\sigma = -Q/4\pi R_2^2$ and $\sigma_{net} = -Q/4\pi\kappa R_2^2$. The capacitance is κ times that of Eq. 2.5–3:

$$C = \frac{4\pi\kappa\epsilon_0 R_1 R_2}{R_2 - R_1} \tag{3.8–3}$$

If R_2 is allowed to go to infinity, we have the case of a sphere embedded in an infinite ideal dielectric. As a special case of this, consider a free point charge q surrounded by a dielectric in the presence of other free charges. We may suppose the point to be inside a small spherical cavity. If the radius of the cavity is small enough, the field at its inside surface produced by the point charge q is very much greater than that produced by distant charges, so that the polarization just outside the cavity surface is effectively that of a single isolated sphere embedded in the dielectric. That is, the

---

[15] The requirement that the materials be ideal is not necessary if the component of **D** parallel to **E** is restricted to being in the same sense as **E**, the materials are linear, and they show no significant relaxation or hysteresis phenomena.

field at a distant point produced by q and by the polarization charge on its cavity is the same as that produced by a charge q/κ at the same place with no dielectric present, i.e., $\mathbf{E} = q\mathbf{1}_r/4\pi\kappa\epsilon_0 r^2$.

By the principle of superposition, we can calculate $\mathbf{E}$ for a collection of free charges immersed in an infinite ideal medium according to the rule

$$\mathbf{E} = \sum_n \frac{q_n \mathbf{1}_r}{4\pi\kappa\epsilon_0 r^2} \qquad (3.8\text{–}4)$$

The appearance of κ in this rule may be described as a device to allow the polarization charges to enter the formula implicitly by means of κ whereas the free charges q_n appear explicitly in the usual way.

If we have many free charges and can consider them close enough to have a continuous density ρ while still actually being separated by enough dipoles that Eq. 3.8–4 is still correct, we can write the Poisson equation for the field and potential in the medium as

$$\nabla \cdot \mathbf{E} = -\nabla^2 V = \rho/\epsilon = \rho/\kappa\epsilon_0 \qquad (3.8\text{–}5)$$

We must be careful, however, in dealing with the force exerted by such a field on another macroscopic charge q' embedded in the same medium. The force on q' depends on the field in the cavity in which it is put. Consider two charges q and q'. Only if q' is in a long needlelike cavity parallel to the radius drawn from q, will the force be given by the formula (sometimes called "Coulomb's law for a dielectric medium"):

$$\mathbf{F} = \frac{qq'\mathbf{1}_r}{4\pi\kappa\epsilon_0 r^2} \qquad (3.8\text{–}6)$$

Since the field in a coin-shaped cavity normal to $\mathbf{D}$ is equal to $\mathbf{D}/\epsilon_0$ or κ times $\mathbf{E}$ in the medium, $F = qq'/4\pi\epsilon_0 r^2$ if q' lies in such a cavity. The case of a spherical cavity will be considered in Section 3.9.

A different situation results if we define "force on a charge in a dielectric" to mean the sum of the electric forces on q' itself and on the surrounding polarization charges, *plus the mechanical forces in the fluid near q'* that are called into play as a reaction to the electric forces in the body of the dielectric. This sum of forces is that which must be balanced if an external agent (e.g., gravity acting on an oil drop in a gaseous dielectric) is to move the charged body through the medium at essentially zero speed (no energy going into friction). That this force must be equal to $q'\mathbf{E}$, with $\mathbf{E}$ the field calculated as above, can be seen if we assume conservation of energy to apply to the motion of q' around an arbitrary closed path, part in the medium and part out. (Any factor multiplying $q'\mathbf{E}$ would lead to a violation of the conservation law, since we know that $\oint \mathbf{E} \cdot \mathbf{dl} = 0$ for *any* path.) Thus Eq. 3.8–6 holds when the force on the medium is included.[16]

Another important restriction on the validity of this modified "Coulomb law" has to do with the presence of boundaries. Our discussion so far has had to do with infinite media so that no extraneous surface polarization charges can add to the fields we have calculated. A specific example to illustrate the effect of a boundary is that of a charge q embedded in a semi-infinite piece of ideal dielectric whose boundary is a plane. The surface distribution and resulting field pattern are calculated in Chapter 4,

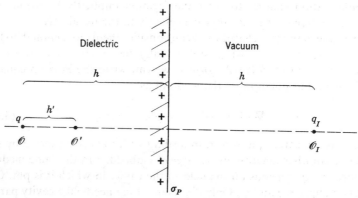

Fig. 3.8a.   A charge q embedded in a dielectric near a boundary. Charge q_I at point $\mathcal{O}_I$ is an "image charge" in terms of which the field can be calculated at a point such as $\mathcal{O}'$.

Section 4.3. It is shown there that if q is at a point $\mathcal{O}$ at a distance h from the plane boundary (Fig. 3.8a), the field $\mathbf{E}$ at points in the dielectric is the same as if there were no medium present but as if a charge q/κ resided at $\mathcal{O}$ and a charge $q_I = q(\kappa - 1)/\kappa(\kappa + 1)$ resided at $\mathcal{O}_I$, which is the mirror image of $\mathcal{O}$ on the other side of the plane. The charge q_I thus produces the same field as is actually made by σ_P on the plane surface of the dielectric. For example, the field at a point $\mathcal{O}'$ nearer the plane whose distance is h' from $\mathcal{O}$ on the perpendicular to the plane is given by

$$E' = q/4\pi\kappa\epsilon_0 h'^2 - q(\kappa - 1)/4\pi\kappa(\kappa + 1)\epsilon_0(2h - h')^2$$

$$= \frac{q}{4\pi\kappa\epsilon_0 h'^2}\left[1 - \frac{\kappa - 1}{\kappa + 1}\frac{h'^2}{(2h - h')^2}\right] \qquad (3.8\text{–}7)$$

For a dielectric of $\kappa = 3$, the correction to the infinite-medium result is 25% when $h' = 0.828h$ and 10% when $h' = 0.618h$.

---

[16] See the Report of the Coulomb's Law Committee, *Am. J. Phys.*, **18**, 6–11 and 83–84 (1950), for a more detailed discussion.

We conclude this section with the calculation of the force on a small dielectric object such as a pith ball, in an external field. We shall consider the object to have a low susceptibility, so that the external field is not appreciably modified by the polarization of the object. Then Eq. 3.7–2 can be written

$$\mathbf{P} = \chi\epsilon_0\mathbf{E}_{ext}$$

and the dipole moment of the small object is

$$\mathbf{p} = \mathbf{P}\tau$$

if its volume is τ.

The force on it by Eq. 3.2–3 is

$$\mathbf{F} = (\mathbf{p}\cdot\nabla)\mathbf{E}_{ext} = \tau\chi\epsilon_0(\mathbf{E}_{ext}\cdot\nabla)\mathbf{E}_{ext}$$

The operator in parentheses calls for a derivative in the direction of $\mathbf{E}_{ext}$; let us call this direction the x-direction. Then we have

$$\mathbf{F} = \mathbf{1}_x\tau\chi\epsilon_0 E_{ext}\frac{\partial}{\partial x}E_{ext} = \tfrac{1}{2}\mathbf{1}_x\tau\chi\epsilon_0\,\partial(E_{ext}^2)/\partial x \qquad (3.8\text{–}8)$$

showing that the force is parallel to the direction of the field and acts in the direction toward which the magnitude of the field increases. That is, a pith ball or similar object is always pulled into a region of stronger field, regardless of the sign of the field or the charge producing it.

Inclusion of the local field produced by the polarization, so that the restriction of low susceptibility can be removed, can be done by methods to be given in Chapter 4.

Problem 3.8a. Use the conditions 3.5–5 and 3.5–6 along with the relation 3.7–3 between **D** and **E** in ideal dielectrics to obtain a "law of refraction" for lines of **D** and **E** at a plane boundary between two dielectrics.

Problem 3.8b. Explain why the "law of refraction" referred to in the previous problem cannot be used with suitably shaped surfaces to "focus" electric fields and so strengthen them.

Problem 3.8c. Consider a long thin rod of ideal dielectric placed in an originally uniform electric field $\mathbf{E}_{dist}$ at an arbitrary angle with the field. Indicate on a sketch (a) the location of the surface polarization charges; (b) the direction of the field $\mathbf{E}_{local}$ produced in the rod by this surface charge (neglect end effects); (c) the direction of the resultant field $\mathbf{E}_{local} + \mathbf{E}_{dist}$; (d) the direction of **P** in the rod; and (e) the direction of the torque, if any, of $\mathbf{E}_{dist}$ on **P**. What does the rod tend to do?

Problem 3.8d. Consider by the method of the previous problem the torque on a thin plane sheet of ideal dielectric, free to rotate about an axis contained in its plane and perpendicular to the external field, and show that this torque is proportional to χ^2 when χ is small.

Problem 3.8e. A layer of neoprene 0.5 cm thick is placed in contact with two metal plates, each of area 30 cm². Find the capacitance of the combination, neglecting edge effects. If a PD of 100 v is placed on the capacitor, find D, E, and P in the neoprene. (See Table 3.7*A*.)

Problem 3.8f. Write formulas for the flux Φ_D produced by a single charge q embedded in an infinite ideal dielectric through an open surface that subtends a solid angle Ω, in both MKS and Gaussian units. Explain why the formula may fail if the dielectric is finite in extent or non-ideal.

Problem 3.8g. A spherical capacitor has an inner sphere of radius 12 cm and an outer sphere of inner radius 17 cm. The inner sphere is covered with 2 cm of dielectric of $\kappa = 2.0$, and the rest of the space is filled with dielectric of $\kappa = 4.0$. If 6×10^{-9} coulomb is placed on the inner sphere, find E, D, and P as functions of r. Find also the polarization charge densities and the total polarization charge at the three boundaries. Calculate the PD between the metal spheres by integration, and find the capacitance.

Problem 3.8h. Find the capacitance of the condenser in Fig. 3.7*a*, if $S = 12$ cm², $d = 1.00$ mm, $d' = 0.75$ mm, and $\kappa = 2.5$.

Problem 3.8i. What would be the difference in capacitance between the two cylinders of Problem 2.7*e* if they were both filled with benzene at 20°C?

Problem 3.8j. If the force exerted on a charge q in a long drill hole oriented in the direction of another distant charge q imbedded in a spherical cavity in an ideal dielectric of permittivity ϵ is $qq'/4\pi\epsilon r^2$, does it follow that the force exerted on q is also of this amount? What other charges take part in each force?

Problem 3.8k. A coaxial cable has an inner conductor of o.d. (outer diameter) 0.250 in., and outer conductor of i.d. 0.600 in., and is filled with dielectric of $\kappa = 2.9$. Find its capacitance per meter.

Problem 3.8l. Find the field strength, potential, displacement, and polarization as a function of distance for a dielectric sphere of radius a and permittivity ϵ which bears a uniform volume distribution of free charge ρ. Find also the distribution of polarization charge.

Problem 3.8m. Derive a formula for the force on a small pith ball in the field of a uniformly charged sphere.

Problem 3.8n. Derive a formula for the force on a small pith ball located at a distance r from a dipole of strength p, on the axis of the dipole.

3.9 Spherical Cavities and Effective Polarizing Fields[17]

Let us now calculate the actual or effective field $\mathbf{E}_{\text{eff}}$ that acts on any chosen spherical piece of material in a uniform polarized dielectric medium. As in Section 3.4 we divide the material up into a small sphere and the remainder. The remainder produces a field within the sphere equal to $\mathbf{E}$ in the medium plus the contribution of the surface charge density P_n on the inside surface of the spherical "cavity" which contains the small sphere.

Now, this surface density is just the opposite of that on a spherical electret of the same dimensions and polarization, for the direction of the outward normals are opposite in the two cases. In fact, the material within the sphere constitutes just such an electret, the internal field of which is just $\mathbf{E}_{\text{sph}} = -\mathbf{P}/3\epsilon_0$ by Eq. 3.6–5a.

Thus the field produced by the remainder is

$$\mathbf{E}_{\text{eff}} = \mathbf{E} + \mathbf{P}/3\epsilon_0 \qquad (3.9\text{–}1)$$

For ideal dielectrics, $\mathbf{P} = (\kappa - 1)\epsilon_0\mathbf{E}$, so $\mathbf{E}_{\text{eff}} = \mathbf{E}[1 + (\kappa - 1)/3]$ or

$$\mathbf{E}_{\text{eff}} = \frac{\kappa + 2}{3}\,\mathbf{E} \qquad (3.9\text{–}2)$$

and also, eliminating $\mathbf{E}$,

$$\mathbf{P} = \frac{3(\kappa - 1)}{\kappa + 2}\,\epsilon_0\mathbf{E}_{\text{eff}} \qquad (3.9\text{–}3)$$

This relation holds for a large enough sphere that the molecules in it have an average uniform behavior. If we let the sphere get smaller and smaller, we may come to a point where effects of local crystal structure produce a lack of spherical symmetry, and the relation ceases to be accurate. For gases and liquids, the average in both space and time of the electrical behavior of a single molecule is probably sufficiently symmetric that the equation continues to hold. In this case, we can find the ratio α between the average moment $\mathbf{p} = \mathbf{P}/N$ for a single molecule, to $\mathbf{E}_{\text{eff}}$. This ratio, called the molecular polarizability, is given by

$$\alpha = \frac{\mathbf{p}}{\mathbf{E}_{\text{eff}}} = \frac{\mathbf{P}}{N\mathbf{E}_{\text{eff}}} = \frac{3(\kappa - 1)\epsilon_0}{(\kappa + 2)N} \qquad (3.9\text{–}4)$$

This relation is called the Clausius-Mossotti equation or sometimes (in works on optics) the Lorenz-Lorentz equation. It is useful chiefly for gases in which κ is close to unity, and α can be written approximately as $(\kappa - 1)\epsilon_0/N = \chi\epsilon_0/N$.

The Field in a Spherical Cavity. Now let us consider what would happen if the material in one of these spherical regions were removed.

---

[17] This section may be omitted without losing continuity.

The field in the remainder of the material will include, in addition to the original $\mathbf{E}$, a contribution equal to that outside of a spherical polarized electret, which as we saw in Section 3.6 is a dipole field. The strength of this field near the sphere is of the same order of magnitude as $\mathbf{P}/\epsilon_0 = \chi\mathbf{E}$ (cf. Problem 3.6f). Thus if χ is not too small, this added field will change $\mathbf{P}$ substantially in the neighborhood of the cavity, and our calculation will be incorrect.

Let us try guessing what the correct field might be near such a spherical cavity, assuming the original $\mathbf{E}$ to be uniform. The resultant surface distribution must produce a field and a polarization that are related by $\mathbf{P} = \chi\epsilon_0\mathbf{E}$, neither of which can be uniform either in magnitude or direction. Perhaps the resultant distribution adds to the original uniform $\mathbf{E}$ a dipole field in the medium of different strength from that just mentioned. Since if this is correct, it will act as a dipole oriented in the opposite direction to $\mathbf{E}$, let us assume that the equivalent dipole is some vector $-\mathbf{p}$. The combination of the field of $\mathbf{E}$ and $-\mathbf{p}$ must produce a surface charge density $P_n = -\mathbf{P} \cdot \mathbf{1}_r$ on the cavity whose resultant field is that of $-\mathbf{p}$.

From the spherical electret calculation, Eq. 3.6–6, we see that $-\mathbf{P} \cdot \mathbf{1}_r$ must equal $-\mathbf{p} \cdot \mathbf{1}_r / \frac{4}{3}\pi a^3$. On the other hand, we know that the radial component of electric field in the medium next to the boundary of the cavity is $-2\mathbf{p} \cdot \mathbf{1}_r / 4\pi\epsilon_0 a^3 + \mathbf{E} \cdot \mathbf{1}_r$, using Eq. 3.1–7$a$ for the dipole field. Then $-\mathbf{P} \cdot \mathbf{1}_r$ is $-\chi\epsilon_0$ times this, giving the radial component equation

$$-\frac{\mathbf{p} \cdot \mathbf{1}_r}{\frac{4}{3}\pi a^3} = -\chi\epsilon_0\left(-\frac{2\mathbf{p} \cdot \mathbf{1}_r}{4\pi\epsilon_0 a^3} + \mathbf{E} \cdot \mathbf{1}_r\right)$$

which will be satisfied if the vectors are related by

$$\mathbf{p} = -\tfrac{2}{3}\chi\mathbf{p} + \tfrac{4}{3}\pi a^3\chi\epsilon_0\mathbf{E}$$

Solving for $\mathbf{p}$, we obtain

$$\mathbf{p} = \frac{\frac{4}{3}\pi a^3\chi\epsilon_0\mathbf{E}}{\frac{2}{3}\chi + 1} = \frac{4\pi a^3\epsilon_0\mathbf{E}(\kappa - 1)}{2\kappa + 1} \tag{3.9–5}$$

and the field in the cavity is

$$\mathbf{E}_{\text{sph cav}} = \mathbf{E} - \left(\frac{-\mathbf{p}}{\frac{4}{3}\pi a^3} \cdot \frac{1}{3\epsilon_0}\right) = \mathbf{E}\left(1 + \frac{\kappa - 1}{2\kappa + 1}\right)$$

$$= \mathbf{E}\left(\frac{3\kappa}{2\kappa + 1}\right) \tag{3.9–6}$$

For $\kappa = 1$, we see that the medium has no effect, whereas for very large κ, $\mathbf{E}_{\text{sph cav}} = \tfrac{3}{2}\mathbf{E}$.

We shall see in Chapter 4 (Problem 4.3n) that the field found by this guesswork process is indeed the correct one.

Problem 3.9a. Find α for diamond (see Problem 3.6*i*).

Problem 3.9b. Two point charges q and q' are located in spherical cavities in a piece of dielectric material, far from any boundaries. The diameters of the cavities are small enough compared to the distances between their centers that the field of each charge and cavity may be treated as uniform at the other cavity. Find the forces on each charge, and account for them in terms of both bound and free charges.

Problem 3.9c. Find $\mathbf{E}_{eff}$ on a small sphere of dielectric (*a*) just inside the end of a long bar electret and (*b*) at the center of a thin disk electret. Such fields in the direction of $-\mathbf{p}$ are called "depolarizing fields."

3.10 Properties of Real Dielectrics

Real dielectrics are characterized by various types of behavior that complicate the simple picture we have presented of ideal dielectrics. We have referred briefly to departures from homogeneity and isotropism, and in this section we wish to consider several other characteristics.

Dielectric Relaxation. It takes a finite time in many polar materials for the polarization to reach its maximum value. This is because the forces between adjacent molecules tend to prevent their being readily turned around under the action of $\mathbf{E}_{eff}$, so that they turn in individual energy exchanges or "quantum jumps," occurring at random times. The average time for this "relaxation" varies from substance to substance over an enormous range, values from 10^{-10} sec to several thousand years having been reported.

One consequence of this effect is that when a condenser containing such materials is suddenly connected to a potential difference V, it will acquire charge at a finite rate, much as if κ and C increased during the charging time from low values, corresponding to polarization only by electron shift, to final higher values, corresponding to polarization by both electron shift and polar molecule rotation. On discharge, an inverse effect occurs. For instance, if a condenser is charged and quickly discharged and then left with terminals open, it will later be found to have acquired a potential difference between its plates (Problem 3.10*c*).

Another consequence of the relaxation time is the phenomenon of hysteresis with alternating fields, namely that the polarization lags behind the field in its variations. Because of the resulting heat transfer in the quantum jumps (a phenomenon that can properly be called "friction"), there is a loss of electric energy, which is of considerable importance at high frequencies.

Finite Conductivity. Some dielectric materials have sufficient conductance for the resulting currents to produce noticeable energy loss in the form of heat. This loss and the hysteresis loss are referred to jointly as "dielectric losses." The term "condenser losses" may also include energy losses due to the resistance of the plates and connecting wires.

Another consequence of finite conductivity is the appearance of an absorption effect in condensers similar to the relaxation phenomenon. If a condenser contains between its plates two layers of material that have different conductivities (even if nominally the same substance), the currents in the two parts will in general be unequal at the start. As a result, charge will pile up at the interface between the two layers until the resulting additional field is enough to balance the currents. Even if the currents are too small to notice, the build up of charge appears as a change in C with time with an opposite effect at the time of discharge. (See Problem 5.2a for details of a calculation.) This effect, together with the similar one resulting from dielectric polarization, is called "dielectric absorption."[18]

Real Electrets. Electrets can be prepared by subjecting to high fields ($\sim 10^6$ v/m) thin layers of various types of waxes, plastics, ceramics, and other inorganic and organic substances. Sometimes the material is molten and allowed to solidify in the field, but this procedure is not necessary. Two effects are produced simultaneously: (a) A volume polarization leading to σ_P on each surface which is, of course, opposite in sign to the electrode placed on that surface and so is called a "heterocharge" and (b) sprayed-on free charge that arises from dielectric breakdown (see below) in the space between electrode and surface. Being of the same sign as the charge on the electrode, this latter charge is called a "homocharge." Both effects may remain for many years, but will vary with temperature, age, and mechanical treatment. An electret tends to lose its strength by a combination of the attraction of ions from the surroundings which neutralize the homocharge and the depolarizing effect of the heterocharge on itself (cf. Problem 3.9c). Therefore a disk electret is usually stored with metal plates placed on each face and connected together, in order to reduce both of these effects.[19]

It is interesting to note that, if the plates are originally uncharged and then placed on opposite sides of the disk, a spark may be obtained when

---

[18] For details on dielectrics used in capacitors of various types, see M. Brotherton, *Capacitors*, D. Van Nostrand, Princeton, 1946; F. E. Terman, *Radio Engineer's Handbook*, McGraw-Hill, New York, 1943, pp. 109–112 and 119–128; and D. E. Gray, ed., *American Institute of Physics Handbook*, 2nd ed., McGraw-Hill, New York, 1963, Sec. 5d. For standard condensers, see F. K. Harris, *Electrical Measurements*, John Wiley, New York, 1952, pp. 673–687.

[19] For further information on electrets, the reader is referred to B. Gross, *J. Chem. Phys.* **17**, 866 (1949); G. G. Wiseman and G. R. Feaster, *J. Chem. Phys.* **26**, 521 (1957); J. W. Wild and J. D. Stranathan, *J. Chem. Phys.* **27**, 1055 (1957), and for a review of earlier literature, F. Gutmann, *Rev. Mod. Phys.* **20**, 457 (1948).

they are connected; also, a spark may be obtained by merely lifting one plate from the electret. However, energy cannot be drawn from the electret as from a battery. The reader will find it instructive to locate the source of energy in the spark. (Problem 3.10a.)

Variations of κ with Temperature and Pressure. It can be shown by use of statistical mechanics that the molecular polarizability α is the sum of a part independent of temperature and one inversely proportional to the absolute temperature:

$$\alpha = \alpha_0 + p^2_{\text{perm}}/3kT \qquad (3.10\text{--}1)$$

In this equation α_0 is the contribution to the polarizability of the electron shifting process, and $p^2_{\text{perm}}/3kT$ is that due to molecular rotation, which is clearly the temperature-dependent part. Careful experiments have verified both the form of Eq. 3.10–1 and the constants.[20] The constant α_0 can be calculated in certain cases from atomic theory, and p_{perm} is the permanent dipole moment of the molecules, also calculable in some instances. The quantity k is the thermodynamic constant known as Boltzmann's constant and T is the absolute temperature. The value of p_{perm} for different substances ranges roughly from 0.10 to 2.0 × 10^{-18} electrostatic unit,[21] corresponding to the displacement of one electronic unit of charge by 0.02 to 0.4 × 10^{-10} m.

Another way to change κ for a given piece of dielectric is to subject it to mechanical stress. Conversely, when dielectrics are polarized by external fields, a change in size is observed unless prevented by mechanical stress. This effect is known as "electrostriction" and must be taken into account in the proper study of the forces on charged conductors embedded in fluids.

Ferroelectricity. Ferroelectricity is a phenomenon that bears at least a superficial resemblance to ferromagnetism (Sections 8.6 and 8.7), after which it takes its name. Typical materials exhibiting this behavior are Rochelle salt and barium titanate. The strong tendency in these materials for the elementary dipoles to hold each other in alignment is shown by hysteresis effects, in which changes in **D** tend to lag behind changes in **E**. Ferroelectric polarization tends to get masked by the absorption of free charge, just as with electrets, so that variations of **P** are more easily observed than absolute values. The phenomenon of pyroelectricity, in which materials become polarized on heating, is an example of ferroelectric behavior in which only the temperature variation is detectable.

Ferroelectric materials, unlike electrets, obtain their behavior from their crystal structure and have a so-called Curie temperature, above which they do not demonstrate their tendency for dipole alignment. These materials

[20] F. Gutmann, *loc. cit.*; W. F. G. Swann, *Journ. Frank. Inst.*, **255**, 513 (1953). Panofsky and Phillips, *op. cit.*, pp. 39–40; Van Vleck, *op. cit.*, Chapter III.
[21] Van Vleck, *op. cit.*, pp. 66, 67.

can show very large polarizations for small applied fields, having effective dielectric constants of several thousand or more. They often show a "domain" structure similar to that of ferromagnetic materials, with different regions in a crystal polarized in different directions.

There also exist materials called "antiferroelectric" which contain lines of ions all polarized in the same direction, but with neighboring lines alternating in their polarity, so that the over-all polarization is held to very low average values.[22]

Piezoelectricity. This is an effect that occurs on the application of mechanical stress to certain anisotropic crystals. Not only does κ change, but also a fixed polarization may result. The mechanical stresses set up in such crystals by electric fields are not isotropic and are quantitatively different from ordinary electrostriction. These last two effects are jointly referred to as "piezoelectricity." Materials showing these effects to a marked degree are called "piezoelectric materials." Quartz and Rochelle salt are the two most important.

Properly cut and ground crystals of quartz, for instance, will develop a polarization along a certain direction when compressed along another axis at right angles to the former. Such crystals can be used to convert sound waves or the mechanical vibration of a phonograph needle into varying currents in and out of a condenser into which the crystal has been inserted. A certain amount of electrical energy can be turned into mechanical energy of vibration by the inverse process, generating sound waves. This process is particularly useful in the field of ultrasonics.[23]

Dielectric Breakdown. This is the last property of real dielectrics we wish to discuss, and indeed one of the most important. For any material there is a maximum field intensity beyond which damage occurs that results in conduction, sparking, and other breakdown phenomena.

At relatively high fields, the electrons in the filled bands (cf. Section 2.1), as well as the few available conduction electrons or ions, can gain enough energy by successive small quantum jumps or single large ones to be able to knock other charged particles loose and make them available for conduction. The process can in some instances reach a constant state of fairly steady current, but usually a multiplying or "cascading" process results, producing an "avalanche" of conducting particles that are produced along certain paths in the material. Local heating also occurs along these paths,

---

[22] Further information on ferroelectricity may be found in G. Shirane, F. Jona, and R. Pepinsky, *Proc. Inst. Radio Engrs.*, **43**, 1738 (1955), C. Kittel, *Introduction to Solid State Physics*, 2nd ed., John Wiley, 1956, Chapter 8, and *American Institute of Physics Handbook*, *op. cit.*, Sec. 9f–14.

[23] For further details on piezoelectricity, see W. G. Cady, *Piezoelectricity*, McGraw-Hill, New York, 1946; Dover, New York, reprint, 1963, 2 vols; also *American Institute of Physics Handbook*, *op. cit.*, Sec. 9f–9.

and permanent damage results. Spark holes or punctures appear and the insulating qualities are greatly impaired.

Electrostatic apparatus that operates at high potentials, as most of it does, depends for its operation on the quality of the insulation with respect to breakdown (and, of course, with respect to conductivity). Air is the most common insulating material. Its breakdown occurs when dry and

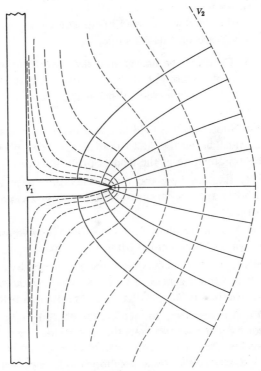

Fig. 3.10a. A conductor with a sharp point showing equipotentials and lines of force.

at standard temperature and pressure (0°C and 760 mm Hg) at fields of about 3×10^6 v/m or 100 statv/cm. Fields somewhat less than this may produce steady discharging currents known as "corona." The value quoted gives roughly the field for which disruptive sparking occurs.

The discharge of electricity is sometimes to be promoted rather than discouraged. For this purpose, conductors with sharp points can be used. We can show readily that the field near a sharp point is much larger than at other places on the conductor, so that corona and sparking most readily occurs at these points. Consider the conductor shown in Fig. 3.10a, with a "point" which is a hemisphere of radius R on the tip of a cone.

It will be observed that the flux density at the surface of the point is much larger than elsewhere in the diagram. Consequently, when the field intensity is not unreasonably large over most of the region, it may nevertheless come to or above the breakdown value near the point. The lines of force near the point are like those for a sphere, and so we can use the result for a sphere (Problem 2.2e) that $E = V/a$ just outside it, where a is the radius. If V is about 300 v, and $a = 0.1$ mm $= 10^{-4}$ m, $E = 3 \times 10^6$ v/m, and breakdown will occur.

The operation of lightning rods and brush discharge points in electrostatic generators is based on this principle.

Problem 3.10a. Describe the charge and field distributions that occur when neutral metal plates are put on both sides of a disk electret. What happens when the plates are joined? What is the source of the energy in the spark that occurs?

Problem 3.10b. Show that the field in a depression on the outer surface of a conductor must be weaker than that at a nearby plane region, in contrast to the strengthening of the field at protuberances.

Problem 3.10c. Explain how the finite relaxation time for dielectric materials can lead to the appearance of a PD across a capacitor after it has been discharged.

Problem 3.10d. Use the result of Problem 1.7n to justify more accurately the use of $E = V/a$ for the spherical tip in Fig. 3.10a.

Problem 3.10e. Calculate the maximum charge carried by a unit area of the belt of a Van de Graaff generator in air at atmospheric pressure if the field just outside the belt is 70% of the mean breakdown field for air.

Problem 3.10f. It is proposed to increase the charging rate of a Van de Graaff generator by using several belts that run inside one another. Show by use of the flux law that, if the belts are to be charged until the maximum field in air is just attained in their neighborhood, improvement can be obtained by neighboring belts running in alternate directions with alternate signs of charge, but not if they all run in the same direction.

Problem 3.10g. The inside of the grounded tank of a Van de Graaff generator near the high voltage end is a spherical surface of radius R. Show that the maximum PD between it and a concentric spherical high-voltage terminal inside the tank can be achieved for a fixed value of the gas-breakdown field strength if the high voltage terminal is a sphere of radius $R/2$.

Chapter 4

FURTHER TOPICS
IN ELECTROSTATICS

4.1 Introduction

There are two general types of calculations in electrostatics that we have not yet discussed and wish to consider in this chapter. These are the question of how the charge is distributed on a given set of conductors when the potential or total charge on each is known and the question of the dependence of the potential energy of a system of charged conductors on their charges, potentials and positions. These problems are related because, first, the theory for each depends on the general uniqueness theorem; second, in each case the potentials V and net charges Q of the conductors are taken to be the determining factors in the situation; and third, the coefficients of capacitance and potential that we shall introduce for the energy considerations are usually calculated by the same methods that solve the distribution problem.

We shall start with a survey of the methods of solving the distribution problem. Next we shall deal with some relatively simple but quite important distribution calculations. Finally we shall take up the general energy problem and arrive at useful methods for finding the forces on charged conductors.

4.2 Application of the Uniqueness Theorem

In Section 1.10, we proved that there is only one solution of Laplace's equation in a given region that reduces to given values of V on the bounding surfaces of the region. In Section 2.2, we showed that given charges Q_1, $Q_2 \cdots Q_n$ on n conductors and potentials $V_{n+1} \cdots V_{n+m}$ on m other conductors, there is only one way in which charge can be distributed on

151

each of the $n + m$ conductors and a unique potential function $V(x, y, z)$ in the space between conductors. Finally, in Section 3.8, we showed that this uniqueness property still holds when the space is filled with ideal dielectric of constant or varying κ.

By means of this theorem, the distribution problem is reduced to that of finding by *any mathematical means available* a potential function $V(x, y, z)$ whose gradient obeys the flux law and which satisfies the proper *boundary conditions*, namely:

1. The approach of V to a constant value over the surface of each conductor.
2. The provision of the proper value of Q or V at each conductor.
3. The provision for the existence of whatever point charges are specified.
4. The proper conditions on **D** and **E** at any dielectric boundary or interface.

Regardless of how we find such a solution, we can be sure it is the correct one. Three general methods for constructing such fields deserve mention here.

A. Fields may be constructed in "patchwork" fashion by finding simple arrangements of point charges that happen to have one or more equipotential surfaces of suitable shapes and then replacing the volumes inside or outside these particular equipotentials with regions of constant potential. A modification consists of matching two different free-space fields at a given surface in such a way as to fit the dielectric interface boundary conditions of the actual problem. This approach is called the "method of images" and will be considered in the next three sections.

B. One may construct solutions by suitable use of the condition that V must obey Laplace's equation $\nabla^2 V = 0$. This approach involves a systematic study of solutions of this equation with various sorts of symmetry and then the selection of solutions that in proper combinations will satisfy the boundary conditions. A brief introduction to this approach is given in Section 4.6.

C. We may use the powerful methods based on the theory of complex variables for the generation of solutions of Laplace's equation in two dimensions,

$$\frac{\partial^2 V}{\partial x^2} + \frac{\partial^2 V}{\partial y^2} = 0 \qquad (4.2\text{--}1)$$

Such methods can provide solutions to problems with cylindrical symmetry in which the potential is not a function of z, and which involve many different shapes of boundaries. However, we shall not take up these methods here, and refer the reader to other books.[1]

4.3 Point and Plane Image Calculations

The simplest application of the method of images has in effect already been presented, namely, the case of the charged spherical conductor of radius R in a vacuum. A field that fits the conditions for this conductor may be invented by taking the field of a point charge Q, placed at the location of the sphere's center, but using this field only at distances equal to or greater than R. An interior region of constant potential (zero field) is then patched on to the point charge field at the radius R. The resultant field satisfies conditions 1, 3, and 4. If the charge Q that generates the fitting field equals the given charge on the conductor, or if $Q = 4\pi\epsilon_0 RV$ where V is the given potential, then condition 2 is also satisfied, as we already know.

We could describe the situation by saying that we start with a point charge and then wipe out the field between it and one of its equipotentials, *transferring the charge to the equipotential surface* since we now must allow the same flux to end or begin there that originally went to or from the point. The charge at the center that appears to be there from the outside, but really is not, is similar to a virtual image in optics and we shall call it an "image charge."

The next simplest case is that of two equal and opposite point charges. One equipotential between them has a simple shape, namely, the plane of symmetry, for which $V = 0$. As shown in Fig. 4.3a, we may take a grounded conductor with a plane surface and place the surface so as to coincide with the plane of symmetry, the remainder of the conductor being on the side that had the negative charge. Charge $-q$ is then all transferred to the conductor, appropriately distributed in accordance with the original flux pattern. The flux pattern in the space above the conductor and around the charge $+q$ will remain unchanged, since it represents the unique field with $+q$ at the given point a height h above the plane, and $V = 0$ on the plane.

The negative charge $-q$ which was removed may be imagined still present in a "virtual" form, like a virtual image in optics, and for this

[1] L. Page and N. I. Adams, Jr., *Principles of Electricity*, 3rd ed., D. Van Nostrand, Princeton, 1958, pp. 92–96; W. K. H. Panofsky and M. Phillips, *Classical Electricity and Magnetism*, 2nd ed., Addison-Wesley, Reading, Mass., 1962, Chapter 4; D. R. Corson and P. Lorrain, *Introduction to Electromagnetic Fields and Waves*, W. H. Freeman, San Francisco, 1962, Appendix D; R. Plosney and R. E. Collin, *Principles and Applications of Electromagnetic Fields*, McGraw-Hill, New York, 1961, Chapter 4.

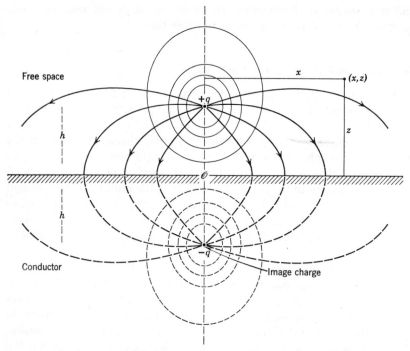

Fig. 4.3a. A charge q outside a conducting plane, and its image.

reason it is called the "image" of $+q$. The potential at a point (x, z) above the conductor is the same as in the original case, so it may be calculated from $+q$ and its image. We have

$$V(x, z) = \frac{q}{4\pi\epsilon_0[x^2 + (z - h)^2]^{1/2}} - \frac{q}{4\pi\epsilon_0[x^2 + (z + h)^2]^{1/2}} \quad (4.3\text{–}1)$$

The value of σ on the surface of the conductor can be found from $\sigma = -\epsilon_0 \left(\dfrac{\partial V}{\partial z}\right)_{z=0}$. The result is

$$\sigma = -\frac{hq}{2\pi(x^2 + h^2)^{3/2}} \quad (4.3\text{–}2)$$

The charge density and potential are of course symmetric with respect to rotation about the line joining q and $-q$.

The force acting on q can be calculated immediately from Coulomb's law and the distance $2h$ between charge and image. That is,

$$\mathbf{F} = -\mathbf{1}_z \frac{q^2}{16\pi\epsilon_0 h^2} \quad (4.3\text{–}3)$$

This case is considered further in Problems 4.3a and b.

If we have two or more point charges outside a plane, we can solve the problem by adding the potentials of the corresponding charge pairs. The images in this case make collectively a mirror image of the original disrtibution of charges.

A more complicated case can be solved by use of the field of the four charges of Fig. 1.6*f*, shown with equipotentials in Figs. 4.3*b* and *c*. The zero equipotential consists of two intersecting planes. The field can be wiped out in three quadrants, leaving us with the case of two conducting half planes intersecting at right angles and having a single point charge located somewhere in the smaller angle between them—it does not have to be on a 45° line (Problem 4.3*d*).

Images with Dielectrics. Let us now show the application of this method to the problem of a point charge in a dielectric medium with a plane

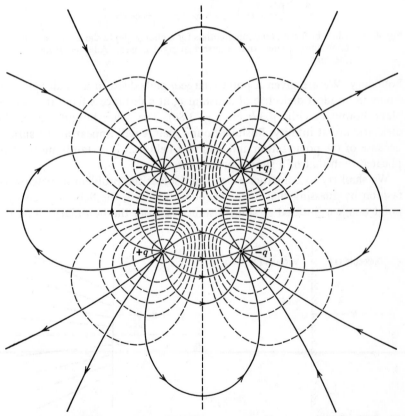

Fig. 4.3*b*. Lines of force and equipotentials for a symmetrical array of two positive and two negative charges. (Adapted from E. Durand, *Électrostatique et Magnétostatique*, Masson et Cie, Paris, 1953, Fig. 37.)

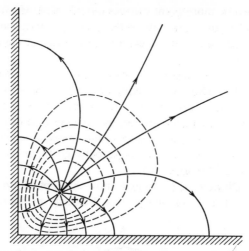

Fig. 4.3c.   Lines of force and equipotentials for a charge $+q$ in the space between two conducting planes that intersect at right angles. (Adapted from Durand, *loc. cit.*)

boundary. We are given a point charge q embedded in a small spherical cavity in an ideal dielectric of constant κ, at a distance h from the infinite plane boundary (Fig. 4.3d; cf. Fig. 3.8a). The other boundaries of the dielectric are at infinity. Positive bound charge will appear at the surface because of the polarization and lead to a field that is certainly more complicated than that of a simple point charge.

We shall try to construct a field that solves the problem in patchwork fashion by guessing that in the vacuum, region 2, the field is given by a point image q_2 located at some distance h_2 from the boundary along the

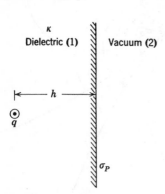

Fig. 4.3d.   A charge imbedded in a dielectric near a boundary.

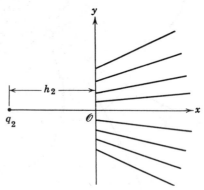

Fig. 4.3e.   Image and field for region 2.

axis of symmetry, as shown in Fig. 4.3e, and that in region 1 the field is produced both by q/κ at h in accordance with the calculation of Section 3.8 and by an image q_1 in the vacuum at distance h_1 from the interface, as in Fig. 4.3f. (This latter image is to have effect only in the region in which it is not located.) We assume that only these particular point images are present—i.e., no polarization charges and no dielectric media add to

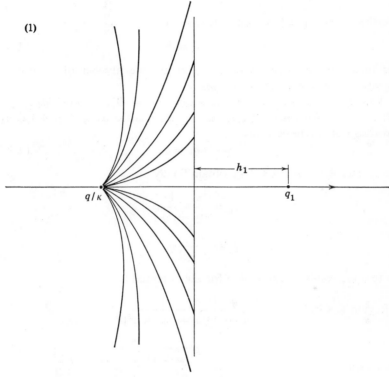

Fig. 4.3f. Image and field for region 1.

our calculated fields. Then we can write for the potential at a point (x, y) in the plane of the paper

Region 1, $x < 0$: $V = \dfrac{q/\kappa}{4\pi\epsilon_0[(x+h)^2 + y^2]^{1/2}} + \dfrac{q_1}{4\pi\epsilon_0[(h_1 - x)^2 + y^2]^{1/2}}$

Region 2, $x > 0$: $V = \dfrac{q_2}{4\pi\epsilon_0[(x+h_2)^2 + y^2]^{1/2}}$

At the interface, we must have the same value of V from the two expressions, a more complicated statement of which is that $-\partial V/\partial y = E_t$

is the same on both sides. Setting the V's equal for $x = 0$ gives

$$\frac{q/\kappa}{(h^2 + y^2)^{1/2}} + \frac{q_1}{(h_1^2 + y^2)^{1/2}} = \frac{q_2}{(h_2^2 + y^2)^{1/2}} \tag{4.3-4}$$

For very large y, we can neglect the h's, so that we must have

$$\frac{q}{\kappa} + q_1 = q_2 \tag{4.3-5}$$

Furthermore, Eq. 4.3–4 cannot hold for all y unless

$$h = h_1 = h_2 \tag{4.3-6}$$

for otherwise we could write down an infinite number of inconsistent equations relating the three charges.

The other boundary condition is that $D_{n1} = D_{n2}$, or $\kappa(\partial V/\partial x)_{x \to 0-} = (\partial V/\partial x)_{x \to 0+}$. We obtain from this equation after using Eq. 4.3–6 and dividing out common terms

$$q - \kappa q_1 = q_2 \tag{4.3-7}$$

From Eqs. 4.3–5 and 4.3–7 we obtain finally

$$q_1 = \frac{\kappa - 1}{\kappa(\kappa + 1)} q$$

$$\tag{4.3-8}$$

$$q_2 = \frac{2}{\kappa + 1} q$$

so that the resultant expression for the potential is

Region 1, $x < 0$: $V = \dfrac{q}{4\pi\kappa\epsilon_0}\Bigg[\dfrac{1}{[(x + h)^2 + y^2]^{1/2}}$

$$+ \dfrac{\kappa - 1}{(\kappa + 1)[(x - h)^2 + y^2]^{1/2}}\Bigg] \tag{4.3-9}$$

Region 2, $x > 0$: $V = \dfrac{2q}{4\pi(\kappa + 1)\epsilon_0[(x + h)^2 + y^2]^{1/2}}$

The reader can readily verify (Problem 4.3g) that the surface density of polarization charge is

$$\sigma_P = \frac{(\kappa - 1)h}{2\pi\kappa(\kappa + 1)(h^2 + y^2)^{3/2}} q \tag{4.3-10}$$

We have thus found the solution to the distribution of polarization and field when a point charge is embedded in a large piece of dielectric near a plane surface, a solution anticipated near the end of Section 3.8. More details for this case are taken up in Problems 4.3h and i.

Problem 4.3a. Prove by direct integration of σ that the total charge on the plane of Fig. 4.3a is $-q$.

Problem 4.3b. Find the work necessary to take an electron from a point 1 angstrom unit (10^{-10} m) outside a metal surface to infinity. Is a factor 2 needed because of the image charge? What is the field E that acts on q? What does the fact that E depends on q signify?

Problem 4.3c. Discuss the point-and-conducting-plane image case when the entire space outside the conductor is filled with an ideal dielectric.

Problem 4.3d. Find the charge densities for an unsymmetrical case of Fig. 4.3c directly under the foot of the perpendicular from the charge q on each plane, where q is one electronic unit, distant 3×10^{-8} m from one surface and 4×10^{-8} m from the other. What is the charge density at the intersection of the planes?

Problem 4.3e. For what other angles than 90° can the method of images be used to find the field when a point charge is placed between two intersecting planes? Discuss and give an example.

Problem 4.3f. Make a sketch showing the images needed when two point charges are arbitrarily located in a 60° angle between two conducting planes.

Problem 4.3g. Verify Eq. 4.3–10.

Problem 4.3h. Calculate the total polarization charge q_P that appears on the surface in Fig. 4.3d, from Eq. 4.3–10. Verify this result by using the flux theorem on q_P and q_1.

Problem 4.3i. Calculate the angle through which a line of force is "refracted" at a point on the plane of Fig. 4.3d whose distance from the origin is 0.40 m, when $h = 0.50$ m, $q = 2 \times 10^{-9}$ coulomb, and $\kappa = 3.0$.

Problem 4.3j. Find the distribution of polarization on the plane surface of a very large piece of ideal dielectric when a point charge q is located a small distance h from the plane, *outside* the material.

Problem 4.3k. Find the force with which the dielectric material attracts q in Problem 4.3j.

Problem 4.3l. Verify that the solution given in Section 3.9 for the field in a spherical cavity in a piece of dielectric is correct in accordance with the method of images.

Problem 4.3m. Part of the work function of a metal is the work done against the image force with which an electron at a distance x outside a piece of metal is attracted inward. Find that potential as a function of x that would give the same force on the electron (this effective potential is sometimes called the "motive"). If this potential is combined with that due to a uniform field E just outside the metal and directed toward it, a maximum of the total potential energy for the electron can be found some-where outside the metal. The work function in the presence of **E** is therefore reduced to the work necessary to get an electron from the Fermi level up to this maximum. Prove that the amount $\Delta\phi$ by which ϕ is reduced is $e(eE/4\pi\epsilon_0)^{1/2}$.

4.4 Point and Sphere Image Calculations

Careful examination of the equipotential diagrams for pairs of opposite but unequal charges, such as Fig. 1.11e, will reveal that one equipotential surface has a simple shape. Specifically, the surface for $V = 0$ is a sphere. To show this, consider the potential produced by charges q_1 and q_2 of opposite signs located on the x-axis at distances x_1 and x_2 from the origin as in Fig. 4.4a. We have at the point (x, y, z)

$$V = \frac{q_1}{4\pi\epsilon_0[(x - x_1)^2 + y^2 + z^2]^{1/2}} + \frac{q_2}{4\pi\epsilon_0[(x - x_2)^2 + y^2 + z^2]^{1/2}} \quad (4.4\text{-}1)$$

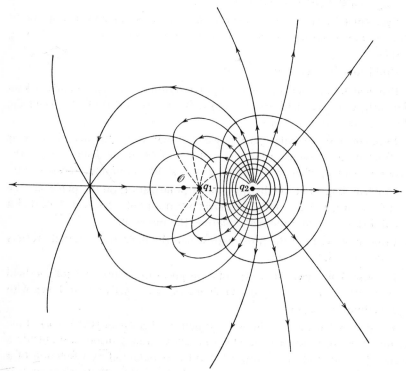

Fig. 4.4a. Lines of force and equipotentials for a positive charge q_2 and a negative charge q_1 where $-q_1 < q_2$. The zero equipotential is a sphere centered at the origin $\mathcal{O}$.

When V is zero, this expression can be considerably simplified, the radicals disappearing with only one operation of squaring. The result can be written

$$q_2{}^2[(x - x_1)^2 + y^2 + z^2] - q_1{}^2[(x - x_2)^2 + y^2 + z^2] = 0$$

which is the equation of a sphere, since the coefficients of x^2, y^2, and z^2 are each equal to $q_2{}^2 - q_1{}^2$. The center of the sphere will be at the origin if the coefficient of x is zero, that is, if $q_1{}^2 x_2 = q_2{}^2 x_1$ or

$$\frac{q_1{}^2}{q_2{}^2} = \frac{x_1}{x_2} \tag{4.4-2}$$

so for convenience we shall assume this to be true; furthermore since x_1 and x_2 are of the same sign, we will take them to be both positive and let $x_1 < x_2$ so that $q_1{}^2 < q_2{}^2$. The equation of the zero equipotential then becomes

$$x^2 + y^2 + z^2 = \frac{x_2{}^2 q_1{}^2 - x_1{}^2 q_2{}^2}{q_2{}^2 - q_1{}^2} = x_2 q_1{}^2 \frac{x_2 - x_1}{q_2{}^2 - q_1{}^2} = x_2{}^2 \frac{q_1{}^2}{q_2{}^2} \tag{4.4-3}$$

simplifying by means of Eq. 4.4–2. The radius R of the sphere is

$$R = x_2\left(-\frac{q_1}{q_2}\right) = (x_1 x_2)^{1/2} = x_1\left(-\frac{q_2}{q_1}\right) \tag{4.4-4}$$

where the minus sign is needed to make R positive. Thus we have $x_2 = -Rq_2/q_1$ and $x_1 = -Rq_1/q_2$, with $x_1 < R$ and $x_2 > R$. We have therefore a spherical equipotential of radius R and potential value $V = 0$, produced by a charge q_1 at a distance $R(-q_1/q_2)$ from the center inside the sphere and a charge q_2 of opposite sign at a further distance $R(-q_2/q_1)$ along the same radius outside the sphere. We can wipe out the field inside and distribute q_1 on the surface of a spherical conductor of radius R, or wipe out the field outside and put q_2 on the inside surface of a spherical cavity of the same dimensions. (In this latter case the potential at "infinity" can be zero or any other value, namely the potential of the conductor in question.) The surface charge density can again be calculated from $\sigma = \epsilon_0 E$, with E at the conducting surface derived from q_1 and q_2. Calculations for these cases are asked for in Problems 4.4b, c, and d.

A more general field with a spherical equipotential may be obtained with three point charges. Let us place q_3 at the center of the sphere of radius R discussed above. At the surface of the sphere we now have the sum of the original value $V = 0$ and the added value $V = q_3/4\pi\epsilon_0 R$. Thus we have, outside the sphere, a field which gives a constant potential $V = q_3/4\pi\epsilon_0 R$ over a sphere of radius R, implies a total charge on the sphere $Q = q_1 + q_3$, and involves a point charge q_2 at a distance $R(-q_2/q_1)$ from the center of the sphere. The field can be calculated from q_2 and the two images, q_3 at the center and q_1 at a radius $R(-q_1/q_2)$ from the center.

If we are given the radius of the sphere and the value and location of q_2, it remains to specify either Q or V on the sphere in order to locate both images and calculate the field and charge distribution.

The problem of two conducting spheres and that of a sphere and a plane, which are of considerable practical interest, can only be solved with an infinite series of images and will not be considered in this book.[2]

Problem 4.4a. Discuss the reasons why spherical equipotentials can only exist in the case of two point charges when these are of opposite sign and why one charge must be inside and one out.

Problem 4.4b. A point charge of 4×10^{-7} coulomb lies outside a grounded conducting sphere. The sphere has a radius of 10 cm and the charge lies at a distance of 25 cm from the center of the sphere. Find the magnitude and location of the image charge inside the sphere that yields the correct distribution, and find the value of σ at the two points of the conductor that are nearest and farthest from q. Also find the value of σ at a point on the sphere midway between these two points.

Problem 4.4c. Write a formula for the force exerted by the charge residing on a grounded conducting sphere of radius R on a point charge q at a distance r from its center ($r > R$).

Problem 4.4d. Find a general expression for the field in a spherical cavity in a conductor when a single charge q is placed in the cavity but not at the center. Find the force on q. Will q be in stable or unstable equilibrium if placed at the center?

Problem 4.4e. A point charge q resides at a distance $r > R$ from the center of an isolated conducting sphere with zero net charge and radius R. Find the force on q.

Problem 4.4f. Consider an isolated conducting sphere and a point charge q outside it. Allow q to recede from the sphere and increase in magnitude so that the field $\mathbf{E}$ it produces by itself at the center of the sphere remains constant. Find the limiting charge distribution and external field around the sphere as $q \to \infty$, thus solving the problem of a conducting sphere placed into a fixed, homogeneous electric field.

Problem 4.4g. A conducting sphere of radius 10 cm is maintained at a potential of $+100$ v by means of a battery. A point charge of -1.1×10^{-9} coulomb resides at 10 cm from its surface. Find the resultant electric field at a point on a radius 10 cm beyond the negative charge.

---

[2] See, for instance, Page and Adams, *op. cit.* section 31; Sir James Jeans, *Mathematical Theory of Electricity and Magnetism*, Cambridge, 1946, paperback 1961, sections 221, 222; J. C. Maxwell, *Treatise on Electricity and Magnetism*, 2nd and 3rd ed., Oxford, 1881 and 1904, Dover, New York, reprint, 1964, articles 165–175; Corson and Lorrain, *op. cit.*, section 4.3.4.

Problem 4.4h. A conducting sphere of radius 1 m is given a charge of 3×10^{-7} coulomb. Find the force exerted on a point charge of 6×10^{-7} coulomb 0.2 m outside its surface.

4.5 Image Calculations for Lines, Cylinders, and Planes

In Section 1.7, we calculated the potential due to two infinite, parallel filaments of charge of linear densities λ and $-\lambda$, namely Eq. 1.7–15:

$$V = (\lambda/2\pi\epsilon_0) \ln (r_2/r_1) \qquad (4.5\text{–}1)$$

In this equation, r_2 is the perpendicular distance from the negative line of charge to the point where V is evaluated, and r_1 is that from the positive.

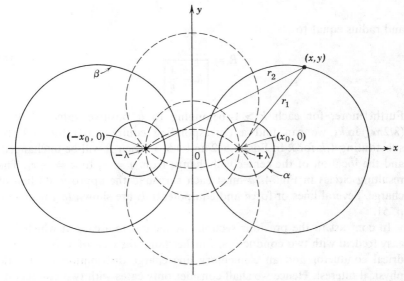

Fig. 4.5a. Variables used for the calculation of the equipotentials (solid) and lines of force (dashed) for two long parallel filaments of charge.

The equipotentials are cylindrical surfaces; that is, they are surfaces composed of lines all parallel to the given lines of charge. We can readily show that they are *circular* cylinders. Figure 4.5a shows a plane perpendicular to the lines of charge.

The equation of an equipotential line in this plane is given by setting r_2/r_1 equal to a constant k. From the figure we have

$$\frac{r_2^{2}}{r_1^{2}} = k^2 = \frac{(x + x_0)^2 + y^2}{(x - x_0)^2 + y^2} \qquad (4.5\text{–}2a)$$

which reduces after rearranging and completing the square to

$$\left[x - \left(\frac{k + \dfrac{1}{k}}{k - \dfrac{1}{k}} \right) x_0 \right]^2 + y^2 = \frac{4x_0^2}{\left(k - \dfrac{1}{k} \right)^2} \qquad (4.5\text{-}2b)$$

Therefore each equipotential is a circular cylinder with center at $x = x_1$, where

$$x_1 = x_0 \frac{\left(k + \dfrac{1}{k} \right)}{\left(k - \dfrac{1}{k} \right)} \qquad (4.5\text{-}3a)$$

and radius equal to

$$R = \frac{2x_0}{\left| k - \dfrac{1}{k} \right|} \qquad (4.5\text{-}3b)$$

Furthermore, for each $k > 1$ belonging to a positive value of $V = (\lambda/2\pi\epsilon_0) \ln k$, we can find a corresponding equipotential for $-V$ by substituting $1/k$ for k in Eqs. 4.5-2 and 4.5-3. Then R will be unchanged, and the location of the center will change from $x = x_1$ to $x = -x_1$. The resulting circles in Fig. 4.5a must each surround the appropriate line of charge. Several lines of force and equipotentials are shown in Fig. 1.11d, p. 51.

In contrast to the previous section, we have here a case in which it is easy to deal with two conductors. Furthermore, the case of a single cylindrical conductor and an elementary line charge distribution is of little physical interest. Hence we shall consider only cases with two conducting surfaces.

Let us consider the general case of two long parallel circular-cylindrical wires of arbitrary diameters, placed an arbitrary distance apart and charged as a capacitor to a potential difference V. We wish to find their capacitance. These two wires might be considered to correspond in Fig. 4.5a to the surfaces labeled α and β.

A field which satisfies the boundary condition for this pair of conductors can be constructed by using line images λ and $-\lambda$ if we can find their locations so that a pair of equipotentials α and β have the correct radii and positions to coincide with the surfaces of the wires and λ has such a value that the correct difference of potential V ensues.

We are given two radii R_α and R_β and a distance between the centers of the wires which we can call D. This distance must equal $x_{1\alpha} - x_{1\beta}$ where $x_{1\alpha}$ and $x_{1\beta}$ are given by Eq. 4.5–3a. Therefore we have enough equations to determine x_0, k_α, and k_β. The potential difference is

$$V = V_\alpha - V_\beta = (\lambda/2\pi\epsilon_0)[\ln k_\alpha - \ln k_\beta] = (\lambda/2\pi\epsilon_0) \ln (k_\alpha/k_\beta)$$

so that we can solve for λ. Finally, the capacitance per unit length is $C_l = \lambda/V$ and can readily be calculated. Note that the location of the zero equipotential cannot be freely taken because of the difficulty at infinity referred

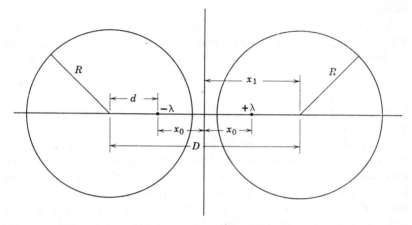

Fig. 4.5b. Application to a pair of wires of radius R and separation D.

to in Section 1.7 but also that the final answer is independent of this difficulty. The answer is, of course, approximate for an actual pair of wires of finite length but may be considered accurate except for end corrections.

The results for two unequal wires are rather complicated and are reserved for those who wish to tackle Problem 4.5h. Let us work out the case of two wires of equal radii R (Fig. 4.5b). Let $k_\alpha = k > 1$, and $k_\beta = 1/k$.

Solving Eq. 4.5–3b for k (taking the positive root of the resulting quadratic equation), we find

$$k = \frac{x_0 + (x_0^2 + R^2)^{1/2}}{R}$$

We have $D = 2x_1$, which is by Eqs. 4.5–3a and 4.5–3b equal to $R[k + (1/k)]$. Using the value of k just obtained, $D = 2(x_0^2 + R^2)^{1/2}$ or

$$x_0 = \tfrac{1}{2}(D^2 - 4R^2)^{1/2}$$

so that

$$k = \frac{D + (D^2 - 4R^2)^{1/2}}{2R} \tag{4.5–4}$$

Now, the potential difference between the wires is

$$V = (\lambda/2\pi\epsilon_0) \ln (k_\alpha/k_\beta) = (\lambda/2\pi\epsilon_0) \ln k^2 = (\lambda/\pi\epsilon_0) \ln k,$$

or $C_l = \lambda/V = \pi\epsilon_0/\ln k$, yielding finally

$$C_l = \frac{\pi\epsilon_0}{\ln \dfrac{D + (D^2 - 4R^2)^{\frac{1}{2}}}{2R}} \tag{4.5-5}$$

for the capacitance per unit length of a parallel pair of wires of radii R and axis-to-axis separation D.

The potential at points in the region between the wires is given by Eq. 4.5–1. The location of the images λ and $-\lambda$ from which the r's are measured is given by the distance d from the wire axis, where $d = \frac{1}{2}D - x_0$ or

$$d = \frac{1}{2}[D - (D^2 - 4R^2)^{\frac{1}{2}}] \tag{4.5-6}$$

The surface charge density on either wire may then be found as in the previous sections.

The result just obtained can be immediately extended by using one-half the resulting field and applying it to the problem of the single wire parallel to a *plane* conductor. One of the two equal wires thus becomes an extended image. (Any other equipotential belonging to the same problem could of course be used for the image.) The only quantitative difference between this calculation and the preceding is that we must have one-half of the potential difference since V now means the PD from wire to central plane. It is convenient to write $D = 2h$ where h is the distance from wire to plane. The capacitance between a wire and a plane parallel to it is then twice the result of Eq. 4.5–5 (inserting $D = 2h$ and simplifying)

$$C_l = \frac{2\pi\epsilon_0}{\ln \dfrac{h + (h^2 - R^2)^{\frac{1}{2}}}{R}} \tag{4.5-7}$$

Note that in both Eq. 4.5–5 and Eq. 4.5–7 the logarithm becomes $\ln (D/R) = \ln 2h/R$ when $R \ll D$, and d becomes very small (approximately R^2/D).

We have not discussed the possible presence of dielectric materials, but it is obvious that, if an ideal dielectric fills all the relevant space, C_l is multiplied by κ.

Problem 4.5a. Show by calculation from Eqs. 4.5–2 and 4.5–3 that the circles described by Eq. 4.5–1 must surround the appropriate lines of charge.

Problem 4.5b. Prove that the lines of force for two parallel charged wires are circles. *Hints:* Calculate dy/dx from Eq. 4.5–2b, eliminate k using 4.5–2a, and show that the equation obtained on replacing dy/dx by $-dx/dy$ is satisfied by any circle passing through ($\pm x_0$, 0).

Problem 4.5c. Find the capacitance per unit length of two parallel #16 (AWG or B & S) copper wires whose centers are 1 in. apart (cf. any convenient handbook with wire tables).

Problem 4.5d. Find the capacitance per centimeter between a #20 copper hook-up wire and a plane metal chassis if the wire runs parallel to the chassis and its center is 0.5 cm away from the plane surface of the chassis. Neglect the influence of any insulating material.

Problem 4.5e. Find a formula for the force per unit length on a charged wire parallel to a grounded conducting plane.

Problem 4.5f. Two long cylinders each of radius 3 cm lie parallel with their axes 10 cm apart. Find the charge densities on their nearest and farthest sides when charged to a PD of 1000 v.

Problem 4.5g. Discuss the application of Section 4.5 to the case of a wire inside a long cylindrical cavity, parallel to the cavity axis but displaced from it.

Problem 4.5h. Find the capacitance of two parallel circular cylinders of radii R and R', with distance D between their axes. *Hint:* Prove first that

$$D = Rk + R'k' = (x_0{}^2 + R^2)^{1/2} + (x_0{}^2 + R'^2)^{1/2}$$

4.6 The Use of Laplace's Equation

We wish now to consider briefly the method of constructing solutions to electrostatic problems by a systematic study of Laplace's equation. The first consideration is to make a proper choice of a coordinate system. We could make some progress with Cartesian coordinates, since the function $V = A/(x^2 + y^2 + z^2)^{1/2}$ is a solution of

$$\frac{\partial^2 V}{\partial x^2} + \frac{\partial^2 V}{\partial y^2} + \frac{\partial^2 V}{\partial z^2} = 0$$

as we saw in Section 1.10 and since derivatives of V with respect to x, y, or z or any combination (and any order of derivative) are also solutions[3] (cf. Problems 1.10a and 3.1b).

However, the most important and useful properties of the method we wish to discuss are not conveniently represented with Cartesian coordinates. We shall therefore consider other appropriate sets of coordinates.

---

[3] This is true because $\partial^2 V/\partial x\ \partial y = \partial^2 V/\partial y\ \partial x$ and so forth for all combinations of partial differentiations, so that $\nabla^2(\partial V/\partial x) = (\partial/\partial x)(\nabla^2 V) = 0$, etc.

By appropriate coordinate systems, we mean the following. Any point $\mathscr{P}(x, y, z)$ is to be located by three new variables. Just as allowing y and z to vary with x kept constant generates a plane, so also will there be sets of coordinate surfaces generated respectively by holding constant each of the three new variables. We require that these surfaces always intersect each other at right angles (that is, are mutually orthogonal) and prefer that they have shapes related to types of conducting or dielectric surfaces of physical interest (spheres, cylinders, cones, ellipsoids, etc.). Finally, and most important, Laplace's equation in the new coordinates shall be "separable," which means that it shall have solutions which are the products of three functions, each depending on one variable only. The great advantage of separability is that the partial differential equation is replaced by three ordinary ones and the many useful techniques available for solving the latter may be employed.

Spherical Coordinates. There are approximately eleven coordinate systems possible which have these properties (the number depends on how they are classified).[4] A simple example, and perhaps the most important, is that spherical coordinates (r, θ, ϕ), in which r is the distance of $\mathscr{P}$ from the origin $\mathcal{O}$, θ is the angle between the line $\mathcal{O}\mathscr{P}$ and a chosen axis, and ϕ represents rotation about this axis (see Fig. A.2d, p. 6 15). It may be shown from the appendix (see Table A.2A and Problem A.2b) that in these coordinates, the Laplace equation becomes

$$\frac{\partial}{\partial r}\left(r^2 \frac{\partial V}{\partial r}\right) + \frac{1}{\sin \theta}\frac{\partial}{\partial \theta}\left(\sin \theta \frac{\partial V}{\partial \theta}\right) + \frac{1}{\sin^2 \theta}\frac{\partial^2 V}{\partial \phi^2} = 0 \qquad (4.6\text{--}1)$$

Let us now assume that V is a product of a function of r and a function of θ and ϕ:

$$V(r, \theta, \phi) = f(r)Y(\theta, \phi) \qquad (4.6\text{--}2)$$

Substitute this expression in Eq. 4.6–1, and then divide by fY, noting that in each term one of the functions is a constant with respect to the differentiation. We have then

$$\left[\frac{1}{f(r)}\frac{d}{dr}\left(r^2 \frac{df}{dr}\right)\right] + \left[\frac{1}{Y\sin\theta}\frac{\partial}{\partial\theta}\left(\sin\theta\frac{\partial Y}{\partial\theta}\right) + \frac{1}{Y\sin^2\theta}\frac{\partial^2 Y}{\partial\phi^2}\right] = 0 \quad (4.6\text{--}3)$$

The first square bracket is a function only of r, and the second only of θ and ϕ. Their sum cannot possibly add to zero for *all* the values of r, θ, and ϕ in the space between the given boundaries, unless each bracket is

---

[4] A systematic discussion of them is given by E. Weber, *Electromagnetic Fields; Theory and Applications;* Vol. I, *Mapping of Fields*, 2nd ed., John Wiley, New York, 1950, pp. 445–446 and by P. M. Morse and H. Feshbach, *Methods of Theoretical Physics*, McGraw-Hill, New York, 1953, Vol. I, p. 655ff.

constant. The most convenient way to write this constant turns out to be to set the first bracket equal to $n(n + 1)$ and the second $-n(n + 1)$.

We have then the ordinary differential equation

$$\frac{d}{dr}\left(r^2 \frac{df}{dr}\right) = n(n + 1)f(r) \tag{4.6-4}$$

and the partial one in two variables

$$\frac{1}{\sin \theta} \frac{\partial}{\partial \theta}\left(\sin \theta \frac{\partial Y}{\partial \theta}\right) + \frac{1}{\sin^2 \theta} \frac{\partial^2 Y}{\partial \phi^2} + n(n + 1)Y = 0 \tag{4.6-5}$$

Solutions of Eq. 4.6–5 are called "surface spherical harmonics" of degree n. We shall not discuss them in general, but shall give some of their properties. Proofs and further details may be found in standard texts in mathematics and mathematical physics.[5] Let us remark in particular that the solutions are finite and continuous for all θ and ϕ only if n is an integer, positive, negative, or zero.

Equation 4.6–4 can be solved by letting f be a power of r. Two such powers prove to be solutions, r^n and r^{-n-1}. By the general properties of second-order differential equations (see Appendix A.3) any solution of the equation must be an arbitrary sum of these two, namely

$$f(r) = Ar^n + Br^{-n-1} \tag{4.6-6}$$

since such a sum contains two adjustable constants. It will be noted that Eq. 4.6–5 is unchanged if we substitute $-n - 1$ for n and $-n$ for $n + 1$, so that the double choice for f is not reflected in a double choice for Y. A general solution for Y may be written $Y_n{}^m$, where m is an integer $(-n \leqslant m \leqslant n)$ that distinguishes the different possible solutions for a given n from each other. Thus we can write solutions of Laplace's equation in the form

$$V(r, \theta, \phi) = (Ar^n + Br^{-n-1})Y_n{}^m(\theta, \phi) \tag{4.6-7}$$

Such functions are called "spherical harmonics."

A theorem of fundamental importance for the present method is the following, which we state without proof: Any arbitrary function of θ and ϕ, suitably well behaved in the mathematical sense, may be represented in a unique way by an infinite series of surface spherical harmonics. That

[5] Cf. R. V. Churchill, *Fourier Series and Boundary Value Problems*, 2nd ed., McGraw-Hill, New York, 1963, Chapter IX; Morse and Feshbach, *loc. cit.*, pp. 1325–1330; Sir E. T. Whittaker and G. N. Watson, *Modern Analysis*, 4th ed., Cambridge, 1927, Chapter XV; A. Erdélyi et al., *Higher Transcendental Functions*, McGraw-Hill, New York, 1953, Vol. I, Chapter III.

is, given any $F(\theta, \phi)$ for the range of these angles over a sphere, we can write

$$F(\theta, \phi) = \sum_{n=0}^{\infty} \sum_{m=-n}^{n} C_{n,m} Y_n^m(\theta, \phi) \tag{4.6-8}$$

where the $C_{n,m}$ are the coefficients in the expansion, that can be determined in a straightforward way from knowledge of F. Furthermore, *any solution of the potential problem* can be written as

$$V(r, \theta, \phi) = \sum_{n=0}^{\infty} \sum_{m=-n}^{n} (A_{n,m} r^n + B_{n,m} r^{-n-n}) Y_n^m(\theta, \phi) \tag{4.6-9}$$

This expansion method is closely analogous to Fourier series expansions, used in the cylindrical case below and discussed in some detail in Section 9.7.

Now, suppose we are given the value of V over the surface of a sphere of radius R, by a function $V = V_0(\theta, \phi)$. We can then find a function V that satisfies $\nabla^2 V = 0$ and reduces to V_0 on the sphere by writing either of two series

$$V_1 = \sum_{n=0}^{\infty} \sum_{m=-n}^{n} (r^n/R^n) C_{n,m} Y_n^m(\theta, \phi) \tag{4.6-10a}$$

$$V_2 = \sum_{n=0}^{\infty} \sum_{m=-n}^{\infty} (R^{n+1}/r^{n+1}) C_{n,m} Y_n^m(\theta, \phi) \tag{4.6-10b}$$

The $C_{n,m}$'s are calculated for $F = V_0$, so that each of the series reduces to $V_0(\theta, \phi)$ when $r = R$. Thus V_1 has positive powers of r and will get very large as $r \to \infty$, so that it is in general only physically meaningful for small r, namely for points inside the sphere. On the other hand V_2 is infinite if $r \to 0$ and constitutes a solution outside the sphere. There are many other ways of solving boundary value problems, but this example will serve to show the general power of the method.

Let us restrict ourselves further to those cases with axial symmetry, namely, those in which V and Y do not depend on ϕ. The middle term of Eq. 4.6-5 drops out, and we have an ordinary differential equation. It turns out that solutions of this equation that have no discontinuities are polynomials in $\cos \theta$. They are generally represented by the notation $P_n(\cos \theta)$ and are called "Legendre polynomials" or "surface zonal harmonics." The expansion theorem 4.6-8 applies to these functions also, for any F that is a function only of θ. Table 4.6A lists the P_n for $n = 0, 1, 2$, and 3. The reader can readily verify that these functions satisfy Eq. 4.6-5 (Problem 4.6f). Corresponding solutions of Eq. 4.6-1 are called "zonal harmonics" or "solid zonal harmonics" and are also listed.

Another general reason for the value of the present approach is that there are many useful ways of calculating or "generating" the functions

Table 4.6A

n	$P_n(\cos\theta)$	Zonal Harmonics	
0	1	1	$\dfrac{1}{r}$
1	$\cos\theta$	$r\cos\theta$	$\dfrac{1}{r^2}\cos\theta$
2	$\frac{1}{2}(3\cos^2\theta - 1)$	$\dfrac{r^2}{2}(3\cos^2\theta - 1)$	$\dfrac{1}{2r^3}(3\cos^2\theta - 1)$
3	$\frac{1}{2}(5\cos^3\theta - 3\cos\theta)$	$\dfrac{r^3}{2}(5\cos^2\theta - 3\cos\theta)$	$\dfrac{1}{2r^4}(5\cos^3\theta - 3\cos\theta)$

P_n. For instance, if any two adjacent ones are known, the next may be found from a general formula (the "recurrence" formula). Values of $P_n(0)$ can be calculated, and the fact that $P_n(1) = 1$ can be proved from such formulas. There are also numerous ways of writing definite integrals which are equal to those functions. The other coordinate systems also lead on separation to differential equations with sets of solutions that can be used to expand arbitrary functions, can be calculated by recurrence relations, and can be represented by definite integrals that are frequently of use for analytic and computational purposes.

Let us construct a solution to the problem of a conducting sphere of radius R in a fixed, uniform external electric field (Fig. 4.6a). We expect to find V as a sum of zonal harmonics. Our boundary conditions are that V is constant on the sphere—we can take the constant conveniently to be

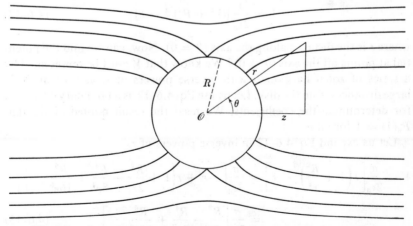

Fig. 4.6a.   A conducting sphere in a fixed, uniform external electric field.

zero—and that far from the sphere E is constant, say in the z-direction so that $-(\partial V/\partial z) = \text{constant} = E_0$ and $V = -E_0 z + V_0$. The extra constant V_0 arising from integration can be set equal to zero by noting that by symmetry the plane through the center of the sphere normal to the z-axis must be an equipotential that intersects the sphere, so that at points far from the sphere in this plane we have $V = V_0 = 0$.

Taking the z-axis as the polar axis, we have $z = r \cos \theta$, so $V = -E_0 r \cos \theta$ for large r. This is proportional to one of the zonal harmonics. We can add to it only inverse powers of r that disappear when $r \to \infty$. However, we must add terms that can yield a constant total V over the surface of the sphere, i.e., we must cancel the $\cos \theta$ variation in the harmonic we have already chosen. There is thus only one other that can be used, namely, $(1/r^2) \cos \theta$, so we must have

$$V = -E_0 r \cos \theta + \frac{B}{r^2} \cos \theta$$

Setting $V = 0$ when $r = R$ yields $B = E_0 R^3$, and we have for the complete solution of the problem

$$V = E \left(\frac{R^3}{r^2} - r \right) \cos \theta \qquad (4.6\text{--}11)$$

Problems 4.6a and b deal with this case; Problems 4.6c and d apply the same considerations to spherical dielectric boundaries.

Let us give one more example of the general power of the spherical harmonic method. Problem 1.7e calls for the potential of a uniformly charged disk of radius R at a point on its axis at a given distance from its center. The result is that

$$V = \frac{\sigma}{2\epsilon_0} [(r^2 + R^2)^{\frac{1}{2}} - r] \qquad (4.6\text{--}12)$$

where r is the distance along the axis ($\theta = 0$). Now, can we find the potential at points off the axis ($\theta \neq 0$)? We know that V must be represented by a series of zonal harmonics with inverse powers of r, at least at fairly large distances from the disk. Let us use Eq. 4.6–12 as a boundary condition for determining the coefficients. We need the result quoted above that $P_n(1) = 1$ for all n.

Let us expand Eq. 4.6–12 in inverse powers of r.

$$V = \frac{\sigma}{2\epsilon_0} \left[r \left(1 + \frac{R^2}{r^2} \right)^{\frac{1}{2}} - r \right] = \frac{\sigma}{2\epsilon_0} \left[-r + r \left\{ 1 + \frac{R^2}{2r^2} - \frac{R^4}{8r^4} + \frac{R^6}{16r^6} \cdots \right\} \right]$$

$$= \frac{\sigma}{2\epsilon_0} \left[\frac{R^2}{2r} - \frac{R^4}{8r^3} + \frac{R^6}{16r^5} \cdots \right] \qquad (4.6\text{--}13)$$

Now, if V is to be a series $\sum\limits_{n=0}^{\infty} B_n P_n(\cos\theta)/r^{n+1}$, we must have this series
fit the expansion just given along the axis where $\theta = 0$. Since $P_n(\cos 0°) = 1$, we see that each B_n can be immediately deduced from Eq. 4.6–13, so
that we have in general, for $r > R$

$$V(r, \theta) = \frac{\sigma}{2\epsilon_0}\left[\frac{R^2 P_0(\cos\theta)}{2r} - \frac{R^4 P_2(\cos\theta)}{8r^3} + \frac{R^6 P_4(\cos\theta)}{16r^5}\cdots\right] \quad (4.6\text{–}14)$$

A similar result could be written for $r < R$ by expanding in positive powers
of r. The two solutions will "match" at the sphere of radius R drawn about
the center of the disk.

Cylindrical Coordinates. Laplace's equation in cylindrical coordinates
reads

$$\frac{1}{r}\frac{\partial}{\partial r}\left(r\frac{\partial V}{\partial r}\right) + \frac{1}{r^2}\frac{\partial^2 V}{\partial\phi^2} + \frac{\partial^2 V}{\partial z^2} = 0 \quad (4.6\text{–}15)$$

We can effect a separation of coordinates by writing the potential $V(r, \phi, z)$
as a product of three functions.

$$V(r, \phi, z) = f(r)\Phi(\phi)Z(z) \quad (4.6\text{–}16)$$

On substitution in the equation and dividing by V we have

$$\frac{1}{rf(r)}\frac{d}{dr}\left(r\frac{df}{dr}\right) + \frac{1}{r^2\Phi(\phi)}\frac{d^2\Phi}{d\phi^2} + \frac{1}{Z(z)}\frac{d^2Z}{dz^2} = 0 \quad (4.6\text{–}17)$$

which can only be true for all r, ϕ, and z if in the first place the z-dependent
term is a constant; let us call it k^2. Therefore, we write

$$\frac{d^2Z}{dz^2} = k^2 Z(z) \quad (4.6\text{–}18)$$

and multiplying Eq. 4.6–17 by r^2

$$\frac{r}{f(r)}\frac{d}{dr}\left(r\frac{df}{dr}\right) + \frac{1}{\Phi(\phi)}\frac{d^2\Phi}{d\phi^2} + k^2r^2 = 0 \quad (4.6\text{–}19)$$

We see now that the ϕ-dependent term is constant; let us call it $-n^2$.
We have then the two equations

$$\frac{d^2\Phi}{d\phi^2} = -n^2\Phi(\phi) \quad (4.6\text{–}20)$$

$$r\frac{d}{dr}\left(r\frac{df}{dr}\right) + (k^2r^2 - n^2)f(r) = 0 \quad (4.6\text{–}21)$$

If k is real and not zero, Eq. 4.6–18 has solutions of exponential type,
i.e., $Z(z) = e^{\pm kz}$. If n is real and not zero, Eq. 4.6–20 has solutions of

trigonometric type, $\Phi(\phi) = \sin n\phi$ or $\Phi(\phi) = \cos n\phi$. Such solutions will give the same result for the physically identical angles ϕ and $\phi + 2\pi$ if, and only if, n is an integer.

Now, if k is not zero, Eq. 4.6–21 is a form of Bessel's equation, which has as solutions the Bessel functions $J_n(kr)$ and $N_n(kr)$. These functions are rather complicated oscillatory functions with many interesting properties, but it would take us too far afield to study them here.[6]

Let us restrict ourselves to the case in which $Z(z)$ is constant, so that we have $k = 0$ and cylindrical symmetry (two-dimensional fields). Then it is clear that $f = r^n$ and $f = r^{-n}$ are solutions of Eq. 4.6–21.

For the special case $n = 0$, a solution of Eq. 4.6–20 is $\Phi = A\phi + B$. Equation 4.6–21 reads then

$$\frac{d}{dr}\left(r \frac{df}{dr} \right) = 0$$

or

$$r \frac{df}{dr} = C$$

or

$$f = C \ln r + D$$

where A, B, C, and D are constants.

We can then make a table of cylindrical harmonics for $V(r, \phi)$ (Table 4.6B).

Let us find the field and polarization in a long thin circular rod of ideal dielectric that is placed in an originally homogeneous field $\mathbf{E}_0$ at right angles to the field direction. As in the example of Fig. 4.6a, the potential far from the rod can be taken as $V = -E_0 r \cos \phi$. We can write V in general as a

Table 4.6B   Cylindrical Harmonics

n	$f(r) \cdot \Phi(\phi)$	
0	$(C_0 \ln r + D_0)(A_0\phi + B_0)$	
1	$r(A_1 \sin \phi + B_1 \cos \phi)$;	$\dfrac{1}{r}(A_1 \sin \phi + B_1 \cos \phi)$
2	$r^2(A_2 \sin 2\phi + B_2 \cos 2\phi)$;	$\dfrac{1}{r^2}(A_2 \sin 2\phi + B_2 \cos 2\phi)$
.	.	.
.	.	.
.	.	.
	$r^n(A_n \sin n\phi + B_n \cos n\phi)$;	$\dfrac{1}{r^n}(A_n \sin n\phi + B_n \cos n\phi)$

[6] All the references on p. 169 treat Bessel functions.

series of cylindrical harmonics, using positive powers of r inside the rod and negative powers, except for $-E_0 r \cos \phi$, outside the rod. The $\ln r$ solution is infinite for both $r = 0$ and $r \to \infty$ and so is not physically meaningful. Thus we write tentatively, using suitable symbols for the various unknown constants:

$$V_{\text{outside}} = -E_0 r \cos \phi + \sum_{n=1}^{\infty} \frac{1}{r^n} (A_n \sin n\phi + B_n \cos n\phi) \quad (4.6\text{-}22)$$

$$V_{\text{inside}} = \sum_{n=1}^{\infty} r^n (a_n \sin n\phi + b_n \cos n\phi)$$

Treated as functions of ϕ alone, these series are the ordinary type of Fourier expansions.

The boundary conditions $D_{1n} = D_{2n}$ and $E_{1t} = E_{2t}$ at the surface of the rod can be written

$$\frac{\partial V_{\text{outside}}}{\partial r} = \kappa \frac{\partial V_{\text{inside}}}{\partial r} \; ; \qquad r = R$$

$$\frac{\partial V_{\text{outside}}}{\partial \phi} = \frac{\partial V_{\text{inside}}}{\partial \phi} \; ; \qquad r = R$$

$$(4.6\text{-}23)$$

The two conditions 4.6–23 yield equations containing all the $\sin n\phi$ and $\cos n\phi$ which must hold for all values of ϕ, so that the coefficients for each of these functions must be the same on each side. For all values of n except 1, the two equations yield a pair of inconsistent equations for A_n and a_n or B_n and b_n that can only be satisfied by setting all these coefficients equal to zero. For $n = 1$, we find $A_1 = a_1 = 0$, and for B_1 and b_1,

$$-E_0 - \frac{B_1}{R^2} = \kappa b_1$$

$$E_0 R - \frac{B_1}{R} = -R b_1$$

$$(4.6\text{-}24)$$

from which we readily find

$$b_1 = - \frac{2E_0}{\kappa + 1} \quad \text{and} \quad B_1 = E_0 R^2 \frac{\kappa - 1}{\kappa + 1} \quad (4.6\text{-}25)$$

so that we have

$$V_{\text{outside}} = E_0 \cos \phi \left(-r + \frac{\kappa - 1}{\kappa + 1} \frac{R^2}{r} \right)$$

$$V_{\text{inside}} = - \frac{2E_0 r \cos \phi}{\kappa + 1}$$

$$(4.6\text{-}26)$$

We can then find **E** inside the cylinder, setting $r \cos \phi = z$,

$$\mathbf{E} = - \frac{\partial V}{\partial z} \mathbf{1}_z = \frac{2E_0}{\kappa + 1} \mathbf{1}_z \quad (4.6\text{-}27)$$

and the rod is uniformly polarized according to

$$\mathbf{P} = (\kappa - 1)\epsilon_0 \mathbf{E} = \frac{2(\kappa - 1)\epsilon_0 E_0}{\kappa + 1} \mathbf{1}_z \qquad (4.6-28)$$

Problem 4.6a. Show that Eq. 4.6–11 agrees with the result of Problem 4.4f, and describe the resulting field in suitable multipole terms.

Problem 4.6b. Find an expression for the charge density on the sphere whose potential is given by Eq. 4.6–11, at an arbitrary angle θ.

Problem 4.6c. Find the potential inside and outside a sphere of ideal dielectric placed in a fixed, uniform electric field. Also find $\mathbf{P}$ at an arbitrary point in the sphere.

Problem 4.6d. Use the result of Problem 4.6c to get a better approximation than that of Eq. 3.8–7 for the force on a sphere of dielectric in an inhomogeneous electric field. (Assume the field to be homogeneous while calculating $\mathbf{P}$; then inhomogeneous for finding $\mathbf{F}$.)

Problem 4.6e. Use the zonal-harmonic method to find the field in a spherical cavity in an ideal dielectric which itself lies in a uniform external field.

Problem 4.6f. Write Eq. 4.6–5 with $\partial^2 Y/\partial\phi^2 = 0$ in terms of the independent variable $\mu = \cos\theta$, and verify that the functions $P_n(\mu)$ of Table 4.6A satisfy this equation.

Problem 4.6g. Find a formula for the surface charge distribution on a long thin circular conducting uncharged rod placed at right angles to an originally uniform field.

Problem 4.6h. Find the field in a long circular cylindrical cavity lying at right angles to an originally homogeneous field in a large piece of ideal dielectric.

Problem 4.6i. Show by calculating the next term of Eq. 3.3–3 that the first four terms of the expansion involve the first four Legendre polynomials of $\cos\theta = \mathbf{1}_r \cdot \mathbf{1}_{r0}$.

Problem 4.6j. Separate the variables in 4.6–5 by writing $Y = \Theta(\theta)\Phi(\phi)$, assuming Φ to be similar to Φ in 4.6–20 with n replaced by another integer m. Find the differential equation for Θ.

4.7 Energy in Systems of Conductors

The general problem of calculating forces in systems of electrostatic conductors—for instance in electrostatic potential-measuring devices—is best solved from the point of view of energy. A number of our previous results could also have been derived from what follows, but we have preferred to emphasize direct use of the force concept, since it leads to a better development of physical intuition. We wish now to derive several different expressions for the total potential energy in a system of conductors, relate these to each other, and show how they may be used to solve a number of force problems.

Let us begin with another expression of the superposition principle. Imagine a number of conductors in a given region that can be charged to arbitrary values of Q and V by means of appropriate batteries. The region may or may not be filled with linear dielectric material. Figure 4.7a shows

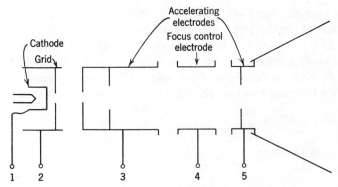

Fig. 4.7a.   Conductors in an electron-beam-forming apparatus.

such a set (part of an electron-beam-forming apparatus). We wish to show that the charge on any one is given by a linear combination of the potentials of all. We shall number the conductors from 1 to n and write summations with letters $i, j, k, l, \cdots$, each of which is to run from 1 to n, also allowing any of these letters to denote a particular conductor. Our assertion is that

$$Q_i = \sum_{j=1}^{n} c_{ij} V_j \tag{4.7-1}$$

where the constants c_{ij} are specific to the given arrangement of conductors and are called "coefficients of induction" when $i \neq j$, "coefficients of capacitance" when $i = j$. We can prove the validity of Eq. 4.7–1 by adding the n separate fields produced by successively connecting only one conductor to a battery, leaving the rest grounded. When the kth conductor· has a potential V_k with all $V_j = 0$ for $j \neq k$, the grounded conductors will in general all have induced charges on their surfaces whose total amounts (again by superposition) are proportional to V_k. The ith conductor will then have a charge which we can write $c_{ik} V_k$, the constant of proportionality having two subscripts to show that it gives the value of charge on the ith conductor when the kth is at unit potential and all others are at zero potential. Adding the fields and σ's for all the separate cases then yields the expression 4.7–1.

Let us now charge up the entire system from neutrality to the chosen set of potentials $V_1 \cdots V_n$ in uniform fractional steps. Specifically if V'_k is the potential on the kth conductor during the charging process, let $V'_k = \eta V_k$, where η (small Greek eta) is the same for all conductors and varies from 0 to 1. For some particular value of η, we will have

$$Q'_i = \sum_{j=1}^{n} c_{ij} V'_j = \sum_j c_{ij} \eta V_j = \eta Q_i$$

Now consider the work done by the batteries in adding charge. The potentials of the batteries are imagined to be controllable and slowly varied as η is changed. When a charge $dQ_i = Q_i \, d\eta$ is transferred from ground to the potential V'_i, the work done will be[7] $V'_i \, dQ' = V'_i Q_i \, d\eta = V_i Q_i \eta \, d\eta$ from the definition of potential and the assumption made above about the charging process. The total potential energy U is thus

$$U = \sum_{i=1}^{n} \int V'_i \, dQ_i = \sum_i V_i Q_i \int_0^1 \eta \, d\eta$$

or

$$U = \tfrac{1}{2} \sum_{i=1}^{n} Q_i V_i \tag{4.7–2}$$

Since the potential energy does not depend on the order in which the conductors are charged, this expression must be true for any method of charging. (See Problem 4.7a for an alternative proof of Eq. 4.7–2.)

Using Eq. 4.7–1, we have

$$U = \tfrac{1}{2} \sum_{i=1}^{n} \sum_{j=1}^{n} c_{ij} V_i V_j \tag{4.7–3}$$

as another expression for the energy.

A third expression can be obtained by inverting the relations 4.7–1. This relation consists of n equations, one for each Q_i, and is therefore adequate to determine the n V's in terms of the Q's. If the determinant of the c_{ij}'s does not vanish and we imagine the equations to be solved, we can write[8]

$$V_l = \sum_{k=1}^{n} p_{lk} Q_k \tag{4.7–4}$$

---

[7] Strictly, the work done is dQ_i times the proper average of V in between V'_i and $V'_i + dV'_i$. The error made here is proportional to $dV'_i \, dQ_i = V_i Q_i (d\eta)^2$ and disappears in the limit on integration.

[8] Equation 4.7–4 can be derived directly from the principle of superposition.

where the p_{lk} are called the coefficients of potential. Thus p_{lk} is the potential attained by conductor l when conductor k bears one unit of charge and all other conductors are neutral. Using this relation in Eq. 4.7–2, we have

$$U = \tfrac{1}{2} \sum_{i=1}^{n} \sum_{k=1}^{n} p_{ik} Q_i Q_k \qquad (4.7\text{–}5)$$

A fourth expression for the energy differs from these three by referring the energy to fields rather than to potentials. Let us include infinity or ground as a conductor in Eq. 4.7–2, even though $V = 0$. Then we can divide all the charge in the system into pairs of equal and opposite elements, each pair being located at the two ends of a tube of displacement flux. For each positive dQ, say dQ_+, there is another negative dQ, say $dQ_- = -dQ_+$. The contribution to the sum in Eq. 4.7–2 from the two is $\tfrac{1}{2}dQ_+(V_+ - V_-) =$ $\tfrac{1}{2}dQ_+\int \mathbf{E} \cdot \mathbf{dl}$, where we shall take the integral from V_+ to V_- along a line of displacement. The cross-sectional area of the tube associated with dQ_+ will be $dS = dQ_+/D$, where D is the magnitude of **D**.

Thus the energy contribution is

$$\tfrac{1}{2}D \, dS \int \mathbf{E} \cdot \mathbf{dl} = \tfrac{1}{2}D \, dS \int \mathbf{E} \cdot \mathbf{1}_l \, dl = \tfrac{1}{2}\int_l (\mathbf{E} \cdot \mathbf{D}) \, dl \, dS$$

where the integral is over dl but *not* over dS ($\mathbf{1}_l$ is a unit vector in the direction of **D**) and where the variation of D is canceled out by a reciprocal variation of dS. We finally add contributions from all tubes of flux—that is, from all the dQ_+'s—and must then integrate the last expression over dS. However, $dl \, dS = d\tau$, an element of volume, so that the complete integration now covers all the space outside the conductors.[9] We arrive at the result

$$U = \tfrac{1}{2} \int_{\text{all space}} \mathbf{E} \cdot \mathbf{D} \, d\tau \qquad (4.7\text{–}6)$$

which reduces in the case of ideal dielectrics to

$$U = \frac{\epsilon_0}{2} \int_{\text{all space}} \kappa E^2 \, d\tau \qquad (4.7\text{–}7)$$

We can say on the basis of Eq. 4.7–6 that each unit volume of an electrostatic field "contains" potential energy $\tfrac{1}{2}(\mathbf{E} \cdot \mathbf{D})$, bearing in mind that it is the system as a whole that really has the energy. Division of potential energy into parts has no strict operational meaning, although the example of Problem 4.7e gives a partial justification to this concept of energy per unit volume.

[9] Space inside the conductors can be included since $E = D = 0$ there.

Let us apply the four expressions above to the simple case of an ideal condenser (cf. Problem 2.5c). The energy is

$$U = \int_c^Q V \, dq = \int_0^Q (q/C) \, dq = \tfrac{1}{2}(Q^2/C) = \tfrac{1}{2}QV = \tfrac{1}{2}CV^2$$

We have two conductors, so that

$$Q_1 = c_{11}V_1 + c_{12}V_2; \qquad Q_2 = c_{21}V_1 + c_{22}V_2$$

and since Q_1 is a function only of $V_1 - V_2$, we must have

$$c_{12} = -c_{11}; \qquad c_{21} = -c_{22}$$

Furthermore, $Q_2 = -Q_1 = -Q$, so that $c_{11}(V_1 - V_2) = c_{22}(V_1 - V_2)$ or

$$c_{11} = c_{22} = C$$

the ordinary capacitance. In this particular case, we cannot solve for the p's since only $V_1 - V_2$ enters the equations with the c's—in fact, the determinant of the c's is zero. However, we must have $V_1 = p_{11}Q_1 + p_{12}Q_2 = (p_{11} - p_{12})Q_1$, and similarly $V_2 = (p_{21} - p_{22})Q_1$, so that

$$V = V_1 - V_2 = (p_{11} + p_{22} - p_{12} - p_{21})Q_1$$

resulting in

$$p_{11} + p_{22} - p_{12} - p_{21} = 1/C$$

Thus

$$U = \tfrac{1}{2}[p_{11}Q_1^2 + (p_{12} + p_{21})Q_1Q_2 + p_{22}Q_2^2]$$
$$= \tfrac{1}{2}[p_{11} + p_{22} - p_{12} - p_{21}]Q_1^2$$
$$= \tfrac{1}{2}Q^2/C$$

as above.

Finally, if the condenser were an ideal plane-parallel condenser with area S, plate separation d, and dielectric constant κ, we would have from 4.7-7,

$$U = \tfrac{1}{2}\int \mathbf{E} \cdot \mathbf{D} \, d\tau = \tfrac{1}{2}\kappa\epsilon_0 E^2 Sd = \frac{\kappa\epsilon_0 S}{2d}(Ed)^2 = \tfrac{1}{2}CV^2$$

again corroborating our original result.

If the condenser is not perfect but has stray flux from each plate to ground, we can write the charge on each plate as a sum of charge whose flux goes to the other plate and charge whose flux goes to ground, yielding

$$Q_1 = C(V_1 - V_2) + C'V_1 = (C + C')V_1 - CV_2$$
$$Q_2 = C(V_2 - V_1) + C''V_2 = -CV_1 + (C + C'')V_2$$

where C' and C'' are the measures of the stray capacitances. That is, we have $c_{11} = C + C'$; $c_{12} = -C$; $c_{21} = -C$; $c_{22} = C + C''$. These equations can be solved for V_1 and V_2, yielding

$$V_1 = \frac{(C + C'')Q_1 + CQ_2}{C(C' + C'') + C'C''}$$

$$V_2 = \frac{CQ_1 + (C + C')Q_2}{C(C' + C'') + C'C''}$$

from which relations the values of p_{11}, p_{12}, p_{21}, and p_{22} can be read.

The energy expression then reads

$$U = \tfrac{1}{2}Q_1V_1 + \tfrac{1}{2}Q_2V_2 = \tfrac{1}{2}[(C + C')V_1^2 - 2CV_1V_2 + (C' + C'')V_2^2]$$
$$= \tfrac{1}{2}[C(V_1 - V_2)^2 + C'V_1^2 + C''V_2^2]$$

with a corresponding expression in the Q's that does not however show so clearly that the effect of the stray capacitance is always to add to the energy.

Problem 4.7a. Consider a system of point charges that are brought into position from infinity one at a time, and prove that Eq. 4.7–2 applies to them when V_i is the potential at the ith charge produced by the other charges.

Problem 4.7b. Prove that the coefficients of capacitance are positive and the coefficients of induction are negative or zero.

Problem 4.7c. Prove that all the coefficients of potential p_{ij} are positive.

Problem 4.7d. Find the energy in the condenser of Fig. 3.7a if the dielectric slab has a constant κ, by the formula $\tfrac{1}{2}Q^2/C$ and by Eq. 4.7–7.

Problem 4.7e. Find the change in energy when one plate of an insulated condenser with fixed charge is allowed to move a small distance toward the other plate. Compare the value you obtain with the work done, finding the force as in Section 2.4.

Problem 4.7f. A 2-μf condenser is charged to 100 v, and a 3-μf condenser is charged to 50 v. The two are disconnected from their respective batteries and are connected to each other, positive terminal to positive and negative to negative. Find the original charges, the final charge, the original energy stored in each and the final energy in the combination. How do you account for the discrepancy?

Problem 4.7g. Use Eq. 4.7–6 to find the potential energy of a uniformly charged spherical conductor. What result do we get if we imagine the conductor to be shrunk to a point, bearing a constant charge Q? Is there any physical meaning to be given to the resulting value for the potential energy of a single point charge?

Problem 4.7h. If the potential produced by a point charge follows a different power law than the minus first, show how the coefficients c_{ij} of a system of conductors will change when all dimensions are changed by the same factor k. Taking as an experimental fact that the c_{ij} always remain in constant ratio to each other when such a scale change by a factor k is made, show that any potential variation other than a power law is not possible.

4.8 Force Calculations

A general method of calculating forces in systems of conductors can readily be derived from the energy expressions of the last section, but there are a number of important properties of the coefficients that we must first discuss.

In the first place, the coefficients p_{ij} and c_{ij} with different subscripts are symmetrical, i.e., $p_{ij} = p_{ji}$, and $c_{ij} = c_{ji}$. To show this, imagine that we make small but *arbitrary* changes in the potentials and charges of each conductor by making small variations in batteries connected to each. Either the dV_i's or the dQ_i's can be taken as arbitrary, but then the other set is related to the chosen one by the c_{ij}'s or p_{ij}'s. The change in energy will then be given, as in the last section (p. 178), by

$$dU = \sum_{i=1}^{n} V_i \, dQ_i \qquad (4.8\text{--}1)$$

However, the expression $U = \frac{1}{2} \sum_i V_i Q_i$ will continue to be valid as the V's and Q's change, so dU is also the differential

$$dU = \frac{1}{2} \sum_{i=1}^{n} (V_i \, dQ_i + Q_i \, dV_i) \qquad (4.8\text{--}2)$$

Comparing Eqs. 4.8–1 and 4.8–2, we see that

$$\sum_i V_i \, dQ_i = \sum_i Q_i \, dV_i \qquad (4.8\text{--}3)$$

for all possible dQ's and dV's. Let us now use Eq. 4.7–1 and its differential in Eq. 4.8–3, obtaining

$$\sum_{i=1}^{n} \sum_{j=1}^{n} c_{ij} V_i \, dV_j = \sum_{k=1}^{n} \sum_{l=1}^{n} c_{kl} \, dV_k V_l \qquad (4.8\text{--}4)$$

where we have used k in place of i and l in place of j on the right to emphasize the fact that all the summations are independent of each other and that the name given to each summation index is unimportant. Suppose now that all V's are zero except one—say V_3—and all dV's are zero except one other—say dV_2. Equation 4.8–4 will then reduce to $c_{32}V_3\,dV_2 = c_{23}\,dV_2 V_3$, so that $c_{32} = c_{23}$. Similarly, every c_{ij} for $i \neq j$ is equal to c_{ji}. An exactly similar proof may be worked out for the p_{ij} by using Eq. 4.7–4 instead of Eq. 4.7–1 in Eq. 4.8–3.

Now let us consider variations of the c_{ij} and p_{ij}. These coefficients depend on the *geometry* (size, shape, position) of the system of conductors and on the geometry and dielectric constants of any dielectric media present. Consequently they will vary if any conductor or piece of dielectric is moved and in general we must assume that all the coefficients change when any one part of the system is displaced.

Let us focus our attention on the force on some part of the system and specifically on some component of this force. Any component of a force on an object at rest has a definite meaning only when we have defined the way in which it might move in the direction indicated, at least infinitesimally—that is, if we can consider the force in question to perform at least an infinitesimal amount of work. The object may of course be in equilibrium under a balance of electric and mechanical forces; by motion we mean motion against the mechanical restraints. Suppose that the possible motion in the given direction is measured by a coordinate ξ (small Greek xi). Then the work done by the electrical force for a displacement $d\xi$ will be $F_\xi\,d\xi$. We shall use this expression as a means of finding F_ξ.

The force F_ξ will not depend on whether V's or Q's are determined on the conductors by batteries or by isolation, since it could in principle be calculated from $f_S = \sigma^2/2\epsilon_0$ as in Section 2.4. However, the energy change accompanying a displacement $d\xi$ will be different according to whether or not energy is available from batteries. Let us then calculate the energy changes for two possibilities—one, that all the charges Q_i are fixed and the other, that all the potentials V_i remain constant.

In the first case, all the energy $F_\xi\,d\xi$ that goes into work must come from the field (no batteries are present), so $F_\xi\,d\xi = -dU$, and

$$F_\xi = -\left(\frac{\partial U}{\partial \xi}\right)_Q$$

where the subscript Q indicates that all the Q's are kept constant in calculating $\partial U/\partial \xi$.

In the second case, some energy may come from the batteries. Let us calculate it by imagining that we first disconnect all the connecting wires so that all the Q's will be constant (each $dQ_i = 0$) and allowing the V's to vary by amounts dV_i during the displacement $d\xi$, so that $dU = \frac{1}{2}\sum_i Q_i\,dV_i$, a negative quantity in this case. Then reconnect the batteries, and bring all the conductors back to their original potentials by the addition of suitable dQ's, which we shall call dQ'_i, $i = 1, 2 \cdots n$. This change is a special case of the arbitrary one we used in the first part of this section, so that

$$\sum_i V_i \, dQ'_i = \sum_i Q_i \, dV'_i = -\sum_i Q_i \, dV_i$$

where we have used the fact that $dV'_i = -dV_i$, since we restored the initial potentials. But $\sum_i V_i \, dQ'_i$ is the energy supplied by the batteries and is seen to constitute an *increase* in U whose magnitude is twice the amount of the first decrease $\frac{1}{2} \sum_i Q_i \, dV_i$. Thus the net change in U with constant potentials is *equal and opposite* to the change when the charges are constant, the batteries supplying *exactly twice as much energy* as is used up in mechanical work. Hence we may write

$$F_\xi = -\left(\frac{\partial U}{\partial \xi}\right)_Q = +\left(\frac{\partial U}{\partial \xi}\right)_V \qquad (4.8\text{--}5)$$

which may be written in the more explicit forms

$$F_\xi = -\frac{1}{2} \sum_{i=1}^n \sum_{j=1}^n \frac{\partial p_{ij}}{\partial \xi} Q_i Q_j \qquad (4.8\text{--}6)$$

$$F_\xi = +\frac{1}{2} \sum_{i=1}^n \sum_{j=1}^n \frac{\partial c_{ij}}{\partial \xi} V_i V_j \qquad (4.8\text{--}7)$$

We can also calculate torques in a similar way, since the work done during a small angular displacement $d\theta$ is $\mathscr{T}_\theta \, d\theta$ where $\mathscr{T}_\theta$ is the torque about the axis to which θ refers. In fact, we need only to read $\mathscr{T}_\theta$ in place of F_ξ and θ in place of ξ in Eqs. 4.8–5, 4.8–6, and 4.8–7 to get the proper torque equations. For reference we shall write out the first one:

$$\mathscr{T}_\theta = -\left(\frac{\partial U}{\partial \theta}\right)_Q = +\left(\frac{\partial U}{\partial \theta}\right)_V \qquad (4.8\text{--}8)$$

As a first example let us consider the force and torque on one plate of a condenser. We have $U = \frac{1}{2}CV^2 = \frac{1}{2}Q^2/C$ so that

$$F_\xi = -\left(\frac{\partial U}{\partial \xi}\right)_Q = +\frac{Q^2}{2C^2}\frac{\partial C}{\partial \xi} ; \qquad \mathscr{T}_\theta = \frac{Q^2}{2C^2}\frac{\partial C}{\partial \theta} \qquad (4.8\text{--}9a)$$

and

$$F_\xi = +\left(\frac{\partial U}{\partial \xi}\right)_V = \frac{1}{2}V^2\frac{\partial C}{\partial \xi} ; \qquad \mathscr{T}_\theta = \frac{1}{2}V^2\frac{\partial C}{\partial \theta} \qquad (4.8\text{--}9b)$$

The two expressions are readily seen to be the same and show that the force and torque are in the direction of increasing capacitance. If the formula is applied to the "absolute" voltmeter discussed in Section 2.5, we have $C = \epsilon_0 S/\xi$, where ξ is the plate separation, earlier called d. Then

$\partial C/\partial \xi = -\epsilon_0 S/\xi^2$ and $F_\xi = -\epsilon_0 SV^2/2\xi^2$, which agrees with Eq. 2.5–8, the minus sign indicating that the force is inward while ξ increases outwardly.

Now suppose that a slab of dielectric of thickness d' is inserted part way between the condenser plates, as indicated in Fig. 4.8a. Let us calculate the force tending to pull the dielectric further in when it is inserted a distance x less than the width w of the plates. If V is the PD between the plates, the field in the space beyond the point to which the slab has been pushed is $E = V/d$. Above and below the slab, we will have a field E' and

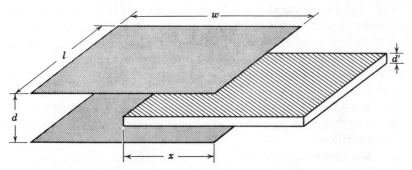

Fig. 4.8a. A slab of dielectric between two condenser plates.

within it a field E'/κ (by the continuity of D_n) where $E'(d - d') + E'd'/\kappa = V$. The total energy in the condenser by Eq. 4.7–7 is then

$$U = \tfrac{1}{2}\epsilon_0[E^2l(w - x)d + E'^2lx(d - d') + \kappa(E'/\kappa)^2lxd'] + U_{\text{corr}}$$

where U_{corr} is the correction to the energy because of the necessary failure of our infinite-plane formulas at the edge of the slab. This term is difficult to calculate but will be independent of x as long as the edge of the slab is not near either edge of the condenser.[10] In terms of V, we have

$$U = \tfrac{1}{2}\epsilon_0\left[\frac{V^2l(w - x)}{d} + lxE'V\right] + U_{\text{corr}}$$

$$= \tfrac{1}{2}\epsilon_0V^2\left[\frac{l(w - x)}{d} + \frac{lx}{d - d' + d'/\kappa}\right] + U_{\text{corr}} \qquad (4.8\text{–}10)$$

and

$$F_x = \left(\frac{\partial U}{\partial x}\right)_V = \tfrac{1}{2}\epsilon_0V^2l\left[\frac{\kappa}{\kappa d - (\kappa - 1)d'} - \frac{1}{d}\right] = \frac{\tfrac{1}{2}(\kappa - 1)\epsilon_0V^2ld'}{\kappa d^2 - (\kappa - 1)dd'}$$

The force is always positive, and so the slab is always pulled *into* the condenser.

[10] The correction at the edges of the slab that are parallel to the motion has not been included but can be made small by a large ratio l/d'.

More complicated applications are to be found, for instance, in connection with the various forms of the quadrant electrometer, described in books on electrical measurements.[11] The generalization of Earnshaw's theorem to the instability of a charged conductor in an electrostatic field is given in the footnote reference on p. 42.

Problem 4.8a. Write out the details of the proof that $p_{ij} = p_{ji}$.

Problem 4.8b. Consider a system of conductors consisting of (1) a conductor with a totally enclosed cavity, (2) an isolated conductor in the cavity, and (3) an isolated conductor outside of (1) but in its vicinity (ground or infinity is not to be enumerated as part of the system but, of course, cannot be overlooked). Show that there are just four independent c_{ij}'s that do not vanish, and describe them in terms of ordinary capacitances. This calculation expresses a more formal theory of electrostatic shielding than that given in Chapter 2.

Problem 4.8c. Find the coefficients of potential from the c_{ij}'s of Problem 4.8b. Show that $p_{21} = p_{11}$ and $p_{31} = p_{32}$, and give a physical interpretation of these relations.

Problem 4.8d. Prove that $(\partial U/\partial \xi)_V = -(\partial U/\partial \xi)_Q$ by differentiating both Eq. 4.7–1 and Eq. 4.7–3.

Problem 4.8e. An air condenser has plates 10 cm square, separated by 1.0 cm. A $\frac{1}{2}$-cm thick slab of Corning 0010 glass, also 10 cm square, is inserted halfway between the plates. Find the electrostatic force on the slab when the condenser is charged to 1000 v.

[11] See, for instance, F. K. Harris, *Electrical Measurements*, John Wiley, New York, 1952, pp. 445–448; L. Page and N. I. Adams, Jr., *op. cit.*, pp. 65–68.

Chapter 5

STEADY
CURRENTS

5.1 Steady-Flow Conditions in a Conductor

The flow of charge in a conductor under the influence of a field was discussed in Chapter 2, and two important facts governing this flow were asserted there. In the first place, the average velocity $\mathbf{v}$ of the electrons in any given region of a conductor is proportional to the average field $\mathbf{E}$ in the region, but of course in the opposite direction. In the second place, any piling up of charge that results from the motion always has the effect of reducing the field. A steady velocity requires a steady field, and therefore there must be some mechanism that prevents the piling up of charge if steady currents are to be realized. We wish to discuss this mechanism and establish in general the conditions necessary for steady flow.

We describe the flow of charge with the concepts of *current* and *current density*. A current is a flow or streaming of charge, measured by the rate at which positive charge passes through any specified surface area (e.g., the cross section of a wire). Current is a scalar quantity denoted by the letter i; its unit, the coulomb per second, is called the *ampere*. The charge that passes the surface area in time t will thus be $Q = it$. The current density at a point in a conducting medium is defined to be a vector $\mathbf{J}$, having the direction of the flow of positive charge and a magnitude equal to the current per unit area through an infinitesimal area normal to the direction of flow. $\mathbf{J}$ is measured in amperes/meter² or coulombs/meter²-second. The current through any small area is to be calculated by $\Delta i = \mathbf{J} \cdot \Delta \mathbf{S}$. The current through ΔS in Fig. 5.1a, for instance, is the same as that through the area $\Delta S \cos \theta$ perpendicular to $\mathbf{J}$, namely $J \Delta S \cos \theta$. For large areas, clearly we must write an integral

$$i = \int_S \mathbf{J} \cdot d\mathbf{S} \tag{5.1–1}$$

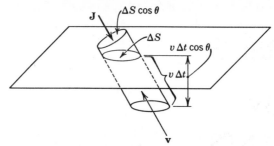

Fig. 5.1a. Illustrating current density **J**.

The sign convention just established maintains consistency with the signs for charge and charge density. The confusion that sometimes results from the fact that electrons flow in the negative direction may be mitigated by use of the hole concept. If electrons are considered to move one after another, like a row of balls, the spaces ("holes") left behind by each electron successively move in the opposite direction as illustrated in Fig. 5.1b. These holes in the cloud of conduction electrons are regions of net positive charge. As was said in Chapter 1, there is no distinction as far as the piling up of charge is concerned between a treatment of current as a motion of

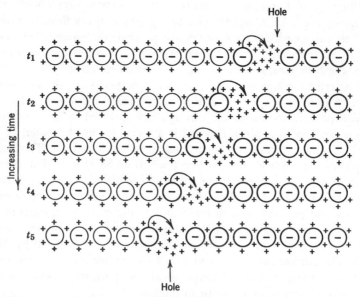

Fig. 5.1b. A row of electrons in a fixed background of positive charge. As electrons move toward the right, the retion of uncanceled positive charge, or "hole," moves to the left.

electrons in the negative direction and as a motion of positive holes in the positive direction.

The first-mentioned property of conduction may be described now in terms of **J**. If there are n conduction electrons per cubic meter traveling with an average velocity **v**, each will travel a distance $l = v\,\Delta t$ in a time Δt, and all those in a cylinder of slant height $v\,\Delta t$ and base ΔS (Fig. 5.1a) will pass through ΔS in Δt. The volume of the cylinder is $v\,\Delta t \cos\theta\,\Delta S$, so that $nv\,\Delta t\,\Delta S \cos\theta$ electrons will cross ΔS in the negative direction, involving a total charge of $-env\,\Delta t\,\Delta S \cos\theta$, where e is the numerical value of the electron charge. Thus **J**, in the opposite direction to **v**, will have the magnitude

$$J = nev \qquad (5.1\text{--}2)$$

Since **v** is proportional to $-\mathbf{E}$ we can write

$$\mathbf{J} = \sigma_c\mathbf{E} = -\sigma_c\boldsymbol{\nabla}V_F = -\sigma_c\,\boldsymbol{\nabla}V \qquad (5.1\text{--}3a)$$

or

$$\mathbf{E} = -\boldsymbol{\nabla}V = \rho_c\mathbf{J} \qquad (5.1\text{--}3b)$$

Although the current in an electrolytic solution is carried by ions and not by electrons, Eq. 5.1–3 applies quite accurately to such a solution.

As stated in Chapter 2, it is the Fermi potential V_F rather than the Volta or cavity potential V that determines current, but for homogeneous, isothermal conductors, the two potentials have the same gradient and need not be distinguished. We shall use the plain symbol V for Fermi potentials in conductors throughout this chapter. The constant σ_c is a scalar called the *conductivity* of the conductor, and its reciprocal ρ_c is called the *resistivity*. The dimensions of $\rho_c = 1/\sigma_c$ are (volts/meter) $\times$ (meter^2/ampere) = meter-volts/ampere, which we shall shortly identify with meter-ohms. The conductivity σ_c is measured in reciprocal ohms (mhos) per meter.

Equation 5.1–2 holds whether or not **E** is constant (at least if it is constant for times long compared with the mean free time t_m between electron collisions, about 10^{-14} sec). Let us see how constant values of **E** and **J** can be maintained. Consider first a particular piece of current-carrying material like the wire in Fig. 5.1c. If at any instant, current is directed toward an insulated boundary of the conductor, charge must be piling up at the boundary, producing a steady increasing added field. Therefore constant **E** and steady flow requires **J** and **E** to be parallel to the conductor boundaries. If we consider any two surfaces S_1 and S_2 everywhere perpendicular to **J**, each bounded by curves lying in the conductor boundaries, we will have currents $i_1 = \int_{S_1}\mathbf{J}\cdot\mathbf{dS}$ and $i_2 = \int_{S_2}\mathbf{J}\cdot\mathbf{dS}$ through them. Then i_1 must equal i_2, for otherwise charge must pile up in between. So the current must be the same through any surface that cuts across the wire. Current behaves mathematically like electric flux, and we can draw lines of flow (everywhere parallel to **J**) that *do not begin or end anywhere in the conductor.* Since $J = \sigma_c E$, the lines of **E** must coincide with the current lines and must also not end in the conductor. (They could so end if σ_c were variable from point to point; cf. Section 5.2.)

Before considering entire circuits, open or closed, let us consider the field and potential patterns in and near conducting wires. We shall assume in this chapter and the next, as we have up to now, that there is no source of electric field other than electrostatic charge distributions. We also assume that the conductors are stationary, so that no non-electric forces

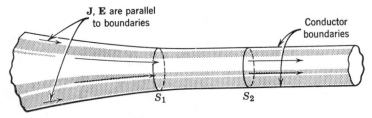

Fig. 5.1c.   Current in a wire.

can act on the electron. (Magnetic sources of electric field and non-electrostatic forces due to motion will be considered in Chapter 7.) Therefore there must reside on the surface of the conductors, and elsewhere in the external neighborhood, just the proper distribution of electric charge to produce a field inside the conductor with *lines of force parallel to the edges, no matter how curved or twisted are the wires.*

By the argument given on p. 121 for the tangential component of electric field at a charged boundary, we see that just outside a wire there must be an electric field whose component parallel to the wire must be the same as that just inside. Since the differences of potential around a circuit imply the passage of electric flux between different points on the wires of the circuit, there must in general be perpendicular components of electric field at the wire surfaces as well. *The resultant electric field just outside a current-carrying wire of finite resistivity can never vanish nor can it be perpendicular to the surface as in the electrostatic case.*

Charge flows through a conductor in the direction of decreasing potential. The two surfaces S_1 and S_2 in Fig. 5.1c are seen to be equipotentials, and the potential *decrease* between S_1 and S_2, commonly called "potential drop" and denoted by a positive number V, is

$$V_1 - V_2 = V = \int_1^2 \mathbf{E} \cdot \mathbf{dl} = \int_1^2 E \, dl = \int_1^2 \rho_c J \, dl \qquad (5.1\text{-}4)$$

where the path of integration is along any line of flow from S_1 to S_2.

Let us consider for a moment the principle of superposition, which applies to Eq. 5.1–2 because it is linear. If we increase the field and potential everywhere in the same ratio, the flow lines will not change their pattern, but $\mathbf{J}$ will increase everywhere in the same proportion, as will i. If we write

$$V/i = \int_{1}^{2} (\rho_c J/i)\, dl$$

we see that the resulting integral is independent of V and i. Thus we can set

$$V = iR \qquad\qquad (5.1\text{–}5)$$

where R is a number that remains constant as V and i change[1] but depends on the location of S_1 and S_2, on the flow pattern between these surfaces, and on the value of ρ_c (which we shall nearly always take as having the same value throughout the conductor, but which sometimes may vary from point to point). The constant R is called the *resistance* of the piece of conductor and is measured in ohms ($=$ volts/ampere), thus allowing us to measure ρ_c in meter-ohms. Equation 5.1–5 is called *Ohm's law;* the name is also given to Eq. 5.1–3.

If the wire is straight and long in comparison to its cross-sectional dimensions, the lines of current flow and of electric field will all be parallel, so that E will be constant along any one line and hence throughout the wire. (The potential drop must be the same along a unit length of any line of flow, so that E must be the same on each line.) With ρ_c constant, $\mathbf{J}$ is also uniform in direction and magnitude. Thus we can write $i = JS$, where S is the cross-sectional area of the wire and $V = \int_{1}^{2} \rho_c J\, dl = (\rho_c i/S)\int_{1}^{2} dl = \rho_c li/S$, where l is the length of wire between two cross sections S_1 and S_2. We see that for this case,

$$R = \rho_c l/S = l/\sigma_c S \qquad\qquad (5.1\text{–}6a)$$

and when ρ_c and S vary along the wire,

$$R = \int \rho_c\, dl/S = \int dl/\sigma_c S \qquad\qquad (5.1\text{–}6b)$$

The resistivities of materials are usually found from this equation by measuring R for samples of the materials in the form of wires. These formulas can be used for curved wires if the radius of curvature is sufficiently large compared to the radius of the wire.[2]

---

[1] Excluding, of course, changes in current sufficient to produce temperature variations.

[2] For details on the construction of resistors, see F. Harris, *Electrical Measurements*, John Wiley, New York, 1952, Chapter 6.

Table 5.1A Properties of Conducting Materials*

	Conductivity (σ_c) Mhos/Meter		Resistivity (ρ_c) Meter-Ohms		Temperature Coefficient (α)
Aluminum	3.54	$\times 10^7$	0.282	$\times 10^{-7}$	0.0039
Bismuth	0.083	$\times 10^7$	12	$\times 10^{-7}$	0.004
Brass (Cu 66%, Zn 34%)	1.39	$\times 10^7$	0.719	$\times 10^{-7}$	0.002
Carbon, 0°	0.00286	$\times 10^7$	349	$\times 10^{-7}$	−0.0005
Carbon, 500°	0.00370	$\times 10^7$	270	$\times 10^{-7}$	−0.0005
Constantan . . .	0.20	$\times 10^7$	4.9	$\times 10^{-7}$	0.00001
Copper, annealed . .	5.8	$\times 10^7$	0.172	$\times 10^{-7}$	0.00393
Copper, hard drawn . .	5.65	$\times 10^7$	0.176	$\times 10^{-7}$	0.00382
Iron, 99.98% pure . .	1.0	$\times 10^7$	1.0	$\times 10^{-7}$	0.005
Lead	0.45	$\times 10^7$	2.22	$\times 10^{-7}$	0.004
Manganin (Cu 84%, Mn 12%, Ni 4%)	0.23	$\times 10^7$	4.35	$\times 10^{-7}$	0.000002
Mercury	0.104	$\times 10^7$	9.62	$\times 10^{-7}$	0.00089
Nichrome	0.1	$\times 10^7$	10.0	$\times 10^{-7}$	0.0004
Silver	6.14	$\times 10^7$	0.162	$\times 10^{-7}$	0.0038
Sodium, 0° (solid) . .	2.3	$\times 10^7$	0.43	$\times 10^{-7}$	0.0044
Sodium, 116° (liquid) .	0.98	$\times 10^7$	1.02	$\times 10^{-7}$	0.0033
Steel (4% Si)	0.161	$\times 10^7$	6.21	$\times 10^{-7}$	0.0008
Wolfram (tungsten) . .	1.81	$\times 10^7$	0.552	$\times 10^{-7}$	0.0045
Zinc	1.72	$\times 10^7$	0.58	$\times 10^{-7}$	0.0037
Amber	2	$\times 10^{-15}$	5	$\times 10^{14}$	
Sealing wax	1.3	$\times 10^{-14}$	8	$\times 10^{13}$	
Hard rubber	1×10^{-16}–5	$\times 10^{-14}$	2×10^{13}–1	$\times 10^{16}$	
Ordinary glass . . .	1.1	$\times 10^{-12}$	9	$\times 10^{11}$	
Mahogany	2.5	$\times 10^{-12}$	4	$\times 10^{11}$	
Commercial plate glass .	5	$\times 10^{-12}$	2	$\times 10^{11}$	
Maple wood	3.3	$\times 10^{-9}$	3	$\times 10^8$	
Red fiber	2	$\times 10^{-8}$	5	$\times 10^7$	
Blue Vermont marble .	1	$\times 10^{-5}$	1	$\times 10^5$	
Bakelite	5×10^{-15}–5	$\times 10^{-6}$	2×10^5–2	$\times 10^{14}$	
Paraffin oil	1	$\times 10^{-14}$	1	$\times 10^{14}$	
Ethyl alcohol	3.3	$\times 10^{-4}$	3	$\times 10^3$	
Distilled water . . .	2	$\times 10^{-4}$	5	$\times 10^3$	
Sodium chloride solution, 10% by weight . .	12		8.33	$\times 10^{-2}$	
Sodium chloride, fused .	3.4	$\times 10^2$	2.94	$\times 10^{-3}$	

* Taken at 20°C unless otherwise indicated.

Table 5.1A gives values of ρ_c for several elements and alloys, selected to show the wide range of values that occur for common materials. The variation of resistance with temperature is comparatively large for pure metallic elements, being approximately 0.4% per degree Centigrade in most cases. Specifically, we can say that, if R_{20} is the resistance of a piece of wire at 20°C, its resistance at t°C is given approximately by

$$R_t = R_{20}[1 + 0.004(t - 20)] \qquad (5.1\text{-}7)$$

where the coefficient 0.004 is called the temperature coefficient, denoted by α in Table 5.1A. Equation 5.1–5 assumes that R_t varies linearly with t, which is not strictly true; for greater accuracy, quadratic terms should be used. For instance, for pure platinum, the relation is[3]

$$R_t = R_0(1 + 0.003985t - 0.000000586t^2) \qquad (5.1\text{-}8)$$

where R_t is given in terms of R_0, the resistance at 0°C.

Along any piece of wire of any shape, charge moves to lower values of potential, so that work is continually being done by the electric field. For each coulomb of charge that moves through one volt of potential drop, one joule of work is performed. The power expended (work per unit time) in a length of wire of resistance R is therefore

$$P = Vi = i^2R = V^2/R \qquad (5.1\text{-}9)$$

in joules/second or watts. Since in steady flow no kinetic energy is gained (**v** at any one point is constant in time) and no charges are redistributed, this power must all go into heat. It is in fact often called the "Joule heating."[4] It is easily understood in terms of our theory of conduction (Section 2.1) as being the transfer of energy to heat in the downward quantum jumps of the electrons. *Note that reversing i or V does not change the sign of P; the Joule heating is irreversible.* We shall treat reversible energy changes in connection with steady currents, when we discuss the source of the energy that goes into heat in Section 5.3.

For a small portion of a wire of cross-sectional area ΔS and length Δl, the Joule heating is $\Delta V J \Delta S$, where ΔV is the PD on the portion. Per unit area, then, we have the heating rate

$$P_S = J \Delta V \qquad (5.1\text{-}10)$$

and per unit volume, using $\Delta V = E \Delta l$, the several expressions

$$P_\tau = J \Delta V/\Delta l = JE = \mathbf{J} \cdot \mathbf{E} = \sigma_c \mathbf{E} \cdot \mathbf{E} = \sigma_c E^2 \qquad (5.1\text{-}11)$$

[3] H. F. Stimson, *National Bureau of Standards Journal of Research*, **42**, 209 (1949).

[4] Some of J. P. Joule's many experiments on the mechanical equivalent of heat were performed with this electrical effect.

The charges that reside on the surfaces of wires carrying steady currents may be discussed in relation to the potential. The amount of charge on any small portion of the surface of a wire is equal to the mean potential of that portion multiplied by its capacitance to ground or to the appropriate nearby conductor. This distributed capacitance (the so-called stray capacitance) is seen to play a fundamental role in the production of steady currents, for it is the source of most of the field that makes the electrons flow. The surface charges must of course be in motion as are those in the interior of the wire, but the amount at any one place must remain constant by replenishment for steady state currents.

5.2 Two- and Three-Dimensional Currents

We focussed our attention in the last section on currents in thin wires where the flow is one-dimensional in character. Let us now consider in more detail the flow of charge in extended media. We treat J therefore as a type of field vector which can vary in magnitude and direction from point to point.

The current through any surface S will be given by the integral 5.1–1. If S is a closed surface, the current out of S will be the rate of decrease of the charge inside (since charge can neither be created nor destroyed):

$$\int_{\text{closed } S} \mathbf{J} \cdot d\mathbf{S} = -\frac{\partial Q}{\partial t}; \qquad Q = \int_{\tau} \rho \, d\tau \qquad (5.2\text{–}1)$$

where τ is the volume bounded by S. If any polarization charge is present, we will not include its motion in J and hence must understand the volume density ρ to mean free charge. The surface integral can be rewritten by use of the divergence theorem, Eq. A.2–22, and the time derivative can be taken inside the integral sign for the τ integration if the boundary of τ is fixed. Thus we have

$$\int_{\text{closed } S} \mathbf{J} \cdot d\mathbf{S} = \int_{\tau} \mathbf{\nabla} \cdot \mathbf{J} \, d\tau$$

$$= -\int_{\tau} \frac{\partial \rho}{\partial t} \, d\tau \qquad (5.2\text{–}2)$$

which must hold for any volume τ whatsoever. It therefore holds for as small a volume as we please surrounding any arbitrary point $\mathscr{P}$, from which fact we can deduce that the integrands are equal, giving the result that

$$\mathbf{\nabla} \cdot \mathbf{J} + \frac{\partial \rho}{\partial t} = 0 \qquad (5.2\text{–}3)$$

This equation is called the "equation of continuity" and is an expression of the conservation of charge.

A steady state is one in which all time derivatives are zero, so we must have $\partial\rho/\partial t = 0$ and

$$\mathbf{V} \cdot \mathbf{J} = 0 \qquad \text{Steady state} \quad (5.2\text{--}4)$$

Now, if the medium obeys Ohm's law, we have $\mathbf{J} = \sigma_c\mathbf{E}$. If σ_c is a constant with respect to position in the medium, we must have div $\mathbf{J}$ proportional to div $\mathbf{E}$, for steady or unsteady states:

$$\mathbf{V} \cdot \mathbf{J} = \sigma_c\mathbf{V} \cdot \mathbf{E} \qquad (5.2\text{--}5)$$

and for a steady state we conclude that $\mathbf{E}$ has zero divergence, so that ρ vanishes and Laplace's equation is valid:

$$-\nabla^2 V = \mathbf{V} \cdot \mathbf{E} = \rho/\epsilon_0 = 0 \quad \text{Steady state} \quad (5.2\text{--}6)$$

(We replace ϵ_0 by ϵ if the material possesses a dielectric constant different from unity.)

On the other hand, if σ_c is a function of position, its variation must be considered in calculating div $\mathbf{J}$:

$$\mathbf{V} \cdot \mathbf{J} = \partial(\sigma_c E_x)/\partial x + \cdots$$
$$= \sigma_c\, \partial(E_x/\partial x) + \cdots + E_x(\partial\sigma_c/\partial x) + \cdots$$

where the dots indicate the y and z terms. In vector form we have

$$\mathbf{V} \cdot \mathbf{J} = \sigma_c\mathbf{V} \cdot \mathbf{E} + \mathbf{E} \cdot \mathbf{V}\sigma_c = \frac{\sigma_c\rho}{\epsilon_0} + \mathbf{E} \cdot \mathbf{V}\sigma_c \qquad (5.2\text{--}7)$$

(cf. Table A.2B, p. 633, item 2) and the vanishing of $\mathbf{V} \cdot \mathbf{J}$ does not ensure the vanishing of ρ. Volume charge density can exist in regions of variable conductivity, and its amount can be calculated from Eq. 5.2–7. Such regions exist in thin layers at the boundary between two materials of different conductivity, and so we see that even in the steady state static charge will be found at such interfaces.

Rather than use Eq. 5.2–7 for ρ in a thin boundary layer, let us assume as usual that the boundary is a surface of infinitesimal thickness, and consider the surface charge density and the "refraction" of flow lines at the boundary for the steady state (Fig. 5.2a). Since charge can neither be piling up or disappearing at a boundary, the current toward the boundary on one side must be equal that away from it on the other side; that is, $\mathbf{J}_1 \cdot \mathbf{dS} = \mathbf{J}_2 \cdot \mathbf{dS}$ or

$$J_{n1} = J_{n2} \qquad (5.2\text{--}8a)$$

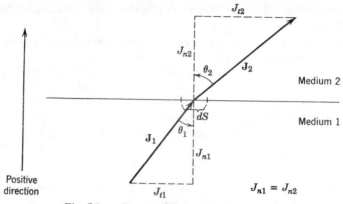

Fig. 5.2a. Current directions at a boundary.

where J_{n1} and J_{n2} are the normal components of **J** in the two cases. Just as in the dielectric case, the tangential component of **E** is the same on both sides, representing the common value of $-\nabla V$ along the boundary:

$$E_{t1} = E_{t2} \tag{5.2–9a}$$

The two conditions just established can be rewritten by use of $\mathbf{J} = \sigma_c\mathbf{E}$:

and

$$\sigma_{c1}E_{n1} = \sigma_{c2}E_{n2} \tag{5.2–8b}$$

$$\frac{J_{t1}}{\sigma_{c1}} = \frac{J_{t2}}{\sigma_{c2}} \tag{5.2–9b}$$

By use of either the J's or the E's we can find the "law of refraction" for the angles made by **E** and **J** with the normal. For instance, divide Eq. 5.2–9b by Eq. 5.2–8a, getting

$$\frac{\tan \theta_1}{\sigma_{c2}} = \frac{\tan \theta_2}{\sigma_{c2}} \tag{5.2–10}$$

The surface charge density σ can be found by the Gauss flux law:

$$E_{n2} - E_{n1} = \sigma/\epsilon_0 \tag{5.2–11}$$

We notice that, if σ_{c2} is relatively very large (medium 2 is highly conducting, and medium 1 is poorly conducting) and θ_2 is some angle between 0 and 90°, $\tan \theta_1$ and θ_1 become very small, which means that the lines of flow in the poorly conducting medium are practically perpendicular to the surface. J_{t1} and E_{t1} hence become essentially zero. Furthermore, from Eq. 5.2–8b we see that large σ_c is accompanied by a very small E_{n2}. The field practically vanishes in the good conductor, although it must be appreciable in the other.

The surface charge density on a very good conductor surrounded by a poor one is then practically the same as for the static case with no current flow, Eq. 2.2–1. The total charge on an ideal conductor of zero resistivity is related to the current into it by a constant involving the conductivity of the surrounding medium (we use ϵ for the permittivity of the medium since some polarization effects are likely to accompany the conduction current):

$$Q = \int_S \sigma \, d\mathbf{S} = \epsilon \int_S \mathbf{E} \cdot d\mathbf{S} = \frac{\epsilon}{\sigma_c} \int_S \mathbf{J} \cdot d\mathbf{S} = \frac{\epsilon i}{\sigma_c} \qquad (5.2\text{–}12)$$

The Resistance-Capacitance Analogy. If current enters and leaves a poorly conducting medium via two good conductors (called "electrodes"), we can write the equivalent resistance in terms of the PD V between the two good conductors:

$$R = V/i$$

which by use of Eq. 5.2–12 becomes

$$R = \frac{\epsilon V}{\sigma_c Q} \qquad (5.2\text{–}13)$$

Now, Q/V is just the capacitance C of the two conductors with a medium of permittivity ϵ between them, so that we have the relation

$$R = \frac{\epsilon}{\sigma_c C} \qquad (5.2\text{–}14a)$$

The definition of C depends on the existence of static charge on the conductors that is proportional to V and is independent of whether or not current also exists. It is however important that all (or practically all) of the flux, and therefore current, that leaves one conductor enters the other.

Suppose now that we have a pair of electrodes that can be placed either in an insulating medium (or a vacuum) or in a conducting medium and that there are no boundary effects which will disturb the field and current patterns. The field pattern must then be the same in the two cases, as charge resides in the same places in each case and div $\mathbf{E}$ is zero in the space between. Thus if we can find the capacitance $C' = Q'/V'$ for the insulating case, which is ϵ'/ϵ times that with the medium in place, we can calculate the resistance when the conducting medium is present by the formula

$$R = \frac{\epsilon'}{\sigma_c C'} \qquad (5.2\text{–}14b)$$

and vice versa. In fact, the proportionality of capacitance and permittivity makes it evident that R in 5.2–14 does not depend on the value of ϵ.

This result is readily verified for the case of a slab of low-conductivity material of thickness l with parallel plane sides of area S and with plane electrodes in contact. The resistance of this arrangement is given according to Eq. 5.1–6 by $R = l/\sigma_c S$, and the capacitance according to Eq. 2.5–4 by $C_0 = \epsilon_0 S/l$ when the slab is replaced by a vacuum, so that Eq. 5.2–14b is seen to hold. The resistance between concentric spheres or cylinders can be found by use of Eqs. 2.5–3 and 2.5–5.

In many cases there is not only a boundary between a metal of negligible resistivity (with σ_c of the order of 10^7 mho/m) and a liquid or solid of fairly high resistivity (σ_c of the order of 1 mho/m), but there is also a boundary between the latter and a gas or other insulator of extremely high resistivity (σ_c roughly of the order of 10^{-10} mho/m).

Let us consider the boundary condition for the second situation. We have already considered this for thin wires, in which **J** is obviously parallel to the surface inside the more conducting substance, and **E** outside (together with the practically negligible **J**) makes an angle of almost any magnitude with the normal in the poorly conducting medium. In a more general case, the normal component of **J** will be so small in the gas or other insulator that its equal in the other medium will be negligible in comparison to the parallel component (cf. Problem 5.2d).

For instance, consider a thin layer of a conducting solution with plane parallel sides—e.g., a surface open to the air and the horizontal bottom of an insulating tray. All the current will be in the plane of the layer, and cylindrical symmetry will result without the necessity of infinitely long electrodes perpendicular to the plane in question. Thus the capacitance formulas for two parallel infinite circular wires or for two concentric cylinders can be used to find the resistance between disk-shaped or ring-shaped electrodes in a tray containing a conducting electrolyte whose depth is not greater than the height of the electrodes.

By placing a conducting liquid in a tray with a tilted bottom, one can treat axially symmetric fields, for which the same pattern occurs in every plane through a given axis and no current flows through any of these planes (no ϕ or "hoop" component in spherical coordinates; cf. Appendix A.2). A wedge-shaped piece of liquid results, and the flow pattern within it will represent a fraction of the complete figure of revolution that is found in the static case.

Lines of force and equipotentials can much more readily be located and graphed for a conducting solution than for a field in vacuo, because a small amount of current can be drawn by the measuring apparatus without making an appreciable disturbance of the field pattern; the usual method that uses the potentiometric-balance principle in fact draws current only when balance is not achieved. The reader is referred elsewhere for the several different techniques for making such measurements.[5]

Another application of the relation between electrostatic and steady-current situations is to the resistance between terminals inserted in the earth for purposes of measuring soil conductivity. If a small spherical electrode is inserted in the ground and a much larger electrode of arbitrary shape is inserted some distance away, the capacitance is like that of a small isolated sphere, with "infinity" the other terminal. Most of the PD and the resistance is to be found in the neighborhood of the small sphere, so the total resistance between it and the distant electrode is a measure of the soil conductivity in the neighborhood of the sphere.

The Relaxation Time. The approach of current in an extended medium to a steady state can be studied by using Eqs. 5.2–3 and 5.2–5 together with $\nabla \cdot \mathbf{E} = \rho/\epsilon_0$, where ρ is the charge density and we assume the medium to be conducting but not *also* polarizable (any appreciable bound charge flow is counted in with the total current). We have then

$$\frac{\sigma_c \rho}{\epsilon_0} + \frac{\partial \rho}{\partial t} = 0 \tag{5.2–15}$$

which is a differential equation that can be written in a form suitable for integration:

$$\frac{d\rho}{\rho} = - \frac{\sigma_c \, dt}{\epsilon_0}$$

We have

$$\int \frac{d\rho}{\rho} = \ln \rho + \text{constant} = - \int \frac{\sigma_c \, dt}{\epsilon_0} = - \frac{\sigma_c t}{\epsilon_0} + \text{constant}$$

which we can write, letting a be the difference of the two constants,

$$\ln \rho = -\sigma_c t/\epsilon_0 + a$$

and

$$e^{\ln \rho} = e^{-\sigma_c t/\epsilon_0 + a}$$

or

$$\rho = e^a \cdot e^{-\sigma_c t/\epsilon_0}$$

The quantity e^a can be evaluated by setting $t = 0$, taking as given the value of ρ_0, the initial charge density as a function of x, y, and z. We have then

$$\rho = \rho_0 \, e^{-\sigma_c t/\epsilon_0} \tag{5.2–16}$$

[5] E. Weber, *Electromagnetic Fields: Theory and Applications;* Vol. I, *Mapping of Fields*, John Wiley, New York, 1950, pp. 189–192.

We see that the time required for an initial charge density to fall to $1/e$ of its value is ϵ_0/σ_c. It is called the "relaxation time." If we use values of σ_c from Table 5.1A, we see that for copper the relaxation time is 1.5×10^{-19} sec, and for pure water it is 4×10^{-8} sec, whereas for plate glass it is about 2 sec and for amber it is about 4×10^3 sec. For metals the time is far too short to measure or observe. It is, in fact, much shorter than the time constants for establishing currents in closed circuits that we shall discuss in the next section and considerably shorter than the mean free time $t_m \simeq 10^{-14}$ sec between electron collisions.

Current with Space Charge. Our considerations in this section have thus far dealt with current in ohmic materials. The law of conservation of charge, Eq. 5.2–3, holds also for the motion of charges in empty space. In this case, we can write Eq. 5.1–2 for any type of charge in motion as

$$\mathbf{J} = \rho\mathbf{v} \qquad (5.2\text{–}17)$$

where ρ is the volume density of the moving charges and is the total or net density if there are no fixed charges present. Then Eq. 5.2–3 reads

$$\mathbf{\nabla} \cdot (\rho\mathbf{v}) + \frac{\partial\rho}{\partial t} = 0 \qquad (5.2\text{–}18a)$$

which can be rearranged to give

$$\rho\mathbf{\nabla} \cdot \mathbf{v} + (\mathbf{v} \cdot \mathbf{\nabla})\rho + \frac{\partial\rho}{\partial t} = 0 \qquad (5.2\text{–}18b)$$

The diode considered in Section 1.10 is an example. In that case, $\mathbf{J}$ is in the x-direction and all quantities are functions of x only. For the steady state, $d(\rho v)/dx = 0$, so $J = \rho v$ is a constant, as was stated in Section 1.10. The existence of a minimum of potential at a point where v is reduced to zero may be inferred from the fact that, if the PD between the electrodes is not too great, the current that reaches the anode is considerably less than that emitted. Therefore some but not all of the electrons must turn back. If we assume them all to have an initial velocity v_0, they will all slow down to rest together. At the rest point, some fraction must be able to drift beyond to a region where they are accelerated, and therefore this rest point is a minimum of V. Generally, the rest point is very near the cathode, so that one can take $x_1 \simeq 0$ in Eq. 1.10–11. Since the constant a is proportional to J, we obtain from this equation the usual result of diode theory that the current is proportional to the $\frac{3}{2}$ power of the PD between the electrodes.[6]

Problem 5.2a. A parallel-plate condenser whose plates are 10 cm square and 0.5 cm apart contains two slabs of dielectric, one 0.3 cm thick with

---

[6] For a good discussion of space-charge-limited current, see L. B. Loeb, *Basic Processes of Gaseous Electronics*, University of California, Berkeley, 1955, pp. 620–625.

$\sigma_c = 6.0 \times 10^{-5}$ mho/m and the other 0.2 cm thick with $\sigma_c = 4.0 \times 10^{-5}$ mho/m. The dielectric constants are 2.0 and 2.5 respectively. Find the current and the free charge density at the interface between the two slabs when a PD of 100 v is applied between the plates and a steady state has been reached. The plate in contact with the thicker slab is positive. Also find the charge densities on each plate.

Problem 5.2b. Use the result of Problem 2.5e to find approximately the resistance between two small metal hemispheres of radii a and b imbedded with their plane faces flush with the ground in level soil at a distance c apart large compared to their radii.

Problem 5.2c. Find the leakage conductance per meter of a cylindrical coaxial cable whose inner conductor has a radius of 0.125 in. and whose outer conductor has an inner radius of 0.500 in. if the space between is filled with material whose conductivity is 6.0×10^{-8} mho/m.

Problem 5.2d. Assume that E_{n1} at a boundary like that in Fig. 5.2a is not very large, and that σ_{c2} is very small. Show that the only important component of current density is J_{t2}.

Problem 5.2e. Modify Eq. 1.10–11 to apply to points $0 \leqslant x \leqslant x_1$. Assume that in this region $J = J_{em} - J_{ret}$, where J_{em} is the emitted current density and J_{ret} that which returns from the rest point. Then find the constant a in terms of the J's for each region, and finally find $V(x_2)$ in terms of J and x_2, where x_2 is the distance from cathode to anode, and x_1 in terms of J, J_{em}, and v_0. Assume that x_1 is very small in comparison to x_2. *Hints:* J_{em} and J_{ret} are each independent of x, and v is the same at a given x for each direction of motion.

5.3   Complete Circuits and Emfs

Let us now ask where the lines of charge flow might begin or end. Any such place would be a location of the piling up or taking away of electrons (or, of course, of positive charge). The field produced by the charge in these regions would then vary in time, so that for flow that is steady for a long or indefinite time there can be no such regions of variable charge, and we shall not consider them here. We shall come back in Section 5.4 to the case of flow that is approximately steady for short times and in which charge is transferred from end to end of the flow lines.

Since circuits do not have infinite extent, the lines of flow in thin wires must form closed loops if they are not to end.[7] *Steady currents require*

---

[7] It is possible to have, in an extended conducting medium, a spiraling or twisted system of non-closed current lines topologically similar to the **D** lines of Fig. 3.8d, but circuits with wires whose thickness is neglected cannot show such behavior.

closed circuits. There may be branches in the circuit where three or more wires are connected together, but any given line of flow will close on itself without branching. Such a closed flow line will be called a *current filament*.

If we follow a current filament along a wire, starting from one point in the circuit, we observe a continual decrease in potential. This cannot go on indefinitely, since $\oint \mathbf{E} \cdot \mathbf{dl} = 0$ here as elsewhere where all fields are electrostatic. There *must* be some portion of the circuit that does not behave like a conductor (does not obey Ohm's law) but where there is a *rise* in potential along the current. There must also, of course, be some place where energy is available to be the source of the Joule heat, since the charge densities on the surfaces of the various conductors do not change and their potential energy cannot be the source.

The most common non-magnetic sources of energy and locations of potential rises are at the electrode-to-solution boundaries in chemical cells. The physical principles of such cells are considered in Chapter 6, but we need to consider here enough of their electrical properties to provide an explanation of their potential rises.

A chemical cell consists of two electrodes in an electrolytic solution (or two adjoining solutions). The most important feature of an electrolytic solution is that although it can conduct current, it contains *no conduction electrons* and therefore *cannot be said to have a Fermi potential in the ordinary sense.* Of course, any portion of it will have a cavity potential, and for each of its ions that are free to move a free energy per ion can be defined that is analogous to V_F but does not refer to electron transfer.

At each electrode, some type of chemical reaction can occur, depending on the type of cell. Every such reaction, simple or complex, can be described or at least summarized in terms of an electron transfer between a level associated with the metal of the electrode and a level in an atom, molecule or ion in the solution. We can attribute a Fermi potential to *each* possible reaction level in the solution and thus say that in place of a single value of V_F for conduction electrons, the solution has several values of V_F for bound electrons, one for each electron transfer that might occur at an interface with an electrode.

If the Fermi level in the electrode is higher than the pertinent reaction level in the solution, the reaction proceeds in the direction that removes electrons from the metal and vice versa. Equilibrium occurs at each metal-solution interface when the Fermi potentials there are equal. Absence of current in the body of the solution means that $\nabla V = 0$ throughout it, i.e., there are no ion potential gradients to produce conduction.

Now, if the electrodes are different, or the solution is not homogeneous and has a different chemical composition at each electrode, the two metallic terminals of the cell will have different values of V_F at equilibrium. The solution will have the same cavity potential outside each electrode, but the different Fermi reaction potentials will have different work functions.

If the equilibrium is changed by allowing electrons to flow momentarily in the external circuit, the more negative electrode will have its V_F increase and its Fermi level become depressed. The chemical reaction at that electrode will then deliver electrons to the metal until the balance is restored. This flow will leave the solution a bit more positive in the neighborhood of the electrode, producing a field in the body of the solution that leads to conduction of ions until this field in turn is brought into balance. Corresponding changes will, of course, occur at the other electrode and the equilibrium will be restored.

A cell, in simple terms, is a chemical device for *putting two conductors into electrical contact while maintaining a Fermi potential difference between them*. The value of this difference when no current is drawn from the cell is called the emf ("electromotive force") $\mathscr{E}$ of the cell.[8]

A steady current requires, as we have just seen, the same current in the external circuit, in the body of the solution, and at each electrode-to-solution interface. The lines of $\mathbf{J}$ will then be continuous, but charge will be carried by electrons in the wires, ions in the solution, and the appropriate chemical species (ions or electrons) at each interface. We know that a definite PD is required around the external circuit for a given current, by Ohm's law. In the body of the solution, a definite difference of cavity potential will be needed to maintain the ion current (again by Ohm's law) and this difference will cause the Fermi levels at the two edges of the solution to change their separation accordingly. Finally, at each interface there will be required an appropriate difference of Fermi potentials to keep the reactions going at the right rate (as long as the chemicals are not used up). Reaction rates do not vary in a precise linear way with differences of Fermi potential, but to rough approximation they do. The changes of external PD required when a current is maintained may thus all be attributed to an internal potential drop ir across a single resistance r.

Thus in the presence of current the PD between the terminals of a cell will be

$$V_+ - V_- = \Delta V = \Delta V_F = \mathscr{E} - ir \qquad (5.3\text{--}1)$$

There is no unambiguous way of assigning part of the emf of a cell to one electrode and part of the other, since the difference of V_F's at the terminal is a difference between V_F's at the two electrode-solution interfaces. However, we can make such a division by convention, by arbitrarily assigning to the solution

---

[8] We shall use only the abbreviation, since the word "force" has come to mean something with definite dimensions different from those of potential difference. Some recent authors use the term "electromotance" for $\mathscr{E}$.

as a whole the Fermi potential that the standard hydrogen electrode would have if placed in contact with the solution in question.

The standard hydrogen electrode involves hydrogen gas at atmospheric pressure bubbling over a strip of platinum in a one-molar solution of hydrochloric acid. Contact with another solution is made by means of an inverted U-tube filled with an appropriate intermediate solution—a so-called salt bridge. The emf produced when any chosen electrode is combined with the standard electrode in a particular solution can then be measured and is referred to as the emf of the chosen electrode with respect to the solution. A table of such single-electrode potentials can then be used by subtraction for the emf when any two electrodes are used together.

We can then consider that the rise in PD produced by the emf $\mathscr{E}$ of a cell occurs in an amount $\mathscr{E}'$ at one electrode and $\mathscr{E}'$ at the other, where $\mathscr{E} = \mathscr{E}' + \mathscr{E}''$.

A most important property of chemical-cell potential difference is that *emfs do not reverse with the current* (that is, if an external source is arranged to make the current pass in the reverse direction). Therefore the power involved *does* reverse, so that electric potential energy can either be produced or used up in a cell. (Actual reversal in many cells leads to extraneous chemical reactions that interfere considerably with the primary ones, but ideal infinitesimal reversals will do for the arguments which follow.)

Let us now use the obvious fact that the net change of V around a circuit is zero and apply it to an unbranched circuit in which all the conduction is ohmic except at two interfaces in a cell, the sum of whose PD's is a constant $\mathscr{E}$. The entire potential drop V must equal the rise $\mathscr{E}$. Since V is the sum of terms iR for all the sections into which we wish to divide the ohmic part of the circuit, we can write

$$\mathscr{E} = i\left(\sum_i R_j + r\right) = i(R_{ext} + r) \qquad (5.3\text{--}1)$$

where $\sum_j R_j = R_{ext}$ is the sum of the external resistances and r is the internal resistance. The generalization of Eq. 5.3–1 to branched circuits will be made in Section 5.6.

From Eq. 5.3–1 we can find the power relation for the circuit, for the power produced by the emf $\mathscr{E}$ is

$$\mathscr{E}i = i^2(R_{ext} + r) \qquad (5.3\text{--}2)$$

The sources of energy for a cell are the energy changes that occur in the chemical reactions. These changes are of electric origin and could be described as charge rearrangements, involving both electrostatic potential energy and molecular (electronic) kinetic energy. A cell has an enormous reservoir of separated positive and negative charges which release energy as they re-arrange themselves but are limited by their atomic and wavelike (quantum) properties to rearranging by means of the relatively slow chemical reactions at the solid-liquid interfaces.

How does the energy "travel" from the interfaces, where it becomes available, to the conducting portions of the circuit, where it appears as heat? The electric field that pushes the electrons can be said to perform the work, although any given charge that produces the field will acquire as much potential energy from charges of the same sign moving toward it as it will lose by charges moving away from it. The energy associated with any given element of surface charge $\sigma \, dS$ will remain constant. These surface charges provide a sort of guiding field for the current without actually performing net work. We shall see later (Section 10.4) that we can account for the flow of energy in terms of both electric and magnetic fields. It will suffice here to point out that since the moving electrons in the body of the wire do *not* push each other along or have any appreciable interactions with each other, other than the preservation of the average electrical neutrality in the metal, it would be incorrect to say that the energy flows along inside the wires.

5.4 The Establishment of Steady Flow, Condenser Charging, and Time Constants

Let us consider the following process in initiating a steady current in a conductor, in order to give a graphic picture of the fields and charges involved in the establishment of steady flow. We start with a cell that has two electrodes projecting at the top with no wires connected. Two long wires are then connected to the two terminals. After charges on them have come to rest, their ends are connected together and the current starts.

The field surrounding the cell and the wires is, of course, to be derived from the cavity potentials rather than the Fermi potentials, but only if there are differences of work functions among the various conductors and the solution will this distinction matter. For the quantitative and approximate analysis of this section we can overlook such possible differences of ϕ, although we might as well assume that the wires at least have the same ϕ throughout.

Before the wires are connected, there will be an electric field between the terminals and from the terminals to the solution, somewhat as in Fig. 5.4a. (Remember that the solution as a whole lies at a potential somewhere between the potentials of the two electrodes.) In the second case, Fig. 5.4b, the two wires become extensions of the equiqotential volumes of each electrode. (There is, of course, nothing to prevent these wires being several miles long or having many bends and twists, etc.) Lines of force proceed from one to the other along their entire lengths, entering and leaving the wire surfaces at right angles. The field is strongest where the wires are closest. In each case, the PD between the electrodes is equal to the sum of the interface PD's, that is, to the emf $\mathscr{E}$ of the cell.

When the ends of the wires are brought together, the field between the ends increases to a large value (same PD, small distance), generally enough to make a spark-over just before they touch. At the instant of contact, electrons move very rapidly under the action of this large field, rapidly

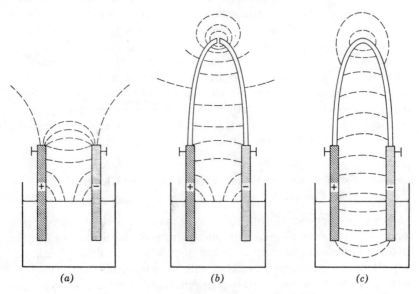

(a)   (b)   (c)

Fig. 5.4a-c.   Lines of force for a chemical cell.

destroying the equipotential nature of the nearby wire interiors. Thus a current is initiated. Much of the flow is likely to have components toward the boundaries, so that charge rapidly gets to the boundaries and redirects the field along the wires.

These effects will spread along the whole length of each wire, and re-adjustments will continue until the conditions of steady flow are reached, as in Fig. 5.4c. Note that the lines of force meet the wires at angles other than 90° because there is now a component of field parallel to the wire. Also, note the lines of force in the solution between the electrodes.

The time taken for the establishment of steady flow is experimentally observed to be very short. To estimate this time, we shall take into consideration the distributed capacitance of the wires. The idea behind the calculation will be clearer if we first deal with the process of charging or discharging a single large condenser (a "lumped" rather than a "distributed" capacitance).

Consider a condenser of capacitance C that is charged to a potential difference $V = V_0$ and connected to wires like those attached to the cell of Figs. 5.4a–c. A very similar set of diagrams can be made for (a) the isolated condenser, (b) the condenser with two pieces of wire connected to its terminals but not to each other, and (c) the condenser and circuit shortly after the wires are joined. The condenser will begin to discharge, with lines of charge flow passing from the positive charges on one plate through the wire to the negatives on the other.

As a first estimate of the time it will take, let R be the total resistance of the two joined wires. Then the current, as soon as the very short time of establishment is over, will be $i = V_0/R$, or nearly so if V has decreased somewhat. If we assumed that V and i did not change, the charge $Q_0 = CV_0$ initially on the condenser would have passed through the wire from positive plate to negative in a time given by writing $Q_0 = it_0$, so that $t_0 = Q_0/i = CV_0/(V_0/R) = RC$.

Now we can specify the conditions of the experiment more carefully in order to make a better calculation. Let us choose C so that RC is very much larger than the experimentally observed time for the establishment of steady current with a *cell* of emf $\mathscr{E} = V_0$ and the same wires with the same R. The discharging can then be considered a slow process, with Q and $V = Q/C$ on the condenser changing slowly with time. In this case, the current will remain steady for any period of time short compared to RC, during which the potential V of the condenser does not change appreciably. We shall call such currents "quasi-steady." Thus we can write

$$V = Q/C = iR$$

and since the current is the rate at which the condenser discharges,

$$i = -dQ/dt$$

so that

$$R \frac{dQ}{dt} = -\frac{Q}{C} \tag{5.4–1}$$

which differential equation is like 5.2–15 and is satisfied by

$$Q = Q_0\, e^{-t/RC} \tag{5.4–2}$$

We then have

$$i = \frac{Q_0}{RC}\, e^{-t/RC} = \frac{V_0}{R}\, e^{-t/RC} = i_0\, e^{-t/RC} \tag{5.4–3}$$

so that, since $V = iR$,

$$V = V_0\, e^{-t/RC} \tag{5.4–4}$$

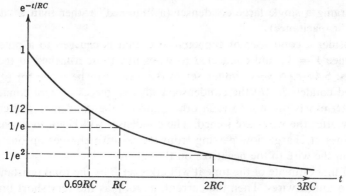

Fig. 5.4d. Exponential-decay curve.

It is seen that Q, i, and V all decrease in the same way with time. The exponential function $e^{-t/RC}$ is plotted in Fig. 5.4d. The value RC is now seen to be the time it takes the potential, charge, or current to drop to $1/e = 0.368$ of its initial value and is called the "time constant" of the circuit containing the capacitance C and resistance R, being the only way in which a meaningful discharge time can be defined (of course, a factor other than $1/e$ could be adopted).

Now if we charge up a capacitance with a cell of emf $\mathscr{E}$ and wires of total resistance R (including the internal resistance r of the cell), we will also have quasi-steady flow. In this case, there are three types of PD around the circuit (see Fig. 5.4e). The rise is the emf $\mathscr{E}$; the potential difference in the condenser is down in the direction of the current (although no actual current exists between the condenser plates), as is the iR drop. Thus we have

$$\mathscr{E} = iR + \frac{Q}{C} = R\frac{dQ}{dt} + \frac{Q}{C} \qquad (5.4\text{--}5)$$

where $i = +dQ/dt$ since the current increases Q in this case. This is a more complicated differential equation than Eq. 5.4–1. It can be reduced to a form similar to the latter if we define $q = \mathscr{E}C - Q$, the difference

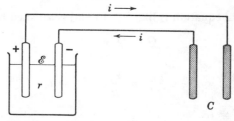

Fig. 5.4e. Charging a capacitance from a cell.

between the final charge $\mathscr{E}C$ on the condenser and its value Q at any time t. Then $Q = \mathscr{E}C - q$, and

$$\frac{dQ}{dt} = -\frac{dq}{dt}$$

so that Eq. 5.4–5 reads

$$\mathscr{E} = -R\frac{dq}{dt} + \frac{\mathscr{E}C - q}{C} = -R\frac{dq}{dt} + \mathscr{E} - \frac{q}{C}$$

or

$$R\frac{dq}{dt} = -\frac{q}{C}$$

We can then repeat the earlier method of solution and obtain

$$q = q_0\,e^{-t/RC}$$

Since in the charging case $Q_0 = 0$ and $q_0 = \mathscr{E}C$, we have

$$\mathscr{E}C - Q = \mathscr{E}C\,e^{-t/RC}$$

which rearranges to

$$Q = \mathscr{E}C[1 - e^{-t/RC}] \qquad (5.4\text{–}6)$$

from which we derive

$$i = \frac{\mathscr{E}}{R}\,e^{-t/RC} \qquad (5.4\text{–}7)$$

and for the PD on the condenser

$$V = \mathscr{E}[1 - e^{-t/RC}] \qquad (5.4\text{–}8)$$

The charge and potential on the condenser increase as shown by the graph of $1 - e^{-t/RC}$ in Fig. 5.4f, whereas the current decreases as in the previous case.

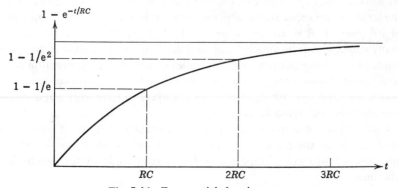

Fig. 5.4f. Exponential-charging curve.

Note that in time $t = 2RC$ the functions in Figs. 5.4d and 5.4f are within $1/e^2$ of their final values, and so forth. Apparently one requires infinite times for complete charge and discharge. However, after sufficiently long times the discrete nature of charge will play a role, and fluctuations due to thermal agitation will end the process. Since the electron charge $e = 1.6 \times 10^{-19}$ coulomb, a typical charge of 10^{-6} coulomb would have to be reduced to about 10^{-13} of itself before the discreteness is important. However, $10^{-13} = e^{-13 \ln 10} = e^{-13 \times 2.3} = e^{-30}$, so that a reduction of 10^{-13} occurs when $t = 30RC$. If RC is 1 sec, the process of charge or discharge is essentially through in one-half a minute ($t = 5RC$ or $6RC$ would generally give a *practically* complete discharge).

The time constant of a resistance–capacitance series circuit plays a fundamental role in alternating-current and pulse circuits, especially those involving vacuum tubes and transistors. We shall return to such matters later (Section 9.8).

Let us reconsider the establishment of a current in a circuit with a cell and wires of resistance R. The capacitance is now distributed rather than lumped, which means that all parts of the circuit charge up simultaneously, and we can only calculate the time constant approximately.

The capacitance of a wire parallel to a plane conductor—in particular a grounded conductor—is given by Eq. 4.5-7. Any piece of our circuit will have approximately a capacitance of $2\pi\epsilon_0/\ln(2h/R_w)$ farads/m to ground, even though the latter only roughly approximates a plane. Here h is the distance from wire to ground, and R_w is the radius of the wire. The ratio $2h/R_w$ is likely to vary from about 4 (when $h \simeq 2R_w$) upwards to, say, 100 or 1000. Its logarithm will then vary from 1.4 to 7 or more. We can thus estimate the capacitance per meter of our circuit at 4×10^{-11} farads (if $\ln(2h/R_w) = 1.4$) down to 0.8×10^{-11} farad (if $\ln(2h/R_w) = 7$). Taking 1×10^{-11} farad/m as an average value, and a circuit of 2 m length, we have a total capacitance of the order of 2×10^{-11} farad = 20 pf. Now, the largest resistances in common use in laboratory circuits are of the order of 10^6 ohms. If $R = 10^6$ and $C = 2 \times 10^{-11}$, then $RC = 2 \times 10^{-5}$ sec. In many cases, R will be smaller and so will C, so that this time is an upper limit. In very long circuits—e.g., the miles of wire from a generating plant to a distant house—the resistance is kept low to reduce power losses, so that if we have, say, 10^4 m of wire we are likely to have only a few ohms, and the time will again be very short.

Calculations of a more exact nature that take into account the distributed nature of the capacitance in a circuit can produce more definite answers but will not change the order of magnitude of the results just obtained.

Problem 5.4a. An insulated sphere 30 cm in diameter is charged to a potential of 300,000 volts. How long will it take to reduce its potential to 600 volts by means of a short-circuiting resistance of 10 megohms?

Problem 5.4b. Find the time constant of a circuit consisting of a metal plane of negligible resistance and 10 cm of #22 copper wire (AWG or B & S) parallel to the plane with the wire axis 0.5 cm from the plane. Use wire tables.

Problem 5.4c. A 1-μf and a 3-μf capacitor are charged respectively to 100 volts and 1000 volts and then connected, positive to positive and negative to negative, by wires whose total resistance is 1500 ohms. How long will it take for the 1-μf capacitor to reach within 1% of its final charge?

5.5   Simple Battery Circuits[9]

In this section we shall consider in detail the current, voltage, and resistance relationships in simple circuits containing resistances and one or more electrochemical cells. Consider first the case already discussed of one cell of emf $\mathcal{E}$ and internal resistance r, with an external conductor whose total resistance is R_{ext}. Let us graph the potential V at points around the circuit as a function of the resistance measured along it from any arbitrary point, such as $\mathscr{P}$ in the schematic circuit in Fig. 5.5a.

$$R_{\text{ext}} = R_a + R_b + R_c + R_d$$

Fig. 5.5a.   Potential-resistance diagram, simple circuit.

[9] The rest of this chapter may be omitted if the circuit details of Chapter 9 are also going to be skipped.

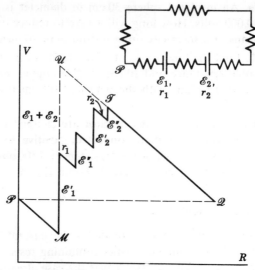

Fig. 5.5b. A circuit with two cells.

The potential falls along the resistive part of the circuit, with a slope $dV/dR = -i$. At the first interface, there is a sudden rise $\mathscr{E}'$ ($\mathscr{M}\mathscr{N}$ in the figure), then a fall in the solution between the plates ($\mathscr{N}\mathscr{S}$), another rise $\mathscr{E}''$, and then a steady fall back to the point $\mathscr{Q}$ which is at the same potential as $\mathscr{P}$ and represents the same point. The reader might imagine the graph to be wound around a cylinder so that $\mathscr{Q}$ and $\mathscr{P}$ coincide. The dotted lines $\mathscr{N}\mathscr{U}$ and $\mathscr{U}\mathscr{T}$ complete a parallelogram that shows that $\mathscr{E}'$

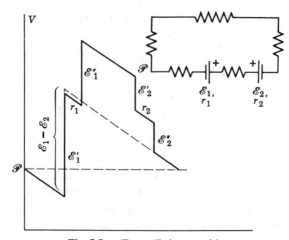

Fig. 5.5c. Two cells in opposition.

and $\mathcal{E}''$ can be considered as acting at one place, with the internal resistance r added to R_{ext}, for purposes of studying the external behavior of the circuit. Figures 5.5b and 5.5c show the results obtained when combining two cells into a battery, first in the usual way with emf's adding, and second with emf's opposing. The dotted lines again show that we may treat any such battery (or any series-connected group of cells) as having a simple emf and internal resistance. Figure 5.5c shows graphically the reversal of

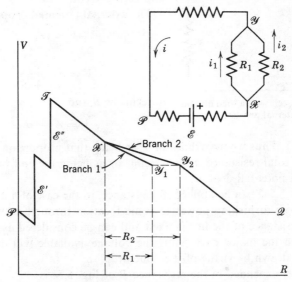

Fig. 5.5d. A circuit with a parallel branch.

emf without reversal of internal-resistance drop when a cell is connected backwards.

Figure 5.5d shows a diagram and graph for a circuit with two elements in parallel. The graph proceeds as in Fig. 5.5a from $\mathcal{P}$ to $\mathcal{X}$, where the current divides. The line $\mathcal{X}\mathcal{Y}_1$ shows the drop from $\mathcal{X}$ to $\mathcal{Y}$ in resistor R_1, and similarly for the line $\mathcal{X}\mathcal{Y}_2$ and resistor R_2. Here $\mathcal{Y}_1$ and $\mathcal{Y}_2$ have the same ordinate because they both represent the same point $\mathcal{Y}$ and the same potential. The rest of the graph could equally well be continued from $\mathcal{Y}_1$ instead of from $\mathcal{Y}_2$ as shown. The lines $\mathcal{X}\mathcal{Y}_1$ and $\mathcal{X}\mathcal{Y}_2$ must each have a less negative slope than $\mathcal{T}\mathcal{X}$ because the current is less in each branch than in the rest of the circuit. Furthermore, the sum of the slopes of $\mathcal{X}\mathcal{Y}_1$ and $\mathcal{X}\mathcal{Y}_2$ must equal that of $\mathcal{T}\mathcal{X}_1$ since $i_1 + i_2 = i$ in order that no charge continue to pile up at $\mathcal{X}$ and $\mathcal{Y}$.

Any battery circuit with elements in series (no branches) can be represented schematically as in Fig. 5.5e, where we use R for R_{ext} to make the writing simpler. The current is given by

$$i = \frac{\mathscr{E}}{r + R} \qquad (5.5\text{-}1)$$

and is a maximum when $R = 0$, a condition known as a "short circuit." When $R = \infty$, we have an "open circuit" and zero current.

The external potential drop is

$$V = iR,$$

or

$$V = \mathscr{E}\,\frac{R}{r + R} \qquad (5.5\text{-}2)$$

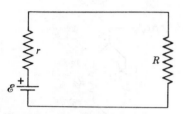

Fig. 5.5e. A cell with a load and an internal resistance.

in terms of R and

$$V = \mathscr{E} - ir \qquad (5.5\text{-}3)$$

in terms of i. Thus we may think of V as being that proportion of $\mathscr{E}$ that R is of the total resistance in the circuit, or as being the emf reduced by the internal potential drop ir.

Equation 5.5–3 can be applied, for instance, to the case of a distant cell (or generator) furnishing power to some location through a long power line. The resistance of the line is fixed and can be considered as part of r, in fact often the major part. Thus the voltage available will depend on the current drawn by virtue of the "line drop" ir.

The power expended in the resistance R of Fig. 5.5e is

$$P = i^2 R = \frac{\mathscr{E}^2 R}{(r + R)^2} \qquad (5.5\text{-}4)$$

Suppose we vary R keeping $\mathscr{E}$ and r fixed. Then P is zero if $R = 0$ and also if $R \to \infty$. It has a maximum which can be found by writing $dP/dR = 0$. It is left to the reader to show that this occurs when $R = r$ (Problem 5.5a). The maximum power that a given battery can furnish to a variable resistance R is furnished when R equals the internal resistance of the battery.[10] This statement is the power-transfer theorem and is of extreme practical importance. We shall see later that it can be applied in the alternating-current case as well (Section 9.6).

[10] For low-resistance sources, such as storage batteries or generators, the maximum power cannot be drawn without serious overheating of connecting wires or damage to battery cells. The theorem as stated is of practical importance only for high-resistance sources.

The efficiency of the power transfer may be defined as the ratio of the power expended in R to the power $\mathscr{E}i$ produced by the emf, so that

$$\text{efficiency} = \frac{P}{\mathscr{E}i} = \frac{iR}{\mathscr{E}} = \frac{R}{R + r} \qquad (5.5\text{–}5)$$

a quantity that varies from 0 to 1 as R varies from 0 to ∞ and is equal to the fraction of the emf that appears as external PD. The efficiency is 50% under the condition of maximum power transfer, and the external voltage is $\mathscr{E}/2$.

The external resistance R is often called a "load" when power transfer is under consideration. The conductance $G = 1/R$ (in mhos) may be taken

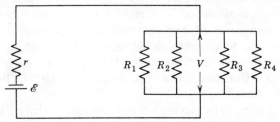

Fig. 5.5f. Resistances in parallel.

as a measure of it, so that "no load" refers to an open circuit ($G = 0$ and $R = \infty$). The "regulation" of a source of power designed for a particular load G is a number expressing the internal drop (or line loss, or difference between PD at rated load and at no load) as a percent of the rated voltage on the load. In our terms, regulation $= ir/V = (\mathscr{E} - V)/V$.

We have indicated that when several resistance elements are connected in series, their total or overall resistance is their sum:

$$R = R_1 + R_2 + R_3 + \cdots \qquad (5.5\text{–}6)$$

On the other hand, when we have several resistors connected in parallel forming several branches, as in the circuit of Fig. 5.5f, we can treat the group as a single resistor by the following considerations. Let V be the common potential difference across all the resistors, and let $i_1, i_2 \cdots$ be the separate currents. Then $i_1 = V/R_1, i_2 = V/R_2$ etc; the separate currents are inversely proportional to the resistances. If i is the current in the rest of the circuit ($\mathscr{E}$ and r in the figure), then since charge does not collect at the junctions,

$$i = i_1 + i_2 + \cdots$$

or

$$i = V/R_1 + V/R_2 + \cdots = V\left(\frac{1}{R_1} + \frac{1}{R_2} + \cdots\right)$$

Thus i and V are proportional, and so the group of resistors acts like a single one. The reciprocal of its resistance, i/V, is given by the symmetrical formula

$$\frac{1}{R} = \frac{1}{R_1} + \frac{1}{R_2} + \cdots \qquad (5.5\text{--}7a)$$

Equation 5.5–7a can be written in terms of conductance:

$$G = G_1 + G_2 + \cdots \qquad (5.5\text{--}7b)$$

A discussion of voltmeter and ammeter measurements will not be out of place in this section, although the electromagnetic forces upon which such meters depend for their operation will not be taken up until Chapter 7, and their actual construction in Section 8.9. Both instruments may be described here in terms of their common central feature—a device that gives a mechanical deflection to an indicating pointer that is proportional to the current through the instrument. This device is generally called a "galvanometer." Common forms require from 5×10^{-5} to 10^{-2} amp for full-scale deflection.

A voltmeter is made by placing a high resistance (called a "multiplier") in series with a galvanometer so that the full-scale current will flow through the instrument when some chosen PD exists between the terminals. Then for any lower potential difference V the current and the deflection will change proportionately, so that the scale can be calibrated directly in volts.

A voltmeter is connected between the two points in a circuit whose PD is desired. The current drawn by the voltmeter generally disturbs the circuit under test, however, and it is usually important to make this disturbance small by making the resistance of the voltmeter large. It is customary to indicate the full-scale current or sensitivity for a given meter by indicating the ratio of the instrument's resistance to the full-scale voltage reading. Thus for a full-scale current of 5×10^{-5} amp, the sensitivity is $1/(5 \times 10^{-5}) = 20{,}000$ ohms/v.

An ammeter is made by putting a small resistance called a "shunt" in parallel with the galvanometer. If the shunt resistance is considerably less than that of the galvanometer, most of the current that enters and leaves the terminals will pass through the shunt. However, the small fraction that passes through the galvanometer will be proportional to the total, so that the scale can be calibrated directly in amperes. It is desirable for an ammeter to have as low a resistance as possible, so as to interfere as little as possible with a circuit in series with which it is inserted.

Problem 5.5a. Prove the statement in the text that the maximum power transfer for a cell with an external resistance R occurs when R is equal to the internal resistance r.

Problem 5.5b. Write the ratio of power expended in a resistance R connected to a cell of emf $\mathscr{E}$ and resistance r to the maximum available for a fixed value of r, in terms of the ratio $K = r/R$. Show the slow variation of this ratio with K by calculating the ratio for $K = 100, 25, 10, 2.5$, and 1.25. Show also that the ratio for any value K' is the same as for $K = 1/K'$.

Problem 5.5c. Two equal resistors R_1, and two others R_2 and R_3 are arranged as shown (Fig. 5.5g). Find the relation that must hold between R_1 and R_2 if the resistance between $\mathscr{A}$ and $\mathscr{B}$ is to be equal to R_3.

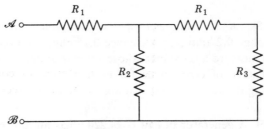

Fig. 5.5g. Circuit for Problems 5.5c and d.

Problem 5.5d. Find the relation between the values R_1, R_2, and R_3 in Fig. 5.5g when an emf $\mathscr{E}$ and series resistance equal to R_3 is connected between $\mathscr{A}$ and $\mathscr{B}$, and the PD across the original R_3 is $\mathscr{E}/100$.

Problem 5.5e. An emf $\mathscr{E}_1$ with resistance r_1 is in parallel with an emf $\mathscr{E}_2$ of resistance r_2. The PD across the combination is V, and the net current entering and leaving is i. Find the relation between V and i involving $\mathscr{E}_1$, $\mathscr{E}_2$, r_1, and r_2, and give a rule for constructing a series circuit with one $\mathscr{E}$ and one r that is equivalent to this parallel circuit (has the same relation between V and i).

Problem 5.5f. A certain resistor is supposed to have a resistance of $10\ K$ (10,000 ohms), but its value is actually 10% too high. What resistance should be put in parallel to correct its value? What tolerance is allowable in the added resistor if the resulting value may be in error by 1% ?

Problem 5.5g. A generator has an emf of 120 v and feeds a certain house with a line whose resistance is 0.13 ohm in each wire. In the house there are three 60-watt, 120-volt lamps connected in parallel on the line. Then an electric iron rated at 120 v and 1500 watts is connected in parallel. Find the drop in voltage at the lamps when the iron is connected. (Assume resistances of lamps and iron to be constant.)

Problem 5.5h. A 500-v generator feeds a trolley line. The overhead wire has a resistance of 0.10 ohm/mile. The return rails have a combined resistance of 0.03 ohm/mile. Two cars are on the line, one 1.0 mile from the power house, and one 3.0 miles away. The motor in each is controlled so as to draw 120 amp. Find the PD at each trolley car.

Problem 5.5i. A battery of emf 120 v and internal resistance 4 ohms is connected to a parallel combination of 10 ohms and a variable resistor R. Find the value of R that will result in an expenditure of 100 watts in itself.

Problem 5.5j. A 20,000-ohm/volt voltmeter of range 300 v is used to test a certain power supply. It reads 280 v. Then a resistance of 6000 ohms is placed in parallel with the voltmeter, which now reads 245 v. If the power supply can be treated as an emf $\mathscr{E}$ with a resistance r in series, find $\mathscr{E}$ and r to 1%.

Problem 5.5k. A 3-v voltmeter of 100-ohms/volt resistance and an ammeter of range 0.2 amp and resistance 0.25 ohm are used along with a 1.5-v cell to measure a resistance whose value is about 12 ohms. Calculate the percentage of error made for each method of connecting the meters in taking the ratio of their readings to be the correct value of the resistance.

Problem 5.5l. A generator of emf $\mathscr{E} = 220$ v has an internal resistance of 0.050 ohm and is rated to deliver 100 kilowatts. Find the percent regulation.

5.6 The Method of Kirchhoff

The rules of the previous section for resistances in series and in parallel can be used to solve a number of circuit problems for the pertinent currents and voltages. However, there are many more complicated cases that cannot be handled this way, and it is important to develop a more general method. For instance, if the connections between the resistances are complicated, as by the 400-Ω connection between two parallel branches in Fig. 5.6a, or

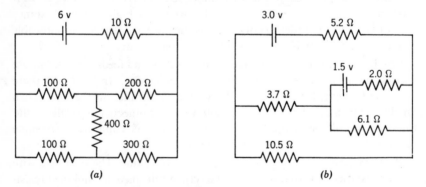

Fig. 5.6a-b. Circuits for which series-parallel calculations do not apply.

if there are emfs in various parts of a circuit, as in Fig. 5.6b, we cannot use the ordinary series-parallel calculation for effective resistance.

The general method for handling such problems must evidently involve writing down suitable simultaneous equations for the various unknown currents and/or voltages. The method is called the method of Kirchhoff and the rules for obtaining equations are the conditions we have already discussed, namely, that no current lines end anywhere and that the total potential drop around any closed path is zero.

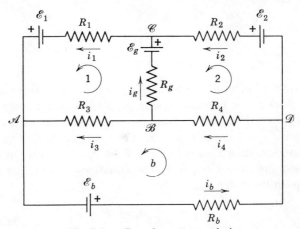

Fig. 5.6.c. Branch-current analysis.

Formal statements of the rules are known as "Kirchhoff's laws":

1. The sum of the currents entering any junction of three or more circuit elements equals the sum of the currents leaving that junction.

2. The sum of the emfs around any closed loop in a circuit, taken with due regard to signs, equals the sum of the ohmic potential drops around that loop.

There are several ways of writing equations from these rules. One may write them in terms of currents or of voltages and one may either construct sets of equations from both laws or define a set of unknowns that automatically satisfy one law, leading to a single set of equations derived from the other law. We shall illustrate by considering the branch-current and the loop-current methods. As an example, we shall take the circuit of Fig. 5.6c, which with certain simplifications will be important for the study of the Wheatstone's bridge in Section 5.8. ($\mathscr{E}_g$ and R_g will become the galvanometer branch; $\mathscr{E}_b$ and R_b the battery branch of the bridge.)

The branch-current method consists in assigning symbols and positive directions for the currents in each distinct branch and writing two sets of equations for these currents. A branch is the complete set of series-connected elements between two junctions (by the word junction we mean a point where three or more elements are connected together). If the number of junctions is j, the first rule will provide us with j equations. However, one of these equations must be derivable from the others, since if charge of either sign does not collect at any $j - 1$ of the junctions, it cannot collect at the jth one. Thus we get $j - 1$ *independent* equations. In our example $j = 4$, and the three equations are for junctions $\mathscr{A}$, $\mathscr{B}$, and $\mathscr{C}$ respectively

$$i_3 + i_1 = i_b \qquad (5.6\text{--}1)$$

$$i_4 = i_3 + i_g \qquad (5.6\text{--}2)$$

$$i_g + i_2 = i_1 \qquad (5.6\text{--}3)$$

The equation for junction $\mathscr{D}$ is evidently just the sum of these three.

Now, if there are m branches in the circuit and m unknown currents, we need $m - (j - 1)$ equations from the second rule, so we choose $m - j + 1$ loops for application of the rule. For each one, a positive direction of circulation is assumed, as indicated by the curved arrows in Fig. 5.6a, where $m = 6$ and $m - j + 1 = 3$. The equations become for this case, taking loops in the order 1, 2, and b,

$$i_1 R_1 + i_g R_g - i_3 R_3 = \mathscr{E}_1 + \mathscr{E}_g \qquad (5.6\text{--}4)$$

$$i_2 R_2 - i_g R_g - i_4 R_4 = \mathscr{E}_2 - \mathscr{E}_g \qquad (5.6\text{--}5)$$

$$i_b R_b + i_4 R_4 + i_3 R_3 = \mathscr{E}_b \qquad (5.6\text{--}6)$$

We now have six equations in the six unknowns i_1, i_2, i_3, i_4, i_g, and i_b, which can be solved by standard methods.

However, let us proceed with the loop-current method. In this method, we consider that there are a set of independent closed currents flowing in $m - j + 1$ loops, so that the first rule of Kirchhoff is satisfied automatically, although we have the non-physical idea of two or more independent currents in some of the branches—frequently in both directions. No difficulty actually results, however, if we add the PD's produced by each current in an element containing two or more, for this corresponds to the proper algebraic addition of the currents to give the actual physical value.[11]

In our example, we can assume that a current i_1 circulates around loop 1, i_2 around loop 2, and i_b around loop b, as in Fig. 5.6d. Note that we have used for the loops currents the same symbols as we used above for those

---

[11] These loop currents were first introduced by J. C. Maxwell, *Treatise on Electricity and Magnetism*, 2nd or 3rd ed., Clarendon Press, Oxford, 1881 and 1904, Dover, New York, reprint, 1962, article 282b.

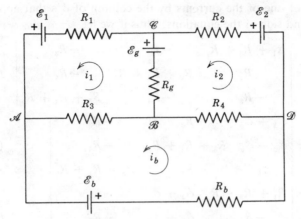

Fig. 5.6d. Loop-current analysis.

branch currents which appear in only one loop apiece. This is done to show the equivalence but is, of course, not necessary, just as it is not necessary to use the particular loops we have chosen. Current i_b, for instance, could have been assumed to pass through R_2 and R_1 instead of R_4 and R_3 as indicated, or it could follow a path through R_4, R_g, and R_1. For our particular choice of loops, the equations from the second rule read

$$i_1(R_1 + R_3 + R_g) - i_2R_g - i_bR_3 = \mathscr{E}_1 + \mathscr{E}_g \qquad (5.6\text{--}7)$$

$$-i_1R_g + i_2(R_2 + R_4 + R_g) - i_bR_4 = \mathscr{E}_2 - \mathscr{E}_g \qquad (5.6\text{--}8)$$

$$-i_1R_3 - i_2R_4 + i_b(R_3 + R_4 + R_b) = \mathscr{E}_b \qquad (5.6\text{--}9)$$

Each equation in this group sets the iR drops equal to the potential rises in the emfs. For each loop, the drop due to the current belonging to that loop involves all the resistance around the loop. Other currents enter only through the resistances of the branches in common with the loop in question and involve potential rises if the currents are opposite to the chosen positive sense around the loop.

We have three equations in the three unknowns i_1, i_2, and i_b, written in the appropriate form for the determinant method of solution (determinants are discussed briefly in Appendix A.6). Note that these equations are just the same as Eqs. 5.6–4, 5.6–5, and 5.6–6 after elimination of i_3, i_4, and i_g by Eqs. 5.6–1, 5.6–2, and 5.6–3. The difference in the two methods lies in the directness with which the equations are obtained, a matter of considerable importance for especially complex circuits.

The determinant method for this case requires the calculation of the determinant Δ formed by all the coefficients of the i's and also of the determinants Δ_1, Δ_2, etc., found from Δ by replacing the column of coefficients of one of the currents by the column of $\mathscr{E}$'s that appears on the right hand side of the equations. Thus if we let

$$\Delta = \begin{vmatrix} R_1 + R_3 + R_g & -R_g & -R_3 \\ -R_g & R_2 + R_4 + R_g & -R_4 \\ -R_3 & -R_4 & R_3 + R_4 + R_b \end{vmatrix} \qquad (5.6\text{–}10)$$

$$\Delta_1 = \begin{vmatrix} \mathscr{E}_1 + \mathscr{E}_g & -R_g & -R_3 \\ \mathscr{E}_2 - \mathscr{E}_g & R_2 + R_4 + R_g & -R_4 \\ \mathscr{E}_b & -R_4 & R_3 + R_4 + R_b \end{vmatrix} \qquad (5.6\text{–}11)$$

$$\Delta_2 = \begin{vmatrix} R_1 + R_3 + R_g & \mathscr{E}_1 + \mathscr{E}_g & -R_3 \\ -R_g & \mathscr{E}_2 - \mathscr{E}_g & -R_4 \\ -R_3 & \mathscr{E}_b & R_3 + R_4 + R_b \end{vmatrix} \qquad (5.6\text{–}12)$$

$$\Delta_b = \begin{vmatrix} R_1 + R_3 + R_g & -R_g & \mathscr{E}_1 + \mathscr{E}_g \\ -R_g & R_2 + R_4 + R_g & \mathscr{E}_2 - \mathscr{E}_g \\ -R_3 & -R_4 & \mathscr{E}_b \end{vmatrix} \qquad (5.6\text{–}13)$$

then according to the theory of determinants, we have

$$i_1 = \Delta_1/\Delta$$
$$i_2 = \Delta_2/\Delta \qquad (5.6\text{–}14)$$
$$i_b = \Delta_b/\Delta$$

We shall not evaluate these expressions without first setting certain terms equal to zero, but before so doing, there are two features of the complete solution we wish to point out.

In the first place, each current is a linear function of the four emfs—e.g., $i_1 = k\mathscr{E}_1 + l\mathscr{E}_2 + p\mathscr{E}_g + q\mathscr{E}_b$, where k, l, p, and q are functions only of the R's. That is, each emf contributes separately and independently to all the currents. We can solve the problem separately for each emf if we wish, setting the other emfs equal to zero but leaving their internal resistances in the circuit, and then adding the separate solutions for each current. This fact is the *superposition theorem*, valid for all d-c circuits with ohmic elements and constant emfs.

In the second place, we can derive a result from the diagonal symmetry of Δ. Note that the element in the first row and second column is the resistance in common between the first and second loops and is equal to the element in the second row and the first column, and so forth. The result we wish to point out is that the current i_1, produced in branch 1 by a unit emf in branch 2 (with other emfs equal to zero), is equal to the current i_2 in branch 2 produced by unit emf in branch 1. Specifically, if we set $\mathscr{E}_2 = 1$ and the other $\mathscr{E}$'s equal to zero, the expression for i_1 becomes

$$i_1 = \frac{1}{\Delta} \cdot \begin{vmatrix} 0 & -R_g & -R_3 \\ 1 & R_2 + R_4 + R_g & -R_4 \\ 0 & -R_4 & R_3 + R_4 + R_b \end{vmatrix}$$

whereas if we set $\mathscr{E}_1 = 1$ with the others zero, we have for i_2

$$i_2 = \frac{1}{\Delta} \cdot \begin{vmatrix} R_1 + R_3 + R_g & 1 & -R_3 \\ -R_g & 0 & -R_4 \\ -R_3 & 0 & R_3 + R_4 + R_b \end{vmatrix}$$

The two expressions are seen to be equal when we pick out the co-factor determinant of the 1 in each case (see Appendix A.6). The same symmetry considerations apply to any two branches in any circuit. This is a statement of the *reciprocity theorem*.

Now let us solve for the currents. We shall restrict ourselves to the case in which $\mathscr{E}_1 = \mathscr{E}_2 = 0$ and $R_b = 0$. We shall show later how to develop a solution for $R_b \neq 0$ from the results we shall now calculate.

Using the rule for evaluating third-order determinants that is given in the Appendix, we obtain the following results:

$$\Delta = R_1 R_2 R_3 + R_2 R_3 R_4 + R_3 R_4 R_1 + R_4 R_1 R_2$$
$$+ R_g (R_1 + R_2)(R_3 + R_4) \quad (5.6\text{--}15)$$

$$i_1 = \frac{1}{\Delta} \{ \mathscr{E}_b [R_g (R_3 + R_4) + R_3 (R_2 + R_4)] + \mathscr{E}_g R_2 (R_3 + R_4) \} \quad (5.6\text{--}16)$$

$$i_2 = \frac{1}{\Delta} \{ \mathscr{E}_b [R_g (R_3 + R_4) + R_4 (R_1 + R_3)] - \mathscr{E}_g R_1 (R_3 + R_4) \} \quad (5.6\text{--}17)$$

$$i_b = \frac{1}{\Delta} \{ \mathscr{E}_b [R_g (R_1 + R_2 + R_3 + R_4) + (R_1 + R_3)(R_2 + R_4)]$$
$$+ \mathscr{E}_g (R_2 R_3 - R_1 R_4) \} \quad (5.6\text{--}18)$$

We can now find the currents in the other branches from Eqs. 5.6–1, 5.6–2, and 5.6–3 or by inspection of Fig. 5.6d. We have

$$i_3 = i_b - i_1 = \frac{1}{\Delta} \{ \mathscr{E}_b [R_g (R_1 + R_2) + R_1 (R_2 + R_4)]$$
$$- \mathscr{E}_g R_4 (R_1 + R_2) \} \quad (5.6\text{--}19)$$

$$i_4 = i_b - i_2 = \frac{1}{\Delta} \{ \mathscr{E}_b [R_g (R_1 + R_2) + R_2 (R_1 + R_3)]$$
$$+ \mathscr{E}_g R_3 (R_1 + R_2) \} \quad (5.6\text{--}20)$$

$$i_g = i_1 - i_2 = \frac{1}{\Delta} \{ \mathscr{E}_b (R_2 R_3 - R_1 R_4) + \mathscr{E}_g (R_1 + R_2)(R_3 + R_4) \} \quad (5.6\text{--}21)$$

Careful inspection of these results will show a complete symmetry of i_1, i_2, i_3, and i_4 with respect to R_1, R_2, R_3, and R_4 which reflects the symmetry of the circuit arrangement. Another result to note is that in the expression for the current in any particular branch, the coefficient of the emf in the same branch will always be positive.

Let us finally show how to modify the solution just obtained so as to include a non-zero value of R_b. We can imagine that, in setting up the determinants, we placed the term $i_b R_b$ of Eq. 5.6–9 on the right-hand side and treated $-i_b R_b$ as if it were an emf added to $\mathscr{E}_b$. Since the solution process is from the algebraic point of view simply an elimination of unknowns, Eqs. 5.6–16 through 5.6–21 will still be valid if we replace $\mathscr{E}_b$ everywhere by $\mathscr{E}_b - i_b R_b$. In Eq. 5.6–18 we will have i_b appearing twice, so that we can solve for it, and then use this value in the other equations. Problem 5.6a asks for a useful and not too tedious calculation with R_b.

This process uses what is frequently called the *compensation theorem*, which like the other theorems is applicable to d-c circuits in general. It says that addition of a resistance δR to any branch is equivalent to adding an emf $-i' \delta R$ to the same branch instead, where i' is the *new* current in that branch.[12]

Problem 5.6a. Find i_b for the circuit of Fig. 5.6d with a battery resistance R_b included, but $\mathscr{E}_1$ and $\mathscr{E}_2$ still zero, by modifying the solution for the case without R_b, as suggested in the text. Verify by inspection of Eqs. 5.6–10 and 5.6–13. Use the solution so obtained and the reciprocity theorem to find the current in R_g when $\mathscr{E}_g = 0$, $\mathscr{E}_b \neq 0$, and $R_b \neq 0$.

Problem 5.6b. Verify that Eqs. 5.6–15 through 5.6–21 have the correct symmetry properties with respect to the exchanges (a) of R_1 with R_2 and R_3 with R_4 and (b) of R_1 with R_3 and R_2 with R_4.

Problem 5.6c. Find the currents in each cell in the circuit of Fig. 5.6e.

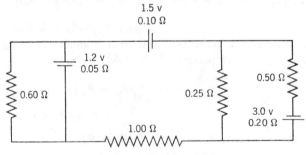

Fig. 5.6e. (Problem 5.6c).

[12] A detailed discussion of several circuit theorems is given by E. A. Guillemin, *Introductory Circuit Theory*, John Wiley, New York, 1953.

Problem 5.6d. Three Edison storage cells in different states of charge are shown in Fig. 5.6*f*, connected in parallel to a common load. Find the current delivered by each and the PD on the load.

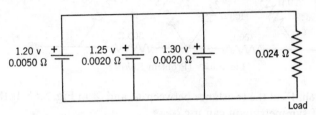

Fig. 5.6*f*. (Problem 5.6*d*)

Problem 5.6e. An east-west trolley line 10 miles long has an overhead wire whose resistance is 0.070 ohm/mile and a return rail of resistance 0.0050 ohm/mile. It is fed at the east end by a generator of emf 500 v and internal resistance 0.02 ohm and at the west end by a generator of emf 490 v and internal resistance 0.03 ohm. At what point on the line would a car drawing 100 amp obtain a minimum of potential difference? What is the value of this minimum PD?

Problem 5.6f. Eight resistors form a square as in Fig. 5.6*g*. Find the resistance between 𝒜 and ℬ, 𝒜 and 𝒞, and 𝒜 and 𝒟.

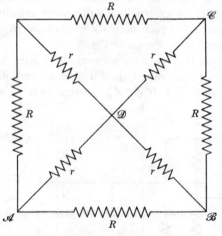

Fig. 5.6g. (Problem 5.6*f*)

Problem 5.6g. Twelve equal resistors lying on the edges of a cube are connected at the corners. Find the resistance between one corner and each of the three unlike other corners.

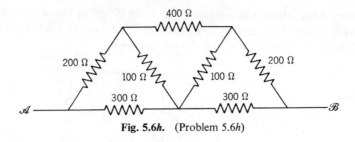

Fig. 5.6h. (Problem 5.6h)

Problem 5.6h. Find the resistance between $\mathscr{A}$ and $\mathscr{B}$ in Fig. 5.6h. Is there a principle of symmetry you can use?

5.7 Thévenin's Theorem

In the last section, we gave illustrations of three circuit theorems of rather general applicability. In this section, we shall prove and illustrate another circuit theorem of considerable interest and importance. The proposition is called "Thévenin's theorem" and asserts that any combination of emfs and resistors connected between two terminals acts like a single effective emf with an effective internal resistance in series. Problem 5.5e gave a simple example.

To prove this theorem for the general case, let us consider an arbitrary network connected between two terminals, with some other equally arbitrary network connected externally to the same terminals. One might imagine, for instance, that each network is enclosed in a box with only the terminals projecting, as shown in Fig. 5.7a.

Now let us imagine that we solve network N by Kirchhoff's laws, using the external potential difference V as if it were an emf, just as we treated $-i_b R_b$ as an emf on p. 224. If $\mathscr{E}_1, \mathscr{E}_2, \cdots$ represent the various emf's in

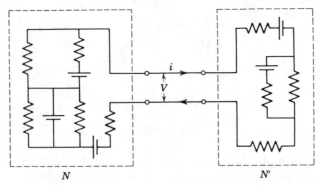

Fig. 5.7a. Two arbitrary two-terminal networks in boxes.

network N, the solution for the current i will be a linear expression in $\mathcal{E}_1, \mathcal{E}_2, \cdots$, and V with coefficients depending on the resistances $R_1, R_2, \cdots$ in N. If V is taken as a potential drop when calculated in the direction chosen as positive for i, the coefficient of V will be negative, since the equivalent emf is $-V$. Thus we shall write

$$i = g_1\mathcal{E}_1 + g_2\mathcal{E}_2 + \cdots - gV \qquad (5.7\text{--}1)$$

where the g's all have the dimensions of mhos and represent a sort of conductance (called "transfer conductance"). Solving for V we obtain

$$V = \frac{g_1}{g}\mathcal{E}_1 + \frac{g_2}{g}\mathcal{E}_2 + \cdots - \frac{i}{g} \qquad (5.7\text{--}2)$$

The relation between V and i becomes exactly that for a cell of emf $\mathcal{E}$ and internal resistance r, namely

$$V = \mathcal{E} - ir \qquad (5.7\text{--}3)$$

if we set

$$\mathcal{E} = \frac{g_1}{g}\mathcal{E}_1 + \frac{g_2}{g}\mathcal{E}_2 + \cdots \qquad (5.7\text{--}4)$$

and

$$r = \frac{1}{g} \qquad (5.7\text{--}5)$$

thus proving the theorem.

We can also solve network N' for i in terms of its emfs $\mathcal{E}_1', \mathcal{E}_2', \cdots$ and resistances $R_1', R_2' \cdots$, and of V as an emf. However, if V is defined as a drop for network N, it acts as a rise for network N', so we have

$$i = g_1'\mathcal{E}_1' + g_2'\mathcal{E}_2' + \cdots + g'V$$

or

$$V = \frac{i}{g'} - \frac{g_1'}{g}\mathcal{E}_1 - \frac{g_2'}{g}\mathcal{E}_2 \cdots$$

which may be written

$$V = ir' - \mathcal{E}' \qquad (5.7\text{--}6)$$

where r' and $\mathcal{E}'$ depend only on $R_1', R_2' \cdots$ and $\mathcal{E}_1', \mathcal{E}_2' \cdots$.

The two Eqs. 5.7–3 and 5.7–6 can now be combined to give an expression for the current i between the networks:

$$i = \frac{\mathcal{E} + \mathcal{E}'}{r + r'} \qquad (5.7\text{--}7)$$

just as if two cells were connected in series, with a combined emf of $\mathcal{E} + \mathcal{E}'$ and a combined resistance of $r + r'$, as in Fig. 5.7b.

Let us see what operational meaning we can attach to $\mathcal{E}$ and r, or $\mathcal{E}'$ and r'. If network N' is removed, so that there is an open circuit at the terminals of N, we will have $i = 0$ and $V = \mathscr{E}$. Thus the effective emf of a two-terminal network is the open-circuit potential difference at the terminals.

Suppose now that all the emfs $\mathscr{E}_1$, $\mathscr{E}_2$, $\cdots$ are removed from N. Any internal cell resistances are to be replaced by equal resistors, so that none of the values R_1, $R_2 \cdots$ are changed. Choose for N' a single cell of emf $\mathscr{E}'$ and negligible resistance. Then $\mathscr{E}$ and r' are zero, and since $i = \mathscr{E}'/r$, we see that the internal resistance of a two-terminal network is just the resultant resistance between the terminals when the emfs are set equal to zero. Such a network without emfs is called a "passive network," as contrasted with an "active network" containing emfs.

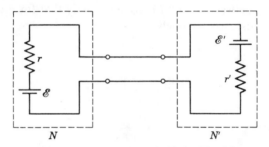

Fig. 5.7b. An equivalent circuit for Fig. 5.7a.

The most important use of Thévenin's theorem comes from its use in the power-transfer theorem which was proved in Section 5.5. If an active network N of equivalent emf $\mathscr{E}$ and resistance r feeds power to a passive network N' of variable effective resistance r', the maximum power transfer will occur when $r' = r$. This condition does not involve the emf's, so it holds true if they vary, as in the a-c case. An important application is to the transfer of a-c power in communication circuits. It is customary to design various pieces of apparatus such as amplifiers, test sources, microphones, loudspeakers, and transmission cables to have effective internal resistances[13] of one or another standard value, e.g., 500 ohms or 200 ohms. Then any active element (source of a communicative "signal") can be connected to any passive element (receiver) of the same design resistance. The proper matching of the elements not only provides for maximum power transfer, but also affects certain other properties, such as frequency response, linearity, maintenance of vacuum-tube or transistor currents within safe limits, etc. Problems 5.7a–f deal with attenuators that provide impedance matching along with reduction in voltage. Problems 5.7g and h

---

[13] In a-c circuits, the concept of impedance usually replaces that of resistance. But in the usual power-transfer case, the relevant impedances generally act like resistances.

call for treatment of two circuits of the previous section by Thévenin's theorem.[14]

Problem 5.7a. A T-section network, shown in Fig. 5.7c, is used to match two networks N and N' each to a resistance R, and at the same time to reduce the voltage on N' by the attenuation factor x_a over what it would

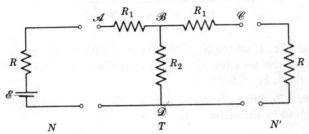

Fig. 5.7c. A T-section attenuator network with input and output circuits N and N' (Problem 5.7a)

be if N and N' were connected directly. Show that for proper matching, R_1 and R_2 are related by

$$R^2 = R_1^2 + 2R_1 R_2 \qquad (5.7\text{–}8)$$

and that

$$x_a = \frac{R_2}{R_2 + R_1 + R} \qquad (5.7\text{–}9)$$

Find R_1 and R_2 in terms of R and x_a.

Problem 5.7b. Show that R_1 of Problem 5.7a increases as x_a decreases from 1 to 0 and that R_2 decreases, when R is constant. Sketch curves showing these variations.

Problem 5.7c. The attenuation α_{db} in decibels is

$$\alpha_{db} = 10 \log_{10} (1/x_a^2)$$

Show for Problem 5.7a that $R_1 = R \tanh (2.303\alpha_{db}/40)$ and $R_2 = R \operatorname{csch} (2.303\alpha_{db}/20)$, so that R_1 and R_2 can be calculated for a given R and α_{db} from a table of hyperbolic functions (these functions are defined in Appendix A.5).

Problem 5.7e. Find R_1 and R_2 for T-section networks designed for 500-ohm input and output resistances, and attenuations of 1 db, 5 db, 10 db, and 50 db.

Problem 5.7f. Find the conditions on R_1 and R_2 in the π-section network of Fig. 5.7d so that it will match resistances R at each pair of terminals and provide a given attenuation α_{db}.

[14] Cf. Guillemin, *op. cit.*, for further details on all these matters.

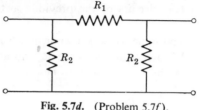

Fig. 5.7d. (Problem 5.7*f*).

Problem 5.7g. Treat the circuit of Fig. 5.6d with $\mathscr{E}_1$, $\mathscr{E}_2$, and R_b all equal to zero by Thévenin's theorem, taking the network N' to be $\mathscr{E}_g$ and R_g, and thus check Eq. 5.6–21.

Problem 5.7h. Treat the circuit of Fig. 5.6d by Thévenin's theorem when N' is taken to be the resistor R_1, and $R_b = 0$.

5.8 Resistance Bridges and Potentiometers

Precision measurements in the field of steady-current circuits involve determinations of emf, current, and resistance. Of these three, the measurement of resistance by comparison with known resistance standards is the most straightforward and direct. Furthermore, accurate resistance values are required for emf and current measurements. Resistance bridges are especially valuable because they allow comparison of resistance values without the necessity of known or constant emfs or currents. The question of the determination of resistance in terms of mechanical units (so-called "absolute" determinations) will be discussed in Section 7.15.

The Wheatstone Bridge. The Wheatstone bridge circuit, shown in Fig. 5.8a, is similar to the circuit of Fig. 5.6d, with all batteries but one removed. We take the case of negligible battery resistance (see Problem 5.8d for the inclusion of R_b). Three of the resistors shown are considered to be known and the fourth is to be found by adjusting one ·or more of the three until the galvanometer deflection is reduced to zero. By an elementary calculation, or from Eq. 5.6–21, we see that a null result on the

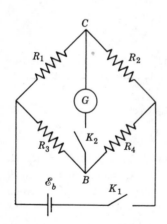

K_1 = Battery key
K_2 = Galvanometer key

Fig. 5.8a. A Wheatstone bridge:
K_1 = battery key,
K_2 = galvanometer
key; the galvanometer
G has resistance R_g.

galvanometer occurs when $R_2R_3 = R_1R_4$ or

$$\frac{R_1}{R_2} = \frac{R_3}{R_4} = n \tag{5.8-1}$$

where n is called the bridge ratio across the galvanometer. This relation is of course valid for steady currents. If there are appreciable inductive or capacitive effects in the circuit, charge may flow in the galvanometer while the current in the rest of the bridge is being established, even if Eq. 5.8-1 holds. Therefore it is necessary to test the balance by closing the battery key K_1 first, allowing the main currents to become established, and then pressing the galvanometer key K_2 to test for balance.

Satisfactory use of such bridges requires a sufficiently good sensitivity. By sensitivity is generally meant the smallest fractional deviation from the balance value of one of the resistance arms that leads to a detectable current in the galvanometer. The smallest detectable current depends on the particular galvanometer and the conditions of its use. We shall only calculate here a bridge sensitivity defined as the ratio of the current through (or PD across) the galvanometer to the fractional change away from balance of one of the resistors.

By Eq. 5.6-21, the current through the galvanometer is in general

$$i_g = \mathscr{E}_b \frac{R_2R_3 - R_1R_4}{R_1R_2R_3 + R_2R_3R_4 + R_3R_4R_1 + R_4R_1R_2 + R_g(R_1 + R_2)(R_3 + R_4)} \tag{5.8-2}$$

Let us consider that $R_2R_3 = R_1R_4$ and that R_2 is replaced in Eq. 5.8-2 by a variable R_2' when the bridge is slightly out of balance. We shall write

$$R_2' = R_2(1 + x)$$

or

$$x = \frac{R_2' - R_2}{R_2}$$

so that x is the fractional deviation of resistor 2 from balance. When we substitute R_2' in Eq. 5.8-2, the numerator will reduce to xR_2R_3. The presence of x in the denominator will on binomial expansion lead to terms in the numerator with x^2, x^3, $\cdots$ which we shall neglect, assuming x to be small (the simplest bridges are easily balanced to within 1%). Therefore we shall not substitute R_2' for R_2 in the denominator of Eq. 5.8-2.

The resulting expression can be easily simplified if we factor R_2R_3 or its equal R_1R_4 out of the first four terms of the denominator. We find

$$i_g \simeq \frac{x\mathscr{E}_b}{(R_1 + R_2 + R_3 + R_4) + R_g\left(\dfrac{R_1}{R_2} + 2 + \dfrac{R_2}{R_1}\right)} \tag{5.8-3}$$

so that

$$\frac{i_g}{x} \simeq \frac{\mathscr{E}_b}{(R_1 + R_2 + R_3 + R_4) + R_g\left(n + 2 + \dfrac{1}{n}\right)} \qquad (5.8\text{-}4)$$

It is easily seen that the same result except for a possible minus sign results if R_1, R_3, or R_4 is taken as the adjustable resistor.

The expression $n + 1/n$ has a minimum value when $n = 1$. Thus the sensitivity ratio i_g/x is a maximum when we have, simultaneously, $n = 1$, the lowest permissible total resistance of the bridge, and the largest permissible emf $\mathscr{E}_b$. Both the upper limit on $\mathscr{E}_b$ and the lower limit on $R_1 + R_2 + R_3 + R_4$ are determined principally by the value of the unknown to be measured and the permissible power dissipation in the various resistors.

The choice of which galvanometer to use for a given bridge depends, of course, on the relation between i_g and the galvanometer deflection (cf. Section 8.9). It also depends on R_g, and on the value of effective resistance to which it should be connected for proper damping. Sometimes, for instance, it is useful to place an external resistance in series with the galvanometer or in parallel with it to make a proper match. The influence of such resistors on the over-all sensitivity is not hard to compute.[15]

Potentiometers. The potentiometer method is the most important technique for comparing potential differences and has a number of applications. It consists fundamentally in balancing two potential differences against each other and detecting their equality when a galvanometer in the circuit connecting them indicates no current flow. Figure 5.8b shows two networks connected with a galvanometer. When no current flows, the open-circuit PD's of the two networks must be equal. One of the networks, say network 2, contains a quantity to be measured in terms of the open-circuit PD V_2, and the other is a measuring circuit with a means for adjusting V_1 and knowing its value.

The types of PD's that can be measured with this method include the emfs of cells and of thermocouples, the PD on a voltmeter carrying sufficient current to make it read some convenient value, and the PD on a resistor carrying a current that passes through an ammeter to be calibrated or through another resistor to be compared with the first. Since at balance no current is drawn from the cell or thermocouple, its external potential difference must equal its emf. Any internal resistance thus does not enter into the measurement, although it may affect the sensitivity. It should be

---

[15] Cf. Harris, *op. cit.*, Chapter 7, for details on precision resistance bridges; also M. B. Stout, *Basic Electrical Measurements*, 2nd ed., Prentice-Hall, Englewood Cliffs, N.J., 1960, Chapter 4.

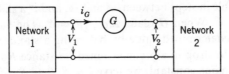

Fig. 5.8b.   Illustrating the potentiometer principle. When $i_G = 0$, $V_1 = V_2$.

noted that in case the measured circuit contains more than one kind of material, it is always the difference in V_F that is actually measured.

The measuring network invariably uses an iR drop for V_1. One method of adjusting V_1, known as Poggendorff's[16] first method, consists in keeping i fixed and varying the portion of the total resistance in network 1 that is connected to the terminals. Poggendorff's second method consists in keeping a fixed resistance between the terminals and varying and measuring the current.

The variation in the amount of resistance required in the first method can be accomplished at one or at both connections. A simple slide wire can be used as a potentiometer, with only one connection variable, but greater precision of reading can be obtained by making one terminal vary in steps and the other along a continuous wire.

Figure 5.8c shows a circuit for comparing the emf $\mathscr{E}$ of a cell with the iR drop in a resistance R which is the resistance between the taps $\mathscr{P}$ and

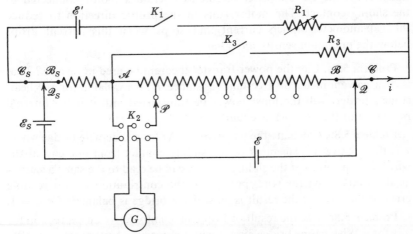

Fig. 5.8c.   A potentiometer circuit, showing a special slide-wire for standard cell adjustment and a parallel circuit for range changing. Switch K_2 is closed to the right for balancing $\mathscr{E}$ and to the left for balancing $\mathscr{E}_S$. In a modern recording instrument, the galvanometer is replaced by a servo amplifier controlling a motor that moves $\mathscr{Q}$ or $\mathscr{Q}_S$ until balance is achieved.

[16] J. C. Poggendorff was the first to use the potentiometer principle, *Ann. Phys. u. Chemie*, **54** (1841).

$\mathscr{Q}$, with $\mathscr{P}$ movable in steps between $\mathscr{A}$ and $\mathscr{B}$, and $\mathscr{Q}$ a sliding tap movable between $\mathscr{B}$ and $\mathscr{C}$. When G reads zero, $iR = \mathscr{E}$. The value of i may be adjusted to a predetermined value by balancing a standard cell of known emf $\mathscr{E}_S$ against the drop in a predetermined resistance R_S between $\mathscr{A}$ and $\mathscr{Q}_S$. Then if i remains constant, we have $i = \mathscr{E}/R = \mathscr{E}_S/R_S$, and $\mathscr{E}$ can be found.

The most serious problem in potentiometer measurements is that of maintaining a constant current in the tapped resistance R. This problem is attacked partly by using a battery $\mathscr{E}'$ of much larger current capacity than actually needed and partly by a rapid switching from standard cell to unknown and back to standard cell.

Also shown in Fig. 5.8c is an arrangement for changing the range of the potentiometer. Many ordinary potentiometers have a maximum range of 1.6 v and can be read to 0.0001 v. Thermocouple measurements, however, involve emfs of a millivolt or so; accurate measurement of such emfs requires a smaller range, say 0.016 v. If resistance R_3 is exactly 1/99 of that in the branch $\mathscr{A}\mathscr{B}\mathscr{C}$, then closing of K_3 and rebalancing the circuit will result in the same current i in $\mathscr{E}_S\mathscr{A}$ but only 1/100 as much in $\mathscr{A}\mathscr{B}\mathscr{C}$, so the potentiometer has 1/100 the range it had before.[17]

Many automatic potential-measuring meters and recorders use the potentiometer principle coupled with a servomechanism that employs a signal from the galvanometer circuit to operate a motor connected to the sliding contact. The motor runs in the proper direction to reduce the galvanometer-branch current and stops when this current drops below the minimum sensitivity value.

Problem 5.8a. Can the power-transfer theorem be used in reverse? That is, if a galvanometer of a certain resistance R_g is available for a Wheatstone's bridge, will the most power be transferred into it if the internal resistance of the network is equal to R_g?

Problem 5.8b. Calculate the sensitivity $i_g/\Delta x$ for a slide-wire bridge where x is the relative displacement of the sliding contact from one end of the wire. If the position of the sliding contact can be read to the same accuracy at all points along the wire, prove that the contribution of this reading error to the error of the result is least if the bridge is balanced for $n = 1$.

Problem 5.8c. Use the result of Problem 5.6a to derive an expression for i_g/x for a Wheatstone bridge circuit with appreciable battery resistance R_b.

Problem 5.8d. Suppose the contact errors at the ends of a slide-wire bridge amount respectively to additional lengths of wire α and β. If the bridge is balanced with a resistor R_1 near the α end and R_2 near the β end, with wire lengths l_1 and l_2, and then rebalanced with R_1 and R_2 interchanged,

[17] For details, see Harris, *op. cit.*, Chapter 12, and Stout, *op. cit.*, Chapter 7.

yielding lengths l_2' and l_1', find α and β in terms of these measured lengths and the ratio $R_2/R_1 = n$. What happens when $n = 1$?

Problem 5.8e. Show that, if R_1 and R_2 are in parallel and an error dR_2 is made in R_2, an error $dR = dR_2[R_1/(R_1 + R_2)]^2$ is made in the value of the parallel resistance. If a switch has an unknown contact resistance of about 0.001 ohm, show how to make a variable resistor of values from 49.50000 to 50.50000 ohms for which the contact resistance error is less than 0.00002 ohm.

Problem 5.8f. Use Thévenin's theorem on a simple potentiometer circuit to find the current through the galvanometer when the setting between $\mathscr{P}$ and $\mathscr{Q}$ (see Fig. 5.8c) is out by ΔV volts. Hence find $i_g/\Delta V$. Show how measurements of i_g can eliminate the necessity of getting an exact balance (this is the principle of the "deflection potentiometer").

Problem 5.8g. What sensitivity must a galvanometer have if it is to be used in a potentiometer with a range of 1.6 v, standard current of 1.0 ma, main battery 5.0 v, when an emf of 1.0 v is to be measured to 0.001%? Take the resistance of galvanometer and standard cell together to be 300 ohms.

Problem 5.8h. Tell how the circuit of Fig. 5.8d can be used to measure the emf of cell $\mathscr{E}$ without drawing current from it. Under what conditions could $\mathscr{E}'$ be measured instead?

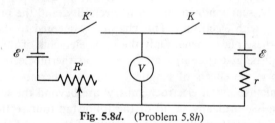

Fig. 5.8d. (Problem 5.8h)

Problem 5.8i. Two standard cells differ in emf by about 300 μv. Show how to measure this difference if you are given a galvanometer, a standard 0.1 ohm resistor, a 10-ma range ammeter, and a battery and controlling resistor.

Problem 5.8j. A high-voltage supply produces between 1250 v and 1350 v and may provide up to 200 μa of current. A battery of constant emf and a galvanometer calibrated to read ± 25 μa are available along with necessary resistors. Show how to measure small variations in the high voltage from an originally set value of 1300 v, using a type of potentiometer.

Chapter 6

PHENOMENA RELATED TO ELECTRON LEVELS

6.1 Introduction

We have seen that the concept of the Fermi level for electrons in a metal is essential for explaining the properties of conductors, chemical cells, and contacts between different materials. There are three other sets of phenomena whose electrical aspects may be adequately understood only in terms of electron levels and which in these aspects form a proper part of our subject, namely, semiconduction, thermoelectricity, and the properties of ionic solutions with electrodes. This chapter is devoted to the electrical principles of these phenomena. Only the basic elements of the physics of each topic will be given; complications, such as thermoelectric effects in semiconductors, the effects of magnetic fields on thermoelectricity, and thermodynamic aspects of electrochemistry, are beyond the scope of this book. The omission of any or all of the following four sections of this chapter will not interfere with the continuity of the rest of the material.

6.2 Semiconductors

Insulators differ from conductors in that the electrons in the atoms or molecules of the former are all in closed shells, largely because they share their outer electrons by chemical combination in covalent bonds just so as to achieve this state. Consequently the lowest energy bands that develop when the units are closely packed are also filled; a relatively large amount of energy is needed for any electron before it can jump into the next higher band. In a diagram like that of Fig. 2.1a (p. 59), an insulator would have the conduction band all filled, in which case it is called a valence band, as in Fig. 6.2a.

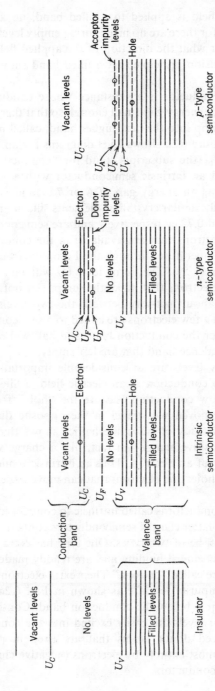

Fig. 6.2a. Energy level diagrams for four types of non-metals, showing the highest level in the valence band U_V, the lowest level in the conduction band U_C, the Fermi level U_F and the donor and acceptor levels U_D and U_A.

When an electric field is applied to a filled band, no acceleration of electrons is possible, for there are no neighboring empty levels for electrons to jump to no matter what the direction of the applied field. It is a consequence of the exclusion principle that a filled band shows no net conduction.

An intrinsic semiconductor is a substance whose conduction band is filled but which has an energy gap small enough so that thermal excitation causes electrons to jump into the next higher band, called in this case the conduction band. Figure 6.2a shows level diagrams for an insulator with a large gap $U_C - U_V$ (the subscripts stand for "conduction band" and "valence band") and an intrinsic semiconductor with a small gap. For instance, diamond has an energy gap of 6 or 7 ev and is an insulator, whereas the chemically similar crystalline elements silicon and germanium have gaps of 1.10 and 0.72 ev respectively and are semiconductors.

The number of electrons that are available in the conduction band is determined by the temperature (through the Fermi distribution function, given in footnote 1 on p. 59). The Fermi level U_F will vary in accordance with the number of electrons that make the jump. For not too high temperatures, it will lie about half-way between the two levels U_V and U_C; this means that when a few electrons are added to a semiconductor, about half of them will enter the conduction band and half will enter the levels near the top of the valence band that are left empty.

These latter empty levels are of considerable importance. Because a filled band shows no conduction in an electric field, a filled band minus one electron will show conduction because the "hole" from which the electron has been removed will travel in the opposite direction to the electrons. A detailed study of wave mechanics shows that such a hole indeed acts like a positive charge—in fact, like a charge whose mass is somewhere near that of an electron. Thus an intrinsic semiconductor has an equal number of holes and electrons that can move under the influence of a field.

This type of semiconductor is called intrinsic to contrast it with impurity semiconductors. The latter class of semiconductors contains foreign atoms or impurities that can be of two types. One type has extra electrons that do not take part in chemical binding and are readily made free to move about. Such atoms are called "donors." Their extra electrons occupy what are called "donor impurity levels"; as shown in Fig. 6.2a, these levels, denoted by U_D, are just below the conduction band. Consequently, electrons from the donor levels are easily excited into the conduction band, leaving behind ionized donor atoms that are fixed in position. Such materials conduct almost entirely by electrons (negative charges) and are called "n-type" semiconductors.

The other type of impurities are atoms that each lack an electron for complete chemical binding and so have vacant levels into which they can accept electrons. They are called "acceptors" and their levels, denoted in Fig. 6.2*a* by U_A, are just above the top of the valence band. Electrons from the valence band are excited by thermal energy into these levels, where they become trapped or localized so that they cannot move. The holes that remain behind can move, so that conduction is by positive charges, and the material is labeled "*p*-type."

Let us now describe the principal electrical properties of semiconductors. In the first place, their conductivity is low because the available carriers, whether electrons or holes, are present in very much smaller density than in metals. This fact, however, means that their conductivity is quite sensitive to factors that tend to change the carrier density. Raising the temperature, for instance, will cause more electrons to jump the appropriate gap ($U_C - U_V$ in intrinsic material, $U_C - U_D$ in *n*-type, and $U_A - U_V$ in *p*-type), and the conductivity will show a marked temperature dependence, increasing with T rather than reducing as for most metals. Semiconducting devices called thermistors make use of this effect for numerous control purposes.[1]

Luminous energy falling on a semiconductor can increase the charge carrier density by a photoelectric effect, in which electrons in the conduction band or in donor levels absorb photons and are excited to the conduction band. This property is called photoconductivity and has numerous applications.[2]

The *p–n* Junction. As we have indicated, the height of the Fermi level in a semiconductor is considerably dependent on the impurity concentration. It can also be modified by changing the temperature or temporarily adding excess charge carriers of one sign or the other. Rectification properties can be derived from these facts. We shall use as a single illustration the so-called *p–n* junction, or boundary between a piece of *p*-type semiconductor and a piece of *n*-type (both usually of germanium). We can suppose that there is a certain density N_0 of acceptors in the *p*-type material, and (for simplicity) the same density of donors in the *n*-type material. The junction will then be assumed to be a region of width $2x_0$, in which the acceptor density N_A varies linearly from N_0 at, say, $x = -x_0$, to 0 at

[1] See J. A. Becker, C. B. Green, and G. L. Pearson, *Bell Sys. Tech. Journ.*, **26**, 170–212 (1947) and *Trans. Amer. Inst. Elec. Eng.*, **65**, 711–725 (1946), for details on thermistors; brief accounts are given by C. L. Alley and K. W. Atwood, *Electronic Engineering*, John Wiley, New York, 1962, p. 45, and A. L. Albert, *Electronics and Electron Devices*, Macmillan, New York, 1956, pp. 380–381.

[2] K. R. Spangenberg, *Fundamentals of Electron Devices*, McGraw-Hill, New York, 1957, pp. 408–414; L. P. Hunter, *Handbook of Semiconductor Electronics*, 2nd ed., McGraw-Hill, New York, 1962, part I, sec. 5.

$x = x_0$, whereas the donor density N_D varies linearly from 0 at $x = -x_0$ to N_0 at $x = x_0$.

Because there are no conduction electrons in the p-type material and no conduction holes in the n-type, holes and electrons will tend to equalize the situation by passing across the boundary, making the p-type material more negative and the n-type material more positive. This will raise the electron energy levels in the former and lower them in the latter; in fact, equilibrium will set in when the Fermi levels come to equilibrium, which requires just this sort of change.

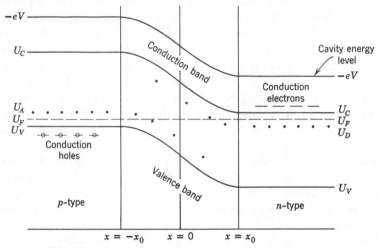

Fig. 6.2b. Level diagram for a p-n semiconductor junction.

Figure 6.2b illustrates this state of affairs, showing the level variation as a function of x. Because the Fermi level drops considerably below the conduction band for x just less than x_0, we can assume that the donors in this region are all ionized and have delivered their electrons to the p-type material. Similarly, on the p side we can assume that for $x > -x_0$, all the acceptor levels are filled. This means that there is a charge density in the transition layer given by

$$\rho = -eN_A + eN_D = eN_0(x - x_0)/2x_0 + eN_0(x + x_0)/2x_0$$

or

$$\rho = eN_0 x/x_0 \qquad (6.2\text{-}1)$$

where we have used the above-mentioned variation of N_A and N_D with x.

It then follows from the one-dimensional Poisson equation (Section 1.10) that

$$\frac{d^2 V}{dx^2} = \frac{-eN_0 x}{\epsilon_0 x_0} \qquad (6.2\text{-}2)$$

Integrating once and using the vanishing of dV/dx for $|x| \geqslant x_0$, we have

$$\frac{dV}{dx} = -\frac{eN_0(x^2 - x_0^2)}{2\epsilon_0 x_0} \qquad (6.2-3)$$

A second integration now gives, letting $V(0) = 0$,

$$V(x) = \frac{-eN_0}{2\epsilon_0 x_0}(\tfrac{1}{3}x^3 - xx_0^2) \qquad (6.2-4)$$

which shows that the cavity potential varies in a cubic fashion between $x = -x_0$ and $x = x_0$. The energy of each electron level will vary in accordance with $-eV(x)$, since the levels are located below the cavity potential-energy value by amounts depending on the local atomic structure, which we assume to be approximately homogeneous throughout.

Let us show that such a junction acts as a rectifier. Current can be most easily passed in the direction that brings the majority carriers in each material toward the junction. This fact can be seen more clearly if we consider what it is that prevents electrons from going to the p-type material and vice versa when the system is in equilibrium. There are relatively few levels available for the conduction electrons of the n-type material to occupy in the p-type.[3] Only if they are thermally excited to a considerable energy above the U_C level on the p side can they then pass over easily. Holes on the p side are similarly situated but need to be "excited downwards" (have electrons from lower levels come up to them). When we make the n-type material more negative and the p-type more positive, the levels will shift so as to reduce these barrier heights and make the transfer easier. In statistical mechanics, it is shown that the resulting currents vary in an exponential way with the applied PD (difference in V_F's).

When current is passed the other way, the levels are depressed, and there are very few carriers available to make the transition. What current there is usually derives from the continual thermal production of carriers in the transition layer and is largely independent of the applied PD. Thus it comes about that the current in many semiconductor rectifiers can be approximately given as a function of applied potential difference V by a formula of the type called the "diode characteristic,"

$$i = i_0(e^{bV} - 1) \qquad (6.2-5)$$

where the first term represents the forward exponentially-varying current and the second the constant reverse current.

Metal-to-semiconductor interfaces can also be rectifying, in case a so-called barrier layer is formed by virtue of electrons leaving the bulk

---

[3] The conduction holes are not easily available as levels into which electrons crossing the junction can fall because of their relative paucity and the way they move around.

material and residing on the surface. (Cf. Problem 1.10*g*.) Formulas similar to the diode characteristic hold in these cases as well. Copper-oxide, selenium, germanium, and silicon plate rectifiers are made by using one such rectifying junction with a metal electrode, and another junction treated so as to avoid the production of a barrier layer.

Photovoltaic cells are sources of emf using *p–n* junctions or barrier layers. Luminous energy falling on such a junction will produce electron-hole pairs, each of which will move under the action of the electric field toward the material for which it is a majority carrier. Consequently the *n*-type will become more negative and the *p*-type more positive. A steady difference of V_F's is maintained which is, of course, an emf. The silicon solar cell, used for satellite power, is an example.

Another aspect of the action of a *p–n* junction is that as current is passed in the forward direction, holes enter the *n*-type material and electrons enter the *p*-type material. These minority carriers are said to be "injected" on each side. It takes a finite time for holes and electrons to meet and recombine on each side—it usually takes an intermediate stage of trapping of the minority carrier at an impurity or dislocation where it waits for a majority carrier to come along and neutralize it. Thus it happens that injected carriers can travel some distance in the material of opposite character.

Transistor action uses a combination of rectification and injection. A thin layer of *p*-type material, for instance, is sandwiched between two pieces of *n*-type. A current is then passed through one of these *p–n* junctions, called the "collector," in the reverse direction. If a forward current is passed through the other junction, called the "emitter," electrons injected into the *p*-type material may diffuse all the way to the reverse-biased junction and act to increase the reverse current by providing the carriers that are otherwise missing for that direction of conduction. Thus a current in the low-resistance forward-biased circuit of the emitter can modulate or control a similar magnitude of current in the high-resistance collector circuit. If external and internal resistances are matched, more power (i^2R) will be developed in the collector circuit than was provided in the emitter circuit.

For many further details on semiconductors, the reader is referred elsewhere.[4]

---

[4] Alley and Atwood, *loc. cit.*; Spangenberg, *loc. cit.*; Hunter, *loc. cit.*; H. K. Henisch, *Rectifying Semi-conductor Contacts*, Clarendon Press, Oxford, 1955; W. Shockley, *Electrons and Holes in Semi-conductors*, D. Van Nostrand, Princeton, 1950; C. Kittel, *Introduction to Solid State Physics*, 2nd ed., John Wiley, New York, 1956, Chapters 13 and 14; R. P. Nanavati, *An Introduction to Semiconductor Electronics*, McGraw-Hill, New York, 1963.

6.3 The Seebeck, Peltier, and Thomson Thermal Effects

If there is a difference in temperature between two metallic conductors in contact, there will be a tendency for electrons to pass from the warmer conductor to the cooler one even when the electrochemical potentials are equal, for electrons excited to higher levels in the warmer piece will jump to lower empty levels in the cooler piece more frequently than the reverse will happen. Thus Ohm's law for homogeneous or inhomogeneous materials, Eq. 5.1–3, needs further modification when the temperature is not uniform.

In fact, differences of temperature T act mathematically like differences of V_F. The current density depends linearly on ∇T as well as on ∇V_F. Such linear dependence is generally to be expected for small gradients and is found experimentally to hold over all temperature gradients normally met with. We shall write the modified form of Ohm's law as follows:

$$J = \sigma_c(-\nabla V_F + S^* \nabla T) \tag{6.3–1}$$

where S^* is the new constant of proportionality and is called, for reasons to be mentioned later, the "entropy transport per unit charge" or more briefly the "S-star."[5] It is always positive. It is a property of the metal in question and is a function of the temperature T.

The Seebeck Effect. Equation 6.3–1 has the consequence that when $J = 0$ in a conductor, a difference of temperature implies a difference of V_F. This difference leads to the appearance of an emf, called the Seebeck emf,[6] in a circuit containing wires of two different materials with the two junctions at different temperatures. Figure 6.3a shows such a circuit opened at a place where the temperature is T_p and connected into a potentiometer which measures the difference in V_F between the opened ends. If $J = 0$, we will have

$$\nabla V_F = S^* \nabla T \tag{6.3–2}$$

which for any displacement $\mathbf{dl}$ along the conductor implies $dV_F = S^* dT$. The net emf around the circuit we shall call $\mathscr{E}_{BA}(T', T'')$ with the positive current direction and the labeling of the materials related as in the figure. We have

$$\mathscr{E}_{BA}(T', T'') = V_{F4} - V_{F1} = \int_{\mathscr{P}_1}^{\mathscr{P}_4} dV_F = \int_{\mathscr{P}_1}^{\mathscr{P}_4} S^* dT \tag{6.3–3}$$

[5] In the first edition of this book, the symbol S^* was used for what here would be S^*e.
[6] Named after its discoverer, T. J. Seebeck, *Abh. d. Konigl. Acad. d. Wiss. Berlin*, 1822–1823, p. 265.

Since the terminals $\mathscr{P}_1$ and $\mathscr{P}_4$ are at the same temperature and since S^* depends only on the kind of material and the temperature, we can write the emf as an integral over the temperature range of the values of S^* around the circuit. We have

$$\mathscr{E}_{BA}(T', T'') = \oint_{\text{circuit}} S^* \, dT \tag{6.3-4}$$

or the equivalent

$$\mathscr{E}_{BA}(T', T'') = \int_{T'}^{T''} (S_A^* - S_B^*) \, dT \tag{6.3-5}$$

The former of these equations is clearly quite general and can be used for any number of materials and any temperature distribution. The latter equation is in a form to help us remember the sign convention of Fig. 6.3a:

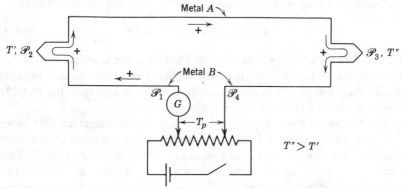

Fig. 6.3a. A thermocouple circuit, illustrating the Seebeck effect.

if S_A^* is greater than S_B^*, electrons are transferred more rapidly along metal A toward lower temperatures than along metal B, and the positive current goes from A to B at the hot junction (i.e., holes go uphill toward higher temperatures, and faster in metal A). The symbol $\mathscr{E}_{BA}(T', T'')$ can be read "emf from B to A at temperature T' less than T''."

When $\mathbf{J}$ is not zero, as in a circuit carrying a steady current, ∇V_F will be equal to $S^* \nabla T + \rho_e \mathbf{J}$. The circulation integral of the second term is just the ordinary potential drop of Ohm's law, and the integral of the first term is still the thermal emf, so that our expression for this emf is correct with or without the presence of currents.

A pair of wires connected as in Fig. 6.3a is called a thermocouple; thermocouples are widely used for temperature measurement and control. The emf of a thermocouple depends on the properties of two materials and on two temperatures, but it is very easy to show from Eq. 6.3–5 that a tabulation of emf's of various substances each paired with one particular standard and each with the same lower temperature $T' = T_0$ (usually 0°C) will allow the prediction of the emf for all the possibilities (see Problem 6.3a).

The quantity $S_A* - S_B*$ for any particular pair of metals is often useful. It can be found by differentiating the emf $\mathscr{E}_{BA}$ with respect to the warmer

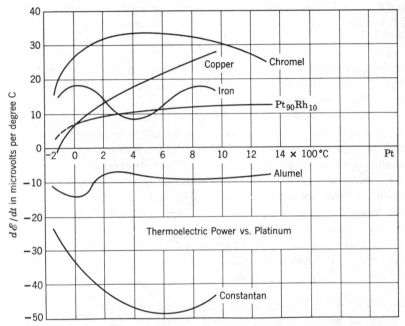

Fig. 6.3b. Thermopowers of various metals referred to platinum. (Taken from P. M. Dike, *Thermoelectric Thermometry*, Philadelphia, 1954, courtesy of Leeds and Northrop, Inc.)

temperature T'' (here we set $T'' = T$). The derivative $d\mathscr{E}_{BA}/dT$ is called, for historical reasons, the "thermoelectric power" or "thermopower." We have

$$\frac{d\mathscr{E}_{BA}}{dT} = S_A*(T) - S_B*(T) \qquad (6.3\text{–}6)$$

It is to be observed that the thermopower depends only on one temperature. Graphs of thermopowers of several substances A with one reference B (usually taken as platinum) present information about the emfs of many possible material and temperature pairs in a very compact way. Figure 6.3b is an example.

For details on the operation of thermocouples, the measurement of thermal emfs, and the reduction of unwanted thermal emfs in other measurements, the reader is referred elsewhere.[7]

The Peltier Effect. The Peltier and Thomson effects involve heat transfer, and so we must consider heat conduction briefly before taking them up. Heat is energy transferred without the performance of any macroscopic work and is thus to be ascribed to the transfer of thermal energies by molecular and electronic collisions. In the absence of electric current, a heat current J_Q joules/m^2-sec will be produced by a temperature gradient ∇T, in accordance with the heat-conduction equation

$$J_Q = -\kappa_Q \nabla T \qquad (6.3\text{-}7)$$

This equation is studied in an elementary way in beginning courses in physics and is called Fourier's law. The constant κ_Q is called the "coefficient of heat conductivity."

It is shown in books on solid-state physics[8] that the electrons in a metal play a major role in heat conduction, their jumps from higher to lower levels in adjacent pieces of material at different temperatures accounting for their activity in this regard. Since without electric current a gradient of V_F exists, this gradient also contributes to J_Q in Eq. 6.3-7.

Now, if there is a current in a wire, ∇V_F and ∇T are differently related than when $J = 0$, and we must write the dependence of J_Q on the two gradients separately. Because the same processes are involved in heat conduction and charge transfer, the quantity S^* appears in the general equation for J_Q.[9] This equation reads

$$J_Q = \sigma_c S^* T \, \nabla V_F - (\kappa_Q + \sigma_c S^{*2} T) \, \nabla T \qquad (6.3\text{-}8)$$

When $\nabla V_F = S^* \, \nabla T$, Eq. 6.3-8 clearly reduces to Eq. 6.3-7.

If we use Eq. 6.3-1, we can write J_Q in terms of J and ∇T:

$$J_Q = S^* T J - \kappa_Q \nabla T \qquad (6.3\text{-}9)$$

[7] R. L. Weber, *Heat and Temperature Measurement*, Prentice-Hall, Englewood Cliffs, N.J., 1950, Chapter 5; P. H. Dike, *Thermoelectric Thermometry*, Leeds and Northrup, Philadelphia, 1954; F. K. Harris, *Electrical Measurements*, John Wiley, New York, 1952, pp. 431–443; E. H. Putley, *The Hall Effect and Related Phenomena*, Butterworths, London, 1960; H. J. Goldsmid, *Applications of Thermoelectricity*, Methuen, London, and John Wiley, New York, 1960.

[8] See, e.g., C. Kittel, *op. cit.*, pp. 138–153.

[9] The fact that S^* relates both ∇V_F to J_Q and ∇T to J is a special case of Onsager's theorem that forms the basis for the theory of the thermodynamics of irreversible processes. Cf. L. Onsager, *Phys. Rev.*, **37**, 405 (1931); *Phys. Rev.*, **38**, 2265 (1931); *Ann. N.Y. Acad. Sci.*, **46**, 241 (1945); H. D. Callen, *Phys. Rev.*, **73**, 1349 (1948); S. R. DeGroot, *Thermodynamics of Irreversible Processes*, Interscience, New York, 1951. C. A. Domenicali, *Rev. Mod. Phys.*, **26**, 237 (1954) has given a detailed review of the applications of this theorem and the concepts of electrochemical potential, etc., to thermoelectricity.

Since $|\mathbf{J}|$ is the number of units of charge passing through a unit area in unit time, we see that the heat transferred per unit charge in the direction of motion of the electrons is S^*T. Since entropy, usually denoted by S, is defined in thermodynamics as heat transfer divided by the absolute temperature at the point of transfer, we see the reason for calling S^* the entropy transport per unit charge. Then, of course, S^*e is the entropy transport per electron.

Now consider a junction between two metals with a steady current across it. If the contact resistance is negligible, V_F will be the same in both metals and no electrical energy is expended at the junction. Both $\mathbf{J}$ and $\mathbf{J}_Q$ will be the same on each side of the junction, for neither charge nor energy will collect there in a steady state. If the two values of S^* are different, the heat transport by the electrons on the two sides will be unequal, and therefore there must also be a difference between the two $\kappa_Q\,\nabla T$ terms.

As far as the external surroundings are concerned, heat can be absorbed or emitted by the junction only through temperature-gradient conduction, for the electrons do not get out of the wires. The difference between the values of $\kappa_Q\,\nabla T$ on each side will in fact lead to such absorption or emission. Specifically, if the two metals are denoted by the letters A and B as before, and S_A^* is greater than S_B^*, then when positive current passes from A to B, electrons carry more heat away from the junction in A than bring it up in B, so that the $\kappa_Q\,\nabla T$ terms must combine to show an absorption of heat from the surroundings. The amount of this absorption per unit charge is denoted by Π_{BA} (Π is a Greek capital pi) and is given by

$$\Pi_{BA} = T[S_A^*(T) - S_B^*(T)] \qquad (6.3\text{–}10)$$

The rate of absorption per unit time is then $\Pi_{BA}i$, where i is the current. It becomes an emission of heat when the current is reversed. This rate of absorption is called the Peltier heat.[10] Since it is a reversible heat exchange, it is sometimes called the Peltier emf, although because V_F is the same in each metal, we cannot properly ascribe any emf to the junction itself.

The Thomson Effect. Finally, let us consider the heat flow along a wire. If there is a temperature gradient in the wire, we expect the heat current, and of course S^* and T, to vary along the wire. Also $\mathbf{J}_Q$ will, in general, have components into or out of the wire. The heat transported by the electrons will not be constant along the wire, and its variation will give rise to compensating changes in the ∇T term that, as in the Peltier effect, result in the absorption or emission of heat. Let us write the component of Eq. 6.3–9 along the wire with ordinary light-face type and calculate

[10] J. C. A. Peltier, *Ann. Chim. Phys.*, **56**, 371 (1834).

the difference of J_Q at the two ends of a uniform piece of wire of length Δl. We have, since S^* is a function of T and J is constant,

$$\Delta J_Q = \Delta l \frac{\partial J_Q}{\partial l} = -J\left(T\frac{dS^*}{dT}\Delta T + S^*\Delta T\right) - \frac{\partial}{\partial l}(\kappa_Q \nabla T)\Delta l \quad (6.3\text{-}11)$$

ΔT represents the temperature difference between the ends of the piece. From Eq. 6.3-1, we see that $S^*\Delta T = J\rho_c \Delta l + \Delta V_F$, so that

$$\Delta J_Q = -JT\frac{dS^*}{dT}\Delta T - J^2\rho_c \Delta l - J\Delta V_F - \frac{\partial}{\partial l}(\kappa_Q \nabla T)\Delta l$$

The quantity $J^2\rho_c \Delta l$ is clearly the Joule heat produced per unit cross section of the segment of wire, and the product $-J\Delta V_F$ represents the net potential energy carried into the segment of wire by the electrons. The last term represents the heat-conduction process that carries away the net heat generated in the wire. Let us examine the first term on the right.

This term evidently represents another component of heat generation beside the Joule heat of amount $-T\Delta T(dS^*/dT)$ per unit charge, or $-iT\Delta T(dS^*/dT)$ per unit time. This heat is called the Thomson[11] heat. It is usually described in terms of the Thomson coefficient σ_{Th}, given by

$$\sigma_{\text{Th}} = -T\frac{dS^*}{dT} \quad (6.3\text{-}12)$$

which is the rate of Thomson heat generation per unit current and per unit temperature difference. It may be said to arise because the rate of heat flow associated with entropy transport is different at different temperatures.

If a current i is established in a wire, the heat generated in a portion with a temperature difference ΔT between its ends is $\sigma_{\text{Th}}i\,\Delta T$, and the rate of heat generation over the entire wire is

$$\frac{dQ_{\text{Th}}}{dt} = i\int_{T'}^{T''}\sigma_{\text{Th}}(T)\,dT \quad (6.3\text{-}13)$$

This heat generation is reversible like the Peltier heat. Its amount per unit charge is often called the Thomson emf, $\mathcal{E}_{\text{Th}}$, so we can write for a single piece of wire

$$\mathcal{E}_{\text{Th}}(T', T'') = -\int_{T'}^{T''}\sigma_{\text{Th}}\,dT \quad (6.3\text{-}14)$$

[11] W. Thomson (Lord Kelvin), *Trans. Roy. Soc. Edinb.*, **21**, 153 (1847); also *Math. Phys. Papers*, **1**, 232 and 266 (1882).

Relations between the three thermoelectric effects are readily obtained. If we integrate Eq. 6.3–5 by parts and use Eqs. 6.3–10 and 6.3–13, we can write

$$\mathscr{E}_{BA}(T', T'') = T''[S_A^*(T'') - S_B^*(T'')] - T'[S_A^*(T') - S_B^*(T')]$$

$$- \int_{T'}^{T''} T\left[\frac{dS_A^*(T)}{dT} - \frac{dS_B^*(T)}{dT}\right] dT$$

$$= \Pi_{BA}(T'') - \Pi_{BA}(T') + \int_{T'}^{T''} [\sigma_{\mathrm{Th},A}(T) - \sigma_{\mathrm{Th},B}(T)] \, dT$$

or

$$\mathscr{E}_{BA}(T', T'') = \Pi_{BA}(T'') - \Pi_{BA}(T') + \mathscr{E}_{\mathrm{Th},A}(T', T'') - \mathscr{E}_{\mathrm{Th},B}(T', T'')$$

$$(6.3\text{–}15)$$

We see that the Seebeck emf can be written as a sum of the Peltier and Thomson emfs. Mathematically this is accomplished by integration by parts; physically it is the heat transported by the electrons that accounts for the different locations of the Seebeck emf and the two heating effects.

Using Eq. 6.3–6 with Eqs. 6.3–10 and 6.3–12, we can readily derive Kelvin's two relations:

$$\Pi_{BA}(T) = T \frac{d\mathscr{E}_{BA}(T_0, T)}{dT} \qquad (6.3\text{–}16)$$

and

$$\sigma_{\mathrm{Th},A}(T) - \sigma_{\mathrm{Th},B}(T) = -T \frac{d^2\mathscr{E}_{BA}(T_0, T)}{dT^2} \qquad (6.3\text{–}17)$$

where the derivatives do not depend on the value of T_0.

The Peltier heat is useful for controlling the heat supply in certain calorimetric studies and of course can be measured in such experiments. Like the Seebeck emf, its measurement always involves the difference between the appropriate quantities for two metals. The Thomson heat is harder to measure but involves a single substance only. It can be measured by establishing a current in a uniform bar of material which is hotter in the middle than it is at the two ends. Then in one half of the bar the current and temperature gradient are in the same direction, and in the other half they are not. Therefore symmetrically situated points on the bar can be found where Joule heating is the same but the Thomson heats are equal and opposite. A thermocouple temperature-difference measurement, coupled with heat conduction information, will suffice to determine σ_{Th}. Careful measurements made on one substance can be used with Seebeck emf measurements and Eq. 6.3–17 to obtain other Thomson coefficients.

For measurement details[12] and for a discussion of the various effects that enter when magnetic fields and crystalline inhomogeneities are present,[13] the reader is referred elsewhere.

Problem 6.3a. Show from Eq. 6.3–5 that the emf of a thermocouple between temperatures T' and T'' can be found from its values between T' and T_0 and between T'' and T_0 and that $\mathscr{E}_{CA} = \mathscr{E}_{BA} + \mathscr{E}_{CB}$ where A, B, and C denote three different materials.

Problem 6.3b. Materials A, B, and C are connected in a circuit, with junctions at temperature $T_{BC} = T_1$, $T_{CA} = T_2$ and $T_{AB} = T_3$. Write the emf as the sum of the emfs of two ordinary thermocouples, using material C as one member of each pair.

Problem 6.3c. Find approximately the emf of a copper-constantan thermocouple operating between 300°C and 600°C, by estimating the appropriate area in Fig. 6.3b.

Problem 6.3d. Find the Peltier heat at the hot junction of the thermocouple in Problem 6.3c. If the thermocouple circuit has a resistance of 2.0 ohms, find how much heat is absorbed at the hot junction owing to the current produced by the Seebeck emf. How much current should be supplied by an external emf to absorb 0.01 watt at the hot junction?

6.4 Electrochemical Effects

All of the principal electrochemical effects occur with electrolytes, which are solutions of ions in water or other solvents, in contact with metallic conductors known as electrodes.[14] The study of such systems is a major item in physical chemistry, and we shall not try to present here a discussion appropriate to texts in that field. However, there are certain fundamental electrical principles involved in these effects, whose elucidation aids materially in the understanding of electrical conduction in solutions and of the operation of electrical cells. Hence we shall give them brief attention in this section.

Ions in Solution. The first consideration concerns the existence of ions in solution. A pair of ions, like Na^+ and Cl^- or Cu^{++} and $SO_4^=$, would be more easily pulled apart in the gaseous state if they were neutral than

[12] Dike, *op. cit.*; Weber, *loc. cit.*; Putley, *op. cit.*; Goldsmid, *op. cit.*; W. Meissner, *Handbuch der Experimentalphysik*, Leipzig, 1935, Vol. XI, Part 2, pp. 458.

[13] See Domenicali, *loc. cit.*; Callen, *loc. cit.*; De Groot, *op. cit.*; Putley, *op. cit.*

[14] The words "electrolyte," "ion," and "electrode" were introduced by M. Faraday, *Experimental Researches in Electricity*, Taylor and Francis or B. Quaritch, London, 1838; Dover, New York, reprint, 1965, §§661–665.

if they were charged. Their potential energy is lowered on neutralization, so that if they had enough energy to move around freely and independently, they would neutralize each other sooner or later. Why do they not do so in solution? One way of answering this is to say that, owing to the large dielectric constant of water, the attraction between two oppositely charged ions is very weak in water solution.

A better but lengthier answer for our purposes is in terms of energy levels. When an atom is positively ionized, the electron most easily removable is taken away. We say that the highest occupied level has been emptied. Thus the highest occupied level of a neutral atom becomes the lowest vacant level of a singly charged positive ion. If the atom can be ionized twice, the highest occupied level of the singly charged atom becomes the lowest vacant level of the doubly charged atom. Similarly, the highest occupied level of a negative ion that has gained an extra electron is the same as the lowest vacant level of the neutral atom, and so on.

Now, the energies of these various levels are changed when the ions are in solution, for each ion will be surrounded by water molecules, these being permanently polarized. The dipoles will line up so as to weaken the field and therefore reduce the amount of energy gained when an electron comes in to neutralize a positive ion. The same reduction will occur when an electron leaves a negative ion. The energies of the empty levels of positive ions are raised in solution, and the energies of the filled levels in negative ions are lowered.

Any ions that can exist in solution make frequent collisions with each other and with other molecules present. In a steady state, we can be sure that there are almost no vacant electron energy levels in some atoms, molecules, or ions that are below any filled levels in the same or other entities, for otherwise electrons would shift into these vacant levels from the higher filled ones.

We therefore answer our question by saying that pairs of ions that can exist in solution must satisfy the condition that all the vacant levels of the positive ions lie above all the occupied levels of the negative ions. It must also be true that the vacant levels referred to are above any filled levels in the water molecules (or molecules of whatever solvent is used) and similarly the occupied levels of the ions must all be below any vacant levels in the solvent.[15] There are no conduction electrons in solutions, and so there are no levels of the metallic sort to consider. Figure 6.4a shows some typical levels for water solutions.

[15] For details on this and other parts of this section, see R. W. Gurney, *Ions in Solution*, Cambridge University Press, Cambridge, 1936; Dover, New York, reprint. A later book by the same author, *Ionic Processes in Solution*, McGraw-Hill, New York, 1953, treats the same material but largely in terms of proton levels.

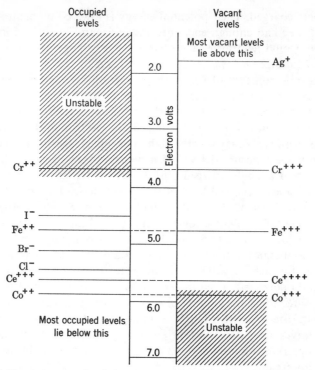

Fig. 6.4a. Electron energy levels in aqueous solutions. (After R. W. Gurney, *Ions in Solution*, Cambridge Univ. Press, Cambridge, 1936, Fig. 43.)

The important quantity for any electron level, vacant or occupied, is the energy required to take an electron from that level to a cavity in the solution. This could be called the work function for the level, but is customarily called the solvated ionization potential and is denoted by $\mathscr{J}_{\pm z}$ where $\pm z$ is the number of electron charges on the ion in question. If V again denotes the cavity potential, we can write for the potential energy of an electron in any particular level an equation like Eq. 2.6–1:

$$-eV_{F,\pm z} = -e\mathscr{J}_{\pm z} - eV \qquad (6.4\text{–}1)$$

Sometimes an electron transfer to or from a molecule is followed immediately by another energy change such as a dissociation or a combination process. In this case, we can define $\mathscr{J}_{\pm z}$ so as to include the overall energy change.

This formula 6.4–1 for the effective Fermi level $V_{F,\pm z}$ is strictly correct only at absolute zero. As the temperature rises and higher levels become partially occupied, $V_{F,\pm z}$ will also rise. At ordinary temperatures however, Eq. 6.4–1 is a fairly good approximation.

Another factor governing the existence of ions in solution is that of the energy with which pairs of ions of opposite sign may come together to form a crystalline solid. If the potential energy per ion pair is less in the crystalline solid than the energy of the same pair in solution, the ions will not remain in the dissolved state.

Electrodes. If a piece of metal is inserted into a solution, there are four elementary possibilities for charge transfer. Electrons may pass from the metal to vacant levels in ions or molecules in the solution, or second, they may pass from filled solution levels into the metal. Third, atoms at the surface of the metal may leave their conduction electrons behind and pass as ions into the solution, and finally ions of the same atomic species may leave the solution and become attached to the surface of the metal. (We say they are "adsorbed" on the surface.) The possibility of a different sort of atoms becoming adsorbed is complicated, because when enough "foreign" atoms have arrived, the surface becomes plated with them and further arrivals find a surface of their own kind. Such cases, along with other cases of two-step chemical reactions, etc., will not be treated here.

We can treat these four possibilities all in terms of energy levels. If electrons transfer in either direction between the metal and a certain electron ("reaction") level in the solution, this level and the Fermi level in the metal will come to equality at equilibrium in the same way as for metal-to-metal contacts. In fact, we can write

$$V_{F,m} = \phi + V_m = V_{F,\pm z} = \mathscr{J}_{\pm z} + V_s \qquad (6.4\text{--}2)$$

where $V_{F,m}$ is the Fermi potential of the metal, V_m its cavity potential, ϕ its work function, and V_s the cavity potential of the solution.

There is, of course, a contact or cavity PD between metal and solution given by

$$V_m - V_s = \mathscr{J}_{\pm z} - \phi \qquad (6.4\text{--}3)$$

(Strictly, a term of the form (kT/e) times the logarithm of a certain concentration ratio must be added on the right side of Eq. 6.4–3, and corresponding terms are needed in Eq. 6.4–2.)

The transfer of an ion from solution to metal can, for the purposes of energy-balance calculations, be thought of as the transfer of an electron from the metal to the ion when it comes near the metal, followed by the adsorption of the neutral atom onto the surface. As indicated above, we can represent the combined action or the reverse transfer by a single work function, which we can also call $\mathscr{J}_{\pm z}$.

The principal transfer that occurs in any particular case is determined by whether the Fermi level of the metal is initially above the lowest vacant level in the solution, below the highest occupied level, or in between these two. In the first two cases, transfers will occur when uncharged metal is put into contact with uncharged solution. In the last case, no change can occur unless $V_m - V_s$ is first adjusted; electrodes in this condition, when no transfer can occur, are called "ideally polarized electrodes." Many electrolytic processes will not take place until a certain minimum cavity or Fermi PD is established.

A chemical cell is a combination of a solution and two electrodes or two solutions and two electrodes. In the latter case, the two solutions are either kept from mixing by a porous diaphragm which allows ions to pass through to establish electrical equilibrium or are separated by a vessel or tube containing a third solution whose mixing with either of the other two does not produce unwanted difficulties. If the charge transfers that occur at the two electrodes are of different types the V_F's in the electrodes will at equilibrium be at different levels, so that an emf will be produced as we indicated in Section 5.3.

Suppose, for instance, that we denote the two electrodes and corresponding reaction levels by single and double primes. Then from 6.4–2 we have for the emf

$$\mathscr{E} = V'_{F,m} - V''_{F,m} = \mathscr{J}_{\pm z'} - \mathscr{J}_{\pm z''} \qquad (6.4\text{–}4)$$

where V_s disappears because it is the same throughout the solution.

When a current is passed from electrode to solution or vice versa, there will be a small shift of the cavity PD from the equilibrium value, for, in order to have a finite rate of charge transfer, there has to be a finite difference ΔV in the V_F's. The relation between ΔV and the resulting current density J in one direction across the interface is exponential in nature, generally of the form

$$J = c \exp \left[\alpha \, \Delta V / kT \right] - c \exp \left[(1 - \alpha) \, \Delta V / kT \right] \qquad (6.4\text{–}5)$$

where c depends on the concentrations and α is a constant between 0 and 1 called the transfer coefficient. Thus it only takes a small difference in the Fermi potentials to produce a considerable current across the interface. This added PD is called the "overvoltage" or "overpotential." For most circuit applications, it can be approximately included in the internal potential drop ir. The exponential character of the current-voltage relation holds only so long as some other process that limits the current does not take effect, such as processes restricting the rate at which ions can get to the interface from the body of the solution. If α for a particular electrode and direction of current is considerably greater than $\frac{1}{2}$, the magnitude of J will be very much greater for positive ΔV's than for negative ones, thus accounting for the asymmetrical or rectification properties of certain cells and of electrolytic condensers.

Electrolytic capacitors are formed by choosing appropriate electrodes and solutions with one rectifying and one non-rectifying pair and running current in the direction of low conductivity long enough to build up a suitable layer of chemical-reaction products at the interface of the rectifying electrode. This will require a large overpotential. If then a considerably smaller overpotential is applied, almost no current will be passed, and the deposited chemical layer will act as a layer of dielectric between the electrode and the solution. On a macroscopic scale, this layer can be extremely thin, leading to very large capacitance values in a small space.

Faraday's Laws. When current passes across a metal-solution boundary, a chemical change occurs. If a current i passes for a time t, then it coulombs pass through, or it/e electrons. If each atom, molecule, or ion involved has a valence z (i.e., carries z electrons), the number of such chemical entities transferred will be it/ze. The mass of each in grams is the molecular weight M divided by Avogadro's number N_0, which is defined as the number of oxygen atoms which have collectively a mass of 16.0000 g ($M = 16.0000$ for oxygen). Therefore, the total mass m deposited or dissolved in the chemical action is

$$m = \frac{it}{ze} \cdot \frac{M}{N_0} = \frac{itM}{z\mathscr{F}} = \frac{Q}{\mathscr{F}} \cdot \frac{M}{z} \qquad (6.4\text{--}6)$$

in grams, where M/z is called the "chemical equivalent" of the molecular species in question, $Q = it$ is the charge in coulombs passed between electrode and solution, and the quantity $\mathscr{F}$, called the "faraday," is given by

$$\mathscr{F} = N_0 e = 6.0228 \times 10^{23} \times 1.60210 \times 10^{-19}$$
$$= 96{,}491 \pm 2 \text{ coulombs}$$

Accurate measurements of the faraday using Eq. 6.4–5 are taken together with a determination of N_0 from X rays to provide one of the most accurate values of e now available.

The two laws of electrolysis discovered by Faraday[16] are both embodied in Eq. 6.4–6—namely, that (1) the mass m deposited or dissolved is proportional to the chemical equivalent, for several cells through which the same Q is passed and (2) m for any one cell is proportional to Q.

Electrolytic Conduction. Although current at a metal-solution interface is usually carried by one type of transfer, current in the body of a solution is transported by all the ionic types that are present. Any ionic species will move under the influence of an electric field at a constant speed proportional to the field strength. We write for the magnitude of the speed of any ion

$$v = uE \qquad (6.4\text{--}7)$$

[16] M. Faraday, *op. cit.*, §§ 713–821.

where the proportionality constant u is called the "mobility." When there are, as in a simple case, one species each of positive and negative ion, the total current density J is given by a sum of terms for each species

$$J = n_+ z_+ eu_+ E + n_- z_- eu_- E \qquad (6.4\text{--}8)$$

where $z_+ e$ and $z_- e$ are the magnitudes of the charge on each species of ion, and n_+ and n_- are the numbers of each per unit volume. Since the solution must be neutral at any interior point, $n_+ z_+ = n_- z_-$. The conductivity $\sigma_c = J/E$ is thus given by

$$\sigma_c = n_+ z_+ e(u_+ + u_-) \qquad (6.4\text{--}9)$$

The fraction of J carried by either ionic species is called the transference number τ for that species. We have clearly

$$\tau_+ = \frac{u_+}{u_+ + u_-} \; ; \qquad \tau_- = \frac{u_-}{u_+ + u_-} \; ; \qquad \tau_+ + \tau_- = 1 \quad (6.4\text{--}10)$$

How can it be that the current is carried by two carrier types in the interior of the solution and by one type only in a discharge process at an electrode? Part of the answer is that the concentration of positive and negative ions near each electrode must change to make up for the difference. Let us call a region near the negative electrode (i.e., the one toward which the positive ions move) within which all the concentration changes occur R_-, and the corresponding region at the other electrode R_+. Then of the current i that enters R_- from the main body of the solution, a fraction τ_+ is carried by the positive ions. If all of the current passing from R_- to the electrode is carried by the same positive ions, an amount of ions corresponding to the current difference $(i - \tau_+ i)$ is removed from R_-. This difference, however, is equal to $\tau_- i$, the amount of negative charge carried out of R_- into the main body of solution by the negative ions. Hence the net result is to reduce the quantity of positive and negative ions in R_- by equal amounts. Measurement of this reduction in quantity constitutes one way of determining τ_+ and τ_-.

This is not all the answer to our question, however. We do not expect τ_+ and τ_- to change very much as the concentration varies, so that except right next to the electrode, the positive and negative ion currents will be uniform and cause no concentration changes. Next to an electrode, however, ions of the same sign as the electrode move away and their concentration near it will get small very rapidly. The region near the electrode then acquires the opposite sign of charge, positive in case the electrode is negative.

Unless negative ions move back into this region, the positive charge there will reduce the field produced by the negative electrode. Positive ions that enter the region will slow down and pile up, so that the current cannot be maintained. Actually, as soon as any species of ion varies considerably in concentration from place to place, thermal diffusion will cause ions to enter the region where the concentration is weak. This diffusion plays an essential and, needless to say, complicated role in readjusting the current at an interface. The exact mechanism of this readjustment is very difficult to calculate even in ideally simplified cases.

Above all, it should be noted that a true steady state is never attainable in electrolysis, because of these progressive concentration changes, as well as the using up of electrode materials. The methods used to maintain a relatively constant emf and internal resistance in practical cells will not be discussed here.

The diffusion tendency just mentioned will produce an emf between different solutions, as in the two-solution cells referred to above. However, a judicious choice of the solution used for connecting two halves of a cell can reduce this emf to almost negligible proportions.

Types of Cells. Of the many types of cells in common use, mention will be made here of only four: the dry cell, fuel cells, the lead storage cell, and the Weston standard cell.

The Leclanche or dry cell consists of a zinc can filled with a paste-like solution of ammonium chloride (NH_4Cl) and zinc chloride ($ZnCl_2$) in water. At the center there is a carbon rod surrounded by a mixture of insoluble manganese oxides, MnO_2 and Mn_2O_3. The solution is a conductor because it contains negative chlorine ions (Cl^-) and positive zinc and ammonium ions (Zn^{++} and NH_4^+) that are free to move as charge carriers. The negative electrode is the zinc can. Since the principal reaction there involves a transfer of zinc ions, it is convenient to describe first the cavity potentials of metal and solution, rather than a balance of electron levels.

Zinc atoms at the electrode surface can fairly easily give up their two valence electrons to the metal and enter the solution as zinc ions. Since water molecules are dipoles, their negative ends can turn to attract the positive zinc ions, so that the dipoles effectively pull zinc ions off the metal surface. Thermal agitation of the zinc atoms assists this process. Every ion that comes off will leave the metal negative, since two electrons are left behind. The cavity potential of the solution becomes positive, and there will be a layer of positive ions just outside the metal, with a corresponding layer of negative charge (electrons) just inside the metal. The process will stop when the electric field is just strong enough to balance the attraction of the water dipoles. Such a pair of layers in a chemical cell is called a double layer. Its thickness is fixed by atomic dimensions, so the definite E at equilibrium corresponds to a definite cavity PD between metal and solution (see Problem 1.7i for a numerical example).

If the cavity PD were reduced, more zinc ions would pass into solution until the PD was restored to its equilibrium value. If electrons were continually removed from the zinc case so that the cavity PD were kept below the equilibrium value, zinc ions would enter into the solution steadily, at a rate depending on the change in PD. Similarly, if the PD were kept larger than the equilibrium value, zinc ions would be continuously pulled back to the case.

Any particular zinc ion at the interface can therefore exist in two different states or levels—as an ion in the double layer or as a neutral atom on the surface. Consideration of an ionization potential and a work function for Zn^{++} can lead to an equation for the cavity PD analogous to Eq. 6.4–3 (cf. Problem 6.4b). However, $\mathscr{J}_{+2}$ can be so defined for this reaction that Eq. 6.4–3, together with ϕ for zinc metal, will give the correct value of $V_m - V_s$.

At the carbon rod, there can occur a fairly complex chemical reaction, involving the transformation of ammonium chloride to ammonium hydroxide and of MnO_2 to Mn_2O_3, accompanied by a transfer of electrons from the carbon rod (the carbon itself is inert).[17] As indicated above, we can treat the electron transfer as a passage from the Fermi level in the carbon to a certain level in the manganese oxide mixture. We can consider all the energy changes involved in the reaction to be lumped together and included in the electron energy jump, leading to an effective $\mathscr{J}_{-2}$ for the manganese oxide mixture. We can then write

$$\mathscr{E} = \mathscr{J}_{-2} - \mathscr{J}_{+2} \tag{6.4–11}$$

where the sign is chosen to give the proper positive polarity to the carbon rod. The reactions are not reversible because reverse currents will introduce still other reactions in the manganese oxide mixture.

Fuel cells involve reactions at neutral electrodes like the carbon rod in the dry cell, but the reacting materials are usually gases brought in continuously. For instance, hydrogen or hydrocarbon molecules might give up electrons (i.e., become "oxidized") at one electrode and oxygen molecules might receive electrons at the other. The result is that energy that

---

[17] The process can be described by three reactions:

$$2MnO_2 + 2NH_4^+ + 2e^- \rightarrow 2MnOOH + 2NH_3$$

$$2MnOOH + 2NH_4^+ \rightarrow MnO_2 + Mn^{++} + 2NH_3 + 2H_2O$$

$$MnO_2 + 4NH_4^+ + 2e^- \rightarrow Mn^{++} + 4NH_3 + 2H_2O$$

For details on this and other so-called primary cells, see the article "Primary Cells," in the *Encyclopedia of Chemical Technology*, 2nd ed., Interscience, New York, 1964, Vol. 3, pp. 111–138; also G. W. Vinal, *Primary Batteries*, John Wiley, New York, 1950.

otherwise could be released on combustion is available electrically, often with quite high efficiency. For details on fuel materials, catalysts, membranes, electrodes, the reader is referred elsewhere.[18]

The lead storage cell involves reversible processes at each plate, there being no secondary reactions to remove the products found when the cell delivers energy. Hence chemical energy can be restored by reversing the current. The reaction at one electrode involves the change of a lead atom with four units of positive charge, Pb^{++++}, to the divalent ion Pb^{++}; at the other plate the reaction is from neutral lead, Pb, to Pb^{++}. For the chemical details, the reader is referred elsewhere.[19] Such a cell is generally characterized in an electrical sense by the charge in ampere-hours it can deliver at a standard current.

The Weston standard cell is used as a reproducible laboratory source of emf for standardization purposes. It contains a solution, saturated or unsaturated, of cadmium sulfate ($CdSO_4$). The positive electrode consists of mercury metal covered with crystals of the nearly insoluble salt mercurous sulfate (Hg_2SO_4). When a mercury ion leaves the metal, it picks up a sulfate ion from the solution and the two deposit together on the salt crystals. Thus the effective reaction is the deposition of $SO_4^=$.

The negative electrode is a solution of cadmium metal in mercury. In the saturated form of the cell, crystals of cadmium sulfate, $CdSO_4$, are placed on the mercury-cadmium solution. As at the other electrode, a transfer of Cd to Cd^{++} results in Cd^{++} and $SO_4^=$ joining the crystal, so the electrode is essentially another form of $SO_4^=$ electrode, involving a different energy change.

The resulting emf turns out to be nearly independent of concentration because the same ion is deposited or dissolved in the two different reactions, so that new cells can be made up to have very closely the same emf as an originally calibrated one. This value, which is temperature dependent, has been determined to be, at $t°C$,

$$\mathscr{E}(t) = 1.018646 - 0.0000406(t - 20)$$

$$- 0.00000093(t - 20)^2 + 0.00000001(t - 20)^3 \text{ v} \quad (6.4\text{--}12)$$

---

[18] *Encyclopedia of Chemical Technology, op. cit.*, pp. 139–160 and references given there; also Morris Eisenberg, "Design and Scale-up Considerations for Electrochemical Fuel Cells," *Advances in Electrochemistry and Electrochemical Engineering*, Vol. 2, Interscience, 1962, pp. 235–291.

[19] Cf. G. W. Vinal, *Storage Batteries*, John Wiley, New York, 4th ed., 1955; *Encyclopedia of Chemical Technology, op. cit.*, pp. 249–271; or a short account in H. J. Creighton and W. A. Koehler, *Principles and Applications of Electrochemistry*, 2nd ed., John Wiley, New York, 1944, Vol. II, Chapter IV.

The unsaturated cell is more portable and has a lower temperature coefficient, but the emf of each new cell has to be calibrated against a standard.[20]

Problem 6.4a. Let the ionization potential (energy necessary to remove one electron) of an atom be $\mathscr{I}$ in vacuo and $\mathscr{J}$ in solution. Let the work done in removing the ion from the solution into a cavity be W and the work of removing a neutral atom be W_0. Find the relation between these four quantities, and give arguments to show that $\mathscr{J} < \mathscr{I}$.

Problem 6.4b. Let the work done in removing an ion of charge $\pm ze$ from the surface of a metal into a cavity within that metal be $\mathscr{I}_{\pm z}$, and the work done in removing the same ion from the solution to a cavity within the solution be $W_{\pm z}$. Find an expression for the cavity PD between metal and solution at equilibrium in terms of these quantities.

Problem 6.4c. Find the number of ampere-hours per cm^2 required to plate a coating of silver 0.1 mm thick on an electrode if the density of the silver layer is 10.50 g/cm^3. (At. wt of silver = 107.88; valence = 1.)

Problem 6.4d. Suppose that at the negative electrode of a cell the current is all carried by the passage of negative ions into the solution. Find out what happens to the number of ions in region R_- as described in the text.

Problem 6.4e. Tell qualitatively why a Daniell cell, consisting of zinc, a solution of zinc sulfate, a porous membrane, a solution of copper sulfate, and copper, will produce an emf with the copper *positive*, whereas when zinc and copper are in direct contact the contact potential difference between them is such as to make the copper *negative*. Assume the solutions on the two sides of the membrane to have negligible cavity PD.

Problem 6.4f. It is observed that if sulfuric acid is dissolved in water to give H^+ and $SO_4^=$ ions, along with a very small concentration of OH^- ions from thermal dissociation of the H_2O water molecules, and a current is passed through the solution between platinum electrodes, H_2 is discharged at the negative electrode in accordance with $2H^+ + 2e \rightarrow H_2$, whereas at the positive electrode, we have $4OH^- \rightarrow 2H_2O + O_2 + 4e$. Nothing appears to happen to the $SO_4^=$. What fact can you infer about the solution that would explain this observation?

Problem 6.4g. Chemists call positive ions "cations" because they migrate toward the electrode that is made negative when an external emf is applied (and is hence called the "cathode" in accordance with standard usage). Similarly, negative ions that proceed toward the positive "anode" are called "anions." Explain why cations migrate toward the positive electrode of a cell that is a source of emf, and vice versa for anions.

---

[20] See references in footnote 17.

6.5 Debye-Hückel Theory for Solutions and Plasmas

We conclude this chapter with a brief version of Debye and Hückel's theory of the way in which the discrete nature of ions in a solution or plasma modifies the charge and field distributions we should expect in a continuous conducting medium.

Consider first the migration of ions toward a plane boundary when a field is initially imposed normal to the boundary, say with a value E normal to the surface and directed away from it. Ions would then migrate to the surface to provide a positive surface charge $\sigma = \epsilon_0 E$ on which the flux of E could terminate, thus adjusting the interior to the zero-field equilibrium conditions. However, individual ions at temperature T will move about randomly, and those in the surface layer will come and go. On the average the field will penetrate a certain distance into the solution or plasma.

To study this penetration, we proceed as follows. Let the normal to the surface be in the x-direction, with $x = 0$ at the surface and the conducting medium on the positive side. In a small volume element $d\tau$ at a depth x not far from the boundary, there would be on the average more positive ions than negative. If the potential is $V(x)$, the excess potential energy of an ion of charge z_+e at that place would be $z_+e[V(x) - V_s]$ where V_s is the cavity potential in the main body of the solution. The potential energy of a negative ion of charge $-z_-e$ would correspondingly be $-z_-e[V(x) - V_s]$. The mean density of ions of a given kind will be the density in the main body of the solution multiplied by the Boltzmann exponential factor $e^{-W/kt}$ that gives the probability for a molecule or ion to have an energy W. Thus, when there are n_+ positive ions and n_- negative ions per unit volume in the body of the solution, we have for the average charge density at x

$$\rho = n_+ z_+ e \exp\left\{-z_+ e[V(x) - V_s]/kT\right\}$$
$$- n_- z_- e \exp\left\{+z_- e[V(x) - V_s]/kT\right\} \quad (6.5\text{--}1)$$

This formula neglects the influence of individual ions on each other and thus will be reasonably correct only for dilute solutions. The degree of dilution necessary for its validity can be estimated by setting the mutual potential energy of two ions separated by their mean distance in the solution equal to a small fraction, say, $\frac{1}{5}$, of the mean thermal energy kT. Thus considering only positive ions, we write

$$\frac{z_+^2 e^2}{4\pi\epsilon_0 \kappa r_m} \lesssim \tfrac{1}{5}kT \quad (6.5\text{--}2)$$

where we can take $r_m = n_+^{-1/3}$, as the mean distance between ions if arranged in a cubic array. The dielectric constant κ is about 80 for water and of course is unity for a completely ionized plasma. The condition for validity of 6.5-1 can then be written[21]

$$n_+ \leqslant \left(\frac{0.8\pi\epsilon_0\kappa kT}{z_+^2 e^2}\right)^3 \tag{6.5-3a}$$

For a binary salt in which $z_+ = z_-$, the concentration c in moles/liter is limited by

$$c \leqslant \frac{1}{10^3 N_0}\left(\frac{0.8\pi\epsilon_0\kappa kT}{z_+^2 e^2}\right)^3 \tag{6.5-3b}$$

For aqueous solutions at 20°C where $\kappa = 80$, we find $c \leqslant 0.03/z_+^6$ moles/liter, whereas for a plasma at 2000°K, the condition is $n_+ \leqslant 4 \times 10^{19}/z_+^6$ particles per m³.

If $V - V_s$ in 6.5-1 is large compared to kT, the effects of thermal motion in spreading out the surface charge will be small but hard to calculate. Let us then consider the case in which $V - V_s$ is small enough that we can replace the exponentials by the first two terms of their expansions. Since overall neutrality requires that $n_+z_+ = n_-z_-$, we have

$$\rho \simeq -n_+z_+e^2(z_+ + z_-)[V(x) - V_s]/kT \tag{6.5-4}$$

Poisson's equation 3.8-5 then gives us an equation we can readily solve for $V(x) - V_s$:

$$\nabla^2 V = \frac{\partial^2 V(x)}{\partial x^2} = -\frac{\rho}{\kappa\epsilon_0} \simeq \frac{n_+z_+(z_+ + z_-)e^2}{\kappa\epsilon_0 kT}[V(x) - V_s] \tag{6.5-5}$$

This equation has solutions that are positive or negative exponentials in x; the negative exponential must be the correct one as $V(x) - V_s$ must go to zero for large x. We have then

$$V(x) - V_s = V_0 e^{-x/\lambda_D} \tag{6.5-6}$$

where λ_D is the so-called Debye length

$$\lambda_D = \left[\frac{\kappa\epsilon_0 kT}{n_+z_+(z_+ + z_-)e^2}\right]^{1/2} \tag{6.5-7}$$

giving a measure of how far the field "penetrates" into the conductor. As an example, for when $T = 293°K$, $\kappa = 80$ (for water), $z_+ = z_- = 1$, and $n = 10^{25}$ m⁻³ ($c = 0.015$ moles/liter), we have $\lambda_D = 22 \times 10^{-10}$ m. For a plasma with $T = 2000°K$, $\kappa = 1$, $z_+ = z_- = 1$, and $n = 10^{18}$ m⁻³, we have $\lambda_D = 2.2 \times 10^{-6}$ m. We can take this value as measuring the thickness of the "sheath" of charge at the boundary of the plasma. When

---

[21] A derivation of this limitation based on correlations between ions and its effect on fluctuations is given by C. L. Longmire, *Elementary Plasma Physics*, Interscience, New York, 1963, pp. 162–8.

more than two ionic species are present, $n_+z_+(z_+ + z_-)$ in 6.5–7 must be replaced by $\sum_i n_i z_i^2$ where the summation is over the different ionic species.

The value of V_0 is related to the surface charge density, since with no flux in the body of the medium, we must have $\sigma = -\epsilon_0(\partial V/\partial x)_{x=0} = \epsilon_0 V_0/\lambda_D$ (assuming no dielectric outside the surface of the fluid). Thus we can finally write for the potential as a function of depth the equation

$$V(x) = V_s + \frac{\sigma \lambda_D}{\epsilon_0} e^{-x/\lambda_D} \qquad (6.5\text{–}8)$$

The potential $V(x)$ is shown graphically in Fig. 6.5a. In order to estimate $V_0 = \sigma \lambda_D/\epsilon_0$, we should first note that σ/ϵ_0 is the value of E outside the

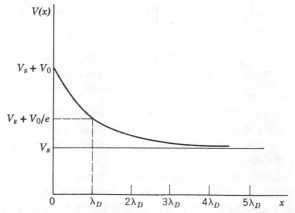

Fig. 6.5a. Distribution of potential with distance from a charged boundary inside a plasma or electrolyte, according to the Debye-Hückel theory (Eq. 6.5-6). The density of charge is proportional to $V(x) - V_s$, according to Eq. 6.5-5.

surface, and that $E\lambda_D$ is the potential drop in a distance λ_D outside the surface. Whether $E\lambda_D$ is large or small compared to kT will depend on the surrounding details, such as the charge distribution in the double layer at an electrode. These details are, however, beyond the scope of this book.

Another application of Debye-Hückel theory is to the average atmosphere of ions of one sign that surround a single one of the other sign. The situation is quite similar to the one we have just tackled, but the geometry is different, for the mean potential around an ion will be a function of the radial distance r from it. (As the ion moves we assume the origin of coordinates to move with it.) Changing $V(x)$ to $V(r)$ in 6.5–5 and using 6.5–7, we have

$$\nabla^2 V = \frac{1}{r^2}\frac{\partial}{\partial r}\left[r^2\frac{\partial V(r)}{\partial r}\right] = \frac{1}{r}\frac{\partial^2}{\partial r^2}[rV(r) - rV_s] \simeq \frac{V(r) - V_s}{\lambda_D^{\,2}} \quad (6.5\text{–}9)$$

It is easy to show that two independent solutions of this equation are given by

$$r[V(r) - V_s] = V_1 \exp(\pm r/\lambda_D)$$

Again we must choose the negative exponential. We have then

$$V(r) - V_s = \frac{V_1}{r} e^{-r/\lambda_D} \tag{6.5–10}$$

To evaluate the constant V_1, we can assume that no ions can approach within a distance a of the central ion, and that the field there is the same as the field of a point charge immersed in a dielectric, Eq. 3.8–4. Thus we have

$$E_r = -\frac{\partial V}{\partial r} = \frac{V_1}{r^2} e^{-r/\lambda_D}\left(1 + \frac{r}{\lambda_D}\right) = \frac{z_+e}{4\pi\kappa\epsilon_0 r^2} \qquad \text{when} \quad r = a$$

or

$$V_1 = \frac{z_+e\ e^{a/\lambda_D}}{4\pi\kappa\epsilon_0(1 + a/\lambda_D)} \simeq \frac{z_+e}{4\pi\kappa\epsilon_0} \tag{6.5–11}$$

since λ_D is usually very much larger than a.

This result may be used to evaluate the contribution of the ionic atmosphere of each charged particle to the work necessary to take it from the solution into a cavity, and thus to calculate activity coefficients, but we shall not work the details out here.[22]

Let us calculate the mean charge residing between r and $r + dr$ of the ion whose atmosphere we have just found. The volume charge density is $-\kappa\epsilon_0$ times the right-hand side of 6.5–9, and the volume in a spherical shell of thickness dr is $4\pi r^2\ dr$. Hence we have

$$f(r)\ dr = -\frac{\kappa\epsilon_0}{\lambda_D{}^2} 4\pi r^2[V(r) - V_s]$$

$$= -\frac{z_+er\ e^{-r/\lambda_D}}{\lambda_D{}^2} \tag{6.5–12}$$

Figure 6.5b shows a graph of $(r/\lambda_D)e^{-r/\lambda_D}$. The maximum occurs at $r = \lambda_D$, so that the important region of the ion atmosphere is in the neighborhood of a radius equal to the Debye length. When r_m is of the order of λ_D or smaller, ions of both signs will be present in the region of the maximum of 6.5–12, and will tend to modify the distribution given by 6.5–12, so we see again that it is accurate only in the limit of very dilute solutions. Finally, the Debye-Hückel theory is derived on the assumption that each ion behaves like a point charge with a Coulomb law field. Within

[22] Cf. R. W. Gurney, *Ions in Solution, loc. cit.*, Chap. XI; T. L. Hill, *An Introduction to Statistical Thermodynamics*, Addison-Wesley, Reading, Mass., 1960, Chapter 18.

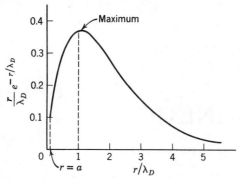

Fig. 6.5b. Distribution function for ions surrounding a given ion in the Debye-Hückel theory for weak electrolytes and dilute plasmas.

distances comparable to a, however, the structure of an ion would make itself felt and the simple Coulomb potential would fail. This is another reason why the theory is only valid for dilute solutions, in which ions very rarely get within a few times a of each other.

Problem 6.5a. Show that the validity condition for 6.5–1 implies that an approximate lower limit for λ_D is $16z_+{}^4$ angstrom units. Assume $z_+ = z_-$.

Problem 6.5b. Find the ion density in a plasma at 2000°K such that $r_m = \lambda_D$.

Problem 6.5c. An aqueous solution of 0.01 molar sodium chloride (NaCl) at 20°C is in contact with an inert metal electrode. Assume that the region between metal and solution can be treated as a "capacitor" of thickness 3.0 Å and dielectric constant 1.0. If a PD of 0.012 volt exists across this "capacitor," find how much PD exists between the surface layer of the solution proper and the main body of the solution. Also find the depth at which V is within $1/e$ of V_s.

Problem 6.5d. If the "capacitor" in Problem 6.5c had a mean dielectric constant of 40, how would Eq. 6.5–8 have to be modified, and how would the answers be affected?

Problem 6.5e. Find the thickness within which 90% of the charge is contained in the sheath of a plasma with 10^{15} electrons per cubic centimeter and an equal number of singly charged positive ions at an effective temperature of 10^6 °K.

Problem 6.5f. A body of gas ceases to function as a plasma if λ_D is of macroscopic dimensions. For what value of n does λ_D become 1 cm when $T = 10^6$ °K, $z_+ = 2$, and $z_- = 1$? When $T = 2 \times 10^3$ °K?

Chapter 7

THE MAGNETIC FIELD

7.1 Introduction

Magnetic forces are forces between currents or moving charges. The most fundamental approach in studying them might be to inquire into the force between a pair of moving charges. However, the expression for this force is too complicated to be made the basis of a simple definition of a magnetic field quantity. We shall take the simpler approach of studying first the forces on a moving charge produced by any unspecified external agent. This force is given by the Lorentz force law, which is not only a physical law but at the same time a definition of a magnetic-field quantity. We shall discuss several straightforward applications of this law.

Our next step will be to specify the way in which magnetic fields are produced, introducing the law due primarily to Ampère, but in certain special forms also to Laplace, Biot, and Savart. Faraday's law for induced emfs will then be taken up as an experimentally verified extension of the Lorentz force law. These laws and their applications will prepare the way for a discussion of magnetic dipoles and magnetized materials in Chapter 8.

7.2 The Force on a Moving Charge and the Definition of B

In Chapter 1, we considered the force on a charge at rest in the observer's or laboratory frame of reference. We saw that we can write the force in a way that separates the properties of the charge, i.e., the magnitude q, from the properties of the surroundings—the vector **E**. Equation 1.2–2, $\mathbf{F} = q\mathbf{E}$, not only expresses the definition of **E**, but also states a law of physics, namely, that the force on a charge at rest at a given point in the vicinity of other charges at rest is proportional to its magnitude q and has a direction that is the same for all positive values of q, being opposite for all negative q's.

Now, if the surroundings contain moving charges (currents) but the test charge q is still at rest, the same law is found to hold, and we make the same definition of $\mathbf{E}$. In this case, however, $\mathbf{E}$ may be no longer given by Coulomb's law, as in Eq. 1.2–3, and of course it may vary in time (Section 7.14 will give the law according to which $\mathbf{E}$ is produced by moving charges).

If, on the other hand, the surrounding charges are stationary and q moves, $\mathbf{F} = q\mathbf{E}$ again holds and $\mathbf{E}$ is of necessity found from Coulomb's law. That is, the expression $q\mathbf{E}$ gives a force that is independent of the velocity $\mathbf{v}$ of the charge. Problems 1.6a and b in Chapter 1, Figures 2.2d to f in Chapter 2, and the diode calculation in Sections 1.10 and 5.2 deal with moving charges in an electrostatic field.

Now let us consider the case in which both the charge q and its neighbors are moving. In order to separate again the effects of the surroundings and the properties of the charge, we shall focus our attention on a particular point $\mathscr{P}$ at a particular time t and ask what force is exerted on q when it is passing through $\mathscr{P}$ at t with some given velocity $\mathbf{v}$. We can imagine an experiment in which particles (electrons and ions) carrying various charges are accelerated by some apparatus which allows them to pass through $\mathscr{P}$ at time t with various speeds and directions. Study of the resulting deflections of these particles will allow a determination of their accelerations when at $\mathscr{P}$ and the force on each can be found by $\mathbf{F} = M\mathbf{a}$.[1]

The results of such experiments and of many other less direct ones is that in addition to the velocity-independent force $\mathbf{F} = q\mathbf{E}$, as seen in a particular reference frame, there is a velocity-dependent force which can always be written in the form

$$\mathbf{F} = q\mathbf{v} \times \mathbf{B} \qquad (7.2\text{–}1)$$

We can then write a general expression for the entire force on a given charge at a given place and time:

$$\mathbf{F} = q\mathbf{E} + q\mathbf{v} \times \mathbf{B} \qquad (7.2\text{–}2a)$$

an equation known as the Lorentz force law.[2] (The entire expression on the right is called the Lorentz force; the second term is called the magnetic

---

[1] To be accurate, our experiments require that the test charges not react appreciably on the surroundings and that the experimental errors in locating the positions of particles near $\mathscr{P}$ and their times of passage be small in comparison to the space and time variations of the effects under study.

[2] This law which we now take as fundamental was derived by H. A. Lorentz from theories of Clausius and others and published in *Archiv. Néerl.* **xxv** 363 (1892), especially Chapter IV, pp. 432 ff. Lorentz usually gets credited with this law, even though it was first found by O. Heaviside, *Phil. Mag.*, **27**, 324 (1889).

force, although occasionally the name of Lorentz is attached to this term alone.)

The vector **B** is independent of q and **v**. It depends only on the moving charges in the surroundings. For historical reasons this vector is called the "magnetic induction"; another common name is "magnetic flux density." We shall use it as our fundamental magnetic field quantity; the simple name "magnetic field" is often adequate.

While Eq. 7.2-1 constitutes a definition of the vector **B**, this formula conceals the symmetry character of the physical situation, which we shall

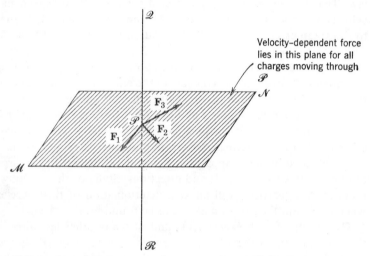

Velocity–dependent force lies in this plane for all charges moving through $\mathscr{P}$

Fig. 7.2a. Velocity-dependent forces on charges moving at $\mathscr{P}$. F_1, F_2, F_3 represent forces for three different q's and v's.

now make explicit. In the first place, note that we could equally well have chosen the opposite direction for **B**, either by writing the vectors in 7.2–1 in reversed order or by defining the vector product with a left-hand instead of a right-hand rule. Let us therefore describe the situation without explicit reference to the vector **B**. In what way does the Lorentz force **F** depend on **v**? Equation 7.2–1 shows us (a) that **F** is zero if **v** is directed in either sense along a certain line in space ($\mathscr{2R}$ in Fig. 7.2a), (b) that the force is always in the plane perpendicular to this line (plane $\mathscr{MN}$ in the figure), (c) that the force is proportional to the projection of **v** in the plane, (v_{proj} in Fig. 7.2b) and (d) that **F** is at right angles to v_{proj}. From (c) the magnitude of **F** can be written

$$F = Bqv_{\text{proj}} \qquad (7.2\text{-}3)$$

To specify its direction without using the direction of **B**, we must first specify the plane $\mathscr{MN}$ or its normal $\mathscr{2R}$, and then tell how its direction is related to that of v_{proj}. A little thought on the vector product in 7.2–1 will show that for all vectors v through $\mathscr{P}$, F and v_{proj} are related in the same sense of circulation or rotation. That is, if as in Fig. 7.2b we draw a circulating arrow showing the direction through which F should be rotated by 90° to get to v_{proj}, this circulating arrow applies to all possible pairs of vectors, except that negative values of q reverse the relationship. We might say that the space has a certain circulating property set up in it. (We shall see in Section 7.6 that this circulation direction is just the direction of circulation of the current that produced the field.)

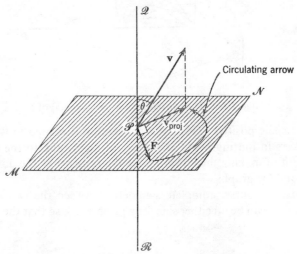

Fig. 7.2b. A charge q moves with velocity v through point $\mathscr{P}$ and experiences a force F perpendicular to v_{proj} in plane $\mathscr{MN}$.

We could try to describe the magnetic field in terms of some type of circulation entity as if the space around $\mathscr{P}$ has some sort of twist to it, with a magnitude B and a direction specified by means of a certain plane and a circular arrow in the plane. But such a description is awkward, is historically unconventional, and does not make use of the relative simplicity of vector analysis. Hence, we shall retain the conventional description of B as a vector directed normally to the plane. We can specify its direction in relation to the circulation by the right-hand screw rule—if the fingers are curled to match the circulating arrow, the thumb points along the normal chosen for B as in Fig. 7.2c. (Of course, the ordinary right-hand rule for vector products is sufficient to determine the direction of B from Eq. 7.2–2.) This convention is arbitrary, but has arisen historically because it fits, as we shall see, the custom of calling the north-seeking end of a

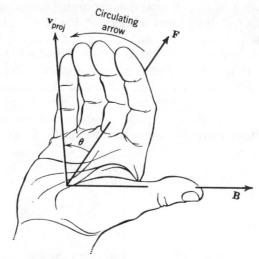

Fig. 7.2c. The convention for the direction of **B**.

compass needle positive. This latter convention is related to the choice of map makers in putting north at the top of maps, and to the mathematicians' habit of making the upward direction rather than the downward the positive one for graphs.

There is, of course, complete symmetry between the two sides of the plane $\mathcal{MN}$ (**v** can be on either side for a given $\mathbf{v}_{\text{proj}}$), so that the assignment

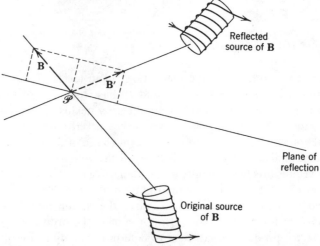

Fig. 7.2d. A source of **B** and its mirror image which would appear to produce a field **B**′. The component of **B** perpendicular to the plane does not change, but the component parallel to the plane is reversed.

of a vector to one of the normals ($\mathscr{P}\mathscr{Q}$ in Fig. 7.2b rather than $\mathscr{P}\mathscr{R}$) conceals this symmetry. There is no physical reason that connects one direction along the line $\mathscr{Q}\mathscr{R}$ with the sign of a charge as there is for the vector **E**.

Consider the reflection properties of **B**. If the physical surroundings were to be viewed as reflected in the plane $\mathscr{M}\mathscr{N}$, no change at all would occur in either v_{proj} or the direction of circulation. The magnitude B will, of course, also remain the same. Thus **B** does not change when seen reflected in a plane normal to itself. A reflection in a plane through the vector **B**, however, would reverse the direction of circulation and hence **B** would reverse its direction. A directed quantity with these properties is called an "axial vector" or a "pseudovector" in contradistinction to a "polar vector" or "true vector" like the electric field E (cf. p. 5). Figure 7.2d shows the behavior of **B** for reflection about an arbitrary plane, and Appendix A.4 contains a general discussion of vectors and pseudovectors.

The Lorentz force law, 7.2–2, has been experimentally verified over a wide range of values of q and v and for a wide variety of values of **E** and **B**. It has also been shown to transform properly between different inertial frames of reference. (Cf. Sections 7.14 and 7.19.) The only limitations on its validity arise from the omission of additional terms related to radiation that depend on the *acceleration* rather than on the velocity of q. We shall limit ourselves whenever necessary to small accelerations so that Eq. 7.2–2 may be considered strictly valid.

In our MKS absolute practical units, we measure F in newtons, q in coulombs, and v in meters/second. Hence B has the units newton-second/coulomb-meter = newton/ampere-meter. This unit is also called the weber/meter², which is the more conventional name (the weber is a flux unit to be introduced shortly).

For a conducting medium with continuous charge density ρ and current density $\mathbf{J} = \rho\mathbf{v}$, the Lorentz force per unit volume is, obviously,

$$\mathbf{f}_r = \rho\mathbf{E} + \mathbf{J} \times \mathbf{B} \qquad (7.2\text{–}4a)$$

Let us also express the magnetic force law in Gaussian units,[3] for which F is in dynes, q in statcoulombs, v in centimeters/second, and B is measured in the electromagnetic unit (emu), known as the gauss or the oersted. (The reason for two names being given to one unit will be discussed in Chapter 8.) In this case, the Lorentz law becomes

$$\mathbf{F} = q\mathbf{E} + \frac{q}{c}(\mathbf{v} \times \mathbf{B}) \qquad \text{Gaussian} \quad (7.2\text{–}2b)$$

$$\mathbf{f}_r = \rho\mathbf{E} + \frac{1}{c}(\mathbf{J} \times \mathbf{B}) \qquad \text{Gaussian} \quad (7.2\text{–}4b)$$

---

[3] Gaussian units are those in which the electrostatic system is used for electric charge, field, potential, and capacitance, and electromagnetic units are used for **B** and the other magnetic quantities to be introduced later. See Appendix A.7.

where c is an experimental constant related to the experimental constant ϵ_0 in the MKS form of Coulomb's law. In fact, $c = 1/(4\pi\epsilon_0 \cdot 10^{-7})^{1/2} = 2.99793 \times 10^{10}$ cm/sec (i.e., the velocity of light). It enters both here and in Ampère's law (cf. section 7.6).

One weber/m² $= 10^4$ gauss; this conversion factor is fairly easy to remember from the fact that 10,000 gauss or 1.00 weber/m² is a round number expressing approximately the largest practicable magnetic field obtainable in ordinary laboratory electromagnets, although steady fields of 2 or even 10 weber/m² are sometimes possible of attainment, and pulsed fields as high as 10^3 weber/m² have been produced.

Problem 7.2a. What would happen to Eq. 7.2–2 if (*a*) the south direction was taken as positive for compasses; (*b*) the left hand was used to define the vector product; (*c*) the left hand was used to relate the circulatory arrow in Fig. 7.2*b* to **B**; (*d*) the circulating arrow was turned around; (*e*) electrons were called positive? Consider these alternatives both separately and in combinations.

Problem 7.2b. Show that the force on a charge q moving through point $\mathscr{P}$ in Fig. 7.2*d* with speed **v** will reflect as a true vector when **v** is reflected along with the source of magnetic field.

7.3 Particle Motions

The value of **B** will in general vary from point to point, so that the motion of a particle in an arbitrary magnetic field can be quite complicated. The only thing we can say in general is that the magnetic force $q\mathbf{v} \times \mathbf{B}$ does no work on the charge q, since **F** is perpendicular to **v**. If no electric field is present, the speed of a particle must necessarily stay constant as it moves regardless of any variations in **B**.

There are, however, a number of reasonably simple cases of particle motions which we now take up. Let us consider as a first example the special case in which **B** is uniform over a certain region in space and is constant in time. Let us also assume that **E** is zero in this region. The magnet of a cyclotron provides a familiar example of such a region.

There are two simple types of particle motion in a uniform magnetic field:

a. If the charge starts to move in the direction of the field **B** or opposite to it, there will be no force and hence the particle will continue to move in this direction without acceleration.

b. If the particle is started in a plane perpendicular to **B**, its acceleration will lie in the same plane, and the particle's path will all be contained in this plane. The speed remains constant, so that as the particle moves, it will change its direction under the action of a *constant* force at right angles to its path. It will, in short, move in a circle and if positive, will circulate in the opposite direction to that of the arrow of Fig. 7.2b.[4] We may find the radius of this circle from $\mathbf{F} = M\mathbf{a}$ by writing

$$F = qvB = Mv^2/R$$

or

$$R = \frac{Mv}{qB} \tag{7.3-1a}$$

R is the radius of the circular path (Fig. 7.3a) and M is the mass of the particle that bears the charge q. If relativistic effects are important, the relativistic value of Mv is to be used (Problem 7.2d).

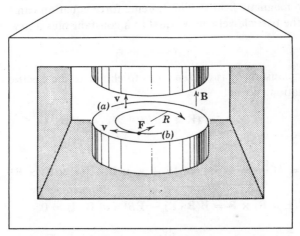

Fig. 7.3a. Motion of positive ions in uniform **B**. (a) **v** is parallel to **B**, leading to straight-line motion. (b) **v** is perpendicular to **B**, leading to circular motion.

The angular frequency ω_c with which a particle circulates in a uniform magnetic field follows readily from 7.3-1 and is seen to be independent of the radius and the speed:

$$\omega_c = \frac{v}{R} = \frac{qB}{M} \tag{7.3-2a}$$

This angular frequency is generally called the "cyclotron frequency," since Eqs. 7.3-1 and 7.3-2 describe the motion of particles in cyclotrons, betatrons, synchrotrons, mass spectrometers, and numerous other devices that involve the magnetic deflection of moving particles. In fact, the success of any of these devices constitutes a verification of the Lorentz force law.

---

[4] This oppositeness is related to Lenz's law. Cf. Section 7.14.

Another use of Eq. 7.3–1 consists in measuring the momentum of particles that make visible tracks in a cloud or bubble chamber. Frequently, the density or origin of the tracks provides sufficient evidence to establish the value of q, whereupon the momentum $Mv = RBq$ may be found from measurements of R and B.

If a particle has an initial velocity at some angle other than 90° or 0° with the direction of **B**, the motion resolves itself into a combination of a constant velocity component in the direction of **B** and a circular motion in the perpendicular plane. The path is thus a helix of constant radius R given by 7.3–1a with v replaced by the component $v_{\text{proj}} = v_\perp$ in the direction perpendicular to **B**.

A second example is that of a uniform electric field **E** perpendicular to a uniform magnetic field **B**. The Lorentz force equation can be simplified if we set the particle velocity **v** equal to a constant plus a new variable **v**

$$\mathbf{v} = \mathbf{v}_d + \mathbf{v}_1 \tag{7.3–3}$$

where the constant $\mathbf{v}_d$ is chosen so as to eliminate the electric term in the force equation. We set

$$\mathbf{v}_d = (\mathbf{E} \times \mathbf{B})/B^2; \qquad v_d = E/B \tag{7.3–4}$$

so that we have

$$\mathbf{F} = M\frac{d\mathbf{v}}{dt} = M\frac{d\mathbf{v}_1}{dt} = q\{\mathbf{E} + \mathbf{v}_1 \times \mathbf{B} + [(\mathbf{E} \times \mathbf{B}) \times \mathbf{B}]/B^2\}$$

or, since $(\mathbf{E} \times \mathbf{B}) \times \mathbf{B} = \mathbf{B}(\mathbf{B} \cdot \mathbf{E}) - \mathbf{E}B^2$ and $\mathbf{B} \cdot \mathbf{E} = 0$,

$$M\frac{d\mathbf{v}_1}{dt} = q\mathbf{v}_1 \times \mathbf{B} \tag{7.3–5}$$

Thus the motion consists of the circular or helical motion described in the previous case superimposed on a constant velocity $\mathbf{v}_d$, called the "electric drift velocity," perpendicular to both **E** and **B**. (We are not now considering any changes to moving frames of reference.) In the absence of any motion parallel to **B**, the resulting orbit is cycloidal (Problem 7.3e). It should be noticed that this result must fail when $E = cB$, for then the drift would be at the speed of light. Our result is, therefore, only valid when $E \ll cB$. A correct relativistic treatment is given in section 7.19.[5]

[5] For further information on particle motions in magnetic fields, see C. L. Longmire, *Elementary Plasma Physics*, Interscience, New York, 1963, Chapter II; also J. R. Pierce, *Theory and Design of Electron Beams*, D. Van Nostrand, Princeton, 1954; and Zworykin, Morton, Ramberg, Hillier, and Vance, *Electron Optics and the Electron Microscope*, John Wiley, New York, 1945.

The Gaussian formulas for orbit radius and cyclotron frequency in a uniform magnetic field are

$$R = \frac{Mvc}{qB} \qquad \text{Gaussian} \quad (7.3\text{-}1b)$$

$$\omega_c = \frac{qB}{Mc} \qquad \text{Gaussian} \quad (7.3\text{-}2b)$$

Problem 7.3a. Find the radius of curvature of an electron in a magnetic field of 5000 gauss if the electron has a kinetic energy of (a) 10 ev, (b) 1000 ev.

Problem 7.3b. Find the value of B in gauss such that the time taken per revolution for a singly-charged ion describing a circular path in a uniform field would be a number of microseconds equal to the ion mass in atomic mass units.

Problem 7.3c. Find B so that an electron will have a frequency of rotation of 2×10^6 cycles per sec, if **B** is uniform.

Problem 7.3d. Deduce from the formula $\mathbf{F} = d(M\mathbf{v})/dt$, which is used in special relativity, that Eq. 7.3-1 is correct for the relativistic value of $M\mathbf{v}$. *Hint:* Prove first that $d(M\mathbf{v})/dt = M\boldsymbol{\omega} \times \mathbf{v}$ for uniform circular motion, where $\boldsymbol{\omega}$ is the angular velocity.

Problem 7.3e. Discuss qualitatively the shape of the path taken by a particle moving perpendicular to **B** when **E** and **B** are uniform and mutually perpendicular by considering the energy and speed changes of the particle as it moves back and forth in the direction of **E**.

Problem 7.3f. Show that the motion given by **v** in Eq. 7.3-3 is cycloidal, i.e., that it follows a path described by a point on the radius of a rolling circle. What is the necessary condition for the path-describing point to reside on the circumference of the circle?

Problem 7.3g. A common velocity filter for ions uses uniform, crossed (mutually perpendicular), **E** and **B** fields. Show that there is just one velocity for which an ion can move in a straight line through such a filter.

Problem 7.3h. Show that if **E** is parallel to **B** and both are uniform, a particle moves around a circle whose center is accelerated.

Problem 7.3i. Show that it is possible for two ions that differ in charge and mass to follow identical paths in an arbitrary magnetic field, provided their momenta or energies are suitably related. Assume no electric fields are present. Show that the ratio of times for two particles to travel a given distance on such a path depends only on properties of the particles themselves.

Problem 7.3j. An electron is projected into a uniform field **B** at an angle to the field such that the kinetic energy associated with the velocity component parallel to the field has the value $K_{\parallel}$, and the remaining energy that is associated with motion in the plane perpendicular to **B** is $K_{\perp}$. Find the radius, pitch, and period of the resulting helical motion.

7.4 The Motor and Generator Rules

The operation of electric motors and generators follows rules derivable from Eq. 7.2–1. The motor rule deals with the force on a thin wire carrying a current. Suppose we consider a section of a wire of length **dl** at rest in a uniform magnetic field of strength **B**, at an angle θ with the wire (Fig. 7.4a).

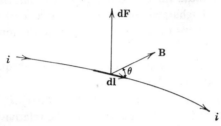

Fig. 7.4a.   A segment of wire of length **dl**, carrying current i, experiences a force **dF** in a field **B**.

Let a current i pass through the wire, and let dq denote the total charge on the conduction electrons in the section of the wire under consideration. If dt is the time required for one electron or electron hole to travel a distance **dl** in the wire (and therefore the time for charge dq to pass the end of the section), we see that the speed of each electron is $\mathbf{v} = \mathbf{dl}/dt$ and also that the current is equal to $i = dq/dt$ from which we can conclude that

$$\mathbf{v}\, dq = i\, \mathbf{dl} \tag{7.4–1}$$

The total force on the charges in the wire is therefore

$$\mathbf{F} = \int \mathbf{dF} = \int dq(\mathbf{v} \times \mathbf{B}) = i \int \mathbf{dl} \times \mathbf{B} \tag{7.4–2a}$$

where the integral is over the entire piece of wire on which we want the force. The increment **dl** is taken in the sense chosen as positive for i.

The force is transmitted to the wire itself by the metallic binding forces. It is directed at right angles to wire and magnetic induction as in Fig. 7.4a (remember that i is positive in the direction of flow of positive charges).[6]

---

[6] There are several right-hand rules for remembering these directions, but since the vector product rule itself is sufficient, we shall not give special rules for motors and generators. The difficulty of memorizing any rule may be appreciated when one realizes that, utilizing both right and left hands, there are twelve ways of associating the three elements, **F**, **v**, and **B**, with three fingers, of which six ways give correct results.

Electric motors are arrangements for utilizing this force to produce torques in rotating machinery.

We have so far considered the wire to be at rest. If the wire moves, the charges it contains will have added velocity components in addition to that due to the current (i.e., convection will occur). The additional force the charges experience is an example of the generator effect. It will be simplest to deal with this latter effect separately before considering it in relation to the motor effect.

Let a thin wire of any shape move through a region where there is a magnetic field that does not vary with time. Let a given element of the

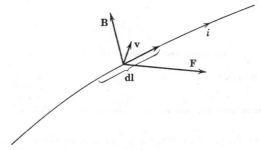

Fig. 7.4b.   Illustrating the magnetic force on charges in a wire when the wire is moved through a field **B** with velocity **v**.

wire **dl** have a velocity **v** (Fig. 7.4b). The positive and negative charges contained in the wire will thus move at velocity **v** and experience magnetic forces. An amount q of these charges will experience a force $\mathbf{F} = q(\mathbf{v} \times \mathbf{B})$, and in general there will be a component of **F** along the wire, oppositely directed for positive and negative charges.

There may also be electric fields present, producing an additional force on q. If the wire obeys Ohm's law, it will be the total force that determines the quantum jumps of the electrons and their average speed. In fact, Ohm's law in the form of Eq. 5.1–3b becomes now[7]

$$\mathbf{J} = \sigma_c(\mathbf{E} + \mathbf{v} \times \mathbf{B}) \tag{7.4–3a}$$

where **v**, the wire velocity, must not be confused with the electron velocity $\mathbf{J}/ne$. The current will be parallel to the sides of the wire—whatever the direction of $\mathbf{v} \times \mathbf{B}$, **E** will become adjusted (in a very short time) so that the resultant $\mathbf{E} + \mathbf{v} \times \mathbf{B}$ is a vector directed along the wire.

In place of a wire, we may consider a body of conducting fluid, such as a plasma. The velocity **v** then becomes the hydrodynamic velocity, which

[7] We have here a different modification of Ohm's law from that expressed in Eq. 6.3–1. We still identify **E** in the wire with $-\nabla \mathbf{V}_F$.

generally varies from point to point in accordance with the laws of fluid dynamics. Plasmas generally have such high conductivities that we can place $\rho_c = 1/\sigma_c$ equal to zero. Thus for highly-conducting plasmas—those that are highly ionized—the electric field is related to the magnetic induction by

$$\mathbf{E} = -\mathbf{v} \times \mathbf{B} \qquad (7.4\text{-}4)$$

regardless of the density of current **J**. This relation does not hold, of course, in the sheath at the edge of the body of ionized gas, where the conductivity falls off to a low value (cf. Section 6.5). In fact, the charge

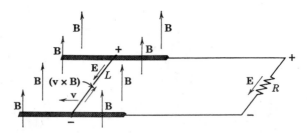

Fig. 7.4c. A wire sliding on rails. When it is moved by an outside force with velocity **v**, an emf $\mathscr{E} = \mathbf{vBL}$ is generated.

density in the sheath will continually adjust itself to help maintain **E** at this value, just as the charge on the surface of a wire in a d-c circuit helps to keep **E** inside the wire parallel to its edges. We shall see in Section 7.14 that variations in **J** will also help to maintain **E** by the process of electromagnetic induction.

Now let us consider the emf produced by motion of a wire in a magnetic field. Suppose the two ends of a generator wire form a closed circuit with an external resistor that is stationary or at least is located outside the magnetic field. Consider as an example the wire shown in Fig. 7.4c. This wire, of length L, can be moved in a uniform field **B** along conducting rails with which it makes electrical contact. Since current will flow only from a more positive potential to a more negative one in the resistor, there must be an electric field along the resistor and therefore one between the rails. We deduce that the potential is higher at the rail toward which the charge moves inside the generator wire. The charge therefore moves against **E** in this latter wire, which means that $\mathbf{v} \times \mathbf{B}$ must be opposite to **E** and greater in magnitude. The integral $\oint \mathbf{E} \cdot \mathbf{dl}$ around the entire circuit is zero here as in the case of the chemical cell, and we again have a situation involving an emf. Since $J = i/S$ and $\rho_c J \, dl = i\rho_c \, dl/S = i \, dR$, where S, dl, and dR are the area, length, and resistance of a small section of the wire, we can write

$$0 = \oint \mathbf{E} \cdot \mathbf{dl} = \oint \rho_c \mathbf{J} \cdot \mathbf{dl} - \oint \mathbf{v} \times \mathbf{B} \cdot \mathbf{dl}$$

$$= \oint i \, dR - \int_{\text{gen wire}} \mathbf{v} \times \mathbf{B} \cdot \mathbf{dl}$$

or

$$\int_{\text{gen wire}} \mathbf{v} \times \mathbf{B} \cdot \mathbf{dl} = i R_{\text{total}} \qquad (7.4\text{--}5)$$

and R_{total} is the total resistance around the circuit.

The energy expended in the circuit is iR_{total} joules per coulomb, which clearly must come from the forces causing the motion of the wire. Furthermore, the work done can be reversed in sign if an external emf is put into

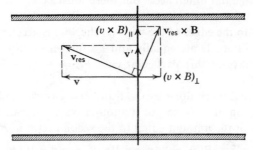

Fig. 7.4d. Showing the velocities of wire and moving charges and the components of the magnetic-force term $\mathbf{v} \times \mathbf{B}$.

the circuit and sets up a current in the opposite direction. The integral on the left of 7.4–5 is therefore an emf, the so-called *motional induced emf*, and we write

$$\mathcal{E} = \oint \mathbf{v} \times \mathbf{B} \cdot \mathbf{dl} \qquad (7.4\text{--}6a)$$

The integral can, of course, be taken around the entire circuit or loop in question since it will only have a value at points where neither $\mathbf{v}$ nor $\mathbf{B}$ vanish.

We have seen in Section 7.3 that magnetic forces do no work for particles moving freely in a field. Then how can it be that they do work in a wire? Strictly speaking, the magnetic force does no work here either—the magnetic field simply deflects charge so that electrical forces can do work (which in turn is derived from mechanical forces).

Figure 7.4d shows the velocity $\mathbf{v}$ of the wire in the previous figure, as well as the velocity $\mathbf{v}'$ of positive charges (electron holes) moving in the wire. Although $\mathbf{v}'$ is usually very small compared to $\mathbf{v}$, we show it as reasonably large for purposes of clarity. The actual magnetic force per unit charge involves the resultant velocity $\mathbf{v}_{res} = \mathbf{v} + \mathbf{v}'$, as shown in the figure. The rate P at which the force $\mathbf{v}_{res} \times \mathbf{B}$ does work on q coulombs of charge in the wire is $q(\mathbf{v}_{res} \times \mathbf{B}) \cdot \mathbf{v}_{res}$, which of course is zero, but which may be written in two parts

$$P = q(\mathbf{v}_{res} \times \mathbf{B}) \cdot \mathbf{v}_{res} = q(\mathbf{v}_{res} \times \mathbf{B}) \cdot (\mathbf{v} + \mathbf{v}')$$
$$= q \, |\mathbf{v}_{res} \times \mathbf{B}|_{\perp} v + q \, |\mathbf{v}_{res} \times \mathbf{B}|_{\parallel} v' \qquad (7.4\text{--}7)$$

referring respectively to motion perpendicular and parallel to the wire. It can be seen that the first term is negative and the second positive for the case shown in Fig. 7.4d.

Now consider the electric field. Any component parallel to the wire is taken into account in the integral $\oint \mathbf{E} \cdot \mathbf{dl}$ around the circuit and in the discussion of potential differences. But there must be an electric field $\mathbf{E}_{tr}$ transverse to the wire to balance out $|\mathbf{v}_{res} \times \mathbf{B}|_{\perp}$ and keep the charges flowing parallel to the edges of the wire. (If the wire is accelerated, charges of both signs will accelerate equally and no further electric force will be involved.) We have in this particular case $E_{tr} = -|\mathbf{v}_{res} \times \mathbf{B}|_{\perp} = v'B$ in the direction of $\mathbf{v}$.

Thus we see that work done by the transverse electric field just cancels the transverse term in P, or to put it another way, the transverse electric field does work of the amount equal to the second term in P,

$$q \, |\mathbf{v}_{res} \times \mathbf{B}|_{\parallel} v' = q(\mathbf{v}_{res} \times \mathbf{B}) \cdot \mathbf{v}' = q(\mathbf{v} \times \mathbf{B} \cdot \mathbf{v}')$$

The transverse electric field E_{tr}, however, is largely produced by charges on the surface of the wire; the force on these charges arises from the mechanical forces introduced in the first place to move the wire.

Thus we see that 7.4–6 gives the correct value of the emf. We can treat it as a magnetic force effect if we consider that the force at right angles to $\mathbf{v}$ does work with respect to the motion $\mathbf{v}'$ of the charges in the wire.

Let us consider another way of describing the motional induced emf. The emf associated with a length $\mathbf{dl}$ of the wire is $\mathbf{v} \times \mathbf{B} \cdot \mathbf{dl}$. By the rules of the triple scalar product (see Appendix A.2–34) we can write it $\mathbf{dl} \times \mathbf{v} \cdot \mathbf{B}$. Write $\mathbf{v} = \mathbf{dl}'/dt$, and note that $\mathbf{dl} \times \mathbf{dl}' = \mathbf{dS}$, the element of area swept cut by $\mathbf{dl}$ in time dt, as shown in Fig. 7.4e. The element of emf can then be written

$$d\mathscr{E} = \mathbf{v} \times \mathbf{B} \cdot \mathbf{dl} = (\mathbf{dS}/dt) \cdot \mathbf{B} = (\mathbf{B} \cdot \mathbf{dS})/dt \qquad (7.4\text{--}8)$$

where we are still assuming that $\partial\mathbf{B}/\partial t = 0$.

The quantity $\mathbf{B} \cdot \mathbf{dS}$ is an element of magnetic flux, in exact analogy to an electric flux element $d\Phi_E = \mathbf{E} \cdot \mathbf{dS}$. We write

$$\mathbf{B} \cdot \mathbf{dS} = d\Phi \qquad (7.4\text{--}9)$$

and can write the integral over the surface S swept out by the motion of the wire as the flux through that surface

$$\Phi = \int_S \mathbf{B} \cdot \mathbf{dS} \qquad (7.4\text{–}10)$$

Magnetic flux Φ is measured in webers in the MKS system.

We see that $d\mathscr{E}$ in 7.4–8 is the rate at which flux is swept out by $\mathbf{dl}$ and the entire $\mathscr{E}$ of 7.4–6 is the rate at which the entire wire sweeps out flux. In order to have the sign of $\mathscr{E}$ be positive for a current in the movable circuit that would generate a flux in the same direction as the given external

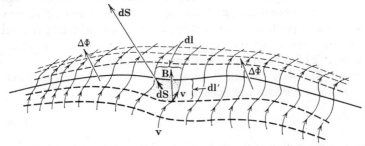

Fig. 7.4e.   Illustrating the production of a motional emf $\mathscr{E}$ in a flexible wire and the accompanying sweeping out of magnetic flux $\Delta\Phi$. The solid and dashed lines show different positions of the wire.

one, we find that we must use a negative sign (cf. Section 7.14 below) and write

$$\mathscr{E} = -\frac{d\Phi}{dt} \qquad (7.4\text{–}11a)$$

for the motional induced emf. Until we prove that magnetic flux is conserved, i.e., that $\nabla \cdot \mathbf{B} = 0$, we cannot show that the flux can be calculated through *any* surface bounded by the final position of the current, rather than just through the actual surface swept out. Furthermore, we cannot deal properly with time-dependent magnetic fields until we are ready to take up moving sources of $\mathbf{B}$ and changes of frame of reference. Hence, the generalization to cases of variable $\mathbf{B}$ (Faraday's Law) will also have to wait.

We assumed in Fig. 7.4d that the charges moved with a speed v' in the wire, where $v' = J/ne$ by Eq. 5.1–2. The emf, however, can be calculated by only asking for the work done *if* charges should move. Let us suppose now that the circuit is open and the current and current density is zero. We have again a case in which $\mathbf{E} = -\mathbf{v} \times \mathbf{B}$ at every point inside the conductor. Hence the potential difference between two points $\mathscr{A}$ and $\mathscr{B}$ is just equal to the induced emf between those two points:

$$V_{ab} = -\int_{\mathscr{A}}^{\mathscr{B}} \mathbf{E} \cdot \mathbf{dl} = \int_{\mathscr{A}}^{\mathscr{B}} \mathbf{v} \times \mathbf{B} \cdot \mathbf{dl} = \mathscr{E} \qquad (7.4\text{--}12)$$

Note that the line integral of the electric field yields the same results regardless of the path, whereas the motional emf must be calculated along the wire at the given instant.

A simple type of generator that can produce steady currents is the Faraday disk. A copper disk is arranged to rotate in a uniform magnetic field, with its axis parallel to $\mathbf{B}$. A circuit is established in the disk between its center and a point on its circumference, by using a sliding contact on the axle and another on the periphery (a cup of mercury into which the disk is inserted a few millimeters is one arrangement).

Then if the disk is rotated at an angular velocity ω, an emf $\mathscr{E}$ will be developed between axle and periphery, given by

$$\mathscr{E} = \tfrac{1}{2}BR^2\omega \qquad (7.4\text{--}13)$$

where R is the radius of the disk (cf. Problem 7.3a). Such a disk can also be run as a motor (Problem 7.3b). Practical motors and generators, including commercially useful Faraday-disk machines (also called homopolar generators), are described in books on electrical engineering.

Now let us consider the generator effect as it occurs in a motor. Suppose an external source of emf replaces the resistor R in Fig. 7.4c, causing a current i to flow in the movable wire from top to bottom of the figure. We assume that the wire is not pushed by an external force. There will be a motor force $F = iLB$ in the direction of $\mathbf{v}$ in the figure. If the wire acquires the velocity $\mathbf{v}$ as a result of this force, the emf $\mathscr{E} = vBL$ will be generated, acting in the direction opposite to that of the current (for this reason it is called a back emf). Some external source of power must thus provide energy at a rate $\mathscr{E}i = ivBL$ to make the charge flow against this back emf. The power exerted mechanically on the wire by the force $\mathbf{F}$ on the charges inside it is $\mathbf{F} \cdot \mathbf{v}$, which is also equal to $ivBL$ since $F = iLB$. Hence we see that the power supplied by a motor is just that which is required by the generator effect occurring in the motor. Of course, the power expended in ohmic heating of the wire must also be supplied by the external sources.

In the general case of variable $\mathbf{B}$ and curved wires, we can write for the force on a piece $\mathbf{dl}$

$$\mathbf{dF} = i\,\mathbf{dl} \times \mathbf{B}$$

and for the power

$$\mathbf{dF} \cdot \mathbf{v} = i\,\mathbf{dl} \times \mathbf{B} \cdot \mathbf{v} = -i\mathbf{v} \times \mathbf{B} \cdot \mathbf{dl} = -i\,d\mathscr{E} \qquad (7.4\text{--}14)$$

leading to the same conclusion as for the straight wire.

In the case of a generator, conversely, a current i leads to the generation of power at the rate $\mathscr{E}i$; the current i produces a motor force on the wire oppositely directed to its velocity $\mathbf{v}$, so that work must be done by an external agent (diesel engine, turbine, etc.) to turn the generator. The two expressions for the power are again equal, as can be seen by reversing the calculation just given.

The formulas of this section require the factor $1/c$ of 7.2–2 when written in Gaussian units. The motor force on a wire becomes

$$\mathbf{F} = \frac{i}{c} \int \mathbf{dl} \times \mathbf{B} \qquad\qquad \text{Gaussian} \quad (7.4\text{--}2b)$$

The generalization of Ohm's law is

$$\mathbf{J} = \sigma_c\!\left(\mathbf{E} + \frac{1}{c}\,\mathbf{v} \times \mathbf{B}\right) \qquad\qquad \text{Gaussian} \quad (7.4\text{--}3b)$$

and for the emf in a circuit, we have the two equations

$$\mathscr{E} = \frac{1}{c} \oint \mathbf{v} \times \mathbf{B} \cdot \mathbf{dl} \qquad\qquad (7.4\text{--}6b)$$

$$\mathscr{E} = -\frac{1}{c}\frac{d\Phi}{dt} \qquad\qquad (7.4\text{--}11b)$$

Problem 7.4a. The magnetic field of the earth at a certain locality has a strength of 0.50 gauss, directed downward at an angle of 65° with the horizontal. Find the force on a straight wire three meters long carrying 100 amp which is (a) vertical, (b) parallel to the horizontal component of the earth's field, and (c) horizontal and perpendicular to the horizontal component of the earth's field.

Problem 7.4b. Derive Eq. 7.4–13 for the emf of a Faraday disk.

Problem 7.4c. Find the torque delivered to a Faraday disk of radius R if a current i is fed in at the periphery and taken out at an axle radius R'. Assume $\mathbf{B}$ to be constant over the disk and perpendicular to it.

Problem 7.4d. A vertical, rectangular U-shaped piece of wire, with the horizontal part 2 cm long and the vertical sides 10 cm long hangs in a magnetic field whose direction is perpendicular to the plane of the U. The field has a value $B = 0.4$ weber/m² within a circle in this plane of diameter 5 cm and is essentially zero outside of this circle. If a current of 7 amp is passed through the loop, find the force on it when the horizontal section is symmetrically located in the center of the circle. Show that if this force is down, a displacement of the loop to either side will result in a force tending to bring the loop back to the center but that the reverse is true if the force on the horizontal path is upward.

Problem 7.4e. The armature of a direct-current motor carries 24 equally spaced coils, each with ten turns, connected in series with their connection points at the 24 segments of the rotating commutator. Sliding carbon "brushes" make contact with the commutator to admit current to the coils; the arrangement of the brushes and the geometry of the magnetic field in which the armature rotates are such that each wire parallel to the axis turns in an average field of 9000 gauss and the torques all are in the same sense. If at any instant the connections are such that there are two equal parallel paths through the combination, and a current of 12 amp is delivered to the brushes, find the average torque developed in the armature. Take each coil as a square 8 cm on each side, with the wires parallel to the axis of the motor at a distance of 5 cm from the axis.

Problem 7.4f. The machine described in Problem 7.4e is run as a generator with the same field. If the armature is turned at 3600 revolutions per minute, find the average emf produced. If a resistance of 12 ohms is connected between the brushes and each ten-turn armature coil has a resistance of 0.100 ohm, find how much power is generated.

7.5   The Hall Effect

We spoke in the last section of a transverse electric field occurring with the generator effect and depending on the value of v'. The Hall effect is the production of a transverse electric field solely from the passage of a current in a conductor placed across a magnetic field. If in a flat rectangular wire, as in Fig. 7.5a, there is a current density $\mathbf{J}$ in the x-direction passing through a magnetic field $\mathbf{B}$ in the y-direction, then, regardless of the sign

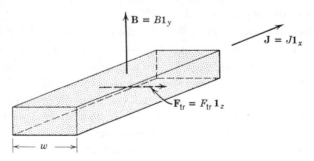

Fig. 7.5a.   Illustrating the Hall effect.

of the current carriers, there will be a force in the positive z-direction as shown.

The carriers will then be deflected toward the positive z side of the bar and will there build up a charge of their own sign until the resulting transverse electric field $\mathbf{E}_{tr}$ across the bar is enough to balance out the magnetic force and restore the flow lines to parallelism with the sides of the bar. That is, the net transverse force in the steady state will be zero and, just as before, we must have

$$\mathbf{E}_{tr} = -\mathbf{v} \times \mathbf{B} = -vB\,\mathbf{1}_z$$

A potential difference will therefore be developed across the width w of the bar equal to

$$V = E_{tr}w = vBw \tag{7.5–1}$$

so that the sign of V measures the sign of v and hence of the charge carriers. A combination of $\mathbf{E}$ and $\mathbf{B}$ can thus provide a distinction which neither can provide while acting alone on a conductor.

Although V and the current i are the quantities actually measured, it is most convenient to describe the Hall effect in terms of E_{tr}, J, and B. Since $J = nqv$ where n is the number of charge carriers per unit volume and q is the charge on each, we have

$$E_{tr} = \frac{JB}{nq} \tag{7.5–2}$$

The constant $1/nq$ is generally called the Hall coefficient R_H, so we write

$$E = R_H JB; \qquad R_H = 1/nq \tag{7.5–3}$$

(Detailed studies of the dynamics of electron motion in metals show that the expression for R_H should be replaced by a value from $1.0/nq$ to $1.5/nq$ or so.

Measurements of R_H have shown that for most metals R_H is negative, and if we assume $q = -e$, we find for n the expected value of one or two times the number of atoms present. However, for some metals R_H is positive, and in some cases n appears to be unusually small. For semiconductors, R_H may be of either sign. Table 7.5A gives a few typical values.

The explanation of these anomalies has to do with the behavior of electron holes in acting like actual positive charges when certain conditions hold for the electronic wave motions. The reader is referred to texts on solid-state physics for details.[8]

[8] C. Kittel, *Introduction to Solid State Physics*, 2nd ed., John Wiley, New York, 1956, pp. 296–298; W. Shockley, *Electrons and Holes in Semiconductors*, D. Van Nostrand, Princeton, 1950; E. H. Putley, *The Hall Effect and Related Phenomena*, Butterworths, London, 1960. The effect was discovered by E. H. Hall, *Phil. Mag.*, **9**, 225 and **10**, 301 (1880).

Table 7.5A   Hall Coefficients for Various Metals*

Hall coefficient (R_H)
volt-meter^3/ampere-weber

Bismuth	-1000×10^{-11}
Beryllium	$+24.4 \times 10^{-11}$
Cadmium	$+6.0 \times 10^{-11}$
Copper	-5.5×10^{-11}
Gold	-7.2×10^{-11}
Lithium	-17.0×10^{-11}
Silver	-8.4×10^{-11}
Sodium	-25.0×10^{-11}
Zinc	$+3.3 \times 10^{-11}$

* Taken from C. Kittel, *loc. cit.*, p. 298.

Problem 7.5a. A bar of annealed copper is used to study the Hall effect and is placed across a magnetic field of 1.20 weber/m². Using values from Tables 5.1A (p. 192) and 7.5A, find the angle which the resultant electric field makes with the sides of the bar. If the bar is 2.0 cm wide (in the direction normal to **B** and **J**), by what distance along the bar must the terminals of a galvanometer circuit be displaced so as to give a null deflection on the galvanometer?

7.6   The Biot-Savart and Scalar-Potential Forms of Ampère's Law

We turn now to a consideration of the law which describes how the magnetic induction **B** at a given point is produced by the external surroundings—that is, by the moving charges in the neighborhood of the point. There are many equivalent forms for this law—we shall give five of them with several variants in this chapter and the next—and although different names are used for different forms, we shall call them all generically Ampère's law, since it was Ampère who gave the law the most thorough treatment at the time of its discovery in 1820.[9] Ampère's law has been experimentally verified by innumerable measurements of the fields produced by many types of current distributions, as well as being verified indirectly through the use of Maxwell's equations.

We start with currents which are steady or slowly varying.[10] Experiment

[9] A. M. Ampère, *Mémoires de l'Academie*, **6**, 175 (Paris, 1823).

[10] The currents may be variable if the time taken for an appreciable variation is large compared with the time necessary to charge up the distributed capacitance of the circuit and also large compared with r/c, where r is the maximum distance from any part of the circuit to points where the magnetic induction is to be computed and c is the velocity of light. (See Sections 10.3 and 10.6.)

shows that the principle of superposition holds here as in the electric-field case, and so we can consider any current to be composed of suitable current elements. Furthermore, any steady current involves a closed circuit, so that we shall first take as a current element a thin filament that makes a closed loop. Complex circuits or current distributions may always be resolved into a sum of such closed filaments.

For an elementary current loop we have the law of Biot and Savart[11] as our first expression of Ampère's law. The magnetic induction at a point outside such a loop is given by

$$\mathbf{B} = \frac{\mu_0 i}{4\pi} \oint \frac{d\mathbf{l} \times \mathbf{1}_r}{r^2} \qquad (7.6\text{--}1a)$$

where r is the distance from a point of integration $\mathscr{Q}$ on the circuit (Fig. 7.6a) to the point $\mathscr{P}$, $\mathbf{1}_r$ is a unit vector in the direction from $\mathscr{Q}$ to $\mathscr{P}$, and $i\,d\mathbf{l}$ is an infinitesimal segment of the current loop.

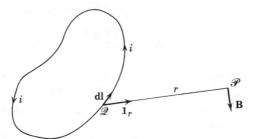

Fig. 7.6a.   Illustrating the law of Biot and Savart.

When several loops are present, Eq. 7.6–1a is of course replaced by a sum of terms for each loop. If we have a volume distribution of steady currents, we replace $i\,d\mathbf{l}$ with $\mathbf{J}\,d\tau$ and write

$$\mathbf{B} = \frac{\mu_0}{4\pi} \int \frac{\mathbf{J} \times \mathbf{1}_r}{r^2} \, d\tau \qquad (7.6\text{--}2)$$

where the integral is taken over all space that contains non-vanishing $\mathbf{J}$.

The quantity μ_0 is introduced in the MKS system to lead later to a symmetry between electric and magnetic quantities when dealing with the magnetic-pole concept. The value of the coulomb as used in the Lorentz force law and also in the current in Ampère's law is defined so as to make

---

[11] J.-B. Biot and F. Savart, *Ann. de Chimie et de Phys.*, **15**, 222 (1820). See also Sir Edmund Whittaker, *A History of the Theories of Aether and Electricity*, Vol. I., *The Classical Theories*, Thomas Nelson, London, 1951 and Harper and Row, New York, 1960, pp. 82–3; and R. A. R. Tricker, "Ampère as a Contemporary Physicist," *Contemporary Physics*, **3**, 453 (1961–2). Other names have been given to Eq. 7.6–1, but "Law of Biot and Savart" seems to be most widely accepted.

μ_0 exactly equal to $4\pi \times 10^{-7}$ weber/meter-ampere, the units of which may also be called henrys per meter and newtons per ampere^2 (cf. Section 7.2).[12]

We cannot infer from Eq. 7.6–1 that each element $i\,\mathbf{dl}$ of a current produces a contribution given by the integrand of this expression, for any expression which is proportional to i and integrates to zero around an arbitrary closed loop can be added to Eq. 7.6–1 without influencing the results. An example of such an expression would be any vector whose separate components are each differentials with respect to $\mathbf{dl}$ of scalar functions of r.[13]

Laplace evidently suggested to Biot and others that the elementary law for production of magnetic field might be just the differential form of 7.6–1, but a great deal of research and controversy went into efforts to find other forms,[14] principally because Laplace's suggestion appeared to violate Newton's law of action and reaction (cf. Problem 7.6a). However, Laplace turns out to have been right. We denote by Laplace's rule the Biot-Savart type of formula for a small segment of current:

$$\mathbf{dB} = \frac{\mu_0 i\,\mathbf{dl} \times \mathbf{1}_r}{4\pi r^2} \qquad (7.6\text{–}3)$$

It is not possible to isolate a current element and test Eq. 7.6–3 directly although in principle one might test the result of replacing $i\,\mathbf{dl}$ by $\mathbf{v}\,dq$ as in 7.4–1 and then replacing dq by the charge q on a small particle. This form of Laplace's rule is

$$\mathbf{B} = \frac{\mu_0 q\mathbf{v} \times \mathbf{1}_r}{4\pi r^2} \qquad (7.6\text{–}4a)$$

This rule is, however, not readily testable, for the magnetic fields produced by moving particles are too small to be easily observed. The justification of 7.6–3 or 7.6–4 will appear when we discuss the appropriate one of Maxwell's equations. The failure of action and reaction to be equal will be cleared up when we consider electromagnetic momentum in Chapter 10.

---

[12] μ_0 is called the "permeability of free space" but the question of whether it represents a real property of "free space" will not be pursued as it is irrelevant to our present study. (The same comments apply to ϵ_0, the "permittivity of free space.") It is, for instance, permissible but not necessary to consider μ_0 a pure dimensionless number (it is after all a defined and not a measured quantity), in which case webers have the same dimensions as meter-amperes, and amperes^2 are dimensionally the same as newtons. We shall for the most part not treat μ_0 this way, however; giving μ_0 dimensions is an aid to clarity in the rest of our subject.

[13] In symbols, $\mathbf{dB}' = i(\mathbf{dl} \cdot \nabla)\mathbf{f}(r)$ or $dB'_x = i\nabla f_x(r) \cdot \mathbf{dl}$; $dB'_y = i\nabla f_y(r) \cdot \mathbf{dl}$, etc.

[14] See A. O'Rahilly, *Electromagnetics, A Discussion of Fundamentals*, Dover, N.Y. 1965; Whittaker, *loc. cit.*, Tricker, *loc. cit.*, W. G. V. Rosser, *Contemporary Physics*, **3**, 28 (1961–2).

In spite of its indirect testability, however, the differential form of the law is perhaps the easiest on the imagination, for it describes the actions at a point $\mathscr{P}$ in terms of specific occurrences at each of a series of points around a circuit. This type of formula may be called "a point-to-point action-at-a distance" formula similar to Coulomb's law for electrostatic fields. It must be noted that Eq. 7.6–4a holds only for speeds much less than that of light. A formula correct for all speeds will be given in Section 10.3.

The vector product in 7.6–3 can be used to verify another use of the right hand for directional purposes. If the hand grasps an element **dl** of a

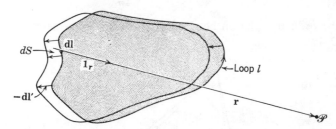

Fig. 7.6b.   A method of deriving the solid angle rule from Laplace's rule.

wire with the thumb pointing along the positive current direction, the fingers go around the wire in the general direction of **dB**.

The Solid-Angle Form and the Magnetic Scalar Potential. We now wish to show that the magnetic field near a current loop is proportional to the gradient of the solid angle subtended by the loop at the point where **B** is to be found. Let us displace the point $\mathscr{P}$ in Fig. 7.6a by an arbitrary amount **dl′**—we use **dl′** for a displacement in space and **dl** for a segment of a current-bearing wire—and find the value of $\mathbf{B} \cdot \mathbf{dl'}$:

$$\mathbf{B} \cdot \mathbf{dl'} = \frac{\mu_0 i}{4\pi} \oint_l \frac{\mathbf{dl} \times \mathbf{1}_r \cdot \mathbf{dl'}}{r^2} \qquad (7.6\text{–}5)$$

where the integral represents a summation around a closed loop l over elements **dl** but not **dl′**. Note that **r** and $\mathbf{1}_r$ both vary along the wire. By the rules of the triple scalar product the integrand may be written $\mathbf{dl'} \cdot \mathbf{dl} \times \mathbf{1}_r/r^2 = \mathbf{dl'} \times \mathbf{dl} \cdot \mathbf{1}_r/r^2$. This expression can be interpreted in terms of solid angles; the interpretation is clearest if we keep $\mathscr{P}$ fixed and move the entire current through the negative displacement $-\mathbf{dl'}$. Then the circuit sweeps out a ribbon-shaped surface as shown in Fig. 7.6b. In this figure, a vector $\mathbf{r} = r\mathbf{1}_r$ has been drawn from a point within a piece of the ribbon dS bounded by **dl** and **dl′** to a point $\mathscr{P}$. The location of $\mathscr{P}$ and the direction of $-\mathbf{dl'}$ are here taken so that the vector leaves the inside of the ribbon. The quantity $\mathbf{dl} \times (-\mathbf{dl'})$ is a vector representing the small area **dS**, directed to the inside of the ribbon; the projection of this area on a plane normal to $\mathbf{r}$ is then $\mathbf{dl} \times (-\mathbf{dl'}) \cdot \mathbf{1}_r$, so that the element of the solid angle subtended at $\mathscr{P}$ by the small piece of ribbon is $\mathbf{dl'} \times \mathbf{dl} \cdot \mathbf{1}_r/r^2$. Thus the integral over the closed loop gives the entire solid angle subtended by the ribbon. This solid angle is shown in a partial view in Fig. 7.6c. It represents the *decrease* of the entire solid angle Ω subtended at $\mathscr{P}$ that occurs when $\mathscr{P}$ moves a distance $\mathbf{dl'}$ away from the loop or the loop moves $-\mathbf{dl'}$ away from $\mathscr{P}$. We therefore write $\oint \mathbf{dl'} \times \mathbf{dl} \cdot \mathbf{1}_r/r^2 = -d\Omega$, and have

$$\mathbf{B} \cdot \mathbf{dl'} = - \frac{\mu_0}{4\pi} i \, d\Omega = - \frac{\mu_0}{4\pi} i \, \nabla\Omega \cdot \mathbf{dl'}$$

using the ordinary relation between gradient and increment (Appendix, Eq. A.2–19).

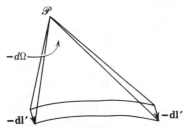

Fig. 7.6c.   A view of part of the solid angle subtended by a ribbon.

Since Eq. 7.6–6 is true for every $\mathbf{dl'}$, we can let $\mathbf{dl'}$ be successively $\mathbf{1}_x \, dx$, $\mathbf{1}_y \, dy$, and $\mathbf{1}_z \, dz$ and show that $\mathbf{B}$ is itself proportional to $\nabla\Omega$:

$$\mathbf{B} = - \frac{\mu_0 i \, \nabla\Omega}{4\pi} \qquad (7.6\text{–}6a)$$

The sign in Eq. 7.6–6a was found by assuming that $\mathscr{P}$ is on the positive side of the circuit, as defined by the right-hand rule shown in Fig. 7.6d. If the fingers of the right hand are directed along the wire pointing in the direction chosen as positive for the current i, the thumb points toward the positive side of the loop. Point $\mathscr{P}$ in Fig. 7.6d is shown as on the positive side of the loop. Then Ω is taken as the interior solid angle subtended at $\mathscr{P}$. (Note that $\nabla\Omega$ is then a vector directed *toward* the loop.) More generally, when a line drawn from the interior of the loop toward $\mathscr{P}$ leaves the former in the positive direction, the solid angle on the loop side of the cone is considered positive and that on the far side negative. If the line to $\mathscr{P}$ leaves the loop in the negative direction, the interior solid angle is negative and the exterior positive. The direction of $\mathbf{B}$ is that of $-\nabla\Omega$, so that $\mathbf{B}$ points away from the loop along its positive normal. This fact is in agreement with the assertion in Section 7.2 that the sense of circulation of the current is the same as that of the rotation of $\mathbf{F}$ to $\mathbf{v}_{\text{proj}}$. As implied earlier, the induction produced by several current loops is given by summing Eq. 7.6–7 for all the loops.

Equation 7.6–6a is the solid-angle form of Ampère's law. It shows that the magnetic induction is derivable from a scalar function $\Omega(x, y, z)$ of the coordinates of $\mathscr{P}$, which is analogous to the electrostatic potential V

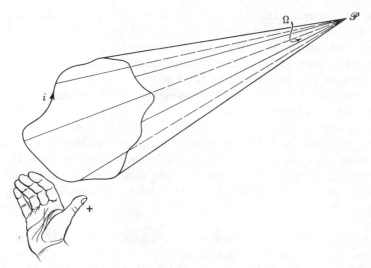

Fig. 7.6d.   The solid angle subtended at $\mathscr{P}$ by a current loop. The hand shows the sign convention for the positive side of the loop.

from which $\mathbf{E}$ can be derived. For convenience in later pursuing the analogy between electric- and magnetic-field quantities, we shall write $\mathbf{B}$ in MKS units as μ_0 times the gradient of a new function V_m, called the "magnetic scalar potential."

$$\mathbf{B} = -\mu_0 \nabla V_m \tag{7.6–7a}$$

Then using Eq. 7.6–6a we can write the magnetic scalar potential for a single current loop

$$V_m = \frac{i\Omega}{4\pi} \tag{7.6–8}$$

and for a collection of loops

$$V_m = \frac{1}{4\pi} \sum_k i_k \Omega_k \tag{7.6–9a}$$

Unlike the electrostatic potential, the potential V_m is not single-valued, since the solid angle Ω is not. Let us consider how Ω varies as $\mathscr{P}$ is moved about a particular loop.

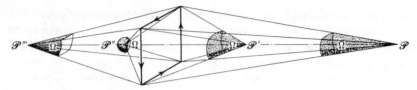

Fig. 7.6e.   Variations of Ω as $\mathscr{P}$ moves through a current loop. The solid angles are positive at each point shown.

As $\mathscr{P}$ recedes indefinitely from the loop in the positive direction (to "$+\infty$"), Ω passes from some positive value less than 2π to zero. If $\mathscr{P}$ approaches the inside of the loop, Ω approaches 2π. If we let $\mathscr{P}$ pass through the loop, Ω will continue to increase and become an exterior angle greater than 2π, approaching 4π as $\mathscr{P}$ goes to "$-\infty$." (Fig. 7.6e.)

On the other hand, if $\mathscr{P}$ is allowed to go around the outside of the loop (Fig. 7.6f) and approach it from the negative side, Ω goes to 0 and must take on negative values since we shall not allow it or its derivative to have a discontinuous jump. (Negative plane angles may be defined by exactly the same argument.) As $\mathscr{P}$ approaches the loop from the back, Ω thus approaches -2π. It will be seen therefore that Ω is not a single-valued function of position. In fact, if $\mathscr{P}$ makes a series of circuits through the loop, Ω will change to $\Omega + 4\pi n$, where n is some positive or negative integer.

Thus the magnetic scalar potential V_m is multiple-valued. If we wish to restrict ourselves to the consideration of points well outside the current circuits under consideration, we can choose that value of Ω and hence of V_m which goes to zero at infinity. Hence V_m can be defined by an equation similar to Eq. 1.7–1 with a reference point chosen at infinity for simplicity:

$$V_m = -\frac{1}{\mu_0} \int_{\infty}^{\mathscr{P}} \mathbf{B} \cdot \mathbf{ds} \qquad (7.6\text{–}10)$$

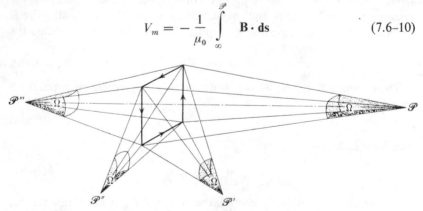

Fig. 7.6f.   Variations of Ω as $\mathscr{P}$ moves around a current loop. The solid angles at $\mathscr{P}$ and $\mathscr{P}'$ are positive, whereas those at $\mathscr{P}''$ and $\mathscr{P}'''$ are negative.

V_m will be multiple-valued unless the path in the integral is not allowed to pass through any current circuits, although it is otherwise arbitrary. The unit for V_m is not commonly given a name, although by Eq. 7.6–8 the MKS unit has the dimensions of amperes.

We have not interpreted V_m as representing energy for the reason that **B** does not directly represent a force on a real entity. If single magnetic poles really existed, then as we shall show in Section 8.2, $\mathbf{B}/\mu_0$ would be the force on a unit pole at the point in question. Hence, we may speak of V_m as a sort of fictional "potential energy per unit pole." This type of energy is not conserved with respect to closed-path motions, as is the genuine electrostatic potential energy, because of the multiple-valued nature of V_m.

This multiple-valuedness results in the complete absence of a scalar potential in a region with a volume current distribution **J**, for in such regions we have to imagine an infinite number of infinitesimal loop filaments, each of which involves multiple values of V_m. (The existence of V_m requires **curl B** $= 0$, and we shall show in Section 7.9 that where **J** is not zero, neither is **curl B**.)

The magnetic induction **B** depends on the gradient $\nabla\Omega$, and this quantity is single-valued, since Ω and $\Omega + 4\pi n$ have the same derivatives.

In Gaussian units, $\mu_0/4\pi$ in the formulas for B is replaced by $1/c$, and the relation between **B** and V_m is defined so as to have no constant multiplier. We have then for current loops

$$\mathbf{B} = \frac{i}{c} \oint \frac{\mathbf{dl} \times \mathbf{1}_r}{r^2} \qquad \text{Gaussian} \quad (7.6\text{–}1b)$$

$$\mathbf{B} = -\frac{i}{c} \nabla\Omega \qquad \text{Gaussian} \quad (7.6\text{–}6b)$$

$$\mathbf{B} = -\nabla V_m \qquad \text{Gaussian} \quad (7.6\text{–}7b)$$

$$V_m = \frac{1}{c} \sum_k i_k \Omega_k \qquad \text{Gaussian} \quad (7.6\text{–}9b)$$

and for a moving charge

$$\mathbf{B} = \frac{q\mathbf{v} \times \mathbf{1}_r}{cr^2} \qquad \text{Gaussian} \quad (7.6\text{–}4b)$$

In the Gaussian system, the esu of charge is defined by Coulomb's law, so that i is measured in statamperes, or statcoulombs/second, one statampere being equal to 3.335×10^{-10} amp. The experimental constant c is defined so as to appear equally in Eqs. 7.2–2b and 7.6–1b; identification with the velocity of light will be made in Chapter 10. An experimentally simpler formulation of the MKS definition of the coulomb and the Gaussian-system definition of c will appear in Section 7.8. Using Gaussian units, it is easy to see that the magnetic force between charges q and q' moving with speeds v and v' is of the order of vv'/c^2 times the Coulomb force, thus explaining the difficulty of measuring the magnetic force between moving charges in a direct way.

Problem 7.6a. Show by an example that the forces according to 7.4–2 and 7.6–3 between two suitably-oriented current elements are not equal and opposite.

Problem 7.6b. Show that the dimensions of the quantity $(\mu_0\epsilon_0)^{-1}$ are (meter/second)^2 regardless of whether μ_0 is taken to be dimensionless.

Problem 7.6c. Show that $\nabla^2 V_m = 0$ in any region free of current by using the results of Problem 1.10d. Then show that div **B** is zero in every such region.

7.7   The Circuital Form of Ampère's Law

The third form of Ampère's law we wish to introduce is a formula for the circulation of **B**, $\oint \mathbf{B} \cdot d\mathbf{l}'$. The formula for a closed loop of current follows easily from the solid-angle form or its equivalent, Eq. 7.6–6. Let

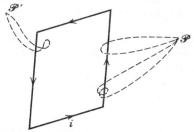

Fig. 7.7a.   Stokesian paths linking a current loop once, twice, and zero times.

us add up the increments $\mathbf{B} \cdot d\mathbf{l}'$ obtained by considering a series of points $\mathscr{P}$ along some arbitrary closed path in space. (Such paths are analogous to the Gaussian surfaces of Section 1.4. They are introduced in locations convenient for calculation and usually do not coincide with any material wires. They can be called Stokesian paths, because of Stokes' theorem, A.3–40.) If the path does not encircle the current, $\oint d\Omega$ is clearly zero, and we have $\oint \mathbf{B} \cdot d\mathbf{l}' = 0$. If the path links the current once, the discussion of solid angle in the previous section shows that Ω must change by 4π. (See Figs. 7.6e and f, and 7.7a.) The sign of the change depends on which way the path goes, i.e., on the directions of the various elements $d\mathbf{l}'$, so that we must specify a positive direction on our arbitrary path. Let us take this path as passing through the loop toward the positive side, which is seen to be the same as passing around the wire in the direction given by the right-hand rule for Eq. 7.6–3. Then the increment of Ω around the path is -4π and using Eq. 7.6–6 we find for the circulation

$$\oint \mathbf{B} \cdot d\mathbf{l}' = \mu_0 i \qquad (7.7\text{–}1)$$

The Stokesian paths can be considered flexible and can be moved around without changing the integrals as long as no currents are cut across. In the general case of a path that links several current loops (or the same one several times), we have

$$\oint \mathbf{B} \cdot d\mathbf{l}' = \mu_0 \sum_k i_k \qquad (7.7\text{–}2a)$$

The summations here include each current once for each time it is linked in the positive sense, and once with the negative sign for each time it is linked in the reverse sense.

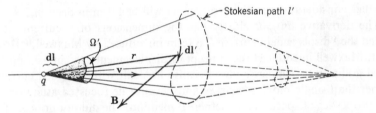

Fig. 7.7b. Illustrating the calculation of the circulation of the field $\mathbf{B}$ produced by a moving charge q around a closed Stokesian path in its neighborhood subtending a solid angle Ω'. The displacement occurs during a time dt given by $d\mathbf{l} = \mathbf{v}\, dt$.

Although the formulas given for $\mathbf{B}$ in Section 7.6 all refer to its value at points not occupied by currents—i.e., at points not *on* any elementary filament—the circuital form allows calculations involving $\mathbf{B}$ to be made at points within continuous current distributions. For instance, the current i in Eq. 7.7–1 can be replaced by $\int \mathbf{J} \cdot d\mathbf{S}$ over a surface bounded by the path for $\oint \mathbf{B} \cdot d\mathbf{l}'$. An example is given in the next section.

Let us now make a calculation of the circulation of $\mathbf{B}$ for a single moving charge, according to Laplace's rule in the form 7.6–4. If we write $\mathbf{v} = d\mathbf{l}/dt$, we can make use of the derivation of 7.6–6 from 7.6–4. We have, in fact,

$$\oint \mathbf{B} \cdot d\mathbf{l}' = \frac{\mu_0 q}{4\pi} \int_{l'} \frac{\mathbf{v} \times \mathbf{1}_r \cdot d\mathbf{l}'}{r^2} = \frac{\mu_0 q}{4\pi} \frac{d}{dt} \int_{l'} \frac{d\mathbf{l} \times \mathbf{1}_r \cdot d\mathbf{l}'}{r^2}$$

where the integral is over $d\mathbf{l}'$ along an arbitrary closed path l' near q, as in Fig. 7.7b. The rules for a triple scalar product allow the numerator of the integrand to be written $-d\mathbf{l}' \times \mathbf{1}_r \cdot d\mathbf{l}$. Thus we can see by comparison with the calculation of Eq. 7.6–6 that the integral is $+d\Omega'$, which is the variation of Ω' in Fig. 7.7b during the time interval dt. Thus we have

$$\oint \mathbf{B} \cdot \mathbf{dl'} = \frac{\mu_0 q}{4\pi} \frac{d\Omega'}{dt} \tag{7.7–3}$$

But according to Eq. 1.4–1b, the electric flux through the circulation path l' is $q\Omega'/4\pi\epsilon_0$, so we have the interesting and simple result

$$\oint \mathbf{B} \cdot \mathbf{dl'} = \mu_0 \epsilon_0 \, d\Phi_E/dt \tag{7.7–4}$$

For charges moving in free space, or in ideal dielectrics, $q\Omega'/4\pi$ is the displacement flux Φ_D through the loop, and we may write

$$\oint \mathbf{B} \cdot \mathbf{dl'} = \mu_0 \, d\Phi_D/dt \tag{7.7–5a}$$

Further consideration of dielectric media will be given in Section 7.9.

The derivative $d\Phi_D/dt$ clearly has the dimensions of a current. It is called the "displacement current," a term introduced by Maxwell.[15] However, Maxwell introduced the concept of displacement current as a postulated addition to Ampère's law. Because he dealt with extended currents rather than single moving charges and because he focussed attention on the properties of space as an "aethereal medium," he did not notice, or at any rate choose to point out, that the circuital law using the displacement current follows from the "action-at-a-distance" Laplace rule.

It should be noted that Ω', as shown in Fig. 7.7b and used in Eq. 7.7–3, obeys the opposite sign convention to Ω in Fig. 7.6d, a fact which is not surprising since Ω' is subtended by a Stokesian path and Ω by a current loop. If q passes through a Stokesian path, Ω' must increase to 2π and become an exterior solid angle as indicated by the dashed lines in Fig. 7.7b. On the other hand, if q passes outside the path, Ω' must go to zero and become negative, as shown in Fig. 7.7c.

The circulation due to a finite segment of current can be found by adding the contribution due to elements $i \, \mathbf{dl}$. Consider a current filament between two points where charge is piling up or leaving, as shown in Fig. 7.7d. The contribution to the circulation around l' of the charge dq in $\mathbf{dl}$ is

$$d \oint \mathbf{B} \cdot \mathbf{dl'} = \frac{\mu_0 \, dq}{4\pi} \frac{d\Omega'}{dt} = \frac{\mu_0 \, dq}{4\pi \, dt} d\Omega' = \frac{\mu_0 \, dq}{4\pi \, dt} \nabla\Omega' \cdot \mathbf{dl}$$

considering that dq travels through $\mathbf{dl}$ in dt and changes its solid angle by $d\Omega' = \nabla\Omega' \cdot \mathbf{dl}$. To add up the contributions from the entire segment of

---

[15] J. C. Maxwell, *Treatise on Electricity and Magnetism*, 2nd or 3rd ed., Clarendon Press, Oxford, 1881 and 1904, Dover, New York, reprint, 1962, articles 607–610.

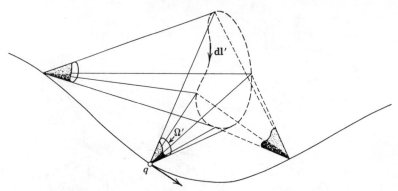

Fig. 7.7c. Variation of Ω' as q passes outside a Stokesian path.

current, we integrate over **dl**. The resulting variation of Ω' that appears will be the difference between Ω_+ and Ω_- as shown in the figure according to the sign convention just described. We have then

$$\oint_{l'} \mathbf{B} \cdot d\mathbf{l}' = \frac{\mu_0 i}{4\pi}(\Omega_+ - \Omega_-) \tag{7.7–6}$$

If the negative end of the segment is extended around a loop to close onto the positive end through the path l', we see in Fig. 7.7e that Ω_- becomes negative and in fact equal to $\Omega_+ - 4\pi$ so that we find Eq. 7.7–1 again. If instead the loop closes outside l', Ω_- becomes just equal to Ω_+ and the circulation is zero as expected.

The resulting equation for the segment, 7.7–6, is thus the appropriate formula for treating the circulation from part of a current filament. How-ever, it may also be considered as an application of the displacement-current rule, Eq. 7.7–5a, since $i = dq/dt$ is the rate of charging and discharging the elementary capacitances at the end of the segment, so that $i\Omega_+/4\pi$ is the rate of change of flux from the positive end of the segment, and $-i\Omega_-/4\pi$ is that from the negative end. Note that if the path l' is

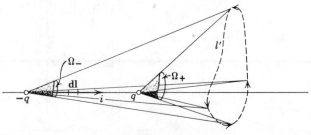

Fig. 7.7d. Illustrating the calculation of $\oint \mathbf{B} \cdot d\mathbf{l}$ for a segment of current between two points where charge piles up or leaves.

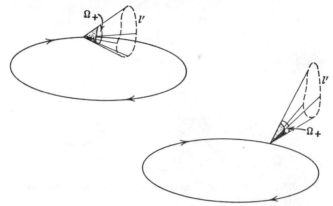

Fig. 7.7e. Closed current loops, one threading *I'* and one bypassing it.

shifted over the segment, so that the positive end has in effect passed through it, we must treat Ω_+ as greater than 2π, and the flux of q as more than $\frac{1}{2}q$ in the positive direction, rather than as less than $\frac{1}{2}q$ in the negative direction.

Let us consider now the circulation of **B** around a circuit containing a capacitor. Each current filament starts at a point on the negative plate and ends at one on the positive plate (Fig. 7.7*f*). If the circulation is taken about a path in the neighborhood of the plates such as 1 in the figure, it

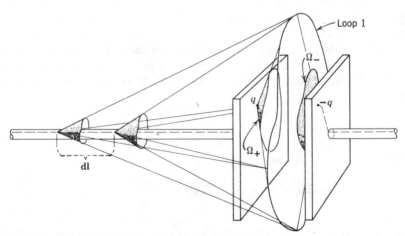

Fig. 7.7f. A current filament between points on the plates of a condenser. The current *i* provides the end points with charges q and $-q$.

is simplest to use Eq. 7.7–5a summed over all filaments and, therefore, involving the total flux Φ_D, which for symmetrical capacitors is usually not hard to calculate.

If, however, the circulation is wanted about a path like 2 in Fig. 7.7g, one would prefer to use the ordinary current form. This can be done by the device of imagining each current filament to be completed across the capacitor, giving the ordinary result 7.7–1, and then subtracting the circulation produced by the added pieces. By this device, the difference $\Omega_+ - \Omega_-$ in 7.7–6 becomes small, rather than being nearly 4π as it would be if

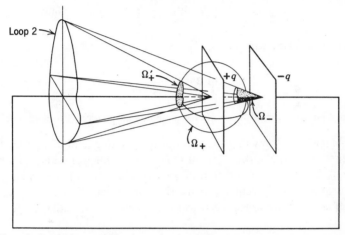

Fig. 7.7g. A circulation path far from the capacitor plates of Fig. 7.7d. Direct use of Eq. 7.7-6 involves the external solid angle Ω_+, but it is simpler to use the internal solid angle $\Omega_+{}'$ and to include a fictional conduction current between the plates.

the solid angles for the nearly closed original filaments were used. Moreover, the corresponding flux then has the ordinary value, rather than having one term referring to more than $\frac{1}{2}q$ in the apparently wrong direction as mentioned above. The circulation around path 2 is thus a sum of the contribution of the whole current i and of the displacement current from the net flux that passes through the path—part of the fringing field that necessarily accompanies every parallel-plate capacitor.

Such considerations show that in general we can write

$$\oint \mathbf{B} \cdot \mathbf{dl'} = \mu_0 \left[\sum_k i_k + \frac{d\Phi_D}{dt} \right] \tag{7.7-7}$$

where the contribution of every closed current filament appears only in the first term and the contribution of every open filament appears either in the first term with a correction for its lack of closure included in the second, or entirely in the second term by a different choice of the signs of the solid angles in calculating the flux Φ_D.[16]

We see that in general a current filament appears in the circuital law either in the ordinary-current form or in the displacement-current form, but not in both ways at once. Note that the correction term in Eq. 7.7–7 goes to zero in each of the limiting cases just discussed.

In Gaussian units, the circuital law has μ_0 replaced by $4\pi/c$. For a set of closed current loops we have

$$\oint \mathbf{B} \cdot d\mathbf{l}' = \frac{4\pi}{c} \sum_k i_k \qquad \text{Gaussian} \quad (7.7\text{–}2b)$$

and for the displacement current

$$\oint \mathbf{B} \cdot d\mathbf{l}' = \frac{1}{c} \frac{d\Phi_D}{dt} \qquad \text{Gaussian} \quad (7.7\text{–}5b)$$

since in Gaussian units, $\Phi_D = q\Omega$ for a single charge q (cf. Problem 3.8f).

Problem 7.7a. Show that the effect of the fringing field of a parallel-plate condenser is to make the value of the circuital integral taken on a path l' just outside the condenser plates less than the value of this integral on a path around the current far from the condenser. Discuss the value of $\oint \mathbf{B} \cdot d\mathbf{l}'$ as the path is moved toward the back side of either plate.

7.8 Applications of Ampère's Law for Steady Currents

There are a limited number of cases in which the calculation of magnetic fields is elementary. A number of these will now be given as examples of the three forms of Ampère's law we have just introduced.

The circuital form can be used easily in those cases in which the field has an appropriate symmetry. Let us consider first a long, straight, thin wire and find $\mathbf{B}$ at a point sufficiently near it that it may be treated as having infinite length (e.g., the effect of the distant return portion of the circuit can be neglected; cf. Problem 7.8c for a proof that this neglect is legitimate). Then $\mathbf{B}$ at a point $\mathscr{P}$ must by symmetry be tangent to a circle l' through $\mathscr{P}$ coaxial with the wire. Let us use such a circle for calculation of the circulation. The magnitude of $\mathbf{B}$ must be the same all around the circle, so that $\oint \mathbf{B} \cdot d\mathbf{s} = 2\pi r B$ where r is the distance of $\mathscr{P}$ from the center of the wire. (Figs. 7.8a and b.)

---

[16] A somewhat different discussion of this development is given by A. P. French and J. R. Tessman, *Am. J. Phys.* **31**, 201 (1963).

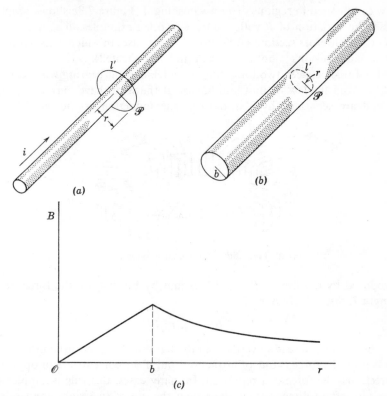

Fig. 7.8a to c. Calculation of **B** inside and outside a long straight wire by the circuital method.

Hence we have the result, due originally to Biot and Savart,[17] for the field outside an infinite straight thin wire:

$$B = \frac{\mu_0 i}{2\pi r} \qquad (7.8\text{--}1a)$$

If the wire has a radius b and the current density J is uniform throughout its interior, the current within a circular cylinder of radius $r < b$ will be $\pi r^2 J = i(r^2/b^2)$ and we have

$$2\pi r B = \mu_0 i(r^2/b^2)$$

or

$$B = \frac{\mu_0 i r}{2\pi b^2}, \qquad r \leqslant b \qquad (7.8\text{--}2)$$

This is the only simple case in which the dimensions of the wire can be taken into account. However, this case does show explicitly how Ampère's

[17] J.-B. Biot and F. Savart, *loc. cit.*

law can be used in regions of non-vanishing **J**. Figure 7.8c shows graphically the variation of B with radius. Our other examples all assume wires of negligible cross section (cf. Section 7.17 for cases in which consideration of wire dimensions is both necessary and complicated).

The force between two long, thin, parallel, current-bearing wires can be found from the law of Biot and Savart. If the wires have currents i_1 and i_2 and are separated by a distance r, the induction at the second one

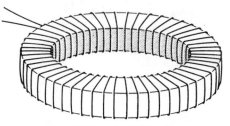

Fig. 7.8d.   A toroidal solenoid.

produced by the first is $B = \mu_0 i_1 / 2\pi r$ and by Eq. 7.4–2a, the force on a length L of the second is

$$F = i_2 BL = \mu_0 i_1 i_2 L / 2\pi r \qquad (7.8\text{–}3a)$$

The reader can readily verify the fact that if the currents are in the same direction, the force is one of attraction; but if the currents are in opposite directions, the force is a repulsion. In many cases, this rule is simpler to use for getting directions or signs than the use of two right-hand rules. Equation 7.8–3a can be used as *an experimental definition of the ampere*, since μ_0 is an exactly defined constant and F and r are measurable in terms of newtons and meters.[18] Actually, as we shall see later, a current balance using the force between circular coils is a more practical device for establishing the unit of current than is a pair of parallel wires.

Another symmetrical case is that of the toroidal solenoid,[19] shown in Fig. 7.8d and e. Regardless of the shape of the cross section of the coil, **B** will be the same at all points on a circle coaxial with the toroid,[20] so that again we can use such a circle for calculation. Through consideration of the solid angles subtended at a point on such a circle by symmetrically placed coils, one can prove that **B** is tangent to the circle (Problem 7.8b). Let us first take a circle l' that lies inside the coil. If the coil has N turns

---

[18] Cf. footnote 12 on p. 288.

[19] A pipelike coil, named from the Greek "solen," a pipe.

[20] This is provided the winding is sufficiently uniform and closely packed. We neglect here the helical nature of solenoid windings, assuming each coil to be in a plane containing the axis (see Problem 7.8q).

and each carries the same current i by virtue of the continuous, helical winding, the path l' surrounds the current Ni and

$$2\pi r B = \mu_0 Ni$$

so that

$$B = \frac{\mu_0 Ni}{2\pi r} \qquad (7.8\text{-}4a)$$

Sometimes it is convenient to describe the coil in terms of the number of turns per unit length n_l measured along a circle drawn through the center

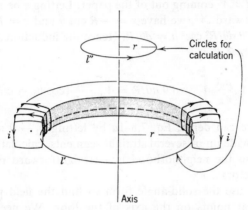

Fig. 7.8e. View of one-half of a toroidal solenoid.

of the cross section. If this circle has a radius b, then $N = 2\pi b n_l$ and

$$B = \frac{\mu_0 b}{r} n_l i \qquad (7.8\text{-}4b)$$

If now the dimensions of the cross section are small compared to b, then r differs from b at most by a small amount, and the value of B at the center may be taken as the value throughout the coil,

$$B = \mu_0 n_l i \qquad (7.8\text{-}5)$$

The field outside the coil is everywhere zero (neglecting effects of winding helicity). This is readily proved by calculating the circulation of $\mathbf{B}$ around a coaxial circle l'' that lies outside the coil and therefore links no current.

The magnetic induction produced by a circuit made up of a number of segments of straight lines, (i.e., a polygon) may be found by the use of Laplace's rule. Let us consider a single segment. In Fig. 7.8f, a segment $\mathcal{MN}$ of a circuit carries a current i. The field at $\mathcal{P}$ produced by this segment is given by integrating Eq. 7.6-2 from $\mathcal{M}$ to $\mathcal{N}$. Let us set $\mathbf{dl} = \mathbf{1}_z\,dz$; then $\mathbf{1}_z \times \mathbf{1}_r = \sin\theta \mathbf{1}_\varphi$ where $\mathbf{1}_\varphi$ is a unit vector at $\mathcal{P}$ perpendicular

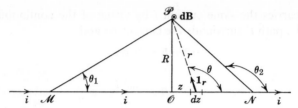

Fig. 7.8f. Illustrating the calculation of **B** at $\mathscr{P}$ produced by a wire segment $\mathscr{MN}$ carrying a current *i*. **dB** is a vector coming out of the page.

to the plane $\mathscr{M} \mathscr{P} \mathscr{N}$ coming out of the paper. Letting z be measured from $\mathcal{O}$ positively toward $\mathscr{N}$, we have $z = -R \cot \theta$ and $r = R \csc \theta$, so that $dz/r^2 = R \csc^2 \theta \, d\theta / R^2 \csc^2 \theta = d\theta / R$. Hence the induction at $\mathscr{P}$ produced by the segment $\mathscr{MN}$ is

$$\mathbf{B} = \mathbf{1}_\varphi \frac{\mu_0 i}{4\pi} \int_{\theta_1}^{\theta_2} \sin \theta \, d\theta / R = \mathbf{1}_\varphi \frac{\mu_0 i}{4\pi R} (\cos \theta_1 - \cos \theta_2) \quad (7.8\text{–}6)$$

from which we can derive Eq. 7.8–1a by letting $\theta_1 \to 0$ and $\theta_2 \to 180°$. For a circuit made up of several straight segments, calculation of the field at any point in the neighborhood is a straightforward problem in the addition of vectors.

Let us now use the solid-angle form to find the field produced by a circular loop at points on the axis of the loop. We need the formula (calculated in Problem 1.4f and g) for the solid angle subtended by a circle of radius a at a point $\mathscr{P}$ on its axis a distance z from its plane (see Fig. 7.8g):

$$\Omega = 2\pi(1 - \cos \theta) = 2\pi\left(1 - \frac{z}{(a^2 + z^2)^{1/2}}\right) \quad (7.8\text{–}7)$$

where θ is the angle indicated in the figure. By symmetry, the field at $\mathscr{P}$ must be along the axis; thus we can find **B** from $-\mu_0 i \, \nabla\Omega/4\pi$ even though we know Ω only on the axis and not at any other point and so cannot calculate derivatives with respect to x and y. We find on differentiating Ω that

$$B_z = \frac{-\mu_0 i}{4\pi} \frac{\partial \Omega}{\partial z} = \frac{\mu_0 i a^2}{2(a^2 + z^2)^{3/2}} \quad (7.8\text{–}8a)$$

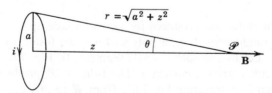

Fig. 7.8g. Calculation of **B** on the axis of a circular loop.

At the center of the circle,

$$B = \frac{\mu_0 i}{2a} \qquad (7.8\text{–}8b)$$

If the loop consists of N turns of wire close together, of average radius a, then i in the last two equations is to be replaced by Ni.

An approximate formula can be found for the solid angle subtended by a current loop at distant points by treating the area of the loop like ΔS in Fig. 1.4d. We have simply

$$\Omega = \mathbf{S} \cdot \mathbf{1}_r / r^2 \qquad (7.8\text{–}9)$$

as in Fig. 7.8h. The magnetic scalar potential of the loop is thus, using 7.6–8,

$$V_m = \frac{i\mathbf{S} \cdot \mathbf{1}_r}{4\pi r^2} \qquad (7.8\text{–}10a)$$

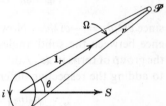

Fig. 7.8h. The solid angle subtended by S at $\mathscr{P}$ is $\mathbf{S} \cdot \mathbf{1}_r / r^2$.

By comparison with Eq. 3.1–4 we see that the magnetic field at a distance from a small current loop is mathematically analogous to the electric field of a dipole since each is the gradient of a potential that has the same variation in space. The analogy is made explicit by defining the vector $i\mathbf{S}$ as the *magnetic dipole moment* of the current loop, denoted by

$$\mathbf{m} = i\mathbf{S} \qquad (7.8\text{–}11a)$$

and measured in meter^2-ampere in the MKS system. We have then

$$V_m = \frac{\mathbf{m} \cdot \mathbf{1}_r}{4\pi r^2} \qquad (7.8\text{–}10b)$$

and we obtain the approximate result

$$\mathbf{B} = -\mu_0 \nabla V_m = \frac{\mu_0 m}{4\pi r^3}(2\cos\theta\mathbf{1}_r + \sin\theta\mathbf{1}_\theta) \qquad (7.8\text{–}12a)$$

(cf. Eqs. 3.1–7 or 1.3–1).

The field inside a circular-cylindrical solenoid may be readily derived from the solid-angle rule. Let us find the component parallel to the axis of the coil. In Figs. 7.8i and j point $\mathscr{P}$ has a coordinate z, measured from the center $\mathcal{O}$. Let the coil have n_l turns per unit length and consider the contribution at $\mathscr{P}$ produced by the turns in a length dz' of the coil at distance z' from $\mathcal{O}$. The solid angle Ω is a function of $z - z'$, and

$$dB_z = \frac{-\mu_0 i n_l\, dz'}{4\pi}\frac{\partial\Omega}{\partial z} = \frac{\mu_0 i n_l\, dz'}{4\pi}\frac{\partial\Omega}{\partial z'}$$

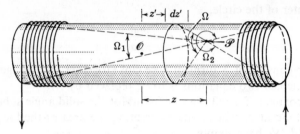

Fig. 7.8i.   Calculation of B_z in a solenoid.

since $\partial\Omega/\partial z = -\partial\Omega/\partial z'$. Now the differential $(\partial\Omega/\partial z')\,dz'$ is just the difference between the solid angles subtended by the front and back sides of the group of turns in dz'. Adding the contributions of all turns thus amounts to adding the respective differences; the result on integration is that

$$B_z = \frac{\mu_0 i n_l}{4\pi} \int_{\text{coil}} \frac{\partial\Omega}{\partial z'}\, dz' = \frac{\mu_0 i n_l}{4\pi}(\Omega_2 - \Omega_1) \qquad (7.8\text{–}13)$$

(Note that we can only get B_z this way; not B_x or B_y.) Now if the coil is long and thin and we consider points $\mathscr{P}$ inside and near the center, Ω_2 is nearly 4π and Ω_1 is nearly 0. Hence for a long thin solenoid, the axial field anywhere inside far from the ends is

$$B_z = \mu_0 n_l i \qquad (7.8\text{–}14a)$$

Thus the axial field inside a long thin solenoid is constant throughout the central region.

For coils of any length, we can evaluate Ω_1 and Ω_2 by Eq. 7.8–7 for points on the axis. The reader will verify that the result is

$$B_z = \tfrac{1}{2}\mu_0 n_l i(\cos\theta_2 + \cos\theta_1) \qquad (7.5\text{–}15)$$

where θ_2 and θ_1 are the angles indicated in Fig. 7.8j. This formula is valid for points both inside and outside the coil. At the center of a long coil, $\cos\theta_1 = \cos\theta_2 \cong 1$, so we get Eq. 7.8–14a again. At the end of a long

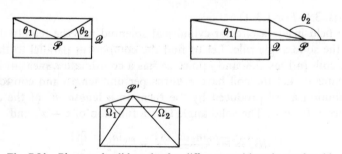

Fig. 7.8j.   Plane and solid angles for different positions in a solenoid.

coil, point $\mathscr{Q}$ in Fig. 7.8j, $\cos \theta_2 = 0$ and $\cos \theta_1 \cong 1$, so the field is one-half the value at the center.

Let us finally consider points outside the solenoid near its center ($\mathscr{P}'$ in Fig. 7.8j). Here Ω_1 of Fig. 7.8i will be a small, positive solid angle while Ω_2 will be a small negative solid angle, as can be seen by following the variation of Ω from one end to the other of the coil. For an infinitely long solenoid, the field is zero anywhere outside. An approximation for long but finite solenoids is considered in Problem 7.8k.

Some Gaussian formulas for the results of this section are as follows. For the field outside a long straight wire,

$$B = \frac{2i}{cr} \qquad \text{Gaussian} \quad (7.8\text{-}1b)$$

and for the force between parallel wires of length L,

$$F = 2i_1 i_2 L / c^2 r \qquad \text{Gaussian} \quad (7.8\text{-}3b)$$

Equation 7.8-3b enables us to evaluate the constant c by measuring the force in dynes, the distance in centimeters. and the current in statamperes. The quantity i/c is the measure of current in electromagnetic units (emu) or abamperes, so that 1 abampere $= c$ statamperes. For the field at the center of a toroid or straight solenoid we have

$$B = 4\pi n_1 i / c \qquad (7.8\text{-}14b)$$

For the magnetic moment of a current loop in Gaussian units we write

$$\mathbf{m} = i \mathbf{S} / c \qquad (7.8\text{-}11b)$$

so that

$$V_m = \mathbf{m} \cdot \mathbf{1}_r / r^2 \qquad (7.8\text{-}10c)$$

and

$$\mathbf{B} = \frac{m}{r^3} (2 \cos \theta \, \mathbf{1}_r + \sin \theta \, \mathbf{1}_\theta) \qquad (7.8\text{-}12b)$$

The Gaussian units of magnetic moment are seen to be gauss-cm^3.

Problem 7.8a. Two flat rectangular current-bearing coils, one slightly larger than the other, are mounted on a common axis which lies in the plane of each. If their sides parallel to the axis are long compared to the other sides, find the torque of each on the other in terms of the dimensions, numbers of turns per coil, and angle of displacement.

Problem 7.8b. Prove as suggested in the text that $\mathbf{B}$ for a toroidal coil is everywhere tangent to a circle coaxial with the coil. *Hint:* Divide the coil into pairs of symmetrically placed coils and show that for each pair, the sum of the solid angle gradients has vanishing components in a plane containing the axis.

Problem 7.8c. Find **B** in the plane of a square wire loop of side a, carrying current i, at a point which is on the perpendicular bisector of one side and at a distance r from the wire toward the center of the square. Show that if $a \to \infty$ while r remains constant, we get as the result Eq. 7.8–1.

Problem 7.8d. Find the acceleration of an electron moving with a speed of 2.0×10^5 m/sec along a radius outside a long straight wire carrying a current of 3.0 amp, when the electron is at a distance of 3.0 cm from the wire.

Problem 7.8e. How close must two parallel wires be if they each carry 25 amp and repel each other with a force of 10 dynes/cm?

Problem 7.8f. Calculate the first and second derivatives of B_z in Eq. 7.8–8a with respect to z, and state a general rule for the symmetry of any derivative with respect to a change from z to $-z$. If two identical coils, each with N turns that are very close together compared to the common coil radius a, are placed with their axes coinciding at a distance apart equal to a, show that the first three derivatives of the combined field of the two coils vanish at the axial point that is equidistant from the two. Such a pair of coils is called a Helmholtz pair. Show that B at this point is equal to $8\mu_0 iN/5^{3/4}a$.

Problem 7.8g. Show why Eq. 7.8–5 can be expected to be the same as Eq. 7.8–14. Find B at the center of a solenoid 70 cm long, 10 cm in diameter, wound uniformly with a total of 300 turns, carrying a current of 6.0 amp.

Problem 7.8h. Use the circuital form of Ampère's law to relate the values of B_z just inside and just outside any point on the winding of a solenoid. Write this result in terms of J_S, the current crossing a unit length of surface. Show that B_z outside the winding near the center of a very long solenoid is equal to zero.

Problem 7.8i. Use a symmetry argument on the variation of Ω in the plane midway between two equal symmetrically placed circular coils to show that **B** in this plane is everywhere perpendicular to it, and hence show that **B** is everywhere parallel to the axis in the perpendicular bisecting plane of a solenoid.

Problem 7.8j. A long straight wire carries a current of 2 amp. A rectangular coil 3 cm × 5 cm lies in a plane containing the long wire, with the 5-cm sides parallel to the wire and the nearest side 3 cm away. Find the force on the rectangle if it carries 10 amp.

Problem 7.8k. Use the approximate formula 7.8–9 for solid angles subtended by the ends of a solenoid to obtain an improved formula for **B** in the mid-plane of a long solenoid at a distance r from the center, both inside and outside the coil.

Problem 7.8l. A solenoid of not especially great length has a single layer of n_t turns per meter over its entire length L and an extra layer covering a short length L' from each end toward the middle. Assuming no increase in diameter for the extra windings, find how to determine L' so that the field at the center will be equal to that for an infinitely long, single-layer coil.

Problem 7.8m. A wire 5 cm long is kept parallel to a long straight wire carrying 20 amp and moved perpendicularly to it, the motion being in the plane of the two wires. If the short wire moves away from the long wire at 10 m/sec, what is the emf induced in the former when the distance between the wires is (a) 1 cm, (b) 1 m?

Problem 7.8n. A square coil 1 cm on a side, with 15 turns, is hung inside the center of a long solenoid with 2000 turns per meter, carrying 300 ma. If the plane of the square coil makes an angle of 25° with the axis of the solenoid and the coil carries 1 ma, find the torque on it.

Problem 7.8o. A steady current of 1000 amp is established in a long, straight, hollow, aluminum conductor of inner radius 0.500 in. and outer radius 0.750 in. Assuming uniform resistivity, calculate **B** as a function of the distance r from the axis of the conductor.

Problem 7.8p. By comparing Eq. 7.8–3b with Coulomb's law written in electrostatic units, show that c has the dimensions of centimeter/second and that a statampere has the dimensions of dyne$^{1/2}$-centimeter/second.

Problem 7.8q. Show that the field on the axis of a toroidal coil, caused by the fact that the winding is helical and not a series of plane loops, is approximately that of a single, coaxial, circular loop of radius b, carrying current i. Discuss the field outside a straight solenoid arising from the helicity·of the winding.

Problem 7.8r. Find **B** at a point $\mathscr{P}$ 5 m from a circular coil of 3 cm diameter, with 30 turns of wire carrying 150 milliamps. The line from $\mathscr{P}$ to the center of the coil makes an angle of 45° with the axis of the coil.

7.9 Differential-Equation Form of Ampère's Law

We have so far presented three forms[21] of the law by which currents produce magnetic fields. These are all of the nature of "action-at-a-distance" formulas, in which the field at one point is related to currents elsewhere. Now, just as we did for Coulomb's law in Section 1.5, we can write a differential equation that expresses Ampère's law in terms of

[21] The law of Biot and Savart 7.6–1, the solid-angle form 7.6–6, and the circuital form 7.7–2. The Laplace rule 7.6–2 may be considered as a modification of 7.6–1 and 7.7–7 a variant of 7.7–2.

currents and fields at a single point. This form is useful in cases of volume distributions of current and also in showing how **B** can be thought of as being "propagated" point by point from the immediate neighborhood of a current to any particular distant point in space. The equation we are to derive is, in fact, the second of Maxwell's equations for electromagnetic radiation.

A volume current distribution is to be described in terms of the current density **J** as described in Chapter 5. Let us first consider the case in which each current filament is a closed loop so that there can be no points at which charge collects. Let us also assume that no dielectric medium is present—the current conductor is in a vacuum. This means that Φ_D is constant, $\partial\rho/\partial t = 0$ and $\nabla \cdot \mathbf{J} = 0$ (Eq. 5.2–4). The case when $\partial\rho/\partial t$ does not vanish will be taken up shortly.

Let us calculate the circulation of **B** around a closed Stokesian path in terms of current density across a surface bounded by the loop. We have, using 7.7–1 and Stokes' theorem,

$$\oint_{l'} \mathbf{B} \cdot \mathbf{dl'} = \mu_0 i = \mu_0 \int_S \mathbf{J} \cdot \mathbf{dS}$$

$$= \int_S \nabla \times \mathbf{B} \cdot \mathbf{dS}$$

This result must hold for any path and surface drawn in the region containing current, which can only mean that the integrands are equal:

$$\nabla \times \mathbf{B} = \mu_0 \mathbf{J} \qquad (7.9\text{–}1)$$

The fact that $\nabla \cdot \mathbf{J} = 0$ is corroborated by noting that the divergence of the curl of any vector is identically zero (cf. Appendix, p. 634).

In case $\partial\rho/\partial t$ is not everywhere negligible—for instance, if there is appreciable capacitance in the circuit and the current is not constant— there will in general be displacement currents through any given closed path, and Eqs. 7.7–5 or 7.7–7 should be used (we still assume no polarizable material to be present). Let us use 7.7–7 and sum over all current filaments, with the understanding that if a given current filament intersects the surface S, it is to be included in the $\sum_k i_k$ term with the flux of displacement from its ends included as a correction. On the other hand, if the filament does not intersect S, its entire contribution is to be included in terms of displacement current. Since Φ_D can be written as an integral over S, we have

$$\oint \mathbf{B} \cdot \mathbf{dl'} = \int_S \nabla \times \mathbf{B} \cdot \mathbf{dS} = \mu_0 \int_S \mathbf{J} \cdot \mathbf{dS} + \mu_0 \frac{d}{dt} \int \mathbf{D} \cdot \mathbf{dS} \quad (7.9\text{–}2)$$

Note that Stokes' law holds for *any* surface S bounded by l'. If as in Fig. 7.9a we have two surfaces S and S', of which one passes between a pair of condenser plates and one cuts a wire, the integrals over S and S' must be equal. Our discussion in Section 7.7 of the shift from the conduction to displacement form of the contribution of any one current filament may be used to show explicitly how the two integrals turn out to be equal. In fact, if all the flux Φ_D from plate $\mathscr{A}$ passes through S', we readily see using $i = dQ/dt = d\Phi_D/dt$ that the integral over S gives i directly, and that over S' it is equal to $d\Phi_D/dt$. A path l'' far enough out to be beyond

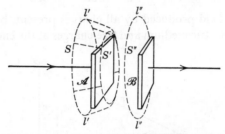

Fig. 7.9a. Two surfaces S and S' whose boundary is path l' and a surface S'' bounded by path e''.

all but a negligible part of the fringing field will also have a circulation equal to $\mu_0 i = \mu_0\, d\Phi_D/dt$.

On interchanging the time derivative and space integration, naturally assuming l' and S to be fixed, and then choosing arbitrarily small loops, we find

$$\nabla \times \mathbf{B} = \mu_0\left(\mathbf{J} + \frac{\partial \mathbf{D}}{\partial t}\right) \tag{7.9–3a}$$

as the Maxwell equation representing Ampère's law. It satisfies the continuity Eq. 5.2–3, for if we take the divergence of each side and divide by μ_0, we have

$$0 = \nabla \cdot \mathbf{J} + \nabla \cdot \frac{\partial \mathbf{D}}{\partial t} = \nabla \cdot \mathbf{J} + \frac{\partial}{\partial t}\, \nabla \cdot \mathbf{D}$$

$$= \nabla \cdot \mathbf{J} + \frac{\partial \rho}{\partial t}$$

using the Gauss flux law for displacement, Eq. 3.5–4.

Now imagine there to be polarizable material present. In time-varying circumstances, the polarization $\mathbf{P}$ will also vary, and one can see by the discussion in Section 3.4 of the transport of charge across a surface as $\mathbf{P}$ is set up or varied, that $\partial \mathbf{P}/\partial t$ is the current density associated with the variation of $\mathbf{P}$. Whatever the variation of $\mathbf{P}$ in space and time, we can

imagine the polarization current to be described in terms of current filaments of finite length, perhaps as short as the length of individual molecules, but of macroscopic length in sufficiently continuous situations. These
polarization currents will also make contributions to the circulation of **B**
around an arbitrary path. Of course as long as we treat them explicitly,
we should use $\epsilon_0 \mathbf{E}$ in place of **D**, as we also should for the conduction
currents. Thus we can write in place of 7.9–3a

$$\mathbf{V} \times \mathbf{B} = \mu_0 \left[\mathbf{J} + \frac{\partial \mathbf{P}}{\partial t} + \epsilon_0 \frac{\partial \mathbf{E}}{\partial t} \right] \qquad (7.9\text{–}4)$$

where $\epsilon_0 \mathbf{E}$ is the field produced by all charges present, both polarization
charges in the dielectric medium and free charges at the ends of conduction

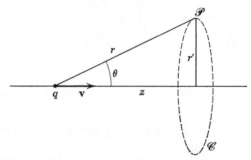

Fig. 7.9b. Calculation of **B** at $\mathscr{P}$ produced by a charge q moving with a velocity **v**.

filaments. However, by definition $\epsilon_0 \mathbf{E} + \mathbf{P} = \mathbf{D}$, regardless of whether or
not the medium is ideal. We are led right back to 7.9–3a as a *general* rule,
when **J** is all the current density present *except* for polarization currents.

Maxwell developed his equations of the electromagnetic field without
benefit of Laplace's rule, for this differential form of the law of Biot and
Savart was not in good repute at the time; consequently he could derive
Eq. 7.9–1, but not 7.9–3a. Maxwell had the genius, however, to see that
7.9–3a was the correct extension of 7.9–1 for varying currents, although
he couched his approach in terms of the aether theories to which he sub-
scribed. We shall see in Chapter 10 that it is just the addition of the displacement current density $\partial \mathbf{D}/\partial t$ to 7.9–1 that makes a theory of electromagnetic waves possible.

We derived 7.9–3a from Laplace's formula for the field of a single moving
charge. Now let us show how to find the latter from the former. In the first
place, we can integrate 7.9–3a over any surface S bounded by a path l' and
obtain 7.9–2.

Let a charge q move with a speed **v** along a straight line. At a fixed point
$\mathscr{P}$ a distance r from q (Fig. 7.9b), **B** is by symmetry tangent to a circle $\mathscr{C}$

of radius r' coaxial with $\mathbf{v}$ and has the same magnitude everywhere on $\mathscr{C}$. Calculating the circulation on $\mathscr{C}$, we have $\oint \mathbf{B} \cdot \mathbf{dl'} = 2\pi r' B$.

Taking any surface S bounded by $\mathscr{C}$ and not passing through or beyond the charge, we have $i = 0$ and Φ_D equal to q times the ratio of the solid angle subtended at q by $\mathscr{C}$, to 4π: $\Phi_D = (q/4\pi)2\pi(1 - \cos\theta) = \frac{1}{2}q\{1 - [z/(r'^2 + z^2)^{\frac{1}{2}}]\}$. Φ_D varies because z varies, with $dz/dt = -v$. Hence,

$$d\Phi_D/dt = \tfrac{1}{2}q \frac{d}{dz}\left(1 - \frac{z}{(r'^2 + z^2)^{\frac{1}{2}}}\right) \cdot \frac{dz}{dt} = \frac{qr'^2 v}{2(r'^2 + z^2)^{\frac{3}{2}}}$$

yielding from Eq. 7.7–7 or 7.9–2

$$B = \frac{\mu_0 q r' v}{4\pi(r'^2 + z^2)^{\frac{3}{2}}}$$

which we may rewrite as

$$B = \frac{\mu_0}{4\pi}\frac{qv\sin\theta}{r^2} \quad \text{or} \quad \mathbf{B} = \frac{\mu_0 q}{4\pi}\frac{\mathbf{v}\times\mathbf{1}_r}{r^2}$$

which is Eq. 7.6–3 back again. Maxwell's introduction of displacement currents into the differential-equation form of Ampère's law allows us to deduce (or verify) the Laplace rule for moving charges.

It should be clear from the derivations that the Gaussian-unit form of 7.9–3a is

$$\nabla \times \mathbf{B} = \frac{4\pi\mathbf{J}}{c} + \frac{1}{c}\frac{\partial \mathbf{D}}{\partial t} \qquad \text{Gaussian} \quad (7.9\text{–}3b)$$

Problem 7.9a. Show explicitly how to deduce from the statement that $\mu_0 \int \mathbf{J} \cdot \mathbf{dS} = \int \nabla \times \mathbf{B} \cdot \mathbf{dS}$ for any surface, the statement that $\mu_0 \mathbf{J} = \nabla \times \mathbf{B}$.

Problem 7.9b. Show explicitly that in the expression $\partial \mathbf{D}/\partial t = \epsilon_0\, \partial \mathbf{E}/\partial t + \partial \mathbf{P}/\partial t$, the term $\partial \mathbf{P}/\partial t$ represents a current associated with the motion of polarization charge as $\mathbf{P}$ varies.

Problem 7.9c. Verify that the induction inside and outside a long straight wire, given by Eqs. 7.8–1 and 7.8–2, satisfies Eq. 7.9–1.

7.10 The Vector Potential

One aspect of the greater complexity of the magnetic field over the electrostatic lies in the existence of two quite different forms of magnetic potential. We have dealt with the magnetic scalar potential in Section 7.6, and turn now to the vector potential, which does not suffer from the multiple-valuedness of V_m and is of great use in deriving certain general and fundamental properties of electromagnetic fields. It is most readily introduced by writing a fifth formulation of Ampère's law. We shall start with the Biot-Savart law, Eq. 7.6–1a, summed over all current loops that contribute to B in a given region.

$$\mathbf{B} = \frac{\mu_0}{4\pi} \sum_k i_k \oint_k \frac{d\mathbf{l} \times \mathbf{1}_r}{r^2}$$

Let us denote the coordinates of the point where $\mathbf{B}$ is to be calculated by (x, y, z), and the coordinates of the varying integration point (the location of $d\mathbf{l}$) by (x', y', z'). Then $r^2 = (x - x')^2 + (y - y')^2 + (z - z')^2$; $d\mathbf{l}$ can be written $\mathbf{1}_x \, dx' + \mathbf{1}_y \, dy' + \mathbf{1}_z \, dz'$, and we have

$$\mathbf{1}_r = \frac{x - x'}{r} \mathbf{1}_x + \frac{y - y'}{r} \mathbf{1}_y + \frac{z - z'}{r} \mathbf{1}_z$$

Now $\mathbf{1}_r/r^2 = -\nabla(1/r)$ (Eq. 3.1–3), where the derivatives in the gradient are taken with respect to the unprimed coordinates. Let us write $d\mathbf{l} \times [-\nabla(1/r)]$ which is the same as $\nabla(1/r) \times d\mathbf{l}$ in the determinant form for the vector product and then rearrange it:

$$\nabla\left(\frac{1}{r}\right) \times d\mathbf{l} = \begin{vmatrix} \mathbf{1}_x & \mathbf{1}_y & \mathbf{1}_z \\ \dfrac{\partial}{\partial x}\left(\dfrac{1}{r}\right) & \dfrac{\partial}{\partial y}\left(\dfrac{1}{r}\right) & \dfrac{\partial}{\partial z}\left(\dfrac{1}{r}\right) \\ dx' & dy' & dz' \end{vmatrix} = \begin{vmatrix} \mathbf{1}_x & \mathbf{1}_y & \mathbf{1}_z \\ \dfrac{\partial}{\partial x} & \dfrac{\partial}{\partial y} & \dfrac{\partial}{\partial z} \\ \dfrac{dx'}{r} & \dfrac{dy'}{r} & \dfrac{dz'}{r} \end{vmatrix}$$

The latter form is the symbolic operator that represents the curl (Appendix, Eq. A.2–39) and follows from the former because the derivatives do not act on dx', dy', and dz', so that, for instance, $(\partial/\partial y)(dz'/r) = dz'(\partial/\partial y)(1/r)$, and so forth. Hence we may write

$$\nabla\left(\frac{1}{r}\right) \times d\mathbf{l} = \nabla \times \left(\frac{d\mathbf{l}}{r}\right) = \text{curl}\,\frac{d\mathbf{l}}{r} \qquad (7.10\text{–}1)$$

The operation **curl** can be interchanged with the integration over x', y', z', so we have

$$\mathbf{B} = \frac{\mu_0}{4\pi} \sum_k i_k \oint_k \nabla\left(\frac{1}{r}\right) \times d\mathbf{l}$$

$$= \nabla \times \left[\frac{\mu_0}{4\pi} \sum_k i_k \oint_k \frac{d\mathbf{l}}{r}\right] \qquad (7.10\text{–}2)$$

The expression in brackets is called the "vector potential" and will be denoted by $\mathbf{A}$. Thus, finally,

$$\mathbf{B} = \text{curl } \mathbf{A} = \nabla \times \mathbf{A} \qquad (7.10\text{–}3)$$

$$\mathbf{A} = \frac{\mu_0}{4\pi} \sum_k \left(i \oint \frac{d\mathbf{l}}{r}\right)_k \qquad (7.10\text{–}4a)$$

In terms of components we have

$$A_x = \frac{\mu_0}{4\pi} \sum_k i_k \oint_k \frac{dx'}{r}$$

$$A_y = \frac{\mu_0}{4\pi} \sum_k i_k \oint_k \frac{dy'}{r} \qquad (7.10\text{--}4b)$$

$$A_z = \frac{\mu_0}{4\pi} \sum_k i_k \oint_k \frac{dz'}{r}$$

We see by comparison with Eq. 1.7–5 that each component of **A** is mathematically similar to the electrostatic potential due to a linear distribution of charge along the various current circuits, with a linear density λ that varies in accordance with the orientation of **dl**. **A** has the MKS dimensions of $\mu_0 i$, namely, webers/meter.

If we think of the current in each conductor as having a finite lateral distribution, each current element $i\,\mathbf{dl}$ can be written $J\,dS\,\mathbf{dl} = \mathbf{J}\,dS\,dl = \mathbf{J}\,d\tau$, since the unit vector along a filament can be associated with **dl** or with **J**. Thus we can write the vector potential as a volume integral over all parts of space in which **J** is not zero:

$$\mathbf{A} = \frac{\mu_0}{4\pi} \int_\tau \mathbf{J} \frac{d\tau}{r} \qquad (7.10\text{--}5a)$$

If currents are restricted to a surface layer and described by a surface current density $\mathbf{J}_S$, we have

$$\mathbf{A} = \frac{\mu_0}{4\pi} \int_S \mathbf{J}_S \frac{dS}{r} \qquad (7.10\text{--}5b)$$

There may, of course, be cases requiring a sum of a surface and a volume integral for **A**.

The volume integrals for each component of **A** are similar to Eq. 1.7–7c for the electrostatic potential due to a distribution of charge density. In Section 1.10 we showed that 1.7–7c is the unique solution of Poisson's equation 1.10–1a, $\nabla^2 V = -\rho/\epsilon_0$, when no surface or line charges are present. Therefore, each Cartesian component of **A**, say, A_x, must obey Poisson's equation with ρ/ϵ_0 replaced by $\mu_0 J_x$.

Thus we can write

$$\nabla^2 \mathbf{A} = -\mu_0 \mathbf{J} \qquad (7.10\text{--}6a)$$

This equation must be interpreted with care if spherical or other non-cartesian coordinates are used, for then the unit vectors will have variable directions and will be acted upon by ∇^2. Hence we shall only use 7.10–6a for cartesian coordinates.

By analogy with the electrostatic potential, we see that the vector potential is readily defined for points in, as well as outside of, a region of continuous current density. Thus the $\mathbf{B} = \mathbf{curl\ A}$ form of Ampère's law can be applied to such cases more easily than can the solid angle rule. Problem 7.10*d* gives an example of the calculation of $\mathbf{A}$ in such a region by the use of a limiting process.

We have defined $\mathbf{A}$ uniquely by Eq. 7.10–4. However, there is more than one vector potential corresponding to a given $\mathbf{B}$ if we use Eq. 7.10–3 to define $\mathbf{A}$. For let $\psi(x, y, z)$ be any suitably continuous function, and calculate **curl** $(\mathbf{A} + \nabla\psi)$:

$$\nabla \times (\mathbf{A} + \nabla\psi) = \nabla \times \mathbf{A} + \nabla \times \nabla\psi = \mathbf{B} + 0 \qquad (7.10\text{--}7)$$

since $\nabla \times \nabla\psi = 0$ for all ψ (cf. Appendix A.2, p. 634). The gradient of any function can thus be added to $\mathbf{A}$ without affecting $\mathbf{B}$. Such a change in the vector potential is called a "gauge transformation." Some authors use the symbol $\mathbf{A}$ for any such generalized function, but we shall stick to the definition Eq. 7.10–4.

The vector potential $\mathbf{A}$ as just defined for closed current loops has the property that its divergence is identically zero:

$$\nabla \cdot \mathbf{A} = \frac{\mu_0}{4\pi} \sum_k i_k \left[\frac{\partial}{\partial x} \oint_k \frac{dx'}{r} + \frac{\partial}{\partial y} \oint_k \frac{dy'}{r} + \frac{\partial}{\partial z} \oint_k \frac{dz'}{r} \right]$$

$$= \frac{\mu_0}{4\pi} \sum_k i_k \left[-\oint \frac{(x - x')\,dx' + (y - y')\,dy' + (z - z')\,dz}{r^3} \right]$$

$$= \frac{\mu_0}{4\pi} \sum_k i_k \left[\oint_k \frac{r\,dr}{r^3} \right] = 0 \qquad (7.10\text{--}8)$$

where dr means the differential of r for variations in x', y', and z'.[22] The integral is equal to the variation of $(-1/r)$ around a closed circuit and thus vanishes.

The vector potential is a type of vector field quantity, for which we can draw field lines. The vanishing of the divergence in the steady current case means that the field lines have no physical beginnings or endings, but only in cases of ideal symmetry will they form closed loops (cf. the discussion of lines of $\mathbf{D}$ in Section 3.6). The general direction of the lines is parallel to the currents, since the vector elements of $\mathbf{A}$ are proportional to current elements.

We have so far considered only closed current loops. For any open current loop, the Laplace rule allows us to make exactly the same calculation as the one above except for the fact that the integrals are to be

---

[22] Since $r^2 = (x - x')^2 + (y - y')^2 + (z - z')^2$, $r\,dr = -(x - x')\,dx' - (y - y')\,dy' - (z - z')\,dz'$.

taken over the actual unclosed current filaments. For each such filament in 7.10–8, the integral gives the variation of $-1/r$ between the end-points of the filament. At the positive end, where the charge q_k obeys the relation $dq_k/dt = i_k$, we have a contribution

$$-\frac{\mu_0}{4\pi}\frac{d}{dt}\left(\frac{q_k}{r}\right) = -\mu_0\epsilon_0\frac{d}{dt}\frac{q_k}{4\pi\epsilon_0 r} = -\mu_0\epsilon_0\frac{dV_{k+}}{dt}$$

where V_{k+} is the electrostatic potential produced by the charge at the positive end of the filament. Similarly the other end will give a contribution $-\mu_0\epsilon_0\, dV_{k-}/dt$. Summing over all the current filaments gives the entire rate of change of V, since charges can only change by means of currents (conduction, polarization, or convection). Thus we find for non-steady situations,

$$\mathbf{\nabla}\cdot\mathbf{A} + \mu_0\epsilon_0\frac{\partial V}{\partial t} = 0 \qquad (7.10\text{–}9a)$$

This relation is called the "Lorentz condition."

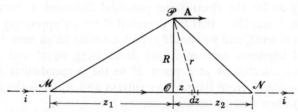

Fig. 7.10a.   Calculation of A produced at $\mathscr{P}$ by a wire segment $\mathscr{M}\mathscr{N}$ carrying a current i.

Equations 7.10–8 and 9 can be used for another derivation of the Poisson equation 7.10–6a and its generalization. From Eq. 7.9–1, the differential form of Ampère's law for steady currents, and 7.10–3 we can write

$$\mu_0\mathbf{J} = \mathbf{\nabla}\times\mathbf{B} = \mathbf{\nabla}\times(\mathbf{\nabla}\times\mathbf{A}) = \mathbf{\nabla}(\mathbf{\nabla}\cdot\mathbf{A}) - (\mathbf{\nabla}\cdot\mathbf{\nabla})\mathbf{A}$$

so that 7.10–6a follows when we put $\mathbf{\nabla}\cdot\mathbf{A} = 0$. It is not hard to show (Problem 7.10d) that 7.10–6a also results when open current loops are considered. However, the Poisson equation 7.10–6a is not correct for rapidly changing currents. The correct form in this case will be found in Section 10.3.

Although the calculation of A is somewhat more complicated than the corresponding calculation of V, there are a few cases in which the vector potential can be calculated fairly easily and which are quite instructive.

The contribution to A of any straight segment of a circuit is a vector parallel to this segment and can be readily calculated. Let the z-axis be taken parallel to the segment in question ($\mathscr{M}\mathscr{N}$ in Fig. 7.10a) and find A at a point located by the perpendicular R and the distances z_1 and z_2, taking the foot of the perpendicular $\mathcal{O}$ as origin. (It is convenient in this calculation to deal with positive numbers for both distances.) Then $dl = \mathbf{1}_z \, dz$, and remembering that r is always a positive number we have

$$\mathbf{A} = \mathbf{1}_z \frac{\mu_0 i}{4\pi} \int_{-z_1}^{z_2} \frac{dz}{(R^2 + z^2)^{\frac{1}{2}}} = \mathbf{1}_z \frac{\mu_0 i}{4\pi} \left[\int_0^{z_1} \frac{dz}{(R^2 + z^2)^{\frac{1}{2}}} + \int_0^{z_2} \frac{dz}{(R^2 + z^2)^{\frac{1}{2}}} \right]$$

$$= \mathbf{1}_z \frac{\mu_0 i}{4\pi} \left[\ln \frac{z_1 + (R^2 + z_1{}^2)^{\frac{1}{2}}}{R} + \ln \frac{z_2 + (R^2 + z_2{}^2)^{\frac{1}{2}}}{R} \right]$$

$$= \mathbf{1}_z \frac{\mu_0 i}{4\pi} \ln \frac{[z_1 + (R^2 + z_1{}^2)^{\frac{1}{2}}][z_2 + (R^2 + z_2{}^2)^{\frac{1}{2}}]}{R^2} \qquad (7.10\text{-}10)$$

The reader should be able to show that this result still holds when $\mathcal{O}$ lies outside of $\mathscr{MN}$ (Problem 7.10a).

The vector potential for any circuit made up of straight segments can be calculated at any point by a straightforward vector addition (Problem 7.10b). On the other hand, we get an infinite result for an infinitely long wire, exactly as for the electrostatic potential discussed in Section 1.7. However, we found there that the potential V for an oppositely charged pair of wires is finite, and we should expect a similar result here. Consider two parallel segments each of length $2z$ carrying equal and opposite currents, and calculate $\mathbf{A}$ at a point $\mathscr{P}$ in the perpendicular bisecting plane, a distance R_1 from the positive current and R_2 from the negative. (Fig. 7.10b.) Then $\mathbf{A}$ at $\mathscr{P}$ becomes, setting $z_1 = z_2 = z$,

$$\mathbf{A} = \mathbf{1}_z \frac{\mu_0 i}{4\pi} \left[\int \frac{dz}{r_1} - \int \frac{dz}{r_2} \right]$$

$$\mathbf{A} = \mathbf{1}_z \frac{\mu_0 i}{4\pi} \left[\ln \frac{[z + (R_1{}^2 + z^2)^{\frac{1}{2}}]^2}{R_1{}^2} - \ln \frac{[z + (R_2{}^2 + z^2)^{\frac{1}{2}}]^2}{R_2{}^2} \right]$$

$$= \mathbf{1}_z \frac{\mu_0 i}{2\pi} \left[\frac{R_2}{R_1} \cdot \frac{z + (R_1{}^2 + z^2)^{\frac{1}{2}}}{z + (R_2{}^2 + z^2)^{\frac{1}{2}}} \right]$$

where the exponent 2 has been removed from the logarithm in the last step. Now if z is allowed to approach infinity (that is, if z is sufficiently large compared to R_1 and R_2), we have a result that is analogous to that of Eq. 1.7-15:

$$\mathbf{A} = \mathbf{1}_z \frac{\mu_0 i}{2\pi} \ln \frac{R_2}{R_1} \qquad (7.10\text{-}11)$$

[23]Thus the equipotentials of Eq. 1.7-15, Section 4.5, and Fig. 1.11d, p. 51, become here the surfaces of constant A_z. Since $\mathbf{B} = \mathbf{curl}\,\mathbf{A}$ and A_x

---

[23] This paragraph may be omitted if Section 4.5 has not been taken up.

and A_y are zero, we have

$$B_x = \partial A_z / \partial y$$
$$B_y = -\partial A_z / \partial x$$
$$B_z = 0$$

(7.10–12)

Now, the vectors **B** and **A** are clearly perpendicular. We can interpret Eq. 7.10–12 simply if we compare **B** with **grad** $A_z = \nabla A_z$ whose components are

$$\left. \begin{array}{l} \text{grad}_x\, A_z = \partial A_z / \partial x \\ \text{grad}_y\, A_z = \partial A_z / \partial y \\ \text{grad}_z\, A_z = \partial A_z / \partial z = 0 \end{array} \right\}$$

(7.10–13)

We see that $B^2 = B_x{}^2 + B_y{}^2 = |\nabla A_z|^2$ and that $\mathbf{B} \cdot \nabla A_z = B_x\, \text{grad}_x (A_x) + B_y\, \text{grad}_y (A_z) = 0$. Hence **B** has the magnitude of the gradient of A_z—proportional to E in the electric case—but is perpendicular to ∇A_z as seen by the vanishing of the scalar product. Since ∇A_z at any point is normal to the surface $A_z = \text{constant}$ through that point, **B** lies on this surface along the circle cut on it by a plane normal to the wires. These circles are therefore the magnetic lines of force. In the electric case, their spacing was shown to be proportional to the gradient of V, so that by the analogous calculation they are seen to be properly spaced in this case, i.e., proportional to B.

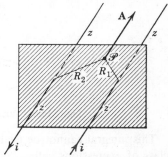

Fig. 7.10b. Calculation of A for two infinite parallel wires.

This case affords an excellent example of varying magnitude and orientation of the circulation density or curl of a vector quantity which is itself everywhere parallel to a given line.

In order to illustrate the difficulty in making exact calculations in cases of even moderate complexity, we shall write an expression for the vector potential produced by a single circular loop of current at an arbitrary point off the axis of the loop.

Consider a loop of current of radius a, and a point $\mathscr{P}$ located at a distance z from the plane of the loop and at a distance R from its axis. (Fig. 7.10c.) Let us locate **dl** at a point $\mathscr{T}'$ by an angle ϕ measured from the line $\mathcal{O}\mathscr{P}'$ in the figure, where $\mathscr{P}'$ is the foot of the perpendicular from $\mathscr{P}$ to the plane of the current. The distance $r = \overline{\mathscr{T}'\mathscr{P}}$ can be found from the law of cosines in triangle $\mathscr{T}'\mathcal{O}\mathscr{P}'$ and the Pythagorean theorem in triangle $\mathscr{T}'\mathscr{P}'\mathscr{P}$, yielding

$$r = (z^2 + a^2 + R^2 - 2aR \cos \phi)^{1/2}$$

Another element **dl**, located at $\mathcal{T}''$ at an angle $-\phi$ in the figure, will be at the same distance from $\mathcal{P}$. The contributions of the two elements to **A** at $\mathcal{P}$ will cancel in the direction $\mathcal{O}'\mathcal{P}$ and add in the direction normal to the plane $\mathcal{P}'\mathcal{O}\mathcal{O}'\mathcal{P}$, the component of dl in this direction being $a\,d\phi\cos\phi$. Thus we can write

$$\mathbf{A} = \frac{\mu_0 i}{4\pi}\,\mathbf{1}_\phi \cdot 2 \int_0^\pi \frac{a\cos\phi\,d\phi}{(z^2 + a^2 + R^2 - 2aR\cos\phi)} \qquad (7.10\text{–}14)$$

where $\mathbf{1}_\phi$ is a unit vector normal to the plane $\mathcal{P}'\mathcal{O}\mathcal{O}'\mathcal{P}$ in the direction corresponding to increasing ϕ.

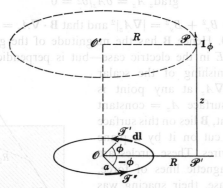

Fig. 7.10c.   Calculation of A for a circular loop.

This integral cannot be evaluated in elementary terms. It belongs to a class of expressions called "elliptic integrals," so called because one of them arises in the calculation of the circumference of an ellipse. The reader is referred to texts on advanced calculus and to mathematical tables, where integrals of this type are reduced to standard forms and tabulated numerically.[24]

There are certain approximately calculable cases. If z is considerably larger than a, the radical can be written by neglect of a^2,

$$\sqrt{z^2 + R^2}\,[1 - (2aR\cos\phi)/(z^2 + R^2)]^{\frac12}$$

and the second factor expanded by the binomial theorem. The results will turn out to agree with a calculation to be made in Section 8.2 (see Problem 8.2a). On the other hand, if z is much smaller than a and R is

[24] Cf. *Handbook of Chemistry and Physics,* Chemical Rubber Publ. Co., Cleveland, mathematical section, any recent edition. W. Kaplan, *Advanced Calculus,* Addison-Wesley, Cambridge, Mass., 1952, pp. 179–181; W. F. Osgood, *Advanced Calculus,* Macmillan, New York, 1925, Chapter IX; Mary L. Boas, *Mathematical Methods,* John Wiley, New York, 1966, Chapter 9.

nearly equal to a, a different expansion can be used, and will be given in Section 7.17 for $z = 0$. It is also possible to make an expansion in terms of Legendre functions, which were considered in Section 4.6.

The vector potential at points far from a small circular loop can be written in terms of the magnetic moment of the loop. We first use the theorem of Eq. A.2–43, $\oint u \, d\mathbf{l} = \int d\mathbf{S} \times \nabla u$, on Eq. 7.10–4 with $u = 1/r$ and find for a single closed loop of any size that the vector potential of an arbitrary current loop can be written as the following integral over any surface bounded by the loop:

$$\mathbf{A} = \frac{\mu_0 i}{4\pi} \int_S d\mathbf{S} \times \nabla'\left(\frac{1}{r}\right) \tag{7.10–15}$$

where the operator ∇' is taken with respect to the coordinates of the point of integration and is the negative of ∇, which operates on the coordinates of the point of observation. When diameter of the loop is small compared to r, $\nabla(1/r)$ can be treated as constant over the surface and we have

$$\mathbf{A} = -\frac{\mu_0}{4\pi} i\mathbf{S} \times \nabla\left(\frac{1}{r}\right) = \frac{\mu_0 \mathbf{m} \times \mathbf{1}_r}{4\pi r^2} \tag{7.10–16a}$$

This formula for the vector potential of a magnetic dipole bears an interesting relation to that for the scalar potential, (7.8–10b).

In Gaussian units, we use $\mathbf{B} = \nabla \times \mathbf{A}$ as in MKS units, but write for current loops

$$\mathbf{A} = \frac{1}{c} \sum_k \left(i \oint \frac{d\mathbf{l}}{r}\right)_k \qquad \text{Gaussian} \quad (7.10–4c)$$

which becomes for volume distributions

$$\mathbf{A} = \frac{1}{c} \int_\tau \mathbf{J} \frac{d\tau}{r} \qquad \text{Gaussian} \quad (7.10–5c)$$

The Lorentz condition in Gaussian units reads

$$\nabla \cdot \mathbf{A} + \frac{1}{c}\frac{\partial V}{\partial t} = 0 \tag{7.10–9b}$$

The vector potential of a small current loop at distant points is (cf. 7.8–11b)

$$\mathbf{A} = \frac{\mathbf{m} \times \mathbf{1}_r}{r^2} \tag{7.10–16b}$$

The Gaussian unit (emu) of vector potential is the maxwell/centimeter or the gauss-centimeter.

Problem 7.10a. Show that Eq. 7.10–10 is correct when $\mathcal{O}$ lies to the left or right of segment $\mathcal{MN}$ in Fig. 7.10b.

Problem 7.10b. Find the vector potential at the same point in the square of Problem 7.8c for which **B** was sought. Show that $\mathbf{A} \to \infty$ as $a \to \infty$. Find its magnitude in webers/meter when $a = 0.50$ m, $r = 0.20$ m, and $i = 16.0$ amp.

Problem 7.10c. Find the vector potential at the center of a cylindrical pipe of length L and inner and outer radii r_1 and r_2, that carries a uniform current density J parallel to its axis. Calculate only that part of **A** produced by the current in this piece of pipe, disregarding the rest of the circuit. Show that as $r_1 \to 0$, **A** remains finite.

Problem 7.10d. Show that Eq. 7.10–6a is valid when open current loops are present.

Problem 7.10e. Show that $\frac{1}{2}\mathbf{r} \times \mathbf{B}$ is a suitable value for **A** when **B** is uniform in a given region, with $\nabla \cdot \mathbf{A} = 0$. What happens if a new origin is chosen? Discuss the uniqueness of this expression for **A**.

7.11 The Vector Potential for an Infinite Solenoid[25]

When we come to consider an infinite, uniformly wound solenoid, we find that we can make an explicit calculation using Eq. 7.10–14. If the solenoid has n_l turns per meter, the contribution to **A** produced by the turns in length dz can be obtained by assuming these turns to act like $n_l\,dz$ circular loops. We have

$$A_\phi = \int_{\text{all loops}} dA_\phi = \frac{\mu_0 a n_l i}{2\pi} \int_{-\infty}^{\infty} dz \int_0^{\pi} \frac{\cos\phi\,d\phi}{(z^2 + a^2 + R^2 - 2aR\cos\phi)^{\frac{1}{2}}}$$

This integral can be evaluated by dividing it into two parts, writing $\pi - \phi$ for ϕ in the angular range between $\pi/2$ and π and then interchanging the order of integration. We have, using the method followed for Eq. 7.10–11 where the z integration is mathematically the same,

$$A_\phi = \frac{\mu_0 a n_l i}{2\pi} \int_{-\infty}^{\infty} dz \int_0^{\pi/2} d\phi \left[\frac{\cos\phi}{(z^2 + a^2 + R^2 - 2aR\cos\phi)^{\frac{1}{2}}} - \frac{\cos\phi}{(z^2 + a^2 + R^2 + 2aR\cos\phi)^{\frac{1}{2}}} \right]$$

$$= \frac{\mu_0 a n_l i}{2\pi} \int_0^{\pi/2} \cos\phi\,d\phi \ln\left(\frac{a^2 + R^2 + 2aR\cos\phi}{a^2 + R^2 - 2aR\cos\phi} \right)$$

Let us denote the ratio $2Ra/(R^2 + a^2)$ by α and use integration by parts, the one part being $\cos\phi\,d\phi$ and the other the logarithm. The integrated

---

[25] This section may be omitted without loss of continuity.

part vanishes and except for the factor $\mu_0 a n_i i / 2\pi$ the integral becomes

$$2\alpha \int_0^{\pi/2} \frac{\sin^2 \phi \, d\phi}{1 - \alpha^2 \cos^2 \phi} = \frac{2}{\alpha}\left[\phi - (1 - \alpha^2)^{1/2}\tan^{-1}\left\{\frac{\tan \phi}{(1 - \alpha^2)^{1/2}}\right\}\right]_0^{\pi/2}$$

as the reader can readily verify by differentiation. The expression $\tan^{-1}\{(\tan \phi)/(1 - \alpha^2)^{1/2}\}$ approaches $\pi/2$ as $\phi \to \pi/2$. Using

$$(1 - \alpha^2)^{1/2} = (R^4 - 2R^2 a^2 + a^4)^{1/2}/(R^2 + a^2) = |R^2 - a^2|/(R^2 + a^2)$$

we have

$$A_\phi = \frac{\mu_0 a n_i i}{2\pi} \cdot \frac{R^2 + a^2}{Ra} \cdot \frac{\pi}{2}\left[1 - \frac{|R^2 - a^2|}{R^2 + a^2}\right]$$

We have for convenience chosen $(1 - \alpha^2)^{1/2}$ to be positive, but the expression $|R^2 - a^2|$ must be taken as positive regardless of which sign is chosen for $(1 - \alpha^2)^{1/2}$. If $R > a$ we have finally

$$A_\phi = \frac{\mu_0 n_i i a^2}{2R} \tag{7.11-1}$$

whereas for $R < a$

$$A_\phi = \tfrac{1}{2}\mu_0 n_i i R \tag{7.11-2}$$

It will be left to the reader to show (Problem 7.11a) that inside the solenoid, when $R < a$, **curl A** yields the value of **B** found earlier and that outside, **curl A** $= 0$. It is especially important to note that we have here a case in which **B** is zero throughout a certain region in which **A** does not vanish. We shall see later (Section 7.15) that this non-vanishing of **A** has considerable physical significance.

Problem 7.11a. Show from Eqs. 7.11–1 and 2 that $\mathbf{B} = \mu_0 n_i i$ inside the solenoid and $\mathbf{B} = 0$ outside it. Show also that although the circulation of **A** does not vanish for a path surrounding the solenoid, its value is independent of the shape of this path (with what restriction?).

Problem 7.11b. Write the vector potential **A** in Eq. 7.6–15 as the sum of two complete elliptic integrals, using a suitable reference work for these integrals.

Problem 7.11c. Discuss **A** outside an infinite solenoid when the winding is taken as helical rather than as a series of true circles.

7.12 Magnetic Flux

The fact that **B** is the curl of another vector leads immediately to a very important conclusion, namely that the divergence of **B** is zero, since the divergence of any curl vanishes identically. Hence

$$\textbf{div B} = \nabla \cdot \mathbf{B} = 0 \tag{7.12-1}$$

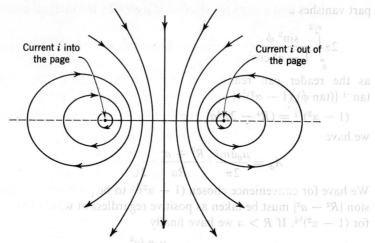

Current *i* into
the page

Current *i* out of
the page

Fig. 7.12a. Lines of **B** for a circular loop. (Adapted from E. Durand, *Électrostatique et Magnétostatique*, Masson et Cie, Paris, 1953.)

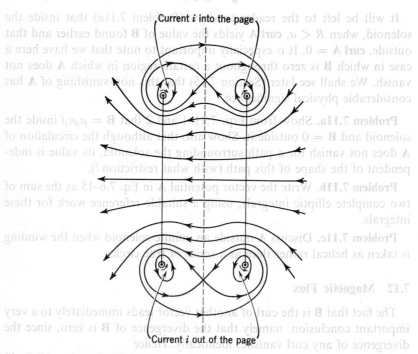

Current *i* into the page

Current *i* out of the page

Fig. 7.12b. Lines of **B** for two circular loops, currents parallel. (Adapted from Durand, *op. cit.*)

everywhere, even at points within continuous current density distributions.

In accordance with study of divergence and flux in Appendix A.2, we see that the flux of **B** through any closed surface is zero.

$$\int_{closed\ S} \mathbf{B} \cdot \mathbf{dS} = 0 \qquad (7.12\text{-}2)$$

It is this fact that allows us to talk of the magnetic flux

$$\Phi = \int_S \mathbf{B} \cdot \mathbf{dS} \qquad (7.12\text{-}3)$$

through any loop or circuit as a definite quantity, for the integral that defines Φ can be taken over any surface bounded by the loop in question.

The flux through any loop can also be calculated from the vector potential. Substituting Eq. 7.10-3 into Eq. 7.12-3 and using Stokes' theorem, we have

$$\Phi = \int_S \mathbf{curl\ A} \cdot \mathbf{dS} = \oint_{boundary\ of\ S} \mathbf{A} \cdot \mathbf{dl} \qquad (7.12\text{-}4)$$

The fact that the flux of induction through any closed surface is zero allows us to construct tubes of magnetic flux, each containing some unit or sub-unit of flux, exactly as in the electric case (Section 1.6). Magnetic lines of induction can, of course, be drawn without the necessity of proving the flux-conservation theorem; however, we have now shown that we can draw lines in such numbers that their density is everywhere proportional to B.

As a simple application of the magnetic-flux law, consider a slender solenoid of cross-sectional area S. The induction at the center is $\mu_0 n_i i$ and is constant over the entire cross section. The induction at one end is one-half this value and is also constant over the cross section. Thus we see immediately that of the flux $\Phi = \mu_0 niS$ in the center of the coil, one-half (nearly) must pass out through the side, leaving one-half to pass out through the end. This result would be awkward to calculate directly from the field at the sides of the solenoid.

Figures 7.12a, b, c, and d show the magnetic lines of induction for a single loop of wire, a pair of Helmholtz coils (Problem 7.8f), a short solenoid, and a long solenoid.

The fact that **div B** $= 0$ everywhere is equivalent to saying that there are no beginnings or ends to lines of induction. This of course was implied in our assertion that **B** is produced by current loops. The existence of free magnetic poles would contradict this statement, but no convincing experimental evidence has ever been found for such poles.

In ideally symmetrical cases, such as those of the long straight wire or the circle, the lines of **B** obviously form closed loops. But this is not generally so. As a simple example, consider a circular current and a long straight wire on the axis of the circle. When the field of the straight wire is superimposed on that of the circular one, it will make the lines near the latter go around it in spiral fashion. Only for very special values of the currents will any of these spiral lines come back to the same point after

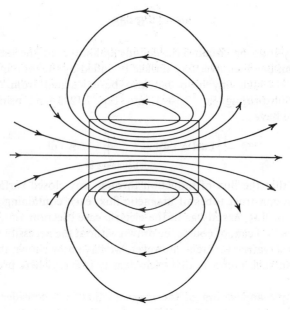

Fig. 7.12c.   Lines of **B** for a short solenoid. (Adapted from Durand, *op. cit.*)

going around the central wire. (Fig. 7.12*e*.) Whether they meet or not, it would be meaningless to talk of flux circulating many times around the circular wire.

Although we must terminate lines in drawing them, if we treated them as physical entities, we would have to say that the lines of **B** in general are infinitely long! The proportionality of the number of lines through a given area to **B** can only be kept meaningful if arbitrary ends and beginnings of lines are introduced in a systematic way.[26]

---

[26] See K. L. McDonald "Topology of Steady Current Magnetic Fields," *Am. Journ. Phys.*, **22**, 586 (1954), Joseph Slepian "Lines of Force in Electric and Magnetic Fields," *Am. J. Phys.*, **19**, 87 (1951), and Mario Iona, "Lines with Ends to Describe div **B** = 0," *Am. J. Phys.*, **31**, 398 (1963).

Even in cases where geometrical symmetry would allow it, actual physical coils cannot have the perfection needed to make the lines close. A similar situation for electrets is discussed on pp. 126–127.

Let us note finally that Eq. 7.12–1 is the third of Maxwell's equations for electromagnetic radiation that we have derived, the first one being Eq. 1.5–1 for div **E**, and the second, Eq. 7.9–3 for **curl B**.

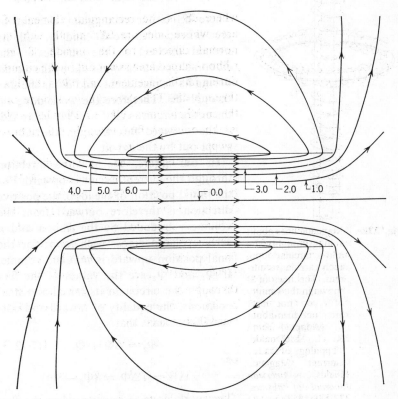

Fig. 7.12d. Lines of **B** for a long solenoid. The numbers represent flux contained in surfaces of revolution (arbitrary scale.)

Flux and Energy. We now wish to show that the externally produced flux through a circuit can be interpreted as an energy function from which forces and torques can be calculated. Let us consider a closed loop l carrying a current i, situated in an external magnetic field of induction **B**. The induction produced by the current i will not be considered, as we are not trying to calculate the force of a circuit on itself. Imagine displacing the circuit by a small amount $\Delta l'$, which need not be a constant around

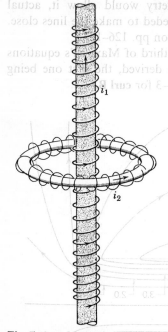

Fig. 7.12e. Magnetic lines about a long straight wire and a circular loop, each carrying a current. The lines of **B** shown in the vicinity of i_2 do not meet after one turn about i_1. (Adapted from K. L. McDonald, "Topology of Steady Current Magnetic Fields," *American Journal of Physics*, 22, 588 (1954), Fig. 1.)

the circuit (Fig. 7.12*f*), and assume that the current i remains constant. The work done by the magnetic force $d\mathbf{F}$ on an element $d\mathbf{l}$ of the wire is then

$$dW = d\mathbf{F} \cdot \mathbf{\Delta l'} = i\, d\mathbf{l} \times \mathbf{B} \cdot \mathbf{\Delta l'}$$
$$= i\mathbf{B} \cdot \mathbf{\Delta l'} \times d\mathbf{l} = i\mathbf{B} \cdot d\mathbf{S} = i\, d\Phi$$

where $d\mathbf{S}$ is the rectangular element of area whose sides are $\mathbf{\Delta l'}$ and $d\mathbf{l}$, with its normal directed to the outside of the ribbon-shaped area swept out by the circuit during its displacement, and $d\Phi$ is the flux through $d\mathbf{S}$. Therefore the work done on the entire circuit is $\Delta W = i\,\Delta\Phi$ where $\Delta\Phi$ is the outward flux through the ribbon swept out by the circuit.

In our figure, the positive direction through the current circuit is upward. For the initial position of the loop, the positive direction is therefore outward from the volume τ bounded by the ribbon and a surface placed across each loop; for the final position upward is *into* the volume. If Φ_1 and Φ_2 are the values of the flux through the circuit in its initial and final positions, the equality of inward and outward flux means that

$$\Phi_2 = \Delta\Phi + \Phi_1 \qquad (7.12\text{–}5)$$

or

$$\Delta W = i\,\Delta\Phi = i(\Phi_2 - \Phi_1)$$

The work done is positive when the flux increases. Since the positive direction is defined by the sign of the current i, we can say that a circuit in an external field tends to move so as to add external flux to its own. The function

$$U = i\Phi \qquad (7.12\text{–}6a)$$

is an energy function whose increase gives the work done by magnetic forces for any displacement of the circuit. We shall see in Section 7.18 that U represents the magnetic potential energy of the current circuit in the field when we take into account the work necessary to establish the current, or to maintain it constant as the circuit is moved into the field. The fact

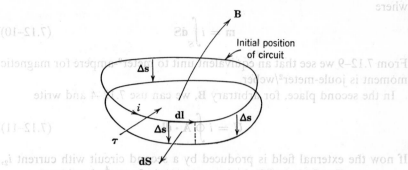

Fig. 7.12 f. Calculation of the work done on displacement of a loop.

that U increases as work is done, in contrast to the reduction of an ordinary potential energy, comes about because, as we shall see, sources of emf must do work to maintain the current.

If $\Delta \mathbf{l}'$ is a constant around the circuit, the work done can be written in terms of the total force $\mathbf{F}$ on the circuit.

$$\Delta U = \mathbf{F} \cdot \Delta \mathbf{l}'$$

If $\Delta \mathbf{l}'$ is successively chosen to be in the x-, y-, and z-directions and the proper limit is taken, we can construct $\mathbf{F}$:

$$\mathbf{F} = \nabla U = i \, \nabla \Phi \qquad (7.12\text{-}7a)$$

The variables x, y, and z of ∇ refer to the coordinates of some chosen point on the current loop.

By considering a rigid rotation of a loop, we can in a similar way calculate the torque. For instance, for a rigid plane loop of area $\mathbf{S}$ in a uniform field $\mathbf{B}$, we have for the torque

$$\mathcal{T} = i\mathbf{S} \times \mathbf{B} \qquad (7.12\text{-}8a)$$

(cf. Problem 7.12c).

Forces and torques calculated from U are independent of the constant-current assumption used in the derivation above, for they depend on instantaneous values of currents and not on how they vary as a displacement is made.

There are two other useful ways of writing U. In the first place, we can define a vector area $\mathbf{S}$ for an arbitrary loop by an integral of vector elements $d\mathbf{S}$ over any surface S bounded by the loop. (That $\mathbf{S}$ is independent of which surface is chosen can be proved from Eq. A.2–24; cf. Problem A.2c.) Then in case $\mathbf{B}$ is constant, we can write U in terms of the magnetic moment of the loop, defined by an extension of 7.8–11:

$$U = i\Phi = i\int_S \mathbf{B} \cdot d\mathbf{S} = i\mathbf{B} \cdot \int_S d\mathbf{S} = \mathbf{m} \cdot \mathbf{B} \qquad (7.12\text{-}9)$$

where

$$\mathbf{m} = i \int_S \mathbf{dS} \qquad (7.12\text{-}10)$$

From 7.12-9 we see that an equivalent unit to meter²-ampere for magnetic moment is joule-meter²/weber.

In the second place, for arbitrary $\mathbf{B}$, we can use 7.12-4 and write

$$U = i \oint \mathbf{A} \cdot \mathbf{dl} \qquad (7.12\text{-}11)$$

If now the external field is produced by a second circuit with current i_2, we can use Eq. 7.10-4 and obtain a symmetric formula for the energy:

$$U = \frac{\mu_0 i_1 i_2}{4\pi} \oint_1 \oint_2 \frac{\mathbf{dl}_1 \cdot \mathbf{dl}_2}{r_{12}} \qquad (7.12\text{-}12)$$

in which we have set $i = i_1$, and denoted by r_{12} the distance from an element $\mathbf{dl}_1$ of circuit 1 to an element $\mathbf{dl}_2$ of circuit 2. The double line integral is extended over both circuits, as indicated. The symmetry of these expressions shows that the force on either circuit can be found from changes in W. Note that r_{12} never becomes zero if the two circuits do not actually intersect.

The coefficient of $i_1 i_2$ is known as the *mutual inductance* M_{12} of the two circuits:

$$M_{12} = \frac{\mu_0}{4\pi} \oint_1 \oint_2 \frac{\mathbf{dl}_1 \cdot \mathbf{dl}_2}{r_{12}} \qquad (7.12\text{-}13a)$$

This formula is known as Neumann's formula.[27] The mutual inductance is clearly equal to the flux through either circuit produced by unit current in the other. The MKS unit of mutual inductance is the henry.[28]

It is clear that the derivatives required for calculating forces and torques from U act on M_{12}. For instance, two parallel current loops will attract each other if the currents are in the same sense, extending an earlier conclusion about parallel straight wires (Section 7.8), for if the loops move toward each other the flux in each will increase. Note that M_{12} will increase as the circuits move together and r_{12} decreases. If the currents are in opposite senses, the flux in each loop will be small because of cancelation

---

[27] F. E. Neumann, *Berlin Abhandlungen*, 1845, p. 1 and *Verhandlung*, 1875, p. 322; 1848, p. 1; reprinted as No. 10 and No. 36 of Ostwald's *Klassiker der Exakten Wissenschuffen* (Leipzig, 1889). Neumann was also the first to introduce the vector potential, in the same publications.

[28] A henry is dimensionally the same as a meter if we assume that μ_0 is dimensionless. Compare this result with the identity of the dimensions of the statfarad and the centimeter in the electrostatic and Gaussian systems of units.

of oppositely-directed contributions, but it will increase as the currents move apart. The decrease of M_{12} in Eq. 7.12–12 is multiplied by the negative sign from the product of i_1 and i_2 and the result again corroborates our conclusion. Further consideration of forces, inductances, and energy will be given in Section 7.18 after we have taken up the general law of induced emfs.

The fact that $\nabla \cdot \mathbf{B} = 0$ and that in current-free regions $\mathbf{B}$ may be derived from a scalar potential V_m means that $\nabla \cdot \nabla V_m = 0$, so that V_m obeys Laplace's equation. If the values of V_m (and thus of $\mathbf{B}$) are wanted in the neighborhood of any particular point, such as a center of symmetry (e.g., the center of a solenoid or the central point of the Helmholtz coils of problem 7.8f), the result can be written as a series expansion in spherical harmonics, in accordance with Section 4.6. In particular, if the coil system has axial symmetry, an expansion in Legendre functions can be used:

$$V_m = a_0 + a_1 r P_1(\cos \theta) + a_2 r^2 P_2(\cos \theta) + \cdots + a_n r^n P_n(\cos \theta) + \cdots$$

$$(7.12\text{–}14)$$

Thus the variation of V_m along the axis ($\theta = 0$) determines the a_n's and hence the variation of V_m for all r and θ. The Helmholtz pair of Problem 7.8f has a field B_z on the axis whose first three derivatives vanish at its central point. Setting $\theta = 0$ and $r = z$ in Eq. 7.12–14 and differentiating to get B_z, we see that a_2, a_3, and a_4 must vanish. Since $P_1(\cos \theta) = \cos \theta$ and $r \cos \theta = z$, the terms $a_0 + a_1 z$ are seen to give the potential for a uniform field. The corrections to this potential involve only the terms $a_5 r^5 P_5(\cos \theta)$ and beyond, so it is clear that the uniformity of the field extends in all directions from the center, to the extent that this first correction term is small.

The various possible arrangements of coils that may be used to produce a uniform field may be classified according to the number of terms beyond a_1 in Eq. 7.12–14 that vanish and may be characterized in detail by the values of the first one or two non-vanishing coefficients. For a survey of various coil arrangements and also of the application of this method to a description of fields at large distances, the reader is referred elsewhere.[29]

The expressions for flux, 7.12–3 and 7.12–4, are the same in all systems of units. The energy function from which forces and torques are found by differentiation becomes in Gaussian units

$$U = \frac{i}{c} \Phi \qquad\qquad \text{Gaussian} \quad (7.12\text{–}6b)$$

The force and torque formulas become

$$\mathbf{F} = \frac{i}{c} \nabla \Phi \qquad\qquad \text{Gaussian} \quad (7.12\text{–}7b)$$

$$\mathscr{T} = \frac{i}{c} \mathbf{S} \times \mathbf{B} \qquad\qquad \text{Gaussian} \quad (7.12\text{–}8b)$$

[29] M. W. Garrett, *J. Appl. Phys.*, **22**, 1091–1107 (1951).

Neumann's mutual inductance formula reads

$$M_{12} = \frac{1}{c^2} \oint_1 \oint_2 \frac{dl_1 \cdot dl_2}{r_{12}} \qquad \text{Gaussian} \quad (7.12\text{–}13b)$$

The relation $U = \mathbf{m} \cdot \mathbf{B}$ (7.12–9) is the same in both systems. We note that the gauss-cm³ unit for magnetic moment is also the erg/gauss.

Problem 7.12a. Write the field B_z on the axis of a solenoid of finite length as a series in powers of z, where z is measured from the center of the coil. Use this series to identify the constants $a_1, a_2, \cdots$ of Eq. 7.12–14 giving two non-vanishing coefficients beyond a_1.

Problem 7.12b. Find the constants a_1 and a_5 for the field at the central point of the Helmholtz pair of Problem 7.8f.

Problem 7.12c. By writing the flux through a rigid plane loop in a uniform field as $\Phi = \mathbf{B} \cdot \mathbf{S}$, prove Eq. 7.12–8.

Problem 7.12d. Prove Eq. 7.12–7 from 7.4–2 by use of the vector theorem A.2–44 and a suitable argument about interchanging the order of the operations $\int$ and ∇.

Problem 7.12e. Find the flux through a square 3 cm on a side produced by a current of 15 amp in a long straight wire if one side of the square is parallel to the wire and 6 cm from it, and the opposite side is (a) 9 cm from the long wire and (b) 8 cm from the long wire.

Problem 7.12f. What is the work required to turn the square coil in Problem 7.8n from a position in which the positive normal to the coil is parallel to the direction of $\mathbf{B}$ in the solenoid to a position reversed by 180°?

Problem 7.12g. A solenoid 50 cm long and 2 cm in diameter has 300 turns and carries 15 amp. A circular coil of 5 turns with an average diameter of 2.5 cm carries a constant current of 0.50 amp. Find the work done when the latter coil is brought up from infinity to a position over the solenoid at its center. Relate the sign of the work done to the relative orientation of the coils.

Problem 7.12h. Prove using results in Section 1.10 that Eq. 7.6–2 is the unique solution of the equations

$$\nabla \times \mathbf{B} = \mu_0 \mathbf{J} \qquad \text{and} \qquad \nabla \cdot \mathbf{B} = 0$$

Problem 7.12i. By the methods of the previous problem, show that the generalization of Eq. 7.6–2 for non-steady currents is

$$\mathbf{B} = \frac{\mu_0}{4\pi} \int \left(\mathbf{J} + \frac{\partial \mathbf{D}}{\partial t} \right) \times \frac{1_r}{r^2} \, d\tau \qquad (7.12\text{–}14)$$

7.13 Magnetic Mirrors and Other Aspects of Particle Motion in Nonuniform Magnetic Fields

The result of the previous section for the force on a current loop can be applied in a rather simple way to the motion of particles in a non-uniform magnetic field. If the induction **B** does not vary too much in a given region of space, a charged particle of mass M and charge q will move approximately in a helix with its axis parallel to **B**, as discussed for a strictly uniform field in Section 7.3. If the helix is a "tight" one, i.e., has a fairly small pitch, we can treat the circulatory motion of the particle as if it were a current loop. As noted in Section 7.3, the direction of this current is negative in respect to the direction of **B**, so U in Eq. 7.12–6 will be negative.

The magnetic moment of the current loop can be found by writing $qv_\perp = 2\pi Ri$ and $m = \pi R^2 i$ where $v_\perp$ is the component of the particle velocity normal to **B**, i is the value of current in the equivalent loop (we may think of the charge q as "smeared out" around the circumference), and R is the radius of the loop. Thus we have

$$m = \pi R^2 q v_\perp / 2\pi R = \tfrac{1}{2} Rq v_\perp \qquad (7.13\text{–}1)$$

which by use of Eq. 7.3–1a becomes

$$m = \tfrac{1}{2} M v_\perp{}^2 / B = K_\perp / B \qquad (7.13\text{–}2)$$

where $K_\perp = \tfrac{1}{2} M v_\perp{}^2$ is the kinetic energy associated with the perpendicular component of the particle's velocity. From Eq. 7.12–9 we see that $U = -mB$, taking the value of B as an average over the particle orbit. The interesting and important effects of non-uniformity of **B** occur with respect to variations of its magnitude along its direction. Taking $\mathbf{1}_z$ along the average direction of **B** over the orbit, we have for the average force parallel to the field

$$F_\parallel = F_z = -m \frac{\partial B}{\partial z} \qquad (7.13\text{–}3)$$

The particle moves along the field at a speed $v_\parallel = dz/dt$ as it circulates. Newton's law of motion reads

$$M \frac{dv_\parallel}{dt} = -m \frac{\partial B}{\partial z}$$

Multiplying both sides of this equation by $v_\parallel$ yields

$$M v_\parallel \frac{dv_\parallel}{dt} = \frac{d}{dt} \left(\tfrac{1}{2} M v_\parallel{}^2 \right) = -m \frac{\partial B}{\partial z} \frac{dz}{dt} = -m \frac{dB}{dt} \qquad (7.13\text{–}4)$$

where dB/dt is the variation of B in time at the position of the particle.

Since the total kinetic energy of the particle, given by

$$K = \tfrac{1}{2}Mv^2 = \tfrac{1}{2}Mv_\parallel{}^2 + \tfrac{1}{2}Mv_\perp{}^2$$

is constant, the time derivative of the parallel part $\tfrac{1}{2}Mv_\parallel{}^2$ is equal and opposite to that of the perpendicular part, given by 7.13-2. Thus Eq. 7.13-4 becomes

$$-\frac{d(mB)}{dt} = -m\,\frac{dB}{dt} \qquad (7.13\text{-}5)$$

showing that *the magnetic moment m remains constant as the particle moves.* We have assumed that the field varies slowly in both magnitude and direction, so the invariance of m is approximate, tending to be stricter as the

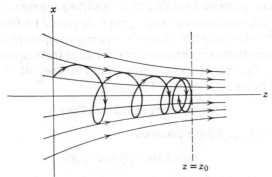

Fig. 7.13a. Reflection of a particle in a "magnetic mirror."

variation of B becomes less. Because such an invariant quantity changes very little per cycle, it is called by analogy with certain calculations in classical statistical mechanics an *adiabatic invariant.*[30]

By eliminating $v_\perp$ in 7.13-1 by 7.3-1a, we find

$$m = \tfrac{1}{2}BR^2q^2/M \qquad (7.13\text{-}6)$$

from which we see that constancy of m implies constancy of $\Phi = \pi R^2 B$. *The particle moves so as to enclose a constant amount of flux.* Still another expression of the same invariant is that since angular momentum is $Mv_\perp R = 2mM/q$, *the angular momentum of the particle remains constant about the field direction.* We note from Equation 7.13-3 that as the particle circulates, *it is forced toward the weaker part of the field.* If a particle enters a field from a region where B is very small, it will execute an ever-tightening spiral around lines of force as it gets into regions of high B, and *may in fact be completely reflected.* The magnetic field acts as a mirror (Fig. 7.13a). We note from Eq. 7.13-2 that as B gets larger, so does $K_\perp$. A larger and

[30] Cf. J. D. Jackson, *Classical Electrodynamics*, John Wiley, New York, 1962, Section 12.10.

larger fraction of the kinetic energy K becomes associated with the circulation and less with motion along **B**. If B becomes so large that $K_\perp = mB$ becomes equal to K, $K_\parallel$ will be zero, and $v_\parallel$ changes its sign—the particle is reflected.

Suppose as a result of scattering, say, a particle starts at an incident value of B_i of B with an initial value $K_{i\perp}$ of $K_\perp$ and a total kinetic energy K. Reflection will occur for a value B_r of B such that

$$\frac{K_{i\perp}}{B_i} = \frac{K}{B_r}$$

or

$$\frac{B_r}{B_i} = \frac{K}{K_{i\perp}} = 1 + \frac{K_{i\parallel}}{K_{i\perp}} = 1 + \frac{v_{i\parallel}^2}{v_{i\perp}^2} \qquad (7.13\text{–}7)$$

where $K_{i\parallel} = K - K_{i\perp}$ and $v_{i\parallel}$ and $v_{i\perp}$ are the initial velocity components. If B_r is the maximum value of B in the field, Eq. 7.13–7 can be used to find the maximum ratio $v_{i\parallel}/v_{i\perp}$ for which a particle can be reflected.

Magnetic mirrors are used in plasma machines to prevent the escape of high-energy charged particles. Only those with initial motion close enough in direction to the axis of B can escape (Problem 7.13a).

We have so far neglected the possibility of any curvature to the lines of force. It is not hard to show that the particles will tend to spiral around lines of force even when they are curved. Consider a region in which lines of **B** curve from the z-direction toward the x-direction as in Fig. 7.13b. Let us also assume that $\partial B_z/\partial z$ is positive. If $B_x \ll B_z$, we can treat B_z as roughly constant, and calculate the curvature of a line of force from

$$\frac{d^2 x}{dz^2} = \frac{d}{dz}\left(\frac{B_x}{B_z}\right) \simeq \frac{1}{B_z}\frac{\partial B_x}{\partial z} = \frac{1}{B_z}\frac{\partial B_z}{\partial x}$$

assuming no conduction or displacement currents to be present so **curl B** = 0 and $\partial B_x/\partial z = \partial B_z/\partial x$.

Positive curvature as shown thus implies that B_z increases with x, so the force tending to repel the circulating charge from regions of strong field will be greater on the upper part of the loop shown than on the lower. The orbit will tend to rotate toward being normal to **B**, regardless of the direction of $v_\parallel$.

The tendency of charged particles to spiral around lines of force is of considerable importance for the motion of ions in the Van Allen radiation belts in the earth's magnetic field, and in many other aspects of space physics. It is also of considerable use in collimating beams of particles in atomic physics experiments.

If such an orbit moves along a line of force of radius R_B, an average centripetal force of amount $mv_\parallel^2/R_B$ will be needed, a force which can only

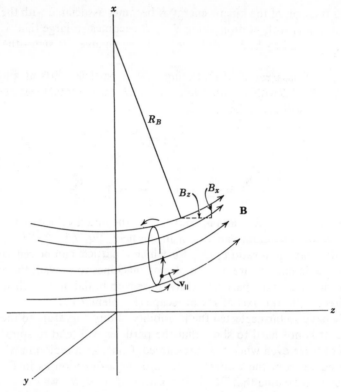

Fig. 7.13*b*. Showing the rotation of a particle orbit in a field of variable direction toward perpendicularity to the direction of **B**.

come from portions of the orbit where the particle is moving in the y-direction, perpendicularly to the x-z plane as shown. That is, the mean velocity component $\bar{v}_y$ cannot average to zero, but we must instead have

$$F_R = q\bar{v}_y B = mv_{\parallel}^2/R_B$$

so that the particle drifts across the field in the y-direction with a mean drift speed $\bar{v}_y = v_{\text{drift}}$ given by

$$v_{\text{drift}} = Mv_{\parallel}^2/qBR_B \tag{7.13--8}$$

where R_B is normally very large and must not be confused with the radius of the orbit. This drift velocity is called the "curvature drift." Since it depends on the sign of q, it can separate charges and produce net currents in a plasma with a curved magnetic field.

We have discussed the invariance of magnetic moment, angular momentum, and flux surrounded in the adiabatic approximation. H. Busch has provided an exact theorem[31] for axially symmetric fields which relates the second two of these quantities, regardless of whether the pitch of the helix is tight or loose.

Let us assume that the cylindrical "hoop" component B_φ is zero and that the components of $\mathbf{A}$ in cylindrical coordinates are not functions of φ. Then we have (cf. Table A.2A)

$$B_r = -\frac{\partial A_\varphi}{\partial z}$$

$$B_z = \frac{1}{r}\frac{\partial}{\partial r}(rA_\varphi)$$

Any contribution of A_r and A_z must have a zero curl and can be neglected. Let us now write for the magnetic force on the particle in the φ direction

$$F_\varphi = q(\mathbf{v}\times\mathbf{B})_\varphi = q(v_z B_r - v_r B_z)$$

$$= -q\left[v_z\frac{\partial A_\varphi}{\partial z} + \frac{v_r}{r}\frac{\partial}{\partial r}(rA_\varphi)\right] \qquad (7.13\text{--}9)$$

where $v_z = dz/dt$ and $v_r = dr/dt$ are components of the particle velocity.

The rate of change of angular momentum of the particle is equal to the torque, so we have

$$\frac{d}{dt}(Mrv_\perp) = rF_\varphi = -q\left[v_z\frac{\partial(rA_\varphi)}{\partial z} + v_r\frac{\partial}{\partial r}(rA_\varphi)\right]$$

$$= -q\left[\frac{dz}{dt}\frac{\partial(rA_\varphi)}{\partial z} + \frac{dr}{dt}\frac{\partial}{\partial r}(rA_\varphi)\right]$$

$$= -q\frac{d(rA_\varphi)}{dt} \qquad (7.13\text{--}10)$$

where the time derivative of rA_φ is taken at the position of the moving particle. Equation 7.13–9 can be integrated immediately. Since the flux through a circle of radius r is $\Phi = 2\pi rA_\varphi$, we have for any two points 1 and 2 on the trajectory

$$\left(Mrv_\perp + \frac{q}{2\pi}\Phi\right)_1 = \left(Mrv_\perp + \frac{q}{2\pi}\Phi\right)_2 \qquad (7.13\text{--}11)$$

as an expression of the Busch theorem. We see that the approximate constancy of angular momentum implies a similar constancy to Φ, provided the hoop component B_φ is negligible.

[31] H. Busch, *Ann. Physik*, **81**, 974 (1926). See also J. R. Pierce, *op. cit.*, pp. 35–37.

The Busch theorem has an application to the case of a magnetic electron lens. Figure 7.13c shows a short solenoid with the trajectory of a particle initially moving away from the axis of the field. First let us consider qualitatively what happens. As the particle gets into the field, it experiences a component B_r which together with its velocity v_z provides a force in the φ direction. Motion in the φ-direction will result in a force in the r-direction which is readily seen to be directed toward the axis regardless of the sign of charge or direction of **B**. After the particle has thus come nearer the axis, the magnitude of B_r will be less and there will be less tendency to leave the axis on the way out of the lens.

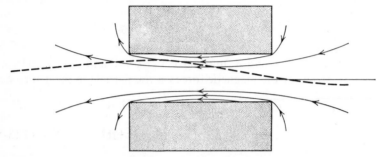

Fig. 7.13c.   A particle trajectory in a magnetic lens. (From J. R. Pierce, *Theory and Design of Electron Beams*, D. Van Nostrand Co., Princeton, N.J., 1954.)

To use the Busch theorem, we assume that far from the lens both $Mv_{\perp}r = Mr^2\omega$ and Φ are zero ($\omega = d\varphi/dt$ is the angular speed of revolution of the particle around the axis). Then at any point in the lens, we have

$$Mv_{\perp}r = -\frac{q\Phi}{2\pi} = -\tfrac{1}{2}qr^2\bar{B}$$

or

$$M\omega = \tfrac{1}{2}q\bar{B} \qquad\qquad (7.13\text{--}12)$$

where $\bar{B}$ is the mean value of B within a circle of radius r at the point in question. The minus sign has been omitted, its significance merely being that, as we know, $v_{\perp}$ is in a direction to produce a field opposite to **B**. The angular velocity of the particle is seen to be just half the ordinary cyclotron frequency. (Note that this result cannot be obtained in the adiabatic approximation where $Mv_{\perp}r$ is taken as invariant.)

Now consider the radial component of Newton's law. We have

$$F_r = M\left[\frac{d^2r}{dt^2} - r\omega^2\right] = -qv_{\varphi}B_z = -qr\omega B$$

where we shall assume that $B_z = \bar{B} = B$. Since $Mr\omega^2 = \tfrac{1}{2}\,qr\omega\bar{B}$, we get simply

$$M\frac{d^2r}{dt^2} = -\tfrac{1}{2}qr\omega B = -\frac{rq^2B^2}{2M} \qquad\qquad (7.13\text{--}13)$$

which shows that the particle is accelerated toward the axis regardless of the sign of q and B.

Problem 7.13a. Suppose the ratio of maximum to minimum axial fields in a magnetic mirror machine is 100/1. For what angle of initial motion with respect to the axis will a particle just be able to escape?

Problem 7.13b. Find the drift velocity for electrons of mean kinetic energy 1 ev in a field of 10^3 gauss in a torus of radius $R_B = 1$ meter.

Problem 7.13c. A particle enters a magnetic lens parallel to its axis with initial speed v. Find the change $\Delta\varphi$ of its azimuth as it passes through the lens in terms of $\int B_z \, dz$. Evaluate the integral for a short solenoid.

7.14   Induced Electric Fields

We are now prepared to generalize the results of Section 7.4 for magnetically induced emf's. We have studied the sources of **B** and deduced the conservation of flux, so that we can partially extend the induction law with this study as a basis. The principal generalization, however, is to a type of induction which cannot be deduced from our previous results although it can be made plausible and can like them be described in terms of flux changes. We shall also discuss the law of induction in terms of non-static electric fields.

The theorem of flux conservation allows us to complete the generator rule of Section 7.4. The flux Φ in Eq. 7.4–11 can be taken as the total flux through the circuit, since by the conservation theorem the latter is a definite number determined only by the location of the circuit. Once a positive direction has been assigned to Φ, there is a positive sign for the motion of current around the circuit according to the conventions of Section 7.6. The emf $\mathscr{E}$ in Eq. 7.4–11 is taken as positive if a current produced solely by its action would run in the positive direction. The reader can readily verify that the negative sign in this equation follows from the Lorentz force law and the above-mentioned right-hand rule for the signs of current and emf.

This negative sign is embodied in the theorem known as Lenz's law: the induced emf is always in such a direction as to produce a current and resulting flux change that counteracts the original flux change responsible for the induction.[32] It will be seen later that this law is a particular case of the law of the conservation of energy.

Now let us ask what happens if the conductors that are the sources of **B** move and the circuit whose emf is being studied is held still. The result is clearly the same as if the circuit moved and the source remained still. In fact, all our experience in the laboratory and on moving vehicles, airplanes, etc., indicates that it is only relative motion that plays a role in electromagnetic phenomena.

[32] H. F. E. Lenz, *Ann. der Phys.*, **31**, 483 (1834).

As a matter of fact, any large effects due to "absolute motion" with respect to the "fixed stars" or any other astronomical frame of reference would show up most strongly in daily and annual variations or strongly directional variations associated with the earth's speed of 19 mi/sec around the sun and tangential velocity of 0.3 mi/sec at the equator due to rotation on its axis. No such effects have ever been found.

This elementary fragment of the theory of relativity[33] leads us to some interesting consequences for the theory of electricity. The first one is that an emf may be produced in a stationary circuit by moving a source of magnetic induction. Since the circuit is stationary, there can be no force of the type $q(\mathbf{v} \times \mathbf{B})$ on the charges in the wire, and the emf must involve a new electric field $\mathbf{E}$. This $\mathbf{E}$ is to be calculated from the changing flux of $\mathbf{B}$; but before we calculate it, let us use its existence to complete our generalization of the law for induced emfs.

Faraday in 1831 discovered by experiment that the emf induced in a closed circuit is given by the negative rate of change of flux through the circuit regardless of how this change is made—whether by motion of the circuit, motion of the source, or change in strength of the source.[34] Faraday's law is the law of induced emf's written with complete generality as

$$\mathscr{E} = -\frac{d\Phi}{dt} \qquad (7.14\text{-}1a)$$

The motional part of the emf can be deduced as above, but the emf produced in one circuit by changing the current in another cannot. It might seem that the change of $\mathbf{B}$ in and around a circuit caused by changing the current in a source coil could be simulated by some complicated type of motion of the source, and there are some cases in which this is so, but there are cases in which it is clearly impossible.

For instance, we showed in Section 7.8 that the magnetic fields outside an idealized toroid and an idealized infinite solenoid are everywhere zero. Yet if a wire is looped around either of these, an emf will be induced when the current in the toroid or solenoid is changed. Since there is at no time any induction $\mathbf{B}$ at any point on the wire loop, the emf could not be found by relative motion considerations and the generator rule of Section 7.4. How can magnetic flux that never touches a wire have an effect on the charges in it?

This question can be properly answered if we now consider the induced electric field. Let us first take up a case of emf induced by relative motion

---

[33] Properly called "Galilean" or "Newtonian" relativity rather than "Einsteinian." Einsteinian relativity is considered briefly in Sections 7.19 and 10.3.

[34] M. Faraday, *Experimental Researches in Electricity*, Taylor and Francis or B. Quaritch, London, 1839, Dover, New York, reprint, 1965, Vol. I, Series I, §§ 1–59.

and apply our elementary relativity to one of the charges in the wire. When the source of magnetic field is stationary and the charge moves with velocity **v**, we have for the force on the charge

$$F = q(\mathbf{E}_0 + \mathbf{v} \times \mathbf{B})$$

where $\mathbf{E}_0$ represents whatever electrostatic field may be present. Now if we observe the force on the charge while we ourselves move with it, so that we observe q to be at rest and the source to move with velocity $-\mathbf{v}$, we will have only an electric force, although it will clearly be the same magnitude and direction of force as before, since **F** is measured by ma and an acceleration is unchanged by addition of a constant velocity. Let us write now

$$\mathbf{F} = q\mathbf{E}'$$

so that we have a new value for the electric field strength[35]

$$\mathbf{E}' = \mathbf{E}_0 + \mathbf{v} \times \mathbf{B} \tag{7.14–2a}$$

A moving source of magnetic field produces an electric field. Since the emf will be the same, being defined as $\oint (\mathbf{F}/q) \cdot \mathbf{dl}$, we must have $\oint \mathbf{E}' \cdot \mathbf{dl} = \oint \mathbf{v} \times \mathbf{B} \cdot \mathbf{dl} = -d\Phi/dt$. This new electric field is not derivable from a potential, since its circulation does not vanish, so that it cannot be called an *electrostatic* field (see Section 1.8). To carry the matter a bit further, we may note that since the wire containing q is at rest, we do not need it. The product $q\mathbf{E}'$ is always the force that *would* be exerted *if* a charge q were put at the point in question (and did not disturb the surroundings). Hence we see that everywhere in the neighborhood of a moving source of **B** there is an induced electric field.

As an example let us consider a body of conducting fluid with essentially zero resistivity that is moving with a velocity **v**. As pointed out in Eq. 7.4–4, $\mathbf{E} = -\mathbf{v} \times \mathbf{B}$ so that $\mathbf{E}' = 0$—there is no electric field to be observed in a frame of reference moving with the fluid. From an observation point at rest in the laboratory, we see that along with the electrostatic effects of charges at the boundaries, the moving currents help to make **E** become equal to $-\mathbf{v} \times \mathbf{B}$.

The most interesting conclusion, however, is that the magnetic flux through any closed loop moving with the fluid must be constant, since $\mathscr{E}' = \oint \mathbf{E}' \cdot \mathbf{dl} = 0$. A high-conductivity plasma carries the magnetic field with it. From the point of view of the laboratory, moving lines of current experience induced emfs that tend to maintain the magnetic fields that those current lines are in. If the resistivity were precisely zero, Lenz's law

[35] Compare with Eq. 7.4–3 where we consider a conductor to be present but do not use Galilean relativity.

would work to keep precisely constant the magnetic field at each current line.

In Section 10.5 a calculation will be given showing how we can treat the magnetic lines of force in a highly-conducting plasma as moving with the fluid, corroborating our above conclusion that the **B** field is "frozen in" the fluid. It is, of course, only a figurative way of speaking to talk of a moving field, for it is not forces that move but objects (e.g., charges) under the influence of the forces. In most cases, it is best to avoid confusion by first considering some single convenient "frame of reference" with respect to which one can then define **E**, **B**, and the velocities of the various charges.[36]

By use of Stokes' theorem, in a similar fashion to its use in Sections 1.8 and 7.9, we can derive a differential equation for **E**. Around any closed *fixed* but otherwise arbitrary path we have

$$\mathscr{E} = \oint \mathbf{E} \cdot \mathbf{dl} = \int_S \boldsymbol{\nabla} \times \mathbf{E} \cdot \mathbf{dS} = -\frac{d\Phi}{dt} = -\frac{d}{dt}\int_S \mathbf{B} \cdot \mathbf{dS}$$

and again the integrands of the surface integrals must be equal, yielding

$$\boldsymbol{\nabla} \times \mathbf{E} = -\frac{\partial \mathbf{B}}{\partial t} \qquad (7.14\text{--}3a)$$

This equation is the last of Maxwell's equations to be developed—the others being Eqs. 1.5–1, 7.9–3, and 7.12–1.

We have shown that **B** and **E** have a particularly intimate relationship beyond that expressed by their both acting on charges and being produced by charges. One seems to turn into the other when we change our velocity relative to the system under observation. Another instance of this relationship is given by considering the magnetic field produced by a moving charge. If we consider the Coulomb law for the field of a stationary charge

$$\mathbf{E} = \frac{q}{4\pi\epsilon_0}\frac{\mathbf{1}_r}{r^2} \qquad (7.14\text{--}4)$$

we see that Eq. 7.6–3a can be written

$$\mathbf{B} = \mu_0\epsilon_0 \mathbf{v} \times \mathbf{E} \qquad (7.14\text{--}5a)$$

where **E** and **B** are both measured at the same point. We can consider Eq. 7.14–5a to apply to the fields produced by a collection of charges with a common velocity **v** and thus assert that *a moving source of electric field produces a magnetic field*. This assertion is, of course, a partial statement of Ampère's law in the Laplace rule form.

---

[36] For a careful discussion of circumstances in which lines of **B** can properly be considered to move, see Longmire, *op. cit.*, pp. 36–40.

Let us take a numerical example. Consider a generator with an induction B of 0.1 weber/m², an armature radius of 0.1 m, and a revolution rate of 1800 rpm or 30 rps. The speed of one of the armature wires will then be $30(2\pi)(0.1) = 19$ m/sec and the force per unit charge will then be $vB = 1.9$ newtons/coulomb. If the magnet rotates instead and the armature is stationary, the induced electric field will then be 1.9 v/m.

Now suppose that we have an electrostatic field of 1.9 v/m and that we move with respect to its source with a velocity of 19 m/sec at right angles to **E**. By Eq. 7.14–5a, the induction will be $\mu_0\epsilon_0 vE = (4\pi \times 10^{-7})$ $(4\pi \times 9 \times 10^9)^{-1}(19)(1.9) = 36.1/(9 \times 10^{16}) = 4 \times 10^{-16}$ weber/m², an extremely small value. Sizable values of B only arise from currents in metallic conductors; in this case, the enormous electrostatic field produced by the moving charges is cancelled by that of stationary charges of opposite sign. This example shows the difficulty involved in making a direct experimental check of Laplace's rule.

On the other hand, a single moving charge is a moving source of **B** and an *induced* electric field should also be present. This in turn may be expected to give rise to another component of **B** and so on. In other words, the fields of a moving charge are rather complicated. As the example above indicates, Eqs. 7.14–4 and 7.14–5 are adequate for all small velocities. More explicitly, let us consider a velocity of 1 m/sec. Then the order of magnitude of the first B we calculate is $1/(9 \times 10^{16})$ times the initial E; the second E is about the same as the first B; the second B is $1/(9 \times 10^{16})$ times the second E and so on. The successive components decrease rapidly for speeds of the order of 1 m/sec. Only for speeds of the order of $1/(\mu_0\epsilon_0)^{1/2} = (9 \times 10^{16})^{1/2} = 3 \times 10^8$ m/sec are all the successive components of importance. This speed is the speed of light, so we can say that when charged particles move with speeds comparable with that of light, the formulas 7.14–4 and 7.14–5a are not accurate, but that for much lower speeds such as are ordinarily encountered, the errors involved in their use are negligible. For calculation at high velocities, other procedures must be used and are considered in Section 7.19.

It should be clear that the division of an electromagnetic interaction into separate **E** and **B** parts is essentially arbitrary, depending as it does on which particular frame of reference is used. Section 7.19 is devoted to an elegant and symmetrical method of displaying this intimate relationship.

We still have one problem to solve. How do we calculate the induced electric field in cases in which relative motion considerations do not work? We make use for this purpose of Eq. 7.12–4

$$\Phi = \int_S \mathbf{B} \cdot d\mathbf{S} = \oint_{\text{boundary of } S} \mathbf{A} \cdot d\mathbf{l}$$

This equation is quite general. It comes from the general relation $\mathbf{B} =$ **curl A** and the use of Stokes' theorem, and holds when the currents are variable.[37] Faraday's law then reads, for fixed circuits,

$$\mathscr{E} = \oint \mathbf{E} \cdot \mathbf{dl} = -\frac{\partial \Phi}{\partial t} = -\oint \frac{\partial \mathbf{A}}{\partial t} \cdot \mathbf{dl}$$

so that

$$\oint \left(\mathbf{E} + \frac{\partial \mathbf{A}}{\partial t} \right) \cdot \mathbf{dl} = 0$$

for any closed path. Now according to the arguments used in Section 1.8, the vanishing of this integral implies the existence of a potential V whose negative gradient gives the sum $\mathbf{E} + \partial \mathbf{A}/\partial t$. Thus

$$\mathbf{E} + \frac{\partial \mathbf{A}}{\partial t} = -\nabla V$$

or

$$\mathbf{E} = -\frac{\partial \mathbf{A}}{\partial t} - \nabla V \qquad (7.14\text{--}6a)$$

The quantity $-\nabla V$ appears to represent any electrostatic field that is present. To test whether this is so, let us calculate $\nabla \cdot \mathbf{E}$ using the Lorentz condition 7.10–9a

$$\nabla \cdot \mathbf{E} = -\frac{\partial}{\partial t}(\nabla \cdot \mathbf{A}) - \nabla^2 V = \mu_0 \epsilon_0 \frac{\partial^2 V}{\partial t^2} - \nabla^2 V \qquad (7.14\text{--}7)$$

If $-\nabla V$ is the electrostatic field, we must have $-\nabla^2 V = \rho/\epsilon_0$, by Eq. 1.10–1, which means that $\nabla \cdot \mathbf{E}$ cannot equal ρ/ϵ_0. This in turn would mean that the electric field of magnetic origin has a non-vanishing divergence even though the field is not produced by charge density. We cannot settle the question without a further assumption (to be justified in Section 7.19 and in Chapter 10), which is that $\nabla \cdot \mathbf{E}$ is always equal to ρ/ϵ_0. This means that $-\nabla V$ includes some magnetically induced field along with the electrostatic field.

However, this last effect is small if the time variations are slow enough. Since $\mu_0 \epsilon_0 = 1/c^2$, we can compare the time and space derivatives in Eq. 7.14–7 by first considering a variation of V with respect to ct and then with respect to x. If time variations of appreciable amount only occur during times long compared to r/c where r is the maximum distance over which V is of interest, we can take $\Delta(ct)$ as much larger than r and Δx as much smaller than r, so that $\partial V/\partial(ct)$ is much less than $\partial V/\partial x$. The second time derivatives will be even smaller in comparison to $\nabla^2 V$. We shall refer to the induced part of ∇V as a radiation term.

For the present we shall assume that ∇V represents any electrostatic field present and omit its consideration here. Except for radiation terms,

---

[37] The application of our equations to cases of *rapidly* varying currents will be discussed in Chapter 10.

the induced electric field produced by motion and/or by change of a current is given by

$$\mathbf{E} = -\frac{\partial \mathbf{A}}{\partial t} \qquad (7.14\text{--}8)$$

This formula expresses Faraday's law for fixed circuits in terms of fields and the directly calculable vector potential $\mathbf{A}$ and is the solution of our problem. In fact, Eq. 7.14–8 is seen to satisfy Eq. 7.14–3a. Lines of $\mathbf{E}$ as given by Eq. 7.14–8 can have no ends if $\nabla \cdot \mathbf{A} = 0$. They will not however be closed except in cases of ideal symmetry (see discussion on p. 326).

Problem 7.12b involves the calculation of the emf induced in a wire surrounding an infinite solenoid and illustrates our solution of the paradox of the induced emf which exists even when $\mathbf{B}$ at the wire is always zero. It remains true that the use of the flux of induction is the easiest way to calculate the emf, but a detailed mental picture of the production of this emf is easier to obtain if the producing current is considered to generate a vector potential $\mathbf{A}$ which acts directly on the charges in the wire through the field of Eq. 7.14–8.

We can go further and write $\mathbf{E}$ directly in terms of the varying current density. By using Eq. 7.10–5 for the vector potential, we have for the electric field of magnetic origin

$$\mathbf{E} = -\frac{\mu_0}{4\pi} \int \frac{\partial \mathbf{J}}{\partial t} \frac{d\tau}{r} \qquad (7.14\text{--}9a)$$

which by the development in Section 7.10 is seen to be valid for open or closed current loops.

Finally, we can write $\mathbf{E}$ as having $\partial \mathbf{B}/\partial t$ as a source. In the case of slowly-varying currents, when displacement currents can be neglected, we can replace $\mu_0 \, \partial \mathbf{J}/\partial t$ with $\nabla \times \partial \mathbf{B}/\partial t$. If we then use the identity given as item 8 in Table A.2B, for the curl of a scalar times a vector, we can write

$$\mathbf{E} = -\frac{1}{4\pi} \int \left(\nabla \times \frac{\partial \mathbf{B}}{\partial t} \right) \frac{d\tau}{r}$$

$$= -\frac{1}{4\pi} \left[\int \frac{\partial \mathbf{B}}{\partial t} \times \nabla \left(\frac{1}{r} \right) d\tau + \int \nabla \times \left(\frac{1}{r} \frac{\partial \mathbf{B}}{\partial t} \right) d\tau \right]$$

The second term can be converted to a surface integral by Eq. A.2–26 and shown to vanish if the surface bounding the volume τ is a sphere of indefinitely increasing radius. We have the result

$$\mathbf{E} = \frac{1}{4\pi} \int \frac{\partial \mathbf{B}}{\partial t} \times \frac{1_r}{r^2} d\tau \qquad (7.14\text{--}10a)$$

This result bears the same relation to Faraday's law in the form 7.14–3a that the Biot-Savart formula 7.6–2 bears to the differential equation 7.9–1. In fact, by using the methods of Problem 7.12–14 we can see that 7.14–10a is the unique solution of the pair of equations $\nabla \times \mathbf{E} = -\partial\mathbf{B}/\partial t$ and $\nabla \cdot \mathbf{E} = 0$, and so properly represents the electric field of magnetic origin in the slowly varying case.

When the currents are rapidly varying, we must add $\partial\mathbf{D}/\partial t$ to $\mathbf{J}$ so that a term proportional to $\mu_0 \partial^2\mathbf{D}/\partial t^2 = \mu_0\epsilon_0 \partial^2\mathbf{E}/\partial t^2$ must be added to the integral of 7.14–10. Just as for the scalar potential, this term is only large when radiation is important. We shall see in Section 10.3 that in this circumstance, the expression 7.10–5 must be modified, so that the proper consideration of displacement-current contributions to 7.14–10 must be deferred to the later chapter.

Faraday's law has already been given in Gaussian units in Eq. 7.4–11b, which we repeat here for the general case

$$\mathcal{E} = -\frac{1}{c}\frac{d\Phi}{dt} \qquad\qquad \text{Gaussian} \quad (7.14\text{–}1b)$$

The electric field that appears because of relative motion is

$$\mathbf{E}' = \mathbf{E}_0 + \frac{1}{c}\mathbf{v} \times \mathbf{B} \qquad\qquad \text{Gaussian} \quad (7.14\text{–}2b)$$

and the differential equation form of Faraday's law reads

$$\nabla \times \mathbf{E} = -\frac{1}{c}\frac{\partial\mathbf{B}}{\partial t} \qquad\qquad \text{Gaussian} \quad (7.14\text{–}3b)$$

Relative motion with respect to a source of $\mathbf{E}$ gives

$$\mathbf{B} = \frac{1}{c}\mathbf{v} \times \mathbf{E} \qquad\qquad \text{Gaussian} \quad (7.14\text{–}5b)$$

and the formula for $\mathbf{E}$ in terms of $\mathbf{A}$ and V reads

$$\mathbf{E} = -\frac{1}{c}\frac{\partial\mathbf{A}}{\partial t} - \nabla V \qquad\qquad \text{Gaussian} \quad (7.14\text{–}6b)$$

In terms of changing current density, we have

$$\mathbf{E} = -\frac{1}{c^2}\int \frac{\partial\mathbf{J}}{\partial t}\frac{d\tau}{r} \qquad\qquad \text{Gaussian} \quad (7.14\text{–}9b)$$

and finally the relation of $\mathbf{E}$ and $\partial\mathbf{B}/\partial t$ is

$$\mathbf{E} = \frac{1}{4\pi c}\int \frac{\partial\mathbf{B}}{\partial t} \times \frac{1_r}{r^2}\,d\tau \qquad\qquad \text{Gaussian} \quad (7.14\text{–}10b)$$

Problem 7.14a. Repeat the calculations of $\mathbf{B}$ and $\mathbf{E}$ in the numerical example in the text involving a generator, using Gaussian units.

Problem 7.14b. Suppose the current in the infinite solenoid whose vector potential is given in Eq. 7.11–1 varies with the time in accordance with $i = f(t)$. Calculate the emf induced in a loop of wire that (a) has n turns inside the solenoid and (b) surrounds the solenoid n times.

Problem 7.14c. The earth's magnetic induction at a certain place is 0.500 gauss, directed downward in a north-south vertical plane, at an angle of 69° with the horizontal. A square coil of 100 turns that is 4 cm on each side is rotated about a vertical axis that bisects two opposite sides of the coil. If the coil turns at 15 revolutions per second, write the induced emf as a function of the time.

Problem 7.14d. Show that Lenz's law can be used to determine the sense of circulation of a charged particle moving normally to a magnetic field **B**.

Problem 7.14e. Show that the radiation term in ∇V in Eq. 7.14–6 cannot influence any emf calculations.

Problem 7.14f. Consider a source of magnetic field, say a solenoid, moving at velocity **v**, and show that $\oint \mathbf{E}' \cdot d\mathbf{l}'$ calculated from 7.14–2 about an arbitrary closed path l' yields Faraday's law for l', in analogy to the derivation of 7.7–4.

Problem 7.14g. Calculate the induced emf from the Lorentz force law for a moving loop of wire when **E** includes magnetically induced electric fields, and show explicitly, by considering the rule for the time derivative of an integral over a region with a moving boundary, that $\mathscr{E} = -d\Phi/dt$.

7.15 Mutual Inductance[38]

In this section, we wish to consider the calculation of emfs induced by one circuit in another and of the currents resulting from them. It will be convenient to take the second aspect first.

Consider a circuit containing a loop of wire in a variable magnetic field and a series resistor R which for definiteness we shall take to be outside the field, as in the case of the generator circuit of Section 7.4. Let the resistance of the loop itself be r, so that $R + r$ is the total resistance in the circuit. Let us assume that a current i flows in the circuit at a given instant when the rate of change of flux is $d\Phi/dt$ and that the time constant of the distributed capacitance of the circuit is small enough that i is constant at any instant throughout the circuit, even though its magnitude may vary with time. For simplicity, we shall consider the loop to be at rest, but similar considerations to those in Section 7.4 will apply if all or part of it is in motion.

---

[38] Sections 7.15 to 7.18 can be postponed until Sections 8.5, 8.8, and 9.2 are to be studied.

There must be a PD across R of magnitude $V = iR$, produced by an ordinary electrostatic field. In the wire of the loop there will be two fields acting, the electrostatic one $\mathbf{E}_{\text{stat}}$ just mentioned and the field $\mathbf{E} = -\partial\mathbf{A}/\partial t$ associated with the magnetic field. The two fields together act to make the current flow, so that Ohm's law becomes for the loop

$$\int_a^b \left(\mathbf{E}_{\text{stat}} - \frac{\partial\mathbf{A}}{\partial t} \right) \cdot \mathbf{dl} = ir$$

where a and b represent the connection points between the loop and the external resistor R. The integral $\int_a^b \mathbf{E}_{\text{stat}} \cdot \mathbf{dl}$ is equal to $-\int_b^a \mathbf{E}_{\text{stat}} \cdot \mathbf{dl}$ taken over R, which is $-V = -iR$. The integral of $-\partial\mathbf{A}/\partial t$, on the other hand, is the induced emf $\mathscr{E}$, so that we have

$$-\int_a^b \frac{\partial\mathbf{A}}{\partial t} \cdot \mathbf{dl} = \mathscr{E} = V + ir = i(r + R) \qquad (7.15\text{--}1)$$

This equation is exactly similar to that for a cell with internal and external resistances.

If an external emf $\mathscr{E}'$, say that of a chemical cell, is present in the circuit, then V for the external part of the circuit will be $iR - \mathscr{E}'$, and we have as to be expected

$$\mathscr{E} + \mathscr{E}' = i(r + R) \qquad (7.15\text{--}2)$$

Now let us consider the induction of an emf in one circuit by a current in another. The flux Φ_{12} through circuit 1 produced by circuit 2 may be written in terms of the mutual inductance (cf. Section 7.12):

$$\Phi_{12} = M_{12}i_2 \qquad (7.15\text{--}3)$$

where M_{12} is given by Neumann's formula, Eq. 7.12–13.

Then the emf $\mathscr{E}_{12} = -d\Phi_{12}/dt$ becomes

$$\mathscr{E}_{12} = -d(M_{12}i_2)/dt \qquad (7.15\text{--}4a)$$

and if both circuits are fixed in position

$$\mathscr{E}_{12} = -M_{12}\,di_2/dt \qquad (7.15\text{--}4b)$$

Equation 7.15–4b may be taken as an alternative definition of the mutual inductance M_{12}. It is the same in all systems of units. The complete symmetry of Eq. 7.12–13 shows that the emf $\mathscr{E}_{21}$ induced in circuit 2 by a changing current in circuit 1, when the circuits do not move, is given by

$$\mathscr{E}_{21} = -M_{21}\,di_1/dt = -M_{12}\,di_1/dt \qquad (7.15\text{--}5)$$

The mutual inductance between two circuits is the same, regardless of which circuit is considered to be the inducing agent and which the circuit acted upon.

The calculation of mutual inductance is quite complicated, even in cases of considerable symmetry. We shall have to restrict ourselves here to three practical applications and one case that illustrates the computational difficulty. Neumann's formula is valuable for showing the symmetry of M_{12} and M_{21}, but rather than start with this formula, we shall use previous calculations of $\mathbf{B}$ and the formula $\Phi = \int \mathbf{B} \cdot d\mathbf{S}$.

Consider first a long solenoid of cross-sectional area S_1 and n_{l1} turns per meter, with a short secondary winding on its outside containing n_{l2} turns per meter, of area S_2 and length l_2 (Fig. 7.15a). If we were to assume

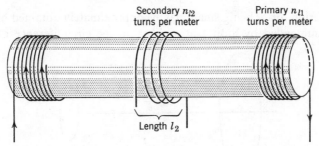

Secondary n_{l2} turns per meter   Primary n_{l1} turns per meter

Length l_2

Fig. 7.15a. A solenoid with a secondary winding for mutual inductance.

unit current in the secondary and to calculate the flux linking the primary, we would have a complicated calculation, for the secondary field will look like Fig. 7.12c, and different amounts of flux will link each different turn of the primary. (The sum of the amounts of flux linking each turn of a coil is called the "flux linkage" in that coil.) On the other hand, if the primary is long and the secondary is located far from the ends of the primary, a unit current in the latter will produce a uniform field through the secondary, and the flux linkage will be easy to calculate. In fact, the flux in the primary when it carries i_1 amperes will be $\mu_0 i_1 n_{l1} S_1$ by Eq. 7.8–14a. Each turn of the secondary will be linked by this flux, so that the total flux linkage will be $n_{l2} l_2 \mu_0 i_1 n_{l1} S_1$. Setting $n_{l2} l_2 = N_2$, the mutual inductance of a long solenoid and a short secondary coil outside it far from its ends is

$$M_{12} = \mu_0 n_{l1} N_2 S_1 \qquad (7.15\text{–}6)$$

Note that the formula involves the turns per unit length and the cross section of the long inside coil and the total number of turns only of the short outside coil.

As a second example, consider two circular loops of wire with a common axis, as in Fig. 7.15b. We shall let one of the loops be small enough that the variation of the field produced by the other over its area is negligible. Let the large circle have a radius a_1, the small one have radius a_2, their distance apart be z, and the positive directions for both be defined in the same sense.

By Eq. 7.8–8a, the field of loop 1 at the center of coil 2 is

$$B = B_z = \frac{\mu_0 i_1 a_1{}^2}{2(a_1{}^2 + z^2)^{3/2}}$$

Since a_2 is small enough, we may assume B_z to have a constant value over the area $\pi a_2{}^2$ of coil 2, so that the mutual inductance is

$$M_{12} = \frac{\pi \mu_0 a_1{}^2 a_2{}^2}{2(a_1{}^2 + z^2)^{3/2}} \tag{7.15–7}$$

The criterion for a_2 being small may be approximately obtained by noting that Ω subtended by loop 1 at a point on the circumference of loop 2

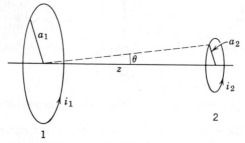

Fig. 7.15b. Illustrating M_{12} between large and small coaxial coils.

differs from that subtended by the center of loop 2 by roughly a factor $\cos \theta$ because of inclination, and by another factor of $\cos^2 \theta$ because the distance to the center of loop 1 increases by $1/\cos \theta$ (as long as z is not too small compared with a_1). Since $\cos^3 \theta \simeq 1 - 3\theta^2/2$ and $\theta \simeq a_2/z$, Ω will vary by less than 1 % if $3\theta^2/2 < 1/100$ or $a_2/z \leqslant \frac{1}{12}$.

If a_1 is small ($a_1/z < \frac{1}{12}$, for instance) we can find M_{12} by finding the flux through loop 1 produced by a unit current in loop 2. The result is

$$M_{12} = \frac{\pi \mu_0 a_1{}^2 a_2{}^2}{2(a_2{}^2 + z^2)^{3/2}}$$

This latter formula differs from Eq. 7.15–7 in assuming a_1 small instead of a_2. If both a_1 and a_2 are sufficiently small compared to z, the two formulas for M_{12} give the symmetrical result

$$M_{12} = \frac{\pi \mu_0 a_1{}^2 a_2{}^2}{2z^3} \tag{7.15–8}$$

A method for deriving Eq. 7.15–7 by calculating the flux through a large loop 1 produced by a small loop 2 is considered in Problem 7.15a. If loop 1 has N_1 closely wound turns and loop 2 N_2 turns, formulas 7.15–7 and 7.15–8 are to be multiplied by N_1N_2.

Finally, note that M_{12} becomes negative if the positive senses of the two coils are oppositely defined. Negative values of mutual inductance are frequently required for consistency in the analysis of the circuits associated with the coils.

The Absolute Measurement of Resistance. As a third example, consider a small rotatable circular coil of N_2 turns and mean radius a_2 located at the center of a pair of Helmholtz coils of N_1 turns each, with mean radius

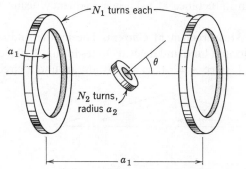

Fig. 7.15c. A variable mutual inductance used in absolute resistance measurements.

a_1, with an angle θ between the two axes (Problem 7.8f and Fig. 7.15c). To a good approximation the flux through coil 2 will be given by using the result of Problem 7.8f, along with the area of coil 2 and $\cos \theta$:

$$M_{12} = \frac{8\pi\mu_0 N_1 N_2 a_2{}^2 \cos \theta}{5^{3/2} a_1} \tag{7.15–9}$$

This arrangement can be used to calibrate a resistance in terms of length and time. Suppose that a current i_1 is passed through the Helmholtz pair and also through a series resistor R. Let the inner coil be rotated at constant angular velocity ω, so that $\cos \theta = \cos \omega t$. Then suppose that an intermittent contact arrangement allows a connection to be made to coil 2 when the induced emf is a maximum. Since $\mathscr{E} = -(d/dt)(M_{12}i_1)$, we have

$$\mathscr{E} = \frac{8\pi\mu_0 N_1 N_2 a_2{}^2}{5^{3/2} a_1} i_1\omega \sin \omega t$$

and $\mathscr{E}$ will have its greatest value $\mathscr{E}_{\max}$ when $\sin \omega t = 1$ or $\theta = 90°$, $450°$, etc. If we balance the drop on the resistor R against $\mathscr{E}_{\max}$, we can get a null result, detectable as usual with a galvanometer, when $i_1 R = \mathscr{E}_{max}$ or

$$R = \frac{8\pi\mu_0 N_1 N_2 a_2{}^2 \omega}{5^{3/2} a_1} \tag{7.15-10}$$

a formula which only involves length and time measurements. In fact, if μ_0 is taken to be dimensionless, we can write the dimensions of ohms as joule-seconds/coulomb² = joules/ampere²-second = joules/newton-second = meters/second in conformity with Eq. 7.15–10. Otherwise we have volts/ampere = (webers/second)/(coulombs/second) = webers/coulomb. This type of resistance measurement is commonly called "absolute." (A more accurate method of measuring a resistance is to compare it with the impedance of a known inductance at a known frequency, using an a-c bridge (Section 9.6).)

The Absolute Measurement of Current. The mutual inductance of two coaxial circular loops (solid and dashed circles in Fig. 7.10c) can be written from Eq. 7.10–14, since $A = A_\phi$ is a constant around a circle of radius R

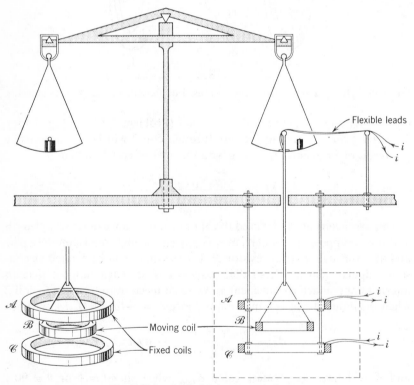

Fig. 7.15d. A Rayleigh current balance.

centered on the axis,

$$M_{12} = 2\pi R A_\phi / i = \mu_0 a R \int_0^\pi \frac{\cos \phi \, d\phi}{(z^2 + a^2 + R^2 - 2aR \cos \phi)^{1/2}} \quad (7.15\text{–}11)$$

We have shown in Section 7.12 that the force between two circuits can be calculated from the mutual inductance. We have, in fact,

$$F_\xi = \frac{\partial U}{\partial \xi} \quad (7.15\text{–}12)$$

where F_ξ is the force in the direction of an arbitrary displacement $\Delta \xi$, and U is given by

$$U = M_{12} i_1 i_2 \quad (7.15\text{–}13)$$

The best way of calibrating an ammeter directly in terms of amperes—i.e., the best way of making an absolute current calibration—is by means of a current balance. Figure 7.15d shows an arrangement for measuring the force exerted on a movable coil between two fixed ones. Coil $\mathscr{B}$ is suspended from the arm of a sensitive balance, between two fixed coils $\mathscr{A}$ and $\mathscr{C}$. The same current i is made to flow through all three coils. The current leads from coil $\mathscr{B}$ must be carefully brought out through flexible leads so as not to disturb the balance, and they must be properly twisted so as not to affect the mutual inductance. If i runs in the same direction in $\mathscr{B}$ and $\mathscr{C}$, and in the opposite direction in $\mathscr{A}$, $\mathscr{C}$ will attract $\mathscr{B}$, and $\mathscr{A}$ will repel $\mathscr{B}$.

The resultant force on $\mathscr{B}$ will be the sum of two. In fact, $\mathscr{A}$ and $\mathscr{C}$ can be treated as parts of the same coil, so that the force can be written

$$F = i^2 \frac{dM_{12}}{dz}$$

where z is measured downward. A precise calculation of M_{12}, then, will allow a standard ammeter to be constructed in the form of a current balance. The details of such calculations are quite involved; the use of Eq. 7.15–11 would give only a first approximation, since the windings on each coil are spaced out. The reader is referred elsewhere for further details.[39]

[39] For measurements of the absolute ampere, see R. W. Curtis, R. L. Driscoll, and C. L. Critchfield, *J. Res. Bur. Stds.*, **28**, 133 (1942) and H. L. Curtis, R. W. Curtis, and C. L. Critchfield, *J. Res. Nat. Bur. Stds.*, **22**, 485 (1939). For the absolute ohm, see H. L. Curtis, C. Moon, and C. M. Sparks, *J. Res. Nat. Bur. Stds.*, **21**, 375 (1938) and **16**, 1 (1936), and J. L. Thomas, C. Peterson, I. L. Cooter, and F. R. Kotter, *J. Res. Nat. Bur. Stds.*, **43**, 291 (1949). A review of both measurements is given by H. L. Curtis, *J. Res. Nat. Bur. Stds.*, **33**, 235 (1944). For inductance calculations in general, see F. W. Grover, *Inductance Calculations*, D. Van Nostrand, Princeton, N.J., 1946. and *Nat. Bur. Stds. Circular 74*.

Problem 7.15a. Calculate the flux produced by a magnetic dipole through an arbitrary circle of radius R coaxial with dipole, whose center is a distance z from the dipole, and use the result to check Eq. 7.15–7.

Problem 7.15b. Find the mutual inductance of two small circular loops separated by a large distance $\mathbf{r}$. Assume that the loops have radii a_1 and a_2 and that their normals make angles θ_1 and θ_2 with $\mathbf{r}$.

Problem 7.15c. A long solenoid which has 15 turns per centimeter and a radius of 9 cm has a short secondary winding of 50 turns that has (a) a radius of 10 cm and (b) a radius of 6 cm. Find the mutual inductance in each case.

Problem 7.15d. Calculate M_{12} from Eq. 7.15–11 for the case that z is much larger than either a or R, by using three terms in the binomial expansion of $[1 + (a^2 + R^2 - 2aR \cos \phi)/z^2]^{-\frac{1}{2}}$, and use the result to check Eq. 7.15–7 together with the remarks on the criterion for a_2 being small.

Problem 7.15e. Find the force exerted by the small coil in Fig. 7.15b on the large one.

Problem 7.15f. Write Eq. 7.15–10 in Gaussian units and describe the dimensionality of the Gaussian unit of resistance.

7.16 Self-inductance

Any closed circuit will be linked by a magnetic flux produced by its own current in addition to any flux produced by neighboring circuits. This flux will be proportional to the current, so that we can write

$$\Phi = Li \qquad (7.16\text{–}1)$$

where L is the constant of proportionality, known as the *self-inductance*, or more briefly, as the inductance.

If there are several loops in the circuit, as in a solenoid, Φ is taken to mean the total flux linkage or the sum of the fluxes through each loop. It is, of course, the quantity whose time derivative gives the emf. By Lenz's law, the emf must be written with a negative sign if current and emf are both assigned the same positive direction. Thus we have

$$\mathscr{E} = -L \frac{di}{dt} \qquad (7.16\text{–}2)$$

which because of the minus sign is often called a "back emf." Self-inductance, like mutual inductance, is measured in henries. Equation 7.16–2 is the same for all systems of units although 7.16–1 is not.

When an external source of emf $\mathcal{E}'$ is used to establish current in a circuit containing, say, a *total* resistance R and an inductance L, we can write as we did in the last section

$$\mathcal{E} + \mathcal{E}' = iR$$

or

$$\mathcal{E}' = iR - \mathcal{E} = iR + L\frac{di}{dt} \qquad (7.16\text{--}3)$$

We may thus treat the induced emf as a potential drop with the positive sign.

Any circuit whatsoever has inductance. Before proceeding to two simplified but nevertheless still complicated calculations of L, let us consider its effect in retarding the establishment of a current. We shall only consider circuits in which this inductive effect is more influential than the effect of the distributed capacitance considered in Section 5.3 so that we can neglect the latter. A typical circuit is conventionally represented as in Fig. 7.16a, where the symbol ⓞⓞⓞⓞ refers to the entire inductance of the circuit, and the

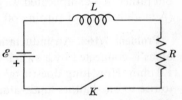

Fig. 7.16a. Circuit with self-inductance.

resistance is correspondingly the total resistance. From Eq. 7.16–3 we see that we may treat these two distributed quantities as if they were two separate series elements, since the potential drops are seen to be additive. Such separated elements are called "lumped" elements. In practical circuits, large values of L and R are generally physically lumped, at least in an approximate sense, whereas small values appear distributed throughout. In ignoring capacitive effects in Eq. 7.16–3 we are assuming that i is the same throughout the circuit at any given instant.

Let us now imagine that at time $t = 0$ the switch K of Fig. 7.16a is closed. The current cannot increase with infinite rapidity since $L\,di/dt$ must be finite. Therefore we can assume that $i = 0$ at $t = 0$ and that after the initial instant, Eq. 7.16–3 must hold. This equation is mathematically identical with Eq. 5.4–5 if we replace Q by i, $1/C$ by R, and R by L. Hence we can use the solution Eq. 5.4–6 for the charging of a condenser to express the rise of current in a self-inductive circuit. The result is

$$i = \frac{\mathcal{E}'}{R}(1 - e^{-(R/L)t}) \qquad (7.16\text{--}4)$$

The current rises in accordance with a curve like that of Fig. 5.4f where now for the time constant we have L/R instead of RC.

For a typical battery circuit without any especially inductive elements in it, L might be of the order of 10^{-6} henry. If R were as low as 1 ohm, the time constant would be 10^{-6} sec, so that the current would be rapidly established. If the capacitance is also important, the equations become more complicated, and must be referred to a later chapter (Section 9.8).

When K is opened, a very large negative di/dt will ensue. If the resulting back emf is large enough (as it frequently is), an arc will be struck across the switch terminals as they are separated, and the current will flow through this arc for a short time. On the other hand, if the key is a rapidly opening kind, for example a toggle or spring-operated switch, or if it is operated in a vacuum so that no arcing can start, the large back emf will lead to the building up of a substantial charge on the condenser formed by the two switch contacts. In either case, the current will not die out instantaneously but rather in a complicated way, which we shall not consider further here. (A modified way of turning off the current is considered in Section 7.18.)

Problem 7.16a. An inductance of 250 millihenrys and resistance of 49 ohms is connected by a switch to a battery of 10 v and internal resistance 1.0 ohm. How long does it take after the switch is closed for the current to rise to one-half its final value? What is the value of the induced emf at this time?

7.17 Calculations of L

The arguments that led to the mutual-inductance formula 7.12–13 can be seen to give a similar value for L, differing only in that the double integral must be taken twice around the single circuit under consideration. However, a serious difficulty arises. The r in the denominator of the integrand becomes zero when $\mathbf{dl}_1$ and $\mathbf{dl}_2$ coincide. The integral turns out on examination to become infinite because of this fact. This can be seen from Eq. 7.10–11 for the vector potential of two long parallel wires. The magnitude of $\mathbf{A}$ becomes infinite at the center of one wire and so does that of $\mathbf{J}$, if we imagine the wire to be an infinitely thin current filament in order to make the equation apply to points as close as we please to its center.

We can describe this result by saying that our theory does not allow us to calculate the inductive effect of a single filament on itself but only that of the various filaments of a current on each other. Self-inductance is thus seen to be a special case of mutual inductance. Any further discussion of this difficulty would involve discussing the action of the individual slowly accelerated electrons on each other and is beyond the scope of this book.

If we take into account the current distribution in a wire, we find that the infinity referred to above reduces to a small and sometimes quite insignificant contribution. We shall illustrate with the case of two long parallel circular wires of equal radius R. In order to avoid end effects, we shall calculate the flux linking a unit length of the circuit far from the ends of the wires. The two wires are shown in cross section in Fig. 7.17a. We assume here that the current is uniformly distributed throughout the wire and shall consider later the extent to which this assumption is justified.

Let us calculate the flux per unit length passing between the wires by an integral of B along a line joining their centers. Because of symmetry, we can calculate twice the flux on one side of the figure. In terms of the

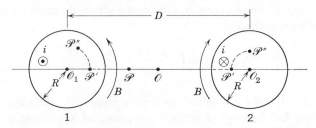

Fig. 7.17a. Illustrating the calculation of L for two parallel wires.

distance r from $\mathcal{O}_1$, the field produced by wire 1 is given inside the wire by Eq. 7.8–2

$$B_1 = \frac{\mu_0 i r}{2\pi R^2} \qquad r \leqslant R$$

and outside the wire by Eq. 7.8–1a

$$B_1 = \frac{\mu_0 i}{2\pi r} \qquad r \geqslant R$$

The field of wire 2 may be written

$$B_2 = \frac{\mu_0 i}{2\pi (D - r)} \qquad r \leqslant D - R$$

Now it will be observed that the flux linking any particular current filament, like that shown entering and leaving the figure at the point pairs $\mathcal{P}'$, is generally not the same as for other filaments. However, if the wires are small, so that $R \ll D$, the amount of flux of wire 2 that passes inside wire 1 will be of insignificant amount. Its average effect on all the filaments in wire 1 can with small error be calculated by integrating from $\mathcal{O}_1$ to $\mathcal{O}$, yielding (note that dS is replaced by dr because we deal with unit length only)

$$\Phi_2 = \int_0^{D/2} \frac{\mu_0 i\, dr}{2\pi (D - r)} = \frac{\mu_0 i}{2\pi} \ln \frac{D}{(D/2)} = \frac{\mu_0 i}{2\pi} \ln 2$$

On the other hand, the contribution of B_1 to the flux will vary considerably over the wire. It will be necessary to calculate it for arbitrary points, like $\mathscr{P}''$ in the figure, and then make a proper average, which is done by considering that the average power is what can be readily measured in such a circuit. Hence we write

$$\mathscr{E}_{\text{av}}i = \int_S \mathscr{E}J \, dS \qquad (7.17\text{--}1)$$

where S is the cross-sectional area of the wire and $\mathscr{E}$ and J are the emf and current density respectively at a variable point in that cross section.

The contribution to Φ_1 from B_1 outside the wire is the same for all points inside the wire, namely

$$\Phi_{1\,\text{outside}} = \int_R^{D/2} \frac{\mu_0 i \, dr}{2\pi r} = \frac{\mu_0 i}{2\pi} \ln \frac{D}{2R}$$

For $\Phi_{1\,\text{inside}}$, linking a filament through a point $\mathscr{P}''$ inside the wire, we can find the flux through a surface composed of a piece of a cylinder coaxial with the wire, connecting $\mathscr{P}''$ with a point $\mathscr{P}'$ on the line $\mathcal{O}_1\mathcal{O}$, and the plane surface $\mathscr{P}'\mathcal{O}$. No flux from wire 1 passes through the cylinder, so that the flux linking the filament through $\mathscr{P}'$ is the same as that through $\mathscr{P}''$, namely

$$\Phi_{1\,\text{inside}}(r) = \int_r^R \frac{\mu_0 i r' \, dr'}{2\pi R^2} = \frac{\mu_0 i (R^2 - r^2)}{4\pi R^2} \qquad (7.17\text{--}2)$$

where r is the distance $\overline{\mathcal{O}_1\mathscr{P}'} = \overline{\mathcal{O}_1\mathscr{P}''}$. Averaging the emf as in Eq. 7.17–1 amounts to averaging the flux over the area, since we are assuming that J is constant (and equal to $i/\pi R^2$). In fact, we only need to average the quantity $(R^2 - r^2)$. For this average, we find

$$\text{average of } (R^2 - r^2) = \frac{1}{S} \int (R^2 - r^2) \, dS$$

$$= \frac{1}{\pi b^2} \int_0^R (R^2 - r^2) 2\pi r \, dr = \frac{R^2}{2}$$

yielding

$$\text{average of } (\Phi_{1\,\text{inside}}) = \frac{\mu_0 i}{8\pi}$$

Now we can find the total flux linking the circuit by combining Φ_2, $\Phi_{1\,\text{outside}}$, and $\Phi_{1\,\text{inside}}$, and multiplying by 2. If we finally divide out i, we have the inductance per unit length of a pair of equal parallel wires, separated by many times their radii:

$$L_i = \frac{\mu_0}{\pi}\left(\ln\frac{D}{R} + \frac{1}{4}\right) \tag{7.17-3}$$

It is interesting to compare this formula with that for the capacitance for wires with similar geometry given in Section 4.5.

For a battery circuit without lumped inductance in which the wires while not parallel are separated by say 100 times their radii, this formula will still give the correct order of magnitude. The logarithm will be of the order of 5, and we have, roughly, 10^{-6} henry or 1.0 microhenry per meter, accounting for the estimate given above in discussing time constants.

As a second example, let us calculate the inductance of a single circular loop that has a radius a and is made of wire of radius b. We shall suppose that b is so much less than a that the field inside the wire is the same as that for a straight wire, allowing us to find the local inside contribution from the average $\Phi_{1\ inside}$ just calculated. In fact, since the wire has a length $2\pi a$, the inside contribution will be $\frac{1}{4}\mu_0 i a$. We shall neglect the contribution inside the wire of the distant portions of the circuit and calculate the external flux by use of the expression for A_ϕ in Section 7.10.

We need A_ϕ for points in the plane of the loop, where $z = 0$, and specifically at the inside edge of the wire where $R = a - b$. Equation 7.10–14 was calculated for a filamentary current, and we shall assume that outside our finite-radius wire we can approximate A_ϕ by considering all the current to be concentrated at the axis of the wire. (Note that for a long straight wire $\mathbf{B} = \nabla \times \mathbf{A}$ outside the wire is strictly independent of how the current is distributed inside the wire so long as the distribution is axially symmetric.) The error made in this assumption will not be greater than the errors made by the approximate expansion we wish to give of Eq. 7.10–14.

Putting $z = 0$ and $R = a - b$ in this equation, we have

$$A_\phi = \frac{\mu_0 i a}{2\pi}\int_0^\pi \frac{\cos\phi\,d\phi}{[(a-b)^2 + a^2 - 2a(a-b)\cos\phi]^{1/2}}$$

Now let us write $\phi/2 = \beta$ and $1 - \cos\phi = 2\sin^2\beta$. The expression can then be rearranged to give

$$A_\phi = \frac{\mu_0 i a}{\pi}\int_0^{\pi/2} \frac{(1 - 2\sin^2\beta)\,d\beta}{[b^2 + 4a(a-b)\sin^2\beta]^{1/2}}$$

$$= \frac{\mu_0 i a}{2\pi[a(a-b)]^{1/2}}\int_0^{\pi/2} \frac{(1 - 2\sin^2\beta)\,d\beta}{[b^2/4a(a-b) + \sin^2\beta]^{1/2}}$$

Let us shorten the writing by setting

$$\frac{b}{2[a(a-b)]^{\frac{1}{2}}} = k$$

The last integral can be evaluated easily but approximately for two ranges of β. If $\sin^2 \beta$ is sufficiently larger than k^2 that we can neglect k^2 altogether, the denominator becomes $\sin \beta$ and the integral can be readily evaluated. On the other hand, if $\sin^2 \beta$ is small enough that it may be replaced by β^2, the integral can also be evaluated simply. If k is small enough, the ranges of β in which the two methods apply will overlap. Since $b \ll a$, $k \simeq b/2a$ and can be considered small.

Let us choose a particular value of β, say β_1, in the region in which both methods overlap. Then for $\beta \geqslant \beta_1$, we can omit k^2 from the integral, and for $\beta \leqslant \beta_1$, we can write $\sin^2 \beta = \beta$. To be specific, suppose that 1% is set as the limit of error. Since $\sin \beta \simeq \beta - (\beta^3/6) = \beta[1 - (\beta^2/6)]$ and 1% in $\sin^2 \beta$ means $\frac{1}{2}\%$ in $\sin \beta$, we can take $\beta_1^2/6 \simeq 0.005$ or $\beta_1 \simeq 0.17$ radian $= 10°$. Then we wish k^2 to be not greater than $0.01 \sin^2 \beta_1 \simeq 0.01\beta_1^2$, or $k \lesssim 0.1\beta_1 \simeq 0.017$, yielding $b/a \lesssim 0.034$ or $1/30$.

Now we can evaluate our integral. We have

$$\int_0^{\pi/2} \frac{(1 - 2\sin^2 \beta)\, d\beta}{(k^2 + \sin^2 \beta)^{\frac{1}{2}}} = \int_0^{\beta_1} \frac{(1 - 2\beta^2)\, d\beta}{(k^2 + \beta^2)^{\frac{1}{2}}} + \int_{\beta_1}^{\pi/2} \frac{(1 - 2\sin^2 \beta)\, d\beta}{\sin \beta}$$

$$= \left\{ (1 + k^2) \ln [\beta + (\beta^2 + k^2)^{\frac{1}{2}}] - \beta(\beta^2 + k^2)^{\frac{1}{2}} \right\}_0^{\beta_1} + \left[\ln \tan \frac{\beta}{2} + 2\cos \beta \right]_{\beta_1}^{\pi/2}$$

as the reader may verify directly by differentiation. When we substitute the limits, we should remember that we have assumed $k^2 \ll \beta_1^2 \ll 1$ so that it would be misleadingly complicated not to omit k^2 from $(\beta_1^2 + k^2)^{\frac{1}{2}}$ or from $(1 + k^2)$, or to retain $\tan (\beta_1/2)$ instead of $\beta_1/2$ and $\cos \beta_1$ instead of $1 - \beta_1^2/2$. (We cannot omit k from the first logarithm when $\beta = 0$, however!) We obtain a result independent f β_1, which further justifies its use. The integral is

$$\left[\ln 2\beta_1 - \beta_1^2 - \ln k + \ln \tan \frac{\pi}{4} - \ln \frac{\beta_1}{2} - 2(1 - \beta_1^2/2) \right] = \ln (4/k) - 2$$

so that, since

$$\Phi_{\text{outside}} = \oint \mathbf{A} \cdot \mathbf{dl} = 2\pi(a - b)A_\phi,$$

$$\Phi_{\text{outside}} = \mu_0 i[a(a - b)]^{\frac{1}{2}} \left\{ \ln \frac{8[a(a - b)]^{\frac{1}{2}}}{b} - 2 \right\}$$

In view of our approximations, only a slight additional error will be made by taking $[a(a - b)]^{\frac{1}{2}} = a$, allowing us to combine Φ_{outside} and

Φ_{inside} to obtain a simple formula for the self-inductance of a circular loop:

$$L = \mu_0 a \left[\ln \left(\frac{8a}{b} \right) - \frac{7}{4} \right] \qquad (7.17\text{-}4)$$

We assumed in the calculation of the inductance of two parallel wires that the current density was uniform over the cross section of each wire. However, we arrived at an expression for the flux enclosed that varied from filament to filament and had to be averaged. Our original assumption is only justified therefore if the variation of the electric field $\mathbf{E} = -\partial \mathbf{A}/\partial t$ over the wire is small enough that the resulting current density variations are negligible. This variation of $\mathbf{E}$ can be estimated from Eq. 7.17-2, by differentiating i with respect to t to get the emf per unit length for one wire only and then finding the derivative with respect to r. The calculation is not strictly accurate because Eq. 7.17-2 assumes a uniform $\mathbf{J}$.

The greatest effect on the current density will occur when the contribution of the static part of $\mathbf{E}$ to the total is negligible. The effect will clearly be small if di/dt is small; that is, uniform $\mathbf{J}$ occurs in the limit of zero rate of change of current. If, on the other hand, di/dt is very large, as in high-frequency circuits, there will be a very large effect. As seen by Eq. 7.17-2, the emf will be largest at the center, and since the emf is directed against the build-up of current, the current will be largest near the edge. As a result of concentrating the current in the outer parts of the wire, the effective resistance of the latter is increased. This phenomenon is called the "skin effect." A calculation of this effect is given in Section 10.8.

Problem 7.17a. A pair of concentric cylindrical shells is used in a circuit, with equal and opposite currents along the two shells. Assume the currents to lie on the outside of the inner shell (radius R_1) and on the inside of the outer shell (radius R_2). Show that the inductance per unit length of this arrangement is

$$L_l = \frac{\mu_0}{2\pi} \ln \frac{R_2}{R_1} \qquad (7.17\text{-}5)$$

Problem 7.17b. Find the mutual inductance of two coaxial circular coils of the same radius a, separated by a distance z much less than a, by use of the same type of expansion and the same integration, as used in the text to derive Eq. 7.17-4. Calculate the force between the coils when they each carry current, and show that the same result could be obtained by using Eq. 7.8-3.

Problem 7.17c. Find the self-inductance of a length l of an infinitely long solenoid, with n_l turns per meter and radius a.

Problem 7.17d. A circular loop of radius 3 cm is made of #18 copper wire (AWG or B&S; consult a handbook for wire sizes). Find its inductance and the flux linking it when it carries 20 amp. What rate of change of current is required to produce a self-induced emf of 1.0 microvolt?

Problem 7.17e. A transmission line consists of two parallel wires of #18 copper, which are 3 in. apart. What is the inductance of a section of length 10 ft of this line?

Problem 7.17f. A toroidal coil of square cross section of side a has a mean radius equal to b, and N turns. Calculate its inductance.

7.18   Energy in Systems of Current-Bearing Circuits

In this section we wish to consider briefly the magnetic-energy relations involved in the establishment of currents and in the relative motion of circuits. Let us consider first a simple circuit with a cell of emf $\mathscr{E}$ volts,

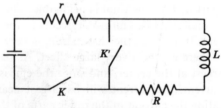

Fig. 7.18a.   Illustrating energy storage in an inductance.

a resistance of r ohms, and an inductance of L henries and R ohms, as in Fig. 7.18a. The extra switch K' is used to short-circuit the inductance before opening the main switch K, so that the decrease of current can be calculated in a more definite way than when K is opened first. The resistor r will protect the cell during this short-circuiting process.

When K is closed, with K' open, the current i obeys the equation

$$\mathscr{E} = i(R + r) + L\frac{di}{dt}$$

During a short time dt, a charge $dq = i\,dt$ passes through the circuit, and work is done by the cell of amount

$$dW = \mathscr{E}i\,dt = i^2(R + r)\,dt + Li\frac{di}{dt}\,dt$$

If we integrate this expression from time $t = 0$ when $i = 0$ to an arbitrary time t_1, we have

$$W = \int_0^{t_1} \mathscr{E}i\,dt = \int_0^{t_1} i^2(R + r)\,dt + L\int_0^{t_1} i\frac{di}{dt}\,dt$$

The integral of $i^2(R + r)$ is just the heat dissipation in the wires and, of course, increases as time goes on. However, the other integral on the right-hand side can be written

$$L \int_{i_1}^{i_1} i\, di = \tfrac{1}{2}L(i_1{}^2 - i_0{}^2) = \tfrac{1}{2}Li_1{}^2$$

where i_0 refers to the current when $t = 0$, which is here taken to be zero, and i_1 refers to the current at $t = t_1$. As time goes on, i_1 approaches the limit $\mathscr{E}/(R + r)$ as we have seen. Thus a certain portion of the chemical energy expended in the cell has not gone into heat but is associated with the inductance. Dropping the subscript, we write the magnetic energy of the coil as

$$U = \tfrac{1}{2}Li^2 \tag{7.18-1}$$

To see that we may treat this energy as stored in the coil and available for transformation into other forms of energy, let us short-circuit the coil by closing K'. Since a jump in the value of i would make an infinite back emf in the coil, we must assume that just after the instant of closing K', the current in L is still i_1. If the distributed capacitances of K' and the connecting wires are small enough, a current i will be established throughout the closed circuit made by K', R, and L, in a very short time. Treating the emf in L as an emf and not as a potential drop, we write for our circuit

$$\mathscr{E} = -L\frac{di}{dt} = Ri \tag{7.18-2}$$

an equation which is just like Eq. 5.4–1 for a discharging condenser. Its solution is therefore like Eq. 5.4–2, namely

$$i = i_1\, e^{-Rt/L} \tag{7.18-3}$$

where $t = 0$ now refers to the time of the closing of K'.

Let us find the amount of heat developed in R. It will be $\int_0^\infty Ri^2\, dt$, a finite integral since the current falls off exponentially. From Eq. 7.18–2, we find

$$\int_0^\infty Ri^2\, dt = -L \int_0^\infty i\frac{di}{dt}\, dt = -\tfrac{1}{2}Li^2\Big|_{t=0}^{t=\infty} = \tfrac{1}{2}Li_1{}^2$$

which is just the extra amount of energy originally provided by the cell. Thus it is quite legitimate to consider the quantity $U = \tfrac{1}{2}Li^2$ as energy stored in the inductance. It may be written $U = \tfrac{1}{2}i\Phi$, where Φ is the flux linking the circuit as a result of i.

Now consider a general system of rigid fixed circuits, which we shall number 1, 2, $\cdots n$. Each will be assumed to contain an emf $\mathscr{E}_j'$ ($j = 1$, $2 \cdots n$), which may be a chemical emf or an isolated generator whose magnetic field we shall not include in our discussion. These $\mathscr{E}$'s do not have to be constant. We denote the total resistances in each circuit by $R_1, R_2, \cdots R_n$, the self-inductances by $L_1, L_2, \cdots L_n$, and the various mutual inductances by $M_{12}, M_{13}, M_{23}, \cdots M_{jk} \cdots$. Each loop must, of course, have its own positive direction assigned. Let us imagine that in all circuits the emfs are turned on simultaneously, with all currents initially zero. We can write for all the circuits

$$\mathscr{E}_1' - L_1 \frac{di_1}{dt} - M_{12}\frac{di_2}{dt} - M_{13}\frac{di_3}{dt} - \cdots - M_{1n}\frac{di_n}{dt} = i_1 R_1$$

$$\mathscr{E}_2' - L_2 \frac{di_2}{dt} - M_{21}\frac{di_1}{dt} - M_{23}\frac{di_3}{dt} - \cdots - M_{2n}\frac{di_n}{dt} = i_2 R_2$$

$$\mathscr{E}_n' - L_n \frac{di_n}{dt} - M_{n1}\frac{di_1}{dt} - M_{n2}\frac{di_2}{dt} - \cdots - M_{nn-1}\frac{di_{n-1}}{dt} = i_n R_n$$

$$(7.18\text{--}4)$$

Let us put all the induced emfs on the right-hand side and simultaneously multiply each equation by its own $i_k\, dt$ for the charge that passes around the corresponding circuit in time dt. Making also the calculus transformation $(di_j/dt)\, dt = di_j$, we have

$$\mathscr{E}_1'i_1\, dt = L_1 i_1\, di_1 + M_{12}i_1\, di_2 + M_{13}i_1\, di_3 + \cdots + M_{1n}i_1\, di_n + i_1{}^2 R_1$$

$$\mathscr{E}_2'i_2\, dt = L_2 i_2\, di_2 + M_{21}i_2\, di_1 + M_{23}i_2\, di_3 + \cdots + M_{2n}i_2\, di_n + i_2{}^2 R_2$$

$$\mathscr{E}_n'i_n\, dt = L_n i_n\, di_n + M_{n1}i_n\, di_1 + M_{n2}i_n\, di_2 + \cdots + M_{nn-1}i_n\, di_{n-1} + i_n{}^2 R_n$$

The sum of the left-hand sides is the entire work done by all the external emfs in time dt. If we add all the right sides together and integrate from $t = 0$ to some upper limit which we can now call t, we will have the total heat developed plus a magnetic energy term U. We shall write down an expression for U by itself. Notice that for each self-inductance we will have a term of the form $\frac{1}{2}Li^2$. For the mutual-inductance terms, note that each mutual inductance comes in twice, once with respect to each of the two currents it links. We have, for instance,

$$M_{12}i_1\, di_2 + M_{21}i_2\, di_1 = M_{12}(i_1\, di_2 + i_2\, di_1) = M_{12}\, d(i_1 i_2)$$

by the usual calculus rule for the differential of a product. When we integrate, we have simply $M_{12}i_1i_2$, evaluated at the time t. Thus we can write

$$U = \tfrac{1}{2}L_1i_1^2 + \tfrac{1}{2}L_2i_2^2 + \cdots + M_{12}i_1i_2 + M_{13}i_1i_3 + \cdots + M_{n-1\,n}i_{n-1}i_n$$

$$(7.18\text{--}5)$$

for the magnetic energy of a system of conductors. In this expression, each pair of currents is written once only.

The function $U = i\Phi$ of Eqs. 7.12–6 and 7.15–3 is seen to be the mutual-inductance part of 7.18–5, just as we predicted. It is now clear that associated with the motion of circuits there will be induced emfs that will change the currents unless control is provided to maintain them, and that in any case energy changes are associated with these emfs.

Before making a specific calculation of this effect, let us consider that peculiarity of the magnetic forces which is reflected in the fact that magnetic forces are derived from the positive rather than the negative gradient of the energy function. We saw in dealing with electrostatics that the motion of charges under the influence of the field is always in such a direction that the field is reduced as the charges get to new positions. The opposite is true for magnetic forces as we showed in Section 7.12. As another example, note that the coils of a loosely wound solenoid will all attract each other and if they come closer together, L will increase as will also $\tfrac{1}{2}Li^2$.

The paradox of work being done by magnetic forces while the field strength increases is resolved by calculating the work done by the energy sources in each circuit as the circuits are allowed to move and the currents are kept constant. Let circuit 1 be fixed, and let circuit 2 be displaced as a whole by a distance $\Delta\xi$ in some chosen direction, changing the mutual inductance by an amount ΔM_{12}. The work done by the magnetic forces will then be $F_\xi\,\Delta\xi = i_1i_2\,\Delta M_{12}$. The flux produced by circuit 2 in circuit 1 will change by an amount $\Delta\Phi_1 = i_2\,\Delta M_{12}$ and that in circuit 2 by $\Delta\Phi_2 = i_1\,\Delta M_{12}$. If the change takes a time Δt, there will be a back emf in circuit 1 of amount $-\Delta\Phi_1/\Delta t$, and extra work will be done by the external source of power in that circuit of amount $(+\Delta\Phi_1/\Delta t)(i_1\,\Delta t) = i_1i_2\,\Delta M_{12}$. The same calculation made for circuit 2 shows that work $i_1i_2\,\Delta M_{12}$ is *also* performed there. We see that, considering both circuits together, *twice as much work is done by the batteries as goes into mechanical work*, so that the magnetic energy of the system of currents increases by just the amount of the work done.

When a circuit is displaced by $\boldsymbol{\Delta\xi}$, the energy *used up* in doing work is $\nabla U \cdot \boldsymbol{\Delta\xi}$ but the energy *added* by the batteries is $2\,\nabla U \cdot \boldsymbol{\Delta\xi}$, so the net *gain* in U is $\nabla U \cdot \boldsymbol{\Delta\xi}$. Energy is in fact conserved!

It will be seen that this establishment of the law of conservation of energy would not have been possible if Lenz's law had had the opposite sign, for then the batteries would be charged up rather than perform work as circuits move under the action of magnetic forces. We have also verified the statement at the end of Section 1.7 concerning the difference between a system of charges at rest and a system of currents with respect to energy conservation.

If the currents are not kept constant, there must be a reduction of the self-energy $\frac{1}{2}L_1i_1{}^2 + \frac{1}{2}L_2i_2{}^2 + \cdots$ to compensate for the increase in the mutual-energy terms. As stated in Section 7.12, the forces for a given set of currents are dependent only on the actual values of those currents at the instant under consideration and do not depend on whether or not an arrangement has been made to keep them constant as the circuits move.

In the case of atoms with electrons circulating in orbits, we have currents with zero resistance and no emfs to maintain them. Consequently, any motion of an atom into an external magnetic field in such a direction as to add to the mutual energy of the atom and the external field source will cause the atomic currents themselves to lose magnetic self-energy, an effect known as diamagnetism. This effect is found in all substances although in many materials it is masked by paramagnetism or ferro-magnetism.

Both paramagnetism and ferromagnetism involve the turning of atomic-current circuits under the action of an applied field. From the considerations above, we see that the turning of a circuit in response to a magnetic torque applied to it will increase the mutual energy, and so add to the field. The strength of the atomic current may tend to decrease by the above-mentioned diamagnetic effect, but if sufficient turning occurs, the paramagnetic effect may overcome it.

We can write two other expressions for U. Let us first divide up the terms of Eq. 7.12–5 in a symmetrical way among all the circuits. We can write

$$U = \tfrac{1}{2}L_1i_1{}^2 + \tfrac{1}{2}M_{12}i_1i_2 + \tfrac{1}{2}M_{13}i_1i_3 + \cdots + \tfrac{1}{2}M_{1n}i_1i_n$$
$$+ \tfrac{1}{2}L_2i_2{}^2 + \tfrac{1}{2}M_{21}i_2i_1 + \tfrac{1}{2}M_{23}i_2i_3 + \cdots + \tfrac{1}{2}M_{2n}i_2i_n + \cdots \text{etc.}$$

so that, on factoring out the appropriate current from each line, we have

$$U = \tfrac{1}{2}(i_1\Phi_1 + i_2\Phi_2 + \cdots + i_n\Phi_n) \qquad (7.18–6)$$

where Φ_1 is the total flux $L_1i_1 + M_{12}i_2 + \cdots + M_{1n}i_n$ through circuit 1, and so forth. This expression might be compared with the electrostatic energy $U = \tfrac{1}{2}(Q_1V_1 + Q_2V_2 + \cdots + Q_nV_n)$ of Eq. 4.7–2.

Now, Φ through any closed circuit can be written in terms of the vector potential produced by all the currents, $\Phi = \oint \mathbf{A} \cdot \mathbf{dl}$. However, we had to calculate the self-inductance by an averaging process, integrating over the cross section of a wire in order to avoid infinities. We can write, then for the expression $\frac{1}{2}i_1\Phi_1 + \cdots + \frac{1}{2}i_n\Phi_n$ the integral

$$U = \tfrac{1}{2} \underbrace{\int J\Phi\, dS}_{\substack{\text{cross section} \\ \text{of each wire}}} = \tfrac{1}{2} \underbrace{\int J\, dS}_{\substack{\text{cross section} \\ \text{of wires}}} \underbrace{\oint \mathbf{A}\cdot \mathbf{dl}}_{\text{filament}} = \tfrac{1}{2} \underbrace{\int \mathbf{J}\cdot\mathbf{A}\, d\tau}_{\substack{\text{vol. of} \\ \text{wire}}}$$

$$(7.18\text{--}7a)$$

In the first expression, Φ represents the flux linking the current filament that passes through the elemental area dS, and the integration over dS can be made at any point along each wire. In the second expression, we have replaced Φ by $\oint \mathbf{A}\cdot\mathbf{dl}$ taken along the given filament. Since $J\, dS$ is constant along a "tube of current," it may be multiplied into the l integration and be taken as applying to all of each wire. For the third expression we write $J\,\mathbf{dl} = \mathbf{J}\, dl$, since $\mathbf{dl}$ was taken along a current filament, and then put $dl\, dS = d\tau$, a volume element.

Now we can replace $\mathbf{J}$ by its value for steady currents given by Eq. 7.9–1

$$\mathbf{J} = \frac{1}{\mu_0}\,\text{curl}\,\mathbf{B}$$

The integrand will then contain

$$(\text{curl}\,\mathbf{B})\cdot\mathbf{A} = \mathbf{A}\cdot(\nabla\times\mathbf{B})$$

which can be related to $\nabla\cdot(\mathbf{B}\times\mathbf{A})$. In fact, in the latter expression ∇ operates on both $\mathbf{A}$ and $\mathbf{B}$, and the rules for rearrangement of the triple scalar product can be used to give formula 7 of Table A.2B:

$$\nabla\cdot(\mathbf{B}\times\mathbf{A}) = \mathbf{A}\cdot(\nabla\times\mathbf{A}) - \mathbf{B}\cdot(\nabla\times\mathbf{A})$$

We recognize $\nabla\times\mathbf{A}$ as $\mathbf{B}$ so we can write

$$U = \tfrac{1}{2} \underbrace{\int \mathbf{J}\cdot\mathbf{A}\, d\tau}_{\substack{\text{vol. of} \\ \text{wires}}} = \frac{1}{2\mu_0}\int [\mathbf{B}\cdot(\nabla\times\mathbf{A}) + \nabla\cdot(\mathbf{B}\times\mathbf{A})]\, d\tau$$

$$= \frac{1}{2\mu_0}\int B^2\, d\tau + \frac{1}{2\mu_0}\int \nabla\cdot(\mathbf{B}\times\mathbf{A})\, d\tau$$

Note now that $\mathbf{J}$ is zero outside the wires, so that the integral of $\mathbf{J}\cdot\mathbf{A}$ could equally well be written over any larger volume containing the wires. However, $\mathbf{B}$ does not in general vanish outside the wires, so that extending the region of integration will amount to reshuffling the contributions of the two integrals on the right without changing their sum. Since the first integral is positive, it will increase as the volume used increases.

The second integral $\int \nabla\cdot(\mathbf{B}\times\mathbf{A})\, d\tau$ can be transformed by the divergence theorem A.2–22 into a surface integral $\int_S (\mathbf{B}\times\mathbf{A})\cdot\mathbf{dS}$ taken over the surface of whatever region we use. It will become zero if we integrate over all space, since there will be no **B** or **A** at infinity. Strictly, we should prove this by showing that the integral approaches zero as the surface expands. The magnitude of **A** will fall off at least as fast as $1/r$, once the surface is far from the currents, and B will decrease at least as rapidly as $1/r^2$. Hence the integrand will fall off at least as fast as $1/r^3$. On the other hand, if the surface S is a large sphere its area will be $4\pi r^2$ and will not increase fast enough to prevent the $1/r^3$ behavior of the integrand from giving a smaller and smaller result.

We can finally write

$$U = \frac{1}{2\mu_0} \int_{\text{all space}} B^2 \, d\tau \qquad (7.18\text{–}8a)$$

and interpret the result by assigning an energy $B^2/2\mu_0$ joules/m³ to each unit volume of a magnetic field, although of course we cannot really locate energy in this fashion. This result is to be compared with Eq. 4.7–6 for the energy in a set of charged conductors, both formulas presenting energy entirely in terms of fields. In Section 10.4 we shall show that Eq. 7.18–8 is also correct for non-steady currents.

Gaussian formulas for the energy integrals are

$$U = \frac{1}{2c} \int_{\substack{\text{vol. of} \\ \text{wire}}} \mathbf{J} \cdot \mathbf{A} \, d\tau \qquad (7.18\text{–}7b)$$

$$U = \frac{1}{8\pi} \int_{\text{all space}} B^2 \, d\tau \qquad (7.18\text{–}8b)$$

Problem 7.18a. A coil of one henry inductance carries a current of one ampere. How many volts would have to be established between the plates of a 1.0 μf capacitor to store as many joules as are stored in the coil?

Problem 7.18b. Find the energy contained in a length l of an infinitely long solenoid, by use of Eq. 7.18–8 and by use of Eq. 7.18–1 together with the answer to Problem 7.17c.

Problem 7.18c. Calculate the rate at which energy is being stored at time t after closing a switch in a circuit containing inductance L and resistance R.

Problem 7.18d. Show that in a highly conductive plasma the energy density of the electric field of magnetic origin is of the order of v^2/c^2 times the magnetic energy density. Assume that Eq. 4.7–7 is valid for all types of electric field.

7.19 Special Relativity[40]

There is an intimate relation between the theory of special relativity and ordinary electromagnetic theory, which we shall demonstrate in this section. We shall not present a detailed argument for, nor an interpretation of, Einstein's theory[41] but shall base our argument on the algebra of invariance as given in Appendix A.4.

We shall assume that the Maxwell equations as we have developed them are valid for all velocities of charges and all rates of change, and find partial justification for this assumption in the elegance of the relativistic formulas. However, complete justification of Maxwell's equations depends on their success in describing radiation, which we shall take up in Chapter 10.

Let us first remark that the velocity of light $c = (\mu_0 \epsilon_0)^{-\frac{1}{2}}$ is a fundamental constant of our theory. The basic principle of special relativity that postulates the equivalence of the laws of physics in any two reference frames moving with a constant relative velocity has as a consequence that c must be the same in each frame. If not, we could distinguish between frames by measuring ϵ_0 or c and thus establish a "favored" one—for instance, that with the smallest value of c.

Einstein showed, by arguments to be found in any elementary account of relativity, that, if c is to be constant, time scales must be relative—i.e., simultaneity is a relative concept.

Furthermore, our laws of physics are basically linear in length and time, at least to a very good approximation. Hence we can postulate that the position and time coordinates x, y, z, and t of an "event" in one frame must be linear combinations of those for another, x', y', z', and t'. Constancy of c can be maintained if we require that the speed recorded for the passage of a beam of light from, say, the origin at time $t = 0$ to a point (x, y, z) at time t will be the same in either frame of reference (allowing the two origins and clocks to coincide at the instant the beam or photon is emitted).

Thus we have

$$c = (x^2 + y^2 + z^2)^{\frac{1}{2}}/t = (x'^2 + y'^2 + z'^2)^{\frac{1}{2}}/t'$$

These relations are more symmetric if we square them and write

$$x^2 + y^2 + z^2 - c^2 t^2 = 0 \quad \text{and} \quad x'^2 + y'^2 + z'^2 - c^2 t'^2 = 0$$

[40] This section may be postponed until Section 10.3 is taken up, although nothing more about electromagnetic radiation than its mere existence is needed for this discussion of relativity.

[41] An excellent discussion is to be found in W. K. H. Panofsky and M. Phillips, *Classical Electricity and Magnetism*, second edition, Addison-Wesley Publishing Co., Reading, Mass., 1962, Chapters 15–18; see also Jackson, *op. cit.*, Chapter 11.

We can find a general condition that these relations hold if we require that the linear transformation we referred to keeps invariant the quantity $x^2 + y^2 + z^2 - c^2t^2$, even if this quantity is not zero. By an argument exactly like that called for in Problem A.4a, p. 644, the "interval" $(x_a - y_a)^2 + (y_a - y_b)^2 + (z_a - z_b)^2 - c^2(t_a - t_b{}^2)$ between any two events will also be invariant, so that, if the events are the emission and the absorption of a photon in vacuo, its speed will be the same in each frame.

We can, in fact, follow Appendix A.4 exactly in a *formal* way if we use four coordinates $x_1 = x$, $x_2 = y$, $x_3 = z$, and $x_4 = ict$ where we use $i = \sqrt{-1}$ in accordance with convention outside the field of a-c circuits. We emphasize the word "formal" because the introduction of the imaginary unit is purely for algebraic simplicity—time is still measured by real numbers. The "four-dimensional rotation" that seems to be involved is just a convenient mathematical construct. We merely assume that all sums run from 1 to 4, instead of from 1 to 3, unless explicitly indicated. (A detailed justification of the transfer of the three-dimensional formulas to the four-dimensional case can be found in books treating the algebra of relativity.)

Let us then write a general linear transformation (neglecting trivial shifts of origin and clock zero) as

$$x_j' = \sum_k a_{jk}x_k \qquad j, k = 1, 2, 3, 4 \qquad (7.19\text{–}1)$$

with the inverse relation

$$x_k = \sum_j x_j' a_{jk} \qquad (7.19\text{–}2)$$

Our invariance requirement is that

$$\sum_j x_j'^2 = \sum_k x_k{}^2 \qquad (7.19\text{–}3)$$

which must entail

$$\sum_k a_{jk}a_{lk} = \delta_{jl} \qquad (7.19\text{–}4a)$$

$$\sum_j a_{jk}a_{jm} = \delta_{km} \qquad (7.19\text{–}4b)$$

Next let us show that this linear transformation represents in general a translatory motion of one frame with respect to the other. Consider the spatial origin in the x_k frame, where $x_1 = 0$, $x_2 = 0$, and $x_3 = 0$. Then we have for the coordinates of this point, viewed in the other system,

$$\left. \begin{aligned} x_1' &= a_{14}x_4 = ica_{14}t \\ x_2' &= a_{24}x_4 = ica_{24}t \\ x_3' &= a_{34}x_4 = ica_{34}t \\ x_4' &= ict' = a_{44}x_4 = ica_{44}t \end{aligned} \right\} \qquad (7.19\text{–}5)$$

Solving the last of these equations for t in terms of t', we have $t = t'/a_{44}$ and find on substitution that the primed coordinates (x_1', x_2', x_3') of the unprimed origin increase uniformly with t', indicating a constant velocity which we shall call $\mathbf{u}$. The components of $\mathbf{u}$ are seen to be

$$u_1 = ica_{14}/a_{44}, \quad u_2 = ica_{24}/a_{44}, \quad u_3 = ica_{34}/a_{44} \quad (7.19\text{--}6)$$

Writing Eq. 7.19–4b for $k = m = 4$, we have

$$a_{14}^2 + a_{24}^2 + a_{34}^2 + a_{44}^2 = 1$$

so that, substituting from Eq. 7.19–6 we have

$$a_{44}^2 \left(-\frac{u_1^2}{c^2} - \frac{u_2^2}{c^2} - \frac{u_3^2}{c^2} + 1 \right) = 1$$

or

$$a_{44} = 1/(1 - u^2/c^2)^{1/2} \quad (7.19\text{--}7)$$

where we have taken the positive root to avoid the consideration of time reversals.

Now, if the two frames of reference are on an equal footing, the speed of the origin in the primed system, as measured in the unprimed system, must also be u, although of course oppositely directed if measured with respect to similarly oriented x, y, and z axes. This means that the coefficients with reversed subscripts must be the negatives of those listed in Eq. 7.19–6. We can finally conclude for six of the a_{jk}'s the following:

$$a_{14} = -a_{41} = \frac{a_{44}u_1}{ic} = \frac{u_1}{ic(1 - u^2/c^2)^{1/2}}$$

$$a_{24} = -a_{42} = \frac{a_{44}u_2}{ic} = \frac{u_2}{ic(1 - u^2/c^2)^{1/2}} \quad (7.19\text{--}8)$$

$$a_{24} = -a_{43} = \frac{a_{44}u_3}{ic} = \frac{u_3}{ic(1 - u^2/c^2)^{1/2}}$$

It is inconvenient to solve for the other coefficients, for the general case involves a pure space rotation between the two sets of axes. However, one can calculate the components of the vector $\mathbf{x}' = \sum_{j=1}^{3} x_j' \mathbf{1}_j'$ in the $\mathbf{u}$ direction. We have for the product of this component of $\mathbf{x}'$ with u,

$$\mathbf{x}' \cdot \mathbf{u} = \sum_{j=1}^{3} x_j' u_j = \sum_{j=1}^{3}\sum_{k=1}^{4} u_j a_{jk} x_k = \sum_{j=1}^{3}\sum_{k=1}^{3} u_j a_{jk} x_k + \sum_{j=1}^{3} u_j a_{j4} x_4$$

Using Eq. 7.19–6 for u_j and Eq. 7.19–4b, we have

$$\mathbf{x}' \cdot \mathbf{u} = \frac{ic}{a_{44}} \sum_{j=1}^{3} \sum_{k=1}^{3} a_{j4} a_{jk} x_k + \frac{ic}{a_{44}} \sum_{j=1}^{3} a_{j4}^2 x_4$$

$$= \frac{ic}{a_{44}} \sum_{k=1}^{3} x_k(-a_{44} a_{4k}) + \frac{ic}{a_{44}} x_4(1 - a_{44}^2)$$

which by Eqs. 7.19–7 and 7.19–8 reduces to

$$\mathbf{x}' \cdot \mathbf{u} = \frac{\mathbf{x} \cdot \mathbf{u} + u^2 t}{(1 - u^2/c^2)^{1/2}} \tag{7.19–9}$$

Using Eq. 7.19–8 on Eq. 7.19–1, written for the fourth component $x_4' = ict'$, we readily find

$$t' = \frac{\mathbf{x} \cdot \mathbf{u}/c^2 + t}{(1 - u^2/c^2)^{1/2}} \tag{7.19–10}$$

It is left to the reader to show that the quantity $(\mathbf{x} \cdot \mathbf{u})^2 - u^2 c^2 t^2$ is invariant under the transformation (Problem 7.19a). Since the first term is u^2 times the square of the component of $\mathbf{x}$ in the direction of $\mathbf{u}$, it follows, using Eq. 7.19–3, that the sum of the squares of the components of $\mathbf{x}$ normal to $\mathbf{u}$ is itself conserved. We can write therefore

$$\mathbf{x}_\perp' = \mathbf{x}_\perp \tag{7.19–11}$$

It is easy to show (Problem 7.19e) that if $\mathbf{u}$ is parallel to the x_1-direction and no space rotation takes place (i.e., so that $x_2' = x_2$ and $x_3' = x_3$), the coefficients a_{jk} become

$$
a_{jk} =
\begin{array}{c|cccc}
j\backslash k & 1 & 2 & 3 & 4 \\
\hline
1 & \gamma & 0 & 0 & \gamma u/ic \\
2 & 0 & 1 & 0 & 0 \\
3 & 0 & 0 & 1 & 0 \\
4 & -\gamma u/ic & 0 & 0 & \gamma
\end{array}
\tag{7.19–12}
$$

where for brevity we have written

$$\gamma = \frac{1}{(1 - u^2/c^2)^{1/2}} \tag{7.19–13}$$

When written in an array like this, the group of coefficients is called a matrix. Note that the first subscript on a_{jk} enumerates the rows and the second one the columns.

Equations 7.19–9, 7.19–10, and 7.19–11, which are equivalent to Eq. 7.19–1, describe what is generally known as a Lorentz transformation.

Any four-component quantity which transforms under a Lorentz transformation in the same way as (x_1, x_2, x_3, x_4) is called a "four-vector." For instance, the space-time interval $(dx_1, dx_2, dx_3, ic\,dt)$ is a four-vector. A theory whose equations are invariant in form under such a transformation is said to be "Lorentz-invariant."[42]

An important example of a four-vector is the so-called "four-velocity." Let us find the transformation law for velocities. When a particle suffers a displacement $\mathbf{dx}$ in time dt as seen in the unprimed frame, we write $\mathbf{dx} = \mathbf{v}\,dt$, with $\mathbf{dx'} = \mathbf{v'}\,dt'$ in the primed reference frame. Then since $(dx_1, dx_2, dx_3, ic\,dt)$ is a four-vector, we can write

$$v_j{}'\,dt' = \sum_{k=1}^{3} a_{jk}v_k\,dt + a_{j4}ic\,dt \qquad j = 1, 2, 3 \qquad (7.19\text{--}14)$$

$$ic\,dt' = \sum_{k=1}^{3} a_{4k}v_k\,dt + a_{44}ic\,dt$$

The invariant form $dx^2 - c^2\,dt^2$ becomes now $(v^2 - c^2)\,dt^2$ so we have

$$(v'^2 - c^2)\,dt'^2 = (v^2 - c^2)\,dt^2$$

or

$$dt'(1 - v'^2/c^2)^{\frac12} = dt(1 - v^2/c^2)^{\frac12} \qquad (7.19\text{--}15)$$

for the ratio of the corresponding time elements for the given displacement. Dividing each of Eqs. 7.19–14 by Eq. 7.19–15, we find that

$$v_j{}'/(1 - v'^2/c^2)^{\frac12} = \sum_{k=1}^{3} a_{jk}v_k/(1 - v^2/c^2)^{\frac12} + a_{j4}ic/(1 - v^2/c^2)^{\frac12}$$

$$j = 1, 2, 3 \quad (7.19\text{--}16)$$

$$ic/(1 - v'^2/c^2)^{\frac12} = \sum_{k=1}^{3} a_{4k}v_k/(1 - v^2/c^2)^{\frac12} + a_{44}ic/(1 - v^2/c^2)^{\frac12}$$

which shows that $v_1/(1 - v^2/c^2)^{\frac12}$, $v_2/(1 - v^2/c^2)^{\frac12}$, $v_3/(1 - v^2/c^2)^{\frac12}$, and $ic/(1 - v^2/c^2)^{\frac12}$ form a four-vector.

The product of each of these components with the rest mass m_0 of the particle forms what is called the four-momentum. The first three components form the ordinary relativistic momentum $\mathbf{p}$, and the fourth may be written as iU/c, where U is the total energy including rest energy. Thus it is seen that conservation of momentum and conservation of energy are linked together in the properties of the four-momentum. We shall not go further into the details of relativistic mechanics.

To demonstrate the Lorentz invariance of Maxwell's equations, we need to express these equations in terms of four-vectors and quantities derived from them. We can get a four-vector from a scalar by the four-component

---

[42] Sometimes called by the technically more accurate term "Lorentz covariant."

gradient (or four-gradient) operation $(\partial/\partial x_1, \partial/\partial x_2, \partial/\partial x_3, \partial/\partial x_4)$ whose components we can denote by ∂_j, $j = 1, 2, 3, 4$. We can, conversely, get a scalar from the scalar product of two four-vectors or from the four-divergence of a four-vector. That is, if A_1, A_2, A_3, and A_4 are the components of a four-vector, the quantity

$$\sum_j \frac{\partial A_j}{\partial x_j} = \frac{\partial A_1}{\partial x_1} + \frac{\partial A_2}{\partial x_2} + \frac{\partial A_3}{\partial x_3} + \frac{1}{ic}\frac{\partial A_4}{\partial t} \qquad (7.19\text{–}17)$$

will be a scalar and will not change its value under a Lorentz transformation.

We can also have entities called "tensors" that transform like products of vectors. Specifically, a four-tensor of the second rank is a collection of 16 numbers which we can denote by a symbol with two subscripts, T_{jk}; the same notation may be used for a three-dimensional tensor with 9 components. A particular component such as T_{23} is associated in some way with both the x_2- and x_3-direction simultaneously. An example of a three-dimensional tensor is the quadrupole moment, defined by Eq. 3.3–5. The electromagnetic stresses to be taken up in Eq. 10.4–10 and Problem 10.4h form another example.

Tensors can also be of third rank—i.e., act like products of three vectors—and so forth. The transformation properties of a Lorentz-invariant tensor are given by a sort of duplication of Eq. 7.19–1. For second-rank tensors, we have

$$T'_{jk} = \sum_{l,m} a_{jl}a_{km}T_{lm} \qquad (7.19\text{–}18)$$

Note that the "scalar product" of a tensor and a vector, such as $B_m = \sum_l A_l T_{lm}$, is itself a vector. In fact, we can write, using Eq. 7.19–2,

$$\sum_m a_{km}B_m = \sum_m a_{km}\sum_l A_l T_{lm} = \sum_m\sum_l a_{km}T_{lm}\sum_j A_j' a_{jl}$$
$$= \sum_j A_j' \sum_m\sum_l a_{km}a_{jl}T_{lm}$$
$$= \sum_j A_j' T'_{jk} = B_k' \qquad (7.19\text{–}19)$$

so that B_m transforms as a four-vector. A clear distinction must be made between a tensor, which may be written for any particular reference frame, and a transformation matrix, such as a_{jk}, which always refers to *two* frames of reference.

We intend to show that Maxwell's equations can be written as one equation relating two four-vectors and another relating two tensors. Let us start by noting that electric charge q must be a scalar, since electric charge is conserved for moving systems. The charge in a small element of volume will thus be the same as seen in different frames of reference. Because of the Lorentz-Fitzgerald contraction (Problem 7.19d), $d\tau$ will contract along the direction of motion when observed in a moving frame, but not transversely. The transformation rule for volume elements from a rest frame to a moving frame is

$$d\tau = d\tau_0(1 - u^2/c^2)^{\frac{1}{2}} \tag{7.19-20}$$

Hence ρ must obey the inverse transformation

$$\rho = \rho_0/(1 - u^2/c^2)^{\frac{1}{2}} \tag{7.19-21}$$

Now if we consider a group of charges first at rest and then moving with a velocity $\mathbf{v}$, we can treat $-\mathbf{v}$ as the velocity $\mathbf{u}$ of a reference frame that reduces the motion to a state of rest. If ρ_0 is the charge density in the rest frame, we can form a four-vector by use of Eq. 7.19–21 and the four-vector velocity given in Eq. 7.19–16. In fact, the quantity

$$J_k = [\rho_0 v_1/(1 - v^2/c^2)^{\frac{1}{2}}, \quad \rho_0 v_2/(1 - v^2/c^2)^{\frac{1}{2}}, \quad \rho_0 v_3/(1 - v^2/c^2)^{\frac{1}{2}},$$
$$ic\rho_0/(1 - v^2/c^2)^{\frac{1}{2}}] = (\rho v_1, \rho v_2, \rho v_3, ic\rho) \tag{7.19-22}$$

is a Lorentz-invariant four-vector called the charge-current density. The first three components are, of course, the ordinary vector $\mathbf{J} = \rho \mathbf{v}$.

The Lorentz condition 7.10–9a relates $\mathbf{A}$ and V in a way that hints at their forming a four-vector. In fact, if we define A_j as the four-vector whose components are given by

$$A_j = (A_1, A_2, A_3, iV/c) \tag{7.19-23a}$$

we can write the Lorentz condition as a four-divergence:

$$\sum_j \partial_j A_j = \frac{\partial A_1}{\partial x_1} + \frac{\partial A_2}{\partial x_2} + \frac{\partial A_3}{\partial x_3} + \frac{\partial A_4}{\partial x_4} = 0 \tag{7.19-24}$$

In this form, the Lorentz condition represents the vanishing of a Lorentz-invariant scalar.

We shall therefore assume that A_j transforms according to

$$A_k' = \sum_j a_{kj} A_j \tag{7.19-25}$$

The justification for this assumption will appear shortly when we consider the transformation rules for $\mathbf{E}$ and $\mathbf{B}$; an additional justification will be given in Section 10.3.

To find these rules, let us write the components of $\mathbf{E}$ and $\mathbf{B}$ in terms of A_j. We have

$$\left.\begin{aligned}
E_x &= E_1 = -\partial A_x/\partial t - \partial V/\partial x = -ic(\partial_4 A_1 - \partial_1 A_4) \\
E_y &= E_2 = -\partial A_y/\partial t - \partial V/\partial y = -ic(\partial_4 A_2 - \partial_2 A_4) \\
E_z &= E_3 = -\partial A_z/\partial t - \partial V/\partial z = -ic(\partial_4 A_3 - \partial_3 A_4)
\end{aligned}\right\} \tag{7.19-26}$$

$$\left.\begin{aligned}
B_x &= B_1 = \partial A_z/\partial y - \partial A_y/\partial z = \partial_2 A_3 - \partial_3 A_2 \\
B_y &= B_2 = \partial A_x/\partial z - \partial A_z/\partial x = \partial_3 A_1 - \partial_1 A_3 \\
B_z &= B_3 = \partial A_y/\partial x - \partial A_x/\partial y = \partial_1 A_2 - \partial_2 A_1
\end{aligned}\right\} \tag{7.19-27}$$

This form for the field components demonstrates in a remarkable form the connection between **B** and **E**. We can write all six components in terms of a single tensor f_{jk}:

$$f_{jk} = \partial_j A_k - \partial_k A_j \tag{7.19–28}$$

This tensor has the property of being anti-symmetric, i.e.,

$$f_{jk} = -f_{kj}; \qquad j, k = 1, 2, 3, 4 \tag{7.19–29}$$

with vanishing values for equal subscripts:

$$f_{jj} = 0 \tag{7.19–30}$$

Then we can write

$$E_j = -icf_{4j} = icf_{j4}; \qquad j = 1, 2, 3 \tag{7.19–31a}$$

$$B_1 = f_{23} = -f_{32}; \qquad B_2 = f_{31} = -f_{13}; \qquad B_3 = f_{12} = -f_{21} \tag{7.19–32}$$

We can express these results most simply by writing the components of f_{jk} in a square array:

$$f_{jk} = \begin{pmatrix} f_{11} & f_{12} & f_{13} & f_{14} \\ f_{21} & f_{22} & f_{23} & f_{24} \\ f_{31} & f_{32} & f_{33} & f_{34} \\ f_{41} & f_{42} & f_{43} & f_{44} \end{pmatrix} = \begin{pmatrix} 0 & B_z & -B_y & -iE_x/c \\ -B_z & 0 & B_x & -iE_y/c \\ B_y & -B_x & 0 & -iE_z/c \\ iE_x/c & iE_y/c & iE_z/c & 0 \end{pmatrix} \tag{7.19–33}$$

This tensor is called the "electromagnetic-field tensor." It will transform as the product of two four-vectors, since it is formed from the two pairs of four-vectors, $\partial_j A_k$ and $\partial_k A_j$. We should reiterate the fact that the presence of the imaginary unit is a formality. The field tensor is a perfectly real physical entity; with a different and more complicated mathematical formalism,[43] it can be written entirely in terms of real numbers.

We are finally ready to consider Maxwell's equations in free space. The equation 1.5–1, div **E** $= \rho/\epsilon_0$, can be written

$$\frac{\partial E_x}{\partial x} + \frac{\partial E_y}{\partial y} + \frac{\partial E_z}{\partial z} = ic\,\partial f_{14}/\partial x_1 + ic\,\partial f_{24}/\partial x_2 + ic\,\partial f_{34}/\partial x_3$$

$$= \rho/\epsilon_0 = \mu_0 c^2 \rho \tag{7.19–34}$$

The expression on the left appears to be the fourth component of the vector formed from the tensor f_{jk} and the vector ∂_j. Since $ic\rho$ is the fourth

[43] Panofsky and Phillips, *op. cit.*, Chapter 18.

component of the charge-current vector, let us seek the other three components in the Maxwell equation containing **J**. Componentwise this equation 7.9–3a reads for free space

$$\left.\begin{array}{l}\dfrac{\partial B_z}{\partial y} - \dfrac{\partial B_y}{\partial z} - \mu_0\epsilon_0\dfrac{\partial E_x}{\partial t} = -\dfrac{\partial f_{21}}{\partial x_2} - \dfrac{\partial f_{31}}{\partial x_3} - \dfrac{\partial f_{41}}{\partial x_4} = \mu_0 J_1 \\[2mm] \dfrac{\partial B_x}{\partial z} - \dfrac{\partial B_z}{\partial x} - \mu_0\epsilon_0\dfrac{\partial E_y}{\partial t} = -\dfrac{\partial f_{32}}{\partial x_3} - \dfrac{\partial f_{12}}{\partial x_1} - \dfrac{\partial f_{42}}{\partial x_4} = \mu_0 J_2 \\[2mm] \dfrac{\partial B_y}{\partial x} - \dfrac{\partial B_x}{\partial y} - \mu_0\epsilon_0\dfrac{\partial E_z}{\partial t} = -\dfrac{\partial f_{13}}{\partial x_1} - \dfrac{\partial f_{23}}{\partial x_2} - \dfrac{\partial f_{43}}{\partial x_4} = \mu_0 J_3 \end{array}\right\} \quad (7.19\text{–}35)$$

To each of these equations, the appropriate term involving the vanishing components f_{11}, f_{22}, or f_{33} can be added to give a four-dimensional divergence. We can then write the single equation

$$\sum_{j=1}^{4} \frac{\partial f_{jk}}{\partial x_j} = -\mu_0 J_k; \qquad k = 1, 2, 3, 4 \qquad (7.19\text{–}36a)$$

which is the clearly Lorentz-invariant expression of the equations div $\mathbf{E} = \rho/\epsilon_0$ and **curl B** $= \mu_0\mathbf{J} + \mu_0\,\partial\mathbf{D}/\partial t$.

The other two Maxwell equations combine to form a tensor of the third rank. For div $\mathbf{B} = 0$, Eq. 7.12–1, we obtain

$$\frac{\partial B_x}{\partial x} + \frac{\partial B_y}{\partial y} + \frac{\partial B_z}{\partial z} = \frac{\partial f_{23}}{\partial x_1} + \frac{\partial f_{31}}{\partial x_2} + \frac{\partial f_{12}}{\partial x_3} = 0 \qquad (7.19\text{–}37)$$

and for the three components of 7.14–3, **curl E** $+ \partial\mathbf{B}/\partial t = 0$, we get

$$\frac{\partial E_z}{\partial y} - \frac{\partial E_y}{\partial z} + \frac{\partial B_x}{\partial t} = ic\frac{\partial f_{34}}{\partial x_2} + ic\frac{\partial f_{42}}{\partial x_3} + ic\frac{\partial f_{23}}{\partial x_4} = 0$$

$$\frac{\partial E_x}{\partial z} - \frac{\partial E_z}{\partial x} + \frac{\partial B_y}{\partial t} = ic\frac{\partial f_{14}}{\partial x_3} + ic\frac{\partial f_{43}}{\partial x_1} + ic\frac{\partial f_{31}}{\partial x_4} = 0 \quad (7.19\text{–}38)$$

$$\frac{\partial E_y}{\partial x} - \frac{\partial E_x}{\partial y} + \frac{\partial B_z}{\partial t} = ic\frac{\partial f_{24}}{\partial x_1} + ic\frac{\partial f_{41}}{\partial x_2} + ic\frac{\partial f_{12}}{\partial x_4} = 0$$

We can summarize all four of these equations by writing, with the understanding that j, k, and l are all different,

$$\frac{\partial f_{jk}}{\partial x_l} + \frac{\partial f_{kl}}{\partial x_j} + \frac{\partial f_{lj}}{\partial x_k} = 0 \qquad (7.19\text{–}39)$$

There are only four possible sets of the three subscripts that are all unequal (each set leaves out one of the integers 1, 2, 3, or 4). If jkl are taken successively as 231, 342, 143, 241, we get the equations above. A change in the order of any of these sets will either give the same equation with the terms rearranged or the negative of the same equation.

Let us now show that the expression in Eq. 7.19–39 represents indeed a tensor of the third rank. The expression $\partial f_{jk}/\partial x_l$, where j, k, and l may now be *any* indices will transform as a tensor of the third rank (cf. Problem 7.19f). Its components will vanish whenever j and k are equal and will change sign when j and k (being unequal) are interchanged. The sum of three such tensors with indices interchanged, as in Eq. 7.19–39, is also a tensor. This sum will vanish when any two of the subscripts are equal, for the term that contains these two subscripts in the numerator will be zero by itself and the other two terms will be equal and opposite.

Therefore we can remove the restriction on the subscripts in Eq. 7.19–39, since the added possibilities are all zero. Consequently, we have written the div **E** and **curl B** equations together as the vanishing of a Lorentz-invariant tensor of the third rank.

We can finally conclude that Maxwell's equations will retain their form when the transformation from one frame of reference to another moving with constant velocity with respect to the first is carried out by the Lorentz rule, Eq. 7.19–1. The way in which the components of **E** and **B** change may be found by applying the transformation matrix in the form of Eq. 7.19–12 to the electromagnetic field tensor, Eq. 7.19–33. It is left to the reader (Problem 7.19g) to show that, using subscripts $\parallel$ and $\perp$ for the fields parallel and perpendicular to the relative velocity **u**,

$$\left.\begin{array}{l} \mathbf{E}_{\parallel}' = \mathbf{E}_{\parallel} \\ \mathbf{B}_{\parallel}' = \mathbf{B}_{\parallel} \end{array}\right\} \tag{7.19–40}$$

$$\left.\begin{array}{l} \mathbf{E}_{\perp}' = \gamma[\mathbf{E}_{\perp} - (\mathbf{u} \times \mathbf{B}_{\perp})] \\ \mathbf{B}_{\perp}' = \gamma[\mathbf{B}_{\perp} + (\mathbf{u} \times \mathbf{E}_{\perp})/c^2] \end{array}\right\} \tag{7.19–41a}$$

When $u \ll c$, γ is very close to unity, and these formulas are seen to agree with the Galilean relativity results of Section 7.14. It should be noted that these formulas relate the field quantities observed in the two frames of reference at the same point of space and instant of time, which of course are measured by different coordinates in the two systems. It is especially important to note by examining the derivation (cf. especially Eq. 7.19–11) that **u** is the velocity of the *unprimed* system as seen in the primed system. If **u** were defined the other way around, its sign would be changed in Eq. 7.19–41a.

Since these transformation rules for **E** and **B** are well verified by many experiments concerning radiation and moving charges, we have justified Eq. 7.19–25 and the rest of the development that led up to them.

Let us apply these equations to the case of crossed electric and magnetic fields discussed in Section 7.3. We start with **E** and **B** uniform and mutually perpendicular in the unprimed system so that $\mathbf{E} \cdot \mathbf{B} = 0$, and transform to a primed system moving at the drift velocity

$$\mathbf{v}_d = (\mathbf{E} \times \mathbf{B})/B^2 \tag{7.19–42}$$

with respect to the unprimed system. We must assume $E/B < c$ if $\mathbf{v}_d$ is to represent a physical velocity. We must then set $\mathbf{u} = -\mathbf{v}_d$ in Eqs. 7.19–41, and since $\mathbf{v}_d$ is perpendicular to both $\mathbf{E}$ and $\mathbf{B}$, we have $\mathbf{E} = \mathbf{E}_\perp$, $\mathbf{B} = \mathbf{B}_\perp$, $\mathbf{E}_\| = \mathbf{B}_\| = 0$.

The result for the fields in the primed system is

$$\mathbf{E}' = \gamma[\mathbf{E} + (\mathbf{E} \times \mathbf{B}) \times \mathbf{B}/B^2] = 0 \tag{7.19–43}$$

$$\mathbf{B}' = \gamma[\mathbf{B} - (\mathbf{E} \times \mathbf{B}) \times \mathbf{E}/B^2 c^2]$$

$$= \gamma\mathbf{B}(1 - E^2/B^2 c^2) \tag{7.19–44a}$$

Note that since $u = v_d = E/B$, γ is given by

$$\gamma = (1 - u^2/c^2)^{-\frac{1}{2}} = (1 - E^2/B^2 c^2)^{-\frac{1}{2}}$$

We conclude that only a magnetic field is found in the primed system, given by

$$\mathbf{B}' = (1 - E^2/B^2 c^2)^{\frac{1}{2}}\mathbf{B} \tag{7.19–44b}$$

As we found before, particle motion in crossed fields consists of a uniform drift $\mathbf{v}_d$ superimposed on helical motion in a pure magnetic field. Our conclusion now, however, is valid for all values of v_d up to as close to c as we please, and for relativistic particle energies.

If $E/B > c$, we make a different transformation. In this case we set

$$\left.\begin{array}{l} \mathbf{u} = -\mathbf{v}_d{}' = -c^2(\mathbf{E} \times \mathbf{B})/E^2 \\ u = v_d{}' = c^2 B/E \end{array}\right\} \tag{7.19–45}$$

$$\gamma = (1 - c^2 B^2/E^2)^{-\frac{1}{2}} \tag{7.19–46}$$

$$\mathbf{E}' = \gamma[\mathbf{E} + c^2(\mathbf{E} \times \mathbf{B}) \times \mathbf{B}/E^2]$$

$$= \gamma\mathbf{E}(1 - c^2 B^2/E^2)$$

$$= (1 - c^2 B^2/E^2)^{\frac{1}{2}}\mathbf{E} \tag{7.19–47}$$

$$\mathbf{B}' = \gamma[\mathbf{B} - (\mathbf{E} \times \mathbf{B}) \times \mathbf{E}/E^2] = 0 \tag{7.19–48}$$

The particle motion in this case may be described as a drift $\mathbf{v}_d{}'$ given by 7.19–45 superimposed on parabolic motion in a pure uniform *electric* field, and the result is again valid no matter how close to c is the value of $v_d{}'$.

In Gaussian units, the four-vector potential becomes

$$A_j = (A_1, A_2, A_3, iV) \qquad \text{Gaussian} \quad (7.19–23b)$$

The electric field components are written as

$$E_j = -if_{4j} = if_{j4}; \quad j = 1, 2, 3 \quad \text{Gaussian} \quad (7.19–31b)$$

and the magnetic induction components are still given by 7.19-32. Thus no factor c appears in the field tensor 7.19-33 in Gaussian units.

The Maxwell four-divergence equation becomes

$$\sum_{j=1}^{4} \frac{\partial f_{jk}}{\partial x_j} = -\frac{4\pi J_k}{c} \; ; \qquad k = 1, 2, 3, 4 \quad \text{Gaussian} \quad (7.19\text{-}36b)$$

The transformation formulas for the transverse components of **E** and **B** are

$$\left.\begin{aligned} \mathbf{E}_\perp' &= \gamma[\mathbf{E}_\perp - (\mathbf{u} \times \mathbf{B}_\perp)/c] \\ \mathbf{B}_\perp' &= \gamma[\mathbf{B}_\perp + (\mathbf{u} \times \mathbf{E}_\perp)/c] \end{aligned}\right\} \quad \text{Gaussian} \quad (7.19\text{-}41b)$$

The drift velocities $\mathbf{v}_d$ and $\mathbf{v}_d'$, Eqs. 7.19-42 and 45, must each have a single factor c on the right in Gaussian units, since **E** and **B** are dimensionally the same.

Problem 7.19a. Prove that $(\mathbf{x} \cdot \mathbf{u})^2 - u^2 c^2 t^2$ is invariant under the transformation Eq. 7.19-1, and hence demonstrate Eq. 7.19-11.

Problem 7.19b. Let **u** and **v** both be along the x-axis. Using the last of Eqs. 7.19-14 together with Eq. 7.19-8 to get $dt'/dt = a_{44}(1 + uv/c^2)$, deduce the relativistic law for the addition of parallel velocities.

Problem 7.19c. Find the law of addition of velocities, as in the previous problem, when **u** and **v** have arbitrary directions.

Problem 7.19d. By considering that a length measurement of an object in a frame of reference in which the object is at rest does not require simultaneous observation of both ends but that measurement in another frame does require simultaneity ($\Delta t' = 0$), show that a moving object always appears shortened along the direction of motion by a factor $(1 - v^2/c^2)^{1/2}$ (Lorentz-Fitzgerald contraction). Show also that no transverse change of length occurs.

Problem 7.19e. Find all the coefficients of a Lorentz transformation for the case in which the origin of the unprimed system moves with speed u along the positive x-axis, as seen in the primed system. Also write down the inverse transformation by inspection. The spatial orientation is the same for the two systems.

Problem 7.19f. Prove explicitly that $f_{jk} = \partial_j A_k - \partial_k A_j$ transforms like a tensor of the second rank and that $\partial f_{jk}/\partial x_l$ transforms like a tensor of the third rank.

Problem 7.19g. Prove Eqs. 7.19-40 and 7.19-41 for the transformation of **E** and **B**.

Problem 7.19h. Write the equations for a Lorentz transformation of the four-vectors J_k and A_k, in terms of **J**, ρ, **A**, and V.

Problem 7.19i. Using 7.19-40 and 7.19-41, show that $\mathbf{E} \cdot \mathbf{B}$ and $E^2 - B^2 c^2$ are Lorentz-invariant.

Chapter 8

MAGNETIC
MATERIALS

8.1 Introduction

In this chapter, we shall discuss magnetic materials and measurements of their properties by combining the material of Chapter 7 with the modern atomic theory of circulating sub-atomic currents. We shall introduce the pole concept and find that there is a close analogy between magnetizable materials and dielectrics; we shall thereby be able to borrow numerous mathematical results from Chapter 3 and obtain relations easily verifiable in the macroscopic realm. Our presentation will be governed largely by a desire to present an orderly arrangement of the material, suitable for clarity and ease in remembering, so that the historical development of the subject will not be followed and only brief consideration will be given to the experimental basis for our assertions about the atomic nature of magnetism.

8.2 Magnetic Dipoles

All atoms are known to contain circulating currents that are sources of magnetic field. These currents are of two types. The circulation around nuclei of electrons in unfilled shells (orbital motion) is an obvious source, such circulation when averaged over sufficiently long times being equivalent to steady currents. (Electrons in filled atomic or molecular shells give collectively a zero magnetic effect.) The other type is involved in the intrinsic magnetic properties of separate electrons, protons, and neutrons. These properties are associated with the particles' intrinsic angular momentum, or spin. The particles act as if they "contained" circulating currents within themselves. No adequate theory of elementary particles now exists (1966), and although the magnetic properties of "elementary" particles seem to be describable in terms of actual currents, for instance of circulating "mesons," the situation is by no means clear. However, the effects are the same as if there really were such currents, and we need not pursue the theoretical question in this book.

What we do require is a formulation of the field produced by a small circulating current, as well as a formulation of the force and torque exerted on such a current by an external field. Both formulations are given in Chapter 7.

The vector potential for a small loop is given by Eq. 7.8–16,

$$\mathbf{A} = \frac{\mu_0 \mathbf{m} \times \mathbf{1}_r}{4\pi r^2} \tag{8.2–1a}$$

and the scalar potential by 7.8–10,

$$V_m = \frac{\mathbf{m} \cdot \mathbf{1}_r}{4\pi r^2} \tag{8.2–2a}$$

By small we mean that the largest dimension of the loop is small compared to the distance from it to a point of observation, a condition very well fulfilled when we wish to calculate the large-scale effects of atomic magnetism, and one that seems to be valid down to distances of the order of nuclear dimensions (10^{-15} m) for the magnetic effects associated with spin.

V_m is actually multiple valued as discussed in Section 7.6. However, the expression given here satisfies the conditions for the integral definition given in Eq. 7.6–10 and remains single valued as long as points within or near the loop are excluded from consideration.

The force and torque on a small loop in an external field $\mathbf{B}$ can be found from Eqs. 7.12–1 to 10. We have for the force

$$\mathbf{F} = \nabla(\mathbf{m} \cdot \mathbf{B}) \tag{8.2–3a}$$

and for the torque

$$\mathscr{T} = \mathbf{m} \times \mathbf{B} \tag{8.2–4a}$$

The only property of an elementary current loop that is needed is the magnetic moment $\mathbf{m}$, so it is not necessary to specify its structure in terms of i and S or a combination or distribution of such elements. The fact that the vector $\mathbf{m}$ enters in a linear way in formulas 8.2–1 to 4 is an expression of the theorem of superposition as applied to Ampère's law and to the Lorentz force law.

Introduction of the Pole Concept. Formulas 8.2–2, 8.2–3, and 8.2–4 are mathematically similar to Eqs. 3.1–4, 3.2–3, and 3.2–4 for an electric dipole. To make the analogy complete we shall write these three results using $\mathbf{B}/\mu_0$ as the field quantity and $\mu_0\mathbf{m} = \mathbf{p}_m$ as the magnetic moment in weber-meters.[1] Except in the interior of magnetized materials, $\mathbf{B}/\mu_0$ is given the symbol $\mathbf{H}$. Then we have

$$V_m = \frac{\mathbf{p}_m \cdot \mathbf{1}_r}{4\pi\mu_0 r^2} \tag{8.2-2b}$$

$$\mathbf{H} = -\nabla V_m \tag{8.2-5}$$

$$U = \mathbf{p}_m \cdot \mathbf{H} = \mu_0 \mathbf{m} \cdot \mathbf{H} \tag{8.2-6a}$$

$$\mathbf{F} = \nabla(\mathbf{p}_m \cdot \mathbf{H}) = \mu_0 \nabla(\mathbf{m} \cdot \mathbf{H}) \tag{8.2-3b}$$

$$\mathscr{T} = \mathbf{p}_m \times \mathbf{H} = \mu_0 \mathbf{m} \times \mathbf{H} \tag{8.2-4b}$$

These formulas are exactly the same as the corresponding equations for electrical dipoles if only we replace $\mathbf{H}$ by $\mathbf{E}$, $\mathbf{p}_m$ by $\mathbf{p}$, μ_0 by ϵ_0, V_m by V, and U by $-U$. On Eqs. 8.2–3a and 8.2–3b we can also make the reverse of the transformation that we made in going from $F = (\mathbf{p} \cdot \nabla)\mathbf{E}$ to $F = \nabla(\mathbf{p} \cdot \mathbf{E})$ in Section 3.2, provided that **curl B** $= 0$ at every point along the current loop (e.g., no current density $\mathbf{J}$ coincident with the loop), and write for the force

$$\mathbf{F} = (\mathbf{m} \cdot \nabla)\mathbf{B} = (\mathbf{p}_m \cdot \nabla)\mathbf{H} \tag{8.2-3c}$$

These equations could be derived if we assumed the existence of magnetic "charges" or poles that have the correct properties in analogy to electric charge. No elementary poles have been found in nature; the experimental evidence against their existence is actually quite strong. However, poles constitute a "useful fiction" and their surface and volume densities can be defined quite precisely, as we shall show. The symbol q_m will be used for magnetic pole strength. We need three equations to introduce this useful fiction; first

$$\mathbf{H} = \frac{q_m \mathbf{1}_r}{4\pi\mu_0 r^2} \tag{8.2-7a}$$

for the field produced by a single pole (Coulomb's law for poles), with the usual rules for attractions and repulsions; second

$$\mathbf{F} = q_m \mathbf{H} \tag{8.2-8}$$

for the force on a pole of strength q_m; and third

$$\mu_0 \mathbf{m} = \mathbf{p}_m = q_m \,\boldsymbol{\delta}\mathbf{l} \tag{8.2-9a}$$

---

[1] It would be simpler if we only used $\mathbf{p}_m = \mu_0 \mathbf{m} = \mu_0 i\mathbf{S}$ as the definition of magnetic moment, as is done in some texts. The practice we follow is that recommended by the Commission of Symbols, Units, and Nomenclature of the International Union of Pure and Applied Physics [SUN commission, see *Physics Today*, **9**, 23–27 (1956) and **10**, 30–34 (1957), except for our use of the letter **m**. In works on atomic physics, the symbol μ is commonly used for magnetic dipole moment, but the traditional use of μ_0 and μ for permeability precludes this choice for this textbook.

for the dipole moment, where $\delta\mathbf{l}$ is a small but fixed separation of two equal and opposite imaginary monopoles.

Although we might *define* magnetic pole strength by an analogy of this kind, we shall be able to define it more directly and satisfactorily in Section 8.4, when we shall justify Eqs. 8.2–7 to 9. In the meantime, we may take the analogy as a working hypothesis. The quantity $\mathbf{H}$ has traditionally been called the "magnetic field intensity," or just the "magnetic field," and where there is no confusion with the more fundamental quantity $\mathbf{B}$, this terminology will be used. An alternative name for $\mathbf{H}$, which is sometimes used and avoids any confusion, is "magnetizing force."[2] It is not difficult to show that in MKS units, $\mathbf{H}$ is measured in amperes/meter.

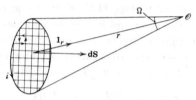

Fig. 8.2a.   Illustrating the dipole form of Ampère's Law.

Before deriving the pole concept for the case of bulk matter, let us consider the case of a large current loop. We have already given five different expressions involving the magnetic field of a closed current, namely, the law of Biot and Savart, Eq. 7.6–1, the solid-angle rule, Eq. 7.6–6, the circuital rule, Eq. 7.7–1, the vector-potential rule, Eq. 7.10–2; and the differential equation 7.9–1. We can now derive a sixth one. Let us calculate Ω for a large circuit by taking an arbitrary surface S whose boundary is the circuit in question, and dividing it into differential elements of area of the sort used for integration. The solid angle at $\mathcal{O}$ (Fig. 8.2a) may be written as a surface integral

$$\Omega = \int_S \frac{d\mathbf{S} \cdot \mathbf{1}_r}{r^2}$$

The magnetic scalar potential is then

$$V_m = \frac{i}{4\pi} \int_S \frac{d\mathbf{S} \cdot \mathbf{1}_r}{r^2} = \int_S \frac{d\mathbf{p}_m \cdot \mathbf{1}_r}{4\pi\mu_0 r^2} \qquad (8.2\text{–}10)$$

where we have written $\mu_0 i \, d\mathbf{S} = d\mathbf{p}_m$, a differential element of magnetic dipole moment. Thus the scalar potential produced by the current is the

---

[2] A. Sommerfeld has suggested calling it the "magnetic excitation." See his *Electrodynamics* (*Lectures on Theoretical Physics*, Vol. III), E. G. Ramberg, trans., Academic Press, New York, 1952.

same as if we substituted for it a physical surface coinciding with S, containing a positive distribution of magnetic poles on its front surface and a negative one on its back surface, separated by a very small distance δl (measured in the direction of the positive normal to S). If we denote the quantity of magnetic pole per unit area by σ_m, we must have

$$d\mathbf{p}_m = \mu_0 i \, d\mathbf{S} = \sigma_m \, dS \, \delta\mathbf{l} = \sigma_m \, \delta l \, d\mathbf{S}$$

We call such a surface a "magnetic shell" and define its strength or magnetic dipole moment per unit area as

$$P_{mS} = \mu_0 M_S = \sigma_m \, \delta l = \mu_0 i \qquad (8.2\text{--}11a)$$

The shell is said to be *equivalent* to the current loop.

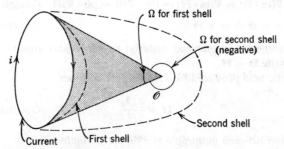

Fig. 8.2b. Two locations for the shell equivalent to a current when the field is desired at point $\mathcal{O}$.

We can equally well derive this result by considering that the current loop is equivalent to the superposition of a large number of loops, namely, the loops formed by the boundaries of all the elements dS. If each loop carries a current i, there will be a cancelation of the contribution from each portion of one loop that abuts on another, for there will be on such portions equal currents in opposite directions. Only on the boundaries of the original loop will there be an uncanceled result. But each separate loop acts like a dipole, and so the sum acts like a magnetic shell. Note the complete analogy to the disk electret, discussed in Section 3.6.

Thus any steady current circuit whatsoever produces a field that could be imagined to have arisen from a collection of magnetic poles. Our derivation requires us to restrict the analogy to calculation of V_m at points far from the alleged dipoles. Hence the equivalent shell must not be passed through any point where we wish to find the field. The shell can, in fact, be taken on either side of the point $\mathcal{O}$, as in Fig. 8.2b. The field calculated from the gradient of Ω will be the same in either case, but V_m will differ by $\pm i$, illustrating again its essential multiple valuedness. (The sign of Ω must be determined in accordance with the rules stated in Section 7.6.)

The relation between current loops and magnetic shells is exemplified by the agreement of Eq. 3.6–9 for the outside value of $\mathbf{D}$ at the center of an electret disk and Eq. 7.8–8b for the value of $\mathbf{B}$ at the center of a circular current.

In Gaussian units, we have for an isolated magnetic dipole

$$\mathbf{A} = \frac{\mathbf{m} \times \mathbf{1}_r}{r^2} \qquad\qquad \text{Gaussian} \quad (8.2\text{–}1b)$$

$$V_m = \frac{\mathbf{m} \cdot \mathbf{1}_r}{r^2} \qquad\qquad \text{Gaussian} \quad (8.2\text{–}2c)$$

$$U = \mathbf{m} \cdot \mathbf{H} \qquad\qquad\qquad \text{Gaussian} \quad (8.2\text{–}6b)$$

$$\mathbf{F} = \nabla(\mathbf{m} \cdot \mathbf{B}) = \nabla(\mathbf{m} \cdot \mathbf{H}) = (\mathbf{m} \cdot \nabla)\mathbf{B} = (\mathbf{m} \cdot \nabla)\mathbf{H} \quad \text{Gaussian} \quad (8.2\text{–}3d)$$

$$\mathscr{T} = \mathbf{m} \times \mathbf{B} = \mathbf{m} \times \mathbf{H} \qquad\qquad \text{Gaussian} \quad (8.2\text{–}4c)$$

where we assume no magnetized material to be present around or near the dipole, and write $\mathbf{B} = \mathbf{H}$.

The magnetic field produced by a single pole becomes

$$\mathbf{H} = \frac{q_m \mathbf{1}_r}{r^2} \qquad\qquad \text{Gaussian} \quad (8.2\text{–}7b)$$

and the relation between monopole and dipole strengths

$$\mathbf{m} = \mathbf{p}_m = q_m \, \boldsymbol{\delta l} \qquad\qquad \text{Gaussian} \quad (8.2\text{–}9b)$$

The strength of a magnetic shell is

$$M_S = \frac{i}{c} \qquad\qquad \text{Gaussian} \quad (8.2\text{–}11b)$$

emn of dipole strength per cm². In Gaussian units, $\mathbf{H}$ like $\mathbf{B}$ is measured in gauss, and for historical reasons connected with the ascribing of properties to empty space, its unit is also called the oersted.[3] The Gaussian unit of pole strength is usually called the electromagnetic unit or emu (Problem 8.26).

Problem 8.2a. Find the flux produced by a circular current of arbitrary radius R through a small loop of radius a coaxial with the first loop and at a distance z from it. If the currents in the two loops are i_1 and i_2, find the force on the small loop.

[3] The International Union of Pure and Applied Physics decided in 1934 to accept the point of view that $\mathbf{B}$ and $\mathbf{H}$ in free space are fundamentally different even if their ratio μ_0 is taken as unity, and hence the oersted was adopted at that time as the unit for $\mathbf{H}$. Inasmuch as we do not wish in this book to ascribe properties to free space, but rather to deal with experimentally verifiable laws of physics, we can consider that "gausses" and "oersteds" are equal and interchangeable. This point of view, applied to MKS units, may be taken to imply that μ_0 is dimensionless (see p. 288. For further details, and a full discussion, see article by R. T. Birge, *Am. Physics Teacher*, 3, 171 (1931).

Problem 8.2b. Show that the MKS unit of q_m is the weber and that of H is the ampere/meter. Show that the emu of pole strength has the dimensions of gauss-centimeter², of abampere-centimeter, and of erg/gauss-centimeter.

Problem 8.2c. If the small loop in Problem 8.2a moves away from the larger one along their common axis with speed v, find the emf induced in it and the emf it induces in the large loop.

Problem 8.2d. Two small loops are a large distance r apart, the second one being on a line making an angle of 45° with the axis of the first one. How is the second one to be oriented so the pair will have zero mutual inductance?

Problem 8.2e. Derive B from Eq. 8.2–1 and show that the result is equivalent to Eq. 8.2–5.

Problem 8.2f. Ten turns of wire are wrapped around the edge of a 6-cm square of plywood, that is hinged so as to fold along a line bisecting two opposite edges. The coil carries a current of 0.40 amp. Find the magnetic moment of the coil when the angle between the two parts of the square is (a) 180°, (b) 120°, (c) 90°, (d) 45°. Describe the direction of **m** in each case.

Problem 8.2g. Find **A** at a point in the plane of one half of the folding square of the previous problem, 10 m away from the hinge line on the perpendicular bisector of the hinge, for each angle given.

Problem 8.2h. How is the field produced by a wire loop arranged in the form of a figure 8 to be described at points far from it in comparison to its dimensions?

8.3   The Current Analysis of Magnetized Material

Magnetized material consists of a collection of atomic currents arranged in a more or less orderly way. Since a single atomic-current loop acts mathematically like an electric dipole, a collection of atoms will be mathematically analogous to a piece of dielectric material. On the other hand, a group of circulating atomic currents can be combined on the macroscopic scale to give a continuous distribution of current density. These two ways of looking at magnetized material lead to two different analyses of the field produced by a magnet and the forces and torques on it, ways that correspond respectively to the use of the scalar and vector potentials. We shall start with the current analysis in this section and develop the pole concept and the analogy with dielectrics in the following.

Both analyses start with combining the effects of all the current loops in a small volume $d\tau$. If there are several current loops in an atom, their resultant field at a great distance can be found by adding their magnetic dipole moments. If these moments add to zero, there may be a higher order contribution of a magnetic quadrupole or higher multipole nature, in exact analogy to the electric multipoles. Also, a more accurate approximation to the field near a loop could be obtained by considering it to be composed of smaller loops and calculating the resultant dipole, quadrupole, and higher moments. We shall be concerned here only with magnetic dipole moments.

Let us consider a group of atomic magnetic dipoles, large enough to be considered as an element of a continuous medium and to average out the variations of **m** from atom to atom, but small enough to be an element of

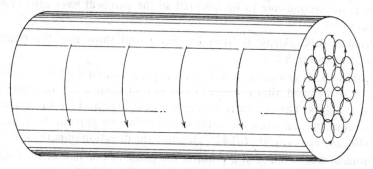

Fig. 8.3a. Resultant currents in a bar magnet.

integration. If $d\tau$ is its volume, we can write the sum of the dipole moments just as in Eq. 3.4–1

$$\sum_i \mathbf{m}_i = \mathbf{M} \, d\tau \tag{8.3–1a}$$

or, multiplying by μ_0

$$\sum_i \mathbf{p}_m = \mu_0 \mathbf{M} \, d\tau = \mathbf{P}_m \, d\tau \tag{8.3–1b}$$

where **M** is a vector which we shall call the magnetization, or magnetic moment per unit volume. The quantity $\mathbf{P}_m$, which is the analog of the electric polarization, may be called the magnetic polarization. The magnetization **M** is measured in ampere/m, and $\mathbf{P}_m$ in webers/m².

The current-analysis method of calculating the combined effects of all the elementary dipoles in a magnet is to generalize the similarity between a solenoid and a uniform magnet (shown in Fig. 8.3a). The current loops in an arbitrary magnetic medium can be added so as to give a net volume current density $\mathbf{J}_m$, with a surface current of surface density J_{Sm} running around the sides of the piece of material. This surface current will give rise to a discontinuity in the component of **B** parallel to the surface, just as occurs for the solenoid. If the magnetization is uniform, all the currents will cancel each other in the interior and only the surface current will be left. The greatest surface density of current will occur for surfaces parallel to **M**, for then the largest uncanceled currents can appear on the surface. (Cf. Fig. 8.3*b*.) A surface perpendicular to **M** will have no surface currents running in one direction along it, but could be thought of as having a current circulating around it, or a distribution of such currents. The discontinuity in the tangential component of **B** for an arbitrarily oriented surface can be found by calculating the surface current density produced

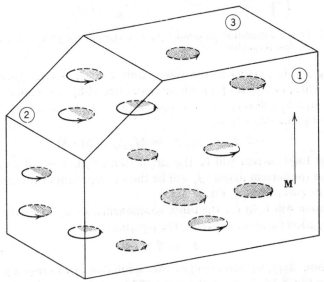

Fig. 8.3*b*. A fragment of magnetized material with a few exaggerated atomic currents. Shown are surfaces: (1) parallel to **M**, (2) at an angle with **M**, (3) normal to **M**.

by the uncanceled atomic currents, and using the result of Problem 7.8*h*, namely, that $B_{t1} - B_{t2} = \mu_0 J_{Sm}$.

The net uncanceled current density $\mathbf{J}_m$ in the interior of a piece of non-uniformly magnetized material may be calculated as follows. We may assume that **M** consists of n elementary loops per unit volume, each having the average value $\mathbf{m} = i\mathbf{S}$ of dipole moment, with components $m_x = iS_x$, $m_y = iS_y$, and $m_z = iS_z$, where i is a suitable average value of current, and S_x, S_y, and S_z are the average projections of the loop areas in the three directions. The net current $J_{mx}\,\Delta y\,\Delta z$ through a small area normal to the x-direction (Fig. 8.3*c*) then comes only from the components of the current loops whose planes are perpendicular to this area. Any loop that both enters and leaves the area contributes no net current; it is only those that circulate about the boundary that count.

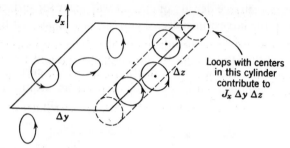

Fig. 8.3c. Only currents that go around the boundary of the area contribute to the current through it.

Along a side parallel to the z-axis, only currents whose normals are along z will count. Every loop whose center lies within a cylinder of length Δz and area S_z will surround the side in question. The total current contributed by this side will be

$$inS_z \, \Delta z = nm_z \, \Delta z = M_z \, \Delta z = \mathbf{M} \cdot \mathbf{\Delta l}$$

Thus the total current will be the circulation of $\mathbf{M}$, $\oint \mathbf{M} \cdot \mathbf{dl}$ around the area, and the current density J_z will be the z-component of the circulation density or curl of $\mathbf{M}$ (cf. Eq. A.2–43).

The same will hold for the other components, so we can write for the magnetization current density $\mathbf{J}_m$ the equation

$$\mathbf{J}_m = \nabla \times \mathbf{M} \tag{8.3–2a}$$

At a boundary, we can calculate the circulation of $\mathbf{M}$ around a path as shown in Fig. 8.3d, drawn in the plane of $\mathbf{M}$ and the normal to the boundary, $\mathbf{1}_n$. Then the circulation is just $M_t \, \Delta x$, plus terms dependent on Δy.

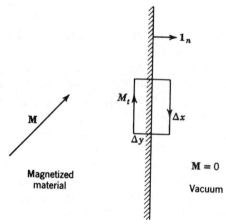

Fig. 8.3d. Calculation of $\mathbf{J}_{sm}$.

If the surface current density is J_{Sm}—it must be normal to the plane of the figure—the current surrounded by the path is $J_{Sm} \Delta x$. Thus letting $\Delta y \to 0$ we have the result for J_{Sm}

$$J_{Sm} = M_t \qquad (8.3\text{–}3a)$$

which confirms the qualitative statements made above about variously oriented boundaries. A vector form for J_{Sm} can be obtained by using the unit vector $\mathbf{1}_n$ normal to the surface. We have

$$\mathbf{J}_{Sm} = \mathbf{M} \times \mathbf{1}_n \qquad (8.3\text{–}3b)$$

(Compare with Problem 7.8h.)

Let us now show that the vector potential produced by magnetized material—e.g., a magnet—at any point is just that which the equivalent current densities $\mathbf{J}_m$ and $\mathbf{J}_{Sm}$ would produce. If in Eq. 8.2–1a we replace $\mathbf{m}$ by $\mathbf{M}\,d\tau$ and integrate, we have an expression for $\mathbf{A}$ as produced by the entire magnet:

$$\mathbf{A} = \frac{\mu_0}{4\pi} \int_\tau \frac{\mathbf{M} \times \mathbf{1}_r \, d\tau}{r^2} = -\frac{\mu_0}{4\pi} \int_\tau \mathbf{M} \times \mathbf{\nabla}\!\left(\frac{1}{r}\right) d\tau = \frac{\mu_0}{4\pi} \int_\tau \mathbf{M} \times \mathbf{\nabla}'\!\left(\frac{1}{r}\right) d\tau$$

$$(8.3\text{–}4)$$

where $\mathbf{\nabla}$ operates on (x, y, z) and $\mathbf{\nabla}'$ on (x', y', z').

Next let us use the identity $\mathbf{M} \times \mathbf{\nabla}'u = u\,\mathbf{\nabla}' \times \mathbf{M} - \mathbf{\nabla}' \times (u\mathbf{M})$ (Table A.2B, item 8) with $u = 1/r$,

$$\mathbf{A} = \frac{\mu_0}{4\pi} \int_\tau \frac{\mathbf{\nabla}' \times \mathbf{M}\, d\tau}{r} - \frac{\mu_0}{4\pi} \int_\tau \mathbf{\nabla}' \times \left(\frac{\mathbf{M}}{r}\right) d\tau$$

which by A.2–26 can be written

$$\mathbf{A} = \frac{\mu_0}{4\pi} \int_\tau \frac{\mathbf{\nabla}' \times \mathbf{M}\, d\tau}{r} + \frac{\mu_0}{4\pi} \int_S \frac{\mathbf{M} \times d\mathbf{S}}{r} \qquad (8.3\text{–}5a)$$

which by 8.3–2 and 8.3–3 is just

$$\mathbf{A} = \frac{\mu_0}{4\pi} \int_\tau \frac{\mathbf{J}_m\, d\tau}{r} + \frac{\mu_0}{4\pi} \int_S \frac{\mathbf{J}_{Sm}\, dS}{r} \qquad (8.3\text{–}6a)$$

as expected (cf. Eqs. 7.10–5). This equation holds for interior as well as exterior points in the neighborhood of a body of magnetic material. It is not, however, especially useful because of the complexity of calculating the vector $\mathbf{A}$ and then taking its curl in order to get the usually-desired $\mathbf{B}$.

The Maxwell-equation form of Ampère's law for points within magnetic material needs no modification if $\mathbf{J}_m$ is included in the total current density

J, but since the symbol **J** is usually reserved for macroscopic flow of charge excluding atomic current loops, we write

$$\mathbf{\nabla} \times \mathbf{B} = \mu_0\left(\mathbf{J} + \mathbf{J}_m + \frac{\partial \mathbf{D}}{\partial t}\right) = \mu_0\left(\mathbf{J} + \mathbf{\nabla} \times \mathbf{M} + \frac{\partial \mathbf{D}}{\partial t}\right) \quad (8.3\text{-}7a)$$

When the conduction and displacement currents are zero, we have $\mathbf{\nabla} \times \mathbf{B} = \mu_0\mathbf{J}_m$ from which we deduce that the quantity $\mathbf{B} - \mu_0\mathbf{M} = \mathbf{B} - \mathbf{P}_m$ has no curl:

$$\mathbf{\nabla} \times (\mathbf{B} - \mu_0\mathbf{M}) = \mathbf{\nabla} \times (\mathbf{B} - \mathbf{P}_m) = 0 \quad (8.3\text{-}8)$$

The quantity in parenthesis is a curl-free or irrotational vector, and is defined to be μ_0 times the magnetic field **H** inside magnetized material:

$$\mu_0\mathbf{H} = \mathbf{B} - \mathbf{P}_m = \mathbf{B} - \mu_0\mathbf{M} \quad (8.3\text{-}9a)$$

Since $\mathbf{\nabla} \times \mathbf{H} = 0$ we know that **H** can be calculated from a potential (cf. Section 1.8). The fact that the potential for **H** is just V_m and that the sources of **H** are magnetic poles will appear when we make the pole analysis in the next section.

Let us note in conclusion that Ampère's law 8.3–7 can be written without explicit reference to the magnetization current by using **H** instead of **B**, for we have in general

$$\mathbf{\nabla} \times \mathbf{H} = \mathbf{J} + \frac{\partial \mathbf{D}}{\partial t} \quad (8.3\text{-}10a)$$

The use of **H** in place of **B** to avoid explicit reference to magnetization is thus seen to be analogous to the case of **D** in place of **E** to avoid explicit reference to dielectric polarization.

The current analysis can also be used, together with $\mathbf{f}_\tau = \mathbf{J} \times \mathbf{B}$, to calculate the force and torque on a piece of magnetized material,[4] but we shall content ourselves with the pole-analysis method, to be given in Section 8.4.

In Gaussian units, **M** and $\mathbf{P}_m$ are taken as equal and are measured in gauss, with $\mathbf{M} = \mathbf{P}_m = i\mathbf{S}/c$, which leads to the magnetization current density

$$\mathbf{J}_m = c(\mathbf{\nabla} \times \mathbf{M}) \qquad \text{Gaussian} \quad (8.3\text{-}2b)$$

and the formulas for **A**:

$$\mathbf{A} = \int_\tau \frac{\mathbf{\nabla}' \times \mathbf{M}\, d\tau}{r} + \int_S \frac{\mathbf{M} \times \mathbf{dS}}{r} \qquad \text{Gaussian} \quad (8.3\text{-}5b)$$

and

$$\mathbf{A} = \frac{1}{c}\int_\tau \frac{\mathbf{J}_m\, d\tau}{r} + \frac{1}{c}\int_S \frac{\mathbf{J}_{Sm}\, dS}{r} \qquad \text{Gaussian} \quad (8.3\text{-}6b)$$

[4] The current-analysis method is worked out in E. R. Peck, *Electricity and Magnetism* McGraw-Hill, New York, 1953, sections 9.14–9.16.

Ampère's law in differential-equation form becomes

$$\nabla \times \mathbf{B} = \frac{4\pi}{c}\mathbf{J} + 4\pi\nabla \times \mathbf{M} + \frac{1}{c}\frac{\partial \mathbf{D}}{\partial t} \qquad \text{Gaussian} \quad (8.3\text{--}7b)$$

The vector $\mathbf{H}$ in Gaussian units is defined as

$$\mathbf{H} = \mathbf{B} - 4\pi\mathbf{M} \qquad \text{Gaussian} \quad (8.3\text{--}9b)$$

so that Ampère's law in terms of $\mathbf{H}$ becomes

$$\nabla \times \mathbf{H} = \frac{4\pi}{c}\mathbf{J} + \frac{1}{c}\frac{\partial \mathbf{D}}{\partial t} \qquad \text{Gaussian} \quad (8.3\text{--}10b)$$

8.4   The Pole Analysis of Magnetized Material

Since magnetized substances are closely similar in behavior to dielectric material, we can borrow the results of Sections 3.4 to 3.6 if we are careful in using the pole analysis to calculate fields far from individual atoms, which means *outside* the material (or in a cavity).[5] The field produced by a piece of magnetic material can be found, in terms of the scalar potential V_m, by substituting $\mathbf{p}_m = \mathbf{P}_m\, d\tau$ in Eq. 8.2–2b and integrating, making the same transformations as in Section 3.4. The result is the analogy of Eq. 3.4–4:

$$V_m = \int_S \frac{\mathbf{P}_m \cdot d\mathbf{S}}{4\pi\mu_0 r} - \int_\tau \frac{\nabla \cdot \mathbf{P}_m\, d\tau}{4\pi\mu_0 r} \qquad (8.4\text{--}1a)$$

which we could describe by saying that (a) the material contains on its surface S a "fictitious" or "effective" magnetic pole strength distribution of magnitude

$$\sigma_m = \mu_0 M_n = P_{mn} \qquad (8.4\text{--}2a)$$

where M_n and P_{mn} are the components of $\mathbf{M}$ and $\mathbf{P}_m$ normal to the surface; and (b) the material contains within its volume τ a distribution

$$\rho_m = -\mu_0 \nabla \cdot \mathbf{M} = -\nabla \cdot \mathbf{P}_m \qquad (8.4\text{--}3a)$$

Positive magnetic poles are called "north" or "north-seeking," and negative ones "south" or "south-seeking." Equations 8.4–2 and 8.4–3 can be said to constitute a definition of magnetic pole strength.

---

[5] The analysis which was given in the first part of Section 3.4 was originally given by Poisson for magnetic materials. See, for instance, Sir. E. T. Whittaker, *A History of Theories of Aether and Electricity*, Thomas Nelson, London, 1951, and Harper and Row, New York, 1960, Vol. I, pp. 63–65.

To find the force exerted by external fields on a magnetized piece of material, we can use the calculation at the end of Section 3.6. Starting with the use of Eq. 8.2–3c for a volume element $d\tau$,

$$\mathbf{dF} = \sum_i (\mathbf{m}_i \cdot \nabla)\mathbf{B} = (\mathbf{M} \cdot \nabla)\mathbf{B}\, d\tau \tag{8.4–4}$$

we end with the resultant force

$$\mathbf{F} = \int_S \mathbf{B}(\mathbf{M} \cdot \mathbf{dS}) - \int_\tau \mathbf{B}(\nabla \cdot \mathbf{M})\, d\tau \tag{8.4–5a}$$

$$= \int_S \mathbf{H}(\mathbf{P}_m \cdot \mathbf{dS}) - \int_\tau \mathbf{H}(\nabla \cdot \mathbf{P}_m)\, d\tau \tag{8.4–5b}$$

showing that we can find the forces on magnetic materials by use of the pole strengths σ_m and ρ_m. The vector $\mathbf{H} = \mathbf{B}/\mu_0$ of course is the externally produced field.

We shall not consider internal stresses and intermolecular forces, so that Eq. 8.4–5 applies only to entire, isolated bodies for which the sum of all internal forces is zero.

The torque on a piece of magnetized material is the sum of the torques on each separate dipole, by Eq. 8.2–4, plus the torque $\mathbf{r} \times \mathbf{dF}$ associated with the force on each dipole in accordance with the mechanical relation A.2–40. We have then

$$\mathbf{d\mathcal{T}} = [\mathbf{M} \times \mathbf{B} + \mathbf{r} \times (\mathbf{M} \cdot \nabla)\mathbf{B}]\, d\tau \tag{8.4–6}$$

which is to be integrated over the volume of the piece of material. The operator $(\mathbf{M} \cdot \nabla)$ is a scalar which can be factored out of the vector product if care is taken to indicate that ∇ operates only on $\mathbf{B}$. If we allow ∇ to operate on both $\mathbf{r}$ and $\mathbf{B}$, we can easily prove the vector relation (item 12 in Table A.2B, p. 633)

$$(\mathbf{M} \cdot \overline{\nabla})(\mathbf{r} \times \mathbf{B}) = [(\mathbf{M} \cdot \overline{\nabla})\mathbf{r}] \times \mathbf{B} + \mathbf{r} \times (\mathbf{M} \cdot \nabla)\mathbf{B}$$

This relation, together with the general relation for any vector $\mathbf{M}$ that $(\mathbf{M} \cdot \nabla)\mathbf{r} = \mathbf{M}$ (Problem A.2r), allows us to rewrite Eq. 8.4–6 as

$$\mathbf{d\mathcal{T}} = (\mathbf{M} \cdot \nabla)(\mathbf{r} \times \mathbf{B})\, d\tau \tag{8.4–7}$$

The same transformation can be made on the integral of this torque element as was made for the force element $\mathbf{dF} = (\mathbf{M} \cdot \nabla)\mathbf{B}\, d\tau$ with the result that the total torque is the sum of the integrals over the volume and surface pole densities multiplied by $\mathbf{r} \times \mathbf{H}$. That is, the torque on an isolated body can be found correctly from the pole strengths and the external field $\mathbf{H}$:

$$\mathscr{T} = \int_S (\mathbf{r} \times \mathbf{B})(\mathbf{M} \cdot d\mathbf{S}) - \int_\tau (\mathbf{r} \times \mathbf{B})(\nabla \cdot \mathbf{M}) \, d\tau \qquad (8.4\text{–}8a)$$

$$= \int_S (\mathbf{r} \times \mathbf{H})(\mathbf{P}_m \cdot d\mathbf{S}) - \int_\tau (\mathbf{r} \times \mathbf{H})(\nabla \cdot \mathbf{P}_m) \, d\tau \qquad (8.4\text{–}8b)$$

In the case of a uniform field a direct calculation is easy, for we need consider no torques to arise from $\mathbf{F} = (\mathbf{m} \cdot \nabla)\mathbf{B}$ (the derivatives in this expression are all zero) and can merely add the torques on each individual dipole. That is $\mathscr{T} = \sum_i \mathbf{m}_i \times \mathbf{B} = \tau\mathbf{M} \times \mathbf{B}$ for a uniform magnet, where τ is the volume.

We conclude that both for calculating fields outside magnetic materials and for finding external forces on them we can use the concept of magnetic pole, taking Eqs. 8.4–2 and 8.4–3 as definitions of pole strength and making calculations by analogy with electrostatics, using Eqs. 8.4–1, 8.4–5, and 8.4–8. In particular, we can use the results of Section 3.6 to get the external fields produced by permanent magnets.

Thus a circular-cylindrical bar of uniform magnetization $\mathbf{M}$ directed parallel to the axis of the bar will have a pole-strength distribution $\sigma_m = \pm(\mu_0 M)$ on each end, and a field on the axis analogous to that of Eq. 3.6–1. If the bar is also sufficiently slender, the total pole strengths $q_m = \sigma_m S$ on the two ends can be treated as point poles, their fields calculated by Coulomb's law, and forces on them found from $\mathbf{F} = q_m\mathbf{H}$. Actual bar magnets are rarely uniform in magnetization near the ends, and in fact $\nabla \cdot \mathbf{M}$ is generally not zero, with the result that there is a volume distribution ρ_m in these regions. For points not too near the magnet, each region can to a good approximation be replaced by a point pole. The field at great distances from any uniform or nearly uniform magnet will be a dipole field, namely that of a dipole located at the center of the magnet of moment given by the integral of $\mathbf{M}$ over the volume:

$$\mathbf{m} = \int_\tau \mathbf{M} \, d\tau \qquad (8.4\text{–}9)$$

For a uniform magnet, $\mathbf{m} = \mathbf{M}\tau$. The torque on it in a uniform field is

$$\mathscr{T} = \tau(\mathbf{M} \times \mathbf{B}) = \mathbf{m} \times \mathbf{B} = \mathbf{p}_m \times \mathbf{H} \qquad (8.4\text{–}10)$$

A uniformly magnetized sphere will have an external field even at points near its surface corresponding to that of a dipole of moment

$$\mathbf{m} = \tfrac{4}{3}\pi R^3 \mathbf{M} \qquad (8.4\text{–}11)$$

located at its center, in accordance with Section 3.6.

The magnetic shell, which is the equivalent of the disk electret, has already been treated. Let us make use of it to compare a solenoid to a bar magnet. If the helical winding of a long uniformly wound solenoid can be replaced without sensible error by a set of closed circular loops, we can then replace each loop by a magnetic disk. The resultant set of disks taken together form a cylindrical bar magnet. If there are n_l turns per meter in the original solenoid, the strength of the shell formed by the disks in a length dx will be $dM_S = n_l i\, dx$. The magnetic moment per unit volume

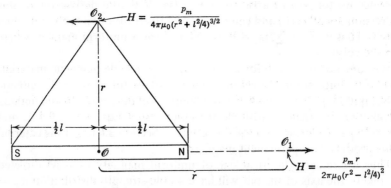

Fig. 8.4a. Illustrating the calculation of H outside a bar magnet.

will then be $dM_S/dx = n_l i$. Thus, the solenoid is equivalent to a uniform magnet whose magnetization is given by

$$M = n_l i \qquad (8.4\text{--}12)$$

We can confirm this statement by finding **H** outside the solenoid, on its axis, both from the direct calculation, Eq. 7.8–15 and by analogy from Eq. 3.6–3. By either method we find

$$H = \frac{M}{2}(\cos\theta_1 + \cos\theta_2) = \frac{n_l i}{2}(\cos\theta_1 + \cos\theta_2) \qquad (8.4\text{--}13)$$

where the angles θ_1 and θ_2 are to be found in Figs. 3.6a and 7.8j.

For a slender magnet or solenoid, the angles of Eq. 8.4–13 can be approximated in terms of the radius a of the bar and the distances $r + l/2$ and $r - l/2$ from the point where H is wanted ($\mathcal{O}_1$ in Fig. 8.4a) to the centers of the two end faces (r is the distance to the center of the bar, and l is its length). Alternatively, the field can be found by use of the pole strengths $q_m = \pm\mu_0 M\pi a^2$. The calculation is left to the reader (Problems 8.4a and b), the result being

$$H = p_m r/[2\pi\mu_0(r^2 - l^2/4)^2] \qquad (8.4\text{--}14)$$

where $p_m = q_m l = \mu_0 M \pi a^2 l$, the magnetic moment of the entire magnet or solenoid. If the pole strength is distributed over small regions near the ends, l represents the distance between the approximate centers of these distributions.

Another simple and useful calculation is that for the field at a distance r from the center of the bar on a line perpendicular to the axis. The pole method is the simplest for this case. We find (Problem 8.4b)

$$H = p_m/[4\pi\mu_0(r^2 + l^2/4)^{3/2}] \tag{8.4–15}$$

The similarity of Eqs. 8.4–14 and 8.4–15 to the expressions for the dipole fields at these points is evident. A dipole at $\mathcal{O}$ directed along SN would have a field at $\mathcal{O}_1$ given by the equivalent of Eq. 3.1–7a

$$H = p_m/2\pi\mu_0 r^3$$

and a field at $\mathcal{O}_2$ given by the equivalent of Eq. 3.1–7b:

$$H = p_m/4\pi\mu_0 r^3 \tag{8.4–16b}$$

We see that the dipole moment of the bar is the main factor in determining the field. The length l is of lesser importance at distances r that are by any appreciable amount larger than l. It is not always easy to locate the proper centers of the pole strengths so as to measure l; $\mathbf{p}_m$ can always be found with greater accuracy. The best way to find q_m is by the formula $q_m = \mathbf{p}_m/l$.[6]

In Gaussian units we have for the pot scalar potential produced by a magnet

$$V_m = \int_S \frac{\mathbf{M} \cdot d\mathbf{S}}{r} - \int_\tau \frac{\nabla \cdot \mathbf{M}\, d\tau}{r} \qquad \text{Gaussian} \quad (8.4–1b)$$

the surface pole density

$$\sigma_m = M_n \qquad \text{Gaussian} \quad (8.4–2b)$$

and the volume pole density

$$\rho_m = -\nabla \cdot \mathbf{M} \qquad \text{Gaussian} \quad (8.4–3b)$$

The force and torque formulas are

$$\mathbf{F} = \int_S \mathbf{H}(\mathbf{M} \cdot d\mathbf{S}) - \int_\tau \mathbf{B}(\nabla \cdot \mathbf{M})\, d\tau \qquad \text{Gaussian} \quad (8.4–5c)$$

$$\mathcal{T} = \int_S (\mathbf{r} \times \mathbf{H})(\mathbf{M} \cdot d\mathbf{S}) - \int_\tau (\mathbf{r} \times \mathbf{H})(\nabla \cdot \mathbf{M})\, d\tau \qquad \text{Gaussian} \quad (8.4–8c)$$

---

[6] For the application of these formulas to magnetometer measurements, see almost any laboratory manual; also F. K. Harris, *Electrical Measurements*, John Wiley, New York, 1952, pp. 356–360.

Problem 8.4a. Approximate $\cos \theta_1$ and $\cos (\pi - \theta_2) = -\cos \theta_2$ in Eq. 8.4–13 for the case of a slender bar of radius $a \ll l$, by using $\tan \theta_1 \simeq \theta_1$ etc, and derive Eq. 8.4–14.

Problem 8.4b. Derive Eqs. 8.4–14 and 8.4–15 by use of the pole concept.

Problem 8.4c. A very small compass is used to plot the lines of force about a horizontal bar magnet, lying approximately east and west on a large sheet of paper. Show about where a point of zero field should occur, taking the earth's field into account, and show how the value of H_e together with the location of this neutral point can provide a value for the magnetic moment of the magnet. Under what conditions would no neutral point be found?

Problem 8.4d. For what current would a needle in the center of a pair of Helmholtz coils (Problem 7.8f) arranged with their axis in the magnetic east-west direction be deflected 30° from the north direction if there are 10 turns in each coil, and the radius is 15 cm? The horizontal component of the earth's field is 0.18×10^{-4} weber/m².

Problem 8.4e. Two magnets of moments m_1 and m_2 are separated by a distance r large enough that each may be treated as a simple dipole. Find the force on each produced by the other if they lie (a) with their axes parallel and along $\mathbf{r}$; (b) if one lies with its axis along $\mathbf{r}$ and one with axis perpendicular to $\mathbf{r}$ and (c) if they are parallel but both axes are perpendicular to $\mathbf{r}$. (Cf. Problem 3.2e.)

Problem 8.4f. Find the torques on each magnet in the circumstances of Problem 8.4e.

Problem 8.4g. Explain why in certain cases in Problem 8.4f the torques are not equal and opposite.

Problem 8.4h. A cylindrical bar of length 8.0 cm and radius 0.5 cm has a magnetization $\mathbf{M}$ that is everywhere parallel to its axis, but whose value depends symmetrically on the distance x from the plane perpendicular to the axis and through its center, as follows: For $-0.030 < x < 0.030$ m, $P_m = 2.5 \times 10^{-2}$ weber/m²; for $0.030 < x < 0.040$ m, $P_m = 2.5 \times 10^{-2}$ $[1 - 0.3 \times 10^4 (x - 0.030)^2]$; and P_m has a similar variation for $-0.040 < x < -0.030$ m. Find the pole strength on the ends of the magnet and the volume density at distance x from the central plane. Find the total amount of positive pole. Find the dipole moment of the bar and hence the distance l to be used if the total pole strength of each sign is to be considered as concentrated at a point.

Problem 8.4i. A bar magnet whose length is 8.0 cm has effectively point poles on its ends of strengths ± 200 emu. Find the magnetic field at points 10 cm from the center of the bar (a) on the axis of the bar; (b) on a perpendicular to the axis; (c) on a line that makes an angle of 30° with the axis.

Problem 8.4j. How far away from the magnet in Problem 8.4i does the dipole formula for H fit the more accurate formula within 1% (a) along the axis and (b) along a perpendicular to the axis?

Problem 8.4k. Show that, if the exponent of $1/r$ in Eq. 8.2–7 is n instead of 2, the ratio of the expressions in Eqs. 8.4–16a and 8.4–16b is similarly modified. (This fact is used in Gauss' method of verifying Coulomb's law for poles.)

Problem 8.4l. A compass needle 3 cm long, 2 mm wide, and 1 mm thick has a uniform magnetization parallel to its length of $M = 0.32 \times 10^6$ amp/m. It is located midway between two parallel wires 12 cm apart, each carrying 30 amp but in opposite directions. Find the torque on the needle when it is parallel to the wires.

Problem 8.4m. Find the force on a thin uniform bar magnet produced by a point pole on the axis at a distance h from the near end of the magnet (a) by direct integration of Eq. 8.4–4 and (b) by use of the poles on the bar.

Problem 8.4n. The magnet of Problem 8.4i is held on the axis of a circular coil bearing 300 amp-turns (powered by a constant-current generator) whose radius is 12 cm. The magnet and the coil are oriented with their north poles towards each other. Find the force on the magnet in terms of the distance z between centers of coil and magnet. Find the work done in bringing the magnet to the center of the coil from infinity. How much work is then done by the generator?

8.5 B and H Inside Magnetic Material

The pole method breaks down when we try to calculate the magnetic induction **B** inside magnetic material, for we no longer deal with points that are far from all sources of field. Furthermore, a field calculated everywhere by the pole theory would have lines with beginnings and endings, which is a property not possessed by **B**. Although we have defined **B** in terms of the Lorentz force on a moving charge, this definition is a rather theoretical one inside matter, for any ordinary measurement of the force $q(\mathbf{v} \times \mathbf{B})$ would involve making a cavity of some sort. The situation is closely analogous to the problem of defining **E** in a dielectric medium by the equation $\mathbf{F} = q\mathbf{E}$. However, there are certain differences. High-speed charged particles can be allowed to pass through a piece of magnetized iron. Their resultant displacement can be measured, leading to a certain average value of **B** over the path taken by the particle. Neutrons, which are electrically neutral although each possesses a magnetic moment $\mathbf{m}_n$, can also be deflected within a piece of magnetic material, and a measure of an average of $(\mathbf{m}_n \cdot \nabla)\mathbf{B}$ thus obtained.

More importantly, the induced emf in a coil of wire around a piece of magnetic material can be readily measured, so that $d\Phi/dt$ can be found, where Φ is given by values of **A** outside the medium but can also be calculated by an integral $\int_S \mathbf{B} \cdot d\mathbf{S}$ over a surface which passes through the medium.

We can say, therefore, that to a limited extent we *can* measure **B** in the medium. We can certainly define it as an average over all points in a region of suitable size of the induction produced by all sources. We are chiefly interested, however, in expressing **B** in the medium in terms of the field in suitable cavities. We maintain the similarity to the electrostatic case by defining **H** as an auxiliary field vector that is calculated from the pole strengths introduced in the last section, as well as from currents in circuits that we do not choose to treat in terms of poles. This auxiliary field, like **D** in the dielectric case, is of considerable use even if it does not give a force on a unit of any existing physical entity.

If we consider a slot or coin-shaped cavity oriented in any direction, we see that the component of **B** normal to the slot surfaces is the same in the slot as in the medium, but the tangential component differs by $\mu_0 J_{Sm}$ in accordance with the result of Problem 7.8h. In fact, we can write boundary conditions in general

$$B_{n1} = B_{n2} \tag{8.5-1}$$

$$B_{t1} - B_{t2} = \mu_0 J_{Sm} = \mu_0 M_t = \mu_0 \left| \mathbf{M} \times \mathbf{1}_n \right| \tag{8.5-2}$$

where in the second equation we have used Eq. 8.3–3 (cf. Problem 3.5a concerning $D_{t1} - D_{t2}$).

The flux through a coil wound around a magnetic core can therefore be calculated by imagining a thin slot to be cut through the core and finding the flux through a surface lying in the slot. Or, we may simply imagine a Gaussian surface passed through the core that does not cut any atoms, as being equivalent to one in a slot. Of course, if we have a slot cut perpendicular to **M**, M_t will be zero, and **B** itself will be the same in the slot as in the medium.

We can calculate **B** in such a slot by the pole method, since points in the slot are removed from the neighborhood of any atom. But by a calculation identical with that for Eq. 3.4–6, the field $\mathbf{B}/\mu_0 = \mathbf{H}_{\text{slot}}$ can be written

$$\frac{\mathbf{B}}{\mu_0} = \frac{\mathbf{B}_{\text{slot}}}{\mu_0} = \mathbf{H}_{\text{slot}} = \mathbf{H} + \frac{\mathbf{P}_m}{\mu_0} = \mathbf{H} + \mathbf{M} \tag{8.5-3}$$

where **H** is the field calculated from all the pole strength on the material except that on the cavity walls and from all other sources of magnetic field outside the piece of material in question. The term **M** in Eq. 8.5–3 gives the contribution from the pole strength $\sigma_m = \pm\mu_0 M_n$ on the surfaces of the cavity.

In a needle-like drill-hole cavity parallel to $\mathbf{M}$, there will be no contribution to $\mathbf{B}$ from local equivalent pole strength. Therefore we have

$$\frac{\mathbf{B}_{hole}}{\mu_0} = \mathbf{H}_{hole} = \mathbf{H} \qquad (8.5\text{-}4)$$

The induction will be reduced from that in the medium, because the equivalent surface current $J_{Sm} = M_t = M$ on the side of the drill hole runs in a direction to produce a field within the cavity in the opposite direction to $\mathbf{M}$. Another way of seeing this result is to consider that such a hole does not pass through any elementary current loop, whereas most of the flux will pass through these currents. The average flux taken across a small drill hole will not be a proper average, for it will overweight the spaces between the atomic currents against their interiors. Furthermore, just as in the dielectric case, the component of $\mathbf{B}/\mu_0$ parallel to the axis of an arbitrarily directed drill hole is seen on the pole analysis to be the component of $\mathbf{H}$ in that direction and is seen to be identical with $\mathbf{H}$ as defined in Eq. 8.3-9.

Finally, consider the average induction $\mathbf{B}$ that acts on a piece of magnetic material. For the dielectric case, we showed in Section 3.9 that for spherical symmetry the average field acting on a piece of material is $\mathbf{E} + \mathbf{P}/3\epsilon_0$. Therefore, by the identical calculation we must have the average field $\mathbf{H}_{eff}$ acting on a spherical piece of magnetic material equal to $\mathbf{H} + \mathbf{P}_m/3\mu_0$.[7] We should expect the properties of the medium to be expressible in terms of a relation between the average moment $\mathbf{m}$ of an atom or molecule and this $\mathbf{H}_{eff}$. Such a relation, can, however, be directly transformed into a relation between $\mathbf{H}$ and $\mathbf{M}$. Thus we see that $\mathbf{H}$ not only appears in the formulas for the cavity fields, but also can be used in a similar way to $\mathbf{E}$ for dielectrics in describing experimental results on magnetizability.

Therefore we see that $\mathbf{H}$ is a vector field calculated *everywhere*, inside a medium and out, from poles on magnetic media and from laboratory or macroscopic currents. Inside a magnet, $\mathbf{H}$ is equal to the value of $\mathbf{B}/\mu_0$ in a thin tunnel parallel to $\mathbf{M}$, and its component parallel to the sides of a tunnel with any orientation is equal to the corresponding component of $\mathbf{B}/\mu_0$.

Our analogy to electrostatics is now complete. The vectors $\mathbf{E}$ and $\mathbf{H}$ can be calculated in the same way for dielectrics and for magnetizable material, and $\mathbf{D}$ and $\mathbf{B}$ can be found from them in the same way. However,

[7] If spherical symmetry does not hold, the factor $1/3$ will be changed. Spherical symmetry may obtain in some cases for regions containing large numbers of elementary crystals, but for smaller regions in iron and similar materials it certainly fails (see Section 8.7).

we should reiterate that the two fundamental vectors are **E** and **B** and that **D** and **H** are auxiliary vectors that are useful but do not represent forces on physical entities. Finally, of course, **E** has contributions from free charges, whereas **H** has contributions from ordinary conduction currents, and also from displacement currents.

Let us, in fact, make another calculation of the curl of **H**. By Eq. 7.9–2, applied to a path lying in a needle-like tunnel through the medium, $\oint \mathbf{H} \cdot \mathbf{dl} = \oint \mathbf{B} \cdot \mathbf{dl}/\mu_0$ is equal to all the current surrounded. But such a tunnel surrounds *no atomic currents*, so that we can write the circuital form of Ampère's law as

$$\mathscr{H} = \oint \mathbf{H} \cdot \mathbf{dl}' = \sum_k i_k + \frac{d\Phi_D}{dt} \qquad (8.5\text{–}4a)$$

where the currents i_k refer to macroscopic currents only, and the displacement current is included for completeness. The quantity $\mathscr{H}$ is called the "magnetomotive force" or mmf, in analogy with induced emf. Its unit in the MKS system is the ampere, more commonly called the ampere-turn because the sum in Eq. 8.5–4a becomes ni for a coil of n turns carrying a current i.

If now Eq. 8.5–4a is applied to an arbitrary infinitesimal loop, we can in the usual way derive again the Maxwell equation 8.3–10a.

The boundary conditions for **B** and **H** are similar to those for **D** and **E**. The tangential component of **H** is the same on both sides of a boundary provided no large-scale currents run along the boundary surface:

$H_{t1} = H_{t2}$ (at a magnetic boundary that
is free of macroscopic currents)   (8.5–5)

The normal components of **H** differ by the difference in M_n's (cf. Problem 3.5a):

$$H_{n1} - H_{n2} = M_{n2} - M_{n1} \qquad (8.5\text{–}6)$$

Gauss' law for **D** in electrostatics has the analogue $\int_{\text{closed } S} \mathbf{B} \cdot \mathbf{dS} = 0$ or div **B** = 0, reflecting of course the fact that no free magnetic poles exist. Another feature of electrostatics whose analogue has not yet been given is Gauss' law for **E**. We can clearly derive a result for **H** that

$$\oint_{\text{closed } S} \mathbf{H} \cdot \mathbf{dS} = \frac{1}{\mu_0} \sum_k q_{m,k} \qquad (8.5\text{–}7)$$

where the sum can be replaced by surface and volume integrals wherever appropriate. The corresponding differential relationship is

$$\nabla \cdot \mathbf{H} = \frac{\rho_m}{\mu_0} \qquad (8.5\text{–}8)$$

which also follows directly from div **B** = 0 and div $\mathbf{P}_m = -\rho_m$.

The H field inside a magnet can be found by comparison with the electret case. In particular, the **H** inside a uniformly magnetized cylindrical bar lies in the opposite direction to **B** and is given in some detail by the formulas for **E** in Section 3.6. The strong reverse field just inside the ends of the bar provides a negative effective field acting on any given atom, of magnitude $\mathbf{H}_{eff} \simeq -\frac{1}{2}\mathbf{M} + \frac{1}{3}\mathbf{M} = -\frac{1}{6}\mathbf{M}$.[8] This field is called the "demagnetizing field" and accounts for the tendency of permanent magnets to lose their magnetization. The same thing of course holds true for electrets. The demagnetizing field will be discussed further in Section 8.7.

Lines of **H** evidently may either end on poles or continuously circulate, only coming back on themselves in ideally symmetric cases. In this respect they resemble lines of **E** that may have both electrostatic and electromagnetic origin.

The Gaussian equation for the circuital law and the magnetomotive force is

$$\mathscr{H} = \oint \mathbf{H} \cdot \mathbf{dl} = \frac{4\pi}{c} \sum_k i_k + \frac{1}{c} \frac{d\Phi_D}{dt} \quad \text{Gaussian} \quad (8.5\text{-}4b)$$

The Gaussian unit of mmf is called the gilbert.

Problem 8.5a. Prove Eqs. 8.5–5 and 8.5–6.

Problem 8.5b. A uniform cylindrical bar magnet, 20 cm long and 4 cm in diameter, has a total magnetic moment p_m equal to 10^{-8} weber-meter. Find the field that acts on a small sphere of material (a) at the center of the bar, and (b) just inside one end. Also find **B** and **H** at each of these positions.

Problem 8.5c. Prove the formula $\mu_0(\mathbf{H} + \mathbf{M})$ for the induction **B** inside a piece of magnetized material by considering first the field due to the material outside a sphere of suitable size, as in Section 3.4, and second the field produced by the sphere itself at its center. For the latter, show that an integral $\int \mathbf{B} \, d\tau$ over the field of a magnetic dipole at the center of a sphere is required, and reduce this integral by use of Eqs. A.2–26 and 8.2–1a.

Problem 8.5d. Find **B** and **H** in the interior and also outside an iron sphere uniformly magnetized parallel to a certain direction. Also find $\mathbf{J}_m$ and $\mathbf{J}_{Sm}$.

Problem 8.5e. Find **B** and **H** inside a uniformly magnetized circular disk with **M** normal to its plane. (Neglect edge effects.)

Problem 8.5f. A spherical shell of internal radius a and external radius b is magnetized along the radius, with $\mathbf{M} = k\mathbf{r}$, where k is a constant. Find ρ_m, σ_m, **B** and **H** wherever they do not vanish.

---

[8] The $\frac{1}{3}$ and $\frac{1}{6}$ will be different for cases without spherical symmetry.

Problem 8.5g. A cylindrical rod of magnetic material whose radius is a and length is l is magnetized so that the lines of $\mathbf{M}$ are circles coaxial with the cylinder, with $M = Kr$, where K is a constant. Calculate ρ_m, σ_m, $\mathbf{J}_m$, and $\mathbf{J}_{Sm}$ wherever they do not vanish, and find $\mathbf{B}$ and $\mathbf{H}$ inside the cylinder.

8.6 Properties of Magnetic Materials

We have seen that the value of $\mathbf{H}$ within a medium is a suitable quantity to which we can relate the production and variation of $\mathbf{M}$. However, it is usually more convenient to relate $\mathbf{B}$ and $\mathbf{H}$ than $\mathbf{M}$ and $\mathbf{H}$, just as we use $\mathbf{D}$ and $\mathbf{E}$ in place of $\mathbf{P}$ and $\mathbf{E}$ for dielectrics.

Let us consider how we can measure $\mathbf{B}$, $\mathbf{M}$, and $\mathbf{H}$ for a given piece of material whose properties are to be studied. Now $\mathbf{H}$ is the field produced by poles and laboratory currents; in order to make meaningful measurements, the effects of poles on the sample in question must be eliminated because knowledge of them depends on knowledge of the properties being measured. The use of poles on other objects, as in permanent magnets or iron cores of electromagnets, is often unsatisfactory since the presence of the sample may alter these other pole strengths.

The simplest way of eliminating poles in the sample is to make the material in question in the form of a ring and magnetize it so that $\mathbf{M}$ is (at least approximately) directed parallel to its surface, making $\sigma_m = 0$. If the ring is homogeneously magnetized, $\nabla \cdot \mathbf{M}$ will also vanish, so that $\rho_m = 0$. Then by the methods of Section 7.8 $\mathbf{H}$ can be found from the current in a coil wrapped uniformly around the ring.

A way of reducing the effect of the poles, while not eliminating them, is to use a piece of material in the form of a very slender rod, so that the pole field over most of the specimen is very small compared with the external field. In this case, it is important either to measure the magnetization M in the center of the rod or to measure an average of M throughout, say by measuring the total moment $\mathbf{m}$ of the specimen.

If the magnetization is very weak, it may be possible to disregard the pole field altogether, so that weakly magnetic materials can be studied in any shapes. In this case, $\mathbf{H}$ may be a field of any sort—e.g., a field between the poles of a strong magnet.

The measurement of $\mathbf{B}$ is made by use of the emf generated in a suitable coil wound around a specimen. The quantity actually detected is of course $d\Phi/dt$, where Φ is the entire flux through the test coil. Thus we do not study $\mathbf{B}$ itself but the rate of change of its average over an appropriate surface in the material. If the material is sufficiently homogeneous, the average will have a good physical meaning, with respect to a study of the intrinsic magnetic properties of the material.

The coil in such a case is usually connected to some type of galvanometer (see Section 8.9). The galvanometer will have a certain resistance and also an inductance. Furthermore, the coil itself will have inductance that is not related to the flux we are measuring. Indeed, if the current that flows in the measuring circuit is not sufficiently small, the measurement will be interfered with. Let us then assume that the current is small, and let L and R be the *total* inductance and resistance in the measuring circuit. The equation for the circuit is then (treating $d\Phi/dt$ as a positive emf)

$$\frac{d\Phi}{dt} = L\frac{di}{dt} + iR \qquad (8.6\text{--}1)$$

Let us multiply both sides of the equation by dt and integrate over an arbitrary time interval (writing $i = dQ/dt$)

$$\int d\Phi = L\int di + R\int dQ$$

$$\Delta\Phi = L\,\Delta i + RQ \qquad (8.6\text{--}2)$$

where $\Delta\Phi$, Δi, and Q are respectively the change in flux, the change in current, and the charge that passed around the circuit, in the arbitrary time interval. We see by Eq. 8.6–2 that it is the change of flux that can be measured and that, if we measure this change from a time when i is zero to another time when i also is zero (so that $\Delta i = 0$), we can reduce the problem of flux measurement to measurement of Q and knowledge of R. The inductance, which even for small currents depends on the specimen being studied, does not appear in the final result. The result is

$$Q = \frac{\Delta\Phi}{R} \qquad (8.6\text{--}3)$$

for the charge Q passing any point of the circuit while Φ changes by $\Delta\Phi$. Methods of measuring Q will be treated in Section 8.9.

Since only changes in flux are measured, there is a constant Φ_0 which is not directly known. This constant is usually made equal to zero by the process of treating the sample symmetrically with respect to two opposite directions by continued reversals of $\mathbf{H}$.

The value of $\mathbf{M}$ for a sample in the form of a slender rod can be measured directly by finding the field produced by its total moment $\mathbf{m}$ at a distant magnetometer. The field $\mathbf{H}$ of the magnetizing coil needs to be balanced out by use of another similar coil on the other side of the magnetometer needle. If the sample is weakly magnetized and sufficiently small, we can measure the force on it when it is placed in an inhomogeneous field, and relate the moment $\mathbf{m}$ calculated from $\mathbf{F} = (\mathbf{m} \cdot \nabla)\mathbf{H}$ to the value of $\mathbf{H}$ at its center or to an average of $\mathbf{H}$ taken over its volume (cf. Problem 8.6a).

Diamagnetic and Paramagnetic Materials. Measurements of the last-mentioned type show that nearly all substances can be classified into two general groups as regards their magnetic properties. One group, comprising the diamagnetic and paramagnetic materials, is very weakly magnetic and is linear and isotropic in behavior, so that **M**, **H**, and **B** are all proportional. The other group, consisting of the ferromagnetic substances, is very strongly magnetic, and its representatives are all decidedly nonlinear. The exceptions consist of some very strongly paramagnetic salts and various substances exhibiting antiferromagnetism and ferrimagnetism (see the end of Section 8.7).

For the linear materials, we can write

$$\mathbf{B} = \mu\mathbf{H} \tag{8.6-4}$$

and by analogy with $\kappa = \epsilon/\epsilon_0$, set

$$\mu_r = \mu/\mu_0 \tag{8.6-5}$$

Furthermore, we shall set for the proportionality of **M** and **H** in both systems of units

$$\mathbf{M} = \chi_m\mathbf{H} \tag{8.6-6}$$

from which with $\mathbf{B} = \mu_0(\mathbf{H} + \mathbf{M})$ we deduce readily that

$$1 + \chi_m = \mu_r \tag{8.6-7a}$$

The quantity μ is called the permeability of the medium, μ_r the relative permeability, and χ_m the magnetic susceptibility.

Diamagnetic substances are those for which $\mu_r < 1$ or χ_m is negative. As indicated in Section 7.18, these substances are those whose atoms or molecules have no appreciable permanent magnetic moments that can line themselves up with an applied field, so that the diamagnetic effect of induced emfs in all the circulating currents prevails. Paramagnetic substances have small positive values of χ_m. Their molecules have permanent magnetic moments, which will precess in gyroscopic fashion about the direction of an applied field. Under the influence of thermal agitation these elementary magnets will undergo a preponderance of quantized energy exchanges that line them up with the field.

Tables 8.6A and 8.6B list the diamagnetic and paramagnetic susceptibilities for a number of common substances. It will be seen that the latter are numerically larger than the former but nevertheless always very small compared to 1.

A small paramagnetic object placed in an inhomogeneous magnetic field will be attracted toward the strongest part of the field, in similar fashion to the small dielectric object considered in Section 3.8, where the force as

Table 8.6A   Susceptibilities of Diamagnetic Materials

	χ_m
Antimony	-7.0×10^{-5}
Bismuth	-1.7×10^{-4}
Copper	-0.94×10^{-5}
Lead	-1.7×10^{-5}
Mercury	-3.2×10^{-5}
Quartz	-1.5×10^{-5}
Silver	-2.6×10^{-5}
Water	-0.88×10^{-5}
Argon (NTP)	-0.95×10^{-8}
Hydrogen (NTP)	-0.21×10^{-8}

NTP = Normal temperature (0°C) and pressure (1 atm)

Table 8.6B   Susceptibilities of Paramagnetic Materials

	χ_m
Aluminum	0.21×10^{-4}
Neodymium	3.0×10^{-3}
Oxygen (liquid at -182°C)	4.0×10^{-3}
Palladium	8.2×10^{-4}
Platinum	2.9×10^{-4}
Air (NTP)	3.6×10^{-7}
Oxygen (NTP)	17.9×10^{-7}

given by Eq. 3.8–8 is proportional to the susceptibility χ. A diamagnetic object, on the other hand, will experience a force toward the weaker part of the field, since χ_m is then negative. It is not easy to measure the small forces involved, but if a small rod of material is suspended on a light thread attached to its center of gravity, the torque on the rod can be observed. When the non-uniformity of the field is of the sort produced by two fairly small poles widely separated and the rod is suspended midway between, it is easy to see that a paramagnetic rod will line up along the field and a diamagnetic one will set itself across the field. (Fig. 8.6a).

On the other hand, a field of the opposite type of inhomogeneity will produce opposite tendencies for the two types of substances (Fig. 8.6b). It is therefore quite easy to test for the sign of χ_m for a given material by delicately suspending a rod made of it in a suitably shaped field of a strong magnet.

The effect on paramagnetic and diamagnetic rods in a uniform field is much weaker. As shown in Problem 3.8c, a dielectric rod will tend to line itself along the lines of a uniform electric field. The magnetization is proportional in the magnetic case to χ_m, and the angle between the resulting magnetization and the external field is nearly proportional to χ_m. Hence,

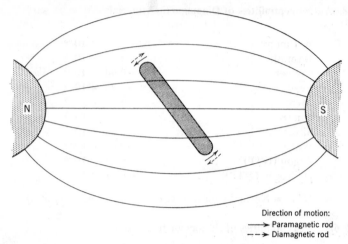

Direction of motion:
———▶ Paramagnetic rod
——▶ Diamagnetic rod

Fig. 8.6a.   An inhomogeneous field weaker in its center. [Adapted from A. R. Laufer, *Am. Journ. Phys.*, **19**, 275 (1951).]

as in Problem 3.8d, the torque is proportional to χ_m^2 and is in the same sense for both types of materials. The small values of χ_m for most materials make this second-order effect hard to observe.

The case of a paramagnetic fluid (e.g., gaseous or liquid oxygen) surrounding a group of permanent magnets is even more difficult to handle than the case of free charges immersed in a dielectric medium, both because the magnetic case is inherently more complicated than the electric and because isolated poles can only be approximately realized by means of very long thin magnets. Therefore the use of Coulomb's law for poles with μ in place of μ_0 is even less meaningful, aside from the fact that relative paramagnetic and diamagnetic permeabilities in most cases differ

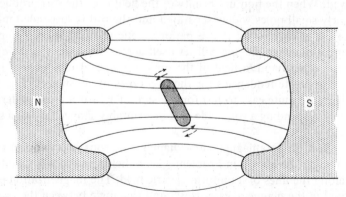

Fig. 8.6b.   An inhomogeneous field stronger in its center. (Adapted from Laufer, *loc. cit.*)

so little from 1. Therefore we shall not treat the case of paramagnetic fluids in the presence of permanent magnets.

However, the case of a magnetic material which behaves at least approximately like an ideal paramagnetic medium and which fills all the field-occupied space near non-magnetic wires carrying currents is quite easy to handle, for in this case B is simply μ_r times the B that would be produced in empty space, or $B = \mu H$. Thus self-inductance and mutual-inductance formulas can all have μ_0 replaced by μ. It should be clear from the discussion in Section 3.8 that this substitution will only be correct if there are no boundaries present that carry poles.

Ferromagnetic Materials. These materials are not only non-linear, but their magnetization also depends on their previous history. Even if the material is prepared in an isotropic way by making it suitably random with respect to crystal structure—relieving strains produced in rolling and cutting by appropriate heat treatments—any magnetization previous to the time that the material is set up for study will be partially retained in both magnitude and direction. Actually, most such materials are not isotropic and are studied with respect to magnetization in one or more directions of interest.

Let us describe the properties of such substances, therefore, by considering first a ring made of an unmagnetized, homogeneous, isotropic piece of iron, cobalt, or nickel or a related alloy. (Some alloys of iron are strongly paramagnetic but *not* ferromagnetic—e.g., certain stainless steels.) Since ferromagnetism always disappears above a certain temperature characteristic of the material in question, it is not hard to obtain such an unmagnetized sample by suitable heat treatment.[9] Let us apply a field H to the ring by means of a current in the coil and increase it steadily to some maximum value H_{max}. By measuring $\Delta \Phi$ and taking Φ_0 to be zero, we can plot B versus H. (Because of the isotropic behavior of the material, B will be parallel to H.) We get an initial magnetization curve somewhat like that labeled 1 in Fig. 8.6c. If now we reduce H to zero and increase it negatively to $-H_{max}$, we get curve 2, showing that B does not go to zero when H does. The material "remembers" its magnetization. Another reversal will yield curve 3, which shows some memory of the negative B. Continued repetition leads ultimately to a symmetrical loop, shown dashed in the figure, which is known as a "hysteresis loop." In practice, 20 or 30 reversals may be necessary to erase any "memory" of previous magnetizations.

The hysteresis loop is the most reproducible indication of the properties of any given magnetic material, so we shall restrict ourselves to descriptions of magnetic properties based on such loops. There is a different loop for

---

[9] Some alloys are permanently changed by such heating and must be demagnetized by the methods described later in this section.

each value of H_{max}; a series of such loops for varying values of H_{max} will describe the behavior of the material in fairly general terms (Fig. 8.6d shows such a series). The curve drawn through the tips of the loops is called a "normal magnetization curve." It is not identical with curve 1 in Fig. 8.5c but differs from it only slightly. In fact, the material cannot be made to follow a normal magnetization curve directly, but this curve provides a very useful approximate account of the behavior of the material.

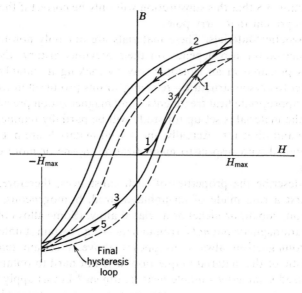

Fig. 8.6c. The development of a regular hysteresis loop.

For any particular loop, there are two points that are of particular interest. The value of $|B|$ for $H = 0$ is called the "residual induction,"[10] B_r. The value of $|H|$ for $B = 0$ is called the "coercive force" H_c, representing the reverse external field needed to reduce B to zero (cf. Fig. 8.6e).

As loops are taken for larger and larger values of H_{max}, their upper ends approach a straight line of the form $B = \mu_0(H + M_{sat})$ where M_{sat} is a constant and must evidently represent a maximum possible value of M for the material in question. The quantity M_{sat} is called the saturation magnetization. The shape of a hysteresis loop except for its tips remains unchanged for values of H_{max} above that for which $M = M_{sat}$. The terms "residual induction" and "coercive force" are commonly taken in the literature to refer to maximum values obtained from any loop involving

---

[10] Also called "retentivity," "remanent induction," or "remanence."

saturation. Substances with large H_c are said to be magnetically "hard," whereas those with small coercive force are called "soft."

The portion of a saturation hysteresis loop for which B is positive but H is negative is called a *demagnetization curve* and is important in the study and design of permanent magnets (cf. Section 8.8).[11]

For purposes of ferromagnetic theory, hysteresis loops are often constructed by plotting M vs H. However, for most materials, μ_r is of the

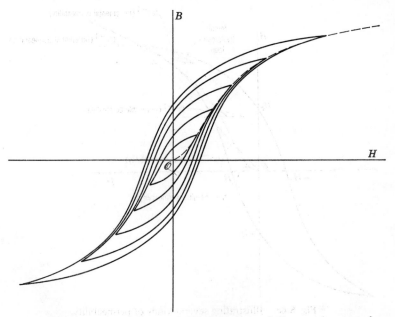

Fig. 8.6d. A set of hysteresis loops of differing values of H_{max}, and a normal magnetization curve (dashed).

order of several hundreds, up to 10^6, and the difference between B and $\mu_0 M$ is negligible, especially in comparison to the variations among samples with composition, heat treatment, and age. Although the shapes of hysteresis loops differ widely from one substance to another, the upper ends of most curves have a hyperbolic shape. The demagnetization curves can also be fitted closely by hyperbolas.

Various kinds of permeability may be defined from a hysteresis loop (see Fig. 8.6e). One may define the *ordinary* or *normal permeability* μ to be B/H for the tip of the loop—that is, for a point on the normal magnetization curve (μ is not used for other points on the loop). Graphs of μ as a

[11] D. E. Gray, ed., *American Institute of Physics Handbook,* 2nd ed., McGraw-Hill, New York, 1963, pp. 5–179, gives demagnetization curves for several materials.

function of H_{max} or B_{max} are frequently given in the literature (see Fig. 8.6j). The *differential permeability* is the slope dB/dH of the magnetization curve. Its value for $H = B = 0$ is called the *initial permeability*. If a steady value of H is applied to a specimen and then a small alternating H is superimposed, a minor hysteresis loop will be followed that has its center near the original point on the B–H graph to which the specimen was taken (approximately but usually not exactly on the normal curve). The slope

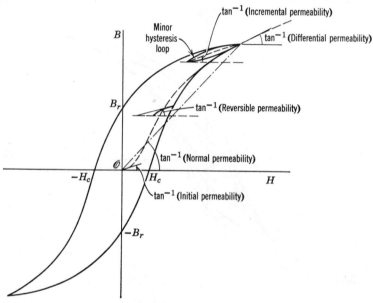

Fig. 8.6e.   Illustrating several kinds of permeability.

of the line connecting the tips of this minor loop is the *incremental permeability*. This quantity is useful for describing the effect of an alternating current in an iron-core coil when a large steady current is also present. A careful measurement of the slope $\Delta B/\Delta H$ of the line obtained by taking the material to a certain point on the hysteresis loop and then reversing the field by a slight amount $-\Delta H$ yields the *reversible permeability* μ_{rev}. It is slightly less than the incremental permeability. The reversible susceptibility $\chi_m = (\mu_{rev}/\mu_0) - 1$ is a quantity important in the development of thermodynamic magnetic theory. The *effective alternating-current permeability* is a suitable average ratio of B/H for the entire loop. One may estimate it by drawing some suitable straight line through the origin roughly parallel to the sides of the loop, or one may calculate an appropriate analytical average, depending on the experimental circuit arrangement for defining and measuring this permeability.

Finally, the area of a hysteresis loop is significant, as it represents the energy used up in carrying a unit volume of material around the loop. To see this, let us magnetize the sample in a coil and calculate the power expended against the back emf produced by the induction B. The work done will be

$$W = -\oint_{\text{one cycle}} \mathscr{E} i \, dt = \oint_{\text{cycle}} dt \cdot i \cdot \frac{d\Phi}{dt} = \oint_{\text{cycle}} i \, d\Phi$$

Let us divide all the flux in the material and surrounding space into tubes, each carrying a small amount $\Phi_1, \Phi_2 \cdots$. Let the kth tube link the circuit n_k times. Then

$$W = \oint_{\text{cycle}} i \, d\left[\sum_k n_k \Phi_k\right] = \oint_{\text{cycle}} \sum_k n_k i \, d\Phi_k$$

We can replace $n_k i$ by the mmf $\oint \mathbf{H}_k \cdot \mathbf{dl}_k$, taken along the kth tube of flux. We can also write $\Phi_k = B_k \, \Delta S_k$, where ΔS_k is the cross-sectional area of the kth tube at any point along it, and B_k is the induction at that point. If we assume $\mathbf{B}$ to be parallel to $\mathbf{H}$, we set $\mathbf{H}_k \cdot \mathbf{dl}_k = H_k \, dl_k$ and can finally write

$$W = \oint_{\text{cycle}} \sum_k \oint_{\text{tube}} H_k \, dl_k \, d(B_k \, \Delta S_k) = \sum_k \oint_{\text{tube}} d\tau \oint_{\text{cycle}} H_k \, dB_k$$

$$= \int_\tau d\tau \oint_{\text{cycle}} H \, dB \qquad (8.6\text{–}8)$$

assuming further that we can take the area of the tubes as constant in time. We have written $dl_k \, \Delta S_k = d\tau$, and by summing over k obtained an integral over the volume τ of the specimen. But, as shown in Fig. 8.6f, the integral $\oint H \, dB$ is the area of the loop, all areas outside it canceling in the calculation.

Thus if a continually alternating current is used to produce H, the energy lost per cycle can be found from the area. This energy goes of course into heating the material. A graph of areas against H or B is another useful representation of the properties of a magnetic substance. The situation is complicated by the fact that induced currents in the material of the core ("eddy currents") will tend to produce an opposite H in the sample and require a larger applied one for the same B, so that a loop measured with alternating currents will be fatter along the H-axis than one measured by the methods of this chapter by an amount that depends on the resistivity and structure of the magnetic material and on the frequency.

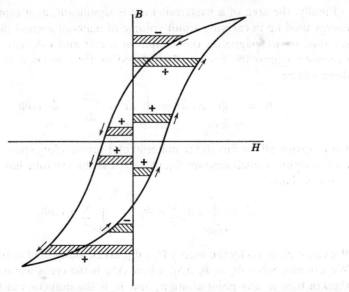

Fig. 8.6f. A hysteresis loop, showing various positions of elements of area $H\,dB$ for the integral $\int H\,dB$. The direction of integration and the signs of the resulting contributions are indicated.

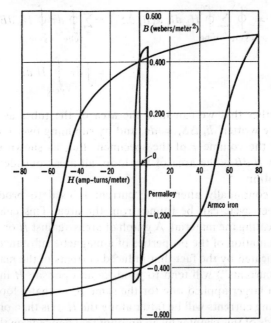

Fig. 8.6g. Hysteresis curves for permalloy and Armco iron. [Adapted from H. D. Arnold and G. W. Elmen, *Journ. Frank. Inst.*, **195**, 630 (1923).]

Figures 8.6g, h, i, and j, show hysteresis loops, magnetization curves, and permeability curves for a selected group of magnetic materials. Tables 8.6C and 8.6D list relevant properties of these materials.[12]

The proper method for demagnetizing a piece of iron is to establish it in a hysteresis loop large enough to erase the memory of previous magnetizations (including any in other directions) and then to continue a great many reversals of H while slowly reducing H_{max} to a low value—that is,

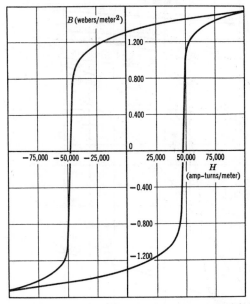

Fig. 8.6h.   A hysteresis curve for Alnico V. [Adapted from P. P. Cioffi, *Rev. Sci. Inst.*, **21**, 624 (1950).]

to a value small compared to subsequent values of H that will be applied. A convenient method for performing this operation is to place the specimen in the field of a strong electromagnet operated on 60-cycle alternating current, and then to remove the specimen slowly from the electromagnet. Sometimes a repetition of this operation will help in reducing more completely the "memory" of magnetizations in various directions.

[12] A more complete description of a variety of steels and alloys is given in S. S. Attwood, *Electric and Magnetic Fields*, 3rd ed., John Wiley, New York, 1949, Chapters 13 and 14; See also *American Institute of Physics Handbook*, op. cit., Section 5g, and A. H. Morrish, *The Physical Principles of Magnetism*, John Wiley, New York, 1965, pp. 407–411. A good summary of the various magnetic properties of use in magnets of all sorts is given in H. C. Roters, *Electromagnetic Devices*, John Wiley, New York, 1941, Chapter II.

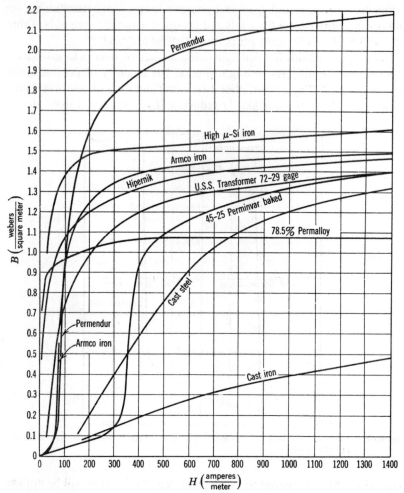

Fig. 8.6i. Magnetization curves for several magnetic materials. (Taken from S. S. Attwood, *Electric and Magnetic Fields*, 3rd ed., John Wiley, New York, 1949, Fig. 13.9.)

The saturable reactor, whose operation is based on the hysteresis properties of iron, is worth mentioning here. This is an iron core equipped with two coils, one of which is designed for a fairly large direct current and the other of which is used as a reactance element in an a-c circuit. The amount of steady current in the first coil determines the degree of saturation of the iron; the a-c reactance depends on the degree of saturation, for the incremental permeability which is the determining quantity will decrease as saturation is approached. Magnetic amplifiers are devices based on saturable reactors as elements.[13]

[13] For details, see W. A. Geyger, *Non-Linear Magnetic Control Devices*, McGraw-Hill, New York, 1964; and H. F. Storm, *Magnetic Amplifiers*, John Wiley, New York, 1955.

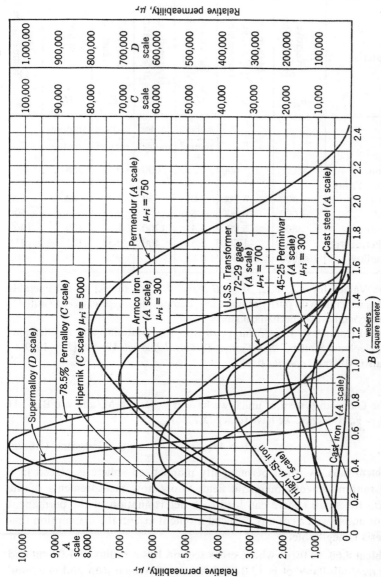

Fig. 8.6j. Normal permeability curves for several magnetic materials (μ_{ri} signifies the initial relative permeability). (Taken from Attwood, *op. cit.,* Fig. 13.12.)

Table 8.6C Properties of Typical Ferromagnetic Materials

Material	Initial Relative Permeability μ_{ri}	Maximum Relative Permeability μ_{rm}	Saturation Magnetization M_{sat}	Hysteresis Loss at Saturation W_∞	Residual Induction B_r	Coercive Force H_c	Curie Temperature T_c
			$\dfrac{\text{webers}}{\text{meter}^2}$	$\dfrac{\text{joules}}{\text{meter}^3}$	$\dfrac{\text{webers}}{\text{meter}^2}$	$\dfrac{\text{amperes}}{\text{meter}}$	°C
Cast iron	. . .	600	. . .	2000	0.53	366	
4 Si-Iron (Transformer)	400	6,700	2.0	350	1.2	40	690
Hipernik	3,000	70,000	1.65	22	0.73	3.2	500
Permendur	800	5,000	2.4	1200	1.4	159	1000
45–25 Perminvar	365	1,800	1.55	400	0.33	111	715
Supermalloy	100,000	1,050,000	0.8	. . .	. . .	0.32	400

Note: Values for μ_{ri}, μ_{rm}, W_∞, B_r, and H_c are subject to considerable variation, depending on purity of materials, composition, type of heat treatment, and final condition of mechanical stress.

Adapted from V. E. Legg, "Survey of Magnetic Materials and Applications in the Telephone System," *Bell System Technical Journal*, **18**, 438 (July 1939). See also Attwood, *op. cit.*, p. 376.

In the Gaussian system of units, we have $\mathbf{B} = \mathbf{H} + 4\pi\mathbf{M}$, and use $\mathbf{B} = \mu\mathbf{H}$ and $\mathbf{M} = \chi_m\mathbf{H}$. Hence, we have (cf. eg. 3.7–5b)

$$1 + 4\pi\chi_m = \mu \qquad \text{Gaussian} \quad (8.6\text{–}7b)$$

Problem 8.6a. A small permanently magnetized sphere is placed in a strong inhomogeneous magnetic field. Show how measurements of the force on the small sphere can lead to a determination of the permanent moment $\mathbf{m}_1$, as well as of any induced moment $\mathbf{m}_2$, on the assumption that hysteresis is negligible.

Problem 8.6b. A torus whose cross section has a radius of 1.00 cm and whose over-all diameter is 17.0 cm is made of Armco iron and is wound uniformly with 350 turns of wire. When 1.5 amp is passed through the winding, what are the values of B and M that would be present if the material followed the normal magnetization curve for this iron in Fig. 8.6i?

Table 8.6D   Properties of Typical Permanent Magnet Materials

Name	Coercive Force (Hc) amperes $\overline{\text{meter}}$	Residual Induction (Br) webers $\overline{\text{meter}^2}$	Energy Product, $(BH)_{max}$ joules
Carbon Steel 1% Mn, 0.9% C	4,000	1.00	1,600
Cobalt Steel 36% Co, 7% W, 3.5% Cr, 0.9% C	18,300	1.00	8,000
Iron (crystalline powder)	37,800	0.60	7,950
Cobalt Ferrite $CoFe_2O_4$ (crystalline powder)	40,000	0.40	7,550
Alnico II 12% Al, 18% Ni, 13% Co, 6% Cu	44,600	0.73	12,700
Alnico V 14% Ni, 8% Al, 24% Co, 3% Cu	52,000	1.27	44,000
Ticonal XX 15% Ni, 7% Al, 34% Co, 4% Cu, 5% Ti	105,000	1.18	88,000
Manganese bismuth (MnBi) (crystalline powder)	291,000	0.48	43,000
Platinax II 50% Pt, 50% Co	380,000	0.64	73,000

From Morrish, *op. cit.*, p. 366.

Problem 8.6c. Using the Armco-iron hysteresis curve in Fig. 8.6g for the torus of Problem 8.6b and assuming a secondary winding on the torus of 50 turns, find the charge in coulombs that passes through the secondary if its circuit resistance is 2.0 ohms and the primary current is changed from +0.075 amp to −0.040 amp on the downward portion of the loop. How much charge would flow in the secondary for the same current change if the iron were replaced by a vacuum?

Problem 8.6d. Find M and H inside a piece of bismuth when it is subjected to an external magnetic induction of 1.50 webers/m². (See Table 8.6A.)

Problem 8.6e. Find the ratio of $\mu_0 M$ to B for permendur, as shown in Fig. 8.6i, when $H = 250$ amp/m.

8.7   Theories of Magnetism[14]

The explanation of the properties of magnetic materials is a complicated subject, involving atomic physics, physics of the solid state, physical chemistry, and some nuclear physics. In a textbook on electricity and magnetism we can only consider certain limited aspects of this complicated problem.

In the first place, all matter should have diamagnetic properties. Atoms or molecules whose atomic currents have zero resultant magnetic-dipole moments will not show any paramagnetic or ferromagnetic effects that mask their diamagnetism.

It is a relatively easy matter to calculate the diamagnetic susceptibility for an atom using the classical Larmor precession for a rotating charge in an external magnetic field.[15] The result gives the susceptibility as proportional to the average moment of inertia of the electrons in the atom or molecule; the modern quantum theory gives the same formula. The calculation of moments of inertia is difficult and the experimental results are generally in good, although approximate, agreement with the calculations. One important result of the theory is that diamagnetism is not associated with thermal agitation and is thus not temperature dependent. This is experimentally verified for most substances. There is a temperature dependence in certain exceptional cases that may be due to a temperature effect on the electron orbits or to a variation in a minor paramagnetic contribution to the susceptibility.

Paramagnetism occurs not only for substances whose atoms or molecules each have a resultant magnetic moment, but also for conductors, since the spins of the conduction electrons can also be rotated by an external field. Resultant magnetic moments of molecules may arise because the orbital motions or the spins of the outer electrons are not completely arranged in equal and opposite pairs.

The complete inner shells of atoms always have a vanishing resultant magnetic moment. It is only incomplete shells that can contribute to

---

[14] This section may be omitted without loss of continuity.

[15] See, for instance, Morrish, *op. cit.*, pp. 27–29 and 38–39; and Attwood, *op. cit.* pp. 252–255. A rather complete account of the experimental facts and a summary of the theory is given by R. M. Bozorth, "Magnetism," *Encycl. Britannica*, Chicago, 1954, Vol. 14, pp. 636–667, reprinted in *Revs. Mod. Phys.*, **19**, 62–65 (1947); see also the more extensive account in R. M. Bozorth, *Ferromagnetism*, D. Van Nostrand, Princeton, 1951.

paramagnetism. The chief examples are some of the so-called transition elements and rare-earth elements which have inner shells with more than the rare-gas complement of 8 but less than their full quota of 18 or 32 electrons. (Outer shell electrons generally get paired off in chemical combination.)

The simplest theory of paramagnetism assumes that each atom with a resultant moment will tend to undergo quantum jumps toward the direction of an applied field, exchanging energy under the influence of thermal agitation. The result is that to a good approximation the susceptibility should be similar to the temperature dependent part of the electric susceptibility (cf. Eq. 3.10–1), namely that

$$\chi_m = \frac{nm^2\mu_0}{3kT} \tag{8.7–1a}$$

where n is the number of atoms or molecules per unit volume and m is the permanent magnetic moment of each atom or molecule.[16]

The paramagnetism of the conduction electrons of metals is temperature independent because of the location of most electrons in the filled levels of the conduction bands that are unaffected by temperature. The quantum theory yields a simple expression if the electrons are assumed to be free and a more complicated one if the actual "binding" in the metal is taken into account. Diamagnetism is also present and reduces the paramagnetic result by about one-third. The resulting susceptibility is a good deal weaker than the paramagnetism resulting from permanent atomic or molecular moments; the calculations agree with experiment to within 10% for lithium and with larger errors for other materials.[17]

The theory of atomic paramagnetism that fits the experiments fairly well assumes that each dipole is acted on by an external field $\mathbf{H}$ but not to any great extent by the fields of neighboring dipoles. Since χ_m is so small, the difference between $\mathbf{H}$ and $\mathbf{H} + \mathbf{M}/3$ (cf. Section 8.5) will be insignificant. Let us try to see why we should expect the local interaction to be weak.

Consider first the potential energy of a pair of dipoles situated at a distance $\mathbf{r}$ from each other. Except for the difference in sign, the energy will have an exactly analogous formula to that for the electrostatic dipole-dipole interaction and, as we have seen, the sign difference does not appear when forces and torques are calculated. (Energy changes in the elementary atomic circuits are to be calculated by quantum theory and do not concern us here.)

---

[16] Cf. Bozorth, "Magnetism," *Revs. Mod. Phys.*, **19**, 65–70 (1947); Morrish, *op. cit.*, pp. 46–54.

[17] Morrish, *op. cit.*, p. 220.

Thus we have for the potential energy, following Eq. 3.2–6,

$$U = \frac{3(\mathbf{p}_{m1} \cdot \mathbf{1}_r)(\mathbf{p}_{m2} \cdot \mathbf{1}_r) - \mathbf{p}_{m1} \cdot \mathbf{p}_{m2}}{4\pi\mu_0 r^3}$$

$$= \mu_0 \frac{3(\mathbf{m}_1 \cdot \mathbf{1}_r)(\mathbf{m}_2 \cdot \mathbf{1}_r) - \mathbf{m}_1 \cdot \mathbf{m}_2}{4\pi r^3} \tag{8.7–2a}$$

giving the magnetic energy for a dipole-dipole interaction.

Let us compare the magnitudes of the electric and magnetic dipole-dipole interactions. If the two dipoles are parallel and each perpendicular to $\mathbf{1}_r$, $U = -\mu_0 m_1 m_2 / 4\pi r^3$. If they are parallel to each other and also to $\mathbf{1}_r$, $U = 2\mu_0 m_1 m_2 / 4\pi r^3$. In any case, it is the magnitude $\mu_0 m_1 m_2 / 4\pi r^3$ that is to be compared with $p_1 p_2 / 4\pi\epsilon_0 r^3$.

The electromagnetic moment of a single circulating electron can be found by comparing it with the angular momentum of the same electron. If the electron has a circular orbit of radius a over which it travels at speed v, its period of revolution is $2\pi a / v$. The average current is the charge divided by the period, so $i = ev / 2\pi a$. Thus for its electromagnetic moment we have

$$m = iS = \frac{ev\pi a^2}{2\pi a} = \tfrac{1}{2} eva \tag{8.7–3a}$$

The angular momentum of the electron is $M_e va$, denoting the electron mass by M_e. The ratio of the magnetic moment of an atomic system to its angular momentum is called the "gyromagnetic ratio" G. For an electron in a circular orbit,

$$G_{\text{orb}} = \frac{m}{M_e va} = \frac{e}{2M_e} \tag{8.7–4a}$$

This ratio is found to hold for non-circular orbital motions as well and is unchanged by the introduction of the wave properties of electrons. The relation between the directions of the magnetic-moment and angular-momentum vectors will be that appropriate to a negative charge.

One of the fundamental principles or theorems of quantum mechanics is that the angular momentum of a circulating electron can only have a magnitude equal to a whole number times $h/2\pi$, where h is Planck's constant, $[h = (6.6256 \pm 0.0001) \times 10^{-34}$ joule-sec]. Associated with one such unit of angular momentum we have therefore an electromagnetic moment

$$m_B = G_{\text{orb}} \frac{h}{2\pi} = \frac{eh}{4\pi M_e} \qquad (8.7\text{-}5a)$$

This number is called the Bohr magneton. Its value is $(0.92732 \pm 0.00002) \times 10^{-23}$ ampere-m$^2 = 0.92732 \times 10^{-20}$ erg/gauss.

The spin of the electron has a magnetic moment associated with it whose value is approximately one Bohr magneton (it is actually 1.00115961 times larger). However, it only has half a unit of angular momentum (i.e., $h/4\pi$). Hence, the gyromagnetic ratio for electron spin is (to a high degree of approximation) twice that for orbital motion:

$$G_{\text{spin}} = \frac{e}{M_e} \qquad (8.7\text{-}6)$$

For any given collection of atoms or molecules, the gyromagnetic ratio can be written

$$G = g \frac{e}{2M_e} \qquad (8.7\text{-}7a)$$

where g is a pure number, which for atomic systems may be expected to be between 1 and 2, depending on the proportion of orbital and spin magnetic moments. For nuclei it may have other values.

We can now compare the electric and magnetic dipole-dipole interactions. Electric dipole moments of permanently polarized molecules are, as indicated in Section 3.10, of the order of magnitude ex where x is 10^{-11} meters. Thus we need to compare

$$\frac{\mu_0}{4\pi r^3}\left(\frac{eh}{4\pi M_e}\right)^2$$

with

$$\frac{(ex)^2}{4\pi\epsilon_0 r^3}$$

at the same distance r. Equivalently, we can compare $\mu_0\epsilon_0(h/4\pi M_e)^2 = (h/4\pi M_e c)^2$ with x^2 ($\mu_0\epsilon_0 = 1/c^2$ as indicated in Section 7.14). But $h/4\pi M_e c$ is the Compton wavelength of the electron, 1.93×10^{-13} meter, so we see that atomic magnetic moments are about 1/50 or 1/100 of atomic electric moments, and the interaction potential energies differ by a factor of 10^3 or 10^4. Paramagnetic interactions are very weak indeed, and the term $\mathbf{M}/3$ referred to above must indeed make a very small contribution.

This result makes a good introduction to the problem of ferromagnetism, for the very large values of M in ferromagnetic materials would seem to imply a very *large* interaction. In fact, when a substance is approximately saturated, nearly all the magnetic moments are lined up, and they tend to remain lined up when **H** is removed. We can easily show that at saturation each atom contributes on the average about one whole Bohr magneton to the magnetization. Inspection of Fig. 8.6*i* shows that saturation values of B range approximately from 1.0 to 2.0 webers/m² or 10,000 to 20,000 gauss. Therefore, M is about $1/\mu_0 = 10^7/4\pi$ ampere/meter. The density of atoms in iron is about $(6.02 \times 10^{23}) \times (7.9 \text{ g/cm}^3)/(56 \text{ g/mole}) \simeq 0.85 \times 10^{23}$ atoms per cubic centimeter, or 0.85×10^{29} per cubic meter so that the average m per atom is $10^7/(4\pi \times 0.8 \times 10^{29}) \simeq 1.0 \times 10^{-23} \simeq m_B$.

If we assume that for some reason peculiar to ferromagnetic materials, there is a very strong local interaction (different from the one we have just calculated) we might describe it by replacing the term $M/3$ by a larger expression γM, with γ to be determined. The paramagnetic susceptibility given in Eq. 8.7–1 is equivalent to

$$M = \frac{nm^2\mu_0 H}{3kT} \tag{8.7–8}$$

but was derived on the assumption of weak local interaction. For strong interactions, H must be replaced by H_{eff}:

$$M = \frac{nm^2\mu_0(H + \gamma M)}{3kT} \tag{8.7–9}$$

If we solve this equation for M, we find

$$M = \frac{nm^2\mu_0 H}{3k(T - \theta)} \tag{8.7–10}$$

where

$$\theta = \frac{nm^2\mu_0\gamma}{3k} \tag{8.7–11a}$$

We notice that, if T is considerably greater than the constant θ, called the Curie temperature,[18] the susceptibility behaves in the usual paramagnetic way, with γ playing no important role. On the other hand, if T is just above the value θ, there will be a large value of M even for a small H,

---

[18] Named for Pierre Curie, who first found experimentally (1895) the relation between paramagnetic susceptibility and temperature given in Eq. 8.7–1.

and for temperatures equal to or less than θ, the formula gives physically meaningless results, indicating that the interaction has become so strong that M can sustain itself without an applied H, and the assumptions underlying Eq. 8.7–1 are no longer valid.

It is in fact true that many substances are paramagnetic above a certain temperature, and follow Eq. 8.7–10 fairly well. Below the temperature θ these substances become ferromagnetic. The theory we have just given is the Weiss theory of ferromagnetism, first announced in 1907.[19] Curie temperatures of iron alloys are of the order of 700 to 1300°K. (See Table 8.6C.) Let us calculate γ for $\theta = 800°K$, and $m = m_B$. The calculation given above for saturation shows that the product nm_B is about $10^7/4\pi$ ampere/meter. Using Boltzmann's constant $k = 1.38 \times 10^{-23}$ joule/degree and $m_B = 10^{-23}$ joule-m²/weber, we find that $\gamma = 4.1\theta$ when θ is in Kelvin degrees. Thus for 800°, γ is about 3300, showing the enormous interaction strengths we must assume to explain ferromagnetism.

Now we must inquire into the relative role of electron spins and electronic orbital motions. This question has a direct experimental answer, provided by experiments first performed by Barnett in 1914 and by Einstein and de Haas in 1915. The gyromagnetic ratio for a single atom can also be applied to a whole specimen. If magnetization consists in turning elementary dipoles toward a particular direction, there must be an increase of total angular momentum about an axis in that direction. If the angular momentum of the specimen is originally zero, the amount gained by all the atomic systems must be compensated by an equal and opposite gain by the specimen as a whole. That is, a delicately mounted specimen should start to rotate when it is magnetized. Einstein and de Haas found this to be so and in fact measured G. So did Barnett by the converse effect of producing magnetization by rotating the specimen.[20] The result is that g of Eq. 8.7–7 is nearly equal to the electron spin value 2, but not quite. (It is about 1.93 for iron.) Thus we can conclude that the electron spin is mainly responsible for ferromagnetism.

Ferromagnetism can be explained in terms of quantum theory, but the explanation is still in a more or less qualitative stage. It is possible to understand why the phenomenon exists and, to a certain extent, the reason that certain particular substances show the effect. It is not yet possible (1966) to calculate the various measurable magnetic properties with any degree of accuracy.

[19] P. Weiss, *J. de Phys.*, **6**, 667 (1907). For a brief account, see Bozorth, "Magnetism," *Revs. Mod. Phys.*, **19**, 73–74 (1947); also Morrish, *op. cit.*, Ch. 6.

[20] For details of the experiments, the reader is referred to a review article by S. J. Barnett, *Revs. Mod. Phys.*, **7**, 129 (1935). S. Chikazumi, *Physics of Magnetism*, John Wiley, New York, 1964, section 3.2, has a brief account.

We shall describe here certain aspects of quantum theory that help to show why ferromagnetism exists. In the first place, electrons in any given atomic or molecular system tend to arrange themselves into the types of allowable motions of lowest energy. In the second place, because of the Pauli exclusion principle, complete shells in atoms always contain even numbers of electrons with their spins and orbits so paired as to have no resultant magnetic moment.

Third, any pair of electrons that can interact will have their spins either parallel or antiparallel (having the same or opposite signs with respect to the direction in space to which they are both parallel). This property is intimately related to their wave nature and is *not* connected with or dependent on the dipole-dipole interaction. The types of motion that are possible for the electrons are different in the two cases, a fact which is a consequence of the exclusion principle. *It is this feature that provides the strong interaction involved in ferromagnetism.*

As an example, consider a pair of electrons that form a covalent bond between two atoms. Various types of motion are possible, including cases in which one electron moves (in the quantum-mechanical sense) around each positive ion, cases in which both move around the same ion, and cases in which each moves around both ions. For each type of motion, the spins may be either parallel or antiparallel. It turns out that the situation in which each electron moves around both ions gives the two states of lowest energy. Detailed calculation of the energies in the parallel and antiparallel arrangements shows that the one with opposite spins has the actual lowest energy and provides for an attraction between the ions. (The motion is such that the electrons spend a good deal of time between the atoms and their attraction for each positive ion leads to a net over-all attraction.)

There are certain cases, however, in which a pair of electrons may have a motion of lowest energy with their spins parallel. This happens in the next-to-outermost electron shells of what chemists call the transition elements and leads to paramagnetism. It also may happen with a pair of electrons that each come from a separate paramagnetic atom, when the two atoms are neither too close nor too far apart.

Ferromagnetic materials are always solids and usually conductors. The important phenomenon for such materials is that of the motion of whole groups of electrons in the resulting energy bands. It seems to be clear from the calculations of several investigators that certain of the conduction and next-to-outer-shell electrons in ferromagnetic materials can have collective motions involving spins all parallel to one given direction. These motions are undoubtedly a combination of the over-all motions of the electrical-conduction sort, and the partially localized ones in which electrons may spend a good deal of time moving around a pair of adjacent atoms.[21] The question of the circumstances under which such motions with parallel spins involve less energy than those with the spins all paired oppositely is a difficult question to answer, for the theory cannot be calculated with sufficient accuracy. However, the two energies are certainly close for the iron group of elements and far apart in most other cases, so that the ferromagnetism is at least not surprising in those cases in which it appears. It is also not hard to show that a Curie temperature should exist, above which a formula like Eq. 8.7-10 will hold for M.

There is, however, a serious difficulty with what we have said so far. Why would not any piece of iron spontaneously become magnetized to saturation? How could we ever demagnetize a ferromagnetic substance?

The answer is provided by the concept of magnetic domains. Suppose that there are many very small regions in a piece of iron within which the spins all cooperate and line up in some particular direction. These directions are likely to have special relations to the crystal axes; they are called the "directions of easy magnetization." Each domain may have several such easy directions. Then demagnetization means that the domains are all magnetized in randomly varying directions.

The boundary between two domains may be the edge of a small crystallite or a region of strain or fracture. However, it is also possible (and has in fact been found experimentally) that a single crystal can have several domains with boundaries that are simply regions separating two groups of atoms with different spin directions. The latter sort of boundary can very well migrate as one domain obtains "converts" from the next one, turning the electron spins from one direction to another.

Two kinds of evidence have been found for these domains. One is that if the coil used in a hysteresis experiment to determine B is connected to a sensitive a-c amplifier and H is slowly increased, many small sudden emfs will be detected, showing that Φ increases by discontinuous jumps. This is just what would be expected if the domains suddenly switched their directions from one at a considerable angle to H to another more nearly parallel to H. This effect is called the "Barkhausen effect."

The other evidence is found by sprinkling some very fine magnetizable powder on the surface of a smooth specimen and observing under a microscope the powder patterns formed as the magnetization is changed. Such

---

[21] The reader with some knowledge of quantum mechanics will find illuminating summaries of ferromagnetic theory in a group of articles by C. Zener and R. R. Heikes, J. C. Slater, E. P. Wohlfarth, J. H. Van Vleck, and R. Smoluchowski in *Revs. Mod. Phys.*, **25**, 191–228 (1953). The last named author gives a summary of the results of the others. Morrish, *op. cit.*, Chapter 6, discusses some of the recent results and gives many references.

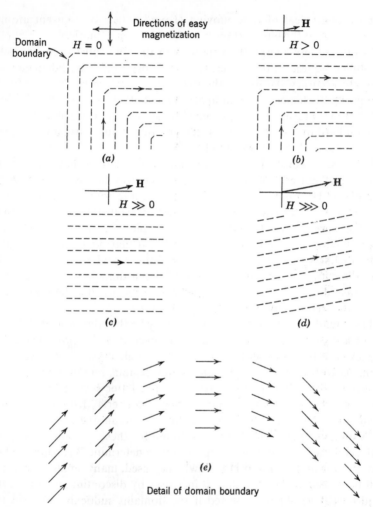

Fig. 8.7a. Schematic diagram of changes in domains at various stages of magnetization. (Adapted from R. M. Bozorth.)

patterns seem to show that there are sharply defined regions of different magnetization. However, it may be that the actual domain sizes are much smaller than the powder-pattern spacings.[22]

[22] For pictures of powder patterns, see F. Bitter, *Introduction to Ferromagnetism*, McGraw-Hill, New York, 1937, pp. 59–66; W. C. Elmore, *Phys. Rev.*, **62**, 486 (1942); R. M. Bozorth, *Ferromagnetism, op. cit.*, pp. 534–538; and K. H. Stewart, *Ferromagnetic Domains*, Cambridge University Press, Cambridge, 1954. For a thorough discussion of recent results, see Morrish, *op. cit.*, Chapter 7; many diagrams and pictures, together with an elementary discussion, are given by Chikazumi, *op. cit.*

It is now possible to describe a hysteresis loop and initial magnetization curves in terms of the domain changes that occur on various parts of them. At the beginning of a magnetization process those domains which have positive components of **M** parallel to **H** will grow at the expense of their neighbors—the boundaries move. The lower bend in the curve represents reversible boundary motion, and the higher portions represent irreversible motion. Finally, for very strong **H**, the spins in each domain rotate together

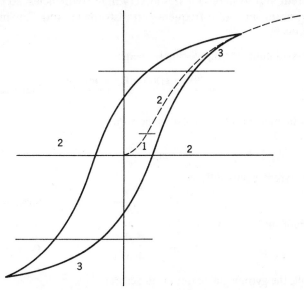

Fig. 8.7b. A hysteresis loop and an initial magnetization curve, showing regions in which different types of domain changes occur. Region 1—reversible motion of domain walls. Region 2—irreversible motion of domain walls. Region 3—rotation of domain magnetizations toward **H**.

toward the **H**, so that at saturation, all the spins are parallel. Figures 8.7a and b illustrate these concepts.

There are a number of materials that show interesting modifications of ferromagnetic behavior. These materials are characterized by containing two interlocking sets of atoms or atom groupings, each of which has the spin-lining-up character of ordinary ferromagnetic substances. In some of these materials the two sub-lattices, as they are called, tend to magnetize in the same direction and to behave a good deal like ferromagnetic substances. In others the two sub-lattices tend to magnetize oppositely. If in these substances the sub-lattices have identical magnetic moments per atom or atomic grouping, there will be a cancellation of the total magnetization to a high order of accuracy, but there will still be a Curie temperature and strong paramagnetic behavior above it. These substances are said to be "antiferromagnetic."

If the two sub-lattices are not identical, there will be a net effect similar to ferromagnetism but considerably weaker. The name for this phenomenon is ferrimagnetism (for emphasis, the second syllable is sometimes pronounced to rhyme with "eye") and substances possessing it are called ferrites. Ferrites are often poor electrical conductors and have very low eddy-current and hysteresis losses at very high frequencies, so they can be used for cores in radio-frequency transformers and for many other applications.[23]

In Gaussian units, the dipole-dipole energy is

$$U = \frac{3(\mathbf{m}_1 \cdot \mathbf{1}_r)(\mathbf{m}_2 \cdot \mathbf{1}_r) - \mathbf{m}_1 \cdot \mathbf{m}_2}{r^3} \qquad \text{Gaussian} \quad (8.7\text{--}2b)$$

the magnetic moment of a circulating electron is

$$m = \frac{eva}{2c} \qquad \text{Gaussian} \quad (8.7\text{--}3b)$$

its orbital gyromagnetic ratio is

$$G_{\text{orb}} = \frac{e}{2M_e c} \qquad \text{Gaussian} \quad (8.7\text{--}4b)$$

and the Bohr magneton is

$$m_B = \frac{eh}{4\pi M_e c} \qquad \text{Gaussian} \quad (8.7\text{--}5b)$$

As a result, the gyromagnetic ratio is in general

$$G = g \frac{e}{2M_e c} \qquad \text{Gaussian} \quad (8.7\text{--}7b)$$

The Curie temperature in terms of the dimensionless constant γ is

$$\theta = \frac{4\pi n m^2 \gamma}{3k} \qquad \text{Gaussian} \quad (8.7\text{--}11b)$$

Problem 8.7a. If an atomic system has an angular momentum $kh/2\pi$ where k is a quantum number (integer or half-odd-integer), show that the magnetic moment can be written $m = gkm_B$. Assume a charge of one electronic unit to be involved.

Problem 8.7b. What is the least value of the dipole-dipole interaction energy for two Bohr magnetons 1.2×10^{-8} cm apart? Give the answer in joules and in electron-volts.

[23] Ferrimagnetism, antiferromagnetism, and still other types of magnetic behavior, are treated in Chikazumi, *op. cit.*, and Morrish, *op. cit.*

Problem 8.7c. Two magnetic dipoles m_1 and m_2 are held a fixed distance r apart and are arranged to rotate while keeping a fixed angle between them. Sketch graphs showing the variation of U with the angle between $\mathbf{m}_1$ and $\mathbf{1}_r$ if (a) $\mathbf{m}_1$ and $\mathbf{m}_2$ are perpendicular; (b) $\mathbf{m}_1$ and $\mathbf{m}_2$ are parallel; (c) $\mathbf{m}_1$ and $\mathbf{m}_2$ are antiparallel.

Problem 8.7d. Show that Eqs. 8.7–1a and 8.7–1b are consistent with each other.

8.8 The Magnetic Circuit and Permanent Magnets[24]

Most applications of ferromagnetic materials involve current-bearing coils containing iron cores which do not lie along the lines of the flux produced by the coils. Permanent magnets are also frequently used with associated pieces of soft iron whose dimensions do not fit the flux patterns produced by the magnets. In both cases the presence of the iron modifies the flux pattern, and the concept of the magnetic circuit is extremely useful in the discussion of these modifications. We shall proceed to develop this concept in the present section.

Consider a coil of wire as shown in Fig. 8.8a, with an inserted bar of soft iron. Although B/H is not constant for the iron, we can take a rough average of μ_r—e.g., 5000 for Armco iron—as adequate for our purposes. The field produced by the coil without iron is shown in dotted lines in the figure.

Now, if the iron should become magnetized along the lines of the original $\mathbf{H}$, north and south poles will appear on the edges of the iron as shown. The $\mathbf{H}$ produced inside the iron by these poles will be approximately normal to the surface and directed away from it. Thus the resultant $\mathbf{H}$ will be altered inside the bar, and $\mathbf{M}$ will change as a consequence. Because of the large value of μ_r, it will take only a weak additional $\mathbf{H}$ to make a substantial readjustment of $\mathbf{M}$. The direction of the adjusted $\mathbf{M}$ will be more nearly parallel to the surface of the iron. In other words, the demagnetizing effect of the poles will be to produce a strong tendency for the magnetic flux to run parallel to the edges of the bar.

The flux must leave the bar near its ends, and there will also be a strong demagnetizing field there. However, the pole strength at the ends cannot disappear the way the pole strength can at the sides, for a small change at the sides will result in a large displacement of the poles, and a small field change at the end can make only a small pole displacement. Consequently, there will be a final state of equilibrium in which the pole density near the ends is a complicated function of the shape of the bar,

---

[24] This section may be omitted without loss of continuity.

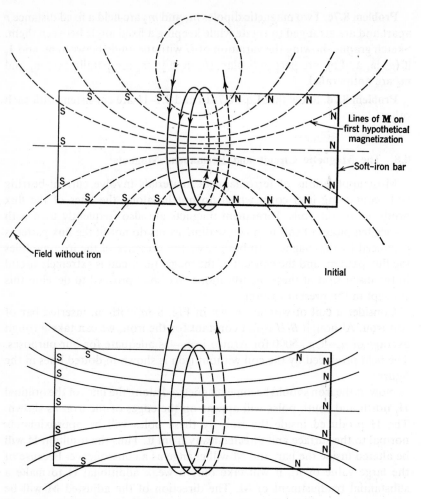

Fig. 8.8a. Initial state (hypothetical) (upper diagram). Equilibrium state of magnetization (lower diagram).

but depends very little on the pattern of the flux produced by the coil alone. In actual practice, the final equilibrium state will be reached almost immediately as the current is turned on or the bar inserted. The process we have imagined is thus rather hypothetical in nature.

Let us now imagine that a closed iron path for the flux is made by adding a U-shaped piece of soft iron to the bar, as shown in Fig. 8.8b. Induced pole strengths on the parts of the U that are adjacent to the ends of the bar will reduce the demagnetizing field materially and make the lines of force in the bar become more nearly parallel to its axis even near its ends.

Poles will also appear on the far side of the U but they will be displaced in the same fashion. They will, in fact, be displaced toward the main body of the U, because any displacement away from it will call into play a further demagnetizing field. The flux will finally be contained within the iron, in almost the same way that a current is contained in an electrical conductor. We call the path followed by the flux in the iron a magnetic circuit.

In close analogy to the case of the **E** in a conducting wire, the field **H** inside the iron is made to be nearly parallel to its edges by small residual amounts of q_m on the various surfaces of the magnetic circuit. At points

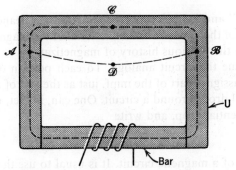

Fig. 8.8b. A closed magnetic circuit.

far from the coil, **H** may be modified considerably. However, the pole part of **H** contributes nothing to $\oint \mathbf{H} \cdot \mathbf{dl}$, so that the mmf $\mathscr{H} = \oint \mathbf{H} \cdot \mathbf{dl} = ni$ produced by the coil is unchanged. Let us consider a tube of flux that lies everywhere within the iron. Along this tube, $\Phi = BS$ if B is sufficiently uniform (S is the cross-sectional area of the tube, which is usually taken to be approximately the area of the specimen itself. It is expected to vary from point to point along the tube). Now, if we treat μ as a constant at any one point in the iron, although it may vary from place to place, we can derive a practical formula from the mmf equation. We calculate $\oint \mathbf{H} \cdot \mathbf{dl}$ along a line of force, and write

$$ni = \mathscr{H} = \oint \frac{B\,dl}{\mu} = \oint \frac{\Phi\,dl}{\mu S} = \Phi \oint \frac{dl}{\mu S} = \Phi \mathscr{R} \qquad (8.8\text{--}1)$$

where the constancy of Φ around the circuit is of course fundamental. (The fact that lines of B do not actually close on themselves does not prevent the flux from forming an essentially closed figure.)

Equation 8.8–1 is the equation of the magnetic circuit. It is analogous to the equation of the simple electric circuit if we compare Φ with i, $\mathscr{H}$ with $\mathscr{E}$, and the quantity $\mathscr{R} = \oint dl/\mu S$ with R. The quantity $\mathscr{R}$ is called

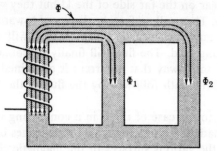

Fig. 8.8c.   A parallel magnetic circuit.

the "reluctance," and its reciprocal is called the "permeance." It is principally a function of the dimensions and material of the magnetic circuit, but
also depends on the previous history of magnetization.

One can pursue the circuit analogy. To each portion of the magnetic
circuit one can assign a part of the mmf, just as the emf of a cell is divided
up into potential drops around a circuit. One can, in fact, use the concept
of magnetic potential drop, and write

$$V_m = \Phi \mathscr{R} \tag{8.8–2}$$

for any portion of a magnetic circuit. It is usual to use the term mmf for
V_m and to consider it as positive in the rising rather than the dropping
sense. One can use series-parallel treatments, since reluctance and mmf
add when in series, and flux can divide and rejoin, as in Fig. 8.8c. More
complicated cases (Fig. 8.8d) require a Kirchhoff's law type of treatment
with junction equations for the flux and loop equations for the mmf, and
they can be handled in exactly the same way as in the electric case.

One important distinction between the magnetic and electric circuits is
that the former always involves some leakage flux, whereas the latter
commonly involves no leakage current. Consider two points $\mathscr{A}$ and $\mathscr{B}$

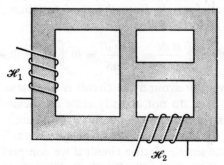

Fig. 8.8d.   A three-loop magnetic circuit.

in the circuit of Fig. 8.8b. The magnetic potential difference $-\int_{\mathscr{A}}^{\mathscr{B}} \mathbf{H} \cdot \mathbf{dl}$ between the two points may be calculated either along a path in the iron, $\mathscr{A}\mathscr{C}\mathscr{B}$, or through the air, $\mathscr{A}\mathscr{D}\mathscr{B}$. The results must be the same, because there is no current passing between the two paths. Therefore there must be a field $\mathbf{H}$ in the space outside the iron and a flux of $\mathbf{B}$ accompanying it. The electric case always involves an external $\mathbf{E}$ by the analogous argument, but there is in general no current accompanying $\mathbf{E}$. The flux leakage will be small, of course, if μ_r is large. One could describe this result by saying that the air (or vacuum) surrounding a magnetic circuit provides a parallel path of high but not infinite reluctance. It is like immersing a coil of wire in a liquid of low, but not zero, conductivity.

This leakage flux is one source of inaccuracy in the magnetic-circuit equation. The other reason for the approximate nature of the equation lies in the expression for the reluctance. The permeability μ is admittedly only an approximate constant. Furthermore, S is the area of a tube of flux. If the tube is chosen to fill out the iron, it will fit well in the straight sections, but poorly at the corners. Thus the integral $\oint dl/\mu S$ is not accurate if S is taken as the cross-sectional area of the entire piece of iron.

However, the reluctance can be defined exactly as the ratio between $\mathscr{H}$ and the flux Φ across the area of a chosen particular part of the circuit for a particular value of Φ. Reluctance can thus be measured for a whole circuit and indeed also for a part (see below). In fact, permeability measurements are actually reluctance measurements.[25] The problem of the variability of μ can be handled for many engineering problems by arranging to have S constant for each part of a given type of material, so that the constancy of Φ insures that $\mathbf{B}$ is constant and the material in different portions of the circuit is operated on the same portion of the magnetization curve (or on the same hysteresis loop in the a-c case). In fact, if S is too small in one portion of the circuit, there may not be enough atomic currents to pass the flux through the circuit and the leakage will be considerable— the effective μ will be small and $\mathscr{R}$ will be large.

The magnetic-circuit equation indicates that the flux depends on the number of ampere-turns of the coil, but not on its location. Actually, moving the coil must change the surface pole strengths, but this of course is a small effect (except near saturation, when coil locations become very important) and will change the reluctance only slightly through alterations of S.

Magnetic shielding of sensitive apparatus is accomplished by surrounding the apparatus with a suitably thick layer of high-permeability soft

[25] For details on magnetic measurements, see the *National Bureau of Standards Circular* C456, "Magnetic Testing," by Raymond L. Sanford, Washington, 1946.

iron. The functioning of such a shield may readily be described in terms of low-reluctance magnetic circuits that "conduct" external flux around rather than through the objects to be shielded. Figure 8.8*e* shows magnetic lines of force for the case of a spherical shell of soft iron of high constant permeability μ_r, placed in an originally uniform field. An analysis of this case by use of Laplace's equation and zonal harmonics shows that the

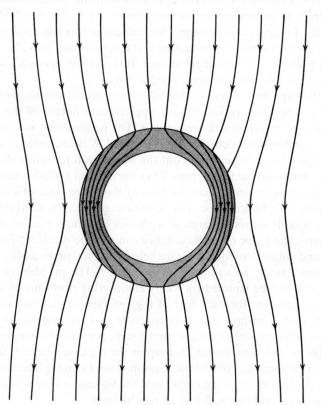

Fig. 8.8*e*.   Shielding effect of a spherical shell of highly permeable material (from Jackson, *loc. cit.*).

field in the cavity is uniform, with intensity approximately $1/\mu_r$ times the original external field.[26]

Let us consider now the case of an air gap in a magnetic circuit. Figure 8.8*f* shows the magnetic circuit of an electromagnet. The reluctance of the gap, of length l_a and area S, is $\mathscr{R}_a = l_a/\mu_0 S$. Let us assume that the iron has a constant cross section also equal to S, a constant value of μ,

[26] J. D. Jackson, *Classical Electrodynamics*, John Wiley, New York, 1962, pp. 162–164.

and an effective length of l_i, so its reluctance is $\mathscr{R}_i = l_i/\mu S$. Then we have

$$\Phi = \frac{\mathscr{H}}{\mathscr{R}_i + \mathscr{R}_a} = \frac{\mathscr{H}}{\dfrac{l_i}{\mu S} + \dfrac{l_a}{\mu_0 S}} \tag{8.8-3}$$

Now, if μ/μ_0 is much greater than l_i/l_a, the reluctance of the iron will be small, and the air gap will be the controlling element in the determination of Φ. The flux will be very much less than if the air gap were not there, and most of the mmf will appear across the gap. We might describe this situation by saying that the field produced by the poles points in the positive direction in the gap and is strong because of the narrowness of

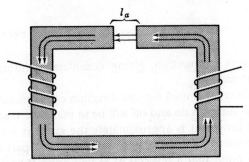

Fig. 8.8*f*. A magnetic circuit with an air gap.

the gap. The pole-produced **H** is in a reversed direction in the rest of the circuit, and although the field produced by the poles at the gap will not of itself conform in shape to the magnetic circuit, it will be made to do so by the presence of additional induced poles on the surface of the iron. Thus **H** and the flux in the iron will be weakened by the presence of the air gap.

It is possible to use normal magnetization curves rather than averages of μ for more precision in the design of magnets. For instance, suppose that certain materials and dimensions have been chosen for an electromagnet, which is to provide a predetermined flux Φ in a given gap. Then S is known for each portion of the circuit, and the value of **B** can be calculated. If this **B** is either to be produced in previously demagnetized materials or represents the maximum to be reached in each cycle of an alternating emf, the **H** needed can be found from the appropriate curve. Therefore the mmf needed for each portion of the magnetic circuit can be separately calculated and the sum found, so that the ampere-turns needed in the coil are established. If such calculations are made for several values of Φ, a graph of flux against magnetomotive force can be made for the

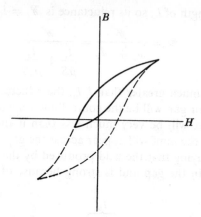

Fig. 8.8g.   An unsymmetrical hysteresis loop for a d-c electromagnet.

particular magnet in question, giving considerable information on the behavior of the magnet.

If an electromagnet is used for one direction of magnetization only, the result of several turnings on and off will be to make the material follow an unsymmetrical loop that is approximately the same as a combination of the normal magnetization curve and the downward part of a hysteresis loop to such a point that a reversal of **H** will bring **B** back through zero (cf. Fig. 8.8g). The reason for the appearance of negative values of H is that residual pole strength is left when the current is turned off.

Demagnetization curves and complete loops of the sort just mentioned can be constructed for the Φ and $\mathscr{H}$ in a particular magnetic circuit. Let us consider a case in which a permanent magnet is made by applying an

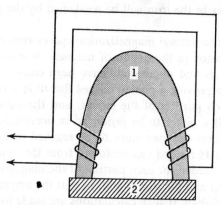

Fig. 8.8h.   Making a permanent magnet. Piece 1—hard magnet steel; Piece 2—soft iron.

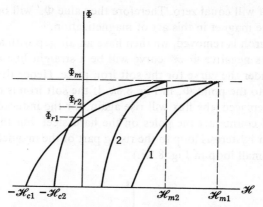

Fig. 8.8i. Showing $\Phi - \mathscr{H}$ curves for pieces 1 and 2 in Fig. 8.8h.

mmf to a circuit containing a piece of hard magnet steel and a removable piece of soft iron (Fig. 8.8h). For each piece (1 and 2) we can construct a curve, as in Fig. 8.8i.[27] We have indicated in the figure that the maximum Φ is the same in both pieces (leakage is considered negligible) and that the $\mathscr{H}_{max}$ needed for piece 2 is smaller than that for piece 1, because of smaller reluctance.

For the combined magnetic circuit, we can add the mmf's on the downward portions of the two curves for the same values of Φ, getting something like Fig. 8.8j. When the current is turned off, the total mmf reduces to zero, and flux Φ_r' remains. It is perhaps easier to picture what happens if the mmf of piece 2 is plotted with reversed sign (as if it were a potential drop), as in Fig. 8.8k. At the point where the two downward curves cross

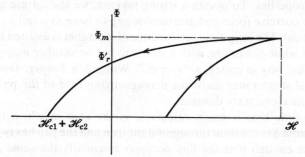

Fig. 8.8j. $\mathscr{H}$ added for same values of Φ, from Fig. 8.8i.

[27] It may take considerable effort to calculate the reluctance of a piece shaped like piece 2 because of uncertainties in the flux pattern. Cf. H. C. Roters, *op. cit.*, Chapters IV and V; and L. W. Matsch, *Capacitors, Magnetic Circuits, and Transformers*, Prentice-Hall, Englewood Cliffs, N.J., 1964, Chapter 3.

the total mmf will equal zero. Therefore the value Φ_r' will be the residual flux left in the magnet in this act of magnetization.

If the soft iron is removed, we then have an air gap with a much larger reluctance; its negative Φ–$\mathscr{H}$ curve will be a straight line and will lie a good deal under the curve for the soft iron piece. Hence the magnet will demagnetize to the point Φ_p in Fig. 8.8k. If the soft iron is demagnetized and then is replaced, the flux will rise again, for the induced poles in the soft iron will counteract the poles on the hard steel, but the rise will be along a minor hysteresis loop to the rising part of the magnetization curve of piece 2. (Small loop in Fig. 8.8k.)

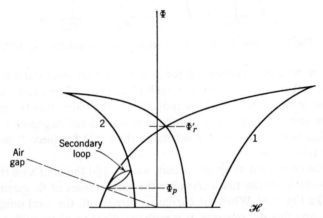

Fig. 8.8k. Showing the soft-iron loop of Fig. 8.8i plotted in reverse.

In this way a fairly complete prediction can be made of permanent-magnet properties. To obtain a strong magnet, we should use a material with large coercive force and arrange the gap to have as small a reluctance as is practical. The long-time permanence of a magnet is assisted by closing the circuit while not in use, with a soft-iron bar or another magnet. A bar used in this way is called a "keeper." Without a keeper, thermal and mechanical shocks may assist the demagnetizing field of the poles in dis-aligning the elementary domains.

An example that is easily calculable is the case in which the cross-sectional area S is constant throughout the iron and the gap has two parallel faces close enough that the flux occupies essentially the same area S in the gap. Then the field H_a in the gap will be uniform, so that the mmf of the gap will be $H_a l_a$ where l_a is its length. Unless the length l_i of the flux path in the iron is very long, H_i in the iron will be essentially uniform, because even for hard steels there cannot be a large amount of leakage flux without surface poles appearing that provide local fields in excess of

H_i. Thus poles will arise to straighten out **B** and **H** inside the iron. We shall have, when the current is turned off, $H_i l_i = H_a l_a$. Since $H_a = B_a/\mu_0 = \Phi/\mu_0 S = B_i/\mu_0$ we can write

$$H_i = \frac{B_i l_a}{\mu_0 l_i} \qquad (8.8-4)$$

and the condition in which the magnet is left will be found by plotting $H_i = -B_i l_a/\mu_0 l_i$ on the demagnetization curve and finding the intersection (note the minus sign for plotting because of the relative directions of H_i and B_i).

Two desirable properties of permanent magnets are large values of the flux Φ in the usable portion of the gap and of the mmf $\mathscr{H}_a$ across this gap. The product of these two is often considered to be a useful single criterion for the "quality" of a magnet. This product is equal to twice the energy stored in the field of the gap, since (taking an integral along a flux line)

$$\mathscr{H}_a \Phi = \int_{\text{gap}} \mathbf{H} \cdot \mathbf{dl} \Phi = \int_{\text{gap}} \mathbf{H} \cdot \mathbf{B} \, dl \, dS = \int_{\text{gap}} \mathbf{H} \cdot \mathbf{B} \, d\tau \qquad (8.8-5)$$

which according to Eq. 7.18–8a is twice the magnetic energy to be assigned to the field in the gap.

For the simple case of the magnet with uniform area and uniform fields, $\mathscr{H}_a \Phi = H_a l_a B_a S = B_i H_i l_i S = B_i H_i \tau_i$, so that for a given value of $\mathscr{H}_a \Phi$, the least volume of iron required can be obtained if the largest value of the product $B_i H_i$ is used. Consequently, curves are frequently given for the product of B and $|H|$ taken along the demagnetization curve.[28] However, it may or may not actually be practical in particular cases to design for the maximum BH product, although the maximum BH is an indication of the general value of a given substance for permanent magnets.[29] Certain aluminum-nickel-cobalt-iron alloys, prepared by a special type of heat treatment, have unusually large BH values and have allowed the construction of powerful magnets of very small size. Alnico V and Ticonal XX are outstanding examples.

The force between two parts of a magnetic circuit that can move relative to one another, as in relays and traction magnets, is a rather complicated function of the flux and the variation of reluctance with displacement. Derivations of the appropriate formulas may be made by considering the energy changes for various portions of the relevant hysteresis loops.[30] The case of two parallel faces with an essentially uniform field and high relative

[28] Attwood, *op. cit.*, pp. 382–386; Morrish, *op. cit.*, p. 365.
[29] The product $B_r H_c$ is also a useful although rough indication of value.
[30] See Roters, *op. cit.*, Chapter VIII, and Matsch, *op. cit.*, Section 3-18.

permeability is quite easy to calculate, and we shall restrict ourselves to this case.

If μ_r is very large, H will be negligibly small inside the iron. Since we can calculate the force on a magnet in terms of poles, we find an analogy with the force on the surface of a conductor, because $E = 0$ inside the conductor. In Eq. 2.4–2, we found the force per unit area to be $\sigma^2/2\epsilon_0$, so that here we should have $\sigma_m^2/2\mu_0$. But $\sigma_m = \mu_0 M_n$, which in the iron is nearly equal to B. Thus for an area S, the force on either surface will be

$$F = \frac{B^2 S}{2\mu_0} = \frac{\Phi^2}{2\mu_0 S} \qquad (8.8\text{–}6)$$

The force will vary with the gap separation, because Φ depends on the reluctance, which is strongly dependent on the separation (cf. Problem 8.8a).

One other example of magnetic forces should be mentioned here. Consider the attraction of a permanent magnet for a distant, unmagnetized object. The field of the magnet will be a dipole field at great distances, with B proportional to r^{-3}. The induced magnetic moment will be roughly proportional to B.

The force on the magnet, $(\mathbf{m} \cdot \nabla)\mathbf{B}$, involves the product of the magnetic moment and the gradient of $\mathbf{B}$, and so it varies like $r^{-3} \times (d/dr)(r^{-3}) \sim r^{-7}$. This inverse seventh-power law explains why magnetic attractions are appreciable over only very short distances. Exact formulas are called for in Problem 8.8b.

Aside from multiplying the left side of Eq. 8.8–1 by $4\pi/c$ and setting $\eta_0 = 1$, the equations for the magnetic circuit are the same in Gaussian as in MKS units.

Problem 8.8a. The magnetic circuit of a certain relay contains a hinge, so that the air-gap length l_a is variable, but the effective path length l_i in the iron is constant. Assuming the cross-sectional area S to be a constant for the entire circuit, find how the force between the poles varies with l_a. Sketch a graph of this force for l_a varying from zero to $10\mu_0 l_i/\mu$, where μ is the average permeability of the iron.

Problem 8.8b. Find the force on a small paramagnetic sphere a distance $r \gg l$ from a uniform bar magnet of length l and moment $\mathbf{m}$, when the sphere is on the axis of the magnet and (b) on its perpendicular bisector.

Problem 8.8c. Write an approximate formula for the self-inductance L of an iron-cored coil of n turns with reluctance $\mathscr{R}$.

Problem 8.8d. Write a formula for the energy stored in a magnetic circuit in terms of flux and reluctance, and discuss the approximations involved.

Problem 8.8e. Find the reluctance of the magnetic circuit shown in Fig. 8.8c, using the value of μ for Armco iron corresponding to an induction on the normal magnetization curve of 9000 gauss. The open rectangles are each 4 cm × 7 cm, and the iron cross section in the straight portions is 1 cm in the plane of the figure by 3 cm in the perpendicular direction. Use center lines for calculating the l's.

Problem 8.8f. It is observed that the force of attraction between two opposite poles of a pair of similar bar magnets, when the poles are in contact, is considerably larger than the force of repulsion when two like poles are forced into contact. Explain.

Problem 8.8g. Use cylindrical harmonics to find the induction **B** in the interior of a circular iron pipe of inner radius a, outer radius b, and permeability μ (assumed constant), placed in an originally homogeneous field $\mathbf{B_0}$ with the axis of the pipe perpendicular to $\mathbf{B_0}$.

8.9 Galvanometers[31]

Current-indicating devices can be made with moving magnets, with wires that change their lengths when heated by the passage of current, and by other means, but by far the most common type of instrument is that with a coil that rotates in a fixed magnetic field. This type of device was invented by Sturgeon in 1836, improved by Thomson in 1867 by use of a fixed soft-iron core within the coil, and brought into essentially its modern form by D'Arsonval[32] in 1882, by the addition of pole pieces to the magnet. Figure 8.9a gives schematic diagrams of side and axial views of two such galvanometers, showing the rectangular coils that can rotate through 90° or so, a pair of coil springs and a wire suspension that exert torques tending to keep the coils in a rest position, and the shaped pole pieces which together with the central iron core make magnetic fields that are accurately radial over the range of motion of the sides of the coils. Current enters and leaves the coil in such an instrument by the suspension springs or wires, and the deflection resulting from the torque of the field on the coil is indicated by either a pointer and scale or a spot of light reflected from the mirror to a distant scale.

We will not concern ourselves here with constructional details[33] but with the principles underlying the motion of the coil. The torque on the coil

---

[31] The results of this section are not needed for the remaining chapters except for references to the differential equations discussed herein. These equations are of considerable importance in the study of transients and pulses in Chapter 9.

[32] A. D'Arsonval, *Comptes Rendus*, **94**, 1347 (1882).

[33] See, for instance, F. K. Harris, *loc. cit.*, Chapter 4, or M. B. Stout, *Basic Electrical Measurements*, 2nd ed., Prentice-Hall, Englewood Cliffs, N.J., 1960, Chapter 5.

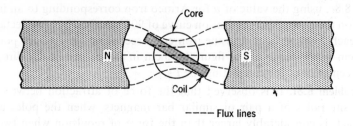

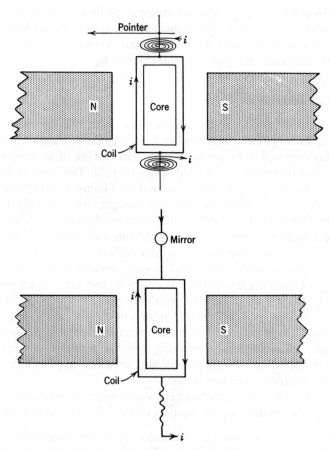

Fig. 8.9a. D'Arsonval galvanometers.

may be found from Eq. 7.12–8. If the coil has n turns, width w, length l, and area $S = wl$, we have

$$\mathcal{T}_m = nBSi = \tau i \qquad (8.9\text{–}1)$$

where $\tau = nBS$ is called the torque constant for the coil.

The mechanical suspension produces a restoring torque that is opposite in sense to the angular deflection θ and generally obeys Hooke's law rather closely. We denote the restoring torque by $\mathcal{T}_r$, and write

$$\mathcal{T}_r = -k\theta \qquad (8.9\text{–}2)$$

where k is the torque constant of the suspension. The angle θ is measured in radians although when static deflections are considered, it is often given in equivalent scale divisions.

The coil can only remain stationary if $\mathcal{T}_m + \mathcal{T}_r = 0$ or $k\theta = \tau i$. The value of θ for which equilibrium holds we will call θ_F, or the final deflection, since we will study at some length the approach of a galvanometer coil to equilibrium. Thus we have the equation

$$k\theta_F = \tau i \qquad (8.9\text{–}3)$$

which, of course, is only meaningful if i is a constant.

Now, we have pointed out in Section 7.4 that the motor effect is always accompanied by the generator effect. Let us calculate the induced emf $\mathcal{E}_b$ accompanying motion of the coil. If θ is the deflection, then $d\theta/dt$ is the angular velocity and $(w/2)\, d\theta/dt$ is the linear velocity of the wires parallel to the axis. Thus by the formula $\mathcal{E} = vBl$, from Eq. 7.4–6a, we have for one wire the emf $\frac{1}{2}Blw\, d\theta/dt$ and for the n turns on the two sides, we have $nBlw\, d\theta/dt = nBS\, d\theta/dt$. Using the appropriate minus sign, the back emf $\mathcal{E}_b$ is given by

$$\mathcal{E}_b = -\tau\, d\theta/dt \qquad (8.9\text{–}4)$$

Another property of the system that we must consider is friction. A coil with an axle that is supported in jewels will have a certain constant amount of frictional torque that changes its direction each time the pointer motion reverses and tends to disappear when the pointer comes to rest. In all well-made galvanometers this torque is small, and its effects are in any case not important to calculate (they are also quite difficult to calculate with accuracy). Hence we shall neglect them. On the other hand, air resistance is always present and may have a considerable frictional effect known as "damping," which is often quite desirable (see below). The torque of air friction is to a good approximation proportional to the angular velocity of the coil, so we write

$$\mathcal{T}_a = -b_a\, d\theta/dt \qquad (8.9\text{–}5)$$

where the minus sign indicates that the torque always opposes the motion. The constant b_a is called the "frictional damping constant."

Now suppose that a constant external emf $\mathscr{E}$ is applied to the coil and that the coil resistance together with any series resistance in the circuit is R. The current that results will depend on the angular velocity of the coil because of the back emf, so that we have

$$\mathscr{E} - \tau \frac{d\theta}{dt} = iR \qquad (8.9\text{–}6)$$

The motion of the coil is determined by Newton's second law in rotational form:

$$\mathscr{T} = I \frac{d^2\theta}{dt^2}$$

where $\mathscr{T}$ is the total torque acting, I is the moment of inertia of the coil and $d^2\theta/dt^2$ represents the angular acceleration. There are three torques that act on the coil, $\mathscr{T}_m$, $\mathscr{T}_r$, and $\mathscr{T}_a$, so that the equation of motion reads

$$\mathscr{T}_m + \mathscr{T}_r + \mathscr{T}_a = \tau i - k\theta - b_a \, d\theta/dt = I \, d^2\theta/dt^2 \qquad (8.9\text{–}7)$$

Using Eq. 8.9–6 to eliminate i and rearranging, we have differential equation for θ:

$$I \frac{d^2\theta}{dt^2} + \left(b_a + \frac{\tau^2}{R}\right)\frac{d\theta}{dt} + k\theta = \frac{\tau\mathscr{E}}{R} \qquad (8.9\text{–}8a)$$

The term $(\tau^2/R)\,d\theta/dt$ acts just like $b_a\,d\theta/dt$ in producing a frictional effect. We will call it the "electromagnetic damping" and write for the combined damping a coefficient b, given by

$$b = b_a + \tau^2/R \qquad (8.9\text{–}8b)$$

Before studying Eq. 8.9–8 in the general case, let us consider two special cases. In the first place, if the coil is at rest with no current in it and $\mathscr{E}$ is then switched on, it is clear that because of friction θ will stop changing after sufficient time has elapsed and its derivatives will become zero. The current will also become a constant, equal to $\mathscr{E}/R$. Setting the derivative terms equal to zero leaves $k\theta = \tau\mathscr{E}/R$, and so after a long time we will have $\theta = \theta_F$, as given by Eq. 8.9–3.

The current sensitivity of a galvanometer S_i is defined as the ratio of the final deflection to the final steady current and is thus seen to be given by $S_i = \tau/k$. It is usually measured in scale divisions per ampere or microampere. For mirror instruments, the scale divisions are commonly taken to be millimeters for a scale at a standard lamp-to-scale distance of 1 m. It is also common to quote sensitivity in reciprocal terms—i.e., microamperes per scale divisions, etc. The voltage sensitivity S_v is the ratio $\theta_F/\mathscr{E} = \tau/kR$ and is measured in corresponding units.

As our second special case, imagine the damping coefficient b to be zero and the external emf $\mathcal{E}$ to have been removed after the coil started moving. The equation of motion reduces to

$$I\frac{d^2\theta}{dt^2} + k\theta = 0 \tag{8.9-9}$$

which is the equation of simple harmonic motion. Any simple harmonic function $\theta(t)$ that satisfies Eq. 8.9-9 will be of the form

$$\theta = \theta_{\max} \sin\left[t\left(\frac{k}{I}\right)^{\!\frac{1}{2}} + \phi\right] \tag{8.9-10}$$

where $\theta_{\max}$ and ϕ can have arbitrary values. The period of the motion, which we shall call T_0, the "undamped period," is given by the relation $T_0(k/I)^{\frac{1}{2}} = 2\pi$, or

$$T_0 = 2\pi\left(\frac{I}{k}\right)^{\!\frac{1}{2}} \tag{8.9-11a}$$

and the angular frequency ω_0 of the motion is related to the frequency f_0 and the period T_0 by

$$\omega_0 = 2\pi f_0 = \frac{2\pi}{T_0} = \left(\frac{k}{I}\right)^{\!\frac{1}{2}} \tag{8.9-11b}$$

Thus, if there were no damping and no external force, the coil once set in motion would continue to oscillate indefinitely with period T_0.

The reader familiar with simple harmonic motion will recognize that Eq. 8.9-10 includes, for suitable values of $\theta_{\max}$ and ϕ, all possible motions that satisfy Eq. 8.9-9—that is, that have the period T_0. It is a general property of second-order differential equations that any function that satisfies such an equation for arbitrary values of two independently adjustable constants is the general solution of the equation, meaning that all possible solutions can be found by suitably adjusting these constants (see Appendix A.3). The two constants for the undamped case are $\theta_{\max}$ and ϕ.

Let us now turn to the general, damped case and seek a solution of Eq. 8.9-8 with two adjustable constants, which we will proceed to adjust so as to fit appropriate physical situations. Since the right-hand side of Eq. 8.9-8a is equal to $k\theta_F$, we can write the equation in the form

$$I\frac{d^2\theta}{dt^2} + b\frac{d\theta}{dt} + k(\theta - \theta_F) = 0 \tag{8.9-12a}$$

Furthermore, since θ_F is a constant, we can use the reduced angle $\theta_r = \theta - \theta_F$ as a variable, obtaining a so-called homogeneous equation (all terms containing the unknown to the first degree)

$$I\frac{d^2\theta_r}{dt^2} + b\frac{d\theta_r}{dt} + k\theta_r = 0 \tag{8.9-12b}$$

To find a solution with arbitrary constants in it, we observe that one way for a constant to enter is by multiplication of θ_r. If a particular θ_r satisfies Eq. 8.9–12b, so will $c\theta_r$ where c is any number. Furthermore, if θ_{r1} and θ_{r2} are two different solutions, their sum is also one, by the rules for differentiating a sum. Hence we will try to find two simple solutions and then add them after multiplying them by adjustable constants.

A function whose derivatives are proportional to itself would be a good one to try. Such a function is $e^{\lambda t}$ where λ is a constant. If we try $\theta_r = e^{\lambda t}$, we have on substitution

$$I\lambda^2 e^{\lambda t} + b\lambda e^{\lambda t} + k e^{\lambda t} = 0$$

and since $e^{\lambda t}$ cannot be zero, we have

$$I\lambda^2 + b\lambda + k = 0 \tag{8.9–13}$$

The roots of this equation are

$$\lambda = -\frac{b}{2I} \pm \frac{1}{2I}(b^2 - 4kI)^{\frac{1}{2}}$$

which we shall write in the form

$$\lambda_1 = -\alpha + \beta \tag{8.9–14a}$$
$$\lambda_2 = -\alpha - \beta \tag{8.9–14b}$$

with

$$\alpha = \frac{b}{2I} = \left(\frac{k}{I}\right)^{\frac{1}{2}} \cdot \frac{b}{2(kI)^{\frac{1}{2}}} = \omega_0 \gamma \tag{8.9–15a}$$

$$\beta = \frac{1}{2I}(b^2 - 4kI)^{\frac{1}{2}} = \left(\frac{k}{I}\right)^{\frac{1}{2}}\left(\frac{b^2}{4kI} - 1\right)^{\frac{1}{2}} = \omega_0(\gamma^2 - 1)^{\frac{1}{2}} \tag{8.9–15b}$$

and

$$\gamma = \frac{b}{2(kI)^{\frac{1}{2}}} = \frac{1}{2(kI)^{\frac{1}{2}}}\left(b_a + \frac{\tau^2}{R}\right) = \gamma_0 + \frac{\tau^2}{2R(kI)^{\frac{1}{2}}} \tag{8.9–16a}$$

where

$$\gamma_0 = b_a/2(kI)^{\frac{1}{2}} \tag{8.9–16b}$$

γ is called the "relative damping" for reasons to be seen later, and γ_0 is the "open-circuit relative damping." Note that β if real is less than α, and that $\alpha^2 - \beta^2 = \omega_0^2$. We observe that $e^{\lambda_1 t}$ and $e^{\lambda_2 t}$ are each solutions of the differential equation for any values of I, b, and k, although β will be real only if γ is greater than 1. We shall assume for the time being that this is so. Let us then add our two solutions, each multiplied by an arbitrary constant, yielding a general solution

$$\theta_r = c_1 e^{\lambda_1 t} + c_2 e^{\lambda_2 t} \tag{8.9–17a}$$

or

$$\theta = \theta_F + c_1 e^{\lambda_1 t} + c_2 e^{\lambda_2 t} \tag{8.9–17b}$$

Now we must ask how c_1 and c_2 are to be specified. There are two simple physical situations that govern most of the cases with which we are concerned. In the first, referred to already, the system starts at $t = 0$ with $\theta = 0$ or $\theta_r = -\theta_F$ and with no initial velocity, so that $d\theta_r/dt = 0$. In the second, we will have $\theta = \theta_r = 0$ at the start and $d\theta/dt$ a certain initial value. This latter case is that of the "ballistic" use of the galvanometer (so called because "ballistics" involves objects—balls, projectiles, etc.—that are given initial velocities and are then subject to Newton's laws of motion) and will be taken up shortly. These two sets of conditions are both referred to as "initial conditions."

Once the dependence of θ on t is determined, the variation of i with t can be found from Eq. 8.9–6 (see Problem 8.9g).

The Approach to a Steady Deflection. For the case of a steady impressed emf, we have

$$\theta_r = -\theta_F; \qquad d\theta_r/dt = 0 \qquad \text{at } t = 0 \qquad (8.9\text{–}18)$$

which yields two equations for c_1 and c_2:

$$-\theta_F = c_1 + c_2 \qquad (8.9\text{–}19)$$

$$0 = \lambda_1 c_1 + \lambda_2 c_2$$

whose solutions are

$$c_1 = \frac{\theta_F \lambda_2}{\lambda_1 - \lambda_2}$$

$$c_2 = \frac{-\theta_F \lambda_1}{\lambda_1 - \lambda_2} \qquad (8.9\text{–}20)$$

as can be easily verified. Using Eqs. 8.9–14 and 8.9–17, we have

$$\theta = \theta_F \left[1 - \frac{\alpha + \beta}{2\beta} e^{-(\alpha-\beta)t} + \frac{\alpha - \beta}{2\beta} e^{-(\alpha+\beta)t} \right] \qquad (8.9\text{–}21)$$

Now, $\alpha - \beta$ and $\alpha + \beta$ are both positive real numbers when $\gamma > 1$, so that the three terms in the brackets represent respectively a constant and two decreasing exponential terms. Thus θ approaches θ_F in exponential fashion, although in a more complicated way than in the cases of the charges and currents of Sections 5.4 and 7.16. If γ is fairly large, α and β will be nearly equal, and the term with $e^{-(\alpha+\beta)t}$ will decrease much more rapidly than $e^{-(\alpha-\beta)t}$ so that after a short time only the latter will be important.

In particular, we can find the time taken for θ to approach within, say, 1% of θ_F. If $\alpha \simeq \beta$, $(\alpha + \beta)/2\beta$ is nearly 1, so that we need only set $e^{-(\alpha-\beta)t} = 0.01$, or $t \simeq 4.6/(\alpha - \beta)$.

Now let us consider what happens if, keeping the initial conditions fixed, the constant b is decreased to the point where $\gamma = 1$. By Eq. 8.9–15, $\beta = 0$, and $\alpha = \omega_0 = 2\pi/T_0$. This situation is often dealt with by an independent solution of the differential equation, but the results are readily obtained by taking a limit in Eq. 8.9–21. The two exponential terms can be written as follows

$$-\frac{\alpha e^{-\alpha t}}{2\beta}(e^{\beta t} - e^{-\beta t}) - \frac{e^{-\alpha t}}{2}(e^{\beta t} + e^{-\beta t}) \qquad (8.9\text{--}22)$$

When β goes to zero, the second term becomes just $-e^{-\alpha t}$. The first term has the form $0/0$ and can be evaluated either by de l'Hôpital's rule (differentiate numerator and denominator with respect to β and then take limits) or by using the Maclaurin series for e^x:

$$e^x = 1 + x + \frac{x^2}{2!} + \cdots$$

The first terms for the two exponentials will cancel; the second terms yield together $2\beta t$, which on dividing by 2β yields the constant t; and the rest of the terms go to zero as $\beta \to 0$. Thus we end up with

$$-\alpha t\, e^{-\alpha t} - e^{-\alpha t}$$

so that

$$\theta = \theta_F[1 - e^{-\alpha t}(\alpha t + 1)]$$
$$= \theta_F[1 - e^{-\omega_0 t}(\omega_0 t + 1)] \qquad (8.9\text{--}23)$$

Again we have an exponential approach of θ to θ_F, but of a different character because of the factor $(\alpha t + 1)$. The reader can verify that if $\alpha t \simeq 6.65$ or $t \simeq 1.06T_0$, θ is about 1% less than θ_F (Problem 8.9l). This case is called that of "critical damping." It will be noted that $2(kI)^{\frac{1}{2}} = b$ for critical damping, which explains why γ is in general called the "relative damping."

Now let us suppose that γ is less than 1. We could also in this case start the solution process over—we might, correctly, guess that the solution had a combined exponential and sinusoidal character, because when $\gamma \to 0$ it must approach the simple harmonic solution, Eq. 8.9–10. However, we can again use our original solution with the same boundary conditions by making use of complex numbers. A considerable use of complex numbers will be required in the next chapter, and many of their properties are taken up in Appendix A.5. Here we need only to quote the relations (see Appendix A.5–11):

$$\sin x = \frac{e^{jx} - e^{-jx}}{2j} \quad \text{and} \quad \cos x = \frac{e^{jx} + e^{-jx}}{2} \qquad (8.9\text{--}24)$$

where we use j for the quantity $\sqrt{-1}$ in accord with current practice in the physics of electromagnetism and in engineering.

When γ is less than one, we shall write

$$\beta = \omega_0(\gamma^2 - 1)^{1/2} = \omega_0(-1)^{1/2}(1 - \gamma^2)^{1/2} = j\omega_0(1 - \gamma^2)^{1/2} = j\omega$$

so that what we shall call the damped angular frequency ω is given by

$$\omega = \omega_0(1 - \gamma^2)^{1/2} \tag{8.9-25}$$

(Note that $\alpha^2 + \omega^2 = \gamma^2\omega_0^2 + \omega^2 = \omega_0^2$.) We can easily rewrite Eq. 8.9–21 with ω instead of β:

$$\theta = \theta_F\left[1 - \frac{\alpha\,e^{-\alpha t}}{2j\omega}(e^{j\omega t} - e^{-j\omega t}) - \frac{e^{-\alpha t}}{2}(e^{j\omega t} + e^{-j\omega t})\right]$$

making use of Eq. 8.9–22. The relations 8.9–24 now yield

$$\theta = \theta_F\left[1 - e^{-\alpha t}\left(\frac{\alpha}{\omega}\sin\omega t + \cos\omega t\right)\right] \tag{8.9-26}$$

which is the solution of Eq. 8.9–12a that satisfies the initial conditions of Eq. 8.9–18 and holds for $\gamma < 1$ or $b < 2(kI)^{1/2}$.

The variable θ now approaches θ_F in an oscillatory fashion, with a steady decreasing amplitude of oscillation about θ_F, proportional to $e^{-\alpha t}$. Figure 8.9b shows the relation between θ and t for particular examples of the three cases we have considered.

The frequency of the oscillating part of Eq. 8.9–26 is $\omega/2\pi$ (the sum of two simple harmonic motions of frequency ω is equal to a simple one of the same frequency) and is less than ω_0. The damping has the effect of slowing down the oscillations from the frequency they would have with

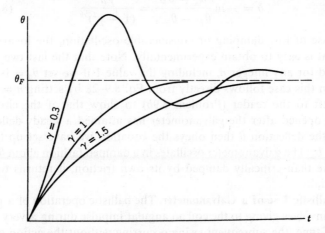

Fig. 8.9b. The approach to equilibrium of a damped galvanometer for three different values of the relative damping.

$\gamma = 0$. When $\gamma \to 1$, $\omega \to 0$; the oscillations disappear as critical damping is approached.

Let us calculate the position of the maxima and minima of the expression 8.9–26. Differentiating with respect to t and canceling two terms, we find

$$\frac{d\theta}{dt} = \theta_F \left(\frac{\alpha^2}{\omega} + \omega \right) e^{-\alpha t} \sin \omega t$$

which is zero when $\sin \omega t$ is 0, or $\omega t = n\pi$ with $n = 1, 2, 3 \cdots$, yielding for t_n, the time of the nth extreme value,

$$t_n = \frac{n\pi}{\omega} = \frac{n\pi}{\omega_0(1 - \gamma^2)^{\frac{1}{2}}} = \frac{nT_0}{2(1 - \gamma^2)^{\frac{1}{2}}} \qquad (8.9\text{–}27)$$

The values of $\theta = \theta_n$ at the maxima and minima are easily found from Eq. 8.9–26. We have $\sin \omega t = 0$ and $\cos \omega t = \cos n\pi = (-1)^n$. Furthermore, we can write $\alpha T_0/2$ as $\pi\gamma$ from Eq. 8.9–15a. Therefore θ_n for the nth extreme value is

$$\theta_n = \theta_F \left\{ 1 - (-1)^n \exp \left[\frac{-\gamma\pi n}{(1 - \gamma^2)^{\frac{1}{2}}} \right] \right\} \qquad (8.9\text{–}28)$$

The ratio of successive (opposite) maximum deviations from the final value θ_F reduces to a simple expression:

$$\frac{\theta_n - \theta_F}{\theta_F - \theta_{n-1}} = \exp \left[\frac{-\gamma\pi}{(1 - \gamma^2)^{\frac{1}{2}}} \right] \qquad (8.9\text{–}29)$$

The negative logarithm of this ratio is called the "logarithmic decrement" δ:

$$\delta = -\ln \frac{\theta_n - \theta_F}{\theta_F - \theta_{n-1}} = \frac{\gamma\pi}{(1 - \gamma^2)^{\frac{1}{2}}} \qquad (8.9\text{–}30)$$

In the case of low damping or considerable oscillation, the logarithmic decrement is easy to obtain experimentally. Note that the last two equations hold for any integer n, including the value 1 if we set $\theta_0 = 0$ (their validity in this case follows directly from Eq. 8.9–28 by setting $n = 1$).

It is left to the reader (Problem 8.9b) to show that if the circuit is suddenly opened after the galvanometer has attained a steady deflection $\theta = \theta_F$, the deflection θ then obeys the equation we have set up for θ_r, with $b = b_a$. The galvanometer oscillates in a damped fashion about $\theta = 0$, or if more than critically damped by its own friction, it returns to zero exponentially.

The Ballistic Use of a Galvanometer. The ballistic operation of a galvanometer involves giving to the coil an angular impulse during a very short period of time, the subsequent swing occurring without the action of any external emf. In other words, the motion after the initial impulse will be governed by Eq. 8.9–8 with $\mathscr{E} = 0$, which is the same as Eq. 8.9–12b for $\theta_r = 0$. The general solution for θ can be written from Eq. 8.9–17a as

$$\theta = c_1' \, e^{\lambda_1 t} + c_2' \, e^{\lambda_2 t} \tag{8.9-31}$$

where c_1' and c_2' are new constants. To find them, we must examine the initial conditions. The ideal case is one in which the initial impulse occurs during a time so short compared to the period T_0 that the deflection during this period is smaller than the errors of measurement. There will, however, be angular velocity $d\theta/dt$ acquired during this time. Let us take the equation of motion in its initial form Eq. 8.9–7, multiply it by dt and integrate over the time Δt of the initial impulse:

$$\tau \int_0^{\Delta t} i \, dt - k \int_0^{\Delta t} \theta \, dt - b_a \int_0^{\Delta t} \frac{d\theta}{dt} \, dt = I \int_0^{\Delta t} \frac{d^2\theta}{dt^2} \, dt$$

Assuming that all quantities are zero at $t = 0$ and that θ is zero throughout the initial time interval, two of the integrals vanish and we have

$$\tau Q = I\left(\frac{d\theta}{dt}\right)_{t=\Delta t}$$

where Q is the total charge passed through the coil. Hence the angular velocity $\hat{\omega}$ acquired with the initial impulse is given by

$$\hat{\omega} = \left(\frac{d\theta}{dt}\right)_{t=\Delta t} = \frac{\tau}{I} Q \tag{8.9-32}$$

(The reader may recognize that τQ represents the angular impulse $\int \mathscr{T} \, dt$ delivered to the coil, and $I\hat{\omega}$ represents the angular momentum acquired.)

Now if Δt is small enough, we can consider that $d\theta/dt = \tau Q/I = \hat{\omega}$ when $t = 0$. Thus we have for the initial conditions for the ballistic galvanometer

$$\theta = 0, \qquad d\theta/dt = \hat{\omega} \qquad \text{when } t = 0 \tag{8.9-33}$$

allowing us to determine c_1' and c_2' in Eq. 8.9–31. The result for θ is (as may be readily verified)

$$\theta = \hat{\omega} \frac{e^{\lambda_1 t} - e^{\lambda_2 t}}{\lambda_1 - \lambda_2} = \frac{\hat{\omega} e^{-\alpha t}}{2\beta} (e^{\beta t} - e^{-\beta t}) \tag{8.9-34}$$

which is the appropriate form of the solution when $\gamma > 0$ and β is real (overdamped case). Letting $\beta \to 0$ as before we find for the critically damped case

$$\theta = \hat{\omega} t \, e^{-\alpha t} = \hat{\omega} t \, e^{-\omega_0 t} \tag{8.9-35}$$

whereas if $\gamma < 1$ and $\beta = j\omega$, we immediately have for the underdamped case

$$\theta = \frac{\hat{\omega}}{\omega} e^{-\alpha t} \sin \omega t \tag{8.9-36}$$

Figure 8.9c shows the variation of θ with t for various values of γ. It will be noted that the coil finally comes to rest in the shortest time when $\gamma = 1$.

The usual method of making observations is to observe the value θ_1 of θ at the first maximum, and so we require formulas for this value and for the time t_1 at which it occurs. The completely undamped case, $\gamma = 0$, gives the equation

$$\theta = \frac{\hat{\omega}}{\omega_0} \sin \omega_0 t$$

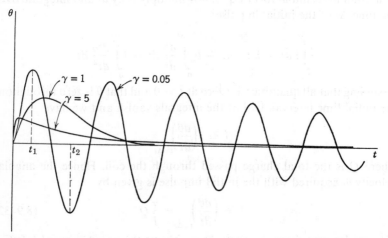

Fig. 8.9c. The deflection of a ballistic galvanometer as a function of time for different amounts of relative damping.

with the values

$$\theta_1 = \frac{\hat{\omega}}{\omega_0} \quad \text{and} \quad t_1 = \frac{\pi}{2\omega_0} = \frac{T_0}{4}; \quad \gamma = 0 \qquad (8.9\text{--}37)$$

When $0 < \gamma < 1$ we set the derivative of Eq. 8.9–36 equal to zero and obtain for any extreme value t_n,

$$\tan \omega t_n = \omega/\alpha \qquad (8.9\text{--}38)$$

The smallest time for which this equation is satisfied is given by the angle ωt_1, shown in Fig. 8.9d, from which we see immediately that $\sin \omega t_1 = \omega/(\omega^2 + \alpha^2)^{1/2} = \omega/\omega_0$ and $\cos \omega_1 t = \alpha/\omega_0 = \gamma$. We have as a result

$$\theta_1 = \frac{\hat{\omega}}{\omega_0} e^{-\alpha t_1} = \frac{\hat{\omega}}{\omega_0} \exp\left[-\frac{\alpha}{\omega} \sin^{-1} \frac{\omega}{\omega_0}\right] = \frac{\hat{\omega}}{\omega_0} \exp\left[\frac{-\gamma \cos^{-1} \gamma}{(1 - \gamma^2)^{1/2}}\right]$$

$$(8.9\text{--}39a)$$

and

$$t_1 = \frac{1}{\omega} \sin^{-1} \frac{\omega}{\omega_0} = \frac{\cos^{-1} \gamma}{\omega_0 (1 - \gamma^2)^{\frac{1}{2}}} = \frac{\sin^{-1}(1 - \gamma^2)^{\frac{1}{2}}}{\omega_0 (1 - \gamma^2)^{\frac{1}{2}}}$$

$$= \frac{T_0}{4} \cdot \frac{2}{\pi (1 - \gamma^2)^{\frac{1}{2}}} \sin^{-1}(1 - \gamma^2)^{\frac{1}{2}}; \quad 0 < \gamma < 1 \quad (8.9\text{-}39b)$$

When γ is very small, the angle ωt_1 is nearly $\pi/2$; in fact, $\sin(\pi/2 - \omega_1 t) = \gamma$, $\frac{\pi}{2} - \omega t_1 \simeq \gamma$, and $\omega \simeq \omega_0$. Then θ_1 is approximately $(\hat{\omega}/\omega_0) e^{-\pi\gamma/2}$. Expanding the exponential to the first-power term, we can write

$$\theta_1 \simeq \frac{\hat{\omega}}{\omega_0}\left(1 - \frac{\pi\gamma}{2}\right) \quad \text{and} \quad t_1 \simeq \frac{T_0}{4}\left(1 - \frac{2\gamma}{\pi}\right); \quad \gamma \ll 1 \quad (8.9\text{-}40)$$

When $\gamma \to 1$, $(1 - \gamma^2)^{\frac{1}{2}}$ becomes small, $\sin^{-1}(1 - \gamma^2)^{\frac{1}{2}} \simeq (1 - \gamma^2)^{\frac{1}{2}}$, and $t_1 = 1/\omega_0$, so that we have a result which can also be obtained from Eq. 8.9-35:

$$\theta_1 = \frac{\hat{\omega}}{\omega_0 e} \quad \text{and} \quad t_1 = \frac{1}{\omega_0} = \frac{T_0}{4} \frac{2}{\pi}; \quad \gamma = 1 \quad (8.9\text{-}41)$$

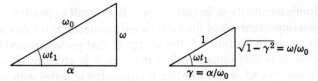

Fig. 8.9d. Illustrating $\tan \omega t_1 = \omega/\alpha$.

For the overdamped case, we differentiate Eq. 8.9-34, getting

$$(-\alpha + \beta) e^{-(\alpha-\beta)t_1} + (\alpha + \beta) e^{-(\alpha+\beta)t_1} = 0,$$

which yields

$$e^{2\beta t_1} = \frac{\alpha + \beta}{\alpha - \beta} = \frac{(\alpha + \beta)^2}{\omega_0^2} = \frac{\omega_0^2}{(\alpha - \beta)^2},$$

the last two forms being obtained from $\alpha^2 - \beta^2 = \omega_0^2$. Thus we have

$$e^{\beta t_1} = \frac{\alpha + \beta}{\omega_0} = \frac{\omega_0}{\alpha - \beta}$$

Furthermore, using $e^{-\beta t_1} = (\alpha - \beta)/\omega_0$,

$$\theta_1 = \frac{\hat{\omega}}{2\beta} e^{-\alpha t_1}\left(\frac{\alpha + \beta}{\omega_0} - \frac{\alpha - \beta}{\omega_0}\right) = \frac{\hat{\omega}}{\omega_0} e^{-\alpha t_1}$$

so we have

$$\theta_1 = \frac{\hat{\omega}}{\omega_0} \exp\left[-\frac{\alpha}{\beta} \ln \frac{\alpha + \beta}{\omega_0}\right] = \frac{\hat{\omega}}{\omega_0} \exp\left\{-\frac{\gamma}{(\gamma^2 - 1)^{\frac{1}{2}}} \ln[\gamma + (\gamma^2 - 1)^{\frac{1}{2}}]\right\}$$

$$(8.9\text{-}42)$$

$$t_1 = \frac{1}{\beta} \ln\left(\frac{\alpha + \beta}{\omega_0}\right) = \frac{1}{\omega_0(\gamma^2 - 1)^{\frac{1}{2}}} \ln[\gamma + (\gamma^2 - 1)^{\frac{1}{2}}]; \quad \gamma > 1$$

Finally, when γ is very large, $(\gamma^2 - 1)^{1/2} \simeq \gamma$, and we have

$$\theta_1 \simeq \frac{\hat{\omega}}{\omega_0} e^{-\ln 2\gamma} = \frac{\hat{\omega}}{2\gamma\omega_0}$$

$$t_1 \simeq \frac{\ln 2\gamma}{\omega_0\gamma} ; \quad \gamma \gg 1 \tag{8.9-43}$$

It will be seen from these various formulas, as well as from Fig. 8.9c, that as γ increases, θ_1 and t_1 both decrease. The question of the proper choice of γ depends on various factors involving the use of the galvanometer.

One use of a ballistic galvanometer is for comparison of capacitances by direct measurement of the charges on two condensers produced by the same charging potential V. However modern bridge methods have largely superseded this method for measuring capacitance. The deflection θ_1 given by Eq. 8.9–39a is a measure of Q, since $\hat{\omega} = \tau Q/I$. We can in fact define the coulomb sensitivity S_Q of the galvanometer as the ratio

$$S_Q = \theta_1/Q = (\tau/\omega_0 I) e^{-\alpha t_1} \tag{8.9-44}$$

The coulomb sensitivity is largest when γ is as small as possible.

The most important use of the ballistic galvanometer is for flux measurements. As shown in Section 9.5, the charge Q that passes around a circuit when a change in flux linkage $\Delta\Phi$ is made in it is given by $Q = \Delta\Phi/R$. Hence if a search coil or test winding is connected in series with a ballistic galvanometer and a flux change is produced by motion or by a change of the magnetic field, a ballistic deflection will occur given by

$$\theta_1 = \frac{\tau\Delta\Phi}{\omega_0 IR} e^{-\alpha t_1} \tag{8.9-45}$$

(a formula valid for any γ) and comparison methods can be used to measure unknown flux changes in terms of known ones. One can also proceed from measurements of R, γ, γ_0, S_i, and T_0 to make absolute measurements. Third, one can use a standard condenser and a known voltage V to measure the coulomb sensitivity S_Q, which together with the value of R gives the flux-linkage sensitivity

$$S_\Phi = \frac{\theta_1}{\Delta\Phi} = \frac{S_Q}{R} \tag{8.9-46}$$

The optimum value of γ for flux measurements—that is, the best value of R—is now not determined by having S_Q large and $\gamma \simeq 0$, but by having γ large (Problem 8.9k). When a galvanometer is used for this purpose with a small resistance R and consequent large damping, a rapid return to zero after a deflection is read is best accomplished by arranging a series key to be opened to start an undamped swing toward 0, which can be arrested by closing the key at 0.

We have assumed in the above an ideal case in which the initial impulse is instantaneous. A careful analysis of the case of a prolonged impulse, which we shall omit here,[34] shows that the error resulting from the finite length of an actual impulse is least for large damping and, as to be expected, for the largest practical period T_0. Hence a ballistic galvanometer for flux-measuring purposes should have both a large relative damping and a long period. Since $\gamma = b/2(kI)^{1/2}$ and $T_0 = 2\pi(I/k)^{1/2}$, the attainment of large T_0 and large γ is aided by the reduction of k, so that a weak suspension is of use for increased sensitivity; so also, by the result of Problem 8.9k, is a low value of the torque constant $\tau = nBS$. Some galvanometers are in fact provided with magnetic shunts for reducing B in the coil gap when extra sensitivity is desired.

The Fluxmeter. This is a galvanometer which is especially arranged for flux measurements with nearly zero restoring torque, and which can be used with slow flux changes as well as fast ones. Let us analyze the system from the original equations in order to appreciate its action. If an emf $d\Phi/dt$ acts in the fluxmeter circuit, we have the circuit equation

$$\frac{d\Phi}{dt} = Ri + L\frac{di}{dt} + \tau\frac{d\theta}{dt}$$

The mechanical equation becomes, with $k = 0$,

$$\tau i = I\frac{d^2\theta}{dt^2} + b_a\frac{d\theta}{dt}$$

Using the latter equation to eliminate i from the former, we have an equation which on integration gives the desired result directly:

$$\frac{d\Phi}{dt} = L\frac{di}{dt} + \frac{RI}{\tau}\frac{d^2\theta}{dt^2} + \left(\frac{b_aR}{\tau} + \tau\right)\frac{d\theta}{dt} \qquad (8.9\text{-}47)$$

We now integrate this equation with respect to dt over a time interval such that both current and coil motion vanish at the ends of the interval. We then obtain, using Δ's for the changes in the quantities over the interval,

$$\Delta\Phi = L\,\Delta i + \frac{RI}{\tau}\Delta\left(\frac{d\theta}{dt}\right) + \left(\frac{b_aR}{\tau} + \tau\right)\Delta\theta$$

which because of the conditions just stated becomes

$$\Delta\Phi = \left(\frac{b_aR}{\tau} + \tau\right)\Delta\theta \qquad (8.9\text{-}48)$$

---

[34] Harris, *op. cit.*, pp. 321–329.

The angular deflection is a direct measure of $\Delta\Phi$, regardless of how fast or slow is the change in Φ. (In practice, changes generally have to be made within five seconds or so to avoid errors due to drifting.) In order to get sensitivity, b_a is made as small as possible, and τ may be reduced by means of magnetic shunts.

It will be noted that the deflection is not measured from zero but may occur at any part of the scale. Arrangements are usually made to provide controllable flux changes in an auxiliary coil to bring the pointer or light spot to a convenient place before making a measurement. The restoring torque of the suspension is sometimes reduced to a very small value by means of an opposing magnetic torque, but it is not usually possible to reduce it altogether to zero; some drift of the coil back to a rest position will generally occur on long standing.

With the exception of replacing the formula for τ by $\tau = nBS/c$, the equations of this section are valid in both MKS and Gaussian units.

Problem 8.9a. Show that Eq. 8.9–23 satisfies Eq. 8.9–12 when $\gamma = 1$.

Problem 8.9b. Discuss the motion of a galvanometer subject to a steady deflection $\theta = \theta_F$ when the circuit is suddenly opened so that i and $\mathscr{E}$ are zero.

Problem 8.9c. If ΔT represents the increase in period over the undamped value T_0 when γ is small, derive an approximate expression for ΔT, showing that it is proportional to b^2.

Problem 8.9d. Find the time in units of T_0 at which the deflection of a galvanometer with $\gamma = 0.825$ first gets to within 1% of θ_F. Show that this value of γ gives the shortest time for the galvanometer to come and remain within 1% of θ_F.

Problem 8.9e. Write a formula for the external critical damping resistance (abbreviation: CDRX) of a galvanometer in terms of τ, k, I, γ_0, and the resistance R_g of the galvanometer itself.

Problem 8.9f. Derive Eq. 8.9–41 from Eq. 8.9–35.

Problem 8.9g. By use of Eq. 8.9–6, write formulas and sketch graphs for the variation of current with time for a galvanometer with a constant impressed emf and values of γ respectively less than, equal to, and greater than 1.

Problem 8.9h. Find θ_1 and t_1 in terms of $\hat{\omega}/\omega_0$ and $T_0/4$ for a ballistic galvanometer with $\gamma = 0.3$, 0.707, 3, and 10.

Problem 8.9i. Show how to find the galvanometer design constants b_a, I, k, and τ from the readily measurable quantities R, γ, γ_0, ω_0, and S_i.

Problem 8.9j. Discuss the influence of a shunt across a galvanometer on its use for the measurement of capacitance.

Problem 8.9k. Show that S_Φ increases steadily with γ as γ ranges from 0 to ∞, with a limiting value $1/\tau$.

Problem 8.9l. Verify the statement following Eq. 8.9–23.

Problem 8.9m. Figure 8.9e gives the circuit of an Ayrton shunt for a galvanometer. If the current i is independent of the switch position (for instance if the line resistance $R_L \gg R_0$), show that i_g is proportional to the fraction x, no matter what constant value of R_g is used.

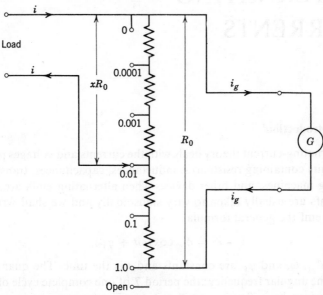

Fig. 8.9e. A circuit for an Ayrton shunt.

Problem 8.9n. A long flexible non-magnetic coil in the form of a ribbon-shaped solenoid has a double layer of windings, wound so that their fields add. The two leads come out at one end and are carefully twisted so as not to enclose appreciable area. Show that if such a coil is connected to a fluxmeter and moved into an arbitrary position in a magnetic field, the deflection resulting will be a measure of $\int \mathbf{H} \cdot \mathbf{dl}$ along the final position of the coil.

Chapter 9

ALTERNATING CURRENTS

9.1 Introduction[1]

Alternating-current theory deals with the currents and voltages produced in circuits containing resistances, inductances, capacitances, transformers, rotating machines, and other devices when alternating emfs are applied. The emfs are usually taken to vary sinusoidally and we shall write for a typical emf the general formula

$$\mathscr{E} = \mathscr{E}_m \cos(\omega t + \varphi_V) \tag{9.1-1}$$

where $\mathscr{E}_m$, ω, and φ_V are constants and t is the time. The quantity ω is called the angular frequency; the period T of one complete cycle of oscillation is given by $\omega T = 2\pi$, or $T = 2\pi/\omega$. The frequency f in cycles per second is therefore $\omega/2\pi$, and $\mathscr{E}_m$ is called the amplitude of the alternating emf.

Other types of variation are also treated in this theory, but we shall emphasize the case of sinusoidal variations and later deal briefly with harmonic analysis and pulse theory, cases that depend on sinusoidal analysis through its use in Fourier series and the Laplace transformation method.

We shall also restrict ourselves for the time being to the case in which emfs of the type of Eq. 9.1-1 have been established for a long enough time that the transient effects due to their establishment have died out. It seems obvious that if the emfs are sinusoidal, the currents will be too, with the same angular frequency ω; we shall show that a solution of the

---

[1] The only part of this chapter that is needed for the study of Chapter 10 is the treatment of the complex-number method in Section 9.4, although a brief reference is made in Chapter 10 to the frequency and pulse analyses of Sections 9.7 and 9.8.

relevant differential equation of this form does in fact exist. The transient treatment in Section 9.8 will provide the proof that it is the *unique* solution and in fact show how rapidly it becomes established.

The main part of our analysis will deal with circuits containing only resistances, capacitances, and inductances, and we shall assume these quantities to be lumped, as in Sections 5.4 (for condensers) and 7.16 (for self-inductances). Our treatment with lumped quantities will lay the foundation for introductory work with distributed quantities in Section 10.2. The fact that all capacitance of any importance in our circuits appears explicitly in the indicated capacitors means that no charging up or discharging occurs at any other place, so that all currents are the same throughout any branch at any given instant, and Kirchhoff's junction law remains valid. Similarly, the lumping of inductance elements means that all the electromagnetically induced emfs are explicitly introduced at the designated inductance coils and can be written as potential drops, as in Section 7.16, so that Kirchhoff's loop rule for emfs also remains valid at any instant.

The final restriction to be kept in mind is that we take R's, L's, M's, and C's to be constants, thus assuming ideal linear behavior of each of these elements. In particular, we shall not consider such high frequencies that the skin effect discussed at the end of Section 7.17 is important. Some reference to non-ideal behavior will be made later.

9.2 Series Circuits

We begin our alternating-current (a-c) theory with a discussion of the circuit of Fig. 9.2*a*, containing a resistance R, a self-inductance L, and a capacitance C in series, to which is applied an alternating emf $\mathscr{E}$ (often called by the redundant expression an "a-c voltage"). By treating the emf $-L(di/dt)$ as a PD, we can write the generalization of Eqs. 5.4–5 and 7.16–3:

$$\mathscr{E} = L\frac{di}{dt} + Ri + \frac{q}{C} \qquad (9.2\text{–}1)$$

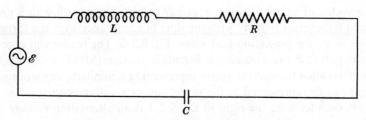

Fig. 9.2*a*. A series circuit with R, L, and C.

where the current i and charge q are related by

$$i = \frac{dq}{dt} \qquad (9.2\text{-}2)$$

As stated above, we shall use Eq. 9.1-1 and assume that i also varies in a sinusoidal way, so that (introducing new constants i_m and φ_i),

$$i = i_m \cos (\omega t + \varphi_i) \qquad (9.2\text{-}3)$$

from which we have

$$L \frac{di}{dt} = -L\omega i_m \sin (\omega t + \varphi_i) \qquad (9.2\text{-}4)$$

and

$$\frac{q}{C} = \frac{1}{C}\int i \, dt = \frac{i_m}{\omega C} \sin (\omega t + \varphi_i) \qquad (9.2\text{-}5)$$

The constant of integration arising from the indefinite integral for q must be zero if Eq. 9.2-1 is to be satisfied. To see this, we integrate both sides

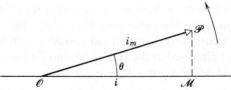

Fig. 9.2b. A graphical representation of an alternating current as the projection of a vector.

of the equation over a period T. The sine and cosine terms will integrate to zero because they are periodic. Thus any constant term in q/C must be zero.

It is a straightforward matter to substitute Eqs. 9.2-3, 9.2-4, and 9.2-5 into Eq. 9.2-1 and evaluate the constants i_m and φ_i by means of suitable trigonometric relations, but we shall leave this method of calculation to the reader in Problem 9.2a. A method more instructive for our purposes is to represent alternating currents and voltages graphically as projections of rotating vectors.

If a vector of length i_m, as in Fig. 9.2b, makes an angle θ with a given line and θ increases steadily with the time in accordance with the formula $\theta = \omega t + \varphi_i$, the projection $\mathcal{OM}$ obeys Eq. 9.2-3. The reader will observe that the point $\mathcal{M}$ executes simple harmonic motion (SHM) about $\mathcal{O}$. The line $\mathcal{OP}$ is called the current vector representing i. Similarly any sinusoidal voltage can be represented as the projection of a voltage vector.

Now, each term on the right in Eq. 9.2-1 is an alternating voltage and can be represented as the projection of an appropriate voltage vector. The sum indicated is thus a sum of projections of appropriate vectors, and we shall express it as the projection of the sum of these vectors.

The quantity Ri is simply R times $\mathcal{OM}$, or the projection of the current vector times R. The term $L(di/dt)$ is equal to

$$-L\omega i_m \sin(\omega t + \varphi_i) = -L\omega i_m \sin \theta$$

and is indicated in Fig. 9.2c as the projection of a vector of length $L\omega i_m$, 90° from $\mathcal{OP}$ in the positive sense.   Since $\cos(\theta + \pi/2)$ is always equal

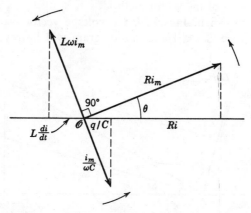

Fig. 9.2c. Voltages in a series circuit as projections.

to $-\sin\theta$, this relation is valid for all values of θ. The term representing q/C, according to Eq. 9.2–5, is $(i_m/\omega C)\sin\theta$, and is shown in Fig. 9.2c as the projection of a vector opposite to that for $L(di/dt)$. We say that the vector for the inductive voltage is ahead of the resistive vector and that the capacitive-voltage vector is behind.

The sum of the three projections is the emf $\mathcal{E}$, so we can construct a vector representation for $\mathcal{E}$ by adding the three vectors already found, as in Fig. 9.2d.

We have, for convenience, performed the vector addition by adding the two oppositely directed vectors first, and combining this result with the Ri_m vector. From Fig. 9.2d we can immediately find the constants $\mathcal{E}_m$ and φ_V of Eq. 9.1–1. We see that $\mathcal{E}_m$ is the hypotenuse of a right triangle and is given by

$$\mathcal{E}_m = \left[(Ri_m)^2 + \left(L\omega i_m - \frac{i_m}{\omega C}\right)^2\right]^{1/2}$$

$$= i_m\left[R^2 + \left(L\omega - \frac{1}{\omega C}\right)^2\right]^{1/2} \qquad (9.2–6)$$

The angles $\omega t + \varphi_V$ and $\omega t + \varphi_i$ are indicated in Fig. 9.2d, so that their difference, the angle $\varphi = \varphi_V - \varphi_i$, is seen to be given by the relation

$$\tan (\varphi_V - \varphi_i) = \tan \varphi = \frac{L\omega - 1/\omega C}{R} \qquad (9.2\text{--}7)$$

Note that these equations could be derived by drawing the vectors of Fig. 9.2d as stationary, with $\omega t + \varphi_i = 0$. It is possible to analyze a-c circuits of considerable complexity by using stationary-vector diagrams. The complex-number type of analysis, to be treated in Section 9.4, is an algebraic extension of the vector method.

In the case shown in Fig. 9.2d, the voltage vector leads the current vector. In the case $L\omega < 1/\omega C$, the diagram will be reversed, and the

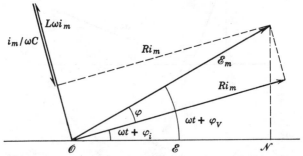

Fig. 9.2d.   The emf $\mathscr{E}$ is the projection $\mathcal{ON}$ of a vector found by adding the three vectors of Fig. 9.2c. Note that the phase angle is $\varphi = \varphi_V - \varphi_L$.

current vector will lead the voltage vector; the angle $\varphi = \varphi_V - \varphi_i$ will become negative. We can also say that in the first case, the current lags behind the voltage, and vice versa for the second case. Either φ_V or φ_i can be taken as zero without loss of generality, since t can be measured from any arbitrary zero of time. The angle φ is sometimes called the phase angle of the emf with respect to the current. The angle $\omega t + \varphi_V$ or $\omega t + \varphi_i$ is sometimes called the phase, but as it is not a constant it is not often referred to.

The square root in Eq. 9.2–6 is a quantity of first importance. It is equal to the ratio $\mathscr{E}_m/i_m$ and is called the impedance,[2] Z. The quantity $L\omega$ is called the inductive reactance X_L; $1/\omega C$ is called the capacitive reactance X_C; and the difference $X_L - X_C$ or $X_C - X_L$ is called the reactance X. (It is not necessary to give a definite sign to X since it appears squared; it may be denoted as principally capacitive or principally inductive depending on which of X_C or X_L is the larger. We shall find it convenient, however, to define X algebraically as $X_L - X_C$.)

[2] "Impedance" and "reactance" are sometimes used to designate *objects* that possess the quantities referred to.

To summarize

$$X_L = L\omega \tag{9.2-8}$$

$$X_C = 1/\omega C \tag{9.2-9}$$

$$X = X_L - X_C \tag{9.2-10}$$

$$Z = (R^2 + X^2)^{1/2} \tag{9.2-11}$$

$$\varphi_V - \varphi_i = \varphi = \tan^{-1}\frac{X}{R} = \sin^{-1}\frac{X}{Z} = \cos^{-1}\frac{R}{Z} \tag{9.2-12}$$

The different expressions for φ in the last line are derived from the right triangle formed by $i_m R$, $i_m X$, and $i_m Z$. Reactance and impedance are, like resistance, measured in ohms.

Although we have made the calculation assuming that an emf is directly applied to the circuit under consideration, the results also give the relation

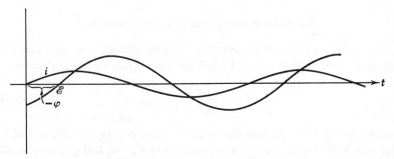

Fig. 9.2e. Phase relations in a capacitive circuit.

between voltage drop and current in the circuit when it is a branch of a more complex circuit.

For a circuit containing only resistance and capacitance, we can set $L = 0$ and obtain

$$i_m = \mathscr{E}_m/(R^2 + 1/\omega^2 C^2)^{1/2} \tag{9.2-13}$$

from which we see that the current decreases with increasing R, as expected, and increases with increasing C and ω. At very high frequencies or for large capacitance values, the impedance reduces essentially to the resistance R. For zero frequency, Z is infinite and i is zero. No direct current will pass through an ideal capacitor.

The phase relation between current and voltage may be represented by a time graph, produced by measuring the current and voltage vertically (i.e., choosing a vertical line for projection) and the time horizontally and to the right. Then it is easy to see that the quantity whose vector leads the other in Fig. 9.2d will arrive at a maximum or a minimum somewhat before the other (to the left in the time graph) as in Fig. 9.2e.[3] The order of the current and voltage graphs in Fig. 9.2e can be remembered from the fact that in a condenser, charge and voltage cannot be acquired until after a current has been established for a period of time. The amount by which one curve is ahead of the other can be measured in seconds or radians, but is usually measured in degrees. The phase angle in a capacitive circuit has the maximum value of 90° when $R = 0$.

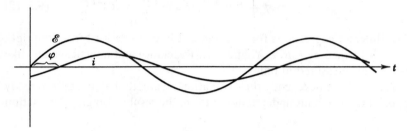

Fig. 9.2f. Phase relations in an inductive circuit.

The case of a circuit with resistance and inductance is to be treated by letting $C \to \infty$ so that q/C and $1/\omega C$ are zero. Then we have, of course,

$$i_m = \frac{\mathscr{E}_m}{(R^2 + L^2\omega^2)^{\frac{1}{2}}} \qquad (9.2\text{--}14)$$

and we see that in this case the largest current occurs for zero ω and L. For very high frequencies, i_m is approximately $\mathscr{E}_m/\omega L$ and gets very small. The phase relation is shown in Fig. 9.2f—in an inductance, the current tends to stay constant and so lags behind the emf that tries to change it. Since (except for superconductors), no actual coil can have zero resistance, the angle by which $\mathscr{E}$ leads i is always less than 90°.

When both C and L are present, the reactance is large and capacitive for low frequencies and large and inductive for high frequencies. There is a particular value ω_0 of ω for which $X = 0$ and hence Z has its minimum value R. A series circuit for which X is zero is said to be resonant. The angle φ must also be zero; we say that the current and voltage are in phase with one another.

To find ω_0 we set

$$X = L\omega_0 - \frac{1}{\omega_0 C} = 0$$

---

[3] The reader should remember that in graphs like this and the next a point representing a time t is to be thought of as moving to the right as time goes on, with the graph remaining stationary. If it is desired to keep the time point fixed and think of the graph as a moving wave, it must be made to move to the left.

which gives $\omega_0^2 LC = 1$ or

$$\omega_0 = \frac{1}{(LC)^{1/2}} \qquad (9.2\text{--}15)$$

For the resonance frequency, we then have

$$f_0 = \frac{\omega_0}{2\pi} = \frac{1}{2\pi(LC)^{1/2}} \qquad (9.2\text{--}16)$$

Figure 9.2g shows the ratio of R to Z as a function of ω/ω_0 for three values of the parameter $\omega_0 L/R$, since the ratio can be written (using $\omega_0 CL = 1/\omega_0$)

$$\frac{R}{Z} = \frac{R}{\left[R^2 + \omega_0^2 L^2 \left(\frac{\omega}{\omega_0} - \frac{1}{\omega\omega_0 CL} \right)^2 \right]^{1/2}}$$

$$= \frac{1}{\left[1 + \frac{\omega_0^2 L^2}{R^2} \left(\frac{\omega}{\omega_0} - \frac{\omega_0}{\omega} \right)^2 \right]^{1/2}} \qquad (9.2\text{--}17)$$

The quantity $\omega_0 L/R = (L/R^2 C)^{1/2}$ is commonly denoted by Q_0 and is sometimes called the "figure of merit" or "quality ratio" but is most often referred to simply as "Q" (not to be confused with charge!). It is here seen as a property of a series circuit and may be defined in general for any resonant type of circuit. In many cases the resistance is that of the coil winding, and for these cases, Q_0 is a property of the coil (and of course is frequency-dependent). For an arbitrary frequency ω it is written simply $Q = \omega L/R$. It is evident from Fig. 9.2g that Q_0 determines the sharpness of the maximum of $i_m = \mathcal{E}_m/Z = (\mathcal{E}_m/R)(R/Z)$ obtained when the frequency is varied.

A method of describing the sharpness is to find the two values of ω for which R/Z is $1/\sqrt{2}$ times its maximum value (the so-called half-power points—see Problem 9.3f and Fig. 9.2g) and to record their difference. The value of Z will be $\sqrt{2}R$ when $X^2 = R^2$ or $X = \pm R$. Hence we can write for these two values, which we call ω_1 and ω_2,

$$\left. \begin{array}{l} \omega_1 L - \dfrac{1}{\omega_1 C} = R \\[2ex] \dfrac{1}{\omega_2 C} - \omega_2 L = R \end{array} \right\} \qquad (9.2\text{--}18)$$

Setting these two expressions equal, we readily obtain

$$(\omega_1 + \omega_2)L = \frac{\omega_1 + \omega_2}{\omega_1 \omega_2 C}$$

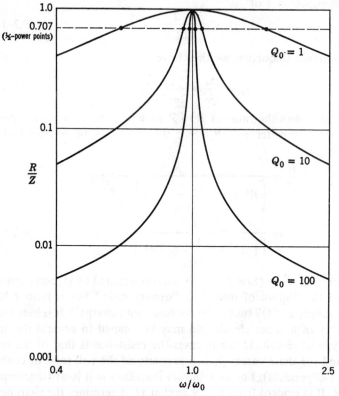

Fig. 9.2g.   The ratio R/Z as a function of ω/ω_0 for a series resonant circuit. The figure of merit is $Q_0 = \omega_0 L/R$. Note that both abscissa and ordinate are plotted on logarithmic scales.

so that

$$\omega_1\omega_2 = \frac{1}{LC} = \omega_0{}^2 \qquad (9.2\text{-}19)$$

Adding the two Eqs. 9.2–18 yields

$$(\omega_1 - \omega_2)L + \frac{\omega_1 - \omega_2}{\omega_1\omega_2 C} = 2R$$

which with Eq. 9.2–19 gives

$$\omega_1 - \omega_2 = \frac{R}{L} \qquad (9.2\text{-}20)$$

and the relative difference in comparison to ω_0 is

$$\frac{\omega_1 - \omega_2}{\omega_0} = \frac{R}{\omega_0 L} = \frac{1}{Q_0} \qquad (9.2\text{-}21a)$$

The difference $f_1 - f_2$ between the two half-power frequencies is frequently called the "bandwidth" BW of the resonant curve. We see that BW is given by the formula

$$f_1 - f_2 = BW = \frac{f_0}{Q_0} = \frac{R}{2\pi L} \qquad (9.2\text{–}21b)$$

Resonant circuits form the basis of oscillators, radio receivers, etc., and for all such that demand sharp resonance curves (sharp "tuning"), a large Q_0 is desirable.

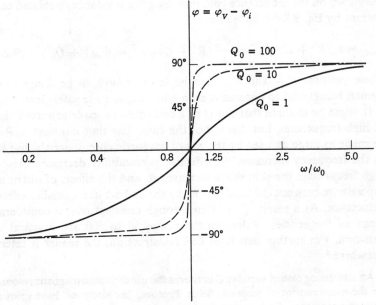

Fig. 9.2h. The variation of phase angle with frequency in a series circuit.

The phase angle φ can be expressed readily in terms of Q_0 and ω/ω_0:

$$\varphi = \tan^{-1}\left(\frac{\omega L - 1/\omega C}{R}\right) = \tan^{-1} Q_0\left(\frac{\omega}{\omega_0} - \frac{\omega_0}{\omega}\right) \qquad (9.2\text{–}22)$$

Figure 9.2h shows this function for three values of Q_0.

Besides the effect of resonance in producing a minimum impedance at a certain frequency, there is also the effect of producing voltage amplitudes on the inductance and capacitor that are considerably larger than the amplitude of the applied emf. It will be noted from Fig. 9.2d that at resonance the inductive and capacitive voltage vector exactly cancel each other, and so each of them can readily be quite large. In fact, for the capacitor voltage amplitude, we have

$$V_m = i_m/\omega C = \frac{\mathscr{E}_m}{\omega CZ}$$

which at resonance is

$$V_m = \frac{\mathscr{E}_m}{\omega_0 CR} = \mathscr{E}_m \frac{\omega_0 L}{R} = Q_0 \mathscr{E}_m \qquad (9.2\text{--}23)$$

and so can be very much larger than $\mathscr{E}_m$. The voltage on the inductance itself has, of course, the same resonance value. The voltage amplitude at resonance on the inductance *coil*, including the resistance, is related to the current by Eq. 9.2–14, so we have

$$V_{mL} = i_m (R^2 + L^2 \omega_0^2)^{\frac{1}{2}} = \frac{\mathscr{E}_m}{R}(R^2 + L^2 \omega_0^2)^{\frac{1}{2}} = \mathscr{E}_m(1 + Q_0^2)^{\frac{1}{2}} \quad (9.2\text{--}24)$$

These voltages V_{mL} and V_{mC} can be large enough to be dangerous to human beings and to apparatus even when $\mathscr{E}_m$ is quite safely low.

It might be thought that the Q of a coil could be made arbitrarily large at high frequencies, but this is not the case. The time constant L/R can be made as large as 1 sec by the use of magnetic core materials, but then as the frequency increases, the effective permeability decreases. Also, at high frequencies the skin effect increases R, and the effects of distributed capacitance between the windings make the coil act like a smaller effective inductance. As a result, Q is often a rough constant over a considerable range of frequencies. Values in the range 50 to 300 are practical and common. For further details of coil construction, the reader is referred elsewhere.[4]

An interesting case of variable Q concerns the use of proton magnetic resonance for the measurement of magnetic fields. Protons, like electrons, have spins and magnetic moments. Each proton has an angular momentum of $h/4\pi$, like that of an electron; its electromagnetic moment, however, is not so simply related to its mass as is true for an electron. The proton magnetic moment m_p has been measured and found to be 2.79275 ± 0.00003 times the nuclear magneton $eh/4\pi M_p$ (5.0505×10^{-27} ampere - m²), where M_p is the proton mass. A proton in a magnetic field can line up with the field or against it, with thus two possible energy values $m_p B$ and $-m_p B$. At any given temperature in a steady field there will be a slightly greater proportion of protons with the lower energy value—the difference in numbers being about 1 part in 10^5 at room temperature.

Now, according to the quantum theory, energy changes can be induced by alternating electric and magnetic fields whose frequency f is related to the energy change U by $U = hf$. So if some proton-bearing material, water for instance, is

[4] G. P. Harnwell, *Principles of Electricity and Electromagnetism*, 2nd ed., McGraw-Hill, New York, 1949, pp. 469–473; F. E. Terman, *Radio Engineer's Handbook*, McGraw-Hill, New York, 1943, pp. 74ff.

inserted in a coil, and the combination is placed in a field of strength B, energy jumps can occur when an alternating current of frequency $f = U/h = m_p B/h$ is passed through the coil. Since there are more protons in the lower energy state, there will result from many random changes a small but finite absorption of energy. The result is just the same as if the resistance of the coil were increased or the Q decreased.

Thus, if a fixed frequency is applied to a coil and B is varied, there will be a change of Q when $B = hf/m_p$, and the alternating PD on the coil will change, although by a very small amount. If a sensitive arrangement, usually an a-c bridge, is made for detecting this change, B can be measured in terms of frequency and m_p. Since frequency can be measured to a part in 10^6, and m_p is known (by use of a calibrated magnet at the National Bureau of Standards) to 1 part in 50,000, very high accuracy in magnetic-field measurements can be attained. Accuracy is especially high in relative determinations of one field with respect to another.

The relations we have calculated in this section can readily be applied to a more complicated series circuit. For instance, if elements R_1, L_1, C_1, and R_2, L_2, C_2 are all connected in series, as indicated in Fig. 9.2i, the current amplitude will be

$$i_m = \frac{\mathscr{E}_m}{[(R_1 + R_2)^2 + (X_1 + X_2)^2]^{1/2}} = \frac{\mathscr{E}_m}{Z}$$

with $\mathscr{E}$ ahead of i by the angle

$$\varphi = \tan^{-1} \frac{X_1 + X_2}{R_1 + R_2}$$

The amplitude of the voltage V_2 on the impedance Z_2 will then be

$$V_{2,m} = i_m(R_2{}^2 + X_2{}^2) = i_m Z_2 = \frac{\mathscr{E}_m Z_2}{Z}$$

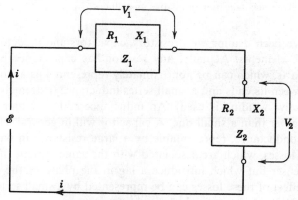

Fig. 9.2i. Two impedances in series.

and the angle of lead of V_2 ahead of i will be

$$\varphi_2 = \tan^{-1}\frac{X_2}{R_2}$$

so that the angle by which $\mathscr{E}$ leads V_2 is

$$\varphi' = \tan^{-1}\frac{X_1 + X_2}{R_1 + R_2} - \tan^{-1}\frac{X_2}{Z_2}$$

Similarly, the relative magnitudes and phase angles of the voltages V_1 and V_2 can be readily calculated.

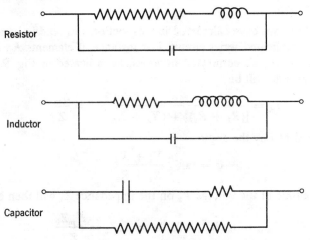

Resistor

Inductor

Capacitor

Fig. 9.2j. Circuit representations of actual elements. The drawings are made so as to give some indication of relative magnitudes.

We have been dealing with resistors, capacitors and inductors as ideal or "pure" elements. Actually, any resistor has capacitance between its various parts, which can be approximately represented as a small capacitance between its ends and a small series inductance (extremely small if a non-inductive winding is used). An inductance coil is similar but has a large Q rather than a small one. A capacitor will in general have a small leakage conductance, representable by a large resistance in parallel, and dielectric losses, which are associated with the same current that charges the condenser but which introduce a lag in the phase of the current so that the effect of these losses can be represented by a small series resistor. Figure 9.2j shows the equivalent circuits.

Problem 9.2a. Set $\varphi_i = 0$ and substitute for $\mathscr{E}$ and i in Eq. 9.2–1. Equate coefficients of sin ωt and cos ωt, and find i_m and φ. Check with the calculation in the text.

Problem 9.2b. Discuss the variation of the ratio $\mathscr{E}/i$ with time and tell why it is not a useful quantity for describing a-c circuits.

Problem 9.2c. In what mathematical way does the current approach zero with ω in a circuit with resistance and capacitance?

Problem 9.2d. Show that the maximum voltage amplitude on the inductance L in a series circuit occurs for a frequency somewhat different from the resonance value, and find a formula for this maximum.

Problem 9.2e. Express the ratio of the voltage amplitude on the condenser in a series circuit to $\mathscr{E}_m$ as a function of Q_0 and ω/ω_0, and sketch graphs of this ratio against ω/ω_0 for $Q_0 = 1$ and $Q_0 = 10$.

Problem 9.2f. Solve Problem 9.2e for the voltage on the inductance coil (L and R together).

Problem 9.2g. Find the capacitances that would resonate with a 12-henry inductance at 60 cycles and at 1000 cycles. What should the resistance be in each case for a Q_0 of 10?

Problem 9.2h. A series circuit is often tuned to resonance by varying the capacitance with ω fixed. Find the values C_1 and C_2 for which the impedance is $\sqrt{2}R$, and express $(C_1 - C_2)/C_0$ in terms of Q, where C_0 is the resonant capacitance. Show how to find C_0 in terms of C_1 and C_2. (C_1 and C_2 are easier to determine with precision than is C_0.) Express L and R in terms of C_1, C_2, and ω.

Problem 9.2i. Write R/Z for a simple series circuit as a function of the relative deviation of the frequency from resonance, $\delta = (\omega - \omega_0)/\omega_0$. Make a simple approximation of this expression for small δ. (This expression is easier to evaluate numerically than Eqs. 9.2–6 or 9.2–17, as it eliminates the subtraction of two nearly equal quantities.)

Problem 9.2j. Two impedances Z_1 and Z_2 are connected in series to a 500-cycle emf of $\mathscr{E}_m = 20$ v. Z_1 consists of a resistance of 50 ohms and an inductance of 20 mh. Z_2 consists of a 20 ohm resistance, a 70-mh inductance, and a 20-μf condenser. Find the voltage amplitudes on Z_1 and Z_2 and the phase angle between them.

Problem 9.2k. Show that a plot of $\mathscr{E}$ vs i, as given by eliminating t from Eqs. 9.1–1 and 9.2–3, is an ellipse. In particular, show that in terms of the variables $x = \mathscr{E}/\mathscr{E}_m$ and $y = i/i_m$, the ellipse has its principal axes at 45° to the x and y axes. Set $\varphi_i = 0$ and show that the shape of the ellipse depends on φ_V.

9.3 Power Relations

The instantaneous rate at which the emf $\mathscr{E}$ of Section 9.2 furnishes energy for the circuit of that section is given by

$$P = \mathscr{E}i = \mathscr{E}_m i_m \cos{(\omega t + \varphi_V)} \cos{(\omega t + \varphi_i)} \qquad (9.3\text{--}1)$$

which by Eqs. 9.2–1, 9.2–3, 9.2–4, and 9.2–5 can be written, setting $\varphi_i = 0$ and $\varphi_V = \varphi$ for convenience,

$$P = -L\omega i_m^2 \sin{\omega t}\cos{\omega t} + R i_m^2 \cos^2{\omega t} + \frac{i_m^2}{\omega C} \sin{\omega t}\cos{\omega t} \qquad (9.3\text{--}2a)$$

By the rules of trigonometry, we can rewrite this as

$$P = -\tfrac{1}{2}L\omega i_m^2 \sin{2\omega t} + \tfrac{1}{2}R i_m^2 (1 + \cos{2\omega t}) + \frac{i_m^2}{2\omega C} \sin{2\omega t} \qquad (9.3\text{--}2b)$$

By combining terms in Eq. 9.3–2, using $X = Z \sin{\varphi}$ and $R = Z \cos{\varphi}$, or by transforming Eq. 9.3–1 directly, we can write finally

$$P = \tfrac{1}{2}i_m^2 Z[\cos{(2\omega t + \varphi)} + \cos{\varphi}] \qquad (9.3\text{--}2c)$$

Figure 9.3a shows time graphs of the separate terms of Eq. 9.3–2, which are of course the powers for the three circuit elements, and the total as calculated from Eq. 9.3–3.

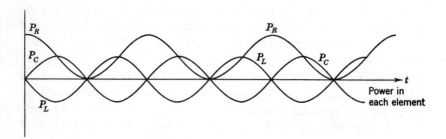

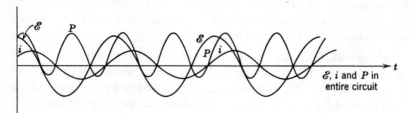

Fig. 9.3a. The power consumption in R, L, C, and in the entire series circuit.

It will be noted that energy alternately enters and leaves the inductance and capacitance in symmetrical fashion with regard to positive and negative power consumption. The power expended in the resistor is always positive, and the total is positive more often than negative (Problem 9.3a).

The energy stored in the inductance is, according to Section 7.18, $U_L = \frac{1}{2}Li^2$. That in the condenser, by Problem 2.5c or Section 4.7, is $U_C = \frac{1}{2}q^2/C$. Utilizing Eqs. 9.2–3 and 9.2–5, we can graph these quantities as shown in Fig. 9.3b. It will be noted that energy flows in and out of these elements but never builds up. We see from both figures that the average power expended in the two reactive elements is zero; this is also clear from Eq. 9.3–2b, since the average value of a sine or cosine is zero. On the

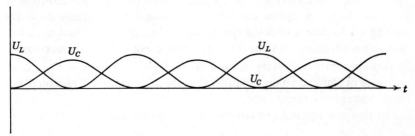

Fig. 9.3b. The energy stored in the inductance and capacitance of a series circuit.

other hand, the average power in the resistor is $\frac{1}{2}Ri_m^2$, which is therefore the entire average power and can in fact be found from Eq. 9.3–3.

The ratio of the energy expended per cycle to the stored energy that flows between L and C is

$$\frac{\frac{1}{2}Ri_m^2 T}{\frac{1}{2}Li_m^2} = \frac{2\pi R}{\omega L} = \frac{2\pi}{Q} \tag{9.3–3}$$

so that a high-Q coil dissipates little of its energy per cycle, and a reduction of Q as in a spin-resonance experiment results in an increased dissipation rate.

The situation bears a striking resemblance to that of forced vibratory SHM of constant amplitude, for instance of a mass m on a spring of force constant k, with displacement x and a frictional force proportional to $v = dx/dt$. In this case, the power expended by the external force all goes into friction; the potential energy $\frac{1}{2}kx^2$ of the spring and the kinetic $\frac{1}{2}mv^2$ continually interchange with each other and with the external power source. To show that the analogy is in fact exact, we replace in Eq. 9.2–1 q by x, i by v, $1/C$ by k, L by m, R by a frictional constant b, and $\mathscr{E}$ by an external force F_{ext}. Then the equation can be rearranged to give

$$F_{\text{ext}} - kx - bv = m\frac{dv}{dt} = m\frac{d^2x}{dt^2}$$

which is Newton's law $F = ma$ written for an external force plus a restoring spring force $-kx$ and an opposing friction force $-bv$. The galvanometer equation of section 8.9 is another example. In fact, any complicated mechanical system with linear elastic behavior and friction forces can be represented by a corresponding a-c network, which in many cases can be studied experimentally so as to solve otherwise difficult mechanical or acoustical problems.

Because of this analogy, the reciprocal of capacitance is sometimes called "elastance."

Because the average power in any circuit is $\frac{1}{2}Ri_m{}^2$, it is convenient to choose as a measure for the current, not the amplitude i_m but $i_e = i_m/\sqrt{2}$, which is called the root mean square (rms) or effective current. In fact, $\frac{1}{2}Ri_m{}^2 = Ri_e{}^2$ is the average of Ri^2, as can be seen from Eq. 9.3–2 (Problem 9.3c), so the mean square current is $\frac{1}{2}i_m{}^2$, and i_e is its square root. By making a-c ammeters read the rms current value, the calculation of power in resistors becomes the same for alternating current as for direct current. It then becomes necessary to use $\mathscr{E}_e = \mathscr{E}_m/\sqrt{2}$ and $V_e = V_m/\sqrt{2}$ as measures of emf and voltage in order that the impedance will remain equal to the voltage-to-current ratio.

The power expended in a circuit can now be written

$$P_{av} = Ri_e{}^2 = i_e{}^2 Z \cos \varphi$$

so that

$$P_{av} = \mathscr{E}_e i_e \cos \varphi \qquad (9.3\text{–}4)$$

This differs from the expression $\mathscr{E}_e i_e$ that would correspond to the d-c case by the factor $\cos \varphi$, which is for this reason called the power factor. For a given emf $\mathscr{E}_e$ and power consumption P_{av}, the required current is the larger the smaller $\cos \varphi$. To reduce heating losses in power transmission lines, it is desirable to have $\cos \varphi$ as near to unity as practicable.

We see that for a purely resistive circuit, the power formulas of d-c analysis are appreciable:

$$P_{av} = i_e{}^2 R = \mathscr{E}_e i_e = \mathscr{E}_e{}^2/R \qquad (9.3\text{–}5)$$

When no ambiguity is involved in what follows, the subscript e will be dropped, and the symbols $\mathscr{E}$, V, and i will be used for rms values instead of for instantaneous values. Likewise P will be used in place of P_{av}. Power is measured in watts or kilowatts, but the measure of the product Ei is referred to as volt-amperes (va) or kilovolt-amperes (kva).

We have referred here only to power in a simple series circuit, and we shall, in the next two sections, take up several more complex circuits. However, in any two-terminal passive network to which an alternating emf $\mathscr{E}$ is applied, there will result a current i with some angle of lag φ.

Equations 9.3–1 and 9.3–3 will apply to this more general case, and Eq. 9.3–4 follows directly.

A pure reactance, like an ideal condenser, takes no power, since cos φ is 0. It is sometimes useful to refer to the product of volts and amperes for a condenser as volt-amperes-reactive (var). In general, the number of var is given by $\mathscr{E}i \sin \varphi$.

A real condenser, in which power is used up in alternating the polarization of the dielectric, must clearly have a phase angle less than $90°$ and a power factor that is different from zero. The effect can be described as a phase-shifting hysteresis.

Problem 9.3a. For what values of t will P as given by Eq. 9.3–3 be negative?

Problem 9.3b. Sketch a graph showing the total energy U delivered to a resistor as a function of the time when an alternating emf is applied, letting $U = 0$ when $t = 0$.

Problem 9.3c. Prove that the average square of a sinusoidal current or voltage is one-half the square of the amplitude by direct use of the integral calculus; e.g., by $(i^2)_{av} = (1/T)\int_0^T i^2 \, dt$.

Problem 9.3d. If a certain piece of apparatus acts like a series circuit with power factor 0.75, and the line has a resistance of 0.02 ohm, calculate the line loss when 10 kw are being supplied at 125 v (rms) and the reduction in this loss that could be achieved if the power factor were changed to 1.00.

Problem 9.3e. A 60-cycle alternating emf of 120 v supplies current to a 120-volt, 400-watt lamp. Assuming the lamp resistance to be constant, find (a) the current required to operate it at 400 watts and at 200 watts. If the current is to be reduced by a series resistor, find (b) the value of this resistor and the power expended in it. If the current is to be reduced by the introduction of a series choke coil, which is an inductance of high Q, find (c) the necessary inductance value taking $Q = 100$, (d) the power expended in the coil, and (e) the power drawn from the line. (*Suggestion:* Disregard the coil resistance when calculating the impedance of the *combination* of coil and lamp.)

Problem 9.3f. Find the three relations corresponding to Eq. 9.3–5 for circuits whose reactance is *not* zero. Justify the reference in Section 9.2 to "half-power" points on the curve of R/Z versus ω/ω_0.

Problem 9.3g. An emf $\mathscr{E}$ feeds two impedances Z_1 and Z_2 in series. Find an expression for the power expended in Z_2.

Problem 9.3h. Show that if an emf $\mathscr{E}$ supplies power P at a power factor cos φ, the resistance of the circuit must be $(\mathscr{E}^2 \cos^2 \varphi)/P$.

9.4   The Complex Number Method for A-C Analysis

The complex-number method for analyzing a-c circuits combines the graphic features of the vector method introduced in Section 9.2 with the simplicity of algebraic calculations. Let us first review some of the features of the vector method.

Any sinusoidally varying current or voltage can be represented as the projection along a given direction of a vector rotating with angular velocity equal to the given angular frequency. The amplitude and phase angle of the motion are given respectively by the length of the vector and its angle with respect to a rotating reference vector. The addition of voltages in series and currents in parallel corresponds to the vector addition of the respective vectors. The relation of current and voltage in a given circuit element involves no phase angle for a pure resistance, an advance of 90° for a pure inductance, and a lag of 90° for a pure capacitance.

The relations between amplitudes and phases are maintained as the vectors rotate, so that the important physical magnitudes can be represented by fixed vectors. The projection which can, of course, be taken in any direction is not needed explicitly; a stationary vector diagram is all that is necessary.

Vector products have no meaning for these vectors, and the only scalar product that appears is the power, $\mathscr{E}i \cos \varphi$. However, current and voltage vectors are related by impedances and phase angles, in a multiplicative sort of way.

Now, it is remarkable that the complex numbers used in algebra have properties exactly like all those mentioned, with the minor exception that scalar products are not readily representable. As we show in what follows, we can make all our calculations with ordinary algebra if we represent our vectors as complex numbers.

The elements of complex-number algebra that we need for electrical quantities are given in Appendix A.5. We shall assume first that the stationary vectors referred to just above are to be written as complex numbers. Then we need only multiply by $e^{j\omega t}$ to represent rotating vectors, since multiplication with a complex number of unit magnitude rotates a vector through the appropriate angle and since in this case the angle is ωt. The actual sinusoidal currents and voltages may be taken as the projections on the x-axis or axis of reals—i.e., the *real parts* of the rotating vectors. (The imaginary parts could equally well be used.) Finally, impedances will be represented by constant complex numbers; the 90° rotations required for inductive and capacitive reactances will involve multiplications by $\pm j = e^{\pm j\pi/2}$.

Instead of using the results of Section 9.2 to derive the complex number that represents an impedance, it is more useful to start directly from the differential equation 9.2–1 for a series circuit. This equation is linear in $\mathscr{E}$ and i, so that the sum of two solutions is also a solution (see Appendix A.3). Conversely, if we find a solution in terms of complex rotating vectors, the real and imaginary parts must separately be solutions. (See Problem 9.4g.) Thus we shall write $\mathscr{E} = \mathscr{E}_m e^{j\omega t}$ and $i = i_m e^{j\omega t}$, and substitute into Eq. 9.2–1, using Eq. 9.2–5:

$$\mathscr{E}_m e^{j\omega t} = L i_m j\omega \, e^{j\omega t} + R i_m e^{j\omega t} + \frac{1}{j\omega C} i_m e^{j\omega t}$$

so that, dividing out $e^{j\omega t}$ and collecting terms (note that $j = -1/j$), we have

$$\mathscr{E}_m = \left[R + j\left(\omega L - \frac{1}{\omega C}\right) \right] i_m \qquad (9.4\text{–}1)$$

We can immediately write this equation in terms of a complex impedance Z (dropping the subscripts so that either amplitudes or rms values can be understood):

$$\mathscr{E} = Z i \qquad (9.4\text{–}2a)$$

$$Z = R + j\left(\omega L - \frac{1}{\omega C}\right) = R + jX \qquad (9.4\text{–}2b)$$

which in exponential form is

$$Z = (R^2 + X^2)^{\frac{1}{2}} e^{j \tan^{-1}(X/R)} \qquad (9.4\text{–}2c)$$

Thus the impedance Z when multiplied into i increases the current magnitude by a factor $Z = (R^2 + X^2)^{\frac{1}{2}}$ and advances its angle on a vector diagram by $\varphi = \tan^{-1}(X/R)$ exactly as in Section 9.2. We see that the real part of the complex impedance is the resistance and the imaginary part is the reactance.

For complicated circuits, we can formulate Kirchhoff's laws in complex terms (since the relations must hold for the real parts of the rotating vectors and also for the imaginary parts):

1. The sum of the complex currents entering any junction of three or more circuit elements equals the sum of the complex currents leaving that junction.

2. The sum of the complex emfs around any closed loop in a circuit, taken with due regard to signs (phases), equals the sum of the complex potential drops around the loop. Emfs due to self and mutual inductances are to be included with the potential-drop terms.

Therefore, we can use the d-c analysis of Sections 5.5 and 5.6 directly. Series impedances add:

$$Z = Z_1 + Z_2 + \cdots \qquad (9.4\text{–}3)$$

and parallel impedances are combined by the reciprocal rule:

$$\frac{1}{Z} = \frac{1}{Z_1} + \frac{1}{Z_2} + \cdots \qquad (9.4\text{--}4)$$

The impedance for two elements in parallel can thus be written

$$Z = Z_1 Z_2 / (Z_1 + Z_2)$$

The reciprocal of an impedance is called an "admittance" and is written Y. Its real and imaginary parts can be found by use of Eq. A.5–10:

$$Y = \frac{1}{Z} = \frac{1}{R + jX} = \frac{R - jX}{R^2 + X^2} = \frac{R}{R^2 + X^2} - j\frac{X}{R^2 + X^2}$$

or

$$Y = G + jB \qquad (9.4\text{--}5)$$

where the real part, called the conductance, is

$$G = \frac{R}{R^2 + X^2} \qquad (9.4\text{--}6)$$

and the imaginary part, called the susceptance, is

$$B = -\frac{X}{R^2 + X^2} \qquad (9.4\text{--}7)$$

(Remember that the sign of X is defined by 9.2–10 or 9.4–2b.) Since $Y = 1/Z$, we can write

$$i = Y\mathcal{E} \qquad (9.4\text{--}8)$$

Let us as a first example treat the parallel circuit of Fig. 9.4a. The admittances of the two branches can be written down immediately and added:

$$Y = Y_1 + Y_2 = \frac{R_1}{R_1^2 + \omega^2 L^2} - \frac{j\omega L}{R_1^2 + \omega^2 L^2}$$

$$+ \frac{R_2}{R_2^2 + \left(\dfrac{1}{\omega C}\right)^2} + \frac{j\left(\dfrac{1}{\omega C}\right)}{R_2^2 + \left(\dfrac{1}{\omega C}\right)^2}$$

$$(9.4\text{--}9)$$

$$= \frac{R_1}{R_1^2 + \omega^2 L^2} + \frac{R_2 \omega^2 C^2}{R_2^2 \omega^2 C^2 + 1} + j\left[\frac{\omega C}{R_2^2 \omega^2 C^2 + 1} - \frac{\omega L}{R_1^2 + \omega^2 L^2}\right]$$

The condition that i and $\mathcal{E}$ are in phase is that Y be a real number. This condition is called "antiresonance" or "parallel resonance." Setting the imaginary part of Y equal to zero yields immediately

$$\frac{\omega L}{R_1{}^2 + \omega^2 L^2} = \frac{\omega C}{R_2{}^2 \omega^2 C^2 + 1} \tag{9.4-10}$$

Dividing both sides by ω and solving for ω^2 we find

$$\omega^2 = \frac{1}{LC} \cdot \frac{L - R_1{}^2 C}{L - R_2{}^2 C} = \frac{1}{LC} \cdot \frac{1 - Q_{10}^{-2}}{1 - Q_{20}^{-2}} \tag{9.4-11}$$

where $Q_{10} = \omega_0 L/R_1 = (L/R_1{}^2 C)^{1/2}$ and $Q_{20} = 1/\omega_0 C R_2 = (L/R_2{}^2 C)^{1/2}$ are the Q-values for each branch at the series-resonant frequency $\omega_0 = (LC)^{-1/2}$. If the Q of each element is large, the parallel resonant frequency is nearly the same as the series resonant frequency for the same two elements.

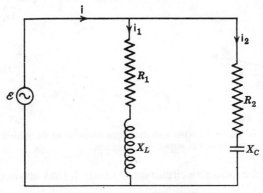

Fig. 9.4a. A parallel circuit.

At parallel resonance, the current being in phase with $\mathcal{E}$ is given by

$$i = \frac{\mathcal{E} R_1}{R_1{}^2 + \omega^2 L^2} + \frac{\mathcal{E} R_2 \omega^2 C^2}{R_2{}^2 \omega^2 C^2 + 1} \tag{9.4-12}$$

It is evident from Eq. 9.4–12 that i is small if R_1 and R_2 are. This apparently strange phenomenon can be understood if it is realized that the oppositely phased (i.e., inductive and capacitive) currents in the two branches at resonance are in the same phase with respect to currents circulating *around* the loop—i.e., when the loop is considered a series circuit. Thus large currents alternate back and forth around the loop and only their small difference enters and leaves at the junctions. If R_1 and R_2 could be both zero, an alternating current of any magnitude could circulate around the loop without any outside contributions, the latter being only necessary to offset the power losses in the resistors.

In particular, if a condenser with negligible resistance is placed in parallel with an inductive circuit, it will make the power factor in the transmission

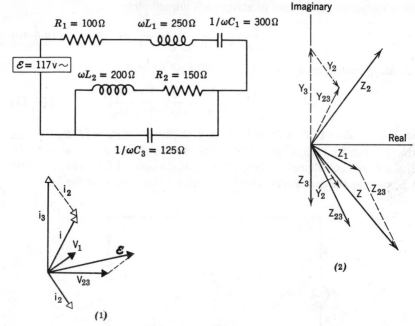

Fig. 9.4b. A series-parallel circuit and diagrams illustrating its solution: (1) voltage-current diagram; (2) impedance diagram.

line supplying the inductive circuit more nearly 1, thus serving to cut down line losses.

The use of algebraic symbols, as in Eq. 9.4–9, yields complicated form-ulae for a-c impedances and admittances; in contrast to most calculations in physics, it is convenient in solving a-c problems to substitute numerical values right at the start. We shall illustrate by giving the results of a slide-rule calculation[5] for the circuit of Fig. 9.4b. We find

$$Z_1 = 100 + (250 - 300)j = 100 - 50j \text{ ohms}$$
$$= 112 \, e^{-26.6°j} \text{ ohms}$$
$$Z_2 = 150 + 200j = 250 \, e^{53.1°j} \text{ ohms}$$
$$Z_3 = -125j = 125 \, e^{-90°j} \text{ ohms}$$

[5] The principle slide-rule operation needed beyond elementary multiplication and division is that of calculating $(a^2 + b^2)^{1/2}$ with the simultaneous finding of $\tan^{-1}(b/a)$. See any slide-rule manual.

The symbol j is generally written before algebraic symbols but after arabic numerals. The angles in the exponents are most conveniently written in degrees, although radian measure is more commonly used in mathematical analysis.

so that for the parallel branch

$$Y_{23} = \frac{1}{Z_2} + \frac{1}{Z_3} = \frac{1}{150 + 200j} - \frac{1}{125j} = \frac{150 - 200j}{150^2 + 200^2} + \frac{j}{125}$$

$$= 0.00240 - 0.00320j + 0.00800j$$

$$= 0.00240 + 0.00480j \text{ ohms,}$$

and

$$Z_{23} = \frac{1}{Y_{23}} = \frac{0.00240 - 0.00480j}{0.00240^2 + 0.00480^2} = 83.3 - 167j \text{ ohms}$$

$$= 186 \, e^{-63.4°j} \text{ ohms}$$

The total impedance is

$$Z = Z_1 + Z_{23} = 183.3 - 217j = 284 \, e^{-49.8°j} \text{ ohms}$$

If we take $\mathscr{E}$ to be $110 \, e^{0.0°j}$ v (rms), the current i will be

$$i = \mathscr{E}/Z = (117/284) \, e^{49.8°j} = 0.412 \, e^{49.8°j} \text{ amp}$$

The current leads the voltage by 49.8° and the power factor is 0.645. The power drawn is then $117 \times 0.412 \times 0.645 = 31.1$ watts (note that the power cannot be found by multiplication of complex numbers).

The analysis can be carried further. For example, the voltage drop on the parallel circuit is

$$V_{23} = Z_{23}i = 186 \, e^{-63.4°j} \times 0.412 \, e^{49.8°j} = 76.6 \, e^{-13.6°j} \text{ v}$$

lagging behind $\mathscr{E}$ by 13.6°. The currents through branches 2 and 3 are $i_2 = V_{23}/Z_2 = 0.307 \, e^{-66.7°j}$ and $i_3 = 0.613 \, e^{76.4°j}$. The voltage V_{C1} on C_1 is $i(-300j) = 124 \, e^{-40.2j}$ v; that on the combination of L_1 and R_1 is $i(100 + 250j) = 111 \, e^{118.0°j}$. These various values are illustrated graphically in Fig. 9.4b. The reader is advised to locate on the voltage-current diagram the appropriate impedance angles.

No mention was made of frequency, since for simplicity the reactance values were given directly in ohms. For a frequency of 60 cycles ($\omega = 377$) it is an easy matter to find what values L_1, C_1, L_2, and C_3 must have in this example. For a different frequency with the same L and C values, the results would be quite different, and the calculation must be gone through again completely from the beginning. It is quite clear that a-c circuit calculations are complicated and lengthy. Although engineering texts give a number of rules for assistance in computation, the only one of use in a physics text is this: in nearly every case, reflection and ingenuity will produce a shorter or easier method of calculation than that which may appear suitable at first glance.

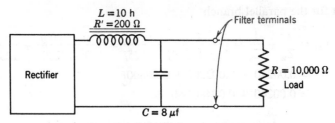

Fig. 9.4c.   A simple filter for a rectifier circuit.

Let us illustrate the simple results that can sometimes be obtained by an approximate calculation. We shall consider a one-stage filter circuit, of the type often used for removing alternating components of the current delivered by a rectifier. Figure 9.4c shows an inductance and a capacitor in a single "L-section" filter, feeding a load resistor.

The aim of the filter is to provide for d-c a low series resistance (in L) and a very high shunt resistance (in C) so that the steady part of the current is little affected by the filter, and to have for alternating current a high series impedance (in L) and a high parallel admittance in C. We shall make an approximate calculation of the ratio of voltage input (voltage output from rectifier) to voltage output (input to load). For 60 cycles, $\omega = 377$ and in the circuit of the figure, $\omega L = 3770$ ohms and $1/\omega C = 332$ ohms. Consequently, the parallel impedance of C and R together is very close to that of the condenser alone, namely $-j/\omega C = -332j$ ohms. The impedance of the inductance coil is, approximately, just its reactance $j\omega L = 3770j$ ohms. The ratio of voltages we seek is the ratio of capacitor impedance to the total, which is

$$\frac{-j/\omega C}{j\omega L - j/\omega C} = -\frac{1}{\omega^2 LC - 1} = \frac{-332j}{(3770 - 332)j}$$

$$= \frac{-332}{3438} = -0.097 \qquad (9.4\text{--}13)$$

The minus sign indicates that the phase of the voltage on the load is just opposite to that on the entire circuit, a fact which is easily understood by considering that the current in the entire circuit is very largely inductive,

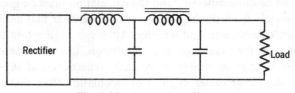

Fig. 9.4d.   A two-stage filter.

lagging the applied voltage by 90°, and that the voltage on the condenser lags the current also by nearly 90°, producing an over-all 180° phase change.

Now if two similar L-section filters are put in tandem, as in Fig. 9.4d, the second section will act on the first in a similar way to the high resistance load, namely, to have an almost negligible effect on the admittance of the first condenser. Its own action will duplicate that of the first and we have just twice the effect of one filter, i.e., the reduction in voltage is the square of Eq. 9.4–13,

$$(\omega^2 LC - 1)^{-2} = (0.097)^2 = 0.0094 \simeq 1\%$$

If, as is frequently the case, the frequency of the most important alternating voltage at the output of the rectifier is 120 cycles, the voltage ratio will be about one-fourth that given for a single section and one-sixteenth for two sections, as can be seen from ω^2 in the denominator of Eq. 9.4–13.

Problem 9.4a. A certain motor acts like an inductance in drawing 800 watts of power with a power factor of 0.80 from a 220-volt line. Find the apparent impedance and resistance of the motor, and the reactance of that capacitor which when put in parallel with the motor will just bring the power factor to 1.00. Find the ratio of the current drawn by the motor to the total current. Line drops are to be neglected.

Problem 9.4b. Show that for a parallel resonant circuit, the circulating current is approximately $Q_1 Q_2 / (Q_1 + Q_2)$ times the net current, for large Q values.

Problem 9.4c. Repeat the calculation in the text for the circuit of Fig. 9.4b for the case in which the frequency is doubled.

Problem 9.4d. For the circuit of Fig. 9.4e, find the currents and also the voltage on the inductance coil.

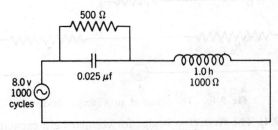

Fig. 9.4e.   (Problem 9.4d).

Problem 9.4e. A resistor R and condenser C are in series with a parallel combination of an equal pair of R and C. Find how the voltage on the parallel combination varies in phase and magnitude as the frequency is varied and the over-all emf is fixed in phase and magnitude (*Hint:* Calculate the ratio $Z_{total}/Z_{parallel}$ first).

Problem 9.4f. An alternating emf $\mathcal{E}$ of 0.100 v is applied to the amplifier network shown in Fig. 9.4g. Find to slide-rule accuracy the voltage between the open-circuited points $\mathcal{A}$ and $\mathcal{B}$ when the frequency is (a) 10 cycles, (b) 500 cycles, and (c) 10,000 cycles.

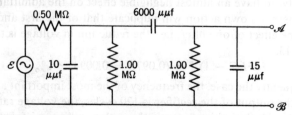

Fig. 9.4f. An R-C coupled amplifier network.

Problem 9.4g. Show that if $\mathcal{E} = \mathcal{E}_0 e^{j(\omega t + \varphi_V)}$ and i satisfy Eq. 9.2–1, the real parts give the solution corresponding to $\mathcal{E} = \mathcal{E}_0 \cos(\omega t + \varphi_V)$ and the imaginary parts give the solution corresponding to $\mathcal{E} = \mathcal{E}_0 \sin(\omega t + \varphi_V)$.

Problem 9.4h. Write and simplify an algebraic formula for the complex impedance Z of two parallel branches, one with $Z_1 = R + jX$ and the other with $Z_2 = -jX'$. What does Z become when $X = X'$?

Problem 9.4i. Solve the circuits of Fig. 9.4c and Fig. 9.4d exactly, for the voltage ratio (output/input).

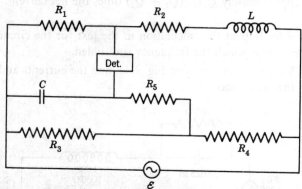

Fig. 9.4g. The circuit of an Anderson bridge.

Problem 9.4j. The Anderson bridge for comparing a capacitance C and an inductance L is shown in Fig. 9.4f. Write equations from which the current in the detector can be determined. Do not solve them, but assume that this current is zero and find two equations that relate C, L, and the resistances and that do not contain the emf $\mathcal{E}$ or the currents.

Problem 9.4k. Prove that the power expended by an emf $\mathcal{E}$ in any circuit is correctly given by $P = \frac{1}{2}(\mathcal{E}\bar{\mathrm{i}} + \bar{\mathcal{E}}\mathrm{i})$, if i is the current delivered by $\mathcal{E}$.

9.5   Circuits with Mutual Inductance

Any two circuits in proximity to each other will have mutual inductance since there will be magnetic flux about all the wires and some interlinking will surely occur. However, it is convenient here as earlier to divide the effects into those big enough to be treated as lumped or localized and those small enough to neglect. (At very high frequencies, this division is inadequate, for distributed effects become very important.) In this section, we shall apply our complex-number analysis to certain types of circuits with specific mutual inductances.

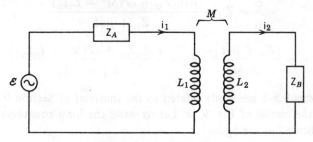

Fig. 9.5a.   A circuit coupled only through a mutual inductance (transformer). The resistances of the coils are included in Z_A and Z_B.

The coupled circuits of Fig. 9.5a are linked only by the mutual inductance indicated by M. The two coils may actually be wound more or less closely together, but are drawn apart for clarity. A current i_1 in circuit 1 will produce flux $\Phi_{11} = L_1 i_1$ in coil 1 and $\Phi_{21} = M i_1$ in coil 2, where L_1 is the self-inductance of coil 1 and M is the mutual inductance of the pair. Similarly, a current i_2 in circuit 2 will make flux $\Phi_{22} = L_2 i_2$ in coil 2 and $\Phi_{12} = M i_2$ in coil 1. It is necessary to specify positive directions for the currents in the two circuits and is convenient to draw the circuit (or choose the definitions) so that, if two adjacent ends of the two coils were connected, one current flows toward the junction and one away, as in Fig. 9.5a. The directions of the coil windings can either be so arranged that when i_1 and i_2 are both positive, Φ_{11} and Φ_{12} are opposite in sign, or so that they are of the same sign. Let us call M positive when Φ_{11} and Φ_{12} are of the same sign. It will then also be true that (for positive currents) Φ_{22} and Φ_{21} are of the same polarity (Problem 9.5h).

Now, if i_1 and i_2 can be written as complex currents $i_1 e^{j\omega t}$ and $i_2 e^{j\omega t}$, the fluxes can be written as $\phi_{11} e^{j\omega t}$, etc. The emf induced in coil 1 will be

$$\mathcal{E}_1 = -\frac{d}{dt}[\phi_{11} e^{j\omega t} + \phi_{12} e^{j\omega t}] = -j\omega[\phi_{11} e^{j\omega t} + \phi_{12} e^{j\omega t}]$$

$$= -j\omega[L_1 i_1 e^{j\omega t} + M i_2 e^{j\omega t}]$$

and the voltage drop across coil 1 will be the same but with a positive sign. The second coil will have a similar emf in it, which we may write either as an emf or as a potential drop, there being no other emf in the circuit.

The equations for the two circuits can thus be written (omitting $e^{j\omega t}$)

$$\mathscr{E} = Z_A i_1 + j\omega L_1 i_1 + j\omega M i_2 \qquad (9.5\text{-}1a)$$

$$0 = Z_B i_2 + j\omega L_2 i_2 + j\omega M i_1 \qquad (9.5\text{-}1b)$$

which can be solved for i_1 and i_2, giving the relations

$$\frac{\mathscr{E}}{i_1} = Z_A + \frac{j\omega L_1 Z_B + \omega^2(M^2 - L_1 L_2)}{Z_B + j\omega L_2} \qquad (9.5\text{-}2)$$

$$\frac{\mathscr{E}}{i_2} = -\frac{(Z_A + j\omega L_1)}{j\omega M}\left[Z_B + \frac{j\omega L_2 Z_A + \omega^2(M^2 - L_1 L_2)}{Z_A + j\omega L_1}\right] \qquad (9.5\text{-}3)$$

Equations 9.5-1 are easily related to the material of Section 9.4, if we consider the circuit of Fig. 9.5b. Let us write the loop equations for the loops indicated in the figure:

$$\mathscr{E} = Z_A i_1 + j\omega L_1' i_1 + Z_M(i_1 - i_2) \qquad (9.5\text{-}4a)$$

$$0 = Z_B i_2 + j\omega L_2' i_2 + Z_M(i_2 - i_1) \qquad (9.5\text{-}4b)$$

which are identical with Eqs. 9.5-1 if we take $Z_M = -j\omega M$, $L_1' = L_1 + M$, and $L_2' = L_2 + M$. Thus a pair of impedances coupled by a mutual inductance behave (at least at a particular frequency) like a single series-parallel combination with an inductance or a capacitance in parallel, depending on whether M is negative or positive. A more complicated circuit like that of Fig. 9.5c can be treated in the same way (Problem 9.5a).

If two inductances in series have mutual flux linkage, we can include this effect in a simple series-circuit calculation. We must have, in fact, for

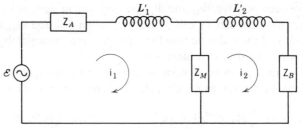

Fig. 9.5b.   A series-parallel circuit that behaves like the coupled circuit in Fig. 9.5a, if $Z_M = -j\omega M$.

the voltage drop on the series combination

$$V = L_1 \frac{di}{dt} + L_2 \frac{di}{dt} \pm 2M \frac{di}{dt} \qquad (9.5\text{--}5)$$

where the factor 2 enters because each coil has an emf induced in it by the other one. For a current of angular frequency ω, we have

$$V = (j\omega L_1 + j\omega L_2 \pm 2j\omega M)i \qquad (9.5\text{--}6)$$

The two coils thus act like a single one. If the effective self-inductance of the combination can be measured with the coils first arranged to produce

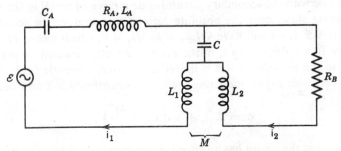

Fig. 9.5c. A coupled circuit of moderate complexity.

flux in the same direction (positive coupling) and then in the same position but with opposite coupling, we can write

$$L_+ = L_1 + L_2 + 2M \qquad (9.5\text{--}7a)$$
$$L_- = L_1 + L_2 - 2M \qquad (9.5\text{--}7b)$$

from which we can find

$$M = \tfrac{1}{4}(L_+ - L_-) \qquad (9.5\text{--}8)$$

If the coils are arranged to rotate with respect to one another, so that M varies continuously from a positive value M_0 to a negative value $-M_0$, the resultant value of L will vary from L_+ to L_-. It is in this way that convenient variable inductors are made.[6]

Since by Lenz's law self-inductance is always a positive quantity, we see by Eq. 9.5–7b that for any two coils whatever, their mutual inductance M is restricted to values less than $\tfrac{1}{2}(L_1 + L_2)$:

$$M < \tfrac{1}{2}(L_1 + L_2) \qquad (9.5\text{--}9)$$

A further and more useful restriction on M is that M is less than the geometric mean of L_1 and L_2:

$$M^2 \leqslant L_1 L_2 \qquad (9.5\text{--}10)$$

[6] See F. K. Harris, *Electrical Measurements*, John Wiley, New York, 1952, p. 667.

which condition we can write

$$M = k(L_1 L_2)^{1/2} \tag{9.5-11}$$

where k is called the coefficient of coupling and is a number between -1 and $+1$.

$$-1 \leqslant k \leqslant +1 \tag{9.5-12}$$

This result is actually a property of Neumann's integral, Eq. 7.12–13, for mutual and self-inductance, but it is not easy to prove directly. One method of verifying it is to consider a rather ideal coupled circuit, namely one like that of Fig. 9.5a in which Z_B is almost exactly zero. A practical case is one with the secondary circuit inside a piece of metal in the super-conducting state, near the absolute zero of temperature. In accordance with Eq. 9.5–1, we will have $j\omega L_2 i_2 + j\omega M i_1 = 0$, which means of course that the flux produced by i_1 in the metal is exactly canceled by that produced in the metal by i_2. (It is indeed a fact that magnetic fields cannot be set up inside superconducting material.) Equation 9.5–2 now becomes

$$\mathscr{E} = Z_A i_1 + j\omega \left(L_1 - \frac{M^2}{L_2} \right) i_1 \tag{9.5-13}$$

showing that the circuit has an effective inductance $L = L_1 - M^2/L_2$. This quantity must be positive, which leads immediately to Eq. 9.5–10. The reference to superconducting material cannot actually be of importance for the proof, since the properties of Neumann's formula have nothing to do with any external resistance or impedance in the circuit.

Equation 9.5–10 can also be proved from the formula 7.18–5 for the magnetic energy of a set of coils (Problem 9.5c). It is more instructive, however, to turn to an approximate proof based on coil structure. Suppose the two coils have, respectively, N_1 turns and N_2 turns and that when i_1 flows in coil 1, the average flux through each turn of the coil is $b_1 i_1$. Then the flux linkage in coil 1 is $\Phi_{11} = N_1 b_1 i_1 = L_1 i_1$. Now, not all of the flux $b_1 i_1$ is likely to link each turn of coil 2. Thus the flux linking all the turns of coil 2 is less than $N_2 b_1 i_1$, so we write

$$\Phi_{21} = \pm k_1 N_2 b_1 i_1 = M i_1 \quad \text{where} \quad 0 \leqslant k_1 \leqslant 1$$

Similarly, when i_2 flows in coil 2, we can write $\Phi_{22} = L_2 i_2 = N_2 b_2 i_2$ and $\Phi_{12} = M i_2 = \pm k_2 N_1 b_2 i_2$, with $0 \leqslant k_2 \leqslant 1$.

From the equations with i_1, we can obtain the ratio $M/L_1 = \pm k_1 N_2/N_1$; from the other equations $M/L_2 = \pm k_2 N_1/N_2$. The product of these ratios eliminates N_1 and N_2, giving the expected result

$$\frac{M^2}{L_1 L_2} = k_1 k_2 \leqslant 1$$

from which we also see that the coefficient of coupling k is $(k_1 k_2)^{1/2}$,the geometric mean of the two fractions that give the flux of one coil linking the other.

The coefficient of coupling will be 1 when $k_1 = 1$ and $k_2 = 1$, that is, when all of the flux produced by either coil links the other. It will be observed that if $k = 1$, the second term in Eq. 9.5–13 vanishes, so that the vanishing of flux in coil 2 is accompanied by zero resultant flux in coil 1. This situation is clearly an ideal limit, which can never be perfectly achieved in practice. Nevertheless, a closely wound pair of coils can have a k very near unity.

Transformers. A transformer is a mutual inductance with k nearly 1 and with large values of L_1 and L_2 in comparison to the circuit components with which it will be used. An ordinary a-c transformer consists of two coils wound on an iron core that "conducts" nearly all its flux through both coils. Both L_1 and L_2 are large because of the iron and because of large numbers of turns on each coil.

The analysis given above with reference to numbers of turns is a good approximation here, so we can write $k_1 = 1$, $k_2 = 1$,

$$\frac{M}{L_1} = \frac{L_2}{M} = \frac{N_2}{N_1} \tag{9.5–14}$$

and

$$\frac{ML_2}{L_1 M} = \frac{L_2}{L_1} = \frac{N_2{}^2}{N_1{}^1} \tag{9.5–15}$$

Neglecting Z_B in the second equation of Eqs. 9.5–1 gives

$$\frac{i_2}{i_1} = \frac{-M}{L_2} = \frac{-N_1}{N_2} \tag{9.5–16}$$

so that the currents have a constant ratio and are 180° out of phase. If we attempt to substitute Eq. 9.5–16 into the first of Eqs. 9.5–1, however, we get no inductive effect at all. When the inductive effect is reduced nearly to zero, Z_B will have an effect on i_1 and we must use a closer approximation. In Eq. 9.5–2, we can neglect Z_B in the denominator where it is added to $j\omega L_2$, but not in the numerator, since $M^2 - L_1 L_2 \simeq 0$. Thus we have

$$\mathcal{E} = \left(Z_A + Z_B \frac{L_1}{L_2} \right) i_1 = \left(Z_A + Z_B \frac{N_1{}^2}{N_1{}^2} \right) i_1 \tag{9.5–17}$$

Assuming that Z_A is small compared to ωL_1, Eq. 9.5–3 yields

$$-\mathcal{E} \frac{M}{L_1} = \left(Z_B + \frac{L_2}{L_1} Z_A \right) i_2$$

or

$$-\mathcal{E}\frac{N_2}{N_1} = \left(Z_B + \frac{N_2{}^2}{N_1{}^2}Z_A\right)i_2 \qquad (9.5\text{--}18)$$

Equation 9.5–17 shows us that viewed from the input end or primary side the transformer has the effect of replacing Z_B by $Z_B(N_1{}^2/N_2{}^2)$—the impedance is "transformed" by the square of the turns ratio. One of the common uses of transformers is for matching impedances by means of this effect.

Equation 9.5–18 shows that on the output or secondary side the input impedance Z_A is also transformed (by the inverse ratio, of course),

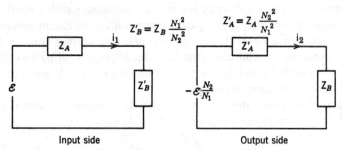

Input side   Output side

Fig. 9.5d. Equivalent circuits for the input and output sides of an ideal transformer.

and that the emf appears multiplied by the ratio N_2/N_1 (as well as being reversed in phase). The voltage drop on the primary side, $\mathcal{E} - Z_A i_1 = Z_B(N_1{}^2 i_1/N_2{}^2) = -Z_B(N_1 i_2/N_2)$, is just equal to $-(N_1/N_2)$ times the secondary voltage drop $Z_B i_2$. Finally, the currents are in the inverse ratio to the emfs, as shown by Eq. 9.5–16.

In many practical cases, the above analysis in terms of an "ideal" transformer is quite adequate. One can write "equivalent" circuits for the input and output ends, in accordance with Eqs. 9.5–17 and 9.5–18, as shown in Fig. 9.5d. It is to be noted that a "transformed" impedance appears larger when looked at from the side of the transformer with the larger number of terms; the same is true of the emf, and the reverse is true for the current. Also note that $\mathcal{E}i_1 = \mathcal{E}_2 i_2$ where $\mathcal{E}_2 = -\mathcal{E}N_2/N_1$ (the power factors are also the same) showing that the assumptions we have made imply no power loss in the transformer.

For any actual transformer there are several factors to consider if it is to be treated in closer approximation than that of ideality. It is convenient to treat these factors as corrections to an ideal transformer. In the first place, we should treat the resistances R_1 and R_2 of the windings as parts of the transformer rather than including them in Z_A and Z_B. Next, k will not be exactly 1. We can correct for this by describing the flux in the primary coil that does not link the secondary as leakage flux, attributing it to an independent series inductance L_1'; similarly there will be an L_2' in the output circuit. Furthermore, there will not be a complete cancellation of the flux in the transformer core, since ωL_2 while large is not infinite in comparison to Z_B. We shall assume that the flux actually present (which of course provides the induced emfs that make the transformer operate) is produced by a small "magnetizing" current in the primary in addition to that which exactly balances the secondary current by Eq. 9.5–16. This requires a shunt inductance L_m in the primary circuit for its representation. Finally, there will be energy losses in the core due to hysteresis and eddy currents, which can be represented by a primary current in phase with the primary voltage—i.e., in a shunt resistor R_c. (The ohmic losses in the windings increase with i_1 and i_2 and can be represented by series resistors. The core losses increase with the rate of change of flux—i.e., with the voltage across the windings—and so must be represented by one or two parallel resistors.)

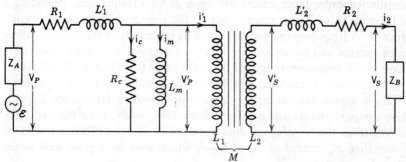

Fig. 9.5e. An actual transformer, drawn as an ideal transformer with modifications.

R_1 = primary resistance	i_c in R_c = core loss current
L_1' = primary leakage inductance	R_2 = secondary resistance
i_m in L_m = magnetizing current	L_2 = secondary leakage inductance

As a result, we draw a diagram like Fig. 9.5e. V_P is the voltage drop on the primary of the actual transformer, and V_P' that at the primary of the ideal one, with a similar notation for V_S and V_S'. If we denote the turns ratio N_2/N_1 by n, we write $V_S' = -nV_P'$ and $i_2 = i_1'/n$. (V_S' is the drop on the load plus that on the correction elements, i.e., it is the emf generated in the secondary coil.) We can then construct equivalent circuits like those in Fig. 9.5d (Problems 9.5d and e).

It is instructive to draw a complex vector diagram for the circuit of Fig. 9.5e. In so doing (see Fig. 9.5f) we can start with an assumed direction for i_2, draw $V_S = i_2 Z_B$, and add $i_2(R_2 + j\omega L_2')$ to get V_S'. The vectors V_P' and i_1' can then be drawn by use of the ratio n in the respective opposite directions. The magnetizing current i_m will be related to V_P' as in a pure inductance; since the drop in L_2 is $-V_S{}'$, the relation of i_m and $V_S{}'$ will, of course, be of the opposite sort. The core-loss current i_c will be in phase with $V_P{}'$, and the three currents i_c, i_m, and $i_1{}'$ can then be added to give i_1. The final construction of $\mathscr{E}$ is then straightforward.

The angles β and $-\gamma$ between the reversed secondary current and voltage vectors and the corresponding (unreversed) primary vectors are called the transformer phase angles. They are shown as respectively positive and negative according to standard convention.

It will be seen from the diagram that an actual transformer approximates ideal behavior if i_m, i_c, $\omega L_1{}'$, and $\omega L_2{}'$ are all small. This requirement puts limitations on the frequency range for which the transformer is useful. At very low frequencies, the inductance L_m will have a very low impedance compared to R_1, so that nearly all of V_P will appear across R_1 (L_m acts like a "short circuit"). For very high frequencies $\omega L_1{}'$ (and also $\omega L_2{}'$) will be large, and again $V_P{}'$ will be only a small part of V_P. In addition, distributed capacitance effects will enter at high frequencies, providing a different type of "short circuit" across the primary. The core-loss resistance R_c is frequency dependent; i_c will be large at high frequencies where eddy-current and hysteresis loss is large. Commercial audio transformers have useful frequency ranges of the order of 20 to 10,000 or 20,000 cycles.

This frequency dependence explains what would otherwise be a paradox. If Z_B is a pure resistance, the transformed primary impedance Z_B/n^2 is also a pure resistance and is independent of frequency. Yet if the frequency is zero (d-c), the transformer does not work at all—the effective resistance being then R_1 instead of $R_1 + Z_B/n^2$, which may be a great deal larger than R_1.

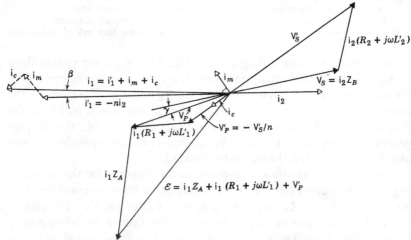

Fig. 9.5f. A vector diagram for the transformer of Fig. 9.5e.

An extreme example of a non-ideal transformer is that of a self-inductance operating at high frequency with considerable eddy-current induction in surrounding pieces of metal. Without an iron core, L_m will be large. The transformer itself, consisting of flux linkage with the metal objects, will act like a resistor in parallel with L_m. For this reason, it is a good approximation to treat an inductance at high frequency as having a resistance in parallel rather than in series.

Coupled Tuned Circuits. Another important application of mutual inductance is that of partially coupled tuned circuits. We shall give here only an approximate treatment and refer the reader elsewhere for more exact (and more complicated) discussions.[7]

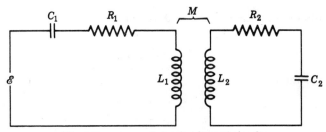

Fig. 9.5g. A coupled pair of tuned circuits.

Let us assume that Z_A in Fig. 9.5a consists of a small resistance and a condenser C_1 which is tuned with L_1 to a resonant frequency ω_0, so that $\omega_0{}^2 L_1 C_1 = 1$. Let us similarly insert for Z_B another condenser and small resistance, tuned also to ω_0, so $\omega_0{}^2 L_2 C_2 = 1$. (See Fig. 9.5g.) We shall take k to be less than 1. For simplicity we shall define X_1 and X_2 by the equations

$$Z_A + j\omega L_1 = R_1 + j\left(\omega L_1 - \frac{1}{\omega C_1}\right) = R_1 + j\omega L_1\left(1 - \frac{\omega_0{}^2}{\omega^2}\right)$$

$$= R_1 + jX_1$$

$$Z_B + j\omega L_2 = R_2 + j\left(\omega L_2 - \frac{1}{\omega C_2}\right) = R_2 + j\omega L_2\left(1 - \frac{\omega_0{}^2}{\omega^2}\right)$$

$$= R_2 + jX_2$$

We can rewrite Eqs. 9.5–2 and 9.5–3 in the forms

$$\frac{\mathcal{E}}{i_1} = Z_A + j\omega L_1 + \frac{\omega^2 M^2}{Z_B + j\omega L_2} = \frac{(R_1 + jX_1)(R_2 + jX_2) + \omega^2 M^2}{R_2 + jX_2}$$

$$= \frac{R_1 R_2 + j(X_1 R_2 + X_2 R_1) - X_1 X_2 + \omega^2 M^2}{R_2 + jX_2} \tag{9.5-19}$$

[7] See for instance, L. Page and N. I. Adams, *Principles of Electricity*, 3rd ed., D. Van Nostrand, Princeton, 1958, Sections 125–127; F. E. Terman, *op. cit.*, pp. 148–169.

and

$$\frac{\mathcal{E}}{i_2} = -\frac{R_1R_2 + j(X_1R_2 + X_2R_1) - X_1X_2 + \omega^2M^2}{j\omega M} \qquad (9.5\text{--}20)$$

If the R's are much smaller than the reactances, the numerators in Eqs. 9.5–19 and 9.5–20 will be almost equal to $\omega^2M^2 - X_1X_2$. At the angular frequency ω_0, when $X_1 = X_2 = 0$, ω^2M^2 will be large compared to R_1R_2. The numerators will be small, implying large currents, when $X_1X_2 = \omega^2M^2$, or

$$\omega^2L_1L_2\left(1 - \frac{\omega_0^2}{\omega^2}\right)^2 = \omega^2M^2 = \omega^2k^2L_1L_2$$

which, discounting the value $\omega = 0$, is true if

$$1 - \frac{\omega_0^2}{\omega^2} = \pm k$$

that is, for the two values

$$\omega_1 = \frac{\omega_0}{(1 + k)^{\frac{1}{2}}} \qquad (9.5\text{--}21a)$$

and

$$\omega_2 = \frac{\omega_0}{(1 - k)^{\frac{1}{2}}} \qquad (9.5\text{--}21b)$$

The frequencies for actual maxima of i_1 and i_2 will differ from these values, but only by a small amount. We see that in place of a single resonant frequency, there are two. The currents as functions of frequency are shown in Fig. 9.5h.

The sharpness of each peak is determined, as to be expected, by the Q's of each circuit, $Q_1 = \omega_0L_1/R_1$ and $Q_2 = \omega_0L_2/R_2$. However, the coupling factor k also enters, for when k is small, M is small, and the numerators of Eqs. 9.5–19 and 9.5–20 are not especially large when $\omega = \omega_0$. Furthermore, the relative influence of the terms in R is greater as X_1X_2 recedes from the (small) value of ω^2M^2. Thus reducing k can broaden the peaks and, as seen in Eqs. 9.5–20, bring them closer together. It is possible so to choose k that the peaks for i_2 just coalesce, giving a flat-topped resonance maximum of a better shape for radio broadcast receivers than is attainable with ordinary series resonance.

If k is very small, there is essentially only one peak, of frequency ω_0. Thus a very loosely coupled secondary circuit can be used to measure the frequency of a current in a primary circuit by ordinary series tuning. Such a device, with a detecting instrument for indicating a current maximum, is called a wavemeter.

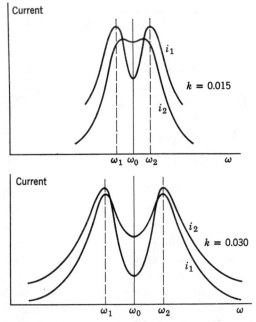

Fig. 9.5h. Primary and secondary currents in a tuned coupled circuit. (Adapted from F. E. Terman, *Radio Engineers' Handbook*, McGraw-Hill, New York., 1943.)

Problem 9.5a. Set up and solve the current equations for the circuit of Fig. 9.5c.

Problem 9.5b. What small but almost unavoidable error limits the accuracy of Eq. 9.5–8?

Problem 9.5c. Use Eq. 7.12–5 for two coils to show that $L_1L_2 \geqslant M^2$. (*Hint:* The energy is always positive; calculate the minimum energy for i_1 fixed and i_2 variable, and set this minimum greater than zero.)

Problem 9.5d. Construct an equivalent primary circuit for the actual transformer of Fig. 9.5e. Characterize the behavior of the transformer when the secondary is open-circuited and when it is short-circuited, as functions of frequency.

Problem 9.5e. Construct an equivalent secondary circuit for the actual transformer of Fig. 9.5e.

Problem 9.5f. The circuit in Fig. 9.5i can be used for an inductor and capacitor in parallel at high frequencies. Set up a differential equation for $V_\parallel$ in terms of $i_\parallel$, compare it with the series circuit Eq. 9.2–1, and show that the two are mathematically equivalent if the correct pairs of quantities are transposed. (*Hint:* $R_\parallel$ and $1/R$ are one pair.) Compare $Z_\parallel$ and Z_{series},

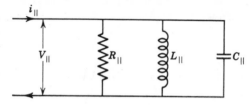

Fig. 9.5i. Three elements in parallel. (Problem 9.5f.)

and write formulas corresponding to Eqs. 9.2–16, 9.2–17, 9.2–21, and 9.2–22. Show that we should write $Q_\parallel = \dfrac{R_\parallel}{X_\parallel}$.

Problem 9.5g. Check Problem 9.5f by direct use of complex analysis.

Problem 9.5h. Prove the statement in the text that if Φ_{11} and Φ_{12} are of the same sign for a given choice of directions for i_1 and i_2, Φ_{22} and Φ_{21} will also be of the same sign.

Problem 9.5i. A dynamic loudspeaker operates by means of a small coil that can vibrate in a permanent magnetic field. Assuming the speaker cone and its attached coil to execute damped SHM with an external force due to the current in the coil, write a differential equation for the coil displacement x. Assuming the coil circuit to contain an applied emf, a resistance, an inductance, and the induced emf produced by the velocity dx/dt of the coil, write a differential equation for the current i in the coil. Show by considering a single angular frequency ω that dx/dt and i are related in the same way as the two currents in a pair of coupled circuits.

9.6 A-C Networks

The treatment of mutual inductance in the last section allows us to complete the statement in Section 9.4 that Kirchhoff's laws can be applied to a-c circuits, for we see that mutual inductance can be treated just like other impedances common to two branches. We can therefore take over in a quite general way the d-c theorems discussed in Chapter 5, namely, the superposition theorem,[8] the reciprocity theorem, the compensation theorem, and Thévenin's theorem.

Thévenin's theorem allows us to represent any two-terminal network by an emf and impedance. Because of the variation of impedance values with frequency, both the equivalent emf and the equivalent impedance of

---

[8] The superposition theorem can be applied to cases of emfs with different frequencies, using the complex method if the factors $e^{j\omega_1 t}$, $e^{j\omega_2 t}$, etc., for the different frequencies are left in the equations. The special case in which some emfs have zero frequency (direct current) is of course included.

an arbitrary network will vary with frequency. If for a fixed frequency, a variable impedance receives power from an arbitrary network, we can calculate the power transfer as we did in the d-c case and inquire into the conditions for it to be a maximum.

Let us represent a two-terminal network by an emf $\mathcal{E}$ and an impedance $z = r + jx$ and imagine it connected to a load impedance $R + jX$. The magnitude of the current will then be $i = \mathcal{E}/[(r + R)^2 + (x + X)^2]^{1/2}$ and the power expended in the load will be

$$P = \frac{\mathcal{E}^2 R}{(r + R)^2 + (x + X)^2} \tag{9.6-1}$$

This expression will vary as both X and R are changed. Setting $X = -x$ will give a zero reactance term and the largest power for any fixed R (i.e., series resonance will occur). Then P is given by exactly the same expression as Eq. 5.4–4 for the d-c case, so that the condition for maximum P when both R and X are varied is that

$$R = r \quad \text{and} \quad X = -x \tag{9.6-2a}$$

which can be written with the complex conjugate notation

$$Z = \bar{z} \tag{9.6-2b}$$

It is not always feasible to adjust both the angle and magnitude of Z. In fact, impedance matching is most important in communications work in which a wide range of frequencies is involved, and only approximate matching is possible over this range. One type of approximate matching occurs when the magnitude Z of Z but not its angle θ is subject to variation. We can then write

$$P = \frac{\mathcal{E}^2 Z \cos \theta}{[(r + Z \cos \theta)^2 + (x + Z \sin \theta)^2]} \tag{9.6-3}$$

and find the maximum of P with respect to Z. It is left to the reader (Problem 9.6a) to show that this maximum occurs for $Z = z = (r^2 + x^2)^{1/2}$ and that the resulting value of P is

$$P = \frac{\mathcal{E}^2 \cos \theta}{4z \cos^2 \frac{1}{2}(\theta - \theta_S)} \tag{9.6-4}$$

if θ_S is the angle of the internal impedance z. As in the d-c case (Problem 5.5b), it can be shown that the power transfer changes rather slowly as Z departs from its optimum value. (See Problem 9.6b.)

An arbitrary two-terminal passive network can have either sign of equivalent reactance but only a positive resistance, since the network will consume power but not produce it. However, vacuum-tube and solid-state circuits that contain power sources can under some circumstances present equivalent input impedances with negative resistance. Our general theory can be extended readily to cover these cases, but of course maximum power transfer is not then of importance.

Let us now consider four-terminal passive networks (or "passive quad-rupoles"). Examples of these are matching networks, attenuators, filters, and phase-shifting networks. One type of four-terminal network was considered in Problem 5.7a, but before we consider the a-c analogue of this, let us consider certain general properties of linear four-terminal networks. Figure 9.6a shows a four-terminal network which has an input emf $\mathcal{E}$ with

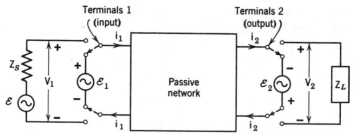

Fig. 9.6a. A passive four-terminal network arranged to connect a source $\mathcal{E}$, Z_S to a load Z_L, or alternatively a fictitious pure emf $\mathcal{E}_1$ to a fictitious pure emf $\mathcal{E}_2$.

impedance Z_S in the source and an output load Z_L. For purposes of calculation, it is convenient to replace each of these by pure emfs, as indicated in the figure.

If we solve the network equations with $\mathcal{E}_1$ and $\mathcal{E}_2$ connected as shown, we can write for the two currents i_1 and i_2 (ignoring all other currents within the network):

$$i_1 = Y_1\mathcal{E}_1 + Y_t\mathcal{E}_2 \qquad (9.6\text{--}5a)$$

$$i_2 = Y_t\mathcal{E}_1 + Y_2\mathcal{E}_2 \qquad (9.6\text{--}5b)$$

where Y_1, Y_t, and Y_2 are constants determined by all the elements within the network. Normally, a general homogeneous linear relation between two currents and two emf's would involve four arbitrary constants, but the reciprocity theorem tells us that the same constant must relate i_1 to $\mathcal{E}_2$ and i_2 to $\mathcal{E}_1$.

These constants have dimensions of mhos and may be called admittances. Any linear four-terminal passive network is thus determined by three quantities, which depend on frequency but are otherwise constant. We can, of course, choose other constants than Y_1, Y_t, and Y_2 to represent the network and will shortly do so, but any other three can always be written as functions of these. Networks that are symmetric with respect to input and output have $Y_1 = Y_2$ and are characterized by two constants only.

An interpretation of the constants Y_1, Y_t, and Y_2 is readily obtained by considering first $\mathcal{E}_2 = 0$ and then $\mathcal{E}_1 = 0$. The condition $\mathcal{E}_2 = 0$ corresponds to a short-circuit at the output or terminal-2 end of the network. It is seen that Y_1 represents the input admittance when the output is short-circuited—it is called for brevity the short-circuit input admittance. Similarly Y_2 is the short-circuit output admittance. When $\mathcal{E}_2 = 0$, there will be a short-circuit current i_2 given by $i_2 = Y_t \mathcal{E}_1$, so we can call Y_t the short-circuit transfer admittance.

It is similarly possible to find the input admittance or impedance when $i_2 = 0$—i.e., when the output is an open circuit. It is left to the reader (Problem 9.6c) to find the three open-circuit quantities analogous to the three short-circuit ones.

Four-terminal networks are frequently used to provide a matching of impedance between source and load or as filters under conditions of impedance matching.[9] That is, when Z_L and the source with $\mathcal{E}$ and Z_S are connected in Fig. 9.6a, the network has an impedance Z_S at terminals 1 and has an impedance Z_L at terminals 2. These two values, Z_S and Z_L, give two conditions on the network parameters, and a third one may also be specified. The usual one is the ratio between the output and input volt-ampere products. Since we have removed the fictitious $\mathcal{E}_1$ and $\mathcal{E}_2$, we must replace them in Eqs. 9.6–5 by V_1 and $-V_2$, as indicated by the signs in the figure. The volt-ampere product ratio is generally expected to be less than one, so we write

$$\frac{V_2 i_2}{V_1 i_1} = \frac{V_2^2/Z_L}{V_1^2/Z_S} = e^{-2\alpha} \cdot e^{-2j\varphi}$$

where 2α is a real positive number (except in cases of resonance, when it may be negative) and 2φ is the phase angle of the ratio. The impedances Z_S and Z_L are in the present case properties of the network and are called the input and output image impedances, Z_{I1} and Z_{I2} respectively. We can also define an image transfer constant Γ (capital Greek gamma) as

$$\Gamma = \alpha + j\varphi \tag{9.6–6}$$

so that the volt-ampere ratio is

$$\frac{V_2^2/Z_{I2}}{V_1^2/Z_{I1}} = e^{-2\Gamma} \tag{9.6–7}$$

[9] The most common case is that in which Z_S and Z_L are purely resistive, so that matching in the conjugate sense of Eq. 9.6–2 is the same as ordinary matching; the more general case is easily handled.

and the voltage ratio is

$$\frac{V_2}{V_1} = \left(\frac{Z_{I2}}{Z_{I1}}\right)^{1/2} e^{-\Gamma} \tag{9.6-8}$$

In the case of filters, designed so as to pass certain frequencies and suppress others, it is common to have two or more networks connected in tandem (cascade) under conditions of impedance matching. Then the voltage ratio at the final output to that at the first input is the product of several factors like Eq. 9.6–8:

$$\frac{V_n}{V_1} = \frac{V_2}{V_1} \cdot \frac{V_3}{V_2} \cdots \frac{V_n}{V_{n-1}} = \left(\frac{Z_{I2}}{Z_{I1}}\right)^{1/2}\left(\frac{Z_{I3}}{Z_{I2}}\right)^{1/2} \cdots \left(\frac{Z_{In}}{Z_{In-1}}\right)^{1/2} e^{-\Gamma_1 - \Gamma_2 \cdots - \Gamma_n}$$

$$= \left(\frac{Z_{In}}{Z_{I1}}\right)^{1/2} e^{-(\Gamma_1 + \Gamma_2 + \cdots + \Gamma_n)} \tag{9.6-9}$$

so that the image transfer constant is additive when networks are connected in cascade. The three image constants describing a single network are thus

$$Z_1 = jX_1 ; \; Z_2 = jX_2$$

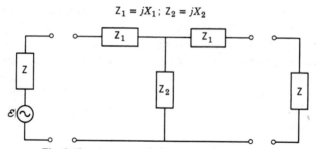

Fig. 9.6b. A symmetrical a-c T-section network.

Z_{I1}, Z_{I2}, and Γ. It is possible, at least in principle, to match any two impedances to each other with any degree of attenuation and any phase shift. However, there are certain restrictive relations between actually attainable values of the constants that are too complicated to consider here.[10] It is generally possible to arrange for approximately zero attenuation ($\alpha = 0$) and a phase shift variable over a considerable range (nearly from $0°$ to $180°$ in case the image impedances are both purely resistive).

Let us now use the a-c analogue of the T-section attenuator of Fig. 5.7c to illustrate the above. We shall first consider strict matching and simply write Z_1, Z_2, and Z in place of R_1, R_2, and R. (Fig. 9.6b.) Furthermore, we shall take the case in which the resistive parts of Z_1 and Z_2 are negligible, so that we can write, to a good approximation,

$$Z_1 = jX_1; \qquad Z_2 = jX_2 \tag{9.6-10}$$

[10] See, for instance, Terman, *op. cit.*, section 3, part 27.

We can take over directly the formulas 5.7–8 and 5.7–9 of Problem 5.7*a*, and shall replace x_a by $e^{-\Gamma}$ since the input and output image impedances are equal (cf. Eq. 9.6–7). We have the matching condition

$$Z^2 = Z_1{}^2 + 2Z_1 Z_2 \tag{9.6–11}$$

the attenuation factor

$$e^{-\Gamma} = \frac{Z_2}{Z_2 + Z_1 + Z} \tag{9.6–12}$$

and the equations for Z_1 and Z_2 (cf. Eq. A.5–12 for hyperbolic functions)

$$Z_1 = \frac{1 - e^{-\Gamma}}{1 + e^{-\Gamma}} Z = Z \tanh \frac{\Gamma}{2} \tag{9.6–13}$$

$$Z_2 = \frac{2e^{-\Gamma}}{1 - e^{-2\Gamma}} Z = \frac{Z}{\sinh \Gamma} \tag{9.6–14}$$

Using Eq. 9.6–10, Eq. 9.6–11 becomes

$$Z^2 = -(X_1{}^2 + 2X_1 X_2) = -X_1(X_1 + 2X_2) \tag{9.6–15}$$

In the case that X_1 and $X_1 + 2X_2$ are both positive or both negative, Z is a pure imaginary number. We can then write $Z = jX$ and

$$X^2 = X_1{}^2 + 2X_1 X_2 \tag{9.6–16a}$$

$$e^{-\Gamma} = \frac{X_2}{X_2 + X_1 + X} \tag{9.6–16b}$$

Equation 9.6–16 then shows that $e^{-\Gamma}$ is a real number, positive or negative, which means that either $\Gamma = \pm\alpha$ or $\Gamma = \pm\alpha \pm j\pi$ where α is positive. Let us consider the various possible cases. If we determine Z by Eq. 9.6–15, either sign of square root may be taken, so that $Z = \pm j(X_1{}^2 + 2X_1 X_2)^{1/2}$; i.e., Z can be a reactance of either sign. Since $(X_2 + X_1)^2 = X^2 + X_2{}^2$, we see that the magnitude of $X_2 + X_1$ is always greater than that of X. Hence if X_1 and X_2 are reactances of the same sign, this sign will also be the sign of the denominator of Eq. 9.6–16 and the entire fraction will be positive, regardless of the sign of X. There will be no voltage phase shift. If X_1 and X_2 are of opposite sign, the magnitude of X_1 must be greater than that of $2X_2$ for Z^2 to be negative, so that the denominator will have the sign of X_1 and the fraction will be negative—the voltage V_2 will be 180° out of phase with V_1.

It is easy to see that when all X's are positive, $e^{-\Gamma}$ is less than 1 and attenuation occurs. It is left to the reader to show (Problem 9.6*e*) that attenuation occurs when X and X_1 have the same sign, whereas voltage multiplication occurs when X and X_1 are of opposite sign (a type of resonance occurs).

Now suppose that $X_1^2 + 2X_1X_2$ is negative and Z is real, thus being equal to a (necessarily positive) resistance R. This will occur if $1 + 2X_2/X_1$ is negative, or $2X_2/X_1 < -1$. Then we can write Eq. 9.6–12 as

$$e^{-\Gamma} = \frac{jX_2}{j(X_2 + X_1) + [-(X_1^2 + 2X_1X_2)]^{\frac{1}{2}}} = \frac{jX_2}{j(X_2 + X_1) + R} \quad (9.6\text{–}17a)$$

For the magnitude of $e^{-\Gamma}$ we have

$$|e^{-\Gamma}| = e^{-\alpha} = \frac{X_2}{[(X_1 + X_2)^2 + (-X_1^2 - 2X_1X_2)]^{\frac{1}{2}}} = \frac{X_2}{X_2} = 1 \quad (9.6\text{–}17b)$$

so $\alpha = 0$ and we have neither attenuation nor multiplication of voltage. The angle of $e^{\Gamma} = e^{j\varphi}$ is, on the other hand, given by

$$\tan \varphi = -\frac{R}{X_2 + X_1} \quad (9.6\text{–}17c)$$

and φ can vary over a wide range.

Now suppose that a group of T-section networks are placed in cascade and terminated by an impedance that is approximately resistive, but which has a reactive component of the same sign as X_1. As the frequency is varied, the end sections will not remain properly matched, but the intermediate ones almost will. For the range of frequencies that gives $(2X_2/X_1) < -1$ or $-1 < (X_1/2X_2) < 0$, there will be no attenuation; the set of networks is said to "pass" this set of frequencies, the range being called the "pass band." For other frequencies, there will be attenuation; the consequence of several sections in cascade will be to add the attenuation constants α; these frequencies are said to be "suppressed." It is in this way that practical filters are designed. Those designed to pass all frequencies below a certain limit are called low-pass filters (the rectifier filter in Section 9.4 is a special example). Those designed to suppress all frequencies below a certain limit are called high-pass filters. If the range of passed frequencies is relatively narrow, we have a band-pass filter, and for the suppression of a narrow band we have band-elimination filters. The pass band can be found by plotting $2X_2$ and $-X_1$ as functions of the frequency and observing where $2X_2/(-X_1) > 1$.

Filters are usually designed to be matched to pure resistive loads. In order to provide suitable approximate matching at a variety of frequencies, L-networks (resembling halves of T-networks) are used between the T's and the source or load. The details are complicated, and the reader is referred elsewhere for them.[11]

[11] See Terman, *loc. cit.*; Page and Adams, *op. cit.*, section 129; also E. A. Guillemin, *Introductory Circuit Theory*, John Wiley, New York, 1953; and H. H. Skilling, *Electrical Engineering Circuits*, John Wiley, New York, 1959.

As another example that shows some of the potentialities of alternating-current circuits, consider Fig. 9.6c, with a fixed frequency, fixed L and C, and variable R. The coil resistance is considered to be negligible. The impedance Z of the entire circuit is:

$$Z = j\omega L + \frac{Z(-j/\omega C)}{R - j/\omega C} = \frac{j\omega L - \omega^2 LCR + R}{1 + j\omega CR} \qquad (9.6\text{--}18)$$

and the current in the resistance R is

$$i_R = i\frac{(-j/\omega C)}{R - j/\omega C} = \frac{\mathcal{E}}{Z} \cdot \frac{1}{1 + j\omega CR} = \frac{\mathcal{E}}{j\omega L - \omega^2 LCR + R} \qquad (9.6\text{--}19)$$

Now, if L and C are tuned to resonance, $\omega^2 LC = 1$ and $i_R = \mathcal{E}/j\omega L$, so i_R is independent of the value of R. This constitutes a constant-current

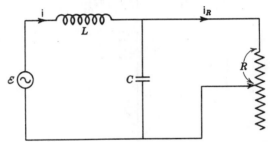

Fig. 9.6c. A circuit for constant-current or variable-phase applications.

circuit. The current will depend slightly on R if the Q of the coil is not extremely high, but for practical purposes this effect is unimportant.

On the other hand, if $\omega^2 LC = 1/2$, Z has interesting properties. We have

$$Z = \frac{j\omega L + \tfrac{1}{2}R}{1 + \dfrac{jR}{2\omega L}} = \omega L\,\frac{j\omega L + \tfrac{1}{2}R}{\omega L + \tfrac{1}{2}jR} \qquad (9.6\text{--}20)$$

so that the magnitude of Z is ωL and is independent of R. The angle of Z, on the other hand, is $\varphi = \tan^{-1}(2\omega L/R) - \tan^{-1}(R/2\omega L) = 2\tan^{-1}(2\omega L/R) - \pi/2$, which varies from $\pi/2$ to $-\pi/2$ when R varies from 0 to ∞. Thus we have an impedance of constant magnitude and variable phase, of use in certain circuit applications.

Another type of four-terminal network is the bridge circuit, which is of such importance for electrical measurements. Using complex analysis, the balance condition for an a-c Wheatstone bridge is found to be directly analogous to that for the d-c bridge, namely

$$\frac{Z_1}{Z_2} = \frac{Z_3}{Z_4} \qquad (9.6\text{--}21)$$

This relation is actually two equations, for the equality of the real and imaginary parts; balancing an a-c bridge involves two adjustments.[12]

Figure 9.6d shows a so-called $Z-Y$ bridge,[13] which is used for measuring either an arbitrary impedance Z introduced in series in arm 4 or an arbitrary admittance Y introduced in parallel in arm 1. We consider it in detail because of the variety of principles it illustrates.

It is convenient in this case to write the balance condition in terms of admittances for branches 1 and 3 and impedances for 2 and 4. We have,

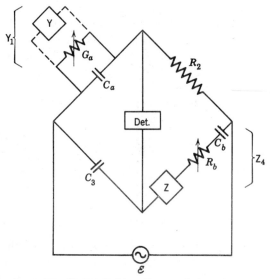

Fig. 9.6d.   The General Radio $Z-Y$ Bridge. (By permission of the General Radio Co., Cambridge, Mass.)

in fact, $Z_2Y_1 = Z_4Y_3$; the quantities $Z_2 = R_2$ and $Y_3 = j\omega C_3$ are considered to be fixed. In general, $Y_1 = G_1 + jB_1$ and $Z_4 = R_4 + jX_4$, so we write for the real and imaginary parts of the balance equation

$$R_2G_1 = -\omega C_3X_4 \qquad (9.6\text{--}22)$$

and

$$R_2B_1 = \omega C_3R_4 \qquad (9.6\text{--}23)$$

The bridge is operated by the substitution method, which has the advantages of balancing out stray capacitances and inductances and the

---

[12] See Harris, *op. cit.*, Chapter 15 for a discussion of a-c bridges and their balancing, particularly the use of the complex-number plane to describe the approach to balance; see also M. B. Stout, *Basic Electrical Measurements*, 2nd ed., Prentice-Hall, Englewood Cliffs, N.J., 1960, Chapter 9.

[13] Stout, *op. cit.*, pp. 298–300.

departures from ideal behavior of the fixed bridge elements. The bridge is first balanced without the unknown in either the Z or Y position. The magnitude of $G_1 = G_a$ is varied to satisfy Eq. 9.6–22, and $R_4 = R_b$ is varied to satisfy Eq. 9.6–23.

Now, if an unknown Z is added to branch 4, the resulting change ΔX_4 in X_4 is compensated by a change ΔG_a in the setting of G_a:

$$\Delta X_4 = -\frac{R_2}{\omega C_3}\Delta G_a$$

The additional resistance in branch 4 is compensated by reducing R_b to maintain R_4 fixed. The unknown Z is thus found from the observed changes ΔG_a and ΔR_b.

On the other hand, if an unknown Y is added to branch 1, the additional conductance is compensated by reduction of G_a to keep G_1 fixed, and the added susceptance is measured by the change needed in the setting of R_b. From Eq. 9.6–23 we have

$$\Delta B_1 = \frac{\omega C_3}{R_2}\Delta R_b$$

and Y is found from ΔR_b and ΔG_a.

It is a straightforward matter to choose the ratio $\omega C_3/R_2$ and the dial calibrations to make the bridge easy to read. It can also be arranged so that if the bridge can handle values of Z up to, say, 1000 ohms, it can handle values of Y up to 0.001 mho—i.e., any element whatsoever will fall into the range of the bridge at either the Y or Z position (of course, the finite sensitivity of the bridge will eliminate very small Z's or Y's). There is a definite advantage to being able to make all adjustments with variable resistors, which are more readily produced and calibrated than variable inductors and capacitors.

Problem 9.6a. Show that the maximum of Eq. 9.6–3 occurs when $Z = (r^2 + x^2)^{1/2}$ if θ is fixed. Also show that for this value of Z, P in Eq. 9.6–3 takes the value given by Eq. 9.6–4.

Problem 9.6b. Show that the ratio of the maximum power transfer from a two-terminal network to the actual value is proportional to $\sec\theta$ times the magnitude of the complex number $(Z + z)^2/Zz = [(Z/z)^{1/2} + (z/Z)^{1/2}]^2$. Show also that because R and r cannot be negative, the positive[14] square root of Z/z or z/Z has a positive real part. Hence show that for any phase angles of Z and z, a power ratio substantially different from 1 is obtained only if the magnitudes of Z and z have a large ratio.

---

[14] The "positive" square root is the one which becomes $+1$ when $Z = z$.

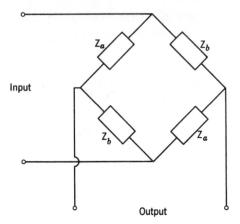

Fig. 9.6e. A four-terminal symmetrical lattice.

Problem 9.6c. Find the open-circuit input and output impedances for Fig. 9.6a in terms of Y_1, Y_t, and Y_2, and also the ratio between the input and output voltages when the output is open-circuited.

Problem 9.6d. Relate the quantity α in Eq. 9.6–6 to the quantity α_{db} of Problem 5.7c.

Problem 9.6e. Consider all eight sign possibilities for X_1, X_2, and X in Eq. 9.6–16, and verify the statements in the text, namely that the sign of $e^{-\Gamma}$ is the same as that of X_2/X_1, and that $e^{-\Gamma}$ is greater than or less than 1 in magnitude according as X/X_1 is negative or positive. (*Hint:* a useful relation for this problem is obtained if we multiply numerator and denominator of 9.6–16b by $X_1 + X_2 - X$.)

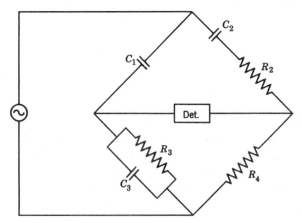

Fig. 9.6f. The Schering bridge circuit.

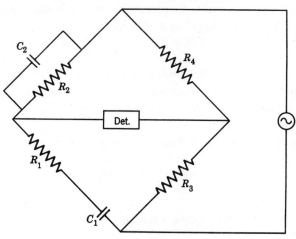

Fig. 9.6g. The Wien bridge circuit.

Problem 9.6f. Consider the four-terminal symmetrical lattice, as in Fig. 9.6e. By use of the appropriate equations in Section 5.5, show that the image impedance is $Z = (Z_a Z_b)^{1/2}$ and that $\tanh \Gamma/2 = (Z_a/Z_b)^{1/2}$. (This arrangement allows Z and Γ to be chosen quite independently of one another.)

Problem 9.6g. If the resistance R_2 of the coil in Fig. 9.6c is not negligible, find a relation between time constants in the circuit that makes i_R nearly independent of R.

Problem 9.6h. Figure 9.6f shows the circuit of a Schering bridge, used for capacitor measurements. Write the balance equations for finding C_2

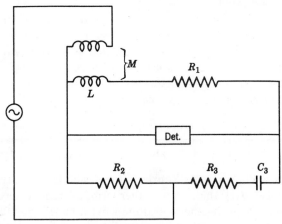

Fig. 9.6h. The Carey-Foster or Heydweiller mutual-inductance bridge.

and R_2. For any reasonable frequency, show which elements should be made variable to give independent adjustments.

Problem 9.6i. The circuit of a Wien frequency-sensitive bridge is shown in Fig. 9.6g. Find the balance equations, show how ω can be determined, and show the relation of this bridge to the circuit of Problem 9.4j. Show what the balance condition becomes in the usual case that C_1 and C_2 are fixed and equal, R_3 and $2R_4$ are likewise fixed and equal, and R_1 and R_2 are kept equal and varied.

Problem 9.6j. The Carey-Foster or Heydweiller mutual-inductance bridge has a circuit as shown in Fig. 9.6h. Analyze this bridge with Kirchhoff's laws, assuming M to have the appropriate sense.

9.7   Non-Sinusoidal Alternating Currents

In this section, we wish to give a brief description of methods used for handling periodic variations of current and voltage that are not sinusoidal in nature. Figure 9.7a shows four simple examples of time variations that might apply to voltages or currents. They are all referred to as "waves" because of the appearance of the various time graphs. Square waves are used in certain pulse circuits and for testing purposes. Saw-tooth waves are used for cathode-ray oscillograph sweep circuits. The full- and half-wave rectifier outputs are the two common varieties of unidirectional voltages applied to the inputs of rectifier filters such as that described at the end of Section 9.4. All these waves are periodic with a period T, which as indicated can be measured from any part of the curve to the next corresponding part. In the rectifier graphs, the period T_0 of the original cosine wave is also indicated.

The general method of handling such non-sinusoidal variations is to make use of the celebrated Fourier expansion theorem, which states that any periodic function $f(t)$ can be represented as a (usually infinite) series of sine and cosine functions whose frequencies are multiples of the frequency of repetition of $f(t)$. Explicitly, if $f(t)$ has the period T and the angular frequency $\omega = 2\pi/T$, we can write

$$f(t) = \tfrac{1}{2}a_0 + a_1 \cos \omega t + a_2 \cos 2\omega t + \cdots + a_n \cos n\omega t + \cdots$$
$$+ b_1 \sin \omega t + b_2 \sin 2\omega t + \cdots + b_n \sin n\omega t + \cdots \quad (9.7\text{-}1)$$

Such a sum is known as a "Fourier series." The term $\tfrac{1}{2}a_0$ represents the average value of $f(t)$, since all the other terms average to zero. The terms in $\cos \omega t$ and $\sin \omega t$ together constitute what is called the "fundamental" or "first harmonic." The terms with $2\omega t$, $3\omega t \cdots$ are called the second

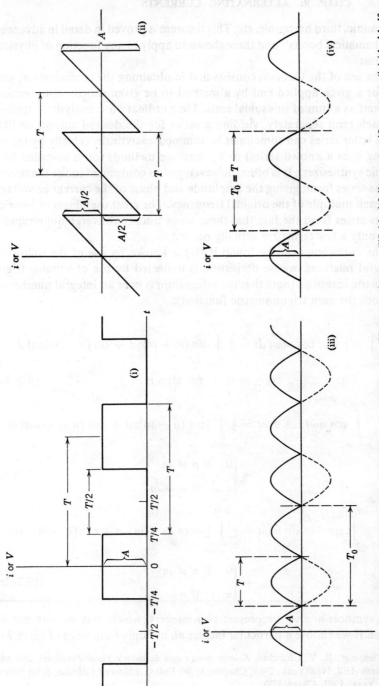

Fig. 9.7a. Some non-sinusoidal periodic functions: (i) square wave, (ii) sawtooth wave, (iii) ideal full-wave rectifier output, (iv) ideal half-wave rectifier output.

harmonic, third harmonic, etc. This theorem is proved in detail in advanced mathematical books[15] and there shown to apply to any function of physical interest.

The use of the theorem consists first in obtaining the coefficients a_n and b_n for a given applied emf by a method to be given shortly, thus writing the emf as a sum of sinusoidal emfs. Then ordinary a-c analysis is applied to each term separately, yielding a series for the desired current or PD. This latter series can sometimes be summed analytically (chiefly by recognizing it as a known series) or by machine methods (on a so-called harmonic synthesizer). It is often, however, just as convenient to use the results in the series form, giving the amplitude and phase of the current or voltage for each multiple of the original frequency. The great usefulness of Fourier series arises from the fact that these series usually converge quite rapidly and only a few terms are actually needed.

The coefficients can be found if $f(t)$ is known by use of the following integral relations, whose derivation is indicated by use of suitable trigonometric identities (note that the integration is over an integral number of periods for each trigonometric function).

$$\int_{-\pi/\omega}^{\pi/\omega} [\sin n\omega t \cos m\omega t \, dt = \tfrac{1}{2} \int_{-\pi/\omega}^{\pi/\omega} \sin (n + m)\omega t + \sin (n - m)\omega t] \, dt$$

$$= 0 \qquad \text{for all } n,m \tag{9.7-2a}$$

$$\int_{-\pi/\omega}^{\pi/\omega} \cos n\omega t \cos m\omega t = \tfrac{1}{2} \int_{-\pi/\omega}^{\pi/\omega} [\cos (n + m)\omega t + \cos (n - m)\omega t] \, dt$$

$$= \begin{cases} 0 & \text{if } n \neq m \\ \pi/\omega & \text{if } n = m \end{cases} \tag{9.7-2b}$$

$$\int_{-\pi/\omega}^{\pi/\omega} \sin n\omega t \sin m\omega t = \tfrac{1}{2} \int_{-\pi/\omega}^{\pi/\omega} [-\cos (n + m)\omega t + \cos (n - m)\omega t] \, dt$$

$$= \begin{cases} 0 & \text{if } n \neq m \\ \pi/\omega & \text{if } n = m \end{cases} \tag{9.7-2c}$$

The symbols m and n represent two integers, which may or may not be equal. If we choose a particular integer m, multiply both sides of Eq. 9.7–1

---

[15] See, e.g., R. V. Churchill, *Fourier Series and Boundary Value Problems*, 2nd ed., McGraw-Hill, New York, 1963, Chapter 4; W. Fulks, *Advanced Calculus*, John Wiley, New York, 1961, Chapter 20.

by $\cos m\omega t$ and integrate over t from $-\pi/\omega$ to π/ω (i.e., $-T/2$ to $T/2$), every term on the right save the one with $\cos m\omega t$ will drop out by Eq. 9.7-2, and we obtain an equation for a_m. Similarly we can obtain b_m by multiplying by $\sin m\omega t$ and integrating. The results are

$$a_m = \frac{\omega}{\pi} \int_{-\pi/\omega}^{\pi/\omega} f(t) \cos m\omega t \, dt \qquad m = 0, 1, 2, \cdots \qquad (9.7\text{-}3a)$$

$$b_m = \frac{\omega}{\pi} \int_{-\pi/\omega}^{\pi/\omega} f(t) \sin m\omega t \, dt \qquad m = 1, 2, 3 \cdots \qquad (9.7\text{-}3b)$$

The factor $\frac{1}{2}$ in front of a_0 in Eq. 9.7-1 is introduced to allow Eq. 9.7-3a to hold as written for the case $m = 0$.

To illustrate, let us consider first the square wave shown in Fig. 9.7a. The function $f(t)$ in the range $-T/2$ to $T/2$ is given by

$$
\begin{aligned}
f(t) &= 0, & -T/2 < t < -T/4 \\
f(t) &= A, & -T/4 < t < T/4 \\
f(t) &= 0, & T/4 < t < T/2
\end{aligned}
\qquad (9.7\text{-}4)
$$

From Eq. 9.7-3a we have for $m > 0$

$$a_m = \frac{\omega A}{\pi} \int_{-\pi/2\omega}^{\pi/2\omega} \cos m\omega t \, dt = \frac{A}{\pi m} \sin m\omega t \Big|_{-\pi/2\omega}^{\pi/2\omega}$$

$$= \frac{2A}{\pi m} \sin \frac{m\pi}{2} = \begin{cases} 0 & m = 2, 4, 6, 8 \cdots \\ 2A/\pi m & m = 1, 5, 9 \cdots \\ -2A/\pi m & m = 3, 7, 11 \cdots \end{cases}$$

For $m = 0$, we have

$$a_0 = \frac{\omega A}{\pi} \Big|_{-\pi/2\omega}^{\pi/2\omega} dt = A$$

From Eq. 9.7-3b, we find

$$b_m = \frac{-A}{\omega m} \cos m\omega t \Big|_{-\pi/2\omega}^{\pi/2\omega} = 0$$

We should, in fact, expect all the b's to be zero since $f(t)$ is an even function, $f(-t) = f(t)$, which property is satisfied by all the cosines and none of the sines. The resulting Fourier series for a square wave is

$$f(t) = \tfrac{1}{2}A + \frac{2A}{\pi} \{\cos \omega t - \tfrac{1}{3} \cos 3\omega t + \tfrac{1}{5} \cos 5\omega t - \tfrac{1}{7} \cos 7\omega t + \cdots\}$$

$$(9.7\text{-}5)$$

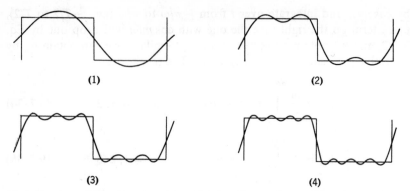

(1)   (2)

(3)   (4)

Fig. 9.7b. The effect of adding successively more terms of Eq. 9.7–5. (1) Two terms. (2) Three terms. (3) Four terms. (4) Five terms.

Figure 9.7b shows the effect of adding successively more terms of this series to approximate the infinite sum.

The sawtooth wave of Fig. 9.7a is an odd function, $f(-t) = -f(t)$. The function $f(t)$ in this case is given by

$$f(t) = \frac{At}{T} = \frac{\omega A}{2\pi} t, \qquad -T/2 < t < T/2 \qquad (9.7\text{--}6)$$

The coefficients b_m are given by

$$b_m = \frac{\omega^2 A}{2\pi^2} \int_{-\pi/\omega}^{\pi/\omega} t \sin m\omega t \, dt = \frac{\omega^2 A}{2\pi^2} \left[\frac{-t \cos m\omega t}{m\omega} + \frac{\sin m\omega t}{m^2 \omega^2} \right]_{-\pi/\omega}^{\pi/\omega}$$

$$= \frac{\omega^2 A}{2\pi^2} \cdot \frac{2\pi}{m\omega^2} (-1)^{m+1} = \frac{A}{\pi m} (-1)^{m+1}$$

so that the sawtooth wave series is

$$f(t) = \frac{A}{\pi} [\sin \omega t - \tfrac{1}{2} \sin 2\omega t + \tfrac{1}{3} \sin 3\omega t - + \cdots] \qquad (9.7\text{--}7)$$

In a similar way, the full-wave rectifier output may be analyzed. In this case, $f(t)$ is given by

$$f(t) = A \cos \frac{\omega t}{2}, \qquad -T/2 < t < T/2 \qquad (9.7\text{--}8)$$

and the resulting series turns out to be (cf. Problem 9.7b)

$$f(t) = \frac{2A}{\pi} \left[1 + \frac{2}{3} \cos \omega t - \frac{2}{15} \cos 2\omega t + \cdots + \frac{2(-1)^{n+1}}{4n^2 - 1} \cos n\omega t + \cdots \right]$$

$$(9.7\text{--}9)$$

It is to be especially noticed that the frequencies appearing in this series are all multiples of twice the frequency of the original cosine wave before rectification (dotted line in Fig. 9.7a). The first harmonic of the rectified voltage is thus the second harmonic of the original alternating current.

The half-wave series can be gotten readily from the full-wave series by the addition of the cosine function $A \cos \omega t/2$, for all t (cf. Problem 9.7c).

To illustrate the use of Fourier series, suppose that an ideal full-wave voltage like that of Eq. 9.7–9 is applied to a simple L–C filter like that of Fig. 9.4c. The nth term of the voltage series is (setting $A = V$)

$$V_n \cos n\omega t = \frac{4V(-1)^{n+1}}{\pi(4n^2 - 1)} \cos n\omega t$$

In accordance with Eq. 9.4–13 the output voltage for this term will be, approximately

$$\frac{-V_n \cos n\omega t}{(n\omega)^2 LC - 1} = \frac{4V(-1)^n \cos n\omega t}{\pi(4n^2 - 1)(n^2\omega^2 LC - 1)}$$

except for $n = 0$, when the result is

$$\frac{V_0 R}{R + R'} = \frac{2VR}{\pi(R + R')}$$

so that the entire voltage is

$$\frac{2VR}{\pi(R + R')} - \frac{4V \cos \omega t}{3\pi(\omega^2 LC - 1)} + \frac{4V \cos 2\omega t}{15\pi(4\omega^2 LC - 1)}$$
$$- \cdots + \frac{(-1)^n 4V \cos n\omega t}{\pi(4n^2 - 1)(n^2\omega^2 LC - 1)} + \cdots \quad (9.7-10)$$

The successive terms decrease very rapidly since the denominator is approximately proportional to n^4, so that the sum of the first two or three makes a very good approximation. The terms beyond the first constitute the "ripple." The percentage of ripple can be defined as 100 times the ratio of the amplitude of the second term to the value of the first:

$$\text{ripple percent} = 100 \cdot \frac{2}{3(\omega^2 LC - 1)} \cdot \frac{R + R'}{R}$$

It is readily seen that the effect of two filter sections in tandem is to reduce the first harmonic considerably and the higher harmonics very much indeed, since each factor $n^2\omega^2 LC - 1$ will then appear squared.

Non-sinusoidal voltages are produced by various means, in addition to the rectifiers and special circuits we have referred to. For instance, a sinusoidal current in the primary of a transformer will produce a non-sinusoidal variation of flux, because of the non-linear shape of the hysteresis loop of the iron core. This fact can be seen quickly without detailed analysis by showing that if the hysteresis curve has, for instance, a dependence on H^2 and therefore on i^2, the flux will have a dependence on, say, $\cos^2 \omega t$. But $\cos^2 \omega t = \frac{1}{2}(1 + \cos 2\omega t)$, so we see that a second-degree term in the equation of the hysteresis loop introduces a second harmonic into the flux variation. Third-degree terms will introduce both third and second harmonics, and so forth. Consequently any complex curve like a hysteresis loop can be expected to introduce a whole series of harmonics although if only the relatively linear portion is used, the higher harmonics may all have small coefficients.

A tungsten lamp filament operated on a-c will have a slight alternating variation in temperature and hence a generally non-sinusoidal variation of resistance, so that the current $i = V/R$ produced by a sinusoidal V will always have some higher harmonics in its variation.

The most important sources of non-sinusoidal voltages and currents, from a practical point of view, are music and speech. Sustained musical tones and vowel sounds are complex periodic variations in air velocity and pressure. By the action of microphones they are converted into similar voltage and current variations. Amplifier circuits that are intended to give accurate reproduction of these sounds are conveniently analyzed in terms of their response to sinusoidal voltages of frequencies over the range of interest; the uniformity of this response gives a measure of the accuracy of the reproduction.

Staccato notes, percussion sounds, and most speech sounds are not sustained periodic vibrations but are better described as "pulses" or "transients." Some consideration will be given to these in the next section, but is should be stated here that a pulse can be analyzed into a continuous range of frequencies by the so-called Fourier integral theorem (which is closely related to the Laplace transform method) so that accurate reproduction of pulses also requires a circuit response that is suitably uniform over the relevant range of frequencies.

Problem 9.7a. Prove that any even $f(t)$ is represented as a Fourier series by cosines alone and that any odd $f(t)$ is represented by sines alone.

Problem 9.7b. Derive the series Eq. 9.7–9 for the full-wave rectifier output.

Problem 9.7c. Derive a series for the half-wave rectifier output (a) by the formulas of the text and (b) by adding $A \cos \omega t/2$ to Eq. 9.7–9 and dividing the sum by two.

Problem 9.7d. If we represent the voltage in a given circuit element by $V = V_0 + V_{1c} \cos \omega t + V_{2c} \cos 2\omega t + \cdots + V_{1s} \sin \omega t + V_{2s} \sin 2\omega t + \cdots$ and the current in the same element by $i = i_0 + i_{1c} \cos \omega t + i_{2c} \cos 2\omega t + \cdots + i_{1s} \sin \omega t + i_{2s} \sin 2\omega t + \cdots$, show that the rms voltage is

$(V_0{}^2 + \frac{1}{2}V_{1c}^2 + \frac{1}{2}V_{1s}^2 + \frac{1}{2}V_{2c}^2 + \frac{1}{2}V_{2s}^2 + \cdots)^{\frac{1}{2}}$, the rms current is $(i_0{}^2 + \frac{1}{2}i_{1c}^2 + \frac{1}{2}i_{1s}^2 + \frac{1}{2}i_{2c}^2 + \frac{1}{2}i_{2s}^2 + \cdots)^{\frac{1}{2}}$, the average power expended is $V_0 i_0 + \frac{1}{2}V_{1c}i_{1c} + \frac{1}{2}V_{1s}i_{1s} + \frac{1}{2}V_{2c}i_{2c} + \frac{1}{2}V_{2s}i_{2s} + \cdots)$ and the nth term of this last equation can be written as the sum of the ordinary power terms for sinusoidal currents, $V_n i_n \cos \varphi_n$ where $\cos \varphi_n$ is the power factor for the nth harmonic.

9.8 Transients and Pulses

Transients are the variations in current or voltage that occur when a system is rapidly changed from one steady state to another, as when a steady or alternating emf is first turned on or a sudden change is made in the amplitude or phase of a steady sinusoidal alternating emf. Pulses are variations that occur for a short time and then disappear. In this section we shall give a brief introduction to methods of handling transients and pulses.

The simplest case to start with is the switching on of a steady emf $\mathscr{E}$ in a series circuit with R, L, and C. We have already considered the special cases of R and C only (Section 5.5) and R and L only (Section 7.16). The equation of a series circuit in its general form is

$$L\frac{di}{dt} + Ri + \frac{q}{C} = \mathscr{E}$$

Since $i = dq/dt$, we can write this as

$$L\frac{d^2q}{dt^2} + R\frac{dq}{dt} + \frac{q}{C} = \mathscr{E} \tag{9.8-1}$$

For constant $\mathscr{E}$, this equation has the same mathematical form as Eq. 8.9–8 or Eq. 8.9–12a. Furthermore, the boundary conditions are the same as for the d-c galvanometer, for if the condenser in the circuit is originally uncharged, we will have $q = 0$ and $i = dq/dt = 0$ at $t = 0$. Consequently we can take over directly the results of Section 8.9. Comparing with Eq. 8.9–12a, and using Eqs. 8.9–15, 8.9–16, and 8.9–25 we can construct the equivalences in Table 9.8A and evaluate the constants α, β, ω, and γ.

Equation 8.9–21 for the solution with the given boundary conditions and damping more than critical can be taken over with only a change in θ and θ_F:

$$q = \mathscr{E}C\left[1 - \frac{\alpha + \beta}{2\beta}e^{-(\alpha-\beta)t} + \frac{\alpha - \beta}{2\beta}e^{-(\alpha+\beta)t}\right] \tag{9.8-2}$$

Table 9.8A   Constants for Galvanometer Motion and for an *R-L-C* Circuit

	Galvanometer	*R-L-C* Circuit
Variable quantity	θ	q
Inertia constant	I	L
Friction constant	b	R
"Restoring force" constant	k	$1/C$
Applied "force"	$k\theta_F$	$\mathscr{E}$
Undamped (natural) angular frequency	$\omega_0 = \left(\dfrac{k}{I}\right)^{\frac{1}{2}}$	$\omega_0 = \dfrac{1}{(LC)^{\frac{1}{2}}}$
Relative damping	$\gamma = b/2(kI)^{\frac{1}{2}}$	$\gamma = R(C/4L)^{\frac{1}{2}}$
Attenuation constant	$\alpha = \omega_0\gamma = b/2I$	$\alpha = R/2L$
Second attenuation constant	$\beta = \omega_0(\gamma^2 - 1)^{\frac{1}{2}} = \dfrac{1}{2I}(b^2 - 4kI)^{\frac{1}{2}}$	$\beta = \dfrac{1}{2L}\left(R^2 - \dfrac{4L}{C}\right)^{\frac{1}{2}}$
Damped angular frequency	$\omega = \omega_0(1 - \gamma^2)^{\frac{1}{2}} = \dfrac{1}{2I}(4kI - b^2)^{\frac{1}{2}}$	$\omega_d = \dfrac{1}{2L}\left(\dfrac{4L}{C} - R^2\right)^{\frac{1}{2}}$

from which we find the current to be

$$i = \frac{dq}{d} = \frac{\mathscr{E}C(\alpha^2 - \beta^2)}{2\beta}[e^{-(\alpha-\beta)t} - e^{-(\alpha+\beta)t}] \qquad (9.8\text{–}3)$$

It is to be noted that $\mathscr{E}C$ is the final charge on the condenser and could as well be written q_F. For the underdamped case, we get from Eq. 8.9–26

$$q = \mathscr{E}C\left[1 - e^{-\alpha t}\left(\frac{\alpha}{\omega}\sin \omega t + \cos \omega t\right)\right] \qquad (9.8\text{–}4)$$

and

$$i = \mathscr{E}C\left(\frac{\alpha^2}{\omega} + \omega\right)e^{-\alpha t}\sin \omega t \qquad (9.8\text{–}5)$$

The critically damped case, from Eq. 8.9–23, gives

$$q = \mathscr{E}C[1 - e^{-\alpha t}(\alpha t + 1)] \qquad (9.8\text{–}6)$$

and

$$i = \mathscr{E}C\alpha^2 t\, e^{-\alpha t} \qquad (9.8\text{–}7)$$

The variation of q with t and thus the variation of the condenser voltage q/C for various values of the relative damping $\gamma = R(C/4L)^{\frac{1}{2}}$ is of the same form as that for θ in Fig. 8.9b. The current will vary like the curves for θ in Fig. 8.9c.

The variations of q and i that occur when a charged condenser is discharged through an *R-L-C* circuit that initially had no current are obtained in the same way as is used to determine the return of a galvanometer to rest. The results are readily obtained from previous results by writing $q_2 = \mathscr{E}C - q_1$, where q_1 is the previous result and q_2 is the discharge result. The current will simply have its sign reversed.

A more complicated case is that of turning on a sinusoidal emf of arbitrary amplitude, frequency, and phase, in a series R-L-C circuit. Since we shall return to using the symbol ω for the angular frequency of an alternating emf, the damped angular frequency ω of Section 8.9 can be called, for instance, ω_d. The equation for the charge on the condenser is now

$$L\frac{d^2q}{dt^2} + R\frac{dq}{dt} + \frac{q}{C} = \mathscr{E}_m \cos{(\omega t + \varphi_V)} \qquad (9.8\text{-}8)$$

subject to the initial conditions $q = 0$ and $i = 0$ when $t = 0$. Let us see how to construct the solution of Eq. 9.8–8 from our previous results. By the complex-number method we know how to find the steady-state solution $q_s = q_{sm} \cos{(\omega t + \varphi)}$. It will not be necessary to specify here the values of q_{sm} and φ. If we write $q = q_t + q_s$, substitute in Eq. 9.8–8, and use the fact that q_s itself satisfies the equation (which we know without calculating derivatives), we see that q_t satisfies the so-called "reduced equation" (see Appendix A.3):

$$L\frac{d^2q_t}{dt^2} + R\frac{dq_t}{dt} + \frac{q_t}{C} = 0 \qquad (9.8\text{-}9)$$

q_t is called the transient part of the solution. Since $q = 0$ and $i = 0$ when $t = 0$, q_t and i_t must have values which are the negatives of q_s and i_s at $t = 0$:

$$q_t(0) = -q_s(0); \qquad i_t(0) = -i_s(0) \qquad (9.8\text{-}10)$$

Now let us write $q_t = q_{t1} + q_{t2}$, specifying that q_{t1} satisfies Eq. 9.8–9 with $q_{t1}(0) = q_t(0)$ and $i_{t1}(0) = 0$, whereas q_{t2} satisfies Eq. 9.8–9 with $q_{t2}(0) = 0$ and $i_{t2}(0) = i_t(0)$. That is, q_t is broken up into a sum of a part with vanishing initial charge and one with a vanishing initial current. It should be evident to the reader that $q = q_s + q_{t1} + q_{t2}$ satisfies our original requirements and that the three parts can be found from, respectively, the steady-state solutions of Sections 9.2 and 9.4, the d-c galvanometer Eqs. 8.9–21, 8.9–23, and 8.9–26 that follow from Eq. 8.9–18, and the ballistic galvanometer Eqs. 8.9–34, 8.9–35, and 8.9–36 that follow from Eq. 8.9–33. It is left to the reader to complete the solution (cf. Problem 9.8a). In the over-damped case, the current approaches its steady-state alternating value in an exponential way. In the under-damped case, transient oscillations of frequency ω_d are superimposed on those of frequency ω. The two frequencies, of course, need not be of the same order of magnitude.

In discussing transients, we are primarily concerned with the establishment of a steady state after a change in the applied emf has been made.

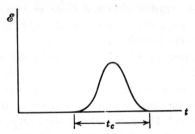

Fig. 9.8a. A simple pulsed emf.

Pulses, on the other hand, are variations of emf or current that start from zero and reduce again to zero after short periods of time and whose effects we wish to study during such short periods. Suppose, for instance, that an emf $\mathscr{E}(t)$ which varies as shown in Fig. 9.8a is applied to the circuit of Fig. 9.8b, and the resulting potential difference on R is observed.

Let us suppose that the time constant RC of the circuit is small compared to the characteristic time t_c of the pulse, meaning the time during which most of the variation occurs. Then we know that the condenser will charge to a potential that is almost equal to $\mathscr{E}(t)$ during the pulse. We can write, therefore,

$$V = q/C \simeq \mathscr{E}(t)$$

and the current i will be given by

$$i = dq/dt \simeq C \frac{d\mathscr{E}}{dt} \qquad (9.8\text{–}10)$$

so that the PD on R is a measure of the derivative of $\mathscr{E}$. Figure 9.8c shows the variation of V. The charging and discharging of the condenser during

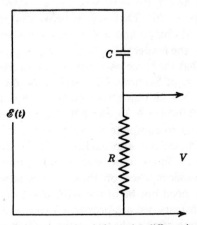

Fig. 9.8b. An a-c circuit for pulse differentiation.

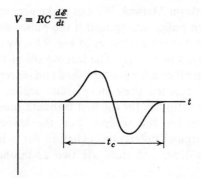

$$V = RC \frac{d\mathscr{E}}{dt}$$

Fig. 9.8c. The derivative of the pulse in Fig. 9.8a.

the pulse are clearly indicated. Such an R-C circuit is called a "differentiating circuit."

If, on the other hand, RC is large compared to t_c, the condenser will have almost no time to charge up, and Ri will be almost equal to $\mathscr{E}$, so that the condenser voltage represents the integral of $\mathscr{E}$:

$$R_i \simeq \mathscr{E}(t)$$

$$V_C = \frac{q}{C} = \frac{1}{C} \int i \, dt = \frac{1}{RC} \int \mathscr{E}(t) \, dt \tag{9.8-11}$$

Appropriate limits can be inserted for the integral in particular cases. If the circuit is not opened after $\mathscr{E}$ becomes zero, the condenser will slowly discharge with the time constant RC, if the impedance of the source is assumed to be small (see Fig. 9.8d). Problem 9.8b deals with similar uses of an inductance and a resistance.

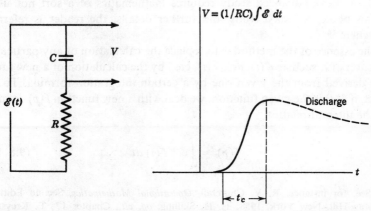

Fig. 9.8d. An integrating circuit and the resulting voltage for $\mathscr{E}(t)$ of Fig. 9.8a.

The Laplace Transform Method. We can make accurate calculations of circuit behavior when pulses are applied if the pulses are of simple form, such as the square or trapezoidal pulses of Fig. 9.8e, by using several steps of the transient analysis just given. The turning off of the square pulse is similar to the turning off of a long-established emf, except that i and q will not in general have reached their steady-state values after the turning on of the pulse. The formulas for the first transient must be used to find the initial conditions for the second. For the trapezoidal pulse, we have to solve the original differential equation for a linearly increasing $\mathscr{E}(t)$, such as $\mathscr{E} = a + bt$, and then use two additional calculations of

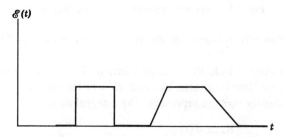

Fig. 9.8e. A square pulse and a trapezoidal pulse.

initial conditions, for the flat part and the decreasing part of the emf, respectively.

The calculations are quite tedious and cumbersome. For this reason, we introduce the reader in the next few paragraphs to the Laplace transform method, which greatly reduces the labor of pulse analysis.

We shall present the method from a relatively elementary point of view. A more advanced study requires mathematics of a sort not used in this book; for such study and further details, the reader is referred elsewhere.[16]

The essence of the method is to replace the calculation of any particular function of t, such as $\mathscr{E}(t)$, $i(t)$, $V(t)$, etc., by the calculation of a new function derived from the given one by a certain integration formula. To be exact, if $F(t)$ is the given function, we deal with a new function $f(p)$ defined by the integral relation

$$f(p) = \int_0^\infty e^{-pt} F(t)\, dt \qquad (9.8\text{--}12)$$

[16] See, for instance, R. V. Churchill, *Operational Mathematics*, Second Edition, McGraw-Hill, New York, 1958; H. H. Skilling, *op. cit.*, Chapter 17; E. Kreyszig, *Advanced Engineering Mathematics*, John Wiley, New York, 1967, Chapter 4.

The new function $f(p)$ is called the Laplace transform of $F(t)$. The symbol p represents a number which may be real or complex, but must have a sufficiently positive real part that the integral is covergent. It will be noted that for any value of p, $f(p)$ depends on *all* the values of $F(t)$. It can be proved quite generally that for all functions of physical interest, the relation 9.8–12 is essentially unique—that is, there is only one $F(t)$ that will yield any particular $f(p)$. Because of the factor e^{-pt}, it is not hard to see that $f(p) \rightarrow 0$ as $p \rightarrow +\infty$.

The point of calculating $f(p)$ instead of $F(t)$ is, first, that a reasonably simple differential equation for $F(t)$ turns into an algebraic one for $f(p)$ and, second, that the initial conditions on $F(t)$ appear explicitly in the equation for $f(p)$, so that the particular solution sought is automatically obtained. The necessary information for using the method is a sufficiently large table of related pairs of functions $F(t)$ and $f(p)$ so that when an $f(p)$ has been found, the corresponding $F(t)$ can be recognized.

Let us consider some special properties of the Laplace transform.

1. The relation between $F(t)$ and $f(p)$ is linear. That is, if $F(t) = aF_1(t) + bF_2(t)$, then $f(p) = af_1(p) + bf_2(p)$, where f_1 and f_2 are respectively the transforms of F_1 and F_2 and a and b are constants. This property allows us to apply the transformation to an entire linear equation.

2. If we replace $F(t)$ by a derivative $F'(t) = dF/dt$, we obtain a formula for the transform of a derivative:

$$\int_0^\infty e^{-pt} \frac{dF}{dt} \, dt = F(t) \, e^{-pt} \Big|_0^\infty + p \int_0^\infty e^{-pt} F(t) \, dt$$

$$= -F(0) + pf(p) \qquad (9.8\text{–}13)$$

A similar result involving $F(0)$ and $F'(0)$ can be calculated for the transform of d^2F/dt^2.

3. For the indefinite integral of F, i.e., $\int_0^t F(t') \, dt'$, we find by the usual rules for interchange of order of integration (Appendix A.1)

$$\int_0^\infty e^{-pt} \, dt \int_0^t F(t') \, dt' = \int_0^\infty dt' F(t') \int_{t'}^\infty e^{-pt} \, dt$$

$$= \int_0^\infty dt' F(t') \frac{e^{-pt'}}{p} = \frac{1}{p} f(p) \qquad (9.8\text{–}14)$$

It is to be noted that $(1/p)f(p)$ is the transform of the integral of $F(t)$ which vanishes at $t = 0$.

4. If $F(t)$ represents a transient that is zero for $t < 0$, we have $F(t - t_1) = 0$ for $t < t_1$ and find, setting $t' = t - t_1$,

$$\int_0^\infty e^{-pt} F(t - t_1)\, dt = \int_0^\infty e^{-pt_1 - pt'} F(t')\, dt'$$

$$:= e^{-pt_1} f(p) \qquad (9.8\text{--}15)$$

so that $e^{-pt_1} f(p)$ is the transform of a function that vanishes for all t before the time $t = t_1$.

5. For certain particular functions $F(t)$, $f(p)$ is easy to find by straight-forward integration. Table 9.8B lists a number of these, which the reader should be able to verify directly or by means of a table of integrals.[17] The

Table 9.8B   Laplace Transforms

$F(t)$	$f(p) = \int_0^\infty e^{-pt} F(t)\, dt$
1	$1/p$
t	$1/p^2$
$t^n \qquad (n > -1)$	$n!/p^{n+1}$
$e^{-at} \qquad (a > 0)$	$1/(p + a)$
$\sin bt$	$b/(p^2 + b^2)$
$\cos bt$	$p/(p^2 + b^2)$
$e^{-at} \sin bt$	$b/[(p + a)^2 + b^2]$
$e^{-at} \cos bt$	$(p + a)/[(p + a)^2 + b^2]$
$aF_1(t)$	$af_1(p)$
$\displaystyle\int_0^t F_1(t')\, dt'$	$f_1(p)/p$
$F'_1(t)$	$-F_1(0) + pf_1(p)$
$\begin{cases} F(t) = 0 & \text{for } 0 < t < t_1 \\ F(t) = 1 & \text{for } t_1 < t < \infty \end{cases}$	$\dfrac{1}{p} e^{-pt_1}$
$\begin{cases} F(t) = 0 & \text{for } 0 < t < t_1 \\ & \text{and } t_2 < t < \infty \\ F(t) = 1 & \text{for } t_1 < t < t_2 \end{cases}$	$\dfrac{1}{p}(e^{-pt_1} - e^{-pt_2})$
$\begin{cases} F_1(t - t_1) & t > t_1 \\ 0 & t < t_1 \end{cases}$	$e^{-pt_1} f_1(p)$

[17] Laplace transform tables are given in the references cited. A large table is available in A. Erdélyi, ed., *Tables of Integral Transforms*, McGraw-Hill, New York, 1954, Vol. I.

square pulse is given in this table, but the trapezoidal pulse has been left as an exercise for the reader (Problem 9.8c).

Let us now see how to apply the method by considering $F(t)$ to represent the current $i(t)$ in an R-L-C circuit to which a square pulse is applied. The equation of the circuit, as before, is

$$\mathscr{E}(t) = L\frac{di}{dt} + Ri + \frac{\int i\, dt}{C}$$

and we shall assume that $q = \int i\, dt$ is zero at $t = 0$; otherwise the initial constant q_0/C should be subtracted from $\mathscr{E}(t)$. Let us multiply both sides of this equation by $e^{-pt}\, dt$ and integrate, letting $g(p)$ be the Laplace transform of $\mathscr{E}(t)$ and $f(p)$ the transform of $i(t)$. We then have

$$g(p) = -Li(0) + Lpf(p) + Rf(p) + \frac{f(p)}{pC} \qquad (9.8\text{–}16)$$

which is easily soluble for $f(p)$. We shall assume here that $i(0) = 0$, but this is not necessary for use of the method. We have

$$f(p) = \frac{g(p)}{Lp + R + \dfrac{1}{pC}} \qquad (9.8\text{–}17)$$

which bears a close resemblance to Eq. 9.4–2 for the complex current in the steady-state case. If we replace $\mathscr{E}$ with $g(p)$, i with $f(p)$, and $j\omega$ with p in Eq. 9.4–2, we get Eq. 9.8–17 exactly. From the derivation it is easy to see that this rule holds for any impedance calculation, so the method can be applied to find the current or PD at any point in any complex a-c circuit when a pulse or transient emf is applied whose Laplace transform can be calculated. Note that the transform of the PD on any element of the circuit can be found from $f(p)$—e.g., the voltage on the condenser corresponds to $f(p)/pC$.

Now, if $\mathscr{E}(t)$ is a square pulse of height $\mathscr{E}_0$, starting for simplicity at $t_1 = 0$, we have from the table

$$g(p) = \mathscr{E}_0 \frac{1 - e^{-pt_2}}{p}$$

and hence

$$f(p) = \mathscr{E}_0 \frac{1 - e^{-pt_2}}{Lp^2 + Rp + 1/C}$$

the denominator of which can be rearranged to give

$$f(p) = \frac{\mathscr{E}_0}{L} \frac{1 - e^{-pt_2}}{\left(p + \dfrac{R}{2L}\right)^2 + \dfrac{1}{LC} - \dfrac{R^2}{4L^2}}$$

With use of the abbreviations in Table 9.8A, this can be written

$$ f(p) = \frac{\mathscr{E}_0}{L} \left\{ \frac{1}{(p+\alpha)^2 + \omega^2} - \frac{e^{-pt_2}}{(p+\alpha)^2 + \omega^2} \right\} $$

Comparison of this formula with Table 9.8B now gives us $i(t)$:

$$ i(t) = \frac{\mathscr{E}_0}{L} \frac{e^{-\alpha t} \sin \omega t}{\omega} \; ; \qquad 0 < t < t_2 \tag{9.8--18} $$

$$ = \frac{\mathscr{E}_2}{L} \left\{ e^{-\alpha t} \frac{\sin \omega t}{\omega} - e^{-\alpha(t-t_2)} \frac{\sin \omega(t - t_2)}{\omega} \right\}; \quad t_2 < t < \infty $$

In case ω is imaginary and β is real, this solution can be directly converted into the overdamped variety. Alternatively, we can treat the denominator by partial fractions as follows

$$ \frac{1}{(p+\alpha)^2 - \beta^2} = \frac{1}{(p+\alpha-\beta)(p+\alpha+\beta)} $$

$$ = \frac{1}{2\beta} \left[\frac{1}{(p+\alpha-\beta)} - \frac{1}{(p+\alpha+\beta)} \right] $$

and each term is now a special case of $1/(p + a)$ in the table (Problem 9.8d).

Figure 9.8f shows the current in an R-L-C circuit when a square voltage pulse is applied.

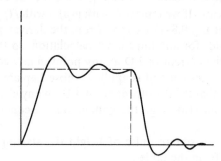

Fig. 9.8f. A square wave applied to an R-L-C circuit.

Problem 9.8a. Find the variation of q and i with time in a series R-L-C circuit when an emf $\mathscr{E} = \mathscr{E}_0 \sin \omega t$ is turned on at time $t = 0$, assuming q and i to be zero at that time.

Problem 9.7b. Show how to use an inductance L and a resistance R as (a) a differentiating circuit and (b) an integrating circuit.

Problem 9.8c. Find the Laplace transform of a trapezoidal pulse which starts at $t = 0$, rises linearly to 1 at $t = t_1$ [$F(t) = t/t_1$ during the rise], is equal to 1 from t_1 to t_2, and drops linearly to 0 at $t = t_3$ [$F(t) = (t_3 - t)/(t_3 - t_2)$ during the fall], bring zero thereafter.

Problem 9.8d. Find the solution corresponding to Eq. 9.8–18 for the overdamped case.

Problem 9.8e. Use the Laplace transform method to show how the PD on R_2 in Fig. 9.4a varies with time after an emf $\mathscr{E} = \mathscr{E}_m \cos \omega t$ is turned on at $t = 0$.

Problem 9.8f. Find the current in an inductance coil of L henrys and R ohms, in parallel with a capacitance of C farads, when the combination is connected at time $t = 0$ to an emf of constant value $\mathscr{E}_0$ volts and internal resistance R_2 ohms.

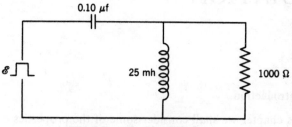

Fig. 9.8g.   (Problem 9.8g.)

Problem 9.8g. A square pulse of 10 v lasting for 1 millisec is applied to the circuit illustrated (Fig. 9.8g). Find the resulting voltage on the 10,000-ohm resistor as a function of time. Sketch a graph of this voltage.

Problem 9.8h. Find the result of applying the trapezoidal pulse of Problem 9.8c, multiplied by a constant $\mathscr{E}_0$, to the differentiating circuit of Fig. 9.8b.

Chapter 10

ELECTROMAGNETIC RADIATION

10.1 Introduction

In this chapter we shall consider some of the properties of electric and magnetic fields that follow from the Maxwell equations which we derived in Sections 1.5, 3.5, 7.9, 7.12, 7.14, and 8.3. We give them here for reference, along with the Lorentz force law which defines $\mathbf{E}$ and $\mathbf{B}$, the equations relating $\mathbf{D}$ with $\mathbf{E}$ and $\mathbf{H}$ with $\mathbf{B}$, and Ohm's law for stationary and moving ohmic conductors (neglecting thermal effects). We use ρ for the density of free charge only and assume that $\mathbf{J}$ is likewise a current of free charges only. We have, therefore,

$$\nabla \cdot \mathbf{D} = \rho \qquad \text{eqs. 1.5-1, 3.5-4} \quad (10.1\text{-}1a)$$

$$\nabla \cdot \mathbf{B} = 0 \qquad \text{eq. 7.12-1} \quad (10.1\text{-}2a)$$

$$\nabla \times \mathbf{H} = \mathbf{J} + \frac{\partial \mathbf{D}}{\partial t} \qquad \text{eqs. 7.9-3, 8.3-10} \quad (10.1\text{-}3a)$$

$$\nabla \times \mathbf{E} = - \frac{\partial \mathbf{B}}{\partial t} \qquad \text{eq. 7.14-3} \quad (10.1\text{-}4a)$$

$$\mathbf{f}_r = \rho \mathbf{E} + \mathbf{J} \times \mathbf{B} \qquad \text{eq. 7.2-4} \quad (10.1\text{-}5a)$$

$\mathbf{D} = \epsilon_0 \mathbf{E} + \mathbf{P}$ (general)　　　eq. 3.5-1

$\mathbf{D} = \epsilon_0 \mathbf{E}$ (free space)　　　$(10.1\text{-}6a)$

$\mathbf{D} = \epsilon \mathbf{E}$ (linear dielectric)　　　eq. 3.7-3

$\mathbf{B} = \mu_0 (\mathbf{H} + \mathbf{M})$ (general)　　　eq. 8.3-9

$\mathbf{B} = \mu_0 \mathbf{H}$ (free space)　　　$(10.1\text{-}7a)$

$\mathbf{B} = \mu \mathbf{H}$ (linear magnetic medium)　　eq. 8.6-4

$\mathbf{J} = \sigma_c\mathbf{E}$ (stationary ohmic medium)   eq. 5.1–3

$\mathbf{J} = \sigma_c(\mathbf{E} + \mathbf{v} \times \mathbf{B})$ (moving ohmic medium)   eq. 7.4–3

$$\left. \begin{array}{l} \mathbf{J} = \sigma_c\mathbf{E}\text{ (stationary ohmic medium)} \quad \text{eq. 5.1–3} \\[2mm] \mathbf{J} = \sigma_c(\mathbf{E} + \mathbf{v} \times \mathbf{B})\text{ (moving ohmic medium)} \quad \text{eq. 7.4–3} \end{array} \right\} \quad (10.1\text{–}8a)$$

The values of ϵ_0 and μ_0 are

$$\left. \begin{array}{l} \epsilon_0 = 8.85417 \times 10^{-12} \text{ coulomb}^2/\text{newton-m}^2 \\[2mm] \mu_0 = 4\pi \times 10^{-7} \text{ newton/ampere}^2 \end{array} \right\} \quad (10.1\text{–}9)$$

from which we find the useful values

$$\left. \begin{array}{l} \dfrac{1}{(\mu_0\epsilon_0)^{1/2}} = c = 2.997925 \times 10^8 \text{ m/sec} \\[3mm] (\mu_0/\epsilon_0)^{1/2} = 119.9\pi = 376.7 \text{ ohms} \end{array} \right\} \quad (10.1\text{–}10)$$

The actual identification of the parameter c with the velocity of light will be made later in this chapter.

Maxwell's equations, as we have pointed out before, relate the field quantities, the charge density, and the current density at one single point in space through their time and space derivatives. They contain all the physical information we have obtained from Coulomb's, Ampère's, and Faraday's laws, including the displacement-current term derived from Laplace's rule and taken as a special assumption by Maxwell.

The equations were all derived for charge and current distributions that are static or slowly varying. Our procedure now is to assume them to be true for all rates of change and to seek solutions in the form of explicit formulas for $\mathbf{E}$ and $\mathbf{B}$ as functions of time and space coordinates. Then we will try to understand the physical significance of these solutions and to see how their consequences are verified experimentally. As the reader is undoubtedly aware, the result of greatest importance is the existence of electromagnetic radiation of a wavelike character.

That the assumption of the validity of Maxwell's equations for all types of time variation constitutes in itself a further physical hypothesis was shown in the discussion of the term $-\nabla V$ in Eq. 7.14–6 and will become especially evident in connection with the retarded potentials in Section 10.3.

We shall begin with the study of the transmission of signals along cables and lines, because by so doing we can provide a rather elementary connection with our earlier discussion of fields near conductors. Then we shall prove general theorems about the propagation of effects with the velocity of light and the transmission of energy by electromagnetic fields. This will allow us to describe radiation from simple antennas and will lead to descriptions of electromagnetic waves and their optical properties. We shall also provide an account of wave guides and cavities and an introduction to magnetohydrodynamics.

Maxwell's equations in Gaussian units read as follows:

$$\nabla \cdot \mathbf{D} = 4\pi\rho \qquad\qquad\qquad \text{Gaussian} \quad (10.1\text{--}1b)$$

$$\nabla \cdot \mathbf{B} = 0 \qquad\qquad\qquad\qquad \text{Gaussian} \quad (10.1\text{--}2b)$$

$$\nabla \times \mathbf{H} = \frac{4\pi}{c}\,\mathbf{J} + \frac{1}{c}\,\frac{\partial \mathbf{D}}{\partial t} \qquad\qquad \text{Gaussian} \quad (10.1\text{--}3b)$$

$$\nabla \times \mathbf{E} = -\frac{1}{c}\,\frac{\partial \mathbf{B}}{\partial t} \qquad\qquad \text{Gaussian} \quad (10.1\text{--}4b)$$

$$\mathbf{f}_\tau = \rho\mathbf{E} + \frac{1}{c}\,\mathbf{J} \times \mathbf{B} \qquad\qquad \text{Gaussian} \quad (10.1\text{--}5b)$$

$$\left.\begin{array}{l} \mathbf{D} = \mathbf{E} + 4\pi\mathbf{P} \text{ (general)} \\ \mathbf{D} = \mathbf{E} \text{ (free space)} \\ \mathbf{D} = \kappa\mathbf{E} \text{ (linear dielectric)} \end{array}\right\} \qquad \text{Gaussian} \quad (10.1\text{--}6b)$$

$$\left.\begin{array}{l} \mathbf{B} = \mathbf{H} + 4\pi\mathbf{M} \text{ (general)} \\ \mathbf{B} = \mathbf{H} \text{ (free space)} \\ \mathbf{B} = \mu\mathbf{H} \text{ (linear magnetic medium)} \end{array}\right\} \qquad \text{Gaussian} \quad (10.1\text{--}7b)$$

$$\left.\begin{array}{l} \mathbf{J} = \sigma_c\mathbf{E} \text{ (stationary ohmic medium)} \\ \mathbf{J} = \sigma_c\left(\mathbf{E} + \dfrac{1}{c}\,\mathbf{v} \times \mathbf{B}\right) \text{ (moving ohmic medium)} \end{array}\right\} \quad \text{Gaussian} \quad (10.1\text{--}8b)$$

10.2 Cables and Lines

Coaxial cables are commonly used to transmit high-frequency alternating currents and fast pulses. Parallel-wire transmission lines also have a number of uses, and both can be treated in the same way by the use of the concepts of distributed inductance and capacitance. Their study forms a convenient bridge between the lumped-constant circuit theory of Chapter 9 and the radiation theory of the rest of this chapter.

Consider a coaxial line consisting of a pair of concentric conducting circular cylinders with inner cylinder of radius a and outer cylinder of inner radius b. We shall assume that the rates of change of the fields are high enough so that the skin effect restricts the current to the surfaces of the conductors.

We saw in Section 2.5 that such an arrangement has a capacitance per unit length C_l given by

$$C_l = \frac{2\pi\epsilon_0}{\ln\,(b/a)} \qquad\qquad (10.2\text{--}1)$$

and in Problem 7.17a that it has an inductance per unit length L_l given by

$$L_l = \frac{\mu_0}{2\pi} \ln \frac{b}{a} \tag{10.2-2}$$

assuming the space between the cylinders to be essentially evacuated. If it is filled with material of uniform linear dielectric and magnetic properties, we must replace ϵ_0 by ϵ and μ_0 by μ. We shall need the product and ratio of L_l and C_l:

$$L_l C_l = \mu\epsilon = \frac{1}{v^2} > \frac{1}{c^2} \tag{10.2-3a}$$

$$\left.\begin{array}{l}\end{array}\right\} \text{uniform linear material}$$

$$\frac{L_l}{C_l} = \frac{\mu}{\epsilon}\left[\frac{\ln (b/a)}{2\pi}\right]^2 \tag{10.2-3b}$$

$$L_l C_l = \mu_0\epsilon_0 = \frac{1}{c^2} \tag{10.2-4a}$$

$$\left.\begin{array}{l}\end{array}\right\} \text{vacuum case}$$

$$\frac{L_l}{C_l} = \frac{\mu_0}{\epsilon_0}\left[\frac{\ln (b/a)}{2\pi}\right]^2 \simeq 3594[\ln (b/a)]^2 \tag{10.2-4b}$$

Let us suppose further that there is a total resistance per unit length R_l including both conductors, and a leakage conductance per unit length G_l of the gas or other dielectric between the conductors. We will assume that R_l is small enough that the current in the outer cylinder will automatically be equal and opposite to that in the inner cylinder—the skin effect functions in this case through the tendency of the magnetic field set up by the inner current to produce an outer current that cancels the field inside the material of the outer cylinder. We shall deal mostly with the case in which R_l and G_l can each be set equal to zero.

Now, if a potential difference between the two conductors is set up at one end of the cable, charge will start to flow. The inductance will oppose the flow of charge, and this effect, coupled with the finite time required for the current to charge up the distributed capacitance, will result in a time lag for the development of voltage across, and current in, the whole of the cable. We might look at the cable as if it were a long series of inductances with interspersed parallel capacitors, forming a cascaded or many-stage filter like a generalization of Fig. 9.4d, with considerable phase shift in each stage. Let us find differential equations for the current i and the potential V_c of the central wire with respect to the outer one, as functions of the distance z along the wire and of the time t (Fig. 10.2a).

The current i and voltage V_c will vary with z in general, so that we can choose an element of length Δz and indicate their increments in Δz by Δi and ΔV_c. There are four physical relations or quantities of importance:

the relation between the average V_c and the charge on the central wire in Δz, the emf associated with the rate of change of the average current in Δz, the iR drop in the conductors, and the leakage current between the conductors due to conductance of the intervening medium.

If we denote by q_l the charge per unit length of the wire (called λ in Chapter 1), we can write using superior bars to represent averages in Δz

$$\bar{V}_c = \bar{q}_l \, \Delta z / C_l \, \Delta z = \bar{q}_l / C_l \tag{10.2-5}$$

The net rate of decrease of the charge in Δz is given by the net current Δi leaving Δz along the wire plus the leakage current $\bar{V}_c G_l \, \Delta z$, so we have

$$\Delta i = -\partial(\bar{q}_l \, \Delta z)/\partial t - \bar{V}_c G_l \, \Delta z$$

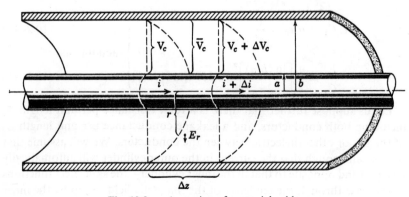

Fig. 10.2a.   A portion of a coaxial cable.

On substituting from Eq. 10.2–5, dividing by Δz, and taking limits, we obtain

$$\frac{\partial i}{\partial z} = -C_l \frac{\partial V_c}{\partial t} - G_l V_c \tag{10.2-6a}$$

The emf associated with L_l will be taken as a voltage drop, as in our previous analysis, so that we have for the total drop in Δz

$$-\Delta V_c = (L_l \Delta z) \frac{\partial i}{\partial t} + i R_l \Delta z$$

(It does not matter how much we ascribe to the central wire and how much to the outer conductor.) We obtain our second differential equation

$$\frac{\partial V_c}{\partial z} = -L_l \frac{\partial i}{\partial t} - i R_l \tag{10.2-7a}$$

These equations as they stand can be applied to a parallel-wire transmission line or, in fact, any form of line, provided the appropriate formulas for L_l and C_l are used.

Let us consider right away the simpler case in which R_l and G_l are negligible. Then we have

$$\frac{\partial i}{\partial z} = -C_l \frac{\partial V_c}{\partial t} \tag{10.2-6b}$$

and

$$\frac{\partial V_c}{\partial z} = -L_l \frac{\partial i}{\partial t} \tag{10.2-7c}$$

To solve these equations, let us differentiate the first with respect to t and the second with respect to z and then eliminate $\partial^2 i/\partial z\, \partial t$ from the results. We obtain

$$L_l C_l \frac{\partial^2 V_c}{\partial t^2} = \frac{\partial^2 V_c}{\partial z^2} \tag{10.2-8}$$

If we reverse the differentiations, we can eliminate $\partial^2 V_c/\partial z\, \partial t$ and obtain

$$L_l C_l \frac{\partial^2 i}{\partial t^2} = \frac{\partial^2 i}{\partial z^2} \tag{10.2-9}$$

Replacing $L_l C_l$ by $1/v^2$ ($1/c^2$ if no material substance is present between the conductors), we have for each quantity an equation which we shall write

$$\frac{1}{v^2} \frac{\partial^2 f}{\partial t^2} = \frac{\partial^2 f}{\partial z^2} \tag{10.2-10}$$

As can readily be checked by substitution, this equation has the solution

$$f(z, t) = f_1(t - z/v) + f_2(t + z/v) \tag{10.2-11}$$

where $f_1(t)$ and $f_2(t)$ are any arbitrary functions whatsoever (as long as they are properly differentiable). From the remarks in Appendix A.3, it is clear that Eq. 10.2–11 represents a *general* solution of Eq. 10.2–10.

Each of these functions represents a traveling wave, the first traveling in the direction of z, and the second in the direction $-z$. To see this, consider a particular value of $f_1(t)$, say $f_1(t')$ for argument t'. Then $f_1(t - z/v)$ has this value for all pairs of t and z for which $t - z/v = t'$. That is, if we consider successive values of t and z which increase together so as to satisfy this relation, we will find the value of f_1 remaining constant. This value thus appears to "travel" with a point whose coordinate z obeys the equation $z = v(t - t')$—i.e., when the point moves with the speed v in the forward direction. The function $f_1(t)$ might, for instance, represent a pulse or sine wave.

Similarly, $f_2(t + z/v)$ represents a wave traveling with speed $-v$. Figure 10.2b illustrates these remarks with space graphs for two different times. Thus we see that both V_c and i may in general have arbitrary wave forms, moving with the speed v in either direction along the cable. It is important to note that if one of these functions is determined as an arbitrary wave, the other is also determined. For instance, if $V_c = f_1(t - z/v)$, then $\partial V_c/\partial t = f_1'(t - z/v)$ and by Eq. 10.2–6b

$$\frac{\partial i}{\partial z} = -C_l f_1'(t - z/v)$$

so that on integration

$$i = vC_l f_1(t - z/v) + g(t) = vC_l V_c + g(t) = vq_l + g(t) \quad (10.2–12)$$

where $g(t)$ can be any function of t but is constant with respect to z. Substitution in Eq. 10.2–7b shows, however, that $g(t)$ must be independent of

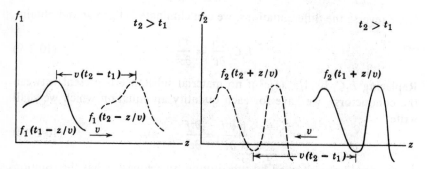

Fig. 10.2b.   Illustrating generalized waves.

t and since we are not considering steady currents, it must be set equal to zero. Thus i, V_c, and q_l are all proportional to each other. A similar result but with a minus sign in front of v holds for the wave traveling in the other direction.

The sign relations to which we have just referred have a simple physical interpretation. When the current in the central wire is positive at a place of maximum positive potential on the wire, charge is being transported in the positive direction so that the position of maximum V_c will shift in that direction, corresponding to positive wave velocity. Conversely, a negative current will carry a positive maximum of V_c in the negative direction.

The proportionality of i and V_c has the consequence that any section of the cable acts to the previous section as if it were a pure resistance of value $V_c/i = 1/vC_l = (L_l/C_l)^{1/2}$. This ratio is called the "characteristic impedance" of the cable Z_c:

$$Z_c = \left(\frac{L_c}{C_l}\right)^{\frac{1}{2}} = \frac{1}{2\pi}\left(\frac{\mu}{\epsilon}\right)^{\frac{1}{2}} \ln\frac{b}{a} \; ; \qquad \text{filled cable} \qquad (10.2\text{--}13a)$$

$$Z_c = \left(\frac{L_l}{C_l}\right)^{\frac{1}{2}} = \frac{1}{2\pi}\left(\frac{\mu_0}{\epsilon_0}\right)^{\frac{1}{2}} \ln\frac{b}{a} \; ; \qquad \text{empty cable} \qquad (10.2\text{--}13b)$$

Let us consider briefly what will happen if a forward-traveling pulse of voltage and current comes to the end of a cable. If the end is open-circuited or has a very high resistance connected between the cylinders, the current at the end when the voltage pulse arrives will be smaller than that which accompanied the pulse on the cable. The inductance of the portion near the end will make the charge tend to keep flowing toward the end, charging up the capacitance of the end portion. This capacitance will then discharge back into the line, and we will have a current of opposite sign to the voltage pulse. A pulse will start back along the cable in the negative direction without reversing the sign of the voltage. All portions of the voltage pulse will be thus reflected, so that the entire reflected pulse has the same time variation as the oncoming pulse.

On the other hand, if the end of the cable is short-circuited (i.e., through a very low resistance), the current at the end will be large and V_c will be small. The effect will be as if another voltage of opposite sign were superimposed on the arriving voltage pulse; this additional voltage and the original current form again a reflected pulse, this time of reversed voltage.

Finally, if the line is terminated with a resistance equal to Z_c, the current and voltage in this resistor will be in exactly the same ratio as if another section of cable were joined, and no reflection will occur. Thus when a coaxial cable is used to transmit pulses, it should be properly terminated to prevent reflections. When a cable is thus terminated in its characteristic impedance, it also presents the same impedance value at its input end. Typical values of Z_c for commercial cables are 52 ohms, 76 ohms, 93 ohms, etc.

Let us now consider a sinusoidal wave and investigate the fields between the cylinders, restricting ourselves for simplicity to the vacuum case. If V_c at any one point on the cable is to alternate with an angular frequency ω, we must have $f_1(t)$ equal to $V_m \sin \omega t$, for instance. Then we can write

$$V_c = V_m \sin \omega\left(t - \frac{z}{c}\right) = V_m \sin\left(\omega t - \frac{z}{\lambda}\right) \qquad (10.2\text{--}14)$$

where λ ("lambda-bar") $= c/\omega = c/2\pi f = \lambda/2\pi$ is called the "reduced wave length." (λ is the distance by which z must increase to make the angle $\omega t - z/\lambda$ decrease by one radian.)

We also have

$$i = \left(\frac{C_l}{L_l}\right)^{\!\frac12} V_c = \frac{2\pi V_m}{\ln(b/a)}\left(\frac{\epsilon_0}{\mu_0}\right)^{\!\frac12}\sin\left(\omega t - \frac{z}{\lambda}\right) \tag{10.2-15}$$

These two quantities are readily seen to satisfy Eq. 10.2–6b and Eq. 10.2–7b if we substitute in them, and use the relation

$$\lambda\omega = c = 1/(L_l C_l)^{\frac12} \tag{10.2-16}$$

The charge per unit length is then

$$q_l = C_l V_c = \frac{2\pi\epsilon_0 V_m}{\ln(b/a)}\sin\left(\omega t - \frac{z}{\lambda}\right) \tag{10.2-17}$$

Let us tentatively assume that we can use the electrostatic Eq. 1.7–14 to find the potential V at a distance r from the axis, a distance z along the cable, and time t. Assuming that $V = 0$ when $r = b$ (outer conductor grounded) we have

$$V(r, z, t) = \frac{q_l}{2\pi\epsilon_0}\ln(b/r) = \frac{\ln(b/r)}{\ln(b/a)}V_m\sin\left(\omega t - \frac{z}{\lambda}\right) \tag{10.2-18}$$

We can now find the components of the "electrostatic" field $\mathbf{E}_{\text{stat}} = -\nabla V$. We find for the radial component the expected result (cf. Eq. 1.3–4)

$$E_{r\,\text{stat}}(r, z, t) = -\frac{\partial V}{\partial r} = \frac{V_m}{r\ln(b/a)}\sin\left(\omega t - \frac{z}{\lambda}\right) \tag{10.2-19}$$

and for the component parallel to the axis

$$E_{z\,\text{stat}}(r, z, t) = -\frac{\partial V}{\partial z} = \frac{V_m\ln(b/r)}{\lambda\ln(b/a)}\cos\left(\omega t - \frac{z}{\lambda}\right) \tag{10.2-20}$$

This perhaps unexpected result for the axial field serves to show that we must use our earlier static formulas with care. Since we do not have a static case because of alternating magnetic fields, let us find $\mathbf{B}$ and $\mathbf{A}$ and see if there is an electric field of magnetic origin. The magnetic field at a given place along the cable can be found from Eq. 7.8–1, which we might expect to hold in this case because it can be derived from the circuital form of Ampère's law even for changing currents. Since by symmetry $\mathbf{B}$ is tangent to a coaxial circle, we have

$$B_\phi(r, z, t) = \frac{\mu_0 i}{2\pi r} = \frac{(\mu_0\epsilon_0)^{\frac12}V_m}{r\ln(b/a)}\sin\left(\omega t - \frac{z}{\lambda}\right) \tag{10.2-21}$$

The flux per unit length of cable Φ_l lying between the radii r and b is found by multiplying B_ϕ by an element of area $dr\,dz$, integrating over r, and dividing out dz:

$$\Phi_l = \int_r^b B_\phi \, dr = \frac{(\mu_0\epsilon_0)^{1/2} \ln (b/r)}{\ln (b/a)} V_m \sin \left(\omega t - \frac{z}{\lambda}\right) \qquad (10.2-22)$$

Finally, we come to the vector potential **A**. In Section 7.10, we saw that when the currents are not steady (but do not vary rapidly), we still have $\mathbf{A} \propto \int i \, d\mathbf{l}/r$, so that **A** here has the direction of all the $d\mathbf{l}$'s, namely the z direction. Now, we can if we wish assume A_z to be zero when $r = b$. To see this, let us recall the Lorentz relation, Eq. 7.10–9:

$$\nabla \cdot \mathbf{A} + \mu_0\epsilon_0 \frac{\partial V}{\partial t} = 0$$

We have $\partial V/\partial t = 0$ when $r = b$ for all z, so $(\text{div } \mathbf{A})_{r=b} = (\partial A_z/\partial z)_{r=b} = 0$. Since A_z, like the other quantities, must be a function of $\omega t - z/\lambda$, we see that $(A_z)_{r=b}$ is a constant with respect to *both* t and z, so that we may set it equal to zero.

Now we can find A_z from Φ_l, since the flux in a length Δz is

$$\Phi_l \Delta z = \oint \mathbf{A} \cdot d\mathbf{l} = \Delta z A_z(r, t, z) - \Delta z A_z(b, t, z)$$

$$= \Delta z A_z(r, t, z)$$

Hence A_z is equal to Φ_l:

$$A_z = \Phi_l = \frac{(\mu_0\epsilon_0)^{1/2} \ln (b/r) V_m}{\ln (b/a)} \sin \left(\omega t - \frac{z}{\lambda}\right) \qquad (10.2-23)$$

It is readily verified that A_z and V satisfy the Lorentz condition.

Let us next calculate $\mathbf{E}_{\text{mag}} = \mathbf{1}_z E_{z \text{ mag}} = -\mathbf{1}_z \, \partial A_z/\partial t$, using the relation $\omega(\mu_0\epsilon_0)^{1/2} = 1/\lambda$:

$$E_{z \text{ mag}} = - \frac{V_m \ln (b/r)}{\lambda \ln (b/a)} \cos \left(\omega t - \frac{z}{\lambda}\right) \qquad (10.2-24)$$

We see that $E_{z \text{ mag}}$ is the exact negative of $E_{z \text{ stat}}$, so that in fact the total z component of **E** is zero:

$$E_z = E_{z \text{ stat}} + E_{z \text{ mag}} = 0 \qquad (10.2-25)$$

This is an expression of the fact that in a resistanceless conductor, the PD set up by charges on its surface exactly counteracts the induced emf, for otherwise with zero resistance there would be infinite current.

At this point, the reader may wonder if there are other components of **B** to consider. How about the displacement current between the conductors? Does it contribute to **B**? Let us answer all questions about possible further components of **B** and **E**, as well as doubts about the use of the steady-state formulas 10.2–18 and 10.2–21, by seeing if the fields we have established in Eqs. 10.2–19, 10.2–21, and 10.2–25 satisfy Maxwell's equations. We see that since $\mathbf{E} = \mathbf{1}_r E_r$ has the radial dependence of the static case, by Eq. 1.3–4, it must satisfy div $\mathbf{E} = 0$ in the space between the cylinders and the Gauss flux law with respect to the charge on the inner wire. Since B_ϕ similarly has the same radial dependence as in the steady current case, $\mathbf{B}$ satisfies div $\mathbf{B} = 0$. The equation with **curl E** must be satisfied, since it expresses the same induced emf law as is involved in Eq. 10.2–24. But we shall check it directly. By symmetry we have $E_\phi = 0$ and all derivatives with respect to ϕ equal to zero. Hence, writing the components of **curl E** in cylindrical coordinates (Table A.2A, p. 633) we see that two of them vanish, so we have

$$
\left.
\begin{aligned}
-\frac{\partial B_r}{\partial t} &= \mathrm{curl}_r\, \mathbf{E} = \frac{1}{r}\frac{\partial E_z}{\partial \phi} - \frac{\partial E_\phi}{\partial z} = 0 \\[2ex]
-\frac{\partial B_z}{\partial t} &= \mathrm{curl}_z\, \mathbf{E} = \frac{1}{r}\frac{\partial (rE_\phi)}{\partial r} - \frac{1}{r}\frac{\partial E_r}{\partial \phi} = 0 \\[2ex]
-\frac{\partial B_\phi}{\partial t} &= \mathrm{curl}_\phi\, \mathbf{E} = \frac{\partial E_r}{\partial z} - \frac{\partial E_z}{\partial r} = \frac{\partial E_r}{\partial z}
\end{aligned}
\right\} \quad (10.2\text{–}26)
$$

The last equation is readily seen to hold by differentiating Eqs. 10.2–19 and 10.2–21.

We can analyze the **curl H** equation similarly. $\mathbf{J}$ is, of course, zero in the space between the cylinders. Thus we can write

$$
\left.
\begin{aligned}
\frac{\partial D_r}{\partial t} &= \epsilon_0 \frac{\partial E_r}{\partial t} = \mathrm{curl}_r\mathbf{H} = \frac{1}{\mu_0}\left(\frac{1}{r}\frac{\partial B_z}{\partial \phi} - \frac{\partial B_\phi}{\partial z}\right) = -\frac{1}{\mu_0}\frac{\partial B_\phi}{\partial z} \\[2ex]
\frac{\partial D_z}{\partial t} &= \epsilon_0 \frac{\partial E_z}{\partial t} = \mathrm{curl}_z\mathbf{H} = \frac{1}{r\mu_0}\left(\frac{\partial (rB_\phi)}{\partial r} - \frac{\partial B_r}{\partial \phi}\right) = 0 \\[2ex]
\frac{\partial D_\phi}{\partial t} &= \epsilon_0 \frac{\partial E_\phi}{\partial t} = \mathrm{curl}_\phi\mathbf{H} = \frac{1}{\mu_0}\left(\frac{\partial B_r}{\partial z} - \frac{\partial B_z}{\partial r}\right) = 0
\end{aligned}
\right\} \quad (10.2\text{–}27)
$$

The first of these is satisfied because of Eqs. 10.2–19 and 10.2–21; the second is satisfied because E_z is zero and rB_ϕ is independent of r; the third contains only vanishing components. Thus the four Maxwell equations for **E** and **B** are satisfied, and we have completed our investigation. There are no extra components of **B** arising from the displacement current—it is evident that the variation of B_ϕ with z accounts for the mmf that could be calculated from $\partial\mathbf{D}/\partial t$. We have here, incidentally, an illustration of the statement made in Section 7.7 that the displacement current *or* the conduction current corresponding to a given filament can be used for calculation, but not both together.

We thus have found a situation in which electric and magnetic fields are propagated with the velocity of light. In the next section, we shall prove a general theorem on such propagation. In the section following we shall study the energy relations in propagated fields and find reasons for focusing more attention on the fields than on the accompanying currents and potential differences.

Attenuation and Reflections. Let us now consider briefly the effects of non-vanishing values of R_l and G_l. We shall consider only the sinusoidal case but shall extend our treatment to consider arbitrary source and load impedances. In so doing we shall give a quantitative account of reflections from cable ends. The complex-number method is useful here. We write as in Section 9.4 $V_c = V_m e^{j\omega t}$ and $i = i_m e^{j\omega t}$ where now V_m and i_m are functions of z. Substituting in Eqs. 10.2–6a and 10.2–7a and dividing out $e^{j\omega t}$, we have:

$$\frac{di_m}{dz} = -(j\omega C_l + G_l)V_m \qquad (10.2\text{–}28a)$$

$$\frac{dV_m}{dz} = -(j\omega L_l + R_l)i_m \qquad (10.2\text{–}28b)$$

Differentiating the first equation and using the second, we have:

$$\frac{d^2 i_m}{dz^2} = (j\omega L_l + R_l)(j\omega C_l + G_l)i_m \qquad (10.2\text{–}29)$$

An identical equation holds for V_m. This equation has two exponential-type solutions which we can readily obtain in terms of the complex number γ defined by:

$$\gamma^2 = (j\omega L_l + R_l)(j\omega C_l + G_l) = -\omega^2 L_l C_l \left(1 + \frac{R_l}{j\omega L_l}\right)\left(1 + \frac{G_l}{j\omega C_l}\right)$$
$$(10.2\text{–}30)$$

It is evident that, if R_l and G_l are very small, γ^2 is nearly equal to

$$-\omega^2 L_l C_l = -\omega^2/c^2 = -1/\lambda^2$$

and Eq. 10.2–29 is a simple harmonic type which will yield the sinusoidal result discussed previously. Let us take γ to be that root of Eq. 10.2–30 which is approximately $+j\omega/c$. We shall write in general

$$\gamma = \alpha + j\beta \qquad (10.2\text{–}31)$$

and take as the general solution for i_m

$$i_m = K_1 e^{-\gamma z} + K_2 e^{\gamma z} \qquad (10.2\text{–}32a)$$

where K_1 and K_2 are arbitrary complex constants which can be found from boundary or initial conditions.

The result for i is then

$$i = K_1 e^{-\alpha z + j(\omega t - \beta z)} + K_2 e^{\alpha z + j(\omega t + \beta z)} \qquad (10.2\text{–}32b)$$

and comparison with f_1 and f_2 as given in Eq. 10.2–11 shows that the first term represents, except for the factor $e^{-\alpha z}$, a forward-traveling wave, and the second similarly a backward-traveling wave. It can also be seen that β represents $1/\lambda$ for these waves, and $\omega/\beta = \omega\lambda$ represents their velocity.

Just as earlier, the current and voltage are proportional. Substituting in the first of Eqs. 10.2–28 and using Eq. 10.2–30 gives

$$V_m = \left(\frac{j\omega L_l + R_l}{j\omega C_l + G_l}\right)^{1/2} (K_1 e^{-\gamma z} - K_2 e^{\gamma z}) \qquad (10.2\text{–}33)$$

The sign relations between V_c and i are the same as for the case of no R_l or G_l.

The square root in the last equation is the new characteristic impedance:

$$Z_c = \left(\frac{j\omega L_l + R_l}{j\omega C_l + G_l}\right)^{1/2} = \left(\frac{L_l - jR_l/\omega}{C_l - jG_l/\omega}\right)^{1/2} \qquad (10.2\text{–}34)$$

Let us consider now the ends of the cable. At the output end where $z = l$, let there be a load impedance Z_l so that for a steady state $V_m/i_m = Z_l$. We have

$$Z_l = Z_c(K_1 e^{-\gamma l} - K_2 e^{\gamma l})|(K_1 e^{-\gamma l} + K_2 e^{\gamma l})$$

from which it is easy to show that

$$K_2 = e^{-2\gamma l}K_1(Z_c - Z_l)/(Z_c + Z_l) \qquad (10.2\text{–}35)$$

This equation relates the backward wave to the forward one and thus describes reflections. The ratio

$$\frac{Z_c - Z_l}{Z_c + Z_l} = \Gamma_l \qquad (10.2\text{–}36)$$

is called the output reflection coefficient. We see again that if $Z_l = Z_c$, there is no reflection.

We note from Eqs. 10.2–32 and 10.2–33 that the ratios of the reflected and incident complex currents and voltages at $z = l$ are

$$\frac{i_{m\,\text{refl}}}{i_{m\,\text{incid}}} = \frac{K_2}{K_1} e^{2\gamma l} = \frac{Z_c - Z_l}{Z_c + Z_l} \qquad (10.2\text{–}37a)$$

$$\frac{V_{m\,\text{refl}}}{V_{m\,\text{incid}}} = -\frac{K_2}{K_1} e^{2\gamma l} = \frac{Z_l - Z_c}{Z_l + Z_c} \qquad (10.2\text{–}37b)$$

These results hold when $\alpha = 0$ and there is no attenuation, in which case Z_c is real.

These relations corroborate our earlier statements that if the line is open-circuited, i.e., $Z_l = \infty$, the current changes sign on reflection and the voltage does not, while the converse holds if $Z_l = 0$. The intimate relation between the Laplace transform method for pulse analysis (Section 9.8) and the complex impedance analysis for sinusoidal currents can be used to show that pulses are reflected with the same changes as given by Eqs. 10.2–37.

Let us now consider the input end, where $z = 0$, which we suppose to be fed by an emf $\mathcal{E}$ with an internal impedance Z_0. We then have at $z = 0$

$$\mathcal{E} - Z_0 i_m = V_m$$

or, substituting,

$$\mathcal{E} = K_1(Z_0 + Z_c) + K_2(Z_0 - Z_c)$$

which with Eqs. 10.2–35 and 10.2–36 gives

$$K_1 = \frac{\mathcal{E}}{Z_0 + Z_c}\left[\frac{1}{1 - \Gamma_l e^{-2\gamma l}(Z_c - Z_0)/(Z_c + Z_0)}\right] \qquad (10.2\text{–}38)$$

This expression contains a ratio called the input reflection coefficient Γ_0

$$\Gamma_0 = \frac{Z_c - Z_0}{Z_c + Z_0} \qquad (10.2\text{–}39)$$

The meaning of Γ_0 is brought out if we expand the bracket in Eq. 10.2–37 by the binomial theorem.

$$[1 - \Gamma_l\Gamma_0\,e^{-2\gamma l}]^{-1} = 1 + \Gamma_l\Gamma_0\,e^{-2\gamma l} + \Gamma_l^2\Gamma_0^2\,e^{-4\gamma l} + \cdots \qquad (10.2\text{–}40)$$

the successive terms of which are seen to represent an unreflected wave, a wave that has traveled down and back suffering one reflection at each end, a wave having had two reflections at each end, and so forth.

The equations given here are sufficient for finding V_m and i_m at any point on a cable and for obtaining the input impedance for any output load, etc. They can, of course, be used for lines of any geometrical arrangement.

The term $e^{-2\alpha l}$ that appears when γ is replaced in these formulas by $\alpha + j\beta$ represents the attenuation associated with R_l and G_l. It is not easy nor useful to write explicit formulas for α and β in general, but if R_l and G_l are small, approximate results can readily be obtained. We have, in fact, by Eq. 10.2–30

$$\begin{aligned}
\gamma &= j\omega(L_l C_l)^{1/2}\left(1 + \frac{R_l}{j\omega L_l}\right)^{1/2}\left(1 + \frac{G_l}{j\omega C_l}\right)^{1/2} \\
&= j\omega(L_l C_l)^{1/2}\left(1 + \frac{R_l}{2j\omega L_l} + \cdots\right)\left(1 + \frac{G_l}{2j\omega C_1} + \cdots\right) \\
&= j\omega(L_l C_l)^{1/2}\left(1 + \frac{R_l}{2j\omega L_l} + \frac{G_l}{2j\omega C_l} + \cdots\right) \\
&\simeq j\omega(L_l C_l)^{1/4} + \frac{1}{2}\left[R_l\left(\frac{C_l}{L_l}\right)^{1/2} + G_l\left(\frac{L_l}{C_l}\right)^{1/2}\right]
\end{aligned} \qquad (10.2\text{–}41)$$

so that a nearly lossless line transmits waves with the same velocity as the ideal line considered earlier and has an attenuation constant α given by

$$\alpha = \frac{1}{2}\left(\frac{R_l}{Z_{c\,\text{ideal}}} + G_l Z_{c\,\text{ideal}}\right) \qquad (10.2\text{--}42)$$

Actual cables can be made with low losses so that these formulas are reasonably accurate. We have of course been assuming the lines to be straight, but the usual bends and curves found in practice have very little influence.

Aside from the transmission of alternating currents and pulses of any frequency up to rather high limits, coaxial cables are useful for introducing short delays into pulse-measuring systems. Because of the high velocity of light, only very short delays, of the order of 10^{-9} to 10^{-7} sec, are practical to obtain in this way. We remarked, however, on the similarity between a cable and a series of L–C filters in tandem. We can make a delay line that acts very much like a cable but allows for longer delays in a given distance by using an actual set of equal inductors in series and capacitors in parallel. Any one pair L and C can be approximately likened to the L_l and C_l for a unit length of the cable we have analyzed. The time delay of the cable, in seconds per meter, is of course $1/c = (L_l C_l)^{1/2}$. Hence the time delay of the series of filters is $(LC)^{1/2}$ per section and can be chosen almost at will. Lines of this sort of 10 or more sections are frequently used for over-all time delays up to 10^{-5} sec. It is also possible to use a continuously wound solenoid with metallic strips on its outside to make a continuous parallel capacitance to ground, with values of $(L_l C_l)^{1/2}$ considerably larger than $1/c$.

The reflecting properties of coaxial or other types of delay lines can be put to a number of uses. For instance, if a cable open at its far end is charged to a constant voltage V_0 and the input end is suddenly connected to a resistance equal to Z_c (for instance by firing a thyratron), the voltage will suddenly drop to $V_0/2$, and a negative step pulse of magnitude $V_0/2$ will travel down the line, reducing V_c all along the wire to $V_0/2$. At the far end, the pulse is reflected without change of sign, and as it passes back it reduces V_c to 0. The PD finally gets to zero at the original end at a time equal to twice the delay time for one passage down the cable, and a rather accurate "step" pulse of amplitude $V_0/2$ has been generated.

The far-reaching success of the theory of coaxial lines in accounting for the many quantitative experimental results that have been obtained is powerful evidence for the correctness of Maxwell's equations, including Maxwell's modification of Ampère's law by means of the displacement current. The success of the theory in dealing with waves in free space, with the optics of reflection, refraction, diffraction, etc, and with waves in pipes and cavities is even more impressive (see the rest of this chapter).

Problem 10.2a. Polyethylene has a dielectric constant $\kappa = 2.29$ and has $\mu_r = \mu/\mu_0 = 1$. Find a numerical formula for the characteristic impedance of lossless coaxial cables filled with polyethylene in terms of b/a. If $a = 0.250$ inches, find b so that $Z_c = 52$ ohms. Find C_l in micromicrofarads per foot for this cable.

Problem 10.2b. Use the formulas 7.17–3 and 4.5–5 to derive a formula for Z_c for a parallel-wire line. If the wires each have diameters of 0.040 in., how far apart must they be for Z_c to be 600 ohms?

Problem 10.2c. Write formulas for i_m and V_m on a cable with attenuation in terms of V_{m0} (for $z = 0$), γ, l, and Z_l.

Problem 10.2d. Find an expression for the input impedance of an improperly terminated cable, with attenuation.

Problem 10.2e. Given the parameters L_l, C_l, R_l, and G_l in microhenries/foot, micromicrofarads/foot, ohms/foot, and mhos/foot, write formulas with numerical constants for Z_c in ohms, α in decibels per foot, and $1/v$ in microseconds/foot.

Problem 10.2f. Discuss the presence or absence of displacement current in a lossless coaxial cable carrying a sinusoidal current.

10.3 Propagation of Electromagnetic Fields

Let us write the field equations for free space and show that the components of **E** and **B** satisfy a wave equation similar to that for V_c and i for the transmission line of the previous section. We have

$$\nabla \cdot \mathbf{E} = 0 \qquad (10.3\text{–}1a)$$

$$\nabla \cdot \mathbf{B} = 0 \qquad (10.3\text{–}1b)$$

$$\nabla \times \mathbf{B} = \mu_0 \epsilon_0 \, \partial \mathbf{E}/\partial t \qquad (10.3\text{–}1c)$$

$$\nabla \times \mathbf{E} = -\partial \mathbf{B}/\partial t \qquad (10.3\text{–}1d)$$

Let us eliminate **B** from the last two equations by taking the curl of the last one:

$$\textbf{curl curl E} = \nabla \times (\nabla \times \mathbf{E}) = -\text{curl}\,(\partial \mathbf{B}/\partial t) = -\partial(\text{curl } \mathbf{B})/\partial t$$

using the interchangeability of space and time derivatives. By item 11, Table A.2*B*, the triple vector product can be simplified:

$$\nabla \times (\nabla \times \mathbf{E}) = \nabla(\nabla \cdot \mathbf{E}) - (\nabla \cdot \nabla)\mathbf{E}$$

and using Eqs. 10.3–1*a* and 10.3–1*c*, together with $\mu_0 \epsilon_0 = 1/c^2$ we have finally

$$\nabla^2 \mathbf{E} = \frac{1}{c^2} \frac{\partial^2 \mathbf{E}}{\partial t^2} \qquad (10.3\text{–}2a)$$

which resembles Eq. 10.2–10 except that it involves all three second derivatives in $\nabla^2 = (\partial^2/\partial x^2 + \partial^2/\partial y^2 + \partial^2/\partial z^2)$ and that it involves a vector $\mathbf{E}$ instead of a scalar f. Each Cartesian component of $\mathbf{E}$, in fact, obeys a three-dimensional wave equation. Exactly the same operation can be carried out starting with Eq. 10.3–1c, yielding the result for $\mathbf{B}$:

$$\nabla^2\mathbf{B} = \frac{1}{c^2}\frac{\partial^2\mathbf{B}}{\partial t^2} \qquad (10.3–2b)$$

There are three fairly simple types of solutions of these wave equations that show the character of electromagnetic waves. In the first place, suppose that within a certain region of space $\mathbf{E}$ and $\mathbf{B}$ are functions of x only. This means that all y and z derivatives must vanish. The equation div $\mathbf{E} = 0$ becomes $\partial E_x/\partial x = 0$, which means that E_x is a constant in x. We set $E_x = 0$, therefore, since uniform fields are not of interest in this section. The other components E_y and E_z obey the one-dimensional wave equation. For E_y we have

$$\frac{\partial^2 E_y}{\partial x^2} = \frac{1}{c^2}\frac{\partial^2 E_y}{\partial t^2}$$

whose solution must be of the form

$$E_y = f_1\left(t - \frac{x}{c}\right) + f_2\left(t + \frac{x}{c}\right)$$

by comparison with Eq. 10.2–11 in the last section. Similar results hold for E_z, B_y, and B_z—all four components undergo wave motion that propagates along the x-axis. Just as for the coaxial line, these four quantities are related to each other. In this case equations 10.3–1c and 10.3–1d reduce to the following:

$$\mathrm{curl}_y\,\mathbf{B} = -\frac{\partial B_z}{\partial x} = \frac{1}{c^2}\frac{\partial E_y}{\partial t} \qquad (10.3–3a)$$

$$\mathrm{curl}_z\,\mathbf{E} = \frac{\partial E_y}{\partial x} = -\frac{\partial B_z}{\partial t} \qquad (10.3–3b)$$

$$\mathrm{curl}_z\,\mathbf{B} = \frac{\partial B_y}{\partial x} = \frac{1}{c^2}\frac{\partial E_z}{\partial t} \qquad (10.3–4a)$$

$$\mathrm{curl}_y\,\mathbf{E} = -\frac{\partial E_z}{\partial x} = -\frac{\partial B_y}{\partial t} \qquad (10.3–4b)$$

From Eqs. 10.3–3 we get a result like that for V_c and i of Section 10.2—namely, the pair of related solutions

$$E_y = f_1\left(t - \frac{x}{c}\right) + f_2\left(t + \frac{x}{c}\right)$$

$$B_z = \frac{1}{c} f_1\left(t - \frac{x}{c}\right) - \frac{1}{c} f_2\left(t + \frac{x}{c}\right) \tag{10.3–5}$$

whereas from Eqs. 10.3–4 we find another, independent pair of solutions

$$E_z = g_1\left(t - \frac{x}{c}\right) + g_2\left(t + \frac{x}{c}\right)$$

$$B_y = -\frac{1}{c} g_1\left(t - \frac{x}{c}\right) + \frac{1}{c} g_2\left(t + \frac{x}{c}\right) \tag{10.3–6}$$

Thus we see that there exist plane wave solutions of Maxwell's equations (called "plane wave" because there is complete uniformity over the y–z plane) that involve *transverse fields*, normal to the direction of travel, with the electric and magnetic vectors mutually perpendicular. The sign relations for f_1, f_2, g_1, and g_2 can all be summarized in a single rule, which says that the vector product $\mathbf{E} \times \mathbf{B}$ formed from the vectors corresponding to any one of these solutions points in the direction of wave propagation. Specifically, for f_1, $\mathbf{E} \times \mathbf{B} = \mathbf{1}_x E_y B_z = \mathbf{1}_x f_1{}^2/c$ whereas for f_2, $\mathbf{E} \times \mathbf{B} = -\mathbf{1}_x f_2{}^2/c$. For g_1, $\mathbf{E} \times \mathbf{B} = -\mathbf{1}_x E_z B_y = \mathbf{1}_x g_1{}^2/c$, and for g_2, $\mathbf{E} \times \mathbf{B} = -\mathbf{1}_x g_2{}^2/c$.

Plane-wave solutions can, of course, be written for the other two planes. They can also be written for an arbitrary direction of propagation. Suppose that $\mathbf{1}_u$ represents an arbitrary unit vector of components u_1, u_2, and u_3: $\mathbf{1}_u = \mathbf{1}_x u_1 + \mathbf{1}_y u_2 + \mathbf{1}_z u_3$. Then, using E_y as an example, consider the possible solution

$$E_y = F\left(t - \frac{\mathbf{r} \cdot \mathbf{1}_u}{c}\right) = F\left(t - \frac{x u_1 + y u_2 + z u_3}{c}\right) \tag{10.3–7}$$

where F is an arbitrary function and $\mathbf{r} = \mathbf{1}_x x + \mathbf{1}_y y + \mathbf{1}_z z$. We have on differentiating

$$\frac{\partial E_y}{\partial t} = F'; \qquad \frac{\partial^2 E_y}{\partial t^2} = F''; \qquad \frac{\partial E_y}{\partial x} = -\frac{u_1}{c} F'; \qquad \frac{\partial^2 E_y}{\partial x^2} = \frac{u_1{}^2}{c^2} F''; \qquad \text{etc.,}$$

so that, since $u_1{}^2 + u_2{}^2 + u_3{}^2 = 1$,

$$\nabla^2 E_y = \frac{\partial^2 E_y}{\partial x^2} + \frac{\partial^2 E_y}{\partial y^2} + \frac{\partial^2 E_y}{\partial z^2} = \frac{u_1{}^2 + u_2{}^2 + u_3{}^2}{c^2} F'' = \frac{1}{c^2} F'' = \frac{1}{c^2} \frac{\partial^2 E_y}{\partial t^2}$$

and E_y satisfies the general wave equation. One can then find relations between solutions for the various field components so as to satisfy Eqs. 10.3–1, but we shall not work them out here.

Note, however, that $\mathbf{r} \cdot \mathbf{1}_u$ has a simple interpretation. It is the projection of $\mathbf{r}$ in the direction of $\mathbf{1}_u$. If the latter were taken as a new x-axis, $\mathbf{r} \cdot \mathbf{1}_u$ would become simply x, and we would have plane waves moving in the x-direction, with their planes perpendicular to it. Thus Eq. 10.3–7 represents plane waves traveling in the $\mathbf{1}_u$-direction.

A third type of solution is one that depends only on t and r, the distance from some particular origin. It is simplest for a scalar, and since we shall show that V obeys the wave equation, we shall use V as an example. We will get to our result most easily if we write

$$V = \frac{f(t, r)}{r}$$

and substitute in the wave equation, utilizing the relations $\partial r/\partial x = x/r$, $\partial r/\partial y = y/r$, and $\partial r/\partial z = z/r$. We have, in fact,

$$\frac{\partial V}{\partial x} = \frac{1}{r}\frac{\partial f}{\partial r}\frac{\partial r}{\partial x} - \frac{f}{r^2}\frac{\partial r}{\partial x} = \frac{x}{r^2}\frac{\partial f}{\partial r} - \frac{xf}{r^3}$$

$$\frac{\partial^2 V}{\partial x^2} = \frac{1}{r^2}\frac{\partial f}{\partial r} - \frac{2x}{r^3}\frac{\partial r}{\partial x}\frac{\partial f}{\partial r} + \frac{x}{r^2}\frac{\partial^2 f}{\partial r^2}\frac{\partial r}{\partial x} - \frac{f}{r^3} - \frac{x}{r^3}\frac{\partial f}{\partial r}\frac{\partial r}{\partial x} + \frac{3x}{r^4}\frac{\partial r}{\partial x}f$$

$$= \left(-1 + \frac{3x^2}{r^2}\right)\frac{f(t, r)}{r^3} + \left(1 - \frac{3x^2}{r^2}\right)\frac{1}{r^2}\frac{\partial f(t, r)}{\partial r} + \frac{x^2}{r^3}\frac{\partial^2 f(t, r)}{\partial r^3}$$

so that adding the corresponding terms in y and z and using $x^2 + y^2 + z^2 = r^2$, we find

$$\nabla^2 V = \left(-3 + \frac{3r^2}{r^2}\right)\frac{f}{r^3} + \left(3 - 3\frac{r^2}{r^2}\right)\frac{1}{r^2}\frac{\partial f}{\partial r} + \frac{r^2}{r^3}\frac{\partial^2 f}{\partial r^2} = \frac{1}{r}\frac{\partial^2 f}{\partial r^2}$$

Hence the wave equation yields for $f(t, r)$

$$\frac{1}{r}\frac{\partial^2 f}{\partial r_2} = \frac{1}{rc^2}\frac{\partial^2 f}{\partial t^2}$$

and f must have the form of an ordinary wave. Thus we can write for V

$$V = \frac{1}{r}f_1\left(t - \frac{r}{c}\right) + \frac{1}{r}f_2\left(t + \frac{r}{c}\right) \tag{10.3–8}$$

The first term represents a diverging wave moving outward from the origin, and the second represents a converging wave moving inward toward the origin. We shall return to spherical waves of this sort later.

The Retarded Potentials. We have shown that Maxwell's equations have wave-type solutions and that the velocity of propagation is c in free space. We have not shown, however, when these solutions are physically relevant or meaningful, nor how they are related to the charges and currents that must be their sources. Our next step is to construct general expressions for the scalar and vector potentials in the presence of free charges and currents that answer these questions.

Let us substitute the expressions for **E** and **B** in terms of **A** and **V**, namely,

$$\mathbf{E} = -\frac{\partial \mathbf{A}}{\partial t} - \boldsymbol{\nabla} V \qquad \text{Eq. 7.14–6}a \text{ (10.3–9)}$$

$$\mathbf{B} = \boldsymbol{\nabla} \times \mathbf{A} \qquad \text{Eq. 7.10–3 (10.3–10)}$$

into the general equations for div **E** and **curl B**, Eqs. 10.1–1a and 10.1–3b, neglecting polarization and magnetization or including them in ρ and **J**. We obtain (cf. Eq. 7.14–7)

$$\boldsymbol{\nabla} \cdot \mathbf{E} = -\frac{\partial}{\partial t}(\boldsymbol{\nabla} \cdot \mathbf{A}) - \boldsymbol{\nabla} \cdot \boldsymbol{\nabla} V = \rho/\epsilon_0$$

$$\boldsymbol{\nabla} \times \mathbf{B} = \boldsymbol{\nabla} \times (\boldsymbol{\nabla} \times \mathbf{A}) = \mu_0 \mathbf{J} + \mu_0 \epsilon_0 \left(-\frac{\partial^2 \mathbf{A}}{\partial t^2} - \boldsymbol{\nabla} \frac{\partial V}{\partial t} \right)$$

Utilizing the Lorentz relation Eq. 7.10–9a and the expansion of $\boldsymbol{\nabla} \times (\boldsymbol{\nabla} \times \mathbf{A})$ we have

$$-\frac{\partial}{\partial t}\left(-\mu_0 \epsilon_0 \frac{\partial V}{\partial t} \right) - \nabla^2 V = \rho/\epsilon_0$$

$$\boldsymbol{\nabla}(\boldsymbol{\nabla} \cdot \mathbf{A}) - \nabla^2 \mathbf{A} + \mu_0 \epsilon_0 \boldsymbol{\nabla} \frac{\partial V}{\partial t} = \mu_0 \mathbf{J} - \mu_0 \epsilon_0 \frac{\partial^2 \mathbf{A}}{\partial t^2}$$

which finally reduce to

$$\nabla^2 V - \frac{1}{c^2}\frac{\partial^2 V}{\partial t^2} = -\rho/\epsilon_0 \qquad (10.3\text{–}11)$$

$$\nabla^2 \mathbf{A} - \frac{1}{c^2}\frac{\partial^2 \mathbf{A}}{\partial t^2} = -\mu_0 \mathbf{J} \qquad (10.3\text{–}12)$$

The similarity between the equation for V and that for each component of **A** suggests that we write these equations in Lorentz-invariant form. They all involve the so-called d'Alembertian operator

$$\square = \nabla^2 - \frac{1}{c^2}\frac{\partial^2}{\partial t^2} = \partial_1^2 + \partial_2^2 + \partial_3^2 + \partial_4^2 \qquad (10.3\text{–}13)$$

which is a four-scalar. The right-hand sides of the two equations are proportional to the components of J_k, given by 7.19–22. Thus the equation for the four-vector A_k, Eq. 7.19–23a, is

$$\square \, A_j = \sum_k \partial^2 A_j / \partial x_k^2 = -\mu_0 J_j, \qquad j = 1, 2, 3, 4 \qquad (10.3\text{–}14a)$$

Since $\square$ is a scalar, we see that 10.3–14a is Lorentz-invariant if *both* J_k and A_k are four-vectors, as was assumed in Section 7.9.

To find general solutions of 10.3–11 and 10.3–12, recall first the similarity between the steady-state formulas for V and A:

$$V = \frac{1}{4\pi\epsilon_0} \int_{\text{all space}} \frac{\rho \, d\tau}{r} \quad \text{Eq. 1.7–7c} \qquad (10.3\text{–}15)$$

$$\mathbf{A} = \frac{\mu_0}{4\pi} \int_{\text{all space}} \frac{\mathbf{J} \, d\tau}{r} \quad \text{Eq. 7.10–5a} \qquad (10.3\text{–}16)$$

If V and ρ are independent of t, we know from Section 1.10 that Eq. 10.3–15 satisfies Eq. 10.3–11, and similarly we can conclude that if $\mathbf{A}$ and $\mathbf{J}$ are constant in time, Eq. 10.3–16 satisfies Eq. 10.3–12. Our desire now is to find expressions for $\mathbf{A}$ and V of a similar nature that satisfy Eq. 10.3–11 and Eq. 10.3–12 when all quantities depend on t.

The calculation in Section 1.10 that verifies 10.3–15 as the solution of Poisson's equation consists first of showing that the operator ∇^2 applied to the integrand gives zero for points not in $d\tau$, and then that an integral over a small region around the point (x, y, z) yields the value $-\rho/\epsilon_0$. For the case with time variations, we seek an integrand to which application of the wave-equation operator $\nabla^2 - (1/c^2) \, \partial^2/\partial t^2$ yields zero for points not in $d\tau$, and for which the second calculation still yields $-\rho/\epsilon_0$.

A solution dependent only on r and t has been found above, namely a converging or diverging wave like Eq. 10.3–8. We choose only the diverging wave since we consider the element to act as a source of V but not as a receiver. The boundary condition is satisfied by noting that as $r \to 0$, $f_1(t - r/c) \to f_1(t)$, so that near the charge we can use the static solution, with $f_1(t) = \rho(t) \, d\tau/4\pi\epsilon_0$. The same treatment can be given to each component of $\mathbf{A}$.

Consequently, if $\rho(x, y, z, t)$ and $\mathbf{J}(x, y \; z, t)$ are functions that give the charge and current densities at each point as functions of the time, the scalar and vector potentials are given by

$$V(x, y, z, t) = \frac{1}{4\pi\epsilon_0} \int_{\text{all space}} \frac{\rho(x', y', z', t - r/c)}{r} \, d\tau \qquad (10.3\text{–}15)$$

$$\mathbf{A}(x, y, z, t) = \frac{\mu_0}{4\pi} \int_{\text{all space}} \frac{\mathbf{J}(x', y', z', t - r/c)}{r} \, d\tau \qquad (10.3\text{–}16)$$

where r is the distance from the volume element $d\tau$ to the point (x, y, z). These quantities are called the retarded potentials and give a general expression for the fields generated by arbitrary charge and current densities. They show that all electromagnetic effects are propagated with the velocity c. A particular motion of charge at a particular time produces potentials and fields at a distance r at time r/c later.[1]

Application of Eqs. 10.3–15 and 10.3–16 to the case of a moving point charge must be made with care, for while it is correct to consider a limiting process in which a spread-out charge of total amount q shrinks to a point, the requirement that the values of ρ and ρv must be calculated at retarded times still has an effect in the limit. Let us make the calculation by assuming a sharply-localized distribution ρ which travels like a wave, with velocity $\mathbf{v}$ along the z-axis. We write

$$\rho(x', y', z', t) = f(x', y', z' - vt) \qquad (10.3\text{–}17)$$

where the constant total charge q can be calculated at $t = 0$:

$$q = \int_\tau f(x', y', z') \, d\tau \qquad (10.3\text{–}18)$$

and the integral can be taken over all space since $f(x', y', z')$ is assumed to differ from zero only in the neighborhood of the origin.

Then we have for V at the point $\mathscr{P}(x, y, z)$ and time t

$$V(x, y, z, t) = \frac{1}{4\pi\epsilon_0} \iiint_\tau \frac{f(x', y', z' - vt + vr/c)}{r} \, dx' \, dy' \, dz'$$

with $r^2 = (x - x')^2 + (y - y')^2 + (z - z')^2$. The integral can be simplified if we carry out the z' integration first, substituting for z' the new variable z'':

$$z'' = z' - vt + \frac{vr}{c} \qquad (10.3\text{–}19)$$

with

$$dz'' = dz' + \frac{v}{c} \frac{\partial r}{\partial z'} \, dz' = dz' + \frac{v}{c} \frac{(z' - z)}{r} \, dz'$$

[1] Expressions satisfying 10.3–11 and 12 can be written for $\mathbf{A}$ and V with $t + r/c$ in place of $t - r/c$, and are called "advanced potentials." Their use appears to violate the law of causality, by making the potentials at a given time and place depend on later events elsewhere. Nevertheless, they are sometimes used in a symmetrical way with the retarded potentials in some theoretical developments. J. A. Wheeler and R. Feynman, *Revs. Mod. Phys.*, **21**, 425 (1949), have given an interesting discussion and resolution of the paradox involved in this approach.

Since, as shown in Fig. 10.3a, $(z - z')/r$ is the cosine of the angle θ between v and 1_r, we have

$$dz' = \frac{dz''}{1 - \mathbf{v} \cdot \mathbf{1}_r/c}$$

The potential then becomes

$$V(x, y, z, t) = \frac{1}{4\pi\epsilon_0} \iiint_{r'} \frac{f(x', y', z'')\, dx'\, dy'\, dz''}{r - \mathbf{v} \cdot \mathbf{r}/c} \tag{10.3-20}$$

Now we can allow f to go to the limit of a point-charge distribution. The integrand will only have a value when each of x', y', and z'' is very close to zero, so the denominator can simply be evaluated at this point and removed from under the integral sign. By Eq. 10.3–19 we see that the point of evaluation is the point at which the charge arrives at a time r/c before the time for which V is desired. The integral is just q by 10.3–18, so we find

$$V = \frac{q}{4\pi\epsilon_0(r - \mathbf{v} \cdot \mathbf{r}/c)}\bigg|_{\text{retarded}} \tag{10.3-21}$$

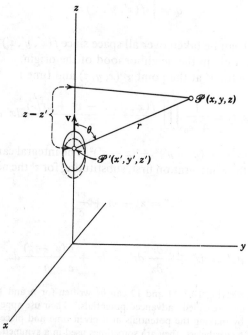

Fig. 10.3a.   Illustrating the calculation of the Liénard-Wiechert potentials. The solid curve is a contour line of the charge distribution at time t; the dashed curve is the same contour for the retarded time $t - r/c$. $\mathcal{P}'(x', y', z')$ is a point of integration.

An exactly similar calculation can be made for **A**, yielding

$$\mathbf{A} = \left.\frac{\mu_0 q \mathbf{v}}{4\pi(r - \mathbf{v} \cdot \mathbf{r}/c)}\right|_{\text{retarded}} \tag{10.3-22}$$

These formulas are called the Liénard-Wiechert potentials.[2] Note that it is not necessary that **v** be constant in magnitude or direction—we need only assume in the derivation just given that **v** is directed along the z-axis at the retarded time in question. The Liénard-Wiechert potentials may be used to calculate **E** and **B** for an arbitrarily-moving point charge, but the

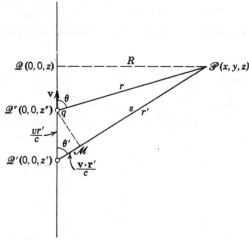

Fig. 10.3b. Illustrating the calculation of the Liénard-Wiechert potentials for a charge q moving at constant velocity **v**. $\mathcal{Q}''$ is its position at time t, for which the potentials at $\mathcal{P}$ are desired and $\mathcal{Q}'$ is the retarded position at time $t - r'/c$.

operations $\nabla \times \mathbf{A}$, $-\partial \mathbf{A}/\partial t$, and $-\nabla V$ must be performed with care because of the retardation.

The calculation for constant **v** can be simplified considerably, however, by rewriting the denominator $s = [r - (\mathbf{v} \cdot \mathbf{r})/c]_{\text{ret}}$ in terms of the unretarded radius. Figure 10.3b shows a charge q, which arrives at $\mathcal{Q}''$ at time t, and is at $\mathcal{Q}'$ at $t' = t - r'/c$. The "retarded radius" is denoted by r', the "present radius" by r, and the perpendicular by R. Note that in time r'/c the particle goes a distance vr'/c from $\mathcal{Q}'$ to $\mathcal{Q}''$. The equation of motion of the particle may be taken simply as $z'' = vt$ or $z' = vt'$.

[2] A. Liénard, *L'Eclairage élect.*, **16**, 5, 53, 106 (1898); E. Wiechert, *Arch. Néerl.* (2) **5**, 549 (1900). A different simple derivation is given by Sir E. T. Whittaker, *A History of the Theories of Aether and Electricity*, Vol. I: The Classical Theories, Thos. Nelson, London, 1951 and Harper, New York, 1960, pp. 407–9. A detailed and clear exposition is given by D. R. Corson and P. Lorrain, *Introduction to Electromagnetic Fields and Waves*, W. H. Freeman, San Francisco, 1962, Chapter 14.

The reduced radius s is seen to be the distance $\mathscr{P}\mathscr{M}$. Its square may be found from the right triangle $\mathscr{P}\mathscr{Q}''\mathscr{M}$ and the relation

$$R = r \sin \theta = r' \sin \theta'$$

We have

$$s^2 = r^2 - (vr' \sin \theta'/c)^2 = r^2 - (vr \sin \theta/c)^2$$
$$= r^2(1 - v^2 \sin^2 \theta/c^2) \tag{10.3–23a}$$

and in terms of x, y, z, and t we have

$$s^2 = x^2 + y^2 + (z - vt)^2 - (v^2/c^2)(x^2 + y^2)$$
$$= (x^2 + y^2)(1 - v^2/c^2) + (z - vt)^2 \tag{10.3–23b}$$

Now we can write V and $\mathbf{A}$ in terms of unretarded quantities:

$$V = \frac{q}{4\pi\epsilon_0 s} = \frac{q}{4\pi\epsilon_0[(x^2 + y^2)(1 - v^2/c^2) + (z - vt)^2]^{1/2}} \tag{10.3–24}$$

$$\mathbf{A} = \frac{\mu_0 q \mathbf{v}}{4\pi s} = \frac{\mu_0 q \mathbf{v}}{4\pi[(x^2 + y^2)(1 - v^2/c^2) + (z - vt)^2]^{1/2}} \tag{10.3–25}$$

If we note that

$$\frac{\partial s}{\partial x} + \frac{x}{s}\left(1 - \frac{v^2}{c^2}\right); \frac{\partial s}{\partial y} = \frac{y}{s}\left(1 - \frac{v^2}{c^2}\right)$$
$$\frac{\partial s}{\partial z} = \frac{z - vt}{s}; \frac{\partial s}{\partial t} = -\frac{v(z - vt)}{s} \tag{10.3–26}$$

and use $\mu_0 = 1/\epsilon_0 c^2$, we can readily calculate $\mathbf{E}$ and $\mathbf{B}$. We obtain

$$\mathbf{E} = \frac{q[x\mathbf{1}_x + y\mathbf{1}_y + (z - vt)\mathbf{1}_z](1 - v^2/c^2)}{4\pi\epsilon_0 s^3}$$
$$= \frac{q\mathbf{1}_r(1 - v^2/c^2)}{4\pi\epsilon_0 r^2[1 - (v^2/c^2)\sin^2 \theta]^{3/2}} \tag{10.3–27}$$

$$\mathbf{B} = \frac{\mu_0 q v}{4\pi s^3}[x\mathbf{1}_y - y\mathbf{1}_x](1 - v^2/c^2) = \frac{1}{c^2}\mathbf{v} \times \mathbf{E}$$
$$= \frac{\mu_0 q v \mathbf{1}_\phi(1 - v^2/c^2)\sin \theta}{4\pi r^2[1 - (v^2/c^2)\sin^2 \theta]^{3/2}} \tag{10.3–28}$$

The magnetic field as expected has only a hoop or ϕ component. These results are exactly the same as those obtained by applying the transformation 7.19–40 and 7.19–41 to the field of a stationary charge (Problem 10.3a).

We note that our calculation which holds for any magnitude of v less than c corroborates the relation 7.14–5a, $\mathbf{B} = \mu_0\epsilon_0\mathbf{v} \times \mathbf{E}$, which was derived only for speeds much less than c. The field $\mathbf{E}$ is radial, but can be described as foreshortened by the following considerations. For $\theta = 0$, the value of r at which a field of a given magnitude E_0 occurs is reduced by $(1 - v^2/c^2)^{\frac{1}{2}}$ over the radius which gives E_0 for a slow charge or one at rest. At $\theta = 90°$, however, the radius for a given E_0 is larger by a factor $(1 - v^2/c^2)^{-\frac{1}{4}}$ over the low-speed value.

The Lorentz-Fitzgerald contraction can thus be described as being an expression of the foreshortening of the electric field of a moving charge. It is not surprising, therefore, that a macroscopic piece of material composed of electric charges will also foreshorten. It was the contribution of Einstein to show that this contraction is general and not just a property of the electric fields of the charged particles. Although his account of the contraction depends on the nature of simultaneous observations of two points on a moving body and thus appears to be quite different than the treatment given here, the fact that a common observation time t is used here and that the fields may be found from a Lorentz transformation of the Coulomb field shows that the two derivations are actually closely related.

These expressions for the potentials produced by continuous or discrete charges are, of course, the generalization of the formulas for V given in Chapter 1, and they have the same limitation as all the material of that chapter—they can only be used if the charge densities and currents are already known. Thus we can use them to find the field radiated by an oscillating dipole, as we will in Section 10.5, but we cannot use them when conductors are present which will contain induced currents and charges dependent on the fields. For this latter purpose, we have to use a generalization of the point of view of Chapters 2 and 4, in which the geometrical arrangements of the conductors determine the boundary conditions. An introduction to the boundary-condition approach will be given in Sections 10.7 and 10.9.

The Gaussian formulas for the retarded potentials are easily obtained by placing $4\pi\epsilon_0 = 1$ in Eqs. 10.3–15 and 10.3–21, and setting $\mu_0/4\pi = 1/c$ in 10.3–16 and 10.3–22.

Problem 10.3a. Derive the fields of a moving charge from those of a stationary one by means of a Lorentz transformation (Section 7.19).

10.4 The Energy and Momentum Theorems

Electromagnetic radiation is a means of transfer of energy and momentum from one set of charges and currents to another. We can in fact attribute definite amounts of energy and momentum to each elementary volume of space occupied by electromagnetic fields. Since we shall need the results in the following sections, we turn now to the relevant theorems.

The Energy Theorem. To study energy transfer, we start with the work done by the fields on charges. The rate of doing work, or power, is given in mechanics as $\mathbf{F} \cdot \mathbf{v}$. Since the magnetic force $q(\mathbf{v} \times \mathbf{B})$ is always perpendicular to the velocity, only the electric force $q\mathbf{E}$ is involved in energy transfer. Let us assume that all charges can be described in terms of a continuous volume density ρ. Then power per unit volume will be $P_\tau = \rho\mathbf{E} \cdot \mathbf{v} = \mathbf{E} \cdot \rho\mathbf{v} = \mathbf{E} \cdot \mathbf{J}$. From the **curl B** equation, we can write

$$P_\tau = \mathbf{E} \cdot \mathbf{J} = \frac{1}{\mu_0} \mathbf{E} \cdot \nabla \times \mathbf{B} - \epsilon_0 \mathbf{E} \cdot \frac{\partial \mathbf{E}}{\partial t} \tag{10.4-1}$$

This equation can be simplified if we use the identity obtained by writing $\nabla \cdot (\mathbf{E} \times \mathbf{B})$ so that the actions of the operator on the two vectors are explicitly separated:

$$\nabla \cdot (\mathbf{E} \times \mathbf{B}) = \overline{\nabla \times \mathbf{E} \cdot \mathbf{B}} = -\overline{\nabla \times \mathbf{B} \cdot \mathbf{E}}$$
$$= \mathbf{B} \cdot \nabla \times \mathbf{E} - \mathbf{E} \cdot \nabla \times \mathbf{B} \tag{10.4-2}$$

The bars over ∇, $\mathbf{E}$, and $\mathbf{B}$ in the first line indicate that the derivatives in ∇ operate on both vectors. Each form of the triple scalar product is then rewritten to show only one derivative operation for each term. If we use Eq. 10.4-2 together with the equation for **curl E**, we can convert Eq. 10.4-1 into

$$P_\tau = -\frac{1}{\mu_0} \nabla \cdot (\mathbf{E} \times \mathbf{B}) - \frac{1}{\mu_0} \mathbf{B} \cdot \frac{\partial \mathbf{B}}{\partial t} - \epsilon_0 \mathbf{E} \cdot \frac{\partial \mathbf{E}}{\partial t}$$
$$= -\frac{1}{\mu_0} \nabla \cdot (\mathbf{E} \times \mathbf{B}) - \frac{1}{2} \frac{\partial}{\partial t} \left(\frac{B^2}{\mu_0} + \epsilon_0 E^2 \right)$$

The theorem we wish to prove is derived by multiplying this result by $d\tau$ and integrating over an arbitrary closed surface. The integral of the divergence of $\mathbf{E} \times \mathbf{B}$ can then be replaced by a surface integral by use of the divergence theorem, Eq. A.2-22. We find for the rate at which work is done on all the charges in an arbitrary volume τ the expression

$$P = \int_\tau P_\tau \, d\tau = -\frac{1}{\mu_0} \int_{\text{surface of } \tau} \mathbf{E} \times \mathbf{B} \cdot d\mathbf{S} - \frac{d}{dt} \int_\tau \left(\frac{B^2}{2\mu_0} + \frac{\epsilon_0 E^2}{2} \right) d\tau \tag{10-3.4}$$

To interpret this result, we consider first a very large volume whose surface lies outside the region in which the fields of interest have any appreciable value. Then the surface integral vanishes, and we see that the rate of doing work is equal to the rate of decrease of a certain volume integral, which can be interpreted as the energy contained in the electro-magnetic field:

$$U = \int_{\tau} \left(\frac{B^2}{2\mu_0} + \frac{\epsilon_0}{2} E^2 \right) d\tau \qquad (10.4\text{-}4a)$$

which is often written in symmetrical fashion as

$$U = \int_{\tau} \tfrac{1}{2}(\mathbf{B} \cdot \mathbf{H} + \mathbf{D} \cdot \mathbf{E}) \, d\tau \qquad (10.4\text{-}4b)$$

This latter equation remains valid for linear dielectric and magnetic materials if we do not count polarization charges and magnetization currents in ρ and $\mathbf{J}$ but include them by using the $\mathbf{D}$ and $\mathbf{H}$ vectors (Problem 10.4e). In this case, P_r represents only the power expected on free charges, the work done in changing polarizations and magnetizations being included in U. For non-linear media, hysteresis and dielectric losses must be included, leading to complexities beyond the scope of this book.

Equations 10.4–4 are seen to be a generalization to the case of arbitrary fields of Eqs. 4.7–6 and 7.18–8. We can always get the correct total amount of energy if we assign an amount $\tfrac{1}{2}(\mathbf{B} \cdot \mathbf{H} + \mathbf{D} \cdot \mathbf{E})$ to each unit volume although there is no way of proving that each unit volume actually contains this energy.

Now if we consider a smaller volume so that the surface integral does not vanish, we can find an interpretation for it as well. Using again a symmetrical notation that holds in general, we have

$$\int_{S} (\mathbf{E} \times \mathbf{H}) \cdot d\mathbf{S} = -P - \frac{dU}{dt} \qquad (10.4\text{-}5)$$

so that the integral is equal to the rate of gain of energy from the charges, $-P$, plus the rate of decrease of the field energy within the surface. That is, if conservation of energy is to be maintained,[3] the surface integral must represent the rate of outflow of energy through the surface. We can then assign to each unit area of the surface a rate of outflow of energy given by

$$\mathbf{N} = \mathbf{E} \times \mathbf{H} \qquad (10.4\text{-}6a)$$

where $\mathbf{N}$ is called the "Poynting vector," happily named after the physicist J. H. Poynting.[4] The quantity $\int \mathbf{N} \cdot d\mathbf{S}$ for any surface is called the Poynting

---

[3] The success of the calculations given below in accounting for the flow of energy in several specific cases is evidence that the law of conservation of energy can be maintained for electromagnetic radiation. There exists, of course, an overwhelming amount of such evidence.

[4] Cf. J. H. Poynting, *Scientific Papers*, Cambridge Univ. Press, Cambridge, 1920, Article 10, pp. 175–193; and *Phil Trans. Roy. Soc.*, **175**, 343 (1884).

flux. Thus we see that the direction rule for plane waves given in the last section also gives the rate of energy flow through a fixed surface.

Note that Eq. 10.4–5 would be satisfied if any quantity which integrates to zero over any closed surface were added to **N**. Experiment rules out such a possibility in most cases, but Problem 10.4*g* gives an example in which Eq. 10.4–6 gives paradoxical results.

An important question arises if we consider what happens to energy transferred to moving charges. They may accelerate, as in the case of ionic beams, with energy going into mechanical form. The charges may be moved into positions of higher potential energy, but only non-electrical energy can be involved, since we saw in Section 4.6 that the energy stored in a condenser may be calculated as if possessed by each charge ($\frac{1}{2} \Sigma qV$) *or* as if located in the field ($\frac{1}{2} \int \epsilon_0 E^2 \, d\tau$), but not in both ways at once. The theorem we have established includes electrostatic potential energy in the volume integral of Eq. 10.4–4, so that we cannot picture an additional gain of energy by the charges. Furthermore, we cannot picture currents as transporting energy directly—the energy associated with currents was calculated in Section 7.18 in terms of $\int (B^2/\mu_0) \, d\tau$.

Another demonstration that we cannot picture energy as being carried by a current is found if we consider the d-c case of a length L of a long straight cylindrical wire, of resistance R, and of radius r. If current i flows in it, the PD between its ends will be $V = iR$, and the electric field component parallel to the wire at its outside will be $E_x = V/L = iR/L$. The magnetic field H at the surface of the wire will be $H_\phi = i/2\pi r$. The Poynting vector **N** will then be directed into the wire, as a little consideration will show, and will have the magnitude

$$N = |\mathbf{E} \times \mathbf{H}| = E_x H_\phi = i^2 R/2\pi r L$$

Since $2\pi r L$ is the area of the outside of the wire, we see that the rate of flow of energy through its sides is

$$\int \mathbf{E} \times \mathbf{H} \cdot d\mathbf{S} = 2\pi r L E_x H_\phi = i^2 R \qquad (10.4–7)$$

which is the rate at which heat is developed. That is, all the Joule heat enters the wire through its sides in the form of Poynting flux and none enters through its two ends. This is actually not surprising when we consider that the current involves a continual jumping of electrons between energy levels, without any significant action of one electron on another. It is the fields that make the charges flow, and it is the fields from which this energy is derived.

As another example, consider the coaxial cable. We saw in Section 10.2 that the electric field is radial and that H has only a circuital component.

Thus $\mathbf{E} \times \mathbf{H}$ lies parallel to the axis of the cable. Taking as an element of area a coaxial ring of radius r and width dr in a plane perpendicular to the axis, we find the total rate of transfer of energy through the plane perpendicular to the axis to be

$$P = \int \mathbf{N} \cdot d\mathbf{S} = \int_a^b 2\pi r E_r H_\phi \, dr$$

which is easily evaluated by using $E_r = -\partial V/\partial r$ and $2\pi r H_\phi = i$, along with $V = 0$ when $r = b$, and $V = V_c$ when $r = a$:

$$P = \int_a^b \left(-\frac{\partial V}{\partial r}\right) i \, dr = i V_c \tag{10.4–8}$$

Thus the expected power transfer along the central wire can be calculated by use of Poynting's vector and can be considered as transferred through the space between the conductors. It is easy to see that the direction of $\mathbf{N}$ corresponds to the direction of progression of the waves, as discussed in Section 10.2.

The Momentum Theorem. Let us now turn to the question of momentum. The force on an object is the rate at which momentum is transferred to that object. The force per unit volume on the charges and currents in a given region is the rate of transfer of momentum per unit volume. We shall see that the total rate of transfer can be interpreted as the rate of decrease of momentum residing in the field. We can find this rate by writing the Lorentz force equation and substituting field expressions for the charge and current densities. We have, in fact,

$$\mathbf{f}_r = \rho\mathbf{E} + \mathbf{J} \times \mathbf{B}$$

$$= \epsilon_0\mathbf{E}(\nabla \cdot \mathbf{E}) + \left(\frac{1}{\mu_0}\nabla \times \mathbf{B} - \epsilon_0\frac{\partial \mathbf{E}}{\partial t}\right) \times \mathbf{B}$$

We shall convert this into an expression involving $\partial(\mathbf{E} \times \mathbf{B})/\partial t$ by adding to this equation another involving $-\epsilon_0\mathbf{E} \times \partial\mathbf{B}/\partial t$, namely, an equation derived from $\nabla \times \mathbf{E} = -\partial\mathbf{B}/\partial t$;

$$0 = -\epsilon_0\mathbf{E} \times (\nabla \times \mathbf{E}) - \epsilon_0\mathbf{E} \times \partial\mathbf{B}/\partial t$$

so that we get

$$\mathbf{f}_r = \epsilon_0\mathbf{E}(\nabla \cdot \mathbf{E}) - \frac{1}{\mu_0}\mathbf{B} \times (\nabla \times \mathbf{B}) - \epsilon_0\mathbf{E} \times (\nabla \times \mathbf{E}) - \epsilon_0\frac{\partial}{\partial t}(\mathbf{E} \times \mathbf{B})$$

All terms but the last can be converted into forms that on volume integration become surface integrals. Let us convert each triple vector product into the sum of two terms and use bars again to indicate the range of action of the derivatives in $\mathbf{V}$. For the $\mathbf{B}$ term, we have

$$\mathbf{B} \times (\mathbf{V} \times \mathbf{B}) = \overline{\mathbf{V}(\mathbf{B} \cdot \mathbf{B})} - (\mathbf{B} \cdot \overline{\mathbf{V}})\mathbf{B}$$
$$= \tfrac{1}{2}\overline{\mathbf{V}(\mathbf{B} \cdot \mathbf{B})} - (\mathbf{B} \cdot \overline{\mathbf{V}})\mathbf{B}$$

Now, since $\mathbf{V} \cdot \mathbf{B} = 0$, we have $\overline{(\mathbf{V} \cdot \mathbf{B})}\mathbf{B} = 0$, so that we can add this expression to $(\mathbf{B} \cdot \overline{\mathbf{V}})\mathbf{B}$ and obtain $\overline{(\mathbf{V} \cdot \mathbf{B})\mathbf{B}}$ in which the derivatives operate on each $\mathbf{B}$ vector. For the $\mathbf{E}$ term there already is an $\overline{(\mathbf{V} \cdot \mathbf{E})}\mathbf{E}$ term in the equation to combine with an $(\mathbf{E} \cdot \overline{\mathbf{V}})\mathbf{E}$ term. The final result for $\mathbf{f}_r$ is

$$\mathbf{f}_r = -\epsilon_0 \frac{\partial}{\partial t}(\mathbf{E} \times \mathbf{B}) - \frac{1}{2\mu_0}\nabla B^2 - \frac{\epsilon_0}{2}\nabla E^2$$
$$+ \frac{1}{\mu_0}\overline{(\mathbf{V} \cdot \mathbf{B})\mathbf{B}} + \epsilon_0\overline{(\mathbf{V} \cdot \mathbf{E})\mathbf{E}} \quad (10.4\text{--}9)$$

Let us integrate this expression over an arbitrary volume τ to find the rate of transfer of momentum to the charges in τ. Using the vector theorems A.2–24 and A.2–27 to convert all but the first term on the right into integrals over the surface S of τ, we obtain

$$\int_\tau \mathbf{f}_r \, d\tau = -\epsilon_0 \frac{d}{d\tau}\int_\tau \mathbf{E} \times \mathbf{B} \, d\tau - \tfrac{1}{2}\int_S \left(\frac{1}{\mu_0}B^2 + \epsilon_0 E^2\right)d\mathbf{S}$$
$$+ \int_S \frac{1}{\mu_0}\mathbf{B}(\mathbf{B} \cdot d\mathbf{S}) + \int_S \epsilon_0\mathbf{E}(\mathbf{E} \cdot d\mathbf{S}) \quad (10.4\text{--}10)$$

Just as in the energy calculation, we get an interpretation of the volume integral by taking a volume so large that the fields are negligible all over its surface.[5] In view of our remarks on momentum we see that each unit volume in the electromagnetic field appears to carry momentum in the amount

$$\mathbf{G}_r = \epsilon_0(\mathbf{E} \times \mathbf{B}) = \frac{1}{c^2}(\mathbf{E} \times \mathbf{H}) \quad (10.4\text{--}11a)$$

in free space. For a linear medium, we can write

$$\mathbf{G}_r = \mathbf{D} \times \mathbf{B} = \epsilon\mu(\mathbf{E} \times \mathbf{H}) \quad (10.4\text{--}12)$$

(Problem 10.4f).

---

[5] In cases in which radiation goes off to "infinity," it is not possible to set the surface integrals equal to zero in either calculation. However, this mathematical difficulty, which is handled in detail in more advanced texts, in no way modifies our interpretations of the vector $\mathbf{E} \times \mathbf{H}$.

The fact that moving charges can exchange momentum with the field shows that the sum of the momenta of a set of charges *per se* is not conserved, and therefore that the law of action and reaction is not valid in general (see Problem 10.4*d*).

If we now consider the surface integrals in cases in which they do not vanish, we interpret these integrals as representing forces per unit area, or stresses, exerted on the region within the surface by the fields without. Considerations of this sort lead to the study of the so-called Maxwell stress tensor but are too complicated to consider in this book (see, however, Problem 10.4*h*).

Let us close with a remark on the relation between G_r and **N**. When an electromagnetic wave travels perpendicularly through a given surface in space at the speed c, a volume of radiation equal in magnitude to c passes each square meter each second. The amount of momentum that passes per square meter per second is therefore equal to N/c, whereas the transport of energy is N per square meter per second. Corresponding to any transported quantity of energy U there is therefore a momentum transport of magnitude U/c. For instance, according to the quantum theory electromagnetic energy is transported in units of $h\nu$, where ν is the frequency of the wave motion. Then each photon of energy $h\nu$ must carry momentum $h\nu/c = h/\lambda$. This result has been verified by experiments such as the Compton effect in which the energy and momentum transferred to an electron by a single X ray photon can be detected.

The Gaussian equations for U, **N**, and G_r are

$$U = \int_\tau \frac{1}{8\pi} (\mathbf{B} \cdot \mathbf{H} + \mathbf{D} \cdot \mathbf{E})\, d\tau \qquad \text{Gaussian} \qquad (10.4\text{--}4c)$$

$$\mathbf{N} = \frac{c}{4\pi} (\mathbf{E} \times \mathbf{H}) \qquad \text{Gaussian} \qquad (10.4\text{--}6b)$$

$$\mathbf{G}_r = \frac{1}{4\pi c} (\mathbf{E} \times \mathbf{H}) \qquad \text{Gaussian} \qquad (10.4\text{--}11b)$$

Problem 10.4a. Use the Poynting vector to calculate the energy flow from a parallel-plate condenser being discharged through a resistor R and draw a sketch showing the paths along which energy flows to R.

Problem 10.4b. Using the surface integrals in Eq. 10.4–10, find the stress (*a*) in the y-direction on a surface whose normal lies in the z-direction and (*b*) in the y-direction on a surface whose normal lies in the y-direction.

Problem 10.4c. Show that the angular momentum about a given origin $\mathcal{O}$ that is carried by electromagnetic radiation is $\mathbf{r} \times \mathbf{G}_r$, by starting with Eq. 10.4–9 and calculating the integral of $\mathbf{r} \times \mathbf{f}_r$. *Hints:* it will be necessary to use Eqs. A.2–26 and A.2–27, and item 13 in Table A.2B, which in turn can be derived from item 4.

Problem 10.4d. Consider two charges separated by a vector distance **r** whose velocities are $\mathbf{v}_1$ and $\mathbf{v}_2$, so oriented that the planes that each makes with **r** are mutually perpendicular, and $\mathbf{v}_1$ is perpendicular to **r** while $\mathbf{v}_2$ makes an angle of $45°$ with **r**. Show that the forces of each on the other fail to obey the law of action and reaction and show without a detailed calculation how the momentum theorem, Eq. 10.4–10, preserves the conservation of momentum in spite of this failure.

Problem 10.4e. Derive Eqs. 10.4–3 and 5 for arbitrary materials, assuming P to be the power expended only on free charges. Show that 10.4–4b is correct for *linear* media.

Problem 10.4f. Verify Eq. 10.4–12 for linear media.

Problem 10.4g. Show that Eq. 10.4–6 implies a steady circulation of energy around a bar magnet that carries a positive electrostatic charge. Discuss the physical significance of this result.

Problem 10.4h. Consider a particular surface element **dS** for the integrals of Eq. 10.4–10, and write the three components of force associated with each of the components of **dS**, in the form of a tensor (cf. Section 7.19).

10.5   Magnetohydrodynamics

The domain of plasma physics is the study of oscillations in an ionized gas of sufficiently high frequency to produce two effects: charge separations such as those described in Section 3.5, and acceleration of electrons and ions in between collisions so that Ohm's law is no longer valid. The domain of magnetohydrodynamics, on the other hand, is the treatment of conducting fluids at low enough frequencies that they remain ohmic and electrically neutral, with sufficiently steady currents that the displacement-current term in Maxwell's equations may be neglected. Needless to say, many magnetohydrodynamic effects are found in actual plasmas. Certain elementary aspects of magnetohydrodynamics follow readily from the material we have discussed above and are of interest to present here.

A fluid of mass density m_r and variable velocity **v** obeys the equation of conservation of mass:

$$\nabla \cdot (m_r \mathbf{v}) + \frac{\partial m_r}{\partial t} = 0 \qquad (10.5\text{–}1)$$

in exact analogy to the equation of continuity of charge (5.2–18a). Newton's law $\mathbf{F} = M\mathbf{a}$ becomes for a unit volume of the fluid

$$\mathbf{f}_r = -\nabla p + \mathbf{J} \times \mathbf{B} + \mathbf{f}_{\text{visc}} + m_r \mathbf{g} = m_r \left(\frac{\partial}{\partial t} + \mathbf{v} \cdot \nabla \right) \mathbf{v} \qquad (10.5\text{–}2)$$

The force terms on the left are $-\nabla p$, the gradient of the hydrostatic pressure in the fluid, the magnetic force $\mathbf{J} \times \mathbf{B}$, the viscous force $\mathbf{f}_{\text{visc}}$ and the force of gravity $m_r\mathbf{g}$. On the right side of the equation, the acceleration $d\mathbf{v}/dt$ must be calculated by a time derivative at the position of the moving volume element, so we use the convective derivative

$$\frac{d}{dt} = \frac{\partial}{\partial t} + \mathbf{v} \cdot \nabla \qquad (10.5\text{-}3)$$

applied to the vector $\mathbf{v}(x, y, z, t)$ as a function of both space and time.[6]

If ρ and $\partial\mathbf{D}/\partial t$ are omitted from the force calculation in Section 10.4, Eq. 10.4–9 may be written

$$\mathbf{J} \times \mathbf{B} = -\frac{1}{2\mu_0}\nabla B^2 + \frac{1}{\mu_0}(\mathbf{B} \cdot \nabla)\mathbf{B} \qquad (10.5\text{-}4)$$

which shows that the quantity $B^2/2\mu_0$ may be added to the mechanical pressure p as a sort of magnetic pressure.[7] The second term of 10.5–4 is a tension along the lines of force. We have then for the net force per unit volume from Eq. 10.5–2,

$$\begin{aligned} \mathbf{f}_r &= -\nabla(p + B^2/2\mu_0) + (\mathbf{B} \cdot \nabla)\mathbf{B}/\mu_0 + \mathbf{f}_{\text{visc}} + m_r\mathbf{g} \\ &= m_r[\partial\mathbf{v}/\partial t + (\mathbf{v} \cdot \nabla)\mathbf{v}] \end{aligned} \qquad (10.5\text{-}5)$$

This result may be used to discuss the pinch effect in a conducting fluid cylinder that carries a current density $\mathbf{J}(r)$ everywhere parallel to the axis. The magnetic induction $\mathbf{B}$ will have only a hoop component $B_\varphi = B(r)$ and since $\partial\mathbf{1}_\varphi/\partial\varphi = -\mathbf{1}_r$ (cf. Appendix A.2, Problem A.2d) we have

$$\mathbf{f}_r(r) = -\left[\frac{dp}{dr} + \frac{B}{\mu_0}\frac{dB}{dr} + \frac{B^2}{\mu_0 r}\right]\mathbf{1}_r \qquad (10.5\text{-}6)$$

where we have neglected viscous and gravitational forces. If we treat the volume force $\mathbf{f}_r$ as produced by an equivalent total pressure p_{eq}, i.e., $\mathbf{f}_r = -\nabla p_{\text{eq}}$, we can integrate Eq. 10.5–6 and obtain

$$p_{\text{eq}} = p + \frac{B^2}{2\mu_0} + \frac{1}{\mu_0}\int_0^r \frac{B^2(r')\,dr'}{r'} \qquad (10.5\text{-}7)$$

where the constant of integration is included in p.

As a special case, let us assume that because the magnetic field and current were built up together in an originally field-free region, the action

---

[6] Two simple applications of convective derivatives were made in Section 7.13.

[7] The connection between this magnetic pressure and the equally valued magnetic energy per unit volume can be made clear if we remember that the ordinary hydrostatic pressure p may be treated as a potential energy per unit volume, for instance in Bernoulli's theorem.

of Lenz's law excluded **B** from the current-carrying region. If r in 10.5–7 is taken as the radius R at the boundary of the conducting cylinder, the integral in the third term will vanish. Furthermore, the hydrostatic pressure will drop just where the magnetic pressure attains appreciable value. We see that the magnetic field excites an inward pressure on the fluid—a fact which follows qualitatively from the Lorentz force law and Ampère's law. Since $B = \mu_d i / 2\pi R$ where i is the total current, we see that if the magnetic pressure exceeds p and compresses the cylinder to a smaller value of R, $B^2/2\mu_0$ will increase and the cylinder will be further compressed with the

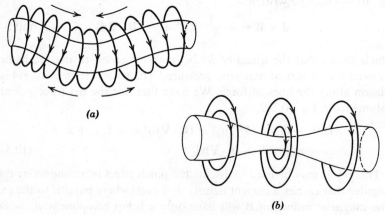

(a)

(b)

Fig. 10.5a.   Instabilities caused by the pinch effect: (a) The expansion of a kink; (b) an unstable contraction or "pinch." (From Jackson, *loc. cit.*, p. 327, Fig. 10.8.)

cycle repeating until the column is cut off, i.e., "pinched." If a balance is obtained between the hydrostatic and magnetic pressures, it will be unstable. Figure 10.5a shows how this instability can either lead to a pinching-off of the current or the expansion of a "kink."

Let us turn now to the trapping of magnetic flux in a magnetohydrodynamic fluid. The assumption of infinite conductivity that was considered in Chapter 7 provides a first approximation. Let us now assume that the conductivity is finite and use Ohm's law for a moving medium, Eq. 10.1–8, to eliminate **E** from $\nabla \times \mathbf{E} = -\partial \mathbf{B}/\partial t$. We have

$$\frac{\partial \mathbf{B}}{\partial t} = -\frac{1}{\sigma_c} \nabla \times \mathbf{J} + \nabla \times (\mathbf{v} \times \mathbf{B})$$

Using now $\nabla \times \mathbf{B} = \mu_0 \mathbf{J}$ (displacement currents are neglected), we get

$$\frac{\partial \mathbf{B}}{\partial t} = \frac{1}{\mu_0 \sigma_c} \nabla^2 \mathbf{B} + \nabla \times (\mathbf{v} \times \mathbf{B}) \tag{10.5–8}$$

For a frame of reference moving with the fluid, **v** is zero and Eq. 10.5–8 resembles the equation for the diffusion of heat,

$$\frac{\partial \mathbf{B}}{\partial t} = \frac{1}{\mu_0 \sigma_c} \nabla^2 \mathbf{B} = \frac{1}{\mu_0 \sigma_c}\left(\frac{\partial^2}{\partial x^2} + \frac{\partial^2}{\partial y^2} + \frac{\partial^2}{\partial z^2}\right)\mathbf{B} \qquad (10.5\text{–}9)$$

In a case in which **B** varies only in the x-direction, it is easy to verify by differentiation under the integral sign that a solution of 10.5–9 is[8]

$$\mathbf{B}(x, t) = \left(\frac{\mu_0 \sigma_c}{4\pi t}\right)^{1/2} \int\limits_{-\infty}^{\infty} dx'\, e^{-\mu_0 \sigma_c (x-x')^2/4t} \mathbf{B}_0(x') \qquad (10.5\text{–}10)$$

When t is very small, the exponent is large and negative unless x' is very near x. Thus as t goes to zero, we can replace $\mathbf{B}_0(x')$ with $B_0(x)$, whereupon the integral can be evaluated as equal to $(4\pi t/\mu_0\sigma_c)^{1/2}$. We see that $\mathbf{B}_0(x)$ is the initial field $\mathbf{B}(x, 0)$. Now if t is large, the exponent in 10.5–10 is small and the result of the integration is to "smear out" the initial field. A criterion for the largeness of t may be derived if we assume that in a region around a given point x, $\mathbf{B}_0$ is essentially constant over a range between $x - l$ and $x + l$. The effect of smearing out will just begin at such a time that $\mu_0\sigma_c l^2/4t$ falls to the order of unity. We shall call this time the diffusion time t_d, and write

$$t_d = \tfrac{1}{4}\mu_0\sigma_c l^2 \qquad (10.5\text{–}11)$$

A magnetic field once set up in a conductor will decay in a time of the order of t_d. For a copper disk 1 cm in diameter, we have by Table 5.1A $t_d \sim \pi \times 10^{-7} \times 6 \times 10^7 \times 10^{-2} \sim 0.2$ sec. For a hydrogen plasma at 3000°K, σ_c is about 250 mhos/m. A magnetic cloud in the sun's corona with $l \sim 10^4$ km would have $t_d \sim \pi \times 10^{-7} \times 250 \times 10^{14} \sim 8 \times 10^9$ secs or about 300 years. Estimations of t_d for the earth's magnetic core and the sun's interior are of the order of 10^4 years and 10^{10} years, respectively.

For times short compared to t_d, the first term in 10.5–8 can be neglected, which amounts to assuming infinite conductivity. Let us use Eq. 10.5–8 with $\sigma_c = \infty$ together with 10.5–1 to show in detail how the magnetic field "moves" with the fluid. From 10.5–1 we find

$$m_\tau \, \mathbf{\nabla} \cdot \mathbf{v} + (\mathbf{v} \cdot \mathbf{\nabla})m_\tau + \frac{\partial m_\tau}{\partial t} = 0$$

and from 10.5–8

$$\frac{\partial \mathbf{B}}{\partial t} = \mathbf{\nabla} \times (\mathbf{v} \times \mathbf{B}) = \overline{(\mathbf{\nabla} \cdot \mathbf{B})\mathbf{v}} - \overline{(\mathbf{\nabla} \cdot \mathbf{v})\mathbf{B}}$$

$$= (\mathbf{B} \cdot \mathbf{\nabla})\mathbf{v} - \mathbf{B}(\mathbf{\nabla} \cdot \mathbf{v}) - (\mathbf{v} \cdot \mathbf{\nabla})\mathbf{B}$$

[8] A clear and careful discussion of the heat equation is given in R. V. Churchill, *Fourier Series and Boundary Value Problems*, 2nd ed., McGraw-Hill, New York, 1963, sec. 66.

If each equation is divided by m_r and $\nabla \cdot \mathbf{v}$ is eliminated, we find after some manipulation

$$\left(\frac{\partial}{\partial t} + \mathbf{v} \cdot \nabla\right)\left(\frac{\mathbf{B}}{m_r}\right) = \left(\frac{\mathbf{B}}{m_r} \cdot \nabla\right)\mathbf{v} \qquad (10.5\text{--}12)$$

However, this equation is the same as the equation for the motion of a short vector of length $\boldsymbol{\delta l}$ connecting two particles of fluid. If the particle at the tail end of $\boldsymbol{\delta l}$ has velocity $\mathbf{v}$, that at its head end has velocity $\mathbf{v} + (\boldsymbol{\delta l} \cdot \nabla)\mathbf{v}$ and the net addition to $\boldsymbol{\delta l}$ in time dt is $(\boldsymbol{\delta l} \cdot \nabla)\mathbf{v}\, dt$. This change is also given by the convective derivative d/dt, so we have in fact

$$\left(\frac{\partial}{\partial t} + \mathbf{v} \cdot \nabla\right)\boldsymbol{\delta l} = (\boldsymbol{\delta l} \cdot \nabla)\mathbf{v} \qquad (10.5\text{--}13)$$

showing that the variation of $\mathbf{B}/m_r$ at the moving position of a particle is the same as that of a vector $\boldsymbol{\delta l}$. If $\boldsymbol{\delta l}$ is originally parallel to $\mathbf{B}$, it will remain so—particles originally on a line of force remain on it. In this sense, then, as well as in the sense of retaining constant flux through any surface moving with the fluid, we can speak of lines of magnetic induction as moving with the fluid.

When the resistivity is not negligible, the fluid does not precisely move with the field. It is clear that magnetic forces can only influence particle motion in directions perpendicular to $\mathbf{B}$. Using Ohm's law, we can write the magnetic force as

$$\mathbf{J} \times \mathbf{B} = \sigma_c[\mathbf{E} \times \mathbf{B} + (\mathbf{v} \times \mathbf{B}) \times \mathbf{B}]$$
$$= \sigma_c B^2(\mathbf{v}_d - \mathbf{v} + \mathbf{v}_\parallel) = \sigma_c B^2(\mathbf{v}_d - \mathbf{v}_\perp) \qquad (10.5\text{--}14)$$

where $\mathbf{v}_d = (\mathbf{E} \times \mathbf{B})/B^2$ is the drift velocity defined in Section 7.3, $\mathbf{v}_\parallel = \mathbf{1}_B(\mathbf{v} \cdot \mathbf{B})/B$ is the component of $\mathbf{v}$ parallel to $\mathbf{B}$, and $\mathbf{v}_\perp = \mathbf{v} - \mathbf{v}_\parallel$ is the perpendicular component. The coefficient $-\sigma_c B^2$ of $\mathbf{v}_\perp$ acts exactly like a viscous-force term in Eq. 10.5–2, showing that the magnetic field tends to modify or "drag" the velocity $\mathbf{v}_\perp$ until it is equal to $\mathbf{v}_d$, which is clearly the value of $\mathbf{v}_\perp$ for the case of infinite conductivity.

To calculate energy transport in a moving conducting fluid, one needs not only Poynting's theorem but also theorems governing both the viscous and thermodynamic properties of fluids. We refer the reader elsewhere for details.[9]

To write the equations of this section in Gaussian units, we may do the following: Multiply $\mathbf{J} \times \mathbf{B}$ in 10.5–2 by $1/c$; replace μ_0 in 10.5–4 with $4\pi/c$; replace μ_0 with 4π in Eq. 10.5–7 so the ordinary magnetic pressure term becomes

[9] L. D. Landau and E. M. Lifshitz, *Electrodynamics of Continuous Media*, Addison-Wesley, Reading, Mass., 1960, pp. 214–5.

$B^2/8\pi$; replace $\mu_0\sigma_c$ in 10.5–8 to 10.5–11 with $4\pi\sigma_c/c^2$; and multiply the left side of 10.5–14 by $1/c$ and the right side by $1/c^2$.

Problem 10.5a. If a current in a cylindrical plasma is to be kept in at least temporary balance by means of the perfect-gas pressure $p = NkT$, find the necessary current i when $N = 10^{21}$ particles/m^3, $R = 5$ cm, and $T = 10^8\ °K$.

Problem 10.5b. Assume that $\mathbf{v}$ is originally parallel to $\mathbf{v}_d$ in a conducting fluid and that no non-magnetic forces act in the $\mathbf{v}$ direction, and find how $\mathbf{v}$ varies in time at a point moving with the fluid. Define an appropriate decay time for the effects of magnetic viscosity.

Problem 10.5c. Show how to relate t_d of Eq. 10.5–11 to the time constant of Eq. 7.16–4.

10.6 Dipole and Plane-Sheet Radiation

Let us now calculate the fields produced at an arbitrary distance from an element of current. It is clear that an isolated current element is not a meaningful concept, since we must either consider a closed circuit or we must take into account the charges on conductors at the ends of the element. We shall use the latter method of constructing a suitable element. Let us suppose we have two small fixed spherical conductors a distance δl apart, connected with a thin straight wire. Let q and $-q$ denote the amounts of charge on the two conductors (together they constitute a dipole), and let $i = dq/dt$ be the current between them. A series of such elements can be added so as to be equivalent to a long antenna with uniform or non-uniform current and charge distributions.

It will be convenient to take a specific frequency and to write charge and current as complex quantities. Vector quantities that are also complex will be written in bold-face sans-serif type, e.g., $\mathbf{E}$. We write the charge as $q = q_{max}\,e^{j\omega t}$ and the current as $i = i_{max}\,e^{j\omega t} = j\omega q_{max}\,e^{j\omega t}$. The dipole moment $\mathbf{p}$ is given by $\mathbf{p} = q\,\delta l = q_{max}\,\delta l\,e^{j\omega t} = p_{max}\,e^{j\omega t}$. Figure 10.5a shows such an oscillating dipole with a set of coordinates for use in describing the potentials and fields.

The vector potential at point $\mathscr{P}$ in the figure is readily found by using Eq. 10.3–16:

$$\mathbf{A} = \frac{\mu_0 i_{ret}}{4\pi r}\,\delta l = \frac{\mu_0 j\omega q_{max}}{4\pi r}\,e^{j\omega(t-r/c)}\,\delta l \qquad (10.6–1)$$

The scalar potential is the difference between the retarded potentials of q and $-q$. By a calculation similar to that of Section 3.1, we have

$$V = -\delta l \cdot \nabla(q_{ret}/4\pi\epsilon_0 r) = \delta l \cdot \nabla(q_{max}\,e^{j\omega(t-r/c)}/4\pi\epsilon_0 r)$$

Now, since the potential $q/4\pi\epsilon_0 r$ is a function of r and t but not of θ or ϕ, the only relevant component of ∇ is $\mathbf{1}_r\,\partial/\partial r$. Thus we have $(\delta\mathbf{l}\cdot\nabla) = \delta l\cos\theta\,\partial/\partial r$, and

$$V = \frac{-\delta l q_{max}\cos\theta}{4\pi\epsilon_0}\frac{\partial}{\partial r}\left[\frac{e^{j\omega(t-r/c)}}{r}\right] = \frac{\delta l q_{max}\cos\theta}{4\pi\epsilon_0\lambda^2}\left[\frac{\lambda^2}{r^2} + \frac{j\lambda}{r}\right]e^{j\omega(t-r/c)}$$

$$(10.6-2)$$

The reader will find it easy to show that $\nabla\cdot\mathbf{A} + \mu_0\epsilon_0\,\partial V/\partial t = 0$ in this case if he notes that only $\partial/\partial r$ can give a non-vanishing result in the divergence and that $\delta\mathbf{l}\cdot\mathbf{1}_r = \delta l\cos\theta$.

Now let us find the field vectors $\mathbf{E}$ and $\mathbf{B}$. Again using only the $\mathbf{1}_r\,\partial/\partial r$ part of ∇ and noting that $\mathbf{1}_r\times\mathbf{1}_z = -\sin\theta\,\mathbf{1}_\phi$, we have $\nabla\times\mathbf{A} = \mathbf{1}_r\times\mathbf{1}_z\,\partial A/\partial r = -\sin\theta\,\mathbf{1}_\phi\,\partial A/\partial r$, or

$$\mathbf{B} = \frac{\mu_0 j\omega\,\delta l}{4\pi}q_{max}\frac{\partial}{\partial r}\left[\frac{e^{j\omega(t-r/c)}}{r}\right]\mathbf{1}_r\times\mathbf{1}_z$$

$$= \frac{\mu_0\omega\,\delta l q_{max}\sin\theta}{4\pi\lambda^2}\left[\frac{j\lambda^2}{r^2} - \frac{\lambda}{r}\right]e^{j\omega(t-r/c)}\mathbf{1}_\phi \qquad (10.6-3)$$

The first term of this expression is easily seen to be just the magnetic induction calculated by Laplace's rule for steady current elements, Eq. 7.6-3. The second arises from the retarded part of the potential and will shortly be seen to involve radiation. Note that the first term is dominant when r/λ is small, and the second when r/λ is large.

The electric field calculation is more complex. We will have a component parallel to $\delta\mathbf{l}$ from $\mathbf{A}$ along with θ and r components from $\nabla V = \mathbf{1}_r(\partial V/\partial r) + \mathbf{1}_\theta(\partial V/\partial\theta)(1/r)$:

$$\mathbf{E} = -\frac{\partial\mathbf{A}}{\partial t} - \nabla V = \frac{\mu_0\omega^3 q_{max}}{4\pi c}\cdot\frac{\lambda}{r}e^{j\omega(t-r/c)}\,\delta\mathbf{l}$$

$$- \frac{\delta l q_{max}\cos\theta}{4\pi\epsilon_0\lambda^3}\left[-\frac{2\lambda^3}{r^3} - \frac{2j\lambda^2}{r^2} + \frac{\lambda}{r}\right]e^{j\omega(t-r/c)}\mathbf{1}_r$$

$$+ \frac{\delta l q_{max}\sin\theta}{4\pi\epsilon_0\lambda^3}\left[\frac{\lambda^2}{r^3} + \frac{j\lambda}{r}\right]e^{j\omega(t-r/c)}\mathbf{1}_0$$

We can combine the term in $\delta\mathbf{l}$ with the other two if we write $\delta\mathbf{l}$ as a sum of vectors along $\mathbf{1}_r$ and $\mathbf{1}_\theta$:

$$\delta\mathbf{l} = (\delta\mathbf{l}\cdot\mathbf{1}_r)\mathbf{1}_r + (\delta\mathbf{l}\cdot\mathbf{1}_\theta)\mathbf{1}_\theta = (\mathbf{1}_r\cos\theta - \mathbf{1}_\theta\sin\theta)\,\delta l$$

as can be seen from Fig. 10.6a. We also need the relation $\mu_0 = 1/c^2\epsilon_0$. Then **E** becomes

$$\mathbf{E} = \frac{q_{max}\,\delta l\,\cos\theta}{4\pi\epsilon_0 \lambda^3}\left(\frac{2\lambda^3}{r^3} + \frac{2j\lambda^2}{r^2}\right) e^{j\omega(t-r/c)}\mathbf{1}_r$$

$$+ \frac{q_{max}\,\delta l\,\sin\theta}{4\pi\epsilon_0 \lambda^3}\left(\frac{\lambda^3}{r^3} + \frac{j\lambda}{r^2} - \frac{\lambda}{r}\right) e^{j\omega(t-r/c)}\mathbf{1}_\theta \quad (10.6\text{-}4)$$

It will be noted that the terms involving $1/r^3$ are exactly the static dipole field expressions, as in Eq. 3.1–7. The $1/r$ term is the largest one at great

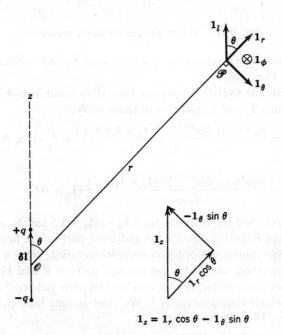

Fig. 10.6a. An oscillating dipole. The vector $\mathbf{1}_\phi$ at $\mathscr{P}$ is directed into the page.

distances. It is readily seen that this term bears a relation to the $1/r$ term in **B** exactly like that for plane waves—namely, that $E_\theta/c = B_\phi$. Furthermore, $E_\theta\mathbf{1}_\theta$ and $B_\phi\mathbf{1}_\phi$ are perpendicular to each other and to $\mathbf{1}_r$ and related so that $\mathbf{E} \times \mathbf{B}$ for these components points outwardly along $\mathbf{1}_r$, (cf. Fig. 10.6b). These components comprise the radiation part of the field. It is interesting to note that the two $\mathbf{1}_r/r$ terms in E_r that come respectively from **A** and V exactly cancel each other, in a similar fashion to the cancellation of the axial field in the coaxial cable.

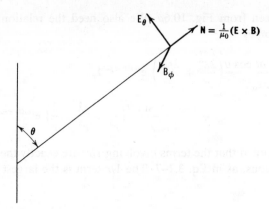

Fig. 10.6b.   Vector relations for dipole radiation.

Curves showing instantaneous lines of force for an oscillating dipole are given in Fig. 10.6c.[10]

Let us write the radiation terms of Eqs. 10.6–3 and 10.6–4 in terms of the unit vectors $\mathbf{1}_z$ and $\mathbf{1}_r$ and also in terms of $\mathbf{A}$:

$$\mathbf{E}_{\text{rad}} = \frac{\mu_0 \omega^2 q_{\max}\, \delta l e^{j\omega(t-r/c)}[(\mathbf{1}_r \times \mathbf{1}_z) \times \mathbf{1}_r]}{4\pi r} = \frac{jc}{\lambda}(\mathbf{1}_r \times \mathbf{A}) \times \mathbf{1}_r$$

(10.6–5a)

$$\mathbf{B}_{\text{rad}} = \frac{\mu_0 \omega^2 q_{\max}\, \delta l e^{j\omega(t-r/c)}(\mathbf{1}_r \times \mathbf{1}_z)}{4\pi c r} = \frac{j}{\lambda}(\mathbf{1}_r \times \mathbf{A})$$

(10.6–5b)

where we have used the relations $\sin\theta\,\mathbf{1}_\phi = (\mathbf{1}_z \times \mathbf{1}_r)$ and $\mathbf{1}_\theta = \mathbf{1}_\phi \times \mathbf{1}_r$.

The average Poynting flux for the radiation part of the field is readily calculated. We cannot use ordinary complex notation, since a power calculation is involved, and so we use the real parts of $\mathbf{E}$ and $\mathbf{H}$. Since the two quantities are in phase, products of the real parts yield $\cos^2 \omega(t - r/c)$, a quantity whose time average is $\frac{1}{2}$. We shall assume that $q_{\max}$ is a real number $q_{\max}$. Thus we can write

$$\mathbf{N}_{\text{rad}} = \mathbf{E}_{\text{rad}} \times \mathbf{H}_{\text{rad}} = \frac{c}{\lambda^2 \mu_0} \sin^2\theta [\text{Re }A]^2 \mathbf{1}_r$$

$$= \frac{\mu_0 c^3 q_{\max}^2\, \delta l^2}{16\pi^2 r^2 \lambda^4} \sin^2\theta \cos^2 \omega(t - r/c)\mathbf{1}_r$$

(10.6–6)

and

$$\mathbf{N}_{\text{rad,av}} = \frac{\mu_0 c^3 q_{\max}^2\, \delta l^2 \sin^2\theta}{32\pi^2 \lambda^4 r^2} \mathbf{1}_r$$

(10.6–7)

[10] See also W. K. H. Panofsky and M. Phillips, *Classical Electricity and Magnetism*, 2nd ed., Addison-Wesley, Reading, Mass., 1962, p. 259. Considerable detail on dipole radiation is given by Corson and Lorrain, *op. cit.*, Chapter 13.

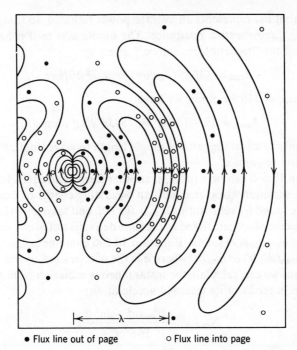

• Flux line out of page   ○ Flux line into page

Fig. 10.6c. Electric field lines and dots indicating magnetic field lines for a radiating dipole. The magnetic lines are circles about an axis through the antenna. (From H. H. Skilling, *Fundamentals of Electric Waves*, 2nd ed., John Wiley and Sons, New York, 1948, p. 169.)

which yields for the time average of the total energy radiated through a sphere of radius r,

$$P_{av} = \left(\int \mathbf{N} \cdot \mathbf{dS} \right)_{av} = \frac{\mu_0 c^3 q_{max}^2 \, \delta l^2}{32 \pi^2 \lambda^4 r^2} \int_0^\pi 2\pi r^2 \sin^3 \theta \, d\theta$$

and since

$$\int_0^\pi \sin^3 \theta \, d\theta = 4/3$$

we have

$$P_{av} = \frac{\mu_0 c^3 q_{max}^2 \, \delta l^2}{12 \pi \lambda^4} = \frac{\mu_0 c^3 p_{max}^2}{12 \pi \lambda^4} = \frac{\mu_0 c i_{max}^2 \, \delta l^2}{12 \pi \lambda^2} \tag{10.6-8}$$

It can be seen that the total rate of radiation depends on the fourth power of the frequency for a given amplitude of oscillation of the dipole and on the square of the frequency for a given current amplitude.

The symbol P_{av} represents an average power radiated, so that the coefficient of $\frac{1}{2}i^2_{max}$ represents a resistance. The dipole acts as if it had a resistance, called the "radiation resistance," given by

$$R_{rad} = (\delta l/\lambda)^2(\mu_0 c/6\pi) = \mu_0\omega^2\,\delta l^2/6\pi c \qquad (10.6\text{--}9a)$$

and since $\mu_0 c = 119.9\pi$ ohms, we have

$$R_{rad} = 19.98(\delta l/\lambda)^2 = 789.0(\delta l/\lambda)^2 \text{ ohms} \qquad (10.6\text{--}9b)$$

We need only to know the ratio of dipole length to wave length to calculate the radiation resistance.

Equation 10.6–6 can be written in another form. The equivalent current and dipole variation associated with an oscillating charge of fixed amount q_{max} can be found by substituting $q_{max}v$ for $i\,\delta l$, and taking v to be a simple harmonic expression, calculated as the time derivative of $\delta l \cos \omega t$. Thus we write $q_{max}v$ as $q_{max}\omega\,\delta l \sin \omega t$. Equation 10.6–6 contains $q_{max}\omega^2\,\delta l \cos \omega t$, which is $q_{max}(dv/dt)$ or $q_{max}a$, where a is the acceleration of the oscillating charge. Thus we can calculate the instantaneous radiation from an oscillating charge in terms of its retarded acceleration:

$$\mathbf{N}_{rad} = \frac{\mu_0 q^2_{max}a^2_{ret}\sin^2\theta}{16\pi^2 cr^2}\mathbf{1}_r \qquad (10.6\text{--}10)$$

with the total instantaneous rate, in all directions:

$$P = \frac{\mu_0 q^2_{max}a^2_{ret}}{6\pi c} \qquad (10.6\text{--}11)$$

Radiation by Accelerated Charges. We have only derived the last two formulas for charges executing SHM; furthermore, the substitution of $q_{max}v$ for $i\,\delta l$ is not easy to justify rigorously. However, the radiation from an accelerated charge may be found exactly from the Liénard-Wiechert potentials given in Section 10.3.

Let us first note that in the calculation on pp. 549–50 of the potentials produced by a uniformly moving charge, the constancy of $\mathbf{v}$ was used only in the interpretation of point $\mathscr{Q}''$ of Fig. 10.3b as the point to which the particle has arrived at time t. If the particle is accelerated it will be at some other point $\mathscr{Q}'''$ at t, although it is still its velocity $\mathbf{v}$ and position $\mathscr{Q}'$ at time t' that determines $\mathbf{A}$ and V (see Fig. 10.6d).

In calculating $\mathbf{E}$ and $\mathbf{B}$ from $\mathbf{A}$ and V we now have the difficulty that $\mathbf{v}$ varies with t' and hence with x, y, z, and t through $t' = t - r/c$. There will still be contributions to $\mathbf{E}$ and $\mathbf{B}$ that do not take this variation into account, but these fields will be respectively oriented radially and hoopwise to a point and a line that no longer represent the actual position and velocity of the charge. The same contributions calculated for a later time

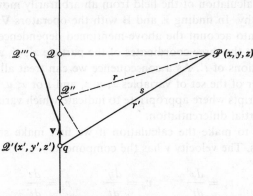

Fig. 10.6d. Illustrating the calculation of the fields of an arbitrarily moving charged particle. $\mathcal{Q}'$ is the retarded position for time t', $\mathcal{Q}''$ the position the particle would have reached at time t, and $\mathcal{Q}'''$ the actual position of the particle at time t.

will then have a different geometrical locations. Roughly speaking we can say that the effect of the acceleration is to curve the lines of **E**, introducing a transverse component that will form part of a radiation field.

If the particle is accelerated for only a short time, the electric lines will have "kinks" in them which constitute the electric part of a radiation field moving outward at the speed c. Figure 10.6e presents such a state of affairs schematically.

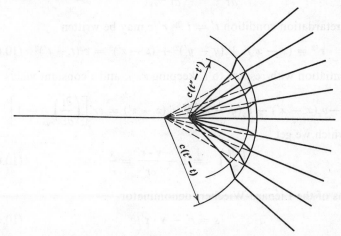

Fig. 10.6e. Lines of force surrounding an accelerated charge. The "kinks" occur at time t'' between the fields produced by motion at constant velocity up to time t and at a greater constant velocity from time t' on. (From R. M. Eisberg, *Fundamentals of Modern Physics*, John Wiley and Sons, New York, 1961, p. 44.)

A detailed calculation of the field from an arbitrarily moving charge is relatively lengthy. In finding $\mathbf{E}$ and $\mathbf{B}$ with the operators ∇ and $\partial/\partial t$, we have to take into account the above-mentioned dependence of $\mathbf{v}$ on t'—in fact, we treat the three coordinates of the particle x', y', and z' each as arbitrary functions of t'. As a consequence we can treat all quantities as functions either of the set of variables x, y, z, and t or x, y, z, and t'. We shall use subscripts where appropriate to indicate which variables are held constant in partial differentiation.

It is easiest to make the calculation if we first make some auxiliary differentiations. The velocity $\mathbf{v}$ has the components

$$v_x = \frac{dx'}{dt'} \qquad v_y = \frac{dy'}{dt'} \qquad v_z = \frac{dz'}{dt'} \qquad (10.6\text{--}12)$$

The vector $\mathbf{v}$ may also be found from the components of the vector $\mathbf{r}'$ directed from $\mathscr{Q}'$ to $\mathscr{P}$:

$$\mathbf{r}' = \mathbf{1}_x(x - x') + \mathbf{1}_y(y - y') + \mathbf{1}_z(z - z') \qquad (10.6\text{--}13)$$

$$\left(\frac{\partial \mathbf{r}'}{\partial t'}\right)_{xyz} = -\mathbf{v} \qquad (10.6\text{--}14)$$

The derivative of $\mathbf{v}$ is the acceleration $\mathbf{a}$:

$$\frac{d\mathbf{v}}{dt'} = -\left(\frac{\partial^2 \mathbf{r}'}{\partial t'^2}\right)_{xyz} = \mathbf{a} \qquad (10.6\text{--}15)$$

The retardation condition $t' = t - r'/c$ may be written

$$r'^2 = (x - x')^2 + (y - y')^2 + (z - z')^2 = c^2(t - t')^2 \qquad (10.6\text{--}16)$$

Differentiation with respect to t' keeping x, y, and z constant yields

$$-v_x(x - x') - v_y(y - y') - v_z(z - z') = cr'\left[\left(\frac{\partial t}{\partial t'}\right)_{xyz} - 1\right]$$

from which we get

$$\left(\frac{\partial t}{\partial t'}\right)_{xyz} = 1 - \frac{\mathbf{v} \cdot \mathbf{r}'}{cr'} = \frac{s}{r'} \qquad (10.6\text{--}17)$$

in terms of the Liénard-Wiechert denominator

$$s = r' - \mathbf{v} \cdot \mathbf{r}'/c \qquad (10.6\text{--}18)$$

The derivative of the scalar r' with respect to t' is then

$$\left(\frac{\partial r'}{\partial t'}\right)_{xyz} = c\left(\frac{\partial t}{\partial t'} - 1\right) = -\frac{\mathbf{v} \cdot \mathbf{r}'}{r'} \qquad (10.6\text{--}19)$$

Differentiation of 10.6–15 with respect to x with y, z, and t constant yields

$$(x - x')\left(1 - v_x \frac{\partial t'}{\partial x}\right) + (y - y')\left(-v_y \frac{\partial t'}{\partial x}\right)$$

$$+ (z - z')\left(-v_z \frac{\partial t'}{\partial x}\right) = c^2(t - t')\left(-\frac{\partial t'}{\partial x}\right)$$

from which we get

$$\left(\frac{\partial t'}{\partial x}\right)_{yzt} = \frac{x' - x}{cr' - \mathbf{v} \cdot \mathbf{r}'} = \frac{x' - x}{sc}$$

Together with the other two components, we can write the gradient of t' with respect to displacement of $\mathscr{P}$

$$(\nabla t')_t = -\frac{\mathbf{r}'}{sc} \tag{10.6-20}$$

The gradient of t' can be used to evaluate $(\nabla \times \mathbf{v})_t$. We have, for instance,

$$\left(\frac{\partial v_x}{\partial y}\right)_{zt} = \frac{dv_x}{dt'}\left(\frac{\partial t'}{\partial y}\right)_{zt}$$

so that

$$(\nabla \times \mathbf{v})_t = (\nabla t')_t \times \mathbf{a} \tag{10.6-21}$$

Finally, we calculate derivatives of s from 10.6–18:

$$\left(\frac{\partial s}{\partial t'}\right)_{xyz} = \frac{\partial r'}{\partial t'} - \frac{\partial \mathbf{r}'}{\partial t'} \cdot \frac{\mathbf{v}}{c} - \frac{\mathbf{r}'}{c} \cdot \frac{\partial \mathbf{v}}{\partial t'}$$

$$= -\frac{\mathbf{r}' \cdot \mathbf{v}}{r'} + \frac{\mathbf{v} \cdot \mathbf{v}}{c} - \frac{\mathbf{r}' \cdot \mathbf{a}}{c} \tag{10.6-22}$$

For $(\nabla s)_t$ we note that s depends explicitly on x, y, and z—i.e. with t' constant—and implicitly on x, y, and z through the variation of t'. We have then

$$(\nabla s)_t = (\nabla s)_{t'} + \left(\frac{\partial s}{\partial t'}\right)_{xyz}(\nabla t')_t$$

or

$$(\nabla s)_t = \mathbf{1}_{r'} - \frac{\mathbf{v}}{c} + \frac{\mathbf{r}'}{sc}\left(\frac{\mathbf{r}' \cdot \mathbf{v}}{r'} - \frac{v^2}{c} + \frac{\mathbf{r} \cdot \mathbf{a}}{c}\right) \tag{10.6-23}$$

Now we can find $\mathbf{E}$ and $\mathbf{B}$. We have

$$\mathbf{E} = -\left(\frac{\partial \mathbf{A}}{\partial t}\right)_{xyz} - (\nabla V)_t$$

$$= -\frac{q}{4\pi\epsilon_0 c^2}\left[\frac{\mathbf{a}}{s} - \frac{\mathbf{v}}{s^2}\frac{\partial s}{\partial t'}\right]\left(\frac{\partial t'}{\partial t}\right)_{xyz} + \frac{q}{4\pi\epsilon_0 s^2}(\nabla s)_t$$

which becomes after substitution

$$\mathbf{E} = \frac{q}{4\pi\epsilon_0}\left[\frac{\mathbf{r}}{s^3}\left(1 - \frac{v^2}{c^2} + \frac{\mathbf{r'}\cdot\mathbf{a}}{c^2}\right) - \frac{\mathbf{a}r'}{s^2c^2}\right] \tag{10.6–24}$$

where we have used the "virtual present radius vector" r from $\mathscr{Q}'''$ to $\mathscr{P}$ in Fig. 10.6d:

$$r = \mathbf{r'} - \frac{r'\mathbf{v}}{c} \tag{10.6–25}$$

and of $\mathbf{v}$ and $\mathbf{a}$ of course are evaluated at the retarded time. By comparison with 10.3–27, we see that the part of $\mathbf{E}$ independent of $\mathbf{a}$ is the same as for constant velocity. If we use the further relation, evident from the figure, that $\mathbf{r'}\cdot\mathbf{r} = \mathbf{r'}s$, we can write the part of $\mathbf{E}$ containing $\mathbf{a}$ as a triple vector product:

$$\mathbf{E}_{\text{accel}} = \frac{q}{4\pi\epsilon_0 c^2 s^3}[\mathbf{r'}\times(\mathbf{r}\times\mathbf{a})] \tag{10.6–26}$$

For $\mathbf{B}_{\text{accel}}$ we find the simple relation

$$c\mathbf{B}_{\text{accel}} = (\mathbf{1}_{r'}\times\mathbf{E}_{\text{accel}}) \tag{10.6–27}$$

with the same relation holding for the velocity-dependent part.

Equations 10.6–26 and 27 give the general relations for the fields of an accelerated charge, calculated in terms of the retarded radius $\mathbf{r'}$, the Lienard-Wiechert distance s, and the virtual present radius $\mathbf{r}$. They can be used for numerous calculations, such as that for the radiation of a suddenly decelerated fast electron ("bremsstrahlung") or of an electron in a circular syncrotron orbit.[11]

If $v \ll c$, r, r', and s are nearly equal (as are $\mathbf{r}$ and $\mathbf{r'}$) and we can write for $\mathbf{E}_{\text{accel}}$ a result similar to 10.6–5a:

$$\mathbf{E}_{\text{accel}} = \frac{\mu_0 q}{4\pi r}[\mathbf{1}_r\times(\mathbf{1}_r\times\mathbf{a})] \tag{10.6–28}$$

If we replace $q\mathbf{a}$ with

$$q_{\max}a e^{j\omega(t-r/c)}\mathbf{1}_z = q_{\max}\omega^2\delta l\, e^{j\omega(t-r/c)}\mathbf{1}_z$$

we find 10.6–5a, showing that the radiating dipole is a special case of 10.6–26. Since Eqs. 10.6–5 satisfy 10.6–27, the same argument holds for the magnetic field, and we have justified Eq. 10.6–11.

The general result that an accelerated charge must radiate was of the first importance in the history of atomic physics, for this consequence of electromagnetism had to be discarded by Niels Bohr in the original form of his famous atomic theory.[12]

---

[11] Panofsky and Phillips, *op. cit.*, Chapter 20.
[12] N. Bohr, *Phil. Mag.*, **26**, 1 (1913).

Multipole Radiation. More complicated forms of radiation than the dipole form just given can be found by the same process used in Section 3.3 for multipole static fields. We can consider two equal and opposite radiating dipoles displaced by a vector $\delta \mathbf{l}'$ and calculate $\mathbf{A}$ and V by use of the operator $-(\delta \mathbf{l}' \cdot \nabla)$, taking care to let the ∇ operate on the r in the retarded sinusoidal factor $e^{j\omega(t-r/c)}$ as well as on the rest of each function. We can then add such quadrupole terms in various ways to represent simple physical cases, as indicated in Fig. 10.6*f*. The calculations of the resulting radiation are lengthy but involve nothing especially new. The results for

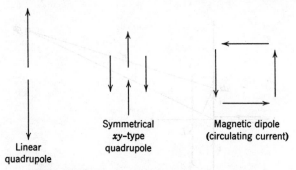

Linear
quadrupole

Symmetrical
xy-type
quadrupole

Magnetic dipole
(circulating current)

Fig. 10.6*f*.   Various quadrupole arrangements.

the "magnetic dipole" combination indicated in Fig. 10.6*f* is the not unexpected one that $\mathbf{H}_{\mathrm{rad}}$ is given by the same formula as $\mathbf{E}_{\mathrm{rad}}$ for the electric dipole case, with ϵ_0 replaced by μ_0 in the denominator, and the magnetic moment $\mu_0 i_{\max} S = \mu_0 i_{\max} \, \delta l \, \delta l'$ in place of $p_{\max} = q_{\max} \, \delta l$ in the numerator. It is easy to calculate the rate of radiation for this case. The new $\mathbf{E}_{\mathrm{rad}}$ will be $c\mu_0 \mathbf{H}_{\mathrm{rad}}$ and will thus differ in magnitude from the dipole electric field by a factor $c\mu_0^2(i_{\max} \, \delta l \, \delta l'/q_{\max} \, \delta l)(\epsilon_0/\mu_0) = \omega \, \delta l'/c = \delta l'/\lambda$. Thus we see that the magnitude of P is reduced by a factor $(\delta l'/\lambda)^2$, which means that for dipoles and current loops that are much smaller in physical dimensions than λ magnetic dipole radiation is very much weaker than electric dipole radiation. Electric quadrupole radiation in general will of course be of the same order of intensity as the magnetic dipole variety.

In fact, it is not hard to show that electric 2^n-pole and magnetic 2^{n-1}-pole radiation have P's of the same order of magnitude. Radiation from atoms or nuclei is called "allowed" if the quantum "jump" corresponds to electric dipole oscillations, "first forbidden" if it corresponds only to electric quadrupole or magnetic dipole, "second forbidden" if electric octupole or magnetic quadrupole radiation is involved, and so forth.

Antennas. An actual radiating antenna behaves like a dipole only if its length is very small compared to a wave length. For longer antennas, the analysis is complicated, because the current will not be uniform in the wire. An antenna wire can in fact sustain running or standing waves, similar to the waves studied in Section 10.2. Such radiating systems must be studied by some analytical or graphical method of summing over elements of the wire's length.

There are numerous methods of getting different patterns of radiated intensity versus direction. There are two cases that can be readily handled—one in which standing wave patterns are set up on the wires, and the other in which the wires are terminated by the appropriate characteristic impedances so no reflections occur. The most common example of the first case

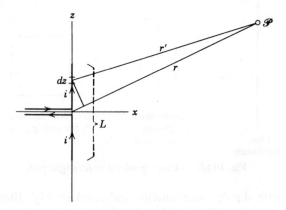

Fig. 10.6g. A center-fed linear antenna.

is the center-fed or doublet antenna—a straight wire usually $\lambda/2$ in length which is broken in the middle to allow current to enter from the transmitter power circuit. An example of the second is the so-called rhombic antenna, consisting of four wires in the shape of a rhombus, fed at one corner from the transmitter and terminated properly at the opposite corner.

Let us consider briefly the radiation from a center-fed linear antenna, as shown in Fig. 10.6g. The two halves of such an antenna will act like a transmission line, similar to the coaxial cable of Section 10.2, even though the capacitance per unit length between corresponding points on the upper and lower halves and the inductance per unit length are quite different than for the cable and not easy to compute. Just as for the coaxial cable, the speed of waves along the wires will be c if the resistance losses are negligible and if the radiation resistance is sufficiently small.

Since the line is open-circuited, there must be reflections; in fact, the only periodic oscillation that can be set up must be a standing wave with current vanishing at the end of each wire. To calculate $\mathbf{E}_{rad}$ and $\mathbf{H}_{rad}$ at a distant point $\mathscr{P}$, we can add the components of $\mathbf{A}$ from each element of the standing current wave and then use 10.6–5. Since r will differ little along the antenna, we shall neglect its variation in the denominator of Eq. 10.6–1. However, when we integrate, we cannot neglect the dependence of the phase of $\mathbf{A}$ on r, so we shall replace r in the exponent by $r' = r - z \cos \theta$, which is seen in the figure to be a sufficient approximation (it is the result obtained by expanding the law of cosines to first order in z/r).

We therefore replace i_{ret} in Eq. 10.6–1 with

$$i = i_m \sin \left[\frac{1}{\lambda} (\tfrac{1}{2} L - |z|) \right] e^{j\omega(t - r'/c)} \qquad (10.6-29)$$

which represents a standing wave that vanishes when $|z| = \tfrac{1}{2}L$. If we are to use the development above, each segment $i \, \delta \mathbf{l} = i\mathbf{1}_z \, dz$ must have appropriate charges associated with it, but we do not need to treat them explicitly. We could find q_l from i and the continuity equation, which would naturally give the same result as adding the charges belonging individually to each $i \, \delta \mathbf{l}$, and then we could find $\mathbf{V}$ as before. However, we have seen that the contribution of $\mathbf{V}$ to the $1/r$ part of the field is merely to cancel the longitudinal contribution from $\mathbf{A}$, so if we consider only the transverse part of $\mathbf{A}$, we need not calculate q_l or $\mathbf{V}$ explicitly.

It is now very simple to find $\mathbf{A}$ for the antenna, by integration over its length:

$$\mathbf{A} = \frac{\mu_0 i_m}{4\pi r} e^{j\omega(t - r/c)} \mathbf{1}_z \int_{-L/2}^{L/2} dz \sin \left[(\tfrac{1}{2} L - |z|)/\lambda \right] e^{jz \cos \theta / \lambda}$$

The integral is lengthy but elementary to perform (hint: use A.5–11b). We find

$$\mathbf{A} = \frac{\mu_0 \lambda i_m}{2\pi r \sin^2 \theta} e^{j\omega(t - r/c)} \left[\cos \left(\frac{L}{2\lambda} \cos \theta \right) - \cos \frac{L}{2\lambda} \right] \mathbf{1}_z \qquad (10.6-30)$$

from which we can find the average Poynting vector according to Eq. 10.6–6,

$$\mathbf{N}_{rad,\,av} = \frac{\mu_0^2 \lambda^2 i_m^2}{8\pi^2 r^2 \sin^2 \theta} \left[\cos \left(\frac{L}{2\lambda} \cos \theta \right) - \cos \frac{L}{2\lambda} \right] \mathbf{1}_r \qquad (10.6-31)$$

For a half-wave antenna we have $L = \lambda/2$, $x = L/\pi$ and

$$\mathbf{N}_{rad,\,av} = \frac{\mu_0^2 \lambda^2 i_m^2}{8\pi^2 r^2} \cdot \frac{\cos^2 \left[(\pi/2) \cos \theta \right]}{\sin^2 \theta} \mathbf{1}_r \qquad (10.6-32)$$

whereas for a full-wave antenna we find with a little trigonometry

$$\mathbf{N}_{rad,\,av} = \frac{\mu_0^2 \lambda^2 i_m^2}{8\pi^2 r^2} \cdot \frac{4 \cos^4 \left[(\pi/2) \cos \theta \right]}{\sin^2 \theta} \mathbf{1}_r \qquad (10.6-33)$$

Problem 10.6 calls for graphical study of the three distributions 10.6–11, 10.6–32, and 10.6–33. For other details on antenna theory, the reader is referred elsewhere.[13]

Plane-Sheet Radiation. The last example of radiation we wish to discuss is that of an idealized plane sheet of alternating current. Suppose that in the x–y plane there is a uniform current in the x-direction (Fig. 10.6h), with a surface current density J_S given by $J_S = J_{S\,max}\,e^{j\omega t}$; J_S is so defined

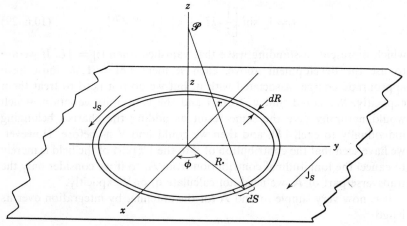

Fig. 10.6h. A plane radiating sheet.

that the current in a strip of surface of width Δy is $J_S\,\Delta y$. Then at a point $\mathscr{P}$ a height z from the plane, the vector potential will be

$$\mathbf{A} = \frac{\mu_0}{4\pi}\,J_{S\,max}\,\mathbf{1}_x\int_{\text{entire plane}} e^{j\omega(t-r/c)}\,dS/r$$

where dS is a unit of area $dx\,dy$ in the plane and r is the distance from dS to $\mathscr{P}$. Let us use polar coordinates R and ϕ in the plane and choose as elements of area rings of radius R and width dR. Then $dS = 2\pi R\,dR$. Next, we can change variables and use r in place of R, where $r^2 = R^2 + z^2$. When R goes from 0 to ∞, r goes from z to ∞; furthermore, $2r\,dr = 2R\,dR$. Thus we have

$$\mathbf{A} = \frac{\mu_0 J_{S\,max}\mathbf{1}_x}{4\pi}\int_z^\infty 2\pi r\,dr\,\frac{e^{j\omega(t-r/c)}}{r} = \frac{\mu_0 J_{S\,max}\mathbf{1}_x}{2}\int_z^\infty dr\,e^{j\omega(t-r/c)} \quad (10.6\text{–}34)$$

[13] S. Ramo and J. R. Whinnery, *Fields and Waves in Modern Radio*, 2nd ed., John Wiley, New York, 1953, Chapter 12; S. A. Schelkunoff and H. T. Friis, *Antennas, Theory and Practice*, John Wiley, New York, 1952.

which gives an undetermined value for the upper limit—we should not be surprised that for an infinite plane the potential involves an uncertain "constant."

We can avoid the difficulty by taking the curl before evaluating the integral. From plane symmetry and the chosen current direction, we have

$$\mathbf{B} = \text{curl } \mathbf{A} = \frac{\partial A_x}{\partial z}\mathbf{1}_y = \frac{\mu_0 J_{S\max}}{2}\mathbf{1}_y \frac{\partial}{\partial z}\int_0^\infty R\, dR\, \frac{e^{j\omega(t-r/c)}}{r}$$

As long as we use R as a variable, we can put the derivative inside the integral sign. Then we have

$$B_y = \frac{\mu_0 J_{S\max}}{2}\int_0^\infty R\, dR\, \frac{\partial}{\partial z}\left[\frac{e^{j\omega(t-r/c)}}{r}\right]$$

$$= \frac{\mu_0 J_{S\max}}{2}\int_z^\infty r\, dr\left(\frac{z}{r}\right)\frac{\partial}{\partial r}\left[\frac{e^{j\omega(t-r/c)}}{r}\right]$$

$$= \frac{\mu_0 J_{S\max}z}{2}\int_z^\infty dr\, \frac{\partial}{\partial r}\left[\frac{e^{j\omega(t-r/c)}}{r}\right] = \frac{\mu_0 J_{S\max}z}{2}\left[\frac{e^{j\omega(t-r/c)}}{r}\right]_z^\infty$$

or

$$B_y = -\frac{\mu_0 J_{S\max}}{2}e^{j\omega(t-z/c)} \tag{10.6–35}$$

Integrating B_y with respect to z, we can find A_x, except for a constant, and thus evaluate the last formula in Eq. 10.6–34:

$$A_x = -\frac{j\mu_0 c J_{S\max}}{2\omega}e^{j\omega(t-z/c)} \tag{10.6–36}$$

from which it is easy to find $\mathbf{E}$:

$$\mathbf{E} = E_x\mathbf{1}_x = -\frac{\partial A_x}{\partial t}\mathbf{1}_x = -\tfrac{1}{2}\mu_0 c J_{S\max}\mathbf{1}_x\, e^{j\omega(t-z/c)} \tag{10.6–37}$$

which has the magnitude of $c\mathbf{B}$ and is so oriented that

$$\mathbf{N} = \mathbf{E} \times \mathbf{H} = \tfrac{1}{4}\mu_0 J_{S\max}^2\mathbf{1}_z\cos^2(\omega t - z/c)$$

represents radiation along the z direction.

In accordance with the remark at the end of Section 10.4, we note that momentum is carried away from the surface at the average rate

$$N_{\text{av}}/c = \mu_0 J_{S\max}^2/8c$$

per unit area. The surface bearing the current must therefore acquire momentum of the same amount in the $-\mathbf{1}_z$ direction—a radiation pressure is exerted on the surface of average amount

$$p_{\text{rad}} = \mu_0 J_{S\,\text{max}}^2/8c = B_{y\,\text{max}}^2/2\mu_0 c \qquad (10.6\text{--}38a)$$

as a consequence of the emission of plane-sheet radiation, where we have found $B_{y\,\text{max}}$ from (10.6–35.)

It will be observed that a plane sheet of current will radiate symmetrically on both sides, just as a plane sheet of static charge produces a field on both sides, and, of course, there will be equal and opposite radiation pressures that just balance. If a conductor is present, there will be other currents present that affect the field inside the conducting material (see Section 10.7).

Receiving Antennas. Let us now consider the reception of electromagnetic radiation. A simple type of receiving antenna is a plane loop. Figure 10.6i shows a rectangular loop arranged to receive energy from a plane

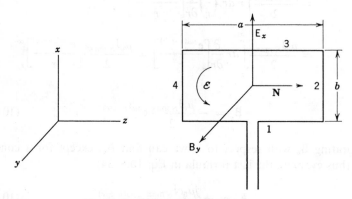

Fig. 10.6i. A loop receiving antenna.

wave like that just discussed. The wave is shown as traveling in the z-direction, with electric field along x given by $E_x = E_{x\,\text{max}}\,e^{j\omega(t-z/c)}$ and the magnetic field by $B_y = E_{x\,\text{max}}\,e^{j\omega(t-r/c)}/c$. We can calculate the emf induced in the loop by finding the flux through it, or by using $\mathbf{A}$:

$$\mathcal{E} = -\frac{d\phi}{dt} = -\frac{d}{dt}\int_S B_y\,dS = -\frac{1}{c}\frac{d}{dt}\int_{z_4}^{z_2} E_{x\,\text{max}}\,e^{j\omega(t-z/c)}b\,dz$$

$$= b\frac{d}{dt}\frac{E_{x\,\text{max}}}{j\omega}[e^{j\omega(t-z_2/c)} - e^{j\omega(t-z_4/c)}]$$

$$= bE_{x\,\text{max}}[e^{j\omega(t-z_2/c)} - e^{j\omega(t-z_4c)}] \qquad (10.6\text{--}39)$$

where the limits of integration refer to the values of z at sides 4 and 2. We also have

$$\mathcal{E} = -\frac{d}{dt}\int_{\text{boundary}} \mathbf{A} \cdot \mathbf{dl} = \int_{\text{boundary}} \mathbf{E} \cdot \mathbf{dl} = b[E_x(z_2) - E_x(z_4)]$$

as another way of getting the same result. The electric and magnetic fields in an electromagnetic wave should be considered as *two aspects of the same entity*, since not only are they each derivable from $\mathbf{A}$ (in the plane-wave case), but *either* can be used to calculate the emf. (If this connection were not made clear, one might be tempted fallaciously to calculate the emf in both ways and add the results.)

It is interesting to calculate the emf induced in a length δl_1 of a receiving antenna by a dipole radiation, using the electric field given by Eq. 10.6-5a. We have

$$d\mathcal{E} = \mathbf{E} \cdot \delta l_1 = \mu_0\omega^2 q_{max}\, e^{j\omega(t-r/c)}[(\mathbf{1}_r \times \delta l) \times \mathbf{1}_r] \cdot \delta l_1/4\pi r$$

$$= \frac{\mu_0\omega^2 q_{max}}{4\pi r}\, e^{j\omega(t-r/c)}(\mathbf{1}_r \times \delta l) \cdot (\mathbf{1}_r \times \delta l_1) \qquad (10.6\text{-}40)$$

This formula is symmetric in δl and δl_1 and shows that the effectiveness of a given receiving antenna with respect to radiation from a given transmitter must be given by the same integrations over Eq. 10.6–40 as the effectiveness for transmission when the antenna roles are reversed. That is, various antennas for a given transmitter will operate as receivers in proportion to their abilities to transmit, so that studies of antenna radiation can be taken over for receivers.[14]

To write the formulas of this section in Gaussian units, we replace $4\pi\epsilon_0$ with 1 and μ_0 with $4\pi/c^2$ in the formulas for V, $\mathbf{E}$, and $\mathcal{E}$; μ_0 with $4\pi/c$ in the formulas for $\mathbf{A}$ and $\mathbf{B}$; and μ_0 with $4\pi/c^2$ in the power formulas—those for $\mathbf{N}$, P, and R_{rad}. The radiation pressure formula reads

$$p_{rad} = 4\pi J_{S\,max}^2/8c^3 = B_{y\,max}^2/8\pi c \qquad \text{Gaussian} \quad (10.6\text{-}38b)$$

Problem 10.6a. Show that in the "near zone" of a radiating dipole where $r \ll \lambda$, the fields are just those expected for a slowly-varying electric dipole and current element.

Problem 10.6b. Show that for the near-zone fields (see previous problem) the electric energy density exceeds the magnetic by a substantial factor, and find the order of magnitude of that factor.

Problem 10.6c. Plot polar graphs of the angular distributions of $\mathbf{N}$ for an electric dipole, a half-wave antenna, and a full-wave antenna in sufficient detail to show differences and similarities.

[14] A detailed account of the reciprocity theorem, covering the interchange of source and detector when frequency and impedances are kept constant, is given in Corson and Lorrain, *op. cit.*, section 13.9.

Problem 10.6d. Show that when L/λ becomes very small, $N_{rad, av}$ in Eq. 10.6–31 has the same angular dependence as N_{rad} in Eq. 10.6–10.

Problem 10.6e. Find by the method outlined in the text the fields produced by a sinusoidally oscillating quadrupole composed of two equal and opposite dipoles with $\delta l = 1_z \, \delta l$ and $\delta l' = 1_z \, \delta l'$.

Problem 10.6f. Find the radiation field of a rectangular-current magnetic dipole by adding quadrupole fields due to (a) dipoles with $\delta l = 1_z \, \delta l$ separated by $\delta l' = 1_y \, \delta l$ and (b) dipoles with $\delta l = -1_y \, \delta l$ separated by $\delta l' = 1_z \, \delta l$. Take the magnetic moment to be $p_m = \mu_0 i_{max} \, e^{j\omega t} \, \delta l^2 1_x$.

10.7 Application to Physical Optics

We wish in this section to give a brief introduction to the treatment of physical optics by means of electromagnetic-radiation theory. Let us first consider plane waves approaching a plane conductor of very small resistivity in the x–y plane, at normal incidence (in the $+z$-direction). The emf induced by the wave in the conductor will at any instant be the same everywhere and will induce a very large current because of the high conductivity. This current will then reradiate a field of its own, as we saw in the last section. Rather than calculate the induced J_S and then the resultant field, we can find the field easily by assuming the ideal case of zero resistivity. The reradiated field must cancel exactly the oncoming field within the metal, for any finite field would produce an infinite current. This allows us to determine J_S, if we wish, and more important to find the reradiated field on the outside of the metal. If the original wave is characterized by, say,

$$\left.\begin{aligned} E_x &= f(t - z/c) \\ B_y &= \frac{1}{c} f(t - z/c) \end{aligned}\right\} \text{original wave} \qquad (10.7\text{–}1)$$

then the reradiated wave inside the metal (for $z > 0$) must be

$$\left.\begin{aligned} E_x &= -f(t - z/c) \\ B_y &= -\frac{1}{c} f(t - z/c) \end{aligned}\right\} \begin{aligned}&\text{reradiated wave,} \\ &\quad z > 0\end{aligned} \qquad (10.7\text{–}2)$$

For $z < 0$, we must have the appropriately symmetrical reradiated wave. $\partial A_x/\partial t$ must be the same at points (x, y, z) and $(x, y, -z)$, but $\partial A_x/\partial z$ must have opposite sign, for it will be seen in the calculation of the last section that the absolute value of z has to be used. Thus B_y changes its sign as we go through the plane, as indeed it must if N is to be directed away from the plane on each side. Thus we have

$$E_x = -f(t + z/c) \left.\right\} \text{reradiated wave,}$$
$$B_y = \frac{1}{c}f(t + z/c) \left.\right\} \quad z < 0 \qquad (10.7\text{-}3)$$

We have thus a reflected wave and have accounted in detail for the reflection of light at normal incidence by a metallic surface. Note in particular that the sum of the two waves just outside the surface gives $E_x = 0$ and $B_y = 2f(t)/c$. The reflected wave reduces the electric field to zero at the surface of the metal as well as in its interior.

The incident wave will carry momentum to the surface of amount $p = B_y^2/2\mu_0 c$ per unit area and unit time and the reradiated wave will carry away a similar amount in the opposite direction, so the total radiation pressure on a reflecting surface at normal incidence will be

$$p_{\text{rad}} = \frac{B_y^2}{\mu_0 c} = \frac{E_x^2}{\mu_0 c^3} \qquad (10.7\text{-}4a)$$

This pressure is, of course, extremely small (Problem 10.7c).

Now consider a plane wave heading for the surface at some angle with the normal, with each field component given by a function like Eq. 10.3-7, namely,

$$F(t - \mathbf{r} \cdot \mathbf{1}_u/c)$$

where $\mathbf{1}_u$ represents a certain unit vector making an angle θ, say, with the normal. This function F might represent the component of $\mathbf{E}$ perpendicular to a plane containing $\mathbf{1}_u$ and the surface normal, or a component in this plane or in some intermediate direction. The surface currents will be more complicated than previously, having certain particular phase variations over the surface (which are actually not hard to calculate). The simplest fact about them is that they will radiate a field inside the metal which exactly cancels the initial wave there and hence by symmetry with respect to the surface plane will radiate a wave on the same side of the normal at the angle θ in the same plane as the incident wave but on the opposite side, thus demonstrating the optical law of reflection (Fig. 10.7a).

Now let us consider radiation incident on an isotropic dielectric medium with, possibly, magnetic properties. We shall assume that ϵ and μ are meaningful constants—in particular that they are evaluated for the frequency or range of frequencies we are considering. At the boundary of the medium (we take a plane again) there will be induced polarization charges and surface currents which oscillate at the frequency of the incident radiation and which thus will also produce reradiated waves. However, polarization and magnetization will appear throughout the medium, so that the situation is not nearly so simple as for the ideal conductor. In fact, the change of velocity from $c = (\mu_0 \epsilon_0)^{1/2}$ to $v = (\mu\epsilon)^{-1/2}$ inside the material can be attributed to a continuous reradiation process. Detailed calculations based on this notion lead to theories of dispersion (meaning the variation of v with ω).

Hence we shall use here only the method of boundary conditions. We assume that we can take over into radiation theory the static boundary conditions, which state that the tangential components of **H** and **E** and

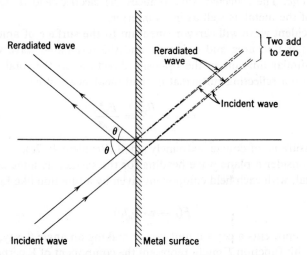

Fig. 10.7a.   Proving the law of reflection by symmetry.

the normal components of **B** and **D** are continuous across the boundary. (The boundary conditions essentially involve only the "near fields" of the surface radiators—cf. Problem 10.6a.) If we have an incident plane wave of effectively infinite extent, we can be sure that the reradiated waves on both sides will be plane waves. Because of different velocities on both sides, we can no longer expect symmetry; instead, we expect the phase variations in P_n and M_n along the surface as a function of time to radiate waves at different angles in the two media.

Without going into detail concerning the directions of the electric and magnetic vectors, we can assert for instance that the function representing the tangential components of **E** must satisfy the boundary condition mentioned above. Thus if we represent the incident wave by $F_{in}[t - (\mathbf{r} \cdot \mathbf{1}_u)/c]$, the other waves must involve the same function F_{in} so that the boundary condition will be satisfied at all times. Let us choose $\mathbf{1}_u$ so that it has just x and z components: $\mathbf{1}_u = u_x \mathbf{1}_x + u_z \mathbf{1}_z$, where $u_x^2 + u_z^2 = 1$. Then the incident wave is $F_{in}[t - (xu_x + zu_z)/c]$ and at the boundary $(z = 0)$ we will have $F_{in}[t - xu_x/c]$. The reflected wave must vary in the same way over the surface, that is with x, and so for this reason also it must be proportional to F_{in}. The refracted wave which travels at velocity v must also be proportional to F_{in} on the boundary.

From these statements, we can find the form of the $\mathbf{r} \cdot \mathbf{1}_u/c$ and $\mathbf{r} \cdot \mathbf{1}_u'/v$ terms in the reflected and refracted wave functions. There can be no y dependence for either function. The reflected wave travels at the speed c, and the requirements that the term be xu_x/c when $z = 0$, that the wave

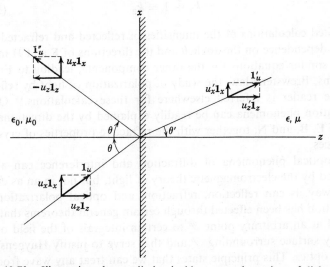

Fig. 10.7b.   Illustrating plane radiation incident on a plane piece of dielectric.

travel on the $-z$ side of the plane, and that $u_x^2 + u_z^2 = 1$ lead to the form $(xu_x - zu_z)/c$.

The refracted wave travels at speed v. Calling the new unit vector $\mathbf{u}'$, we have within the material the term $(xu_x' + zu_z')/v$; the condition at the boundary yields $u_x'/v = u_x/c$, and u_z' can be found if we wish from $u_z' = (1 - u_x'^2)^{1/2}$. Since $\mathbf{1}_u$ and $\mathbf{1}_u'$ are unit vectors, we see from Fig. 10.7b, which shows the x–z plane, that $u_x = \sin \theta$ and $u_x' = \sin \theta'$, leading us directly to Snell's law for refraction:

$$\sin \theta'/\sin \theta = v/c = 1/n \qquad (10.7\text{-}5)$$

where n is c/v, a number greater than unity called the "index of refraction." Note that we do not need the form of $F(t)$ to prove Snell's law, although the frequency enters into the value of v.

In terms of F_{in} given above, we can write expressions for the reflected and refracted waves:

$$F_{refl} = k_1 F_{in}[t - (xu_x - zu_z)/c] \qquad (10.7\text{--}6)$$

$$F_{refr} = k_2 F_{in}[t - (xu_x' + zu_z')/v] \qquad (10.7\text{--}7)$$

where k_1 and k_2 are constants that determine the phases and amplitudes of the waves. The condition that the tangential components of **E** at the boundary are the same on the two sides leads to the equation

$$k_1 + 1 = k_2 \qquad (10.7\text{--}8)$$

Detailed calculations of the intensities of reflected and refracted waves in their dependence on the angle θ and the directions of **E** and **H** involves writing similar equations for the other components, leading to Fresnel's equations, Brewster's law, the study of polarization of light by reflection, etc. The reader is referred elsewhere for these calculations.[15] Optical-polarization phenomena can be readily explained by the directional relations of **E**, **B**, and **N**, together with the refractive properties of crystalline substances.

The optical phenomena of diffraction and interference can also be explained by the electromagnetic theory of light, but not in an as elementary a way as can reflection, refraction, and optical polarization. The explanation has been effected through certain general theorems that relate the field at an arbitrary point $\mathscr{P}$ to certain integrals of the field over an arbitrary surface surrounding $\mathscr{P}$ and that serve to justify Huygens' principle in optics. This principle states that we can treat any wave front as a surface distribution of infinitesimal sources radiating in phase to produce a wave front by constructive interference. It nevertheless is difficult to calculate diffraction patterns rigorously except for certain special cases.[16]

The radiation pressure equation for normal incidence and perfect reflection reads

$$P_{rad} = \frac{B_y{}^2}{4\pi c} = \frac{E_x{}^2}{4\pi c} \qquad \text{Gaussian} \quad (10.7\text{--}4b)$$

[15] Panofsky and Phillips, *op. cit.*, pp. 176–181. R. M. Whitmer, *Electromagnetics*, Prentice-Hall, Englewood Cliffs, 1952, Chapter 12; B. Rossi, *Optics*, Addison-Wesley, Cambridge, 1957; Jackson, *op. cit.*, pp. 216–222; Corson and Lorrain, *op. cit.*, Chapter 11; Landau and Lifschitz, *op. cit.*, pp. 272–279 and Chapter XI.

[16] J. A. Stratton, *Electromagnetic Theory*, McGraw-Hill, New York, 1941, pp. 460–470 and 570; P. M. Morse and H. Feshbach, *Methods of Theoretical Physics*, McGraw-Hill, New York, 1953, Vol. I., pp. 847–848; M. Born and E. Wolf, *Principles of Optics*, Pergamon Press, New York, 1959, Chapters VIII, IX, and XI; Jackson, *op. cit.*, Chapter 9.

Problem 10.7a. Find the amplitudes of reflected and refracted waves when plane waves are incident at angle θ on a plane piece of dielectric, with the electric vector perpendicular to the plane containing the wave vector and the surface normal.

Problem 10.7b. Solve Problem 10.7a when $\mathbf{E}$ lies *in* the plane mentioned.

Problem 10.7c. 10 watts per cm² of light energy is reflected at normal incidence from a metal surface. Find the radiation pressure in dynes/cm², assuming the reflection to be perfect. What acceleration could this pressure develop in a vane made of foil of 1 mg/cm² mass?

10.8 Skin Depth and Skin Effect

Let us now consider briefly how to treat wave propagation within a conductor with a finite conductivity and also, perhaps, appreciable paramagnetism. We shall follow the treatment of Section 10.3. Equation 10.3–1c is the only one of Eqs. 10.3–1 that needs modifying. We write in place of it, using Ohm's law:

$$\mathbf{\nabla} \times \mathbf{B} = \mu \, \mathbf{\nabla} \times \mathbf{H} = \mu\epsilon_0 \frac{\partial \mathbf{E}}{\partial t} + \mu \mathbf{J} = \mu\epsilon_0 \frac{\partial \mathbf{E}}{\partial t} + \mu\sigma_c \mathbf{E} \quad (10.8\text{–}1)$$

Then when we calculate **curl curl** $\mathbf{E}$ and need $\partial(\text{curl } \mathbf{B})/\partial t$, we use Eq. 10.8–1 and obtain in place of Eq. 10.3–2

$$\nabla^2 \mathbf{E} = \mu\epsilon_0 \frac{\partial^2 \mathbf{E}}{\partial t^2} + \mu\sigma_c \frac{\partial \mathbf{E}}{\partial t} \quad (10.8\text{–}2)$$

The identical equation can readily be found to hold for $\mathbf{B}$. Let us consider plane solutions, with $\mathbf{E} = E_x \mathbf{1}_x$ varying only in the z-direction and in time, and let us see if a wave solution exists. The differential equation becomes

$$\frac{\partial^2 E_x}{\partial z^2} = \mu\epsilon_0 \frac{\partial^2 E_x}{\partial t^2} + \mu\sigma_c \frac{\partial E_x}{\partial t} \quad (10.8\text{–}3)$$

We shall try a solution of the form

$$E_x = E_m \, e^{j\omega(t - z/v')} \quad (10.8\text{–}4)$$

On substitution, we find after dividing out E_x

$$-\frac{\omega^2}{v'^2} = -\mu\epsilon_0\omega^2 + j\omega\mu\sigma_c$$

which can be written using $v = (\mu\epsilon_0)^{-\frac{1}{2}}$

$$\frac{v^2}{v'^2} = 1 - \frac{j\sigma_c}{\omega\epsilon_0} \quad (10.8\text{–}5)$$

which shows that such a solution exists, but that v' is not a real number. Now, we saw in Section 5.2 that the relaxation time of a conductor is ϵ_0/σ_c (it is ϵ/σ_c if there is an appreciable molecular polarization in the conductor) and is of the order of 10^{-19} sec for many conductors. Therefore for frequencies of visible light (about 6×10^{14} sec^{-1}) $\sigma_c/\omega\epsilon_0$ is enormous compared to 1, and we can neglect the latter. Since

$$(-j)^{1/2} = \pm (j-1)/2^{1/2}$$

we can write

$$\frac{1}{v'} = \pm \frac{1}{v}\left(\frac{\sigma_c}{2\omega\epsilon_0}\right)^{1/2}(j-1) = \pm \left(\frac{\mu\sigma_c}{2\omega}\right)^{1/2}(j-1) \qquad (10.8\text{-}6)$$

Since $\sigma_c/\omega\epsilon_0$ is a very large number, we see that the magnitude of v' is very much less than v. Let us choose the negative sign in front so that v' will have a positive real part. We can then finally write for E_x the expression

$$E_x = E_m \exp\left\{-z(\mu\omega\sigma_c/2)^{1/2} + j[\omega t - z(\mu\omega\sigma_c/2)]^{1/2}\right\} \qquad (10.8\text{-}7)$$

The relation between E_x and B_y will be just as in Section 10.3 since we can derive it from Eq. 10.3-1d which is still valid. Therefore in the conductor we will have

$$B_y = E_x/v' \qquad (10.8\text{-}8)$$

Now let us consider the boundary conditions for oncoming plane waves normal to a metal surface, using subscripts i, r, and t for the amplitudes of incident, reflected, and transmitted waves, we have

$$E_i + E_r = E_t \qquad (10.8\text{-}9a)$$

$$H_i + H_r = H_t \qquad (10.8\text{-}9b)$$

but $H_i = E_i/\mu_0 c$; $H_r = -E_r/\mu_0 c$; and $H_t = E_t/\mu v'$. Thus we get from Eq. 10.8-9b

$$E_i - E_r = \frac{\mu_0 c}{\mu v'} E_t \qquad (10.8\text{-}10)$$

Adding Eqs. 10.8-9a and 10.8-10 we get

$$E_t = \frac{2\mu v'}{\mu_0 c} E_i \qquad (10.8\text{-}11)$$

which shows that E_t is very small compared to E_i, since at high frequencies μ/μ_0 cannot be very large, and v'/c is very small. Thus nearly all the energy is reflected, and the wave inside the metal is small at the boundary. The factor $\exp\left\{-z(\mu\omega\sigma_c/2)^{1/2}\right\}$ in Eq. 10.8-7 makes E_x fall off exponentially with increasing depth. The constant δ defined by

$$\delta = (2/\mu\omega\sigma_c)^{1/2} \qquad (10.8\text{-}12a)$$

is the depth at which the amplitude of E_x has fallen to $1/e$ of its value just inside the boundary and is called the "skin depth." The reduced wavelength of the radiation inside the conductor is also seen to be δ. The magnitude of δ gives a measure of the accuracy of our idealized boundary condition, which says that the field does not penetrate the conductor at all.

In Section 7.17 we discussed in a qualitative way how alternating current in a wire tends to be concentrated near the surface as the frequency increases. We are now in a position to calculate the current distribution for the relatively simple case of a long straight cylindrical wire of radius a.

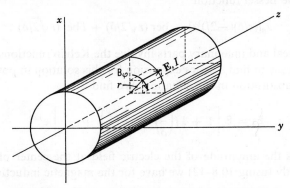

Fig. 10.8a.   Illustrating the calculation of the skin effect.

We assume that **E** is parallel to the axis of the wire, which we take as in the z direction, and is only a function of r and t (cf. Fig. 10.8a). The current density **J** will vary with E according to $\mathbf{J} = \sigma_c\mathbf{E}$. **B** will have only a hoop component B_φ which also is a function of r and t.

The neglect of the 1 in Eq. 10.8–5 is equivalent to omitting the $\partial^2\mathbf{E}/\partial t^2$ term in 10.8–2, i.e., neglecting the displacement current. For frequencies lower than those for which wave propagation in conductors is important, the neglect of this term is even more justified. Hence we can write for all frequencies of interest

$$\nabla^2\mathbf{E} = \mu\sigma_c\,\partial\mathbf{E}/\partial t \tag{10.8–13}$$

and take the electric field to be of the form

$$\mathbf{E} = \mathbf{1}_zE_m(r)\,e^{j\omega t} \tag{10.8–14}$$

The magnetic induction can then be written

$$\mathbf{B} = \mathbf{1}_\phi B_m(r)\,e^{i\omega t} \tag{10.8–15}$$

The fields are related by $\nabla \times \mathbf{E} = -\partial\mathbf{B}/\partial t$ or

$$-\frac{\partial E_m}{\partial r} = -j\omega B_m \tag{10.8–16}$$

so it will suffice to calculate E_z.

Using the cylindrical-coordinate form of ∇^2 (Table A.2A) we find

$$\frac{1}{r}\frac{\partial}{\partial r}\left(r\frac{\partial E_m(r)}{\partial r}\right) = j\omega\mu\sigma_c E_m(r)$$

or

$$\frac{\partial^2 E_m}{\partial r^2} + \frac{1}{r}\frac{\partial E_m}{\partial r} - \frac{2j}{\delta^2}E_m = 0 \qquad (10.8\text{-}17)$$

This equation is a form of Bessel's equation, with a regular solution given by the Bessel function[17]

$$J_0[(r/\delta)(-2j)^{1/2}] = \text{ber}\,(r\sqrt{2}/\delta) + i\,\text{bei}\,(r\sqrt{2}/\delta) \qquad (10.8\text{-}18)$$

where the real and imaginary parts involve the Kelvin functions ber x and bei x. It is easy to find a series expansion for this solution in powers of r/δ by direct substitution in the equation. We find

$$E_z = E_c\left[1 + \tfrac{1}{2}j\left(\frac{r}{\delta}\right)^2 - \frac{1}{16}\left(\frac{r}{\delta}\right)^4 + \cdots\right]e^{j\omega t} \qquad (10.8\text{-}19)$$

where E_c is the amplitude of the electric field at the center of the wire. Consequently (using 10.8-12) we have for the magnetic induction

$$B_\phi = \mu\sigma_c r E_c\left[1 + \tfrac{1}{4}j\left(\frac{r}{\delta}\right)^2 \cdots\right]e^{j\omega t} \qquad (10.8\text{-}20)$$

It is not hard to show that a second solution of Eq. 10.8-15 is a series starting with $\log(r/\delta)$, which must be excluded because it becomes infinite at $r = 0$.

For low frequencies δ is large, and the series give small corrections to the static result for which E is uniform and B proportional to r. It is interesting to note that the first correction terms give field values which are 90° out of phase with the static values.

For high frequencies and small values of δ, it is necessary to use the asymptotic expansion of the Bessel function. This expansion is not easy to obtain, but we can combine a simple approximation with a physical argument as follows.

Two approximate solutions of 10.8-17 are

$$\frac{e^{(1+j)(r/\delta)}}{(r/\delta)^{1/2}} \quad \text{and} \quad \frac{e^{-(1+j)(r/\delta)}}{(r/\delta)^{1/2}}$$

[17] R. V. Churchill, *op. cit.*, Chapter 8. For tables and formulas for *ber* x and *bei* x see M. Abramowitz and I. A. Stegun, *Handbook of Mathematical Tables*, U.S. National Bureau of Standards, Washington, D.C., 1964, pp. 379–385 and pp. 430–433.

as can be seen by substituting in the equation and neglecting a term proportional to $(\delta/r)^{5/2}$ which is much smaller than the rest if $\delta \ll r$. (An improvement in the approximation could be made by adding terms in higher powers of δ/r to the solution above). It happens that the asymptotic form of the Bessel function in Eq. 10.8–18 is given by a linear combination of the two solutions with coefficients 1 and j, respectively. Rather than pursue the mathematical proof of this assertion, we merely note that even at high frequencies E will continue to increase with r near the edge of the wire, so on physical grounds we choose the increasing exponential. The decreasing exponential will be so small for large r/δ that we can safely neglect it.

If we let $\mathbf{E}_{m0}$ be the value of the field just outside the wire, we can write

$$E_z \simeq \frac{E_{m0}\, e^{(1+j)(r-a)/\delta + j\omega t}}{(r/a)^{1/2}} \qquad (10.8\text{–}21a)$$

$$B_\varphi \simeq \frac{1-j}{\omega\delta}\, E_z \qquad (10.8\text{–}21b)$$

where we have neglected the variation of $(r/a)^{1/2}$ in calculating B_φ.

For small values of δ we see, just as before, that the fields fall off to $1/e$ of their surface values at a depth δ below the surface. Equation 10.8–20 can be derived (approximately) by treating the outer surface of the wire as a plane and solving 10.8–2 for $\mathbf{E}$ parallel to the boundary (Problem 10.8c).

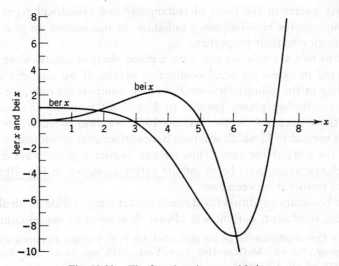

Fig. 10.8b. The functions ber x and bei x.

Note that the functions in Eq. 10.8–21 oscillate very rapidly with r when δ is small, so it is not practical to graph the *ber* and *bei* functions for large argument. The approximation given in 10.8–21 is quite good, however, for $r/\delta > 7$. Figure 10.8*b* shows curves of the Kelvin functions that can be used to get the variation of current density with r for relatively large δ.[18]

The expression for skin depth in Gaussian units has the form

$$\delta = c/(2\pi\mu\omega\sigma_c)^{\frac{1}{2}} \qquad \text{Gaussian} \quad (10.8\text{–}12b)$$

Note also that in Gaussian units, Eq. 10.8–21*b* requires a factor c on the right-hand side.

Problem 10.8a. Write δ in Eq. 10.8–12 in terms of the vacuum wave length λ of the incident waves, and find it for (*a*) copper ($\mu_r = 1$, $\sigma_c = 5.80 \times 10^7$ mhos/m) and (*b*) iron ($\mu_r = 600$, $\sigma_c = 1.00 \times 10^7$ mhos/m) for wave lengths of 400 m, 4 m, 0.4 mm, and 5×10^{-5} cm.

Problem 10.8b. Find the skin depth for sea water, with $\rho_c = 0.20$ m-ohm, for frequencies of 30 kilocycles and 30 megacycles. How practical is radio communication with submarines?

Problem 10.8c. Solve Eq. 10.8–2 for the case with **E** parallel to the conducting surface and a function only of distance along the normal, and compare the results with 10.8–21.

Problem 10.8d. Discuss the relation between the skin depth and the diffusion time given in Eq. 10.5–11. How are their derivations related?

10.9   Radiation in Pipes and Cavities

Wave guides in the form of rectangular and cylindrical pipes are in common use for high-frequency radiation. In this section we give a brief introduction to their properties.

Let us first see how we can have a plane electromagnetic wave that is restricted in extent by ideal conducting planes. If we consider a wave traveling in the z-direction with E_x and B_y components only, we cannot place conducting planes parallel to **E** without violating the boundary conditions discussed in the Section 10.7. We can, however, introduce planes normal to **E**, which will then have surface charges induced on them as in the coaxial-line case. Thus we can restrict a plane wave between two planes which must be of infinite extent as shown in Fig. 10.9*a*, but cannot restrict it between four.

The boundary condition for **B** needs further study. Inside an ideal resistanceless conductor, current will always flow so as to cancel completely

---

[18] For further information on the skin effect, see F. E. Terman, *Electronic and Radio Engineering*, 7th ed., McGraw-Hill, New York, 1955, pp. 21–24, and Ramo and Whinnery, *op. cit.*, Chapter 6.

any external magnetic field. Thus **B** will be zero in the conductor. Since however the normal component of **B** is continuous across any boundary, B_n will be zero just outside the metal, and there can only be a tangential component there. The discontinuity in the latter will be produced by surface currents, whose amount J_S per unit width of surface can be found from the circuital form of Ampère's law. A suitable path is shown in Fig.

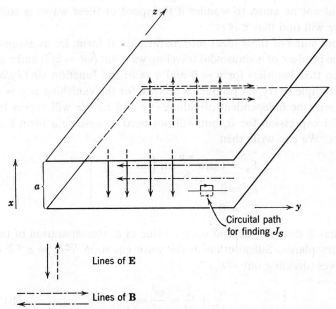

Fig. 10.9a. A plane wave restricted between two infinite planes.

10.9a. If its length parallel to B_y in the figure is one unit, and its x-dimension is negligible, we have immediately (cf. Problem 7.8h)

$$\mu_0 i = \oint \mathbf{B} \cdot \mathbf{dl} = B_y = \mu_0 J_S \tag{10.9-1}$$

Just as in the coaxial-line case, the resulting current will be found to account exactly for the changing charge density on which the electric flux begins and ends.

If we are to have a wave enclosed between four walls in a rectangular pipe, we must have a more complicated field than the plane-wave type. Let us show by an example how one can be constructed. If, in Fig. 10.9a, E_x varied with y so that it was zero at two places, say $y = 0$ and $y = b$, and remained zero at these y values for all z and all t, then a pair of planes perpendicular to the y-axis could be inserted without violating the boundary condition on **E**.

It would, however, then be necessary to have B_y equal to zero at the same planes. Since the lines of **B** have no ends, they must turn out of the y-direction. If the pattern of Fig. 10.9a is not to be modified too drastically, they must bend into the z-direction and surround lines of **E**. Since there will then be components of **B** along the direction of travel of the wave, it would not be amiss to wonder if the speed of these waves is still c; in fact, we will find that it is not.

To put some of these ideas into mathematical form, let us assume that E_x is the product of a sinusoidal traveling wave $\sin(\omega t - z/\lambda)$ and a simple function that vanishes for $y = 0$ and $y = b$; the function $\sin(\pi y/b)$ is a good example to try. (A product is needed, for the vanishing at $y = 0$ and $y = b$ must be independent of values of t and z.) We will expect to find a similar expression for B_y but will not need to assume a form for it in advance. We can write then

$$\left. \begin{aligned} E_x &= C \sin \frac{\pi y}{b} \sin \left(\omega t - \frac{z}{\lambda} \right) \\ E_y &= 0 \\ E_z &= 0 \end{aligned} \right\} \tag{10.9-2}$$

Note that **E** does not depend on the value of a, the separation of the y–z boundary planes. Substitution in the wave equation $\nabla^2 E_x = c^{-2}\, \partial^2 E_x/\partial t^2$ then gives (dividing out $-E_x$)

$$\frac{\pi^2}{b^2} + \frac{1}{\lambda^2} = \frac{\omega^2}{c^2} = \frac{1}{\lambda_0{}^2} \tag{10.9-3a}$$

where λ is the free-space reduced wave length. In terms of actual wave length and frequency we have

$$\frac{1}{4b^2} + \frac{1}{\lambda^2} = \frac{f^2}{c^2} = \frac{1}{\lambda_0{}^2} \tag{10.9-3b}$$

Furthermore, writing the velocity of the waves in the pipe (the so-called "phase velocity") as $v = f\lambda = \omega\lambda$, we have

$$v^2 = \left[\frac{1}{c^2} - \frac{1}{4b^2 f^2} \right]^{-1} = \frac{4b^2 f^2 c^2}{4b^2 f^2 - c^2} = c^2 + \frac{c^4}{4b^2 f^2 - c^2} \tag{10.9-4}$$

which can yield a real velocity only if v^2 is positive or

$$f > \frac{c}{2b} \tag{10.9-5}$$

so that a field of the sort we are seeking can only exist for frequencies above a certain limit. Since $c = f\lambda_0$, we see that the free-space wave length λ_0 must be less than $2b$. We shall shortly give a geometrical justification for this cutoff.

Let us now find the components of **B**. We have from curl $\mathbf{E} = -\partial \mathbf{B}/\partial t$,

$$-\frac{\partial B_x}{\partial t} = \frac{\partial E_z}{\partial y} - \frac{\partial E_y}{\partial z} \equiv 0$$

$$-\frac{\partial B_y}{\partial t} = \frac{\partial E_x}{\partial z} = -\frac{C}{\lambda} \sin \frac{\pi y}{b} \cos \left(\omega t - \frac{z}{\lambda} \right)$$

$$-\frac{\partial B_z}{\partial t} = -\frac{\partial E_x}{\partial y} = -\frac{C\pi}{b} \cos \frac{\pi y}{b} \sin \left(\omega t - \frac{z}{\lambda} \right)$$

from which on integration and setting of constants equal to zero we find

$$\left. \begin{aligned} B_x &= 0 \\[4pt] B_y &= \frac{C}{\lambda\omega} \sin \frac{\pi y}{b} \sin \left(\omega t - \frac{z}{\lambda} \right) \\[4pt] B_z &= -\frac{C\pi}{b\omega} \cos \frac{\pi y}{b} \cos \left(\omega t - \frac{z}{\lambda} \right) \end{aligned} \right\} \qquad (10.9\text{--}6)$$

Let us see how the magnetic lines of force are curved. The ratio B_z/B_y will give their slope in the z–y plane. This ratio is

$$\frac{B_z}{B_y} = -\frac{\pi\lambda}{b} \cot \frac{\pi y}{b} \cot \left(\omega t - \frac{z}{\lambda} \right) \qquad (10.9\text{--}7)$$

For, say, $t = 0$, we have the result that for $z = 0$ and $z = \pi\lambda$ the ratio is infinite, so all lines for these values of z are in the z-direction; for $z = \pm\pi\lambda/2$, the ratio is zero and the lines are in the y-direction. For intermediate values of z, we can conclude from the factor $\cot(\pi y/b)$ that for $y = 0$ and $y = b$ the lines again are in the z-direction, whereas for $y = b/2$ they are in the y-direction. The result is evidently as shown in Fig. 10.9b.

Now let us examine the velocity formula 10.9–4 a bit further. It is evident that, besides being dependent on the frequency, v is greater than c. This seems to contradict the well-established principle of relativity, and needs further investigation. We begin by using some elementary trigonometry to rewrite Eqs. 10.9–2 and 10.9–6. Using the formulas for $\cos (a \pm b)$, we have

$$E_x = \frac{C}{2}\left[\cos\left(\omega t - \frac{z}{\lambda} - \frac{\pi y}{b}\right) - \cos\left(\omega t - \frac{z}{\lambda} + \frac{\pi y}{b}\right)\right]$$

$$E_y = 0$$

$$E_z = 0 \qquad\qquad (10.9\text{–}8)$$

$$B_x = 0$$

$$B_y = \frac{C}{2\lambda\omega}\left[\cos\left(\omega t - \frac{z}{\lambda} - \frac{\pi y}{b}\right) - \cos\left(\omega t - \frac{z}{\lambda} + \frac{\pi y}{b}\right)\right]$$

$$B_z = -\frac{C\pi}{2b\omega}\left[\cos\left(\omega t - \frac{z}{\lambda} - \frac{\pi y}{b}\right) + \cos\left(\omega t - \frac{z}{\lambda} + \frac{\pi y}{b}\right)\right] \qquad (10.9\text{–}9)$$

We have resolved our simple wave into two of a more familiar variety, namely sinusoidal waves of the form 10.3–7. Comparing the expression

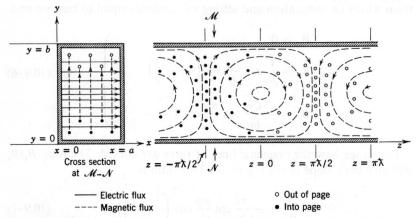

Electric flux ———   o Out of page
Magnetic flux – – –   • Into page

Fig. 10.9b. Field lines for a $TE_{0,1}$ mode in a rectangular wave guide, for $t = 0$. (Taken from Skilling, *op. cit.*, p. 200, Fig. 74, modified.)

$\omega t - (z/\lambda) \pm (\pi y/b)$ with $\omega(t - \mathbf{r} \cdot \mathbf{1}_u/c)$ we find that the vector corresponding to $\mathbf{1}_u/c$ has components 0, $\mp(\pi/b\omega)$, and $1/\lambda\omega$ and magnitude given by

$$\left[\frac{\pi^2}{b^2\omega^2} + \frac{1}{\lambda^2\omega^2}\right]^{1/2} = \frac{1}{c} \qquad (10.9\text{–}10)$$

by use of Eq. 10.9–3a. Hence each of the two component waves travels with the velocity c; the vector $\mathbf{1}_u$ has components

$$u_x = 0; \qquad u_y = \mp\frac{\pi c}{b\omega} = \mp\frac{\lambda_0}{2b};$$

$$u_z = \frac{c}{\lambda\omega} = (1 - u_y^2)^{1/2} = \left[1 - \left(\frac{\lambda_0}{2b}\right)^2\right]^{1/2} \qquad (10.9\text{–}11)$$

Our new waves therefore travel along lines in the y–z plane making angles α with the z-axis given by

$$\cot \alpha = \frac{u_z}{u_y} = \frac{2b}{\lambda_0}\left[1 - \left(\frac{\lambda_0}{2b}\right)^2\right]^{1/2} \qquad (10.9\text{--}12)$$

The effective reduced wave length of these waves is given by ω/c and is thus equal to the free-space value λ_0. These waves do not travel straight down the pipe but criss-cross back and forth. At each reflection the waves with the plus and minus signs must exchange places, in accordance with our study of reflection in the previous section. Figure 10.9c illustrates the two waves in their zigzag behavior.

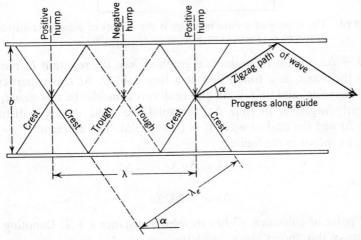

Fig. 10.9c. The zigzag passage of plane waves down a pipe. (Taken from Skilling, *op. cit.*, Fig. 75.)

The meaning of the cutoff for free-space wave length equal to $2b$ becomes clear from Eq. 10.9–12. At this wave length $\cot \alpha = 0$ and the waves reflect back and forth in the y-direction without traveling down the tube at all. The meaning of the phase velocity greater than c for the resultant of the two reflected waves is that the positions where constructive interference occurs travel at this speed (see Fig. 10.9d).

Note that the phase velocity v depends on the frequency. If any actual pulse or finite wave train is introduced into the wave guide, an analysis like that of Section 9.8 shows that it must always contain effectively a series of wave lengths. We wish to show that the velocity of such pulses of energy down the pipe is always less than c. Consider two signals of frequencies f and $f + \Delta f$. They will reflect back and forth at different angles and have different velocities, v and $v + \Delta v$, and wave lengths, λ

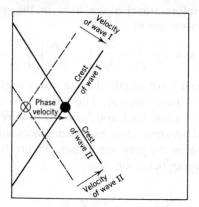

Fig. 10.9d. The velocity of a wave in a pipe is the velocity of points of constructive interference. (Taken from Skilling, *op cit.*, Fig. 76.)

and $\lambda + \Delta\lambda$. Figure 10.9e shows a graph of, say, the resultant E_x plotted along the z-axis, at a time t and at a time $t + \Delta t$. At t, two particular crests coincide, and at $t + \Delta t$, the next two coincide. In this figure, Δv is clearly negative. In time Δt, the solid-line wave travels a distance $s = v\,\Delta t$ and the dashed wave $s' = (v + \Delta v)\,\Delta t$. The difference $s' - s$ is $-\Delta\lambda$, as shown in the figure:

$$s' - s = \Delta v\,\Delta t = -\Delta\lambda$$

so that

$$\Delta t = -\Delta\lambda/\Delta v$$

The "point of coincidence" has traveled a distance $s + \lambda$. Denoting the velocity of this "point" by v_g, we have

$$v_g\,\Delta t = s + \lambda$$

or

$$v_g = \frac{v\,\Delta t + \lambda}{\Delta t} = v - \lambda\frac{\Delta v}{\Delta\lambda}$$

Now, if we consider a group of waves of nearly equal characteristics in which v is a continuous function of λ, the ratio $\Delta v/\Delta\lambda$ can be taken as the derivative $dv/d\lambda$. The "point of coincidence" for the group of waves becomes the place of maximum constructive interference—i.e., the center of the pulse—and the speed v_g becomes the pulse speed, generally called the group velocity. We have then

$$v_g = v - \lambda\frac{dv}{d\lambda} = \lambda f - \lambda\frac{d(\lambda f)}{d\lambda} = -\lambda^2\frac{df}{d\lambda} = \frac{df}{d(1/\lambda)} = \frac{d\omega}{d(1/\lambda)}$$

$$(10.9\text{--}13)$$

From Eq. 10.9–3 we find

$$v_g = (c/\lambda)\left[\frac{\pi^2}{b^2} + \frac{1}{\lambda^2}\right]^{-\frac{1}{2}} = \frac{c^2}{\omega\lambda} = \frac{c^2}{v} \qquad (10.9\text{–}14)$$

which says that when $v > c$, $v_g < c$, so that all pulses and in fact all communications travel with a velocity less than that of light. The values of λ, ω, and v used in calculating v_g must, of course, be the average or central

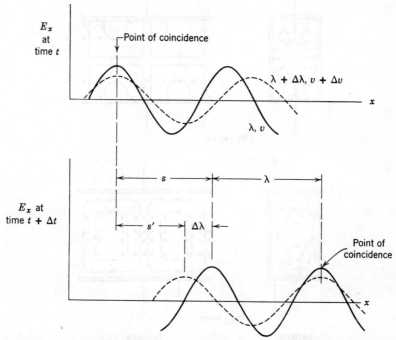

Fig. 10.9e. Two waves whose coincidence point moves forward. The ratio $\Delta v/\Delta\lambda$ is negative in this diagram but is positive for electromagnetic waves in pipes.

values for the pulse. A pulse with a wide range of ω's and v's will consequently have a spread of v_g's and must spread out and become distorted as it travels.

We have described thus far only one arrangement, or mode, of wave propagation in rectangular pipes. There are many possible modes, which we shall only briefly describe. If E_x varies sinusoidally in y in such a way as to vanish one or more times between the walls, the resulting field will have a pattern like two or more of the kind just described, compressed in the y-direction and placed side by side. We can also have the electric field only in the y-direction, with one or more "repeats" of our standard pattern. And we can have any combination of these patterns based on E_x and on E_y. All such patterns are called "transverse electric" modes and are designated by the symbols $TE_{m,n}$ where m and n tell the number of half-cycles of E-pattern there are in the wider and narrower dimensions, respectively. The mode we have described is a $TE_{1,0}$ mode, and is called the dominant mode (in case $b > a$) for it has the lowest cutoff frequency.

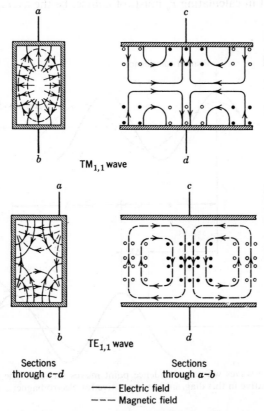

Fig. 10.9f. The field patterns for the $TM_{1,1}$ and $TE_{1,1}$ modes. (Taken from Skilling, *op. cit.*, p. 213, Fig. 79.)

We can also have a purely transverse magnetic field. Since, however, the magnetic lines cannot end, we must start patterns in the x–y plane involving closed loops like those for the magnetic lines in the y–z plane of Fig. 10.9b. The electric lines will curve around the magnetic lines, as well as beginning and ending on the metal surface. We can then have, for instance, an array of $m \times n$ such patterns, where m and n are any two integers, giving us the transverse magnetic or $TM_{m,n}$ modes. Figure 10.9f shows the field patterns for the $TM_{1,1}$ and $TE_{1,1}$ modes.

In cylindrical pipes there can also exist a series of TE and TM modes. Their mathematical description involves the use of Bessel functions, and we shall not attempt it here. For details on these modes as well as the rectangular ones, the reader is referred elsewhere.[19] The mode of propagation in the coaxial line described in Section 10.2 can be called a TEM mode (transverse electric and magnetic fields). TE and TM modes can also exist in coaxial cables but are usually avoided by operating below the cutoff frequency (the TEM mode has no cutoff, as is evident from the derivation in Section 10.2).

The introduction of radiation into a wave guide in a particular mode can be affected by using a small "antenna" in the form of a loop or probe or combination of such elements arranged to produce a field of approximately the same pattern as that desired. Reception can be made with the same sort of elements. The radiation can also be allowed to leave the open end of the pipe and travel in free space. However, a simple open end will reflect a good deal of energy, just as for a coaxial cable, so that radiating ends should be "matched" to free space with suitable horn shapes. Bends, corners, and junctions used in wave-guide "plumbing" must be carefully designed to allow the desired mode to pass through and prevent the excitation of others.

We have neglected the effect of finite conductivity of the metal sides of the pipe, but naturally there must be attenuation because of this effect. Its calculation is more complicated than that for the coaxial line and will not be carried out here.[20] For most modes, the attenuation is very high near cutoff, decreases to a minimum at some two or three times the cutoff frequency, and then increases roughly with $f^{\frac{1}{2}}$.

If a wave guide is closed at both ends, it becomes a cavity that can have standing wave patterns in it, but only of wave lengths properly related to its dimensions. For such a cavity, there is therefore only *one* allowable frequency for each mode. Cavity resonators are used in high-frequency oscillating circuits to produce good frequency control. In place of the use of an antenna, a large cavity can be arranged so as to radiate a small portion of its energy into a wave guide in an appropriate mode.

A precisely constructed cavity resonator can be used to furnish a value of c, for the wave length of a given mode will be related to the dimensions, which can be measured with great precision by optical interferometry; the frequency can be measured quite precisely by the use of a frequency divider and scaling circuit.[21]

[19] Skilling, *op. cit.*, pp. 207–218; F. E. Terman, *op. cit.*, Chapter 5; Ramo and Whinnery, *op. cit.*, Chapters 8 and 9.

[20] Skilling, *op. cit.*, pp. 220–225; Corson and Lorrain, *op. cit.*, pp. 429–433.

[21] For more information about cavity resonators, see Ramo and Whinnery, *op. cit.*, Chapter 10.

Problem 10.9a. Write formulas for the electric and magnetic field components for a TE_{21} wave in a rectangular pipe.

Problem 10.9b. Write formulas for the electric and magnetic field components for a TM_{11} wave in a rectangular pipe.

Problem 10.9c. Find the cutoff frequencies for the $TE_{1,0}$ modes in wave guides whose dimensions are 6 cm × 4 cm and 3 cm × 2 cm.

Problem 10.9d. Prove that for the $TE_{1,0}$ mode discussed in the text, we can have div $A = 0$ and $V = 0$ by proper choice of constants. Find A for this example.

Problem 10.9e. Construct a diagram like Fig. 10.9e for the case that $\Delta v/\Delta \lambda > 0$.

Problem 10.9f. Calculate the Poynting vector for a $TE_{1,0}$ mode, and correlate its space and time variations with Figs. 10.9b and c.

10.10 Magnetohydrodynamic Waves

The tendency of magnetic lines of force to "follow" the motion of a body of conducting fluid leads to a type of oscillatory wave-motion in such fluids. To see qualitatively how this comes about, consider a fluid originally at rest in a uniform magnetic field B_0 and imagine giving a portion of it a small displacement transverse to B_0. The Lorentz force $\rho(v \times B)$ will temporarily set up currents in the moving portion with returning currents in the surrounding medium. By Lenz's law these currents will call into play restoring forces on the portion and opposite forces on the surrounding material, tending to drag it along with the original portion. Thus the displaced portion will tend to be pulled back toward its original position and its displacement will be transferred to neighboring portions. As shown in Fig. 10.10a, displacement will tend to propagate along the direction of B_0. Waves of this type are called "Alfvén waves."[22]

Another way to observe the same phenomenon is to note that part of the magnetic force on a conducting fluid, discussed in Section 10.5–4, consists of a tension $(B \cdot \nabla)B/\mu_0$ along the lines of force. If a line of force is distorted by a small magnetohydrodynamic displacement, this tension will make the distortion propagate along a line of force very much like the way a wave moves along a stretched spring. Let us take $B^2/2\mu_0$ as the value of an equivalent negative pressure along the lines of force from which the tension could be derived with a gradient calculation, and let us borrow the result from elementary physics that the speed of a wave on a string is $(F/m_l)^{1/2}$ where F is the force and m_l the mass per unit length. If we take a "string" of cross-sectional area ΔS, we can replace $F/\Delta S$ with $B^2/2\mu_0$

[22] Cf. H. Alfvén, *Cosmical Electrodynamics*, Oxford University Press, 1950.

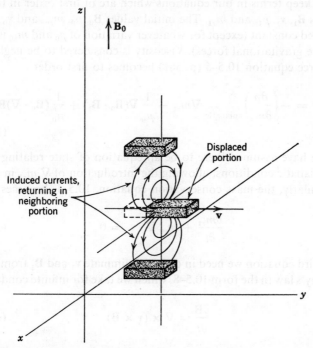

Fig. 10.10a. Illustrating how an initial displacement of a portion of a conducting fluid can initiate an Alfvén wave propagating along the direction of $\mathbf{B}_0$.

and $m_l/\Delta S$ with m_r, the fluid density, and find as a guess for the velocity v_A of Alfvén waves

$$v_A \sim \left(\frac{B_0{}^2}{2\mu_0 m_r}\right)^{\frac{1}{2}} \tag{10.10-1}$$

This result bears a resemblance to the formula for the velocity of sound in the fluid which is

$$v_s = \left(\frac{\partial p}{\partial m_r}\right)^{\frac{1}{2}}_{\text{adiabatic}} \tag{10.10-2}$$

where the derivative is taken under adiabatic conditions.

Now let us make a rigorous derivation of the properties of these waves. We consider that the displacements are always small, and that pressure, density, and magnetic induction only differ by a small fraction of their initial values as the wave passes. We write therefore

$$\left.\begin{aligned}
\mathbf{B} &= \mathbf{B}_0 + \mathbf{B}_1(x, y, z, t) \\
\mathbf{v} &= \mathbf{v}_1(x, y, z, t) \\
p &= p_0 + p_1(x, y, z, t) \\
m_r &= m_{r0} + m_{r1}(x, y, z, t)
\end{aligned}\right\} \tag{10.10-3}$$

and only keep terms in our equations which are of first order in the small quantities B_1, v_1, p_1, and m_{r1}. The initial values B_0, p_0, m_{r0}, and $v_0 = 0$ are all assumed constant (except for whatever variation of p_0 and m_{r0} is needed to balance gravitational forces). Viscosity is considered to be negligible.

The force equation 10.5–5 (p. 561) becomes to first order

$$m_{r0} \frac{\partial v_1}{\partial t} = -\left(\frac{\partial p}{\partial m_r}\right)_{\text{adiabatic}} \nabla m_{r1} - \frac{1}{\mu_0} \nabla(B_0 \cdot B_1) + \frac{1}{\mu_0}(B_0 \cdot \nabla)B_1$$

$$(10.10\text{–}4)$$

where we have assumed there to be an equation of state relating p to m_r under adiabatic conditions, allowing the introduction of ∇m_{r1} in place of ∇p_1. Similarly, the mass conservation equation, 10.5–1, becomes

$$\frac{\partial m_{r1}}{\partial t} + m_{r0} \nabla \cdot v_1 = 0 \qquad (10.10\text{–}5)$$

The third equation we need in order to eliminate v_1 and B_1 from 10.10–4 is Faraday's law in the form 10.5–8, which we take for infinite conductivity:

$$\frac{\partial B}{\partial t} = \nabla \times (v \times B) \qquad (10.10\text{–}6)$$

or to first order (remembering that B_0 is constant)

$$\frac{\partial B_1}{\partial t} = (B_0 \cdot \nabla)v_1 - B_0 \nabla \cdot v_1 \qquad (10.10\text{–}7)$$

In order to eliminate B_1 and m_{r1}, we differentiate Eq. 10.10–4 with respect to t and then substitute from Eqs. 10.10–5 and 7. We find (also using Eq. 10.10–2)

$$m_{r0} \frac{\partial^2 v_1}{\partial t^2} = v_s^2 m_{r0} \nabla(\nabla \cdot v_1) - \frac{1}{\mu_0}[\nabla(B_0 \cdot \nabla)(B_0 \cdot v_1)$$

$$- B_0^2 \nabla(\nabla \cdot v_1) - (B_0 \cdot \nabla)^2 v_1 + B_0(B_0 \cdot \nabla)(\nabla \cdot v_1)] \quad (10.10\text{–}8)$$

Let us see if this formidable-looking equation has solutions representing plane transverse waves propagating in the direction of B_0. We take B_0 in the z-direction, assume that

$$B_0 \cdot v_1 = 0 \qquad (10.10\text{–}9)$$

and also that

$$\frac{\partial v_1}{\partial x} = \frac{\partial v_1}{\partial y} = 0 \qquad (10.10\text{–}10)$$

Since $v_{1z} = 0$, $\nabla \cdot \mathbf{v}_1 = 0$ and only one non-vanishing term remains on the right hand side of 10.10–8. We find

$$\frac{\mu_0 m_{r0}}{B_0{}^2} \frac{\partial^2 \mathbf{v}_1}{\partial t^2} = \frac{\partial^2 \mathbf{v}_1}{\partial z^2} \tag{10.10–11}$$

showing that indeed there exists waves of the expected type, whose velocity is given by the Alfvén velocity

$$\mathbf{v}_A = \frac{\mathbf{B}_0}{\sqrt{\mu_0 m_{r0}}} \tag{10.10–12a}$$

The guess of Eq. 10.10–1 was incorrect, but only by a factor $\sqrt{2}$.

It is also possible to have *longitudinal* waves propagating along the magnetic field at the speed of sound—all the terms in $\mathbf{B}_0$ can be shown to cancel in this case—and longitudinal waves propagating at right angles to $\mathbf{B}_0$ at a higher speed (cf. Problems 10.10b and c). Even more complex are the effects of initial inhomogeneities in density and $\mathbf{B}$, but we shall not enter into their details here.[23]

The Alfvén velocity in Gaussian units is given by

$$\mathbf{v}_A = \frac{\mathbf{B}_0}{\sqrt{4\pi m_{r0}}} \tag{10.10–12b}$$

Problem 10.10a. Find the relation between the amplitudes of $\mathbf{B}_1$, $\mathbf{v}_1$, and m_{r1} for an Alfvén wave of angular frequency ω.

Problem 10.10b. Show that longitudinal waves propagate along the direction of $\mathbf{B}_0$ at the speed of sound and that $\mathbf{B}_1 = 0$ for these waves which are thus pure sound waves.

Problem 10.10c. Show that longitudinal waves propagate at right angles to $\mathbf{B}_0$ with a speed $(v_S{}^2 + v_A{}^2)^{1/2}$. Find the relation between the amplitudes of $\mathbf{B}_1$, $\mathbf{v}_1$, and m_{r1} for a given angular frequency ω.

Problem 10.10d. Find the speed of Alfvén waves in liquid mercury in a field of 1.0 weber/m². and compare with the speed of sound in mercury, 1.45×10^3 m/sec. Make the same calculation for the sun's photosphere where there are about 6×10^{22} hydrogen atoms/m³ and the speed of sound is 10^4 m/sec. Consider a region near a sunspot where $B = 0.1$ weber/m².

[23] Cf. F. Winterberg, "On the Propagation of Alfvén waves in Inhomogeneous Magnetic Fields," *Developments in Mechanics*, Pergamon, London and New York, 1965, pp. 173–183. A somewhat more detailed account of waves in homogeneous fields is given by Landau and Lifshitz, *op. cit.*, pp. 218–223.

APPENDIX

A.1 Notes on Calculus

Taylor's theorem for functions of one variable says that if we are given the value of a function $g(x)$ and its derivatives for $x = x_0$, we can find $g(x)$ for a neighboring value of x from a suitable number of terms of the series

$$g(x) = g(x_0) + (x - x_0)g'(x_0) + \frac{1}{2!}(x - x_0)^2 g''(x_0)$$

$$+ \frac{1}{3!}(x - x_0)^3 g'''(x_0) + \cdots \qquad \text{(A.1--1)}$$

The textbooks that prove this theorem give formulas for the upper limit of the error made by stopping with any particular number of terms.

If we wish similarly to evaluate $f(x, y)$ at points (x, y) in the neighborhood of a point (x_0, y_0), we can write Taylor's theorem in two variables (the generalization to more variables is obvious)

$$f(x, y) = f(x_0, y_0) + (x - x_0)\left(\frac{\partial f}{\partial x}\right)_{\substack{x=x_0 \\ y=y_0}} + (y - y_0)\left(\frac{\partial f}{\partial y}\right)_{\substack{x=x_0 \\ y=y_0}}$$

$$+ \frac{1}{2}\left[(x - x_0)^2\left(\frac{\partial^2 f}{\partial x^2}\right)_{\substack{x=x_0 \\ y=y_0}} + 2(x - x_0)(y - y_0)\left(\frac{\partial^2 f}{\partial x\,\partial y}\right)_{\substack{x=x_0 \\ y=y_0}} \right.$$

$$\left. + (y - y_0)^2\left(\frac{\partial^2 f}{\partial y^2}\right)_{\substack{x=x_0 \\ y=y_0}}\right] + \cdots \qquad \text{(A.1--2)}$$

This formula can be derived from Eq. A.1–1 if we set

$$G(\theta) = f[x_0 + \theta(x - x_0), y_0 + \theta(y - y_0)] \qquad \text{(A.1--3)}$$

so that $G(0) = f(x_0, y_0)$ and $G(1) = f(x, y)$. Then writing a Taylor's series for $G(\theta)$ with $\theta_0 = 0$, we have

$$(\theta - \theta_0)G'(\theta_0) = \theta G'(0) = (x - x_0)\left(\frac{\partial f}{\partial x}\right)_{\substack{x=x_0 \\ y=y_0}} + (y - y_0)\left(\frac{\partial f}{\partial y}\right)_{\substack{x=x_0 \\ y=y_0}}$$

and so on for the higher terms. The rule that

$$\partial^2 f / \partial x\, \partial y = \partial^2 f / \partial y\, \partial x$$

etc., is required for this calculation.

The increment of a function $g(x)$ of one variable is written $\Delta g(x)$ and is related to the increment Δx of x by

$$\Delta g(x) = g(x + \Delta x) - g(x)$$

By Eq. A.1–1, we can write

$$\Delta g(x) = \Delta x g'(x) + \tfrac{1}{2} \Delta x^2 g''(x) + \cdots \qquad \text{(A.1–4)}$$

The differential dg of a function $g(x)$ is defined as the principal part of the increment, or the first term in Eq. A.1–4; the differential dx of an independent variable x is defined to be equal to its increment Δx. Thus we write

$$dg = g'(x)\, dx \qquad \text{(A.1–5)}$$

For a function of several variables, say $f(x, y, z)$, we can write from the three-variable form of Eq. A.1–2

$$\Delta f(x, y, z) = f(x + \Delta x, y + \Delta y, z + \Delta z) - f(x, y, z)$$

$$= \Delta x \frac{\partial f}{\partial x} + \Delta y \frac{\partial f}{\partial y} + \Delta z \frac{\partial f}{\partial z} + \tfrac{1}{2}\bigg[(\Delta x)^2 \frac{\partial^2 f}{\partial x^2}$$

$$+ 2\Delta x\, \Delta y \frac{\partial^2 f}{\partial x\, \partial y} + (\Delta y)^2 \frac{\partial^2 f}{\partial y^2} + 2\Delta y\, \Delta z \frac{\partial^2 f}{\partial y\, \partial z} + (\Delta z)^2 \frac{\partial^2 f}{\partial z^2}$$

$$+ 2\Delta x\, \Delta z \frac{\partial^2 f}{\partial x\, \partial z} \bigg] + \cdots \qquad \text{(A.1–6)}$$

and for the differential of $f(x, y, z)$ we write again the principal part of the increment

$$df = \frac{\partial f}{\partial x}\, dx + \frac{\partial f}{\partial y}\, dy + \frac{\partial f}{\partial z}\, dz \qquad \text{(A.1–7)}$$

If x, y, and z are all functions of another variable u, then from Eq. A.1–7 (more strictly from Eq. A.1–6) we can show that

$$\frac{\partial f}{\partial u} = \frac{\partial f}{\partial x} \frac{\partial x}{\partial u} + \frac{\partial f}{\partial y} \frac{\partial y}{\partial u} + \frac{\partial f}{\partial z} \frac{\partial z}{\partial u} \qquad \text{(A.1–8)}$$

An application of Taylor's theorem that is of particular importance is to the binomial series. By means of the theorem we can establish the series expansion for an arbitrary power α of $1 + x$:

$$(1 + x)^\alpha = 1 + \alpha x + \frac{\alpha(\alpha - 1)}{1 \cdot 2} x^2 + \frac{\alpha(\alpha - 1)(\alpha - 2)}{1 \cdot 2 \cdot 3} x^3 + \cdots$$

$$\text{(A.1–9)}$$

which converges if $|x| < 1$. The first few terms represent a good approximation if $|x|$ is considerably less than one. Table A.1A gives for reference the coefficients for several values of α (other than positive integers) which are of use in this book.

An ordinary integral (so-called Riemann integral) of a function $g(x)$ of one variable between limits a and b is defined as the limit of a sum found by dividing the interval ab into small parts Δx_i, all of which approach zero in the limit. We write

$$\int_a^b g(x)\,dx = \lim_{n \to \infty} \sum_{i=1}^n g(x_i)\,\Delta x_i \qquad (A.1\text{--}10)$$

where x_i is a value of x within the range Δx_i. Then it is proved in calculus that the integral may be evaluated by finding a function $G(x)$ whose derivative is $g(x)$, $G'(x) = g(x)$.

Table A.1.A   Coefficients for the Binomial Expansion $(1 + x)^\alpha$

α		power of x			
	0	1	2	3	4
$\frac{1}{2}$	1	$\frac{1}{2}$	$-\frac{1}{8}$	$\frac{1}{16}$	$-\frac{5}{128}$
$-\frac{1}{2}$	1	$-\frac{1}{2}$	$\frac{3}{8}$	$-\frac{5}{16}$	$\frac{35}{128}$
-1	1	-1	1	-1	1
$-\frac{3}{2}$	1	$-\frac{3}{2}$	$\frac{15}{8}$	$-\frac{35}{16}$	$\frac{315}{128}$
-2	1	-2	3	-4	5

An integral of a function $f(x, y)$ of two variables, taken over an area S, is defined as the limit of a single sum formed by dividing S into infinitesimal elements ΔS_i and evaluating $f(x, y)$ at an arbitrary point in each ΔS_i. We write

$$\int_S f(x, y)\,dS = \lim_{n \to \infty} \sum_{i=1}^n f(x_i, y_i)\,\Delta S_i \qquad (A.1\text{--}11)$$

using a single integral sign to indicate the single sum.

Then it is proved in advanced calculus books that the integral may be evaluated as an iterated integral, for instance over x and y:

$$\int_S f(x, y)\,dS = \int_{x_1}^{x_2} dx \int_{y_1}^{y_2} dy\, f(x, y) \qquad (A.1\text{--}12)$$

where in this order of integration (the y integration is to be evaluated first) y_2 and y_1 are generally functions of x. The possibility of using either order of integration sometimes leads to useful transformations of complicated expressions. The following transformation is fairly common and should be illustrated by the reader with a suitable sketch of the region S:

$$\int_a^b dx \int_a^x dy\, f(x, y) = \int_a^b dy \int_y^b dx\, f(x, y) \tag{A.1-13}$$

The generalization to multiple integrals in three or more variables is straightforward. It can be seen from the definition that integrals representing physical quantities can readily be defined in a physically meaningful way without reference to axes or coordinates that may be required for their evaluation. One of the principal exercises required in the application of integral calculus to physics is the choosing of suitable variables and the writing of the various physical quantities in terms of them, in order to evaluate the integrals.

The law of the mean for integrals states that, if the integrand is continuous and the range of integration finite, the value of an integral can always be set equal to the product of the interval (length, area, or volume) integrated over, times the value of the integrand taken at some (generally unknown) point in the interval. That is, for a surface integral we have

$$\int_S f(x, y)\, dS = f(x', y')S \tag{A.1-14}$$

where S is the area integrated over and (x', y') is that point within S which makes the equality hold.

The reader is assumed to be familiar with the ordinary definition of a derivative as the limit of a difference quotient. The definition of a continuously variable density is related but not the same. For instance, the volume charge density ρ is defined as the limit of the ratio of a small amount of charge Δq to the volume element in which it is contained, as the element goes to zero:

$$\rho = \lim_{\Delta \tau \to 0} \frac{\Delta q}{\Delta t} \tag{A.1-15a}$$

This limiting quotient resembles a derivative, but is not one since there is no function q that is being differentiated.

We can similarly define surface and linear densities by

$$\sigma = \lim_{\Delta S \to 0} \frac{\Delta q}{\Delta S} \tag{A.1-15b}$$

$$\lambda = \lim_{\Delta l \to 0} \frac{\Delta q}{\Delta l} \tag{A.1-15c}$$

Application of these strictly limiting processes to the physics of media composed of discrete particles may be done by assuming that we can stop short of the limit in such a way that large numbers of atoms remain in each element of volume, surface, or length and yet the elements have become very small compared to the errors of macroscopic position measurement.

Problem A.1a. Show that the nth term of Eq. A.1–2 can be written

$$\frac{1}{n!}\left[(x - x_0)\frac{\partial}{\partial x} + (y - y_0)\frac{\partial}{\partial y}\right]^n f(x, y)$$

where the derivatives in the expanded nth power act on $f(x, y)$ but not on $(x - x_0)$ or $(y - y_0)$ and x and y are replaced by x_0 and y_0 in $f(x, y)$ after the derivatives are calculated.

Problem A.1b. Illustrate the order change in Eq. A.1–13 by a suitable sketch of the region of integration in the x–y plane.

A.2   Vectors

Introduction. The ordinary symbols of physics, such as m (mass), t (time), p (pressure) etc. are *algebraic* quantities which can take on any real values, positive or negative. We can call them *scalars* because their values can be represented on a one-dimensional scale. An *arithmetic* quantity is one which takes on only positive values, such as kinetic energy or the radius in polar coordinates.

There are, however, many physical entities which are measurable in a more complex way, namely in terms of arithmetic quantity (magnitude) and direction, and are called vectors. Displacement, velocity, acceleration, and force are the basic vectors of mechanics, and others can be derived from them (e.g., torque as a vector). We also represent plane surfaces, or infinitesimal surfaces of any shape, as vectors, whose magnitudes are the areas and whose directions are along the normals (see below). We represent vectors by bold-faced letters, as **r**, **F**, **v**, **E**, **S**, etc., with the understanding that each vector symbol represents both the magnitude and direction of the physical entity. Light-face type is used for the magnitude of the quantity; (the magnitude may also be denoted by vertical bars: $F = |\mathbf{F}|$). The direction may be specified by a suitable angle or set of angles, but we shall not need a general symbol for direction—the use of components will obviate this need.

Two vectors are equal if their magnitudes are equal and they lie in parallel directions. Vectors can be combined by addition and subtraction and by two kinds of multiplication. Before giving the rules for vector combination, let us write down for comparison the combining rules of algebra. Algebraic quantities, denoted by a, b, c, etc., can be added and multiplied; the result of these operations or any combination of them is another algebraic quantity. There are five rules or laws for combination from which (along with some definitions) all of algebra can be constructed:

$$a + b = b + a \qquad \text{The commutative law of addition}$$
$$a + (b + c) = (a + b) + c \qquad \text{The associative law of addition}$$
$$ab = ba \qquad \text{The commutative law of multiplication}$$
$$a(bc) = (ab)c \qquad \text{The associative law of multiplication}$$
$$a(b + c) = ab + ac \qquad \text{The distributive law}$$

Vector Addition; Components and Coordinate Systems. Vectors can be added graphically or by analytic procedures derived from graphical addition by geometry and trigonometry. We represent a vector graphically as an arrow with the appropriate direction whose length on a suitable scale represents the magnitude.

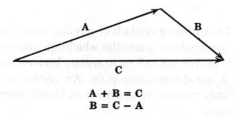

$$A + B = C$$
$$B = C - A$$

Fig. A.2a. Addition and subtraction of vectors.

Figure A.2a represents the summation $A + B = C$ and also of course the subtraction $B = C - A$. If $A = C$, B is a vector of zero length and unspecified direction called a "null vector." If $A = B$, $C = A + A = 2A$, a vector collinear with A of twice the length. We can extend this process of doubling a vector so that a vector can be multiplied by any scalar whether dimensionless or not—e.g., the acceleration a can be multiplied by the scalar m to give the force $F = ma$, a vector in the same direction as a but measured in different physical units. It is obviously also possible to divide a vector by a scalar. Vector addition obeys the same commutative and associative laws as ordinary addition, as is evident from geometry.

Any vector can be represented as the sum of three at right angles (or any number at more or less arbitrary angles). There are three systems of coordinates to which we make reference and which specify convenient directions into which we can resolve vectors. The Cartesian system uses three perpendicular axes labeled x, y, and z. For reasons to appear shortly, we always use a right-handed system, in which, if the fingers of the right hand are pointed from the positive x-axis to the positive y-axis through the 90° angle separating them, the thumb will be found to point on the side of the x–y plane that contains the positive z-axis.

Cylindrical coordinates are those in which one Cartesian axis, usually the z-axis, is retained, and points are located in planes perpendicular to this axis by polar coordinates r and ϕ. In spherical coordinates a point is located by its distance r from the origin, by the angle θ between a chosen polar axis and the radius vector (line from origin to the point), and by the angle ϕ between the plane containing the polar axis and the radius vector and an arbitrary fixed plane through the polar axis.

Vectors are conveniently resolved in any of these systems by the use of coordinate unit vectors, which are vectors of unit (dimensionless) length, directed at any given point along the three perpendicular directions that correspond to infinitesimal motions of the point when each variable respectively is allowed to increase. Each unit vector is represented in this book by a bold-face figure **1**, with an appropriate subscript. For the coordinate unit vectors, the variable that is allowed to change is used as a subscript. Figures A.2b, c, and d represent the three above-mentioned coordinate systems with their associated unit vectors.

A vector **A** can thus be represented as the sum of three vectors, each of which is a scalar (called a component) multiplied by a unit vector. For the three systems, we have

$$\left. \begin{aligned} \mathbf{A} &= A_x\mathbf{1}_x + A_y\mathbf{1}_y + A_z\mathbf{1}_z \quad \text{Cartesian} \\ \mathbf{A} &= A_r\mathbf{1}_r + A_\phi\mathbf{1}_\phi + A_z\mathbf{1}_z \quad \text{Cylindrical} \\ \mathbf{A} &= A_r\mathbf{1}_r + A_\theta\mathbf{1}_\theta + A_\phi\mathbf{1}_\phi \quad \text{Spherical} \end{aligned} \right\} \qquad \text{(A.2–1)}$$

Note that a subscript on a light-face letter signifies a part or component of a vector, whereas a subscript on a **1** signifies the direction of a whole unit vector.

By the theorem of Pythagoras, the magnitude A of **A** is equal to the square root of the sum of the squares of the three components in any system,

$$A = |\mathbf{A}| = (A_x{}^2 + A_y{}^2 + A_z{}^2)^{\frac{1}{2}}$$

with a similar formula for the other coordinate systems. It is easy to see by suitable constructions in the figures that the cosine of the angle between **A** and any of the unit vectors is given by the ratio of the component of A in that direction to the magnitude of A itself. The cosines for the Cartesian case are called the direction cosines, A_x/A, A_y/A, and A_z/A. It is evident that the sum of the squares of the direction cosines is unity.

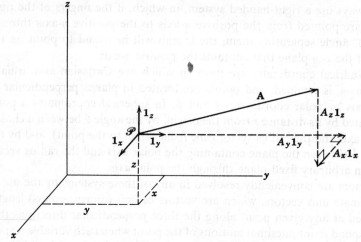

Fig. A.2b. Cartesian coordinates.

The equality of two vectors implies agreement in direction and magnitude, which in turn requires the equality of the corresponding components in any coordinate system.

The radius vector **r** or **R**, representing a displacement from the origin to a given point $\mathscr{P}$, is one of the simplest vectors. In Cartesian coordinates it is

$$\mathbf{r} = x\mathbf{1}_x + y\mathbf{1}_y + z\mathbf{1}_z \tag{A.2–2a}$$

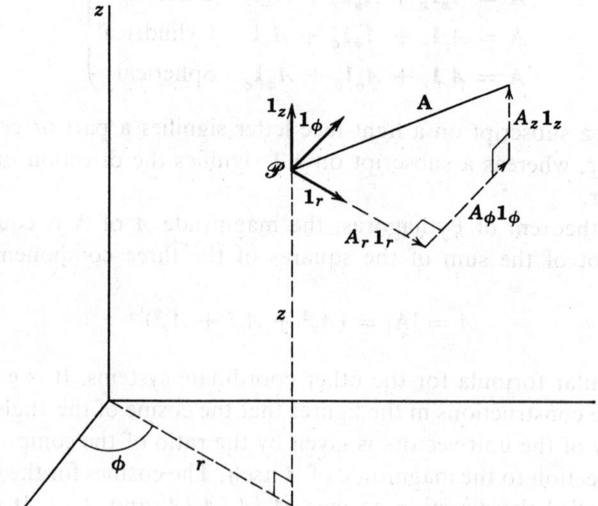

Fig. A.2c. Cylindrical coordinates.

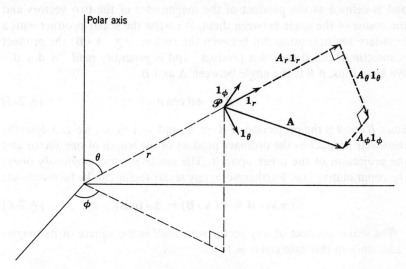

Fig. A.2d. Spherical coordinates.

In cylindrical coordinates, where r has a different significance, we write

$$\mathbf{R} = r\mathbf{1}_r + z\mathbf{1}_z \qquad (A.2-2b)$$

and in spherical coordinates it is simply

$$\mathbf{r} = r\mathbf{1}_r \qquad (A.2-2c)$$

A unit vector in the direction of a vector A is clearly

$$\mathbf{1}_A = \frac{\mathbf{A}}{A} = \frac{A_x}{A}\mathbf{1}_x + \frac{A_y}{A}\mathbf{1}_y + \frac{A_z}{A}\mathbf{1}_z \qquad (A.2-3)$$

The spherical coordinate unit vector $\mathbf{1}_r$ thus is given from Eqs. A.2–2a and 2c by

$$\mathbf{1}_r = \frac{\mathbf{r}}{r} = \frac{x}{r}\mathbf{1}_x + \frac{y}{r}\mathbf{1}_y + \frac{z}{r}\mathbf{1}_z \qquad (A.2-4)$$

in Cartesian coordinates. Any unit vector is thus equal to the sum of the products of each direction cosine with the corresponding Cartesian unit vector.

It should be remarked that the coordinate unit vectors in other systems than the Cartesian are variables, for directions of these unit vectors are dependent on the coordinates themselves (cf. Problem A.2d). This fact makes Cartesian coordinates preferable for most of our development, along with the ease in Cartesian coordinates of making a transfer of origin.

The Scalar Product. Two vectors may be "multiplied" together to give a scalar or a vector. The former type of product is called a scalar product and is defined as the product of the magnitudes of the two vectors and the cosine of the angle between them. We write the scalar product with a bold-face multiplication dot between the vectors, e.g., $\mathbf{A} \cdot \mathbf{B}$; the product is sometimes called the "dot product" and is generally read "A dot B." We have thus, if θ is the angle between $\mathbf{A}$ and $\mathbf{B}$,

$$\mathbf{A} \cdot \mathbf{B} = AB \cos \theta \qquad (A.2\text{--}5)$$

Since $B \cos \theta$ is the projection of $\mathbf{B}$ on $\mathbf{A}$, and vice versa, we can describe the scalar product as the ordinary product of the length of one vector and the projection of the other upon it. The scalar product obviously obeys the commutative law. Furthermore, any scalar factor can be factored out:

$$(m\mathbf{A}) \cdot \mathbf{B} = m(\mathbf{A} \cdot \mathbf{B}) = \mathbf{A} \cdot (m\mathbf{B}) \qquad (A.2\text{--}6)$$

The scalar product of any vector with itself is the square of its magnitude, since in this case $\cos \theta = 1$:

$$\mathbf{A} \cdot \mathbf{A} = A^2 \qquad (A.2\text{--}7)$$

The scalar products of the unit vectors of any of the coordinate systems are either unity or zero:

$$\mathbf{1}_x \cdot \mathbf{1}_x = \mathbf{1}_y \cdot \mathbf{1}_y = \mathbf{1}_z \cdot \mathbf{1}_z = 1 \qquad (A.2\text{--}8)$$
$$\mathbf{1}_x \cdot \mathbf{1}_y = \mathbf{1}_y \cdot \mathbf{1}_x = \mathbf{1}_y \cdot \mathbf{1}_z = \mathbf{1}_z \cdot \mathbf{1}_y = \mathbf{1}_z \cdot \mathbf{1}_x = \mathbf{1}_x \cdot \mathbf{1}_z = 0$$

with corresponding results for the other two systems.

The scalar product of a vector $\mathbf{A}$ with a unit vector $\mathbf{1}_l$ in any direction is the component of $\mathbf{A}$ in the direction of l:

$$\mathbf{A} \cdot \mathbf{1}_l = A_l \qquad (A.2\text{--}9)$$

By a theorem of geometry concerning projections, it is easy to see that the scalar product obeys the distributive law (see Fig. A.2e):

$$\mathbf{A} \cdot (\mathbf{B} + \mathbf{C}) = \mathbf{A} \cdot \mathbf{B} + \mathbf{A} \cdot \mathbf{C} \qquad (A.2\text{--}10)$$

A consequence of Eq. A.2–10 is that we can calculate $\mathbf{A} \cdot \mathbf{B}$ in terms of components by use of Eqs. A.2–1 and A.2–8:

$$\begin{aligned}
\mathbf{A} \cdot \mathbf{B} &= (A_x \mathbf{1}_x + A_y \mathbf{1}_y + A_z \mathbf{1}_z) \cdot (B_x \mathbf{1}_x + B_y \mathbf{1}_y + B_z \mathbf{1}_z) \\
&= A_x B_x + A_y B_y + A_z B_z \qquad \text{Cartesian} \\
&= A_r B_r + A_\phi B_\phi + A_z B_z \qquad \text{Cylindrical} \\
&= A_r B_r + A_\theta B_\theta + A_\phi B_\phi \qquad \text{Spherical}
\end{aligned} \right\} \qquad (A.2\text{--}11)$$

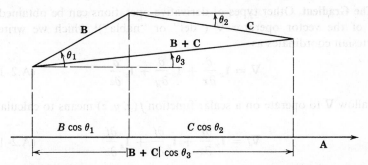

Fig. A.2e. The projection of the sum is the sum of the projections. $\mathbf{A} \cdot (\mathbf{B} + \mathbf{C}) = A(|\mathbf{B} + \mathbf{C}| \cos \theta_3) = A(B \cos \theta_1 + C \cos \theta_2) = \mathbf{A} \cdot \mathbf{B} + \mathbf{A} \cdot \mathbf{C}$. •

Derivatives and Integrals. From the definitions of the difference of two vectors and of division by a scalar, it is easy to derive the concept of the derivative of a vector with respect to a scalar variable. The derivative $d\mathbf{A}/dt$ is thus defined as the limit of $(\mathbf{A}_2 - \mathbf{A}_1)/(t_2 - t_1)$ when $t_2 \rightarrow t_1$.

Similarly, the concept of the integral can be extended to vectors. The integral $\int_l \mathbf{F} \cdot d\mathbf{l}$ represents the work done on an object by a force $\mathbf{F}$ when the object moves along a path l and is defined by

$$\int_l \mathbf{F} \cdot d\mathbf{l} = \lim_{n \to \infty} \sum_{i=1}^{n} \mathbf{F}_i \cdot \Delta\mathbf{l}_i$$

$$= \lim_{n \to \infty} \sum_{i=1}^{n} F_i \Delta l_i \cos \theta_i \qquad (A.2\text{–}12)$$

in accordance with the usual definition of an integral.

A surface integral of the scalar product of a variable vector and a differential of area is called a flux. The flux of $\mathbf{A}$ through a surface $\mathbf{S}$ is written

$$\int_S \mathbf{A} \cdot d\mathbf{S} = \lim_{n \to \infty} \sum_{i=1}^{n} \mathbf{A}_i \cdot \Delta\mathbf{S}_i = \lim_{n \to \infty} \sum_{i=1}^{n} A_i \Delta S_i \cos \theta_i \qquad (A.2\text{–}13)$$

The integrands in the last two expressions are scalars. An example of an integral over vector elements is the one involved in Eq. 7.10–4 for the vector potential,

$$\oint \frac{d\mathbf{l}}{r} = \lim_{n \to \infty} \sum_{i=1}^{n} \frac{\Delta\mathbf{l}_i}{r_i}$$

$$= \lim_{n \to \infty} \sum_{i=1}^{n} \left[\mathbf{1}_x \frac{\Delta x_i}{r_i} + \mathbf{1}_y \frac{\Delta y_i}{r_i} + \mathbf{1}_z \frac{\Delta z_i}{r_i} \right] \qquad (A.2\text{–}14)$$

The Gradient. Other types of derivative operations can be obtained by use of the vector operator ∇ ("del" or "nabla")[1] which we write in Cartesian coordinates as

$$\nabla = 1_x \frac{\partial}{\partial x} + 1_y \frac{\partial}{\partial y} + 1_z \frac{\partial}{\partial z} \qquad \text{(A.2–15a)}$$

To allow ∇ to operate on a scalar function $f(x, y, z)$ means to calculate

$$\nabla f = 1_x \frac{\partial f}{\partial x} + 1_y \frac{\partial f}{\partial y} + 1_z \frac{\partial f}{\partial z} \qquad \text{(A.2–15b)}$$

This vector is called the gradient of f, written sometimes as **grad** f instead of ∇f.

To derive the properties of the gradient, consider an arbitrary straight line in space and let l be the distance measured along it from some reference point. Then when the distance increases by dl, the corresponding variations dx, dy, and dz in the coordinates are equal to the products of dl with the respective direction cosines. Hence we can write these cosines as

$$\frac{\partial x}{\partial l}, \frac{\partial y}{\partial l}, \frac{\partial z}{\partial l}; \qquad \text{direction cosines of line } l \qquad \text{(A.2–16)}$$

where the partial derivative notation is used to imply that variation along this line is being considered. The unit vector along the line is therefore

$$1_l = 1_x \frac{\partial x}{\partial l} + 1_y \frac{\partial y}{\partial l} + 1_z \frac{\partial z}{\partial l} \qquad \text{(A.2–17)}$$

and the scalar product with ∇f is

$$\nabla f \cdot 1_l = \frac{\partial f}{\partial x} \frac{\partial x}{\partial l} + \frac{\partial f}{\partial y} \frac{\partial y}{\partial l} + \frac{\partial f}{\partial z} \frac{\partial z}{\partial l} \qquad \text{(A.2–18)}$$

which is according to Eq. A.1–8 the rate of change of f with l.

The component of the gradient of a function taken in a given direction is thus the rate of change of the function in that direction. The greatest component of a vector is that taken parallel to itself, so we can say that the gradient of a particular scalar function is the vector that represents the direction and magnitude of the greatest space rate of increase of that scalar function.

The expressions for ∇f as given in Table A.2A at the end of this section should be easily derivable by the reader (Problem A.2a).

---

[1] The name "del" is derived from "delta"; "nabla" comes from a Hebrew word for a triangular-shaped harp or psaltery.

Finally, the differential of f corresponding to a vector displacement $\mathbf{dl} = \mathbf{1}_x\,dx + \mathbf{1}_y\,dy + \mathbf{1}_z\,dz$ is clearly

$$df = \nabla f \cdot \mathbf{dl} = \frac{\partial f}{\partial x}\,dx + \frac{\partial f}{\partial y}\,dy + \frac{\partial f}{\partial z}\,dz \qquad \text{(A.2–19)}$$

From this formula we can write the difference between the values of $f(x, y, z)$ at two different points as a line integral over the gradient:

$$f(x_2, y_2, z_2) - f(x_1, y_1, z_1) = \int_1^2 df = \int_1^2 \nabla f \cdot \mathbf{dl} \qquad \text{(A.2–20)}$$

where the scalar-product integral is to be taken from point 1 to point 2 over any path connecting the two (provided f is properly defined, etc., along this path).

The Divergence and the Divergence Theorem. The scalar product of ∇ and a vector $\mathbf{A}$ yields another type of derivative quantity called the divergence, written div $\mathbf{A}$ or $\nabla \cdot \mathbf{A}$:

$$\text{div } \mathbf{A} = \nabla \cdot \mathbf{A} = \frac{\partial A_x}{\partial x} + \frac{\partial A_y}{\partial y} + \frac{\partial A_z}{\partial z} \qquad \text{(A.2–21)}$$

It is understood that A_x, A_y, and A_z are each in general functions of x, y, and z, a fact which we can denote by writing them $A_x(x, y, z)$, $A_y(x, y, z)$, and $A_z(x, y, z)$.

We shall now show that div $\mathbf{A}$ represents the outward flux of $\mathbf{A}$ per unit volume, leaving any infinitesimal volume surrounding the point at which div $\mathbf{A}$ is evaluated. Consider a rectangular box, as shown in Fig. A.2f with sides Δx, Δy, and Δz and one point $\mathcal{B}$ whose coordinates are (x, y, z). The flux of $\mathbf{A}$ out from this box is conveniently calculated by taking the faces in opposite pairs. For faces $\mathcal{CDHG}$ and $\mathcal{BEIF}$, the flux is given by the product of the area $\Delta y\,\Delta z$ and $\bar{A}_x$, the average value of A_x over the respective face. For $\mathcal{CDHG}$, the positive value of $\bar{A}_x$ is needed, and for $\mathcal{BEIF}$, the negative of $\bar{A}_x$. The net flux is thus $\Delta y\,\Delta z$ times the difference of $\bar{A}_x$ on the two faces.

Although A_x will vary over the two faces in question, if the box is small enough the difference between the two averages will be very closely equal to the difference between the values of A_x at $\mathcal{C}$ and at $\mathcal{B}$. This difference is $A_x(x + \Delta x, y, z) - A_x(x, y, z)$, which is an increment of A_x with respect to a small change in x only. Using the calculus expression for the differential, Eq. A.1–7, we can write this difference as $(\partial A_x/\partial x)\,\Delta x$ and the net flux out of the two faces normal to the x-axis as $(\partial A_x/\partial x)\,\Delta x\,\Delta y\,\Delta z$, where the derivative is evaluated at (x, y, z). This result is only approximate, because of the difference between the differential and the increment and because the value of A_x at the corner of a face is not generally equal to the average over the face.

The approximate value for the flux out through all the faces is seen to be

$$\left(\frac{\partial A_x}{\partial x} + \frac{\partial A_y}{\partial y} + \frac{\partial A_z}{\partial z}\right) \Delta x \, \Delta y \, \Delta z$$

if points $\mathcal{B}$ and $\mathcal{E}$ are used for the difference of two values of A_y, and points $\mathcal{B}$ and $\mathcal{F}$ for A_z.

The flux out per unit volume is equal to this result divided by $\Delta \tau = \Delta x \, \Delta y \, \Delta z$. If, after dividing, we allow Δx, Δy, and Δz to approach zero,

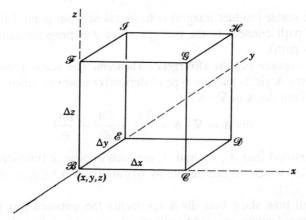

Fig. A.2f. An element of volume for calculating flux.

the inaccuracies referred to all disappear, and we see that $\nabla \cdot \mathbf{A}$ represents exactly the flux out per unit volume.[2]

If in place of the vector $\mathbf{A}$ we use a hydrodynamic velocity $\mathbf{v}$, we have a quantity div $\mathbf{v}$ that represents the outflowing fluid per unit volume, thus accounting for the name "divergence" and that of its negative, the "convergence." Such an outflowing must (except for a creation of matter) be accompanied by a time rate of decrease in the density of that fluid. This concept is used in Section 10.5; its application to the flow of charge is taken up in Section 5.2.

Let us now apply the theorem we have just proved to the calculation of the flux out of an arbitrary volume of any size. If we divide the arbitrary volume into infinitesimal, rectangular volume elements $d\tau = dx \, dy \, dz$ and add the net flux out of each element, we obtain an integral which represents the net flux out of the surface bounding the volume, since every pair of

---

[2] For a calculation that shows more explicitly how the errors disappear in the limit, see E. R. Peck, *Electricity and Magnetism*, McGraw-Hill, New York, 1953, pp. 38–40.

adjacent faces of two volume elements will have equal and opposite fluxes that cancel. The effect of "left-over" pieces of irregular shape just inside the boundary will disappear in the limit.

Thus the flux out through the surface becomes the volume integral

$$\int_\tau \mathbf{\nabla}\cdot\mathbf{A}\,d\tau$$

But the same flux can be found by the surface integral

$$\int_S \mathbf{A}\cdot d\mathbf{S}$$

in which S is the bounding surface of the volume τ. Hence the two integrals must be equal, and we arrive at a purely mathematical relation between the divergence of any vector $\mathbf{A}$ and the values of its normal component on the surface:

$$\int_S \mathbf{A}\cdot d\mathbf{S} = \int_\tau \mathbf{\nabla}\cdot\mathbf{A}\,d\tau \qquad (A.2\text{-}22a)$$

or, without using vector notation,

$$\int_S A_n\,dS = \int_\tau \left(\frac{\partial A_x}{\partial x} + \frac{\partial A_y}{\partial y} + \frac{\partial A_z}{\partial z}\right)d\tau \qquad (A.2\text{-}22b)$$

This theorem is sometimes known as Gauss' theorem, and is proved by direct integration in books on advanced calculus. We shall call it the divergence theorem.

We can use the divergence theorem to define the divergence for general coordinates by a limiting process, taking an infinitesimal volume $\Delta\tau$ and its surface S,

$$\mathbf{\nabla}\cdot\mathbf{A} = \text{div }\mathbf{A} = \lim_{\Delta\tau\to 0}\frac{1}{\Delta\tau}\int_S \mathbf{A}\cdot d\mathbf{S} \qquad (A.2\text{-}23)$$

The expressions of div $\mathbf{A}$ in cylindrical and spherical coordinates can be found by similar processes to that used for Cartesian coordinates if care is taken to note that, in calculating the difference between the fluxes through two opposite faces, the variation in the product of the relevant component of $\mathbf{A}$ and the area must be considered. For instance, the face in a cylindrical coordinate box whose vector lies along $\mathbf{1}_r$ has an area $r\,d\phi\,dz$. We will end up with an expression involving $(1/r)\,\partial(rA_r)/\partial r)$ for this term. It is left to the reader (Problem A.2b) to derive these expressions in detail.

There are several theorems of a similar nature to the divergence theorem that can in fact be derived from it. Six of them are the following, each relating an integral over a volume τ and one over the bounding surface S of τ:

$$\int_S u \, d\mathbf{S} = \int_\tau \nabla u \, d\tau \qquad \text{(A.2–24)}$$

$$\int_S \mathbf{r}(\mathbf{M} \cdot d\mathbf{S}) = \int_\tau [\mathbf{r}(\nabla \cdot \mathbf{M}) + \mathbf{M}] \, d\tau \qquad \text{(A.2–25)}$$

$$\int_S d\mathbf{S} \times \mathbf{A} = \int_\tau \nabla \times \mathbf{A} \, d\tau \qquad \text{(A.2–26)}$$

$$\int_S \mathbf{A}(\mathbf{M} \cdot d\mathbf{S}) = \int_\tau \overline{(\nabla \cdot \mathbf{M})\mathbf{A}} \, d\tau \qquad \text{(A.2–27)}$$

$$\int_S u(\mathbf{M} \cdot d\mathbf{S}) = \int [u(\nabla \cdot \mathbf{M}) + (\mathbf{M} \cdot \nabla u)] \, d\tau \qquad \text{(A.2–28)}$$

$$\int_S u \, \nabla v \cdot d\mathbf{S} = \int [u \, \nabla^2 v + (\nabla u) \cdot (\nabla v)] \, d\tau \qquad \text{(A.2–29)}$$

This last identity is a form of Green's theorem. The proofs of these theorems involve simple vector identities discussed later in this appendix and are left as exercises for the reader (suitable hints are given in Problems A.2*f*, A.2*g*, A.2*h*, and A.2*i*). In these formulas, u and v are variable scalars, $\mathbf{M}$ and $\mathbf{A}$ are variable vectors, and $\mathbf{r}$ is the displacement vector from an arbitrary origin. The bar over the integrand in Eq. A.2–27 signifies that ∇ operates derivativewise on both $\mathbf{M}$ and $\mathbf{A}$.

The various quantities we have introduced up to now either have been defined in a way independent of the coordinate system or, as in the case of the gradient, are easily seen to be independent of the coordinates. It is less evident in the case of the divergence; the various physical applications serve intuitively to make it clear that, if $\nabla \cdot \mathbf{A}$ were calculated with a differently oriented set of axes, the same value would result. A formal proof is given in Appendix A.4.

The Vector Product. The other type of vector multiplication is called the vector product. The vector product (or "cross product") of two vectors $\mathbf{A}$ and $\mathbf{B}$ is written $\mathbf{A} \times \mathbf{B}$, read "$A$ cross B." It is a vector whose magnitude is $AB \sin \theta$, where θ is the angle between $\mathbf{A}$ and $\mathbf{B}$, and whose direction is normal to the plane of $\mathbf{A}$ and $\mathbf{B}$, related to $\mathbf{A}$ and $\mathbf{B}$ as z is to x and y in a right-handed system (stated shortly: rotate $\mathbf{A}$ toward $\mathbf{B}$ with the fingers of the right hand, and the thumb will point along $\mathbf{A} \times \mathbf{B}$). As shown in Fig. A.2*g*, $\mathbf{A} \times \mathbf{B}$ has the magnitude of the area of the parallelogram constructed on $\mathbf{A}$ and $\mathbf{B}$ and may in fact be taken to represent that area. The product $\mathbf{B} \times \mathbf{A}$, from its definition, is oppositely directed to $\mathbf{A} \times \mathbf{B}$, and

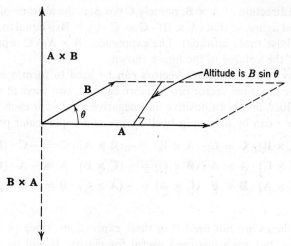

Fig. A.2g. Illustrating the vector product.

so the vector produced does not obey the commutative law; we have instead

$$\mathbf{A} \times \mathbf{B} = -\mathbf{B} \times \mathbf{A} \tag{A.2–30}$$

It is clear that, if m is a scalar,

$$(m\mathbf{A}) \times \mathbf{B} = \mathbf{A} \times (m\mathbf{B}) = m(\mathbf{A} \times \mathbf{B}) \tag{A.2–31}$$

If $\mathbf{A}$ and $\mathbf{B}$ are parallel, $\mathbf{A} \times \mathbf{B} = 0$; a special case of this is

$$\mathbf{A} \times \mathbf{A} = 0 \tag{A.2–32}$$

From the unit coordinate vectors $\mathbf{1}_x, \mathbf{1}_y, \mathbf{1}_z$ we get immediately the results

$$\left.\begin{aligned}
\mathbf{1}_x \times \mathbf{1}_x = \mathbf{1}_y \times \mathbf{1}_y = \mathbf{1}_z \times \mathbf{1}_z = 0 \\
\mathbf{1}_x \times \mathbf{1}_y = -\mathbf{1}_y \times \mathbf{1}_x = \mathbf{1}_z \\
\mathbf{1}_y \times \mathbf{1}_z = -\mathbf{1}_z \times \mathbf{1}_y = \mathbf{1}_x \\
\mathbf{1}_z \times \mathbf{1}_x = -\mathbf{1}_x \times \mathbf{1}_z = \mathbf{1}_y
\end{aligned}\right\} \tag{A.2–33}$$

The right-handed nature of the coordinate system becomes evident in the locations of the minus signs in these equations. Exactly similar relations can be written for the unit vectors of cylindrical and spherical coordinate systems.

Before we prove the distributive law for the vector product, it is convenient to consider the triple scalar product, which is the scalar product of one vector with the vector product of two others. In Fig. A.2h we show a parallelepiped constructed on three vectors $\mathbf{A}$, $\mathbf{B}$, and $\mathbf{C}$. The component of $\mathbf{C}$ in the direction of $\mathbf{A} \times \mathbf{B}$, namely $C \cos \phi$, is the altitude of the three-dimensional figure, so that $(\mathbf{A} \times \mathbf{B}) \cdot \mathbf{C} = \mathbf{C} \cdot (\mathbf{A} \times \mathbf{B})$ is equal to its volume τ (area of base times altitude). The expression $(\mathbf{B} \times \mathbf{A}) \cdot \mathbf{C}$ represents the negative of the volume in the figure shown.

Since any two of the three vectors can be used to form a base of the figure, there are three vector products we can use, two ways of writing the scalar product, and both positive and negative results for each way. Thus the volume τ can be written in twelve ways as a triple scalar product:

$$\tau = (\mathbf{A} \times \mathbf{B}) \cdot \mathbf{C} = \mathbf{C} \cdot (\mathbf{A} \times \mathbf{B}) = -(\mathbf{B} \times \mathbf{A}) \cdot \mathbf{C} = -\mathbf{C} \cdot (\mathbf{B} \times \mathbf{A})$$
$$= (\mathbf{B} \times \mathbf{C}) \cdot \mathbf{A} = \mathbf{A} \cdot (\mathbf{B} \times \mathbf{C}) = -(\mathbf{C} \times \mathbf{B}) \cdot \mathbf{A} = -\mathbf{A} \cdot (\mathbf{C} \times \mathbf{B})$$
$$= (\mathbf{C} \times \mathbf{A}) \cdot \mathbf{B} = \mathbf{B} \cdot (\mathbf{C} \times \mathbf{A}) = -(\mathbf{A} \times \mathbf{C}) \cdot \mathbf{B} = -\mathbf{B} \cdot (\mathbf{A} \times \mathbf{C})$$

$$(A.2\text{--}34)$$

The parentheses are not needed in these expressions, since $(\mathbf{A} \cdot \mathbf{B}) \times \mathbf{C}$ is meaningless, but are sometimes useful for clarity. It will be noted that

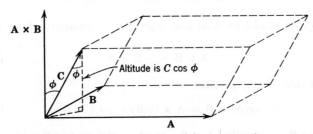

Fig. A.2h.   Illustrating the triple scalar product.

equal expressions are always obtained by interchanging the dot and the cross. This operation, together with the commutation for the dot product and the "anti-commutation" relation for the cross product, will serve to transform any given triple scalar product into any other desired form.

Since $\mathbf{A} \times \mathbf{A} = 0$, it follows that if any two of the members of a triple scalar product are equal, the triple product vanishes. The volume of Fig. A.2h is then zero.

Now let us prove the distributive law for vector products. We wish to show that

$$\mathbf{A} \times (\mathbf{B} + \mathbf{C}) = \mathbf{A} \times \mathbf{B} + \mathbf{A} \times \mathbf{C} \qquad (A.2\text{--}35)$$

This relation will hold if it is true for each component of the two sides of the equation—that is, if it is true for the scalar product of each side with each of the unit vectors in any coordinate system. Thus it will be adequate to prove the relation derived by taking the dot product of Eq. A.2-35 with an arbitrary vector $\mathbf{D}$ (the scalar product is distributive), which is

$$\mathbf{D} \cdot \mathbf{A} \times (\mathbf{B} + \mathbf{C}) = \mathbf{D} \cdot \mathbf{A} \times \mathbf{B} + \mathbf{D} \cdot \mathbf{A} \times \mathbf{C}$$

But by Eq. A.2–34, we have

$$\mathbf{D} \cdot \mathbf{A} \times \mathbf{B} + \mathbf{D} \cdot \mathbf{A} \times \mathbf{C} = (\mathbf{D} \times \mathbf{A}) \cdot \mathbf{B} + (\mathbf{D} \times \mathbf{A}) \cdot \mathbf{C}$$

$$= (\mathbf{D} \times \mathbf{A}) \cdot (\mathbf{B} + \mathbf{C})$$

and the latter, again by Eq. A.2–34, is equal to $\mathbf{D} \cdot \mathbf{A} \times (\mathbf{B} + \mathbf{C})$. Letting $\mathbf{D}$ represent in succession $\mathbf{1}_x$, $\mathbf{1}_y$, and $\mathbf{1}_z$, we see that Eq. A.2–35 is proved.

A consequence of this proof is that the sum of the vectors representing two areas with a common side is equal to the vector of the area produced by the common side and the vector sum of the other two sides as shown in Fig. A.2i. The vectors $\mathbf{A} \times \mathbf{B}$ and $\mathbf{A} \times \mathbf{C}$ represent the areas $\mathcal{MN2P}$

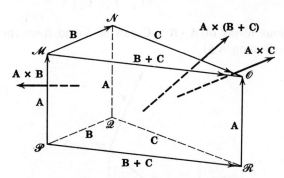

Fig. A.2i. The addition of area vectors.

and $\mathcal{NOR2}$ respectively. Their sum is equal to the vector representing the area $\mathcal{MORP}$. This result is a proof that the area vectors can be added in the ordinary way, corresponding to the result that one would obtain by projecting the areas on the three coordinate planes. (If this property were proved first from geometrical considerations, Eq. A.2–35 will follow immediately.)

With the distributive law and Eqs. A.2–33 we can write the vector product in terms of Cartesian components

$$\mathbf{A} \times \mathbf{B} = (A_x \mathbf{1}_x + A_y \mathbf{1}_y + A_z \mathbf{1}_z) \times (B_x \mathbf{1}_x + B_y \mathbf{1}_y + B_z \mathbf{1}_z) \quad \text{(A.2–36)}$$

$$= (A_y B_z - A_z B_y)\mathbf{1}_x + (A_z B_x - A_x B_z)\mathbf{1}_y + (A_x B_y - A_y B_x)\mathbf{1}_z$$

which can be written in a symmetric way in determinant form (see Appendix A.6):

$$\mathbf{A} \times \mathbf{B} = \begin{vmatrix} \mathbf{1}_x & \mathbf{1}_y & \mathbf{1}_z \\ A_x & A_y & A_z \\ B_x & B_y & B_z \end{vmatrix} \quad \text{(A.2–37)}$$

A similar determinant can be written for the other two coordinate systems provided the unit vectors are written in such an order that they form a right-handed system.

This determinant form is convenient for writing the triple scalar product, for the scalar product of one vector with another can be found by replacing the unit vectors in the Cartesian expression of the former by the corresponding components of the latter. Thus we can write

$$\mathbf{A} \cdot \mathbf{B} \times \mathbf{C} = \begin{vmatrix} A_x & A_y & A_z \\ B_x & B_y & B_z \\ C_x & C_y & C_z \end{vmatrix} \tag{A.2–38}$$

and the various forms of $\mathbf{A} \cdot \mathbf{B} \times \mathbf{C}$ can be found from the rules for determinants (Section A.6).

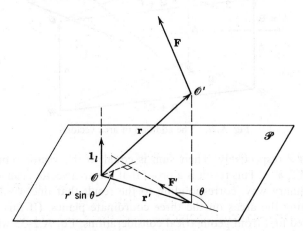

Fig. A.2j. Illustrating torque as a vector.

As an example of a vector product different from most of the examples in the text, consider the torque produced by a force $\mathbf{F}$ acting on an object at a point $\mathcal{O}'$ whose displacement is $\mathbf{r}$ from a point $\mathcal{O}$ on an axis about which the torque is desired. The direction of the axis we shall denote by $\mathbf{1}_l$ (Fig. A.2j). Let us first consider the torque produced by $\mathbf{r}'$ and $\mathbf{F}'$ in the plane $\mathscr{P}$ normal to $\mathbf{1}_l$. As shown in the figure, the moment arm for $\mathbf{F}'$ is $r' \sin \theta$, and the torque is $F'r' \sin \theta = |\mathbf{r}' \times \mathbf{F}'|$, which we can write $\mathbf{r}' \times \mathbf{F}' \cdot \mathbf{1}_l$ since $\mathbf{r}' \times \mathbf{F}'$ is in the direction of $\mathbf{1}_l$.

Now, for $\mathbf{F}$ which is not in $\mathscr{P}$, we need consider only the component of $\mathbf{F}$ in $\mathscr{P}$, which we can obtain as a vector $\mathbf{F}'$ by subtracting from $\mathbf{F}$ the vector $\mathbf{1}_l(\mathbf{1}_l \cdot \mathbf{F})$ which is parallel to $\mathbf{1}_l$ and of length equal to the component of **F** in that direction. We can find the projection **r′** of **r** on $\mathscr{P}$ in the same way. Thus

$$\mathbf{F'} = \mathbf{F} - \mathbf{1}_l(\mathbf{1}_l \cdot \mathbf{F})$$

$$\mathbf{r'} = \mathbf{r} - \mathbf{1}_l(\mathbf{1}_l \cdot \mathbf{r})$$

Now we can find the torque as

$$\mathscr{T} = \mathbf{r'} \times \mathbf{F'} \cdot \mathbf{1}_l = \mathbf{r} \times \mathbf{F} \cdot \mathbf{1}_l \qquad (A.2\text{–}39)$$

by use of the distributive law and the vanishing of the triple scalar product with two equal vectors. Since Eq. A.2–39 holds for any $\mathbf{1}_l$, we are justified in writing a torque as a vector:

$$\mathscr{T} = \mathbf{r} \times \mathbf{F} \qquad (A.2\text{–}40)$$

whose component in any direction gives the torque about an axis through the origin of **r** in that direction.

The Curl and Stokes' Theorem. The curl of a vector **A** is defined in terms of the operator ∇ as $\nabla \times \mathbf{A}$. By reference to Eqs. A.2–36 and A.2–37, we see that it may be written in the forms

$$\mathbf{curl\ A} = \nabla \times \mathbf{A} = \left(\frac{\partial A_z}{y\partial} - \frac{\partial A_y}{\partial z}\right)\mathbf{1}_x + \left(\frac{\partial A_x}{\partial z} - \frac{\partial A_z}{\partial x}\right)\mathbf{1}_y$$

$$+ \left(\frac{\partial A_y}{\partial x} - \frac{\partial A_x}{\partial y}\right)\mathbf{1}_z \qquad (A.2\text{–}41a)$$

$$= \begin{vmatrix} \mathbf{1}_x & \mathbf{1}_y & \mathbf{1}_z \\ \dfrac{\partial}{\partial x} & \dfrac{\partial}{\partial y} & \dfrac{\partial}{\partial z} \\ A_x & A_y & A_z \end{vmatrix} \qquad (A.2\text{–}41b)$$

where the determinant form must be understood as a symbolic abbreviation for the other form.

We shall now show that the component of **curl A** in any direction represents the circulation per unit area of the vector **A**, taken around a small area of any shape in a plane normal to the given direction. Let us choose first a rectangular area parallel to the x–y plane, whose sides are Δx and Δy and one of whose corners is at the point (x, y, z), as in Fig. A.2k. Next we must choose a positive direction for the calculation of the circulation $\oint \mathbf{A} \cdot \mathbf{dl}$. We use the right-hand rule whereby the fingers are directed around the periphery in the positive direction while the thumb points along the normal to the area selected as positive. In the figure, the choice of the

z-direction as positive for the normal to the area leads to the order of circulation $\mathscr{BCDE}$.

Along paths $\mathscr{BC}$ and $\mathscr{DE}$, the component A_x is required in the integral. Since **dl** is $\mathbf{1}_x\, dx$ on $\mathscr{BC}$ and is $-\mathbf{1}_x\, dx$ on $\mathscr{DE}$, the difference between the averages of A_x on the two segments will enter the calculation when the contributions of $\mathscr{BC}$ and $\mathscr{DE}$ are added. Exactly as in the divergence calculation, we can approximate this difference by evaluating A_x at $\mathscr{B}$ and at $\mathscr{E}$ instead of averaging along the paths. The difference between A_x at $\mathscr{E}$ and that at $\mathscr{B}$ can be written as a differential.

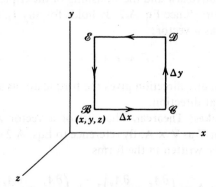

Fig. A.2k. An element of area for calculating circulation.

The part of $\oint \mathbf{A} \cdot \mathbf{dl}$ arising from the two paths parallel to the x-axis is then

$$\bar{A}_{x\mathscr{BC}}\, \Delta x - \bar{A}_{x\mathscr{DE}}\, \Delta x \simeq (A_{x\mathscr{B}} - A_{x\mathscr{E}})\, \Delta x$$

$$= -(A_{x\mathscr{E}} - A_{x\mathscr{B}})\, \Delta x \simeq -\left(\frac{\partial A_x}{\partial y}\, \Delta y\right) \Delta x$$

where the derivative is evaluated at (x, y, z).

Similarly, the contribution from sides $\mathscr{CD}$ and $\mathscr{EB}$ involves A_y. We have

$$\bar{A}_{y\mathscr{CD}}\, \Delta y - \bar{A}_{y\mathscr{EB}}\, \Delta y \simeq (A_{y\mathscr{C}} - A_{y\mathscr{B}})\, \Delta y \simeq \left(\frac{\partial A_y}{\partial x}\, \Delta x\right) \Delta y$$

so the total circulation is, approximately,

$$\oint \mathbf{A} \cdot \mathbf{dl} \simeq \left(\frac{\partial A_y}{\partial x} - \frac{\partial A_x}{\partial y}\right) \Delta x\, \Delta y = (\mathbf{curl\ A})_z\, \Delta x\, \Delta y$$

and the z component of the curl as given in Eq. A.2–41a is seen to be, accurately, the circulation per unit area around a rectangle of sides $\Delta x\ \Delta y$ in the limit when the sides go to zero.

This proof is immediately extendable to the other two components. The method of proving formally that these three components form a vector is indicated in Section A.4. Let us now consider an arbitrary area of any size lying in the x–y plane and calculate the circulation around it. We first divide it into small rectangular areas of sides Δx and Δy, as shown in Fig. A.2l. Then the sum of the circulations around all the small rectangles, plus that around the left-over pieces at the edges, will add up to the circulation around the periphery l, since each interior segment is included once in each direction with a resultant cancellation.

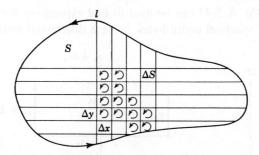

Fig. A.2l.   Illustrating a method of proving Stokes' theorem.

Since the circulation about the ith area is $(\mathbf{curl\ A})_{zi}\,\Delta x_i\,\Delta y_i$, approximately, the sum is also a sum of the type used in a surface integral. We have

$$\oint_l \mathbf{A}\cdot\mathbf{dl} \simeq \sum_i \oint_i \mathbf{A}\cdot\mathbf{dl} \simeq \sum_i (\mathbf{curl\ A})_{zi}\,\Delta x_i \Delta y_i$$

and in the limit in which all the Δx_i and Δy_i go to zero, we have

$$\oint \mathbf{A}\cdot\mathbf{dl} = \int_S (\mathbf{curl\ A})_z\,dS$$

This is a statement of Stokes' theorem, applied to one component of the curl. From this result, we can say that around any small area ΔS, the circulation is a scalar product $\mathbf{curl\ A}\cdot\mathbf{\Delta S}$. Furthermore, we can treat Fig. A.2l as showing a general area that need not be a plane. The rectangles can become small areas of any shape and orientation. In place of the one-component equation just given, we can write the general form of Stokes' theorem

$$\oint_l \mathbf{A}\cdot\mathbf{dl} = \int_S (\nabla\times\mathbf{A})\cdot\mathbf{dS} = \int_S \mathbf{curl\ A}\cdot\mathbf{dS} \qquad (A.2\text{–}42)$$

where the surface integral is over any surface whose boundary is a given closed path l.

We can now write a general definition for any component of **curl A**, by applying Stokes' theorem to any small area ΔS whose normal is along the unit vector $\mathbf{1}_n$:

$$(\text{curl } \mathbf{A})_n = \nabla \times \mathbf{A} \cdot \mathbf{1}_n = \lim_{\Delta S \to 0} \frac{1}{\Delta S} \oint_{\substack{\text{boundary} \\ \text{of } \Delta S}} \mathbf{A} \cdot d\mathbf{l} \qquad (A.2\text{–}43)$$

where again the right-hand rule is used to relate the direction of circulation to $\mathbf{1}_n$. A convenient and graphic synonym for the curl of a vector is "circulation density."

The rule of Eq. A.2–43 can be used to find expressions for the curl in cylindrical and spherical coordinates, using a differential method similar

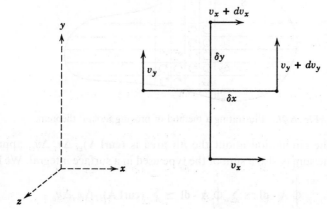

Fig. A.2m.   Illustrating the calculation of mean angular velocity in a fluid.

to that used for Cartesian coordinates. Care must be taken that when two opposite sides of an elementary area are unequal—e.g., $r \, d\theta$ and $(r + dr) \, d\theta$—this difference is considered when differentials are written. We must, for instance, write $d(rE_\theta)$ in place of $r \, d(E_\theta)$. The results are listed in Table A.2A (p. 633) and are left to the reader for verification.

The hydrodynamic significance of the curl is useful for illustrating its meaning. Consider **curl v** where **v** is the vector representing the velocity of the fluid at any point. We wish to show that $\frac{1}{2}$ **curl v** represents the angular velocity of a small portion of the fluid. Consider two short lines of length δx and δy in the x- and y-direction connecting particles in the fluid at a certain point (Fig. A.2m). Each line will tend to rotate in a plane parallel to the x–y plane if the components of velocity perpendicular to it are different at each end. The angular velocity of δx, for example, is given by dv_y, the relative y velocity of the forward end with respect to the rear end, divided by δx, namely, $[(\partial v_y/\partial x) \, \delta x]/\delta x = \partial v_y/\partial x$. Similarly, the angular velocity of δy is $-\partial v_x/\partial y$ (the negative sign is evident from the figure; positive is taken as rotation from x toward y). Thus the average angular velocity for the two lines is

$$\omega_z = \tfrac{1}{2}(\partial v_y/\partial x - \partial v_x/\partial y) = \tfrac{1}{2}(\text{curl } \mathbf{v})_z$$

It is not hard to prove that we get the same result if we consider a variable line of length δl at an arbitrary angle θ with the x-axis, and average over θ (Problem A.2n). The generalization to the other components of angular velocity is straightforward. Because of this connection with angular velocity, the curl is sometimes called the "rotation"; the symbol **rot** A is often used in place of **curl** A in European textbooks.

There are four theorems readily derivable from Stokes' theorem, corresponding to four of those derived from the divergence theorem:

$$\oint u\mathbf{dl} = \int_S \mathbf{dS} \times \nabla u \tag{A.2–44}$$

$$\int_S \mathbf{r}(\nabla \times \mathbf{A} \cdot \mathbf{dS}) - \oint \mathbf{r}(\mathbf{A} \cdot \mathbf{dl}) = \int_S \mathbf{dS} \times \mathbf{A} \tag{A.2–45}$$

$$\oint \mathbf{dl} \times \mathbf{A} = \int_S \nabla(\mathbf{A} \cdot \mathbf{dS}) - \int_S \mathbf{dS}(\nabla \cdot \mathbf{A}) \tag{A.2–46}$$

$$\oint \mathbf{A}(\mathbf{M} \cdot \mathbf{dl}) = \int_S \mathbf{dS} \times \overline{(\nabla \cdot \mathbf{M})\mathbf{A}} \tag{A.2–47}$$

Proofs are called for and hints given in Problems A.2o, A.2p, A.2q, and A.2s. Theorems corresponding to A.2–28 and A.2–29 are also easy to write down.

The Triple Vector Product. Another vector quantity of some importance is the triple vector product, $(\mathbf{A} \times \mathbf{B}) \times \mathbf{C}$. The parentheses are needed for this product, for $\mathbf{A} \times (\mathbf{B} \times \mathbf{C})$ is quite a different quantity. The product $(\mathbf{A} \times \mathbf{B}) \times \mathbf{C}$ is a vector perpendicular to $\mathbf{C}$ and to $\mathbf{A} \times \mathbf{B}$; since the latter is normal to the plane of $\mathbf{A}$ and $\mathbf{B}$, the triple product $(\mathbf{A} \times \mathbf{B}) \times \mathbf{C}$ lies in the plane of $\mathbf{A}$ and $\mathbf{B}$. On the other hand $\mathbf{A} \times (\mathbf{B} \times \mathbf{C})$ lies in the plane of $\mathbf{B}$ and $\mathbf{C}$.

We are thus led to expect that:

$$(\mathbf{A} \times \mathbf{B}) \times \mathbf{C} = m\mathbf{A} + n\mathbf{B}$$

where m and n are scalars. If we take the scalar product of each term with $\mathbf{C}$, the quantity on the left will vanish and we will have

$$m(\mathbf{A} \cdot \mathbf{C}) + n(\mathbf{B} \cdot \mathbf{C}) = 0$$

Letting $n/(\mathbf{A} \cdot \mathbf{C}) = -m/(\mathbf{B} \cdot \mathbf{C}) = k$, where k is another scalar, we have

$$(\mathbf{A} \times \mathbf{B}) \times \mathbf{C} = k[\mathbf{B}(\mathbf{A} \cdot \mathbf{C}) - \mathbf{A}(\mathbf{B} \cdot \mathbf{C})]$$

Since the magnitudes of the vectors appear equally in all terms, k must be independent of them. It is not hard to show by expansion in terms of Cartesian coordinates that $k = 1$. Thus we have

$$(\mathbf{A} \times \mathbf{B}) \times \mathbf{C} = -\mathbf{C} \times (\mathbf{A} \times \mathbf{B}) = \mathbf{C} \times (\mathbf{B} \times \mathbf{A}) = \mathbf{B}(\mathbf{A} \cdot \mathbf{C}) - \mathbf{A}(\mathbf{B} \cdot \mathbf{C})$$

$$(\text{A.2--48})$$

A useful mnemonic rule for these relations is that the first term in the expansion of the triple scalar product contains as a factor the vector that lies in the middle of the product multiplied by the scalar product of the other two, and that the second term is the product of the other vector inside the original parentheses by the scalar product of the remaining two vectors.

Vector Identities. There are a number of vector identities involving ∇ that are of importance. Let us first consider expressions involving one application of the operator ∇ and two scalar or vector variables. We shall denote arbitrary scalars by u and v and vectors by $\mathbf{A}$ and $\mathbf{B}$. The various possible combinations are:

1. $\nabla(uv)$	7. $v\,\nabla u$	13. $\mathbf{A} \cdot \nabla \times \mathbf{B}$	19. $\overline{(\nabla u) \cdot \mathbf{A}}$
2. $\overline{\nabla(\mathbf{A} \cdot \mathbf{B})}$	8. $\mathbf{A} \cdot \nabla u$	14. $\mathbf{A} \times (\nabla \times \mathbf{B})$	20. $\overline{(\nabla u) \times \mathbf{A}}$
3. $\overline{\nabla(\mathbf{A} \cdot \mathbf{B})}$	9. $\mathbf{A} \times \nabla u$	15. $(\mathbf{A} \cdot \nabla)\mathbf{B}$	21. $\overline{\nabla \times u\mathbf{A}}$
4. $\nabla \cdot (\mathbf{A} \times \mathbf{B})$	10. $u(\nabla \cdot \mathbf{B})$	16. $\overline{\nabla \cdot (\mathbf{B} \times \mathbf{A})}$	22. $\overline{(\nabla \cdot \mathbf{A})\mathbf{B}}$
5. $\overline{\nabla \times (\mathbf{A} \times \mathbf{B})}$	11. $\mathbf{A}(\nabla \cdot \mathbf{B})$	17. $(\mathbf{A} \times \nabla) \cdot \mathbf{B}$	23. $\overline{(\nabla \times \mathbf{A}) \cdot \mathbf{B}}$
6. $\overline{\nabla \times (\mathbf{A} \times \mathbf{B})}$	12. $u(\nabla \times \mathbf{B})$	18. $(\mathbf{A} \times \nabla) \times \mathbf{B}$	24. $\overline{(\nabla \times \mathbf{A}) \times \mathbf{B}}$

Many of these can be reduced to simpler forms by combining the vector rules established above with the rule for differentiation of products.[3] We have to keep in mind that the vector and derivative characters of ∇ are essentially independent. When it is not clear upon which vectors written after ∇ the derivatives operate, a superior bar as in certain items above can be used to show "how far" the ∇ operates—e.g., we can write $\overline{\nabla \times (\mathbf{A} \times \mathbf{B})} = \overline{\nabla \times (\mathbf{A} \times \mathbf{B})} - \overline{\nabla \times (\mathbf{B} \times \mathbf{A})}$, where the order of the vectors in the last term has been interchanged to put the vector acted on adjacent to ∇. As an example we have $\overline{(\nabla u) \cdot \mathbf{A}} = (\partial/\partial x)(uA_x) + (\partial/\partial y)(uA_y) + (\partial/\partial z)(uA_z)$, but $\overline{(\nabla u)} \cdot \mathbf{A} = A_x(\partial u/\partial x) + A_y(\partial u/\partial y) + A_z(\partial u/\partial z)$.

Of the expressions listed above, several cannot be reduced to simpler terms. The third one can be written as a fairly complicated expression, involving terms like items 14 and 15 in the list, if we first write $\nabla(\mathbf{A} \cdot \mathbf{B}) = \overline{\nabla(\mathbf{A} \cdot \mathbf{B})} + \overline{\nabla(\mathbf{B} \cdot \mathbf{A})}$ and then compare with expansions of $\mathbf{A} \times (\nabla \times \mathbf{B})$

[3] The simpler forms can also be established by writing in terms of Cartesian components.

Table A.2A   Expressions with ∇ in Cylindrical and Spherical Coordinates

u is an arbitrary scalar function of coordinates,
A is an arbitrary vector function of coordinates.

Cylindrical Coordinates	Spherical Coordinates

$$\nabla u = \frac{\partial u}{\partial r}\mathbf{1}_r + \frac{1}{r}\frac{\partial u}{\partial \phi}\mathbf{1}_\phi + \frac{\partial u}{\partial z}\mathbf{1}_z \qquad \nabla u = \frac{\partial u}{\partial r}\mathbf{1}_r + \frac{1}{r}\frac{\partial u}{\partial \theta}\mathbf{1}_\theta + \frac{1}{r\sin\theta}\frac{\partial u}{\partial \phi}\mathbf{1}_\phi$$

$$\nabla \cdot \mathbf{A} = \frac{1}{r}\frac{\partial(rA_r)}{\partial r} + \frac{1}{r}\frac{\partial A_\phi}{\partial \phi} + \frac{\partial A_z}{\partial z} \qquad \nabla \cdot \mathbf{A} = \frac{1}{r^2}\frac{\partial(r^2 A_r)}{\partial r} + \frac{1}{r\sin\theta}\frac{\partial(\sin\theta\, A_\theta)}{\partial \theta}$$

$$+ \frac{1}{r\sin\theta}\frac{\partial A_\phi}{\partial \phi}$$

$$\nabla \times \mathbf{A} = \left(\frac{1}{r}\frac{\partial A_z}{\partial \phi} - \frac{\partial A}{\partial z}\right)\mathbf{1}_r \qquad \nabla \times \mathbf{A} = \frac{1}{r\sin\theta}\left(\frac{\partial(\sin\theta\, A_\phi)}{\partial \theta} - \frac{\partial A_\theta}{\partial \phi}\right)\mathbf{1}_r$$

$$+ \left(\frac{\partial A_r}{\partial z} - \frac{\partial A_z}{\partial r}\right)\mathbf{1}_\phi \qquad + \left(\frac{1}{r\sin\theta}\frac{\partial A_r}{\partial \phi} - \frac{1}{r}\frac{\partial(rA_\phi)}{\partial r}\right)\mathbf{1}_\theta$$

$$+ \frac{1}{r}\left(\frac{\partial(rA_\phi)}{\partial r} - \frac{\partial A_r}{\partial \phi}\right)\mathbf{1}_z \qquad + \frac{1}{r}\left(\frac{\partial(rA_\theta)}{\partial r} - \frac{\partial A_r}{\partial \theta}\right)\mathbf{1}_\phi$$

$$\nabla^2 u = \frac{1}{r}\frac{\partial}{\partial r}\left(r\frac{\partial u}{\partial r}\right) \qquad \nabla^2 u = \frac{1}{r^2}\frac{\partial}{\partial r}\left(r^2\frac{\partial u}{\partial r}\right) + \frac{1}{r^2\sin\theta}$$

$$+ \frac{1}{r^2}\frac{\partial^2 u}{\partial \phi^2} + \frac{\partial^2 u}{\partial z^2} \qquad \times \frac{\partial}{\partial \theta}\left(\sin\theta\frac{\partial u}{\partial \theta}\right) + \frac{1}{r^2\sin^2\theta}\frac{\partial^2 u}{\partial \phi^2}$$

Table A.2B   Some Vector Identities

1. $\nabla(uv) = u\nabla v + v\nabla u$
2. $\nabla \cdot u\mathbf{A} = u\nabla \cdot \mathbf{A} + \mathbf{A} \cdot \nabla u$
3. $\overline{(\nabla \cdot \mathbf{A})\mathbf{B}} = (\mathbf{A} \cdot \nabla)\mathbf{B} + \mathbf{B}(\nabla \cdot \mathbf{A})$
4. $(\mathbf{A} \cdot \nabla)\mathbf{r} = \mathbf{A}; \qquad \mathbf{r} = \mathbf{1}_x x + \mathbf{1}_y y + \mathbf{1}_z z$
5. $\nabla(\mathbf{C} \cdot \mathbf{r}) = \mathbf{C}$ if $\mathbf{C}$ is constant
6. $\mathbf{A} \times (\mathbf{B} \times \mathbf{C}) = (\mathbf{C} \times \mathbf{B}) \times \mathbf{A} = \mathbf{B}(\mathbf{A} \cdot \mathbf{C}) - \mathbf{C}(\mathbf{A} \cdot \mathbf{B})$
7. $\nabla \cdot (\mathbf{A} \times \mathbf{B}) = \mathbf{B} \cdot \nabla \times \mathbf{A} - \mathbf{A} \cdot \nabla \times \mathbf{B}$
8. $\nabla \times (u\mathbf{A}) = u\nabla \times \mathbf{A} - \mathbf{A} \times \nabla u$
9. $\nabla(\mathbf{A} \cdot \mathbf{B}) = \mathbf{A} \times (\nabla \times \mathbf{B}) + (\mathbf{A} \cdot \nabla)\mathbf{B} + \mathbf{B} \times (\nabla \times \mathbf{A}) + (\mathbf{B} \cdot \nabla)\mathbf{A}$
10. $\nabla \times (\mathbf{A} \times \mathbf{B}) = (\mathbf{B} \cdot \nabla)\mathbf{A} + \mathbf{A}(\nabla \cdot \mathbf{B}) - (\mathbf{A} \cdot \nabla)\mathbf{B} - \mathbf{B}(\nabla \cdot \mathbf{A})$
11. $\nabla \times (\nabla \times \mathbf{A}) = \nabla(\nabla \cdot \mathbf{A}) - (\nabla \cdot \nabla)\mathbf{A}$
12. $\overline{(\mathbf{M} \cdot \nabla)(\mathbf{A} \times \mathbf{B})} = \mathbf{A} \times (\mathbf{M} \cdot \nabla)\mathbf{B} - \mathbf{B} \times (\mathbf{M} \cdot \nabla)\mathbf{A}$
13. $\mathbf{r} \times \overline{(\nabla \cdot \mathbf{A})\mathbf{B}} = (\nabla \cdot \mathbf{A})(\mathbf{r} \times \mathbf{B}) - \mathbf{A} \times \mathbf{B}$

and $\mathbf{B} \times (\nabla \times \mathbf{A})$. An example of item 15 is found in Eq. 3.2–2. Some of the resulting identities are listed in Table A.2*B*.

Another set of identities is that with two applications of ∇ on one scalar or vector. The various possible combinations are $\nabla \cdot \nabla \varphi$, $(\nabla \cdot \nabla)\mathbf{A}$, $\nabla \times (\nabla \varphi)$, $\nabla(\nabla \cdot \mathbf{A})$, $\nabla \cdot \nabla \times \mathbf{A}$, $\nabla \times (\nabla \times \mathbf{A})$, and $(\nabla \times \nabla) \times \mathbf{A}$, where φ is an arbitrary scalar function and $\mathbf{A}$ an arbitrary vector function. Of these, the third, fifth, and last are zero because the symmetry considerations which lead to the vanishing of $\mathbf{A} \times \mathbf{A}$ and $\mathbf{B} \cdot \mathbf{B} \times \mathbf{A}$ apply also to the expressions with ∇. The fourth operation is not generally reducible to a simpler form, and the result of the sixth one is given in Table A.2*B*.

The first two operations are by far the most important. The operation $\nabla \cdot \nabla$ is often written ∇^2, and sometimes Δ, and is called the Laplacian operator. Its form in Cartesian coordinates is simple (cf. Section 1.10):

$$\nabla^2 u = \frac{\partial^2 u}{\partial x^2} + \frac{\partial^2 u}{\partial y^2} + \frac{\partial^2 u}{\partial z^2} \qquad \text{(A.2–49)}$$

For the other coordinate systems, $\nabla^2 u$ can be found by combining the expression for $\nabla \cdot \mathbf{A}$ and that for $\mathbf{A} = \nabla u$. The results are given in Table A.2*A* and can be derived by inspection.

Problem A.2a. Derive expressions for the gradient in cylindrical and spherical coordinates.

Problem A.2b. Derive expressions for the divergence in cylindrical and spherical coordinates, and for $\nabla^2 u$.

Problem A.2c. Derive expressions for the curl in cylindrical and spherical coordinates.

Problem A.2d. Write the spherical coordinate unit vectors in terms of $\mathbf{1}_x$, $\mathbf{1}_y$, $\mathbf{1}_z$, and suitable functions of θ and ϕ. Construct a table of all the derivatives of $\mathbf{1}_r$, $\mathbf{1}_\theta$, and $\mathbf{1}_\phi$ with respect to r, θ, and ϕ. Use this table to show that ∇ may be treated as an operator in spherical coordinates, by deriving ∇u, $\nabla \cdot \mathbf{A}$, and $\nabla \times \mathbf{A}$ with its use.

Problem A.2e. Same as Problem A.2*d*, for cylindrical coordinates.

Problem A.2f. Apply the divergence theorem A.2–22 to the vector $u\mathbf{C}$, where u is a given variable scalar and $\mathbf{C}$ is an arbitrary constant vector, and prove Eq. A.2–24. (*Hint*: See method of proving Eq. A.2–35.)

Problem A.2g. Apply the divergence theorem in succession to the vectors $x\mathbf{M}$, $y\mathbf{M}$, and $z\mathbf{M}$, and prove Eq. A.2–25.

Problem A.2h. Apply the divergence theorem to the vector $\mathbf{A} \times \mathbf{C}$ where $\mathbf{A}$ is a given variable vector and $\mathbf{C}$ is an arbitrary constant vector, and prove Eq. A.2–26.

Problem A.2i. Apply the divergence theorem to the vector $M(A \cdot C)$ where M and A are given variable vectors and C is an arbitrary constant vector, and prove Eq. A.2–27. Then derive Eqs. A.2–28 and 29.

Problem A.2j. Write and simplify the result of applying the divergence theorem to a vector $A \times B$, where A and B are both variable.

Problem A.2k. Write an expression for $\overline{(\nabla \times A)} \times B$ involving terms in each of which ∇ operates on one vector only.

Problem A.2l. Simplify $(A \times \nabla) \times B$ and $A \times (\nabla \times B)$.

Problem A.2m. Find all the ways of writing $A \cdot (\nabla \times B)$.

Problem A.2n. Prove that the average angular velocity in a fluid for lines at arbitrary angles with the x-axis lying in the x–y plane is $\frac{1}{2}(\text{curl } v)_z$.

Problem A.2o. Prove Eq. A.2–44 using Stokes' theorem on the vector uC where C is an arbitrary constant vector.

Problem A.2p. Prove Eq. A.2–45 using Stokes' theorem on the vectors xA, yA, and zA.

Problem A.2q. Prove Eq. A.2–46 using Stokes' theorem on the vector $A \times C$, where C is an arbitrary constant vector.

Problem A.2r. Prove that for any vector A we have

$$(A \cdot \nabla)r = A$$

if r is the displacement vector from the origin.

Problem A.2s. Prove Eq. A.2–47 using Stokes' theorem on the vectors MA_x, MA_y, and MA_z.

A.3   Notes on Differential Equations

An ordinary differential equation of the first order for a function $g(x)$ is a relation connecting dg/dx with g and x. We may always imagine it to be solved for dg/dx:

$$dg/dx = F_1(g, x) \qquad\qquad (A.3–1)$$

A solution of this equation is a function $g(x)$ which may be plotted as a curve in a plane. We can imagine finding this curve directly, but approximately, from Eq. A.3–1 by starting at any value of x, say $x = 0$, choosing g at will for this x, and with the value of dg/dx thus determined finding the differential of g for some chosen increment in x (see Eq. A.1–5). With the new values of g and x we can repeat the process. We can get different curves by choosing different values of g at $x = 0$. Since in general every solution will have a value $g(0)$ for $x = 0$, we get all solutions this way. Any function $g(x, a)$ that satisfies Eq. A.3–1 and contains an adjustable constant a that allows $g(0, a)$ to take on any chosen value is called a general solution, since by the above argument all particular solutions may be obtained from it.

A second-order differential equation for $g(x)$ is one that contains d^2g/dx^2 as well as (in general) dg/dx, g, and x. We may imagine it solved for d^2g/dx^2, and write

$$d^2g/dx^2 = F_2(dg/dx, g, x) \qquad \text{(A.3–2)}$$

We now need, in order to find an appropriate solution, to assume both a value for g and a value for dg/dx for $x = 0$ or any arbitrary starting point. Once started, we can find the increment in dg/dx and the increment in g for a chosen Δx, and get to a new point from which to start again. The general solution of Eq. A.3–2 will thus be a function $g(x, a, b)$ with two adjustable constants for determining g and dg/dx at $x = 0$. It is easy to see that an nth-order differential equation will have n adjustable constants in its general solution.[4]

A partial differential equation of the first order in two variables, for instance for a function $f(x, y)$, is a relation connecting the derivatives $\partial f/\partial x$ and $\partial f/\partial y$ with the values of the function f and the two independent variables x and y. If we solve for one of the derivatives, say $\partial f/\partial x$, we can write

$$\partial f/\partial x = F_3(f, \partial f/\partial y, x, y) \qquad \text{(A.3–3)}$$

An argument like that given for Eq. A.3–1 can be constructed here if we temporarily think of y as a kind of auxiliary parameter. Then we have to specify f and x at the starting point of an approximate calculation for all the values of y of interest, and also of course $\partial f/\partial y$. Then for a slightly larger x, we can use the value of $\partial f/\partial x$ from Eq. A.3–3 to find the new f for all y. The new value of $\partial f/\partial y$ can then be found by differentiation, and we can proceed another step. As a practical procedure the process is even less accurate than the one for ordinary equations, but it serves to demonstrate that we can specify an arbitrary function $f(0, y)$ for a specific value of x. It is easy to see that the starting "point" could be an arbitrary line in the x–y plane, and f can be arbitrarily specified all along this line. The general solution thus is expected to contain one arbitrary, adjustable function.

A second-order partial differential equation will have a general solution that involves two arbitrary functions. Such an equation can be written, for a function $f(x, y)$

$$\partial^2 f/\partial x^2 = F_4(f, \partial f/\partial x, \partial f/\partial y, \partial^2 f/\partial y^2, \partial^2 f/\partial x\,\partial y, x, y) \qquad \text{(A.3–4)}$$

---

[4] This type of argument can be developed into a set of rigorous existence theorems, in which case it is called the "Cauchy-Lipschitz Method."

The specification of f and $\partial f/\partial x$ as functions of y for $x = 0$ will allow the calculation of $\partial f/\partial y$, $\partial^2 f/\partial y^2$ and $\partial^2 f/\partial x\,\partial y$ for all y, and so again we can start to calculate $f(x, y)$ by a stepwise approximation method.

These remarks are intended to make the above-mentioned properties of differential equations geometrically evident but are not intended as proofs or as exhaustive of special cases that might be exceptions. Rigorous discussions are to be found in books on differential equations.

There are two more properties of differential equations we shall state here, the details of solutions being given where needed in the text. A linear differential equation is one in which the function and its derivatives appear to the first or zero powers in every term. If only first-power terms appear, the equation is also homogeneous. The homogeneous equation obtained on omitting the zero-power term from an inhomogeneous equation is called the "reduced equation."

The first property we wish to state is that any linear combination of two solutions of a homogeneous equation is also a solution of the equation. For instance, if we have the equation

$$A \frac{\partial^2 f}{\partial x\,\partial y} + Bx^2 \frac{\partial f}{\partial x} + Cxyf = 0 \tag{A.3-5}$$

and $f_1(x, y)$ and $f_2(x, y)$ are separately solutions, we have

$$A\, \partial^2[af_1(x, y) + bf_2(x, y)]/\partial x\,\partial y + Bx^2\, \partial[af_1(x, y) + bf_2(x, y)]/\partial x$$
$$+ Cxy[af_1(x, y) + bf_2(x, y)]$$
$$= a[A\, \partial^2 f_1(x, y)/\partial x\,\partial y + Bx^2\, \partial f_1(x, y)/\partial x + Cxyf_1(x, y)]$$
$$+ b[A\, \partial^2 f_2(x, y)/\partial x\,\partial y + Bx^2\, \partial f_2(x, y)/\partial x + Cxyf_2(x, y)] \tag{A.3-6}$$
$$= a \cdot 0 + b \cdot 0 = 0$$

The second property is that the general solution of an inhomogeneous linear equation can be written as the sum of the general solution of the reduced equation and any particular solution of the complete inhomogeneous equation. For instance, if the equation reads

$$A(x) \frac{d^2 g}{dx^2} + B(x) \frac{dg}{dx} + C(x)g = R(x) \tag{A.3-7}$$

and if $g_1(x, a, b)$ and $g_2(x)$ satisfy respectively

$$A(x) \frac{d^2 g_1(x, a, b)}{dx^2} + B(x) \frac{dg_1(x, a, b)}{dx} + C(x)g_1(x, a, b) = 0 \tag{A.3-8a}$$

where a and b are adjustable constants, and

$$A(x)\, d^2 g_2(x)/dx^2 + B(x)\, dg_2(x)/dx + C(x)g_2(x) = R(x) \tag{A.3-8b}$$

it is easy to see by adding the last two equations that a solution of Eq. A.3–7 with two adjustable constants is

$$g(x, a, b) = g_1(x, a, b) + g_2(x) \qquad \text{(A.3–9)}$$

A.4 Vector Invariance

The vector relations developed in Appendix A.2 were derived in a largely geometric fashion that makes evident their independence of particular coordinate systems. In this section, we wish to prove this invariance in a formal algebraic fashion for Cartesian coordinates, not only to complete the discussion in Section A.2 but to provide a basis for the discussion of relativity in Section 7.19. The extension of this discussion to curvilinear coordinates would take us beyond the scope of this book.

The invariance we wish to consider is the independence of the various vector relations with respect to translations, rotations, and reflections of the coordinate axes. Translations—shifts of the origin without rotation—produce an almost trivial effect, and we shall not treat them. Reflections will be treated briefly after we have discussed rotations.

A rotation can be defined by starting with a set of orthogonal axes and unit vectors $\mathbf{1}_x$, $\mathbf{1}_y$, $\mathbf{1}_z$, and then relating a new set $\mathbf{1}_x{}'$, $\mathbf{1}_y{}'$, and $\mathbf{1}_z{}'$ to the old set. To shorten our writing and make the formulas easier to remember, let us rename the coordinates, using x_1, x_2, and x_3 in place of x, y, and z, and $\mathbf{1}_1$, $\mathbf{1}_2$, and $\mathbf{1}_3$ in place of $\mathbf{1}_x$, $\mathbf{1}_y$, and $\mathbf{1}_z$. Then we can use letter subscripts, as $i, j, k \cdots$, to indicate sums over the three coordinates. Each sum we indicate will run from 1 to 3, so we do not need to write the limits explicitly.

Now we can write a relation between the new unit vectors and the old in the compact form

$$\mathbf{1}_i{}' = \sum_k a_{ik} \mathbf{1}_k \qquad \text{(A.4–1)}$$

where the nine numbers a_{ik}—i.e., a_{11}, a_{12}, etc.—are the components of the three new unit vectors along the three original axes. Any other letters can, of course, be used for the i and k here; Eq. A.4–1 clearly represents three separate equations. In accordance with Eq. A.2–3, these constants are the direction cosines between the respective unit vectors to which their subscripts refer. Since a_{ik} is the cosine of the angle between $\mathbf{1}_i{}'$ and $\mathbf{1}_k$, we can write $\mathbf{1}_k$ as a sum over the $\mathbf{1}_i{}'$, with the same coefficients

$$\mathbf{1}_k = \sum_i \mathbf{1}_i{}' a_{ik} \qquad \text{(A.4–2)}$$

(for mnemonic purposes we write the factors in such an order that the summed-over index appears in two adjacent places).

The same coefficients allow us to relate the components of any vector **A** in the new system to those in the old system. Denoting the components in the old system with subscripts, and those in the new system with both subscripts and primes, we have

$$A_i' = \mathbf{A} \cdot \mathbf{1}_i' = \mathbf{A} \cdot \sum_k a_{ik} \mathbf{1}_k = \sum_k a_{ik} A_k \qquad (A.4\text{--}3)$$

In particular, if $\mathbf{A} = \mathbf{r}$, the displacement vector from the origin, we have a relation between the new coordinates and the old

$$x_i' = \sum_k a_{ik} x_k \qquad (A.4\text{--}4)$$

and using Eq. A.4–2

$$x_k = \sum_i x_i' a_{ik} \qquad (A.4\text{--}5)$$

The components of the gradient of any scalar f can now be determined with respect to the new axes:

$$\frac{\partial f}{\partial x_i'} = \sum_k \frac{\partial f}{\partial x_k} \frac{\partial x_k}{\partial x_i'} = \sum_k a_{ik} \frac{\partial f}{\partial x_k} \qquad (A.4\text{--}6)$$

where the derivatives $\partial x_k/\partial x_i'$ are determined from Eq. A.4–5. Thus we see that the components of the gradient transform in exactly the same way as the components of the vector **r**. We can in fact use this transformation property as *defining* a vector.

Let us now use the facts that each set of unit vectors have unit length and are mutually perpendicular to get relations among the coefficients. These facts can be succinctly written as

$$\mathbf{1}_k \cdot \mathbf{1}_l = \delta_{kl} \qquad (A.4\text{--}7a)$$

$$\mathbf{1}_i' \cdot \mathbf{1}_j' = \delta_{ij} \qquad (A.4\text{--}7b)$$

where the symbol δ_{kl} called the "Kronecker delta" stands for 1 when the two subscripts are equal and for 0 when they are not:

$$\delta_{kl} = \begin{cases} 1 & \text{if } k = l \\ 0 & \text{if } k \neq l \end{cases} \qquad (A.4\text{--}8)$$

Using Eqs. A.4–7b and A.4–1 we have (taking care not to use the same subscript letter in more than one summation)

$$\delta_{ij} = \mathbf{1}_i' \cdot \mathbf{1}_j' = \left(\sum_k a_{ik} \mathbf{1}_k \right) \left(\sum_l a_{jl} \mathbf{1}_l \right)$$

$$= \sum_k \sum_l a_{ik} a_{jl} \delta_{kl} = \sum_k a_{ik} a_{jk}$$

where the last reduction arises because in summing over l, only the term for $l = k$ gives a non-vanishing contribution. Using Eq. A.4–2 we get a relation involving a sum over the first subscripts, and so together we have

$$\sum_k a_{ik}a_{jk} = \delta_{ij} \tag{A.4-9a}$$

$$\sum_j a_{jk}a_{jl} = \delta_{kl} \tag{A.4-9b}$$

The scalar product of two vectors can now be shown to be invariant (have the same value) when expressed in the two systems in terms of components. We have

$$\mathbf{A} \cdot \mathbf{B} = \sum_k A_k B_k = \sum_k \left(\sum_i A_i' a_{ik} \right) \left(\sum_j B_j' a_{jk} \right)$$
$$= \sum_i \sum_j A_i' B_j' \, \delta_{ij} = \sum_i A_i' B_i' \tag{A.4-10}$$

In particular, the length of a vector $(\mathbf{A} \cdot \mathbf{A})^{1/2}$ remains the same.

The constancy of length of a radius vector $\mathbf{r}$ can in fact be used to *define* a rotation. If we require that the x_i' are linear functions of the x_k, with the same origin, we are led to write Eqs. A.4–4 and then to require that

$$\sum_i x_i'^2 = \sum_i \left(\sum_k a_{ik}x_k \right) \left(\sum_l a_{il}x_l \right)$$
$$= \sum_k \sum_l x_k x_l \sum_i a_{ik}a_{il}$$
$$= \sum_k x_k^2 \tag{A.4-11}$$

which can only hold for all points (x_1, x_2, x_3) if Eq. A.4–9b holds for the sum over i. From this we conclude that the vectors formed by Eqs. A.4–1 are indeed orthogonal unit vectors and the a_{ik} are direction cosines. It can be shown then that the distance between any two points is invariant (Problem A.4a) and thus triangles and angles are preserved, which must be true for a rotation of coordinates.

It is easy to prove that $\nabla \cdot \mathbf{A}$ is invariant for any vector $\mathbf{A}$:

$$\sum_k \frac{\partial A_k}{\partial x_k} = \sum_k \sum_i \frac{\partial A_k}{\partial x_i'} \frac{\partial x_i'}{\partial x_k} = \sum_k \sum_i \sum_j \frac{\partial}{\partial x_i'} (A_j' a_{jk}) \frac{\partial x_i'}{\partial x_k}$$
$$= \sum_k \sum_i \sum_j \frac{\partial A_j'}{\partial x_i'} a_{jk}a_{ik} = \sum_i \sum_j \frac{\partial A_j'}{\partial x_i'} \delta_{ij}$$
$$= \sum_i \frac{\partial A_i'}{\partial x_i'} \tag{A.4-12}$$

The vector nature of the cross product is a little more complicated to show. Let us introduce another symbol that shortens the writing much as does the Kronecker delta, namely, the epsilon symbol, ε_{ijk}, which is zero if any two or three of the subscripts are equal and is ± 1 when they are all different. The plus sign belongs to values i, j, k that are cyclic permutations of 1, 2, 3 and the minus sign to cyclic permutations of 3, 2, 1. That is

$$\left.\begin{array}{l} \varepsilon_{ijk} = 0 \quad \text{unless } i \neq j \neq k \\[4pt] \varepsilon_{123} = \varepsilon_{231} = \varepsilon_{312} = 1 \\[4pt] \varepsilon_{321} = \varepsilon_{132} = \varepsilon_{213} = -1 \end{array}\right\} \qquad (A.4\text{--}13)$$

Then we can write the vector product of **A** and **B** in a short form:

$$\mathbf{A} \times \mathbf{B} = \mathbf{1}_1(A_2 B_3 - A_3 B_2) + \mathbf{1}_2(A_3 B_1 - A_1 B_3) + \mathbf{1}_3(A_1 B_2 - A_2 B_1)$$

$$= \sum_i \sum_j \sum_k \mathbf{1}_i A_j B_k \varepsilon_{ijk} \qquad (A.4\text{--}14)$$

The property of the unit vectors of being mutually perpendicular and forming a right-handed system can be written

$$\mathbf{1}_j \times \mathbf{1}_k = \sum_i \mathbf{1}_i \varepsilon_{ijk} \qquad (A.4\text{--}15)$$

(If j and k are equal, all terms on the right vanish. If they are unequal, only one term on the right is not zero, and it has the proper sign.) This property can be proven in a formal way from Eq. A.4–7a, but we shall leave this as an exercise for the reader (Problem A.4b).

Now we can write Eq. A.4–15 for the new system of vectors and use Eq. A.4–1. We get

$$\sum_m \sum_n a_{jm} a_{kn}(\mathbf{1}_m \times \mathbf{1}_n) = \sum_i \mathbf{1}_i' \varepsilon_{ijk}$$

$$= \sum_p \sum_m \sum_n a_{jm} a_{kn} \mathbf{1}_p \varepsilon_{pmn} = \sum_i \sum_p a_{ip} \mathbf{1}_p \varepsilon_{ijk}$$

and comparing the coefficients of $\mathbf{1}_p$ on each side, we have

$$\sum_m \sum_n a_{jm} a_{kn} \varepsilon_{pmn} = \sum_i a_{ip} \varepsilon_{ijk} \qquad (A.4\text{--}16a)$$

as a new set of relations among the a_{ik}'s. These relations constitute a form of solution of the set of equations A.4–9a for the a_{ik} with a particular first subscript in terms of the coefficients with the other two first subscripts. (See Problem A.4c.) It must be assumed that the new set of vectors is a right-handed system like the old set—i.e., the rotation does not also involve a reflection (see below).

A similar set can be obtained by interchanging the original and new sets of unit vectors. We get

$$\sum_j \sum_k a_{jm} a_{kn} \varepsilon_{ijk} = \sum_p a_{ip} \varepsilon_{pmn} \qquad (A.4\text{--}16b)$$

Now we can use Eqs. A.4–16 to show that the expression **A × B** transforms as a vector. We have, using Eqs. A.4–14, A.4–16b, and A.4–9b,

$$
\begin{aligned}
\sum_i \sum_j \sum_k \mathbf{1}_i' A_j' B_k' \varepsilon_{ijk} &= \sum_i \sum_j \sum_k \sum_l \sum_m \sum_n a_{il} \mathbf{1}_l a_{jm} A_m a_{kn} B_n \varepsilon_{ijk} \\
&= \sum_i \sum_l \sum_m \sum_n \sum_p a_{il} \mathbf{1}_l A_m B_n a_{ip} \varepsilon_{pmn} \\
&= \sum_l \sum_m \sum_n \sum_p \mathbf{1}_l A_m B_n \varepsilon_{pmn} \, \delta_{lp} \qquad \text{(A.4–17)} \\
&= \sum_l \sum_m \sum_n \mathbf{1}_l A_m B_n \varepsilon_{lmn}
\end{aligned}
$$

which shows that the vector product as defined by Eq. A.4–14 yields the same vector in either system of coordinates.

The calculations above on ∇f and $\nabla \cdot \mathbf{A}$ show that for these quantities the components of $\nabla = \sum_i \mathbf{1}_i (\partial/\partial x_i)$ transform just like the components of a vector. Hence it follows that $\nabla \times \mathbf{A}$ transforms like a vector; the demonstration is algebraically just like Eq. A.4–17, and we shall not write it out explicitly. The same argument can be used for the vector operations $(\mathbf{A} \cdot \nabla)$ and $(\mathbf{A} \times \nabla)$ and, of course, for all the more complicated vector combinations given in Section A.2.

Let us now consider reflections. A simple example would be reflection in the y–z plane, in which we change x to $-x$ and $\mathbf{1}_x$ to $-\mathbf{1}_x$ but leave y, z, $\mathbf{1}_y$, and $\mathbf{1}_z$ unchanged. A reflection in any plane can be reduced to a reflection in the y–z plane by use of a rotation, so our example will cover all such reflections.

When we change x to $-x$, we change the sign of the x-component of any vector such as $\mathbf{F}$ or $\mathbf{v}$ whose definition does not involve the right-hand rule. If in the original system we have $\mathbf{F} = \mathbf{1}_x F_x + \mathbf{1}_y F_y + \mathbf{1}_z F_z$, in the new system we have $\mathbf{F} = \mathbf{1}_x' F_x' + \mathbf{1}_y' F_y' + \mathbf{1}_z' F_z' = (-\mathbf{1}_x)(-F_x) + \mathbf{1}_y F_y + \mathbf{1}_z F_z$. The vector is the same as before. Similarly, the scalar product $\mathbf{A} \cdot \mathbf{B}$ is unchanged; and furthermore, since if $x' = -x$, $\partial/\partial x' = -\partial/\partial x$, ∇f and $\nabla \cdot \mathbf{A}$ are unchanged.

The situation is different for the vector product. The x-component of $\mathbf{A} \times \mathbf{B}$ remains unchanged and the y and z components each change sign. In the expression Eq. A.4–14 for $\mathbf{A} \times \mathbf{B}$, every term has either $\mathbf{1}_x$, A_x, or B_x in it and so every term changes sign, which is, of course, a result of a right-hand rule turning into a left-hand rule in a mirror image.

We call a vector which does not change sign on reflection, while one component does, a "polar vector" or a "true vector," and a vector which does change, while the corresponding component does not, an "axial vector" or a "pseudovector." An example of a pseudovector is the area vector associated with a parallelogram constructed on two vectors **A** and

B. If we did not associate a vector with the area, we might describe its (component) sign as follows. Suppose the plane of **A** and **B** to be the y–z plane. We can call the area positive if a rotation of **A** toward **B** through the smaller angle between them is in the same sense of rotation as that obtaining in rotating 1_y toward 1_z. A reflection of the x-axis will not change this sign. If the area were located in the x–y or the z–x plane, the sign defined by the appropriate rotation would change, and the situation would still be like that of the vector product (see Problem A.4f).

Similarly, a vector defined as the curl of a polar vector is an axial vector and has the same properties as the area vector. The circulation density in the y–z plane can be given a sign in the same way as for the area vector.

It will be noted that the magnetic induction **B** is defined in Section 7.2 in a way that makes clear its pseudovector character. This is also evident in the derivation of **B** from the curl of the vector potential **A**, which by *its* definition is clearly a true or polar vector. The vector product **v** × **B** on the other hand is a true vector since **B** is a pseudovector (cf. Problem A.4e).

It will also be noted that if **A**, **B**, and **C** all represent true vectors, the triple scalar product **A** · (**B** × **C**) is not a true scalar, for it will change signs with a reflection. Such a product is called a "pseudoscalar."

If two reflections are considered, say in both the x and y axes, we get a right-handed system back, and there are no sign changes in pseudovectors and pseudoscalars. Three reflections, however, have the same effect as one. The reflection of x to $-x$, y to $-y$ and z to $-z$ is called a "reflection through the origin." Since atomic and nuclear forces seem generally to be symmetric with respect to such reflections, the invariance or non-invariance of the physical quantities entering into theories of these systems is of considerable interest and importance. Invariant quantities are said to have even parity, and those that change sign are said to have odd parity. "Parity conservation" refers to the idea that physical forces do not display the arbitrary right- or left-handedness of axial vectors and that therefore any right- or left-handed character of a physical system must arise because of some initial state into which it was put. Symmetric physical forces cannot then change the parity initially acquired. The discovery of a physical effect related to the direction of an axial vector (e.g., the magnetic moment vector for certain radioactive nuclei) was a dramatic denial of this assertion.[5] However, the discovery seems to be related to non-electromagnetic forces and hence is beyond the scope of this book.

[5] L. S. Rodberg and V. F. Weisskopf, "Fall of Parity," *Science*, **125**, 627–33 (1957); C. S. Wu, E. Ambler, R. W. Hayward, D. D. Hoppes, R. P. Hudson, *Phys. Rev.*, **105**, 1413–1415 (1957).

Problem A.4a. Show that from the requirement that the distance $(x_1^2 + x_2^2 + x_3^2)^{1/2}$ of a point from the origin be invariant under a rotation one can deduce that the distance between any two points (x_1, x_2, x_3) and (X_1, X_2, X_3) is also invariant.

Problem A.4b. Three vectors $\mathbf{A}$, $\mathbf{B}$, and $\mathbf{C}$ satisfy the equations $\mathbf{A} \cdot \mathbf{A} = \mathbf{B} \cdot \mathbf{B} = \mathbf{C} \cdot \mathbf{C} = 1$ and $\mathbf{A} \cdot \mathbf{B} = \mathbf{B} \cdot \mathbf{C} = \mathbf{C} \cdot \mathbf{A} = 0$. Consider equivalent expressions for $\mathbf{A} \times (\mathbf{B} \times \mathbf{C})$, $(\mathbf{B} \times \mathbf{C}) \cdot (\mathbf{B} \times \mathbf{C})$ and $[\mathbf{A} \times (\mathbf{B} \times \mathbf{C})] \cdot [\mathbf{A} \times (\mathbf{B} \times \mathbf{C})]$, and show that $\mathbf{A} \cdot (\mathbf{B} \times \mathbf{C}) = \pm 1$. By considering expansions of $[\mathbf{A} \mp (\mathbf{B} \times \mathbf{C})] \cdot [\mathbf{A} \mp (\mathbf{B} \times \mathbf{C})]$, show that $\mathbf{A} = \pm \mathbf{B} \times \mathbf{C}$, $\mathbf{B} = \pm \mathbf{C} \times \mathbf{A}$, and $\mathbf{C} = \pm \mathbf{A} \times \mathbf{B}$. Show that the choice of signs determines whether the system of vectors is right handed or left handed.

Problem A.4c. Show that if $p = 1$, $j = 2$, $k = 3$, Eq. A.4–16a becomes $a_{11} = a_{22}a_{33} - a_{23}a_{32}$, and find similar equations for $a_{12}, a_{13}, \cdots a_{33}$.

Problem A.4d. Write Eq. A.4–9a for (i, j) respectively equal to $(1, 1)$, $(1, 2)$, and $(1, 3)$. Solve the second two equations for a_{11} and a_{12}, obtaining the ratios $a_{11}:a_{12}:a_{13}$. Use the first equation to get values of a_{11}, a_{12}, and a_{13} and verify Eq. A.4–16a. Show that a choice of signs enters that can be settled by consideration of right- and left-handedness.

Problem A.4e. Show that the vector product of a polar vector and an axial vector is itself a polar vector. Which of Maxwell's equations involve on each side (a) a true vector, (b) a pseudovector, (c) a true scalar, (d) a pseudoscalar?

Problem A.4f. Show what happens to the y- and z-components of $\mathbf{A} \times \mathbf{B}$ when $\mathbf{A}$ and $\mathbf{B}$ are polar vectors and a reflection is made in the y–z plane.

A.5 Complex Numbers

The complex-number system in algebra is based on the quantity $\sqrt{-1}$, which we shall call j in accordance with engineering usage, except in Section 7.19 (the mathematician's symbol i conflicts with our symbol for current). This quantity j is not definable in terms of any ordinary "real" number and so is called "imaginary." Its relation to real numbers is simply that $j^2 = -1$, which of course implies that $j^{-1} = -j$. We combine j with real numbers (represented here by x and y) to form complex numbers, which obey the rules of ordinary algebra (see Appendix A.2), and which we denote by symbols like $\mathbf{z}$, $\mathscr{E}$, i, etc.[6] We then write for a general complex number

$$\mathbf{z} = x + jy \qquad (A.5–1)$$

[6] A special type face ("sans serif" in this book) is used in electrical theory although it is not necessary in mathematical analysis to distinguish the complex and ordinary numbers that refer to the same physical quantities.

and add or subtract numbers by the rules

$$\begin{aligned}
\mathbf{z}_1 + \mathbf{z}_2 &= (x_1 + jy_1) + (x_2 + jy_2) = x_1 + x_2 + j(y_1 + y_2) \\
\mathbf{z}_1 - \mathbf{z}_2 &= (x_1 + jy_1) - (x_2 + jy_2) = x_1 - x_2 + j(y_1 - y_2)
\end{aligned} \qquad \text{(A.5-2)}$$

The numbers x, x_1, and x_2 are called the *real parts* of their respective numbers, and the numbers y, y_1, and y_2 are called the *imaginary parts*. Either part may of course be positive or negative. The real and imaginary parts do not combine directly with each other. They act like the x and y components of a vector in a plane; the addition of two complex numbers

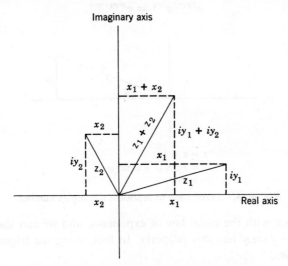

Fig. A.5*a*. The addition of two complex numbers.

involves the addition of the separate components. Therefore we can represent the numbers as vectors or, if we please, as points at the heads of the vectors. Figure A.5*a* shows the addition of two complex numbers in graphical form.

The length of a vector $\mathbf{z} = x + jy$, which we can call its magnitude (amplitude or rms value for electrical quantities), is obviously given by $(x^2 + y^2)^{1/2}$, which we can write as $|\mathbf{z}|$ or as plain z in ordinary type.

We can multiply complex numbers in the ordinary algebraic way, replacing j^2 where it appears by -1. Thus we have

$$\mathbf{z}_1\mathbf{z}_2 = (x_1 + jy_1)(x_2 + jy_2) = x_1x_2 - y_1y_2 + j(x_1y_2 + x_2y_1) \quad \text{(A.5-3)}$$

This expression shows that the product of two complex numbers is another one but does not immediately show any geometrical relation of the product to the factors. There is, indeed, a simple relationship which it is easiest to derive by first representing complex numbers in terms of their magnitudes and the angles they make with the axis of reals.

In Fig. A.5b, we have shown the magnitude z and angle φ of a complex number $\mathbf{z}$. Evidently we can write

$$\mathbf{z} = z(\cos \varphi + j \sin \varphi) \tag{A.5–4}$$

Now we should like to show that $\cos \varphi + j \sin \varphi$ can be written as $e^{j\varphi}$. One property of $e^{j\varphi}$ that we need here is that

$$e^{j\varphi_1} \cdot e^{j\varphi_2} = e^{j(\varphi_1+\varphi_2)}$$

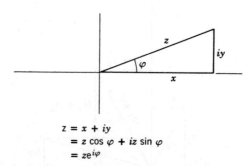

$$z = x + iy$$
$$= z \cos \varphi + iz \sin \varphi$$
$$= z e^{i\varphi}$$

Fig. A.5b. Three ways to represent a complex number.

in accordance with the usual law of exponents, and we can show readily that $\cos \varphi + j \sin \varphi$ has this property. In fact, using the trigonometrical addition rules,

$$(\cos \varphi_1 + j \sin \varphi_1)(\cos \varphi_2 + j \sin \varphi_2)$$
$$= \cos \varphi_1 \cos \varphi_2 - \sin \varphi_1 \sin \varphi_2 + j(\sin \varphi_1 \cos \varphi_2 + \cos \varphi_1 \sin \varphi_2)$$
$$= \cos (\varphi_1 + \varphi_2) + j \sin (\varphi_1 + \varphi_2) \tag{A.5–5}$$

so that we are entitled to use the shorthand formula

$$\cos \varphi + j \sin \varphi = e^{j\varphi} \tag{A.5–6}$$

or

$$\mathbf{z} = z e^{j\varphi} \tag{A.5–7}$$

It is left to the reader in Problems A.5a and b to show that $e^{j\varphi}$ as thus defined possesses the other properties of the exponential function ($d e^{j\varphi}/d\varphi = j e^{j\varphi}$; $e^{j \cdot 0} = 1$; and the proper series expansion).

Now we can give a simple interpretation of the product of two complex numbers, for we have

$$\mathbf{z}_1 \mathbf{z}_2 = z_1 e^{j\varphi_1} z_2 e^{j\varphi_2} = z_1 z_2 e^{j(\varphi_1+\varphi_2)} \tag{A.5–8}$$

so that the product of two given complex numbers is seen to be another complex number whose magnitude is the product of the two given magnitudes and whose angle is the sum of the two given angles. This result can also be obtained directly from Eq. A.5–3, with some algebra (Problem A.5c).

One special type of multiplication should be pointed out. Suppose that $z_1 = x + jy$ and $z_2 = x - jy$. We call z_2 the complex conjugate of z_1, and write it $\bar{z}_1$. Then if the angle of z_1 is $\varphi = \tan^{-1}(y/x)$, the angle of $\bar{z}_1$ is $-\varphi = \tan^{-1}(-y/x)$; the magnitudes are each equal to $(x^2 + y^2)^{1/2}$. By Eq. A.5–8 we then have, dropping subscripts,

$$z\bar{z} = z^2 e^{j(\varphi - \varphi)} = z^2 = x^2 + y^2 \qquad (A.5-9)$$

which result also comes immediately from Eq. A.5–3. We can use Eq. A.5–9 to find z by purely algebraic means, and we also can use it for division, as we now show. Consider the quotient

$$\frac{z_1}{z_2} = \frac{x_1 + jy_1}{x_2 + jy_2} = \frac{z_1 e^{j\varphi_1}}{z_2 e^{j\varphi_2}} = \frac{z_1}{z_2} e^{j(\varphi_1 - \varphi_2)}$$

Sometimes, if the real and imaginary parts are given, it is desirable to reduce the second ratio directly to an expression without j in the denominator. The way to do this is to multiply numerator and denominator by $\bar{z}_2 = x_2 - jy_2$:

$$\frac{z_1}{z_2} = \frac{(x_1 + jy_1)(x_2 - jy_2)}{x_2{}^2 + y_2{}^2} = \frac{x_1 x_2 + y_1 y_2}{x_2{}^2 + y_2{}^2} + \frac{j(y_1 x_2 - x_1 y_2)}{(x_2{}^2 + y_2{}^2)} \qquad (A.5-10)$$

which has the desired form.[7]

A word might be said about approximations. Sometimes one of the parts of a complex number is considerably bigger than the other. Then one can neglect the smaller part. What is the extent of the error? Suppose that in the number $z = x + jy$, $y = mx$ where m is a number, say 10 or larger. Then we have $z = jy + (y/m) \simeq jy$; in magnitude and angle,

$$z = y\left(1 + \frac{1}{m^2}\right)^{1/2} e^{j\tan^{-1} m} = y\left(1 + \frac{1}{m^2}\right)^{1/2} e^{j[\pi/2 - \tan^{-1}(1/m)]}$$

since the tangent of the complement of an angle is the reciprocal of the tangent of the angle. For a small angle, the angle in radians equals the tangent, so that

$$\tan^{-1}(1/m) \simeq (1/m) \text{ radians} \approx 57/m \text{ degrees}$$

---

[7] By analogy to the process of rationalizing the denominator of a fraction involving quadratic surds, like $4/(3 + 2\sqrt{5})$, one is tempted to call this process "realizing the denominator!"

The radical $(1 + 1/m^2)^{\frac{1}{2}}$ is approximately $1 + 1/2m^2$. Hence $\mathbf{z} \simeq jy(1 + 1/2m^2)$ $e^{-(57/m)j}$; the error made in the magnitude of $\mathbf{z}$ by neglecting x is very small $-\frac{1}{2}\%$ or less if $m > 10$ and that in the angle is a matter of less than $6°$. Similar calculations with the same results can be made for $x = my$.

We conclude this appendix with the formulas for the sine and cosine in terms of exponentials, which are readily derivable from Eq. A.5–6, and the corresponding relations for the hyperbolic functions, used in the text in Section 9.6 and in the problems of Section 5.7:

$$\cos \varphi = (e^{j\varphi} + e^{-j\varphi})/2 \tag{A.5–11a}$$

$$\sin \varphi = (e^{j\varphi} - e^{-j\varphi})/2j \tag{A.5–11b}$$

$$\tan \varphi = -j(e^{j\varphi} - e^{-j\varphi})/(e^{j\varphi} + e^{-j\varphi}) \tag{A.5–11c}$$

$$\cosh x = (e^x + e^{-x})/2 \tag{A.5–12a}$$

$$\sinh x = (e^x - e^{-x})/2 \tag{A.5–12b}$$

$$\tanh x = (e^x - e^{-x})/(e^x + e^{-x}) \tag{A.5–12c}$$

Problem A.5a. Show that if $e^{j\varphi}$ is defined by Eq. A.5–6, it satisfies $d\,e^{j\varphi}/d\varphi = j\,e^{j\varphi}$, $\int e^{j\varphi}\,d\varphi = e^{j\varphi}/j = -j\,e^{j\varphi}$, and $e^{j\cdot 0} = 1$.

Problem A.5b. Show by use of the MacLaurin series expansion for $\sin \varphi$, $\cos \varphi$, and e^u where $u = j\varphi$ that Eq. A.5–6 is correct.

Problem A.5c. Show from Eq. 9.5–3 and the addition theorem for tan $(\varphi_1 + \varphi_2)$ that $|\mathbf{z}_1\,\mathbf{z}_2| = |\mathbf{z}_1| \cdot |\mathbf{z}_2|$ and that the angle of $\mathbf{z}_1\,\mathbf{z}_2$ is the sum of the angles of $\mathbf{z}_1$ and $\mathbf{z}_2$.

Problem A.5d. Show that $e^{j\pi/2} = j$; $e^{\pi j} = e^{-j\pi} = -1$ and that $e^{2j\pi n} = 1$ when n is any integer, positive, negative, or zero.

A.6 Notes on Determinants[8]

A determinant is a number formed from a square array of n^2 numbers. This number is formed as a sum of $n!$ distinct products, each one of which has n factors. Each factor is drawn from a different row in the square array and also from a different column. The sign attached to each term of n factors may be found by a number of equivalent rules, one of which is this:

Arrange the factors in the order of the rows to which they belong (counting down), and then inspect their arrangement with respect to the

---

[8] Proofs of the statements made here, and many more details, are to be found in many textbooks; see for instance, E. Kreyszig, *Advanced Engineering Mathematics*, John Wiley, New York, 1962, section 0.3; and Mary L. Boas, *Mathematical Methods*, John Wiley, New York, 1966, Chapter 3.

columns. If an even number of interchanges of adjacent factors will put them in order of the columns from which they come (counting from the left), the sign is positive; if odd, it is negative.

As a consequence, if any two columns or any two rows of a determinant are interchanged, the sign of the determinant will be changed. If two rows or columns are identical or proportional, the determinant will be zero.

If a constant factor is introduced (or removed) from all the elements of one row or column, the determinant is multiplied (or divided) by that factor.

A determinant is unchanged in value if any fixed multiple of the terms of one row (or column) is added to the respective terms of another row (or column), while leaving unaltered the rest of the determinant including the row (or column) first mentioned. This rule can often be used to transform a determinant into another with all the terms of one column or row save one equal to zero.

A determinant can be evaluated by the cofactor rule: Choose any row or column, and successively multiply each term by the positive or negative value of the determinant formed by striking out of the array the row and column that intersect at that term. The sign to be attached to the reduced determinant in each case is determined by the evenness $(+)$ or oddness $(-)$ of the sum of the row number and column number of the term, counting from the upper left-hand corner. This rule combined with the previous one can make a fairly easy reduction of a fourth- or fifth-order determinant $(n = 4$ or $5)$ to one of a lower order.

A second order determinant is easily evaluated:

$$\begin{vmatrix} a_{11} & a_{12} \\ a_{21} & a_{22} \end{vmatrix} = a_{11}a_{22} - a_{21}a_{12} \qquad (A.6–1)$$

A third-order determinant can be evaluated by a simple rule that associates the positive terms with groups of factors two or three of which lie parallel to the main diagonal (down from the left) and the negative terms with the other diagonal. The solid curves in the array shown in Fig. A.6a connect the factors of the positive terms and the dashed lines the negative.

We have the result:

$$\begin{vmatrix} a_{11} & a_{12} & a_{13} \\ a_{21} & a_{22} & a_{23} \\ a_{31} & a_{32} & a_{33} \end{vmatrix} = a_{11}a_{22}a_{33} + a_{12}a_{23}a_{31} + a_{21}a_{32}a_{13} \\ - a_{13}a_{22}a_{31} - a_{12}a_{21}a_{33} - a_{23}a_{32}a_{11} \qquad (A.6–2)$$

There is no similar simple rule for fourth- and higher-order determinants. The rule for solving simultaneous linear equations with determinants

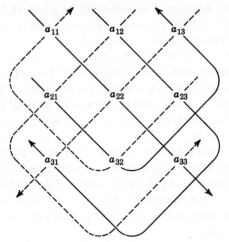

Fig. A.6a.   Illustrating the evaluation of a third-order determinant.

is given in the text (Section 5.5) for the case of three unknowns, but the generalization to the case of more unknowns is immediate.

A.7 Electrical Units

Table A.7A lists the units in which each important electrical quantity is measured in both the MKS and Gaussian systems. Equivalences are given between different units for the same quantity. In some cases, more than one equivalent set of dimensions for a unit is given; different forms are more convenient for checking equations in differing circumstances. A consistent set of dimensions without fractional exponents requires the use of four "basic" quantities, such as length, mass, time, and current. For this reason, both systems are sometimes called "four-dimensional."

This table is also useful for determining how the magnitude of any electrical quantity would change if any of the fundamental units of mass, length, and time were to be modified in the future. From the point of view of such possible changes, each system may be called "three-dimensional."

Relations between units that are written as equations may be treated as such—i.e., direct substitutions can be made for any quantity by its equal in the units attached to any physical quantity. For instance,

$$2.0 \times 10^{-2} \text{ mho/m} = 2.0 \times 10^{-2} \text{ amp/m-v}$$
$$= 2.0 \times 10^{-2} \text{ coulombs}^2/\text{newton-m}^2\text{-sec}$$
$$= 2.0 \times 10^{-2} \times 9 \times 10^{18} \text{ statcoulombs}^2/10^9 \text{ dyne cm}^2 \text{ sec}$$
$$= 18 \times 10^7 \text{ statcoulombs}^2/\text{dyne cm}^2 \text{ sec, etc.} \text{ (cont. on p. 656)}$$

Table A.7A

Physical Concept	MKS Unit	Defining Equation MKS	Defining Equation Gaussian	Gaussian Unit	Equivalence
1. Mass, length, time	kilogram, meter, second			gram, centimeter, second	$1\ kg = 10^3\ gm$ $1\ m = 10^2\ cm$
2. Force	newton = kilogram-meter/second²	$F = ma$		dyne = gram-centimeter/second²	$1\ newton = 10^5\ dyne$
3. Work, energy	joule = newton-meter	$W = \int \mathbf{F}\cdot\mathbf{ds}$		erg = dyne-centimeter	$1\ joule = 10^7\ erg$
4. Power	watt = joule/second	$P = dW/dt$		erg/second	$1\ watt = 10^7\ erg/sec$
5. Charge	coulomb = ampere-second	$q = \int i\,dt$	$F = qq'/r^2$	statcoulomb; [statcoulomb] = [dyne]^½ [centimeter]	$1\ coulomb = (c/10)$ statcoulomb $\simeq 3 \times 10^9$ statcoulomb
6. Current	ampere; [ampere] = [newton]^½/μ_0^½	$F = \mu_0 ii'L/4\pi r$	$i = dq/dt$	statampere = statcoulomb/second = $(1/c)$ abampere	$1\ amp = (1/10)$ abamp = $(c/10)$ statamp $\simeq 3 \times 10^9$ statamp
7. Volume charge density	coulomb/meter³	$\rho = \lim \Delta q/\Delta\tau$		statcoulomb/centimeter³	$1\ coulomb/m^3 = (10^{-7}c)$ statcoulomb/cm³ $\simeq 3 \times 10^3$ statcoulomb/cm³
8. Surface charge density	coulomb/meter²	$\sigma = \lim \Delta q/\Delta S$		statcoulomb/centimeter²	$1\ coulomb/m^2 = (10^{-5}c)$ statcoulomb/cm² $\simeq 3 \times 10^5$ statcoulomb/cm²
9. Linear charge density	coulomb/meter	$\lambda = \lim \Delta q/\Delta l$		statcoulomb/centimeter	$1\ coulomb/m = (10^{-3}c)$ statcoulomb/cm $\simeq 3 \times 10^7$ statcoulomb/cm
10. Current density	ampere/meter²	$J = \lim \Delta i/\Delta S$		statampere/centimeter²	$1\ amp/m^2 = (c/10^5)$ statamp/cm² $\simeq 3 \times 10^5$ statamp/cm²

Table A.7A (*Continued*)

Physical Concept	MKS Unit	Defining Equation MKS / Gaussian	Gaussian Unit	Equivalence
11. Surface current density	ampere/meter	$J_S = \lim \Delta i/\Delta l$	statampere/centimeter	1 amp/m = $(c/10^3)$ statamp/cm $\simeq 3 \times 10^7$ statamp/cm
12. Electric field intensity	newton/coulomb = volt/meter	$\mathbf{E} = \lim \Delta\mathbf{F}/\Delta q$	dyne/statcoulomb = statvolt/centimeter	1 newton/coulomb = $(10^6/c)$ dynes/statcoulomb $\simeq (10^{-4}/3)$ dynes/statcoulomb
13. Electric field flux	newton meter²/coulomb	$\Phi_E = \int \mathbf{E} \cdot d\mathbf{S}$	dyne-centimeter²/statcoulomb; $[\Phi_E]$ = [statcoulomb]	1 newton-m²/coulomb = $(10^{10}/c)$ dyne-cm²/statcoulomb $\simeq (1/3)$ dyne-cm²/statcoulomb
14. Potential, emf, Peltier heat	volt = joule/coulomb	$\mathscr{E}, V = W/q = \int \mathbf{E} \cdot d\mathbf{l}$	statvolt = erg/statcoulomb	1 v = $(10^8/c)$ statv $\simeq (1/300)$ statv
15. Capacitance	farad = coulomb/volt; [farad] = ϵ_0[meter]	$C = Q/V$	statfarad = statcoulomb/statvolt; [statfarad] = [centimeter]	1 farad = $(10^{-9}c^2)$statfarad $\simeq 9 \times 10^{11}$ statfarad
16. Electric dipole moment	meter-coulomb	$\mathbf{p} = q\boldsymbol{\delta}\mathbf{l}$	centimeter-statcoulomb	1 m-coulomb = $(10c)$ cm-statcoulomb $\simeq 3 \times 10^{11}$ cm-statcoulomb
17. Electric quadrupole moment	meter²-coulomb	$Q = q\,\delta l\,\delta l'$ or $Q_{xx} = \int \rho x^2\, d\tau$, etc.	centimeter²-statcoulomb	1 m²-coulomb = (10^3c) cm²-statcoulomb $\simeq 3 \times 10^{13}$ cm²-statcoulomb
18. Electric polarization	coulomb/meter²	$\mathbf{P} = \lim \Delta\mathbf{p}/\Delta\tau$	statcoulomb/centimeter²	1 coulomb/m² = $(10^{-5}c)$ statcoulomb/cm² $\simeq 3 \times 10^5$ statcoulomb/cm²

		MKS unit	Equation	Gaussian unit	Conversion
19.	Permittivity ϵ_0, ϵ	coulomb²/newton-meter² = farad/meter	$\epsilon_0 = qq'/4\pi r^2 F$ $= 10^7/4\pi c^2\}$ $\simeq 10^{-9}/36\pi$	not used in Gaussian system	*1 coulomb²/newton-m² = $(4\pi c^2/10^{11})$ statcoulomb²/ dyne-cm² $\simeq 36\pi \times 10^9$ statcoulomb²/dyne-cm² of κ
20.	Relative permittivity or dielectric constant; electric susceptibility	dimensionless ratio	$\kappa = D/(\epsilon_0 E)$ $= \epsilon/\epsilon_0$ $\chi = \kappa - 1$; $\kappa = D/E$ $\chi = \dfrac{(\kappa - 1)}{4\pi}$	dimensionless ratio (statcoulomb²/ dyne-cm)	κ same in both systems; *1 unit of χ (MKS) = $(1/4\pi)$ unit of χ (Gaussian)
21.	Displacement	coulomb/meter²	$D = \epsilon_0 E + P$ $D = E + 4\pi P$	dyne/statcoulomb	*1 coulomb/m² = $(4\pi \times 10^{-5}c)$ dyne/statcoulomb $\simeq 12\pi \times 10^5$ dyne/statcoulomb of D
22.	Displacement flux	coulomb	$\Phi_D = \int D \cdot dS$	dyne-centimeter²/statcoulomb; $[\Phi_D]$ = [statcoulomb]	*1 coulomb = $(4\pi c/10)$ dyne-cm²/statcoulomb $\simeq 12\pi \times 10^9$ dyne-cm²/ statcoulomb of Φ_D
23.	Resistance	ohm = volt/ampere $[ohm] = [second/meter]/\epsilon_0 = \mu_0[meter/second]$	$R = V/i$	statohm = statvolt/ statampere; [statohm] = [second/ centimeter]	1 ohm = $(10^9/c^2)$ statohm $\simeq (10^{-11}/9)$ statohm
24.	Conductance	mho = ampere/volt	$G = i/V$	statmho = statampere/ statvolt	1 statmho = $(c^2/10^9)$ statmho $\simeq 9 \times 10^{11}$ statmho
25.	Resistivity	meter-ohm	$\rho_c = E/J$	statohm-centimeter	1 m-ohm = 100 ohm-cm = $(10^{11}/c^2)$ statohm-cm $\simeq (10^{-9}/9)$ statohm-cm
26.	Conductivity	mho/meter	$\sigma_c = J/E$	statmho/centimeter	1 mho/m = $(c^2/10^{11})$ statmhos/cm $\simeq 9 \times 10^9$ statmhos/cm

Table A.7A (*Continued*)

Physical Concept	MKS Unit	Defining Equation MKS	Defining Equation Gaussian	Gaussian Unit	Equivalence
27. Magnetic induction (**B**)	weber/meter² = newton/ampere-meter	$F = q(\mathbf{v} \times \mathbf{B})$	$F = (q/c)(\mathbf{v} \times \mathbf{B})$	gauss = (c) dyne/stat-ampere-centimeter (= oersted); [gauss] = μ_0[oersted] = $\mu_0^{1/2}$[dyne$^{1/2}$/cm]	1 weber/m² = 10⁴ gauss
28. Magnetic flux	weber = volt-second = joule/ampere = ampere-henry; [weber] = $\mu_0^{1/2}$[newton$^{1/2}$-meter]	$\Phi = \int \mathbf{B} \cdot d\mathbf{S}$		maxwell = gauss-centimeter² = (c) erg/stat-ampere (= oersted/centimeter²)	1 weber = 10⁸ maxwells
29. Permeability μ_0, μ	weber/meter-ampere = henry/meter = newton/ampere²	$\mu_0 = 4\pi \times 10^{-7}$ henry/m	$\mu_0 = 1$ gauss/oersted = $cB/i\nabla\Omega$	gauss/oersted (=1)	*1 henry/m = $(10^7/4\pi)$ gauss/oersted of μ
30. Relative permeability; magnetic susceptibility	dimensionless ratio	$\mu_r = \mu/\mu_0$, $\chi_m = \mu_r - 1$	$\mu_r = \mu$, $\chi_m = \dfrac{\mu - 1}{4\pi}$	dimensionless ratio	μ_r same in both systems; *1 unit of χ_m (MKS) = $(1/4\pi)$ unit of χ_m (Gaussian)
31. Inductance	henry = weber/ampere; [henry] = μ_0[meter]	$\left\{ L = \Phi/i,\quad \mathcal{E} = -L\,di/dt \right\}$	$\left\{ L = \Phi/ic,\quad L = -L\,di/dt \right\}$	statvolt-second/statampere = erg/statampere²	1 weber/amp = $(10^9/c^2)$ statv-sec/statamp $\simeq$ $(10^{-11}/9)$ statv-sec/statamp
32a. Vector potential 32b. Circulation of **B**	weber/meter	$\left\{ \mathbf{A} = (\mu_0 i/4\pi) \int d\mathbf{l}/r,\quad \text{circulation of } \mathbf{B} = \oint \mathbf{B} \cdot d\mathbf{l} \right\}$	$\mathbf{A} = (i/c) \int d\mathbf{l}/r$	gauss-centimeter (= gilbert)	1 weber/m = 10⁶ gauss-cm
33. Magnetic moment	$\left\{ \begin{array}{l} \text{ampere-meter}^2 \\ \text{weber-meter} \end{array} \right.$	$\mathbf{m} = i\mathbf{S}$ $\mathbf{p}_m = \mu_0 i\mathbf{S}$	$\mathbf{m} = (i/c)\mathbf{S}$	gauss-centimeter³ (= erg/oersted = erg/gauss)	*1 amp-m² = $4\pi \times 10^{-7}$ weber-m = 10³ gauss-cm³ of **m**

No.	Quantity	Equation	MKS unit	Gaussian unit	Conversion
34.	Magnetization	$M = \lim \Delta m/\Delta_\tau$ $P_m = \mu_0 M = \lim \Delta p_m/\Delta_\tau$	{ampere/meter (weber/meter²)	gauss (= oersted)	*1 amp/m = $4\pi \times 10^{-7}$ weber/m² = 10^{-3} gauss (= 10^{-3} oersted) of M
35.	Magnetic intensity (H)	$H = B/\mu_0 - M$ $H = B - 4\pi M$ $= i\nabla\Omega/c$	ampere/meter	oersted (= gauss) = $(1/c)$ statampere/centimeter; [oersted] = [dyne^{1/2}/centimeter]	*1 amp/m = $4\pi \times 10^{-3}$ oersted of H
36.	Magnetic scalar potential and mmf	$V_m = \int H \cdot dl$ $\mathscr{H} = \oint H \cdot dl$	ampere (ampere-turn)	oersted-centimeter = gilbert (= gauss-centimeter)	*1 amp-turn = $(4\pi/10)$ gilberts of $\mathscr{H}$
37.	Surface pole density	$\sigma_m = \mu_0 M_n = M_n$ P_{mn}	weber/meter²	gauss = emu/centimeter² (= oersted)	1 weber/m² = $(10^4/4\pi)$ emu/cm²
38.	Volume pole density	$\rho_m = -\nabla \cdot P$	weber/meter³	gauss/centimeter = emu/cm³ (= oersted/centimeter)	1 weber/m³ = $(10^2/4\pi)$ emu/cm³
39.	Pole strength	$q_m = \int \sigma_m \, dS$	weber	gauss-centimeter² = emu (= oersted-centimeter²)	*1 weber = $(10^8/4\pi)$ emu of q_m
40.	Reluctance	$\mathscr{R} = \mathscr{H}/\Phi$	ampere/weber (ampere-turn/weber)	gilbert/maxwell	*1 amp/weber = $(4\pi/10^9)$ gilbert/maxwell of $\mathscr{R}$
41.	Hall coefficient	$R_H = E/JB$	volt-meter³/ampere weber = meter³/ coulomb	statvolt-centimeter statampere-gauss = centimeter³/(c) statcoulomb	1 v-m³/amp-weber = $(10^7/c^2)$ statv-cm/statamp-gauss ≃ $(10^{-13}/9)$ statv-cm/statamp-gauss
42.	Thermopower, Thomson heat, entropy transport per unit charge	$(d\mathscr{E}/dT = S^*$ $\sigma_{Th} = T \, dS^*/dT$ $S^* = J_Q/JT)$	volt/degree Celsius = joule/coulomb-degree Celsius	statvolt/degree Celsius	1 v/°C = $(10^8/c)$ statv/°C ≃ (1/300) statv/°C

Relations between quantities in brackets give correct dimensional relationships but have no meaning when used as numerical equalities. They can, of course, be used to check the dimensional correctness of equations. For this purpose μ_0 may be treated as a dimensional quantity, although its definition as having the exact MKS value $4\pi \times 10^{-7}$ or exact Gaussian value unity would not be affected by any future change in the adopted units for mass, length, and time. Similar considerations hold for the quantity $\epsilon_0 = 1/4\pi$ in the Gaussian system.

Numerical relations that are starred involve quantities defined differently in the two systems and cannot in general be modified by substitution of equivalent units.

The electrostatic system of units (esu) is based on the statcoulomb; the electromagnetic system (emu) on the abampere, which is the unit of current for which the force in dynes between two parallel wires is $2i_1i_2L/r$. The ratio of the abampere and the statampere is c in centimeters/second. From the table it is seen that 1 abamp is 10 amps.

The Gaussian system uses esu for electrical quantities and emu for magnetic quantities. This system seems likely to be used for some time to come in atomic and nuclear physics, and so it is used as a secondary system throughout the book. Although no distinction is made in the main part of the text between the gauss and the oersted, the distinction is maintained in the table for purposes of comparison. Parentheses are used to indicate the equivalences we have adopted.

The quantity c when written in parentheses represents the velocity of light in cm/sec. The approximate numbers 3 and 9 following the $\simeq$ signs represents actually the numbers 2.99793 and $(2.99793)^2 = 8.98758$. The quantity c written in braces { } represents the velocity of light in meters/second.

Relations between quantities measured in the two systems can be easily read from the table in a "reciprocal" sort of way. For instance, if E_G and E_M represent the electric field intensity in the Gaussian and MKS systems, we have $E_G = (10^{-4}/3)E_M$, since if E_M is 1 newton/coulomb, E_G is $(10^{-4}/3)$ dynes/statcoulomb, as given in item 12 of the table.

Problem A.7a. Write dimensions for all the MKS quantities in Table A.7A in terms of length L, mass M, time T, and μ_0.

Problem A.7b. Force is more frequently used in electromagnetism than is mass. Take μ_0 as dimensionless and write FLT-dimensional formulas for all the MKS quantities in the table.

Problem A.7c. Write FLT formulas for all the Gaussian formulas in the table, taking both $\epsilon_0 = 1/4\pi$ and μ_0 as dimensionless.

A.8 Physical Constants[9]

1. Charge on the electron $e = (1.60210 \pm 0.00007) \times 10^{-19}$ coulomb
   $= (4.80298 \pm 0.00020) \times 10^{-10}$ statcoulomb (esu)
2. Mass of the electron $m_0 = (9.1091 \pm 0.0004) \times 10^{-31}$ kg
3. Mass of the proton $M_p = (1.67252 \pm 0.00008) \times 10^{-27}$ kg
4. e/m for the electron $e/m_0 = (1.75880 \pm 0.00002) \times 10^{11}$ coulombs/kg
   $= (5.27274 \pm 0.00006) \times 10^{17}$ statcoulombs/g
5. Velocity of light $c = (2.997925 \pm 0.000003) \times 10^8$ m/sec
6. Avogadro's Number[10] $N_0 = (6.0228 \pm 0.0003) \times 10^{26}$ per kilogram molecule
   $= (6.0228 \pm 0.0003) \times 10^{23}$ per gram molecule
7. Faraday constant[10] $\mathscr{F} = 96491 \pm 2$ coulombs per chemical equivalent
8. Planck's constant $h = (6.6256 \pm 0.0005) \times 10^{-34}$ joule-sec
9. Boltzmann's constant $k = (1.3805 \pm 0.0002) \times 10^{-23}$ joule/deg
   $= (8.6168 \pm 0.0010) \times 10^{-5}$ ev/deg
10. Bohr magneton $m_B = (0.92732) \pm 0.00006) \times 10^{-23}$ amp-m^2
    $= (0.92732 \pm 0.00006) \times 10^{-20}$ erg/gauss
11. Electron magnetic moment $m_e = (0.92839 \pm 0.00006) \times 10^{-23}$ amp-m^2
12. Proton magnetic moment $m_p = (1.41049 \pm 0.00013) \times 10^{-26}$ amp-m^2
13. Permittivity of free space $\epsilon_0 = (8.85417 \pm 0.00003) \times 10^{-12}$ farad/m
    $= 1/4\pi$ (Gaussian system)
14. Permeability of free space $\mu_0 = 4\pi \times 10^{-7}$ (MKS system)
15. 1 electron volt (ev) $1 \text{ ev} = 1.60210 \times 10^{-19}$ joule $= 1.60210 \times 10^{-12}$ erg

A.9 Lists of Symbols and Abbreviations

Reference is given for the first use of each symbol or abbreviation, or of each particular meaning of a symbol. Page numbers in italics indicate that the symbol is used in that sense only in that section. Numbers marked with p refer to problems.

Subscripts are given only when their presence significantly modifies the meaning of the symbol to which they are attached.

Omitted are script letters used for points in space or on circuits, letters used for objects (as K for key), arbitrary function symbols, $f(p)$, $F(x)$, $g(x, a, b)$, etc., summation indices ($i, j, k, \cdots$), and other letters used only as subscripts.

Roman Alphabet Symbols

A, A_k arbitrary vector 33, 612
A   expansion coefficient 174

[9] From "New Values for the Physical Constants as Recommended by the NAS-NRC," *Physics Today*, **17**, 48 (1964); see also E. R. Cohen and J. W. M. Dumond, "Present Status of Our Knowledge of the Numerical Values of the Fundamental Physical Constants," *Proceedings of the Second International Conference on Nuclidic Masses*, Springer-Verlag, Vienna, 1964; also *Revs. Mod. Physics*, **37**, 537 (1965).

[10] Avogadro's number and the Faraday constant are given here on the chemical scale, for which the mean isotopic constitution of oxygen is taken as having atomic weight 16.0000. On the physical scale, on which C^{12} has weight 12.0000, the significant digits are 6.02252 and 96487, respectively.

G	gravitational constant	6p
G	conductance	215
G	gyromagnetic ratio	422
G_l	conductance per unit length	531
$\mathbf{G}_r, G_r$	momentum per unit volume	558
$\mathbf{g}$	acceleration of gravity	560
g	conductance	227
g	g-number for atomic system	423
$\mathscr{H}$	mmf (magnetomotive force)	402
$\mathbf{H}, H$	magnetic field intensity	383
H_e	earth's field	398p
H_c	coercive force	410
$\mathbf{H}$	complex magnetic field vector	568
h	height or distance	14p
h	Planck's constant	422
$\mathscr{I}$	ionic work function	260p
I	moment of inertia	446
i	current	187
$\mathbf{i}$	complex current	479
i	$(-1)^{\frac{1}{2}}$ (Sections 7.19 and 10.3 only)	370
J_n	Bessel function	174
$\mathbf{J}, J$	current density	187
J_Q	heat current density	*296*
$\mathscr{J}$	solvated ionization potential	252
$\mathbf{J}_m, J_m$	magnetization current density	390
J_S	surface current density	308p
$\mathbf{J}_S$	vector surface current density	315
J_S	complex magnitude of surface current density 578	
j	integer	220
j	$(-1)^{1\,2}$	478, 644
K	constant	*102, 404p*
K	kinetic energy	275p, 333
K	constant for waves on cables and lines	*539*
k	Boltzmann constant	59n
k	scale factor	*98p*
k	constant	*163, 173, 403p, 631*
k	function of resistances	*222*
k	integer	295
k	quantum number	*430*
k	torque constant	445
k	force constant	*475*

k	coefficient of coupling 490
k_1, k_2	relative amplitudes *586*
L	self-inductance 354
L_l	inductance per unit length 359
L	length 8
$\mathbf{l}, l$	length, distance 6
l	function of resistances *222*
M	molecular weight 255
M	mutual inductance 330
M	particle mass 267
M_S	surface density of electromagnetic moment 385
$\mathbf{M}, M$	magnetization 388
M_p	proton mass 6p
M_e	electron mass 6p, 47
m	scalar constant *75, 616, 647*
m	integer 220
m	mass deposited *255*
$\mathbf{m}, m$	electromagnetic moment 305
m_B	Bohr magneton 423
m_p	proton magnetic moment 470
m_l	mass per unit length 602
m_r	mass per unit volume (mass density) 560
N	density of electrons *121*
N	density of molecules 113
N	number of turns 302
$\mathbf{N}, N$	Poynting vector 555
N_n	Bessel function *174*
N_0	Avogadro's number 255
N_0	density of acceptors and donors *239*
N_A	density of acceptors *239*
N_D	density of donors 240
n	arbitrary multiple *39p, 631*
n	integer 169
n	degree of harmonic 169
n	charge carrier density 189
n	bridge ratio *231*
n	number of turns 402
n	atom or ion density 256
n	turns ratio 493
n	index of refraction *585*
n_l	number of turns per unit length 303

$\mathbf{P}, P$	electric polarization	113
P	power	474
P_S	electric dipole moment per unit area	128
P_S	power per unit area	*193*
$P_n(\cos\theta)$	Legendre polynomial	170
P_r	power per unit volume	*193*
P_{mS}	surface density of magnetic dipole moment	385
$\mathbf{P}_m, P_m$	magnetic polarization	388
$\mathbf{p}, p$	electric dipole moment	101
p	pressure	560
p	function of resistances	*222*
p	variable used in Laplace transform method	*522*
p_{lk}	coefficients of potential	*178*
$\mathbf{p}_m, p_m$	magnetic dipole moment	382
P, p	complex dipole vector	565
Q	charge	8
Q	figure of merit	467
Q_{xx}, Q_{xy}, etc.	components of quadrupole tensor	110
Q_{Th}	heat	*248*
q	charge	2
q	function of resistances	*222*
q	complex charge	565
q_m	magnetic pole strength	383
q_l	charge per unit length	*532*
R	radial distance	8
R	resistance	191
$\mathscr{R}$	reluctance	433
R_B	radius of line of force	*335*
R_H	Hall coefficient	*285*
R_l	resistance per unit length	531
r	distance	2
r	resistance	203
S	surface, surface area	10
S^*	entropy transport per unit charge	*243*
S	entropy	*247*
S_i	current sensitivity	*446*
S_V	voltage sensitivity	*446*
S_Q	Coulomb sensitivity	*456*
S_Φ	flux-linkage sensitivity	*456*
s	Liénard-Wiechert denominator	551
T	absolute temperature	59n

T	period 447
T_0	undamped period 447
T_{jk}	tensor component *374*
$\mathscr{T}, \mathscr{T}$	torque 106
t	thickness of disk electret *128*
t	time 187
t_c	characteristic time of pulse 520
t_d	diffusion time 563
t_m	mean free time 189
U	energy 328
U_F	energy of Fermi level 60
u	ionic mobility 256
$\mathbf{u}, u$	velocity vector *371*
$u_1, u_2, u_3; u_x, u_y, u_z$	components of unit vector $\mathbf{1}_u$ *371, 584*
V	potential 30
V_F	Fermi potential 60
V_m	magnetic scalar potential 291
V	complex scalar potential 565
v'	complex velocity-like quantity *587*
$\mathbf{v}, v$	velocity 15
v_A	Alfvén velocity *603*
$\mathbf{v}_d, v_d$	electric drift velocity 274
v_s	velocity of sound *603*
W	work, energy 261
W_∞	hysteresis loss at saturation *418*
w	width *285*
X	reactance 464
x	coordinate 8
x	fractional deviation from balance *231*
x	relative displacement of sliding contact *234p*
$\mathbf{x}, x$	space vector *371*
x_a	attenuation factor *229p*
$Y(\theta, \phi)$	surface spherical harmonic 169
Y	complex admittance 480
y	coordinate 8
Z	function of z *173*
Z	impedance 464
Z	complex impedance 479
z	coordinate 8
z	valence 252
$\mathbf{z}$	arbitrary complex number *644*

Greek Alphabet Symbols

α (alpha)	deviation of Coulomb exponent	*97*
α	molecular polarizability	143
α	temperature coefficient of resistance	*193*
α	transfer coefficient	*254*
α	ratio $2Ra/(R^2 + a^2)$	*322*
α	attenuation constant	501
α	angle	6
α	exponent	448
α_{db}	attenuation	229p
β (beta)	constant in exponent	539
β	transformer phase angle	*493*
β	reciprocal wave length	*540*
Γ (gamma)	image transfer constant	*501*
Γ	reflection coefficient	*540*
γ (gamma)	magnetic interaction factor	*424*
γ	relative damping	448
γ	transformer phase angle	*493*
γ	propagation constant for cables and lines	539
γ	value of $(1 - u^2/c^2)^{-\frac{1}{2}}$	372
Δ	determinant	*221*
δ (delta)	logarithmic decrement	*452*
δ	relative frequency deviation	*473p*
δ	skin depth	588
δ_{ij}	Kronecker symbol	639
ϵ_0 (epsilon)	permittivity of free space	2
ϵ	permittivity	134
ε_{ijk}	epsilon symbol	641
η (eta)	dimensionless variable, range 0 to 1	*178*
θ (theta)	angle	6
θ	Curie temperature	424
κ (kappa)	dielectric constant	134
κ_Q	coefficient of heat conductivity	246
λ (lambda)	linear charge density	8
μ_0 (mu)	permeability of free space	287
λ	constant in exponent	448
λ_D	Debye length	262
$\bar{\lambda}$ (lambda-bar)	reduced wave length $(\lambda/2\pi)$	535
μ_0(mu)	permeability of free space	287
μ	permeability	406

μ_r	relative permeability 406
ν (nu)	frequency *559*
ξ, ξ (xi)	general displacement coordinate *121, 365*
Π (pi)	Peltier heat *247*
ρ (rho)	volume charge density 12
ρ_c	resistivity 189
ρ_m	volume pole density 393
σ (sigma)	surface charge density 10
σ_c	conductivity 189
σ_{Th}	Thomson coefficient 248
σ_m	surface density of pole strength 393
τ (tau)	volume 12
τ	transference number *256*
τ	torque constant for coil 445
Φ	function of ϕ *173*
Φ	magnetic flux 281
Φ_E (phi)	electric flux 14
Φ_v	volume flow *15*
Φ_D	flux of displacement 120
Φ_l	magnetic flux per unit length 536
ϕ (phi)	complex magnetic flux 487
ϕ	angle 11
ϕ	work function 61
φ	phase angle 460
χ (chi)	chi potential 84
χ	electric susceptibility 134
χ_m	magnetic susceptibility 406
Ω (omega)	solid angle 16
ω (omega)	angular velocity 282
ω	angular frequency 447
$\hat{\omega}$	angular velocity of galvanometer 453
ω_p	plasma frequency 122

Abbreviations

abamp	abampere 651
amp	ampere 216
BW	bandwidth 469
cm	centimeter 13
emf	electromotive force 203
emu	electromagnetic unit 271
esu	electrostatic unit 3

ev	electron volt 31
exp	exponential function of 452
gm	gram 651
kg	kilogram 3
kva	kilovolt-amperes 476
L-section	circuit elements arranged as letter L 484
ln	natural logarithm 199
m	meter 3
ma	milliampere 235p
mv	millivolt 234
mmf	magnetomotive force 402
μa	microampere 235p
μf	microfarad 75
$\mu\mu$f	micromicrofarad 75
μv	microvolt 235p
n-type	negative-carrier semiconductor 238
PD	potential difference 31
pf	picofarad $= \mu\mu$f 75
p-type	positive-carrier semiconductor 239
π-section	circuit elements arranged as letter π 229p
rms	root mean square 476
sec	second 3
statamp	statampere 651
statv	statvolt 652
SUN	Commission on Symbols, Units, and Nomen-clature 383n
T-section	circuit elements arranged as letter T 229p
$TE_{m,n}$; $TM_{m,n}$; TEM	modes in wave guides 600
v	volt 38
va	volt-ampere 476
var	volt-ampere-reactive 477

Operational and Other Symbols

1	unit vector 2
Σ	summation sign 4
Δ	increment of 15
$\mathbf{A} \cdot \mathbf{B}$	scalar product 15, 616
∇	del or nabla 22, 618
div $\mathbf{A} = \nabla \cdot \mathbf{A}$	divergence of $\mathbf{A}$ 22, 619
δ	small but not infinitesimal increment 6
curl $\mathbf{A} = \nabla \times \mathbf{A}$	curl of $\mathbf{A}$ 40, 627

$\mathbf{A} \times \mathbf{B}$ vector product   106, 622

grad $V = \nabla V$ gradient of V 42, 618

$\overline{(\nabla \cdot \mathbf{M})\mathbf{A}}$ bar signifies that ∇ operates on both vectors 131, 632

F', F'' first and second derivatives   523, 545

∂_j partial derivative   374

$\square$ d'Alembertian operator   547

$\bar{A}$ average of A 619

A.10 Answers to Selected Problems

Problem 1.2a. 8.25×10^{-8} newton; $F_{\text{grav}}/F_{\text{elec}} = 4.42 \times 10^{-40}$.

Problem 1.3a. 9.86×10^4 newton/coul at $9°42'$ with vertical; 2.52×10^5 newton/coul horizontal; 1.905×10^5 newton/coul at $28°30'$ below x-axis.

Problem 1.3f. See p. 123; $E = 200$ newton/coul; cf. Problems 1.7e and 3.4e.

Problem 1.3i. $E_z = ab/4\epsilon_0 z(a^2 + z^2)^{1/2}$.

Problem 1.4h. $\Phi_E = qz/\epsilon_0(z^2 + a^2)^{1/2}$.

Problem 1.5d. $\rho = (\tfrac{1}{3})\epsilon_0 b_3(x \cos \alpha + y \sin x)^{-2/3}$.

Problem 1.6a. 1.24×10^{-4} m at edge of field, $1°25'$ below horizontal.

Problem 1.7a. 9.508×10^4 V; 1.44×10^5 V; 1.27×10^5 V.

Problem 1.7h. 7.66×10^{-10} coul/m².

Problem 1.7k. -91.5 V.

Problem 1.8e. $b_1/\epsilon_0[6xyz + \tfrac{3}{2}(yz)^{1/2}(y^2 + z^2)]$; 0; 0.

Problem 1.9d. $E = -1.00 \times 10^5$ newton/coul.

Problem 1.10e. As the $\tfrac{1}{3}$, $-\tfrac{2}{3}$, and $+\tfrac{2}{3}$ powers of $x - x_1$.

Problem 1.11g. $V \simeq -14 + 3(x^4 - 3x^2y^2 + 3y^4/8)/x_1^4$; lines of steepest descent at $\pm 40.9°$ from x-axis.

Problem 2.4a. 9.64×10^{-2} coul/m² $= 6.02 \times 10^{-3}$ electrons/angstrom²; 3.23×10^{-3} coul; 1.09×10^{10} newtons/coul.

Problem 2.6a. 30 angstroms.

Problem 2.5f. $\Delta C = 177$ pf.

Problem 2.5h. $r^2(\theta) = 4ad/\epsilon_0(b + \theta)^3$.

Problem 3.1d. $\tan \theta = \tfrac{1}{2}(\sqrt{17} - 3)$.

Problem 3.2e. (a) $\mathbf{F} = -8.1 \times 10^{-8}\, \mathbf{1}_r$ newton. (b) $\mathbf{F} = 4.05 \times 10^{-8}\, \mathbf{1}_\theta$ newtons. (c) and (d) $\mathbf{F} = \pm 4.05 \times 10^{-8}\, \mathbf{1}_r$ newtons.

Problem 3.2f. (b) 5.4×10^{-10} newton-m and 2.7×10^{-10} newton-m in the same sense.

Problem 3.4a. 1.15×10^4 statcoul/cm² $= 3.84 \times 10^{-2}$ coul/m².

Problem 3.4d. $\delta l = 1.647 \times 10^{-16}$ m.

Problem 3.6f. $-3k$, 0, $-kr/\epsilon_0$ for $r < a$. All zero for $r > a$.

Problem 3.8h. 19.3 pf.

Problem 3.8k. 184.5 pf/m.

Problem 3.9a. $\alpha = 9.04 \times 10^{-41}$ f-m²/molecule.

Problem 3.10e. $\sigma = 3.72 \times 10^{-5}$ coul/m².

Problem 4.3d. -2.75×10^{-5} coul/m^2; -1.32×10^{-5} coul/m^2; 0.

Problem 4.3i. $\theta = \tan^{-1}\left(\frac{12}{5}\right) - \tan^{-1}\left(\frac{4}{5}\right) = 15°48'$.

Problem 4.4b. $q_1 = -1.6 \times 10^{-7}$ coul, 4 cm from center; $\sigma_{\text{near}} = -4.25 \times 10^{-6}$ coul/m^2; $\sigma_{\text{far}} = -3.90 \times 10^{-7}$ coul/m^2; $\sigma_{\text{midway}} = -8.25 \times 10^{-7}$ coul/m^2.

Problem 4.4c. $F = -Rrq^2/4\pi\epsilon_0(r^2 - R^2)^2$.

Problem 4.4h. 1.71×10^2 newton.

Problem 4.5c. 7.57 $\mu\mu$f/m $= 2.31$ $\mu\mu$f/ft.

Problem 4.5f. $(26.6$ and $6.70) \times 10^{-8}$ coul/m^2.

Problem 4.6g. $\sigma = 2\epsilon_0 E_0 \cos \phi$.

Problem 4.6h. $V = -2E_0\kappa r \cos \phi/(\kappa + 1)$ for $r < R$; $V = -E_0 \cos \phi[r - (\kappa - 1) \cdot R^2/(\kappa + 1)]$.

Problem 4.7b. Consider the flux when only one $V_\kappa \neq 0$.

Problem 4.7g. $U = Q^2/8\pi\epsilon_0 a$.

Problem 4.8e. 2.12×10^{-5} newton (cf. Fig. 4.8a).

Problem 5.2a. 2.96×10^{-7} coul/m^2 and -5.54×10^{-7} coul/m^2 on plates; 2.58 coul/m^2 at interface; $i = 1.0$ ma.

Problem 5.4a. 2.07×10^{-3} sec.

Problem 5.5d. $98R_2R_3 = 2R_2R_1 + (R_1 + R_3)^2$.

Problem 5.5g. $\Delta V = -3.14$ V.

Problem 5.5i. 69.5 ohms or 0.1205 ohm.

Problem 5.5j. $\mathscr{E} = 280$ V; $r = 852$ ohms.

Problem 5.6c. 1.954 amp, -0.116 amp, 3.31 amp.

Problem 5.6e. 4.267 miles from west end. $V = 474.7$ volts.

Problem 5.6i. 282 ohm, $i = 0$ between either 100-ohm and either 300-ohm resistor.

Problem 5.7e. $R_1 = 28.77, 140, 260, 497$ ohms. $R_2 = 4340, 825, 352, 301$ ohms.

Problem 5.7f. $R^2 = R_1R_2^2/(R_1 + 2R_2)$; $x_a = (R_2 - R)/(R_2 + R) = 10^{-\alpha/20}$.

Problem 5.8e. Put R_2 which can vary between 354 and 400 ohms in parallel with a fixed $R_1 = 58$ ohms.

Problem 5.8g. Min. detectable current $= 0.91 \times 10^{-8}$ amp.

Problem 6.3c. 19.6 mv.

Problem 6.3d. 61.1 mv, 598 μwatts, 0.163 amp.

Problem 6.4c. 0.0261 amp-hr/cm^2.

Problem 6.4f. Highest occupied level of OH$^-$ above that of SO$_4^=$.

Problem 6.5b. 1.14×10^{20} m^{-3}.

Problem 6.5e. 3.55×10^{-4} cm.

Problem 7.3a. 2.13×10^{-5} m, 2.13×10^{-4} m.

Problem 7.3c. 0.714 gauss.

Problem 7.4d. 0.056 newton.

Problem 7.4e. 10.36 newton-m.

Problem 7.5a. $\theta = \tan^{-1}(R_H\sigma_o B) = 0.2195°$; distance $= 7.66 \times 10^{-3}$ cm.

Problem 7.8d. 7.036×10^{11} m/sec^2.

Problem 7.8j. -0.333 dynes.

Problem 7.8m. 2×10^{-4} V; 2×10^{-6} V.

Problem 7.8r. $B_\theta = 1.8 \times 10^{-13}$ weber/m^2; $B_r = 3.6 \times 10^{-13}$ weber/m^2; $B = 4.04 \times 10^{-13}$ weber/m^2 at angle of 26.6°.

Problem 7.10b. 9.25×10^{-7}.

Problem 7.11c. Consider a set of circles and a single axial wire. Correction small if solenoid is finite and pitch of helix is small.

Problem 7.12e. (a) 3.645×10^{-8} weber; (b) 2.412×10^{-8} weber.

Problem 7.12g. 8.9×10^{-6} joules.

Problem 7.13a. 5.75°.

Problem 7.14c. $2.7 \times 10^{-4} \sin (94.2t)$ V.

Problem 7.15c. (a) 2.405 mh; (b) 1.068 mh.

Problem 7.15d. $M_{12} = (\mu_0 a^2 R^2 \pi / 2z^2)[1 - 3(a^2 + R^2)/2z^2 \cdots]$.

Problem 7.16a. 3.465×10^{-3} sec; -5 V.

Problem 7.17b. $M = \mu_0 a[\ln (8a/z) - 2]$.

Problem 7.17d. $L = 0.164 \ \mu h$, $\phi = 3.28 \times 10^{-6}$ weber.

Problem 7.18c. Rate $= \mathscr{E}^2(e^{-Rt/L} - e^{-2Rt/L})/R$.

Problem 7.19b. $v_x' = (v_x + u)/(1 + uv/c^2)$.

Problem 8.2f. $(1.44, 1.25, 1.018,$ and $0.551) \times 10^{-2}$ amp/m.

Problem 8.4d. 0.174 amp.

Problem 8.4i. (a) 4.54 gauss; (b) 2.56; (c) 3.32 at 25.18° from line to center of magnet. (Dipole approximation answers: (a) 3.2 gauss; (b) 3.2; (c) 3.03 at 15.4°.)

Problem 8.4m. $(q_m SM/4\pi)(2lh + l^2)/h^2(h + l)^2$.

Problem 8.5b. (a) at the center $H = -0.604$ amp/m, $B = 3.918 \times 10^{-5}$ weber/m², $H_{ett} = 10.0$ amp/m. (b) just inside one end $H = -16.65$ amp/m, $B = 1.898 \times 10^{-5}$ weber/m², $H_{ett} = -6.1$ amp/m.

Problem 8.5g. $\rho_m = 0$, $\sigma_m = 0$, $\mathbf{J}_m = 2K\mathbf{1}_z$, $\mathbf{J}_{sm} = -Ka\,\mathbf{1}_z$, $\mathbf{H} = 0$, $\mathbf{B} = \mu_0 \mathbf{M} = \mu_0 Kr\,\mathbf{1}_\phi$.

Problem 8.6b. $B = 1.475$ weber/m²; $M = 1.176 \times 10^6$ amp/m; $H = 1115$ amp/m.

Problem 8.6d. $M = -203$ amp/m; $H = 1.19 \times 10^6$ amp/m.

Problem 8.7b. -0.996×10^{-23} joule.

Problem 8.8e. 8.72×10^4 amp/webers.

Problem 8.9c. $\Delta T = b^2 T_0/8Kl$.

Problem 8.9d. $t = 0.665T_0$.

Problem 8.9h. For $\gamma = 0.3$, $\theta_1 = 0.67\hat{\omega}/\omega_0$, $t_1 = 0.85(T_0/4)$. For $\gamma = 10$, $\theta = 0.0496\hat{\omega}/\omega_0$, $t_1 = 0.191(T_0/4)$.

Problem 8.9j. S_Q is reduced both by a factor $R_S/(R_S + R)$ and by an increase in γ.

Problem 9.2f. Ratio $= [1 + Q_0^2\omega^2/\omega_0^2]^{1/2}/[1 + Q_0^2(\omega/\omega_0 - \omega_0/\omega)^2]^{1/2}$.

Problem 9.2j. $V_{m_1} = 5.82$ V, $V_{m_2} = 14.8$ V, $\Delta\phi = 39°10'$.

Problem 9.3d. $i = 106.5$ amp, line loss $= 227$ watts; if pf $= 1.00$, $i = 80$ amp, reduction in loss $= 99$ watts.

Problem 9.3g. $P = \mathscr{E}_e^2 R_2/[(R_1 + R_2)^2 + (X_1 + X_2)^2]$.

Problem 9.4a. $X_L = 29.04$ ohms, $R = 38.72$ ohms, $X_C = 80.7$ ohms; ratio $= 1.25$.

Problem 9.4d. $i_L = (0.291 - 1.28j)$ ma, $i_C = 0.1015 + 0.01j$ ma. $i_R = 0.1895 - 1.29j$ ma. $V_L = 7.94e^{4.5°j}$.

Problem 9.4i. Figure 9.4c, $-0.0964e^{5.43°j}$; Fig. 9.4d, $0.01035^{9.10°j}$.

Problem 9.6g. $R_G \ll L/R_L$.

Problem 9.6h. $C_2 = C_1 R_3/R_4$, $R_2 = C_3 R_4/C_1$; vary C_3 and R_3.

Problem 9.6j. $C_3 = M/R_1 R_2$, $R_3 M = R_2(L - M)$.

Problem 9.8c. $f(p) = (1 - e^{-pt_1})/p^2 t_1 + (e^{-pt_3} - e^{-pt_2})/p^2(t_3 - t_2)$.

Problem 9.8f. $i(t) = \mathscr{E}_0/(R_2 + R) + \mathscr{E}_0 R[e^{-\alpha t} \cos \omega t + (R/2L\omega - 1/RC\omega - \frac{1}{2}R_2 C\omega) \times e^{-\alpha t} \sin \omega t]/R_2(R_2 + R)$; $a = (L + R_2 RC)/2R_2 LC$; $\omega^2 + a^2 = (R_2 + R)/R_2 LC$.

Problem 10.2b. $Z_e = 119.9\{[\ln (D/b) + \frac{1}{4}] \cosh^{-1} (D/2b)\}^{1/2}$; $\cosh^{-1} (D/2b) \simeq \ln (D/b)$; $D \simeq 2.6$ m.

Problem 10.5a. 4.65×10^5 amp.

Problem 10.8a. $\delta = 3.82 \times 10^{-6}\lambda^{1/2}$; (a) 7.64 × 10 m, 7.64 × 10⁻⁶ m, 7.64 × 10⁻⁸ m, 2.70 × 10⁻⁹ m; (b) 7.5 × 10⁻⁶ m, 7.5 × 10⁻⁷ m, 7.5 × 10⁻⁹ m, 2.67 × 10⁻¹⁰ m.

Problem 10.9c. 2.5×10^9, 5.0×10^9.

Problem 10.10d. 7.7 m/sec; 8940 m/sec.

NAME INDEX

SUBJECT INDEX

In this index certain page numbers are followed by ff, n, and p: ff following a page number means that page to the end of the section in which it lies; n refers to a footnote or figure reference on the page; p refers to one or more problems on the page.

John Wiley & Sons Limited

International publishers

Baffins Lane · Chichester
Sussex · England
Telephone: Chichester 84531

Telegrams and Cables:
Wilebook Chichester
Telex: 86290

with compliments

Sh. 55.   MR. 64.00